Fundamentals of Insurance
for Financial Planning

Huebner School Series

Walt J. Woerheide, Editor

Huebner School Series

Fundamentals of Insurance for Financial Planning
Fourth Edition

Burton T. Beam, Jr.
Barbara S. Poole
David L. Bickelhaupt
Robert M. Crowe

The American College/*Bryn Mawr, Pennsylvania*

This publication is designed to provide accurate and authoritative information about the subject covered. While every precaution has been taken in the preparation of this material, the authors and The American College assume no liability for damages resulting from the use of the information contained in this publication. The American College is not engaged in rendering legal, accounting, or other professional advice. If legal or other expert advice is required, the services of an appropriate professional should be sought.

Library of Congress Control Number 2003104309
ISBN 1579960774

Printed in the United States of America

To
Lindsay and Chris
BTB

To my mother, Ruth B. Sawtelle
BSP

To my wife, Lee,
and to all insurance
students and their teachers
DLB

To my children and grandchildren
and to Pat,
who made them all possible
RMC

Contents

Preface

Few fields have changed as dramatically over the last few years as insurance. New life insurance and annuity products have been developed. Medical expense insurance has evolved rapidly in a largely managed care environment. Long-term care insurance is becoming increasingly common. Disability income insurance continues to change as a result of underwriting results. And property and liability policies continue to be adapted to changing family and legal environments. In addition, the structure of the industry has become much different with the growth of large financial services conglomerates. We have made every attempt to capture these changes in this book.

This book is a basic text in insurance and, like most other "fundamentals" or "principles" books, covers theory as well as current products and practices. However, many of these other books focus on what is needed by a college student who is going to become an insurance consumer, a risk manager, or an insurance company employee. We have taken a different approach and have emphasized what we feel is necessary for a financial services professional to know about insurance in order to best serve clients. This service can be in the form of either product sales or analysis and evaluation of existing insurance programs. We have attempted to cover all of the insurance topics that a financial planner must master in order to become a Certified Financial Planner (CFP^{TM}) or a Chartered Financial Consultant (ChFC). We have also tried to provide the foundation necessary for life insurance professionals who will pursue further insurance studies to become a Chartered Life Underwriter (CLU).

Following introductory chapters on risk, insurance, the insurance industry, and basic legal principles and contract analysis, the book's focus turns to the various types of insurance by first looking at Social Security, Medicare, and other government programs. For most clients, these and employer-provided benefits are the foundation on which an individual insurance program is built. This is followed by an in-depth discussion of life insurance, annuities, medical expense insurance, disability income insurance, long-term care insurance, homeowners insurance, automobile insurance, and other property and liability insurance coverages. Both the personal and business needs of clients are addressed.

This fourth edition is a modest revision of the third edition. We have updated material where necessary, corrected a few errors that crept into the earlier edition, and rewritten a few sections for clarity as a result of comments from readers and reviewers. The most significant changes include the following:

- a substantial rewrite of chapter 12 on medical expense insurance as an employee benefit
- new material in chapter 15 on long-term care coverage
- the relocation of the case study and appendices to the student syllabus

Chapters 7 and 12–19 have been the primary responsibility of Burton T. Beam, Jr., since the inception of this book.

Chapters 1–6 and 8–11 were originally written by Robert M. Crowe and have been updated and revised as necessary for this edition by Barbara S. Poole.

We continue to include two special features from the earlier editions of this book that have been of value to students. The first is a series of checklists for evaluating and comparing insurance products. The second is a list of up-to-date sources for further in-depth study. This is not a traditional bibliography that identifies other sources that cover essentially the same material as the text. Rather, the sources listed enable a financial services professional to obtain a much more comprehensive understanding of a topic than we can cover in one book.

Writing a book of this nature and length requires a lot of hard work by a lot of people. However, we as authors have the ultimate responsibility for providing you with the best book possible. It would be foolish to believe that any book is the perfect book. Please take some time to give us your constructive comments on how we can better improve future editions. Also, if this book contains any errors, we apologize, and each of the authors acknowledges that the errors are the fault of one of the other authors.

Burton T. Beam, Jr.
Barbara S. Poole

Acknowledgments

The American College wishes to acknowledge the following people for their contributions to *Fundamentals of Insurance for Financial Planning*. With the possible exception of the authors, no one else has spent more time working on this book than Lynn Hayes, editorial director, and Charlene McNulty, production group leader. We owe them a debt of gratitude for putting up with frequent manuscript revisions and the usual annoyances of dealing with authors and tight deadlines.

We gratefully thank other members of The American College's production, editorial, and graphics departments who have worked on some aspect of the fourth edition.

We thank Deborah A. Jenkins, librarian at The American College, and her staff for their support in finding all the information we requested.

Finally, we acknowledge and thank those who have reviewed portions of the manuscript during the production process for one or more of its four editions. Their comments have been of great value:

- Bob Cooper, Employers Mutual Distinguished Professor of Insurance at Drake University
- Arthur Flitner, assistant vice president and senior director of curriculum design at the American Institute for Chartered Property Casualty Underwriters
- Ed Graves, Charles J. Zimmerman chairholder at The American College
- Tom O'Hare, adjunct professor of insurance at The American College
- Chuck Soule, retired vice president and CEO of the Paul Revere Life Insurance Company
- Kenn Tacchino, associate professor of taxation at Widener University
- Eric Wiening, assistant vice president and ethics counsel at the American Institute for Chartered Property Casualty Underwriters
- Walt J. Woerheide, vice president and dean of academic affairs at The American College

- Bruce Worsham, associate vice president and director of educational development at The American College
- the students and instructors who provided us with valuable suggestions

In addition, we must recognize the many sources from which we have drawn material. These include:

- *General Insurance* by David L. Bickelhaupt. We greatly value his contributions to this book and to the field of insurance education.
- *McGill's Life Insurance*, edited by Edward E. Graves
- *McGill's Legal Analysis of Life Insurance*, edited by Edward E. Graves and Burke A. Christensen
- *Disability Income Insurance: The Unique Risk* by Charles F. Soule
- *Group Benefits: Basic Concepts and Alternatives* by Burton T. Beam, Jr.

The last four books listed are published by The American College.

All of these individuals and source materials have made this a better book, and we are grateful.

About the Authors

Burton T. Beam, Jr., CPCU, CLU, ChFC, is associate professor of insurance at The American College. Prior to joining The American College, Mr. Beam was on the faculties of the University of Florida and the University of Connecticut. He has written extensively in the areas of group and health insurance and has had articles published in several professional journals. He is the author of *Group Benefits: Basic Concepts and Alternatives* and *Group Health Insurance*, published by The American College. He is also coauthor of *Employee Benefits*, a textbook used at many colleges and universities. Mr. Beam is an assistant editor of the *Journal of Financial Service Professionals*. He is a member of the National Association of Health Underwriters and the International Association for Financial Planning.

Barbara S. Poole, PhD, CFP™, ChFC, CLU, FLMI, is associate professor of finance and insurance at The American College. Prior to joining The American College, Dr. Poole was on the faculties of Central Connecticut State University and St. Joseph's College (CT). She has won numerous awards for her research in the areas of financial psychology and behavior, and has published many articles in academic publications, including *Journal of Retirement Planning*, *Financial Services Review*, *Benefits Quarterly*, and *Personal Finances and Worker Productivity*. Dr. Poole currently serves on the editorial boards of *Financial Services Review* and the *Journal of Financial Planning*. In addition to her work in the academic field, Dr. Poole has provided various financial consulting services to business and financial professionals.

Dr. David L. Bickelhaupt, CLU, ChFC, CPCU, ARM, is professor emeritus of insurance and finance, College of Business, Ohio State University. He is the author of *General Insurance*—from which the roots of this textbook stem. Through its 11 editions, more than one million students of insurance in 300 colleges and many professional insurance courses have used this book. Among numerous articles he has written are those appearing annually in the *Encyclopaedia Britannica.* Over the course of his career as a leading insurance educator, Dr. Bickelhaupt has been a member of the Insurance Institute of America's National Examination Committee, president of the American Risk and Insurance Association, executive director of the Griffith Foundation for Insurance Education (OSU), and on the boards of State Auto Insurance Companies, the International Insurance Seminars, and the Insurance Hall of Fame.

Dr. Robert M. Crowe, CLU, ChFC, CFP™, CPCU, spent his entire career in the field of higher education for business. The late Dr. Crowe was a faculty member of several universities including two, the University of Tulsa and the University of Memphis, where he was dean of the College of Business Administration. He was also an academic vice president and professor of finance and insurance at The American College. Among the several books he wrote or edited is *Time and Money: Using Time-Value Analysis in Financial Planning,* currently in its seventh edition. Later in his career, Dr. Crowe was vice president of Keir Educational Resources.

Fundamentals of Insurance
for Financial Planning

1

Basic Concepts of Risk and Insurance

Learning Objectives

An understanding of the material in this chapter should enable the student to

---

1-1. Define risk, uncertainty, and risk-related terms.

1-2. Describe the measurement and classification of risks.

1-3. Describe how individuals may respond to risk.

1-4. Explain the costs of pure risks and how insurance can treat pure risks.

1-5. Describe the benefits and costs of insurance.

1-6. List and describe the major categories of insurance.

1-7. Define key terms in insurance terminology.

Chapter Outline

This book focuses on what the financial planner needs to know about insurance. Every financial planner worthy of the name needs a good background in insurance because no client's financial plan can be complete, or even adequate, if it does not include a properly designed program of insurance.

Financial planning for a client consists of three coordinated components: insurance planning, investment planning, and tax planning. Appropriate insurance planning should precede the other two components. In recognition of this, one of the recommended early courses in both the Chartered Financial Consultant and the Certified Financial Planner professional educational programs focuses on the subject of insurance.

In chapters 1 and 2, we will review some basic concepts associated with risk. Financial planners need to understand these concepts as a foundation for assessing their clients' risk exposure and discussing those exposures with their clients. Later chapters will describe specific risks, and their management in detail.

RISK AND RELATED TERMS

Risk

Insurance professionals often use the word "risk" to describe the object of potential loss, or the object insured. Thus, a building may be referred to as "the risk" in a fire insurance contract. Or an agent may put his or her company "on the risk" when he or she issues a binder of insurance covering a client's automobile.

Rather than using the term risk in a trade jargon sense, insurance scholars have argued for years about an accurate and precise definition of the term. They have posed various alternatives that are not within the scope of this book. Readers who wish to explore these definitions will find a reference work on the subject listed at the end of this chapter.

risk

For purposes of this book, *risk* is defined as the *possibility of loss*. Note that the definition of risk adopted here refers to the *possibility*, not the probability or chance, of loss. Possibility means that something could occur, but the chances of the occurrence cannot be measured or even estimated. Probability or chance of loss, on the other hand, does suggest an element of measurability. As we will see later in this chapter, insurance is concerned primarily with risks that can be measured, at least in a rudimentary fashion.

Examples of risks are everywhere, ranging from unavoidable risks to those that are assumed by choice. Examples of risks assumed by choice include forming a business enterprise, drilling an oil well, or investing in real estate. Anyone who owns property automatically assumes the risks from perils such as fire, windstorm, theft, or liability lawsuits. The inability to predict when or whether these perils may cause losses is a fact of life inherent to property ownership.

Loss

To further understand risk and insurance, we should look more closely at the notion of loss. As we have said, loss is the undesirable end result of risk—a decline in value, usually in an unexpected or relatively unpredictable manner. In general terms, not all losses are closely related to risk; some losses are the result of intentional actions, as, for example, the gift of property to someone. Other losses can be predicted fairly accurately because they are known to always occur to some extent such as depreciation of physical properties, or depletion of resources. Many losses, however, cannot be predicted. Illustrations include loss of property value due to fire, theft, or other causes; loss of income due to property destruction, death, or disability; increased expenses such as medical costs; and loss of assets due to legal liability for injury or damage to other persons.

loss exposure

There are two types of losses: (1) losses that actually occur and (2) losses that might occur. Losses that might occur are often called *loss exposures* and include, for example, financial losses that would arise if a fire or death were to occur. Loss exposures are much more numerous than actual losses that result from the different possibilities of loss. Both types of loss must be considered because the cost of treating risks includes not only the actual losses but also the cost of dealing with the losses that might occur.

direct loss

Losses may be direct or indirect. *Direct losses* are the first or immediate losses that arise from an event. To illustrate, if a client is found guilty of negligently driving an automobile and causing bodily injury to another, the direct

indirect (consequential) loss

loss is the damage award levied against the client. An *indirect loss*, sometimes called a *consequential* loss is a loss that occurs only as a secondary result following the occurrence of a peril. An indirect loss may be the income the client loses while attending court proceedings leading up to the damages award.

As another example, if a client's home is severely damaged by fire from defective wiring, the direct loss is the cost to repair the damage to the home. The client and his or her family will also experience an indirect loss if they must incur extra living expenses to live in a motel and eat meals in restaurants while their home is being repaired. In fact, indirect loss may result for a client even when there is no direct loss for that client.

Example: A client owns a small manufacturing company that depends on the sole supplier of a component used in the client's manufacturing operation. A fire totally destroys the component supplier's premises some miles away. While this fire entails no direct loss for the client, the unavailability of the necessary component may require the client to shut down the manufacturing company and thus result in lost profits.

Uncertainty

uncertainty

While some insurance authors equate the term *risk* with "uncertainty," we believe that risk and uncertainty are separate but often related concepts. *Uncertainty* is a state of mind, typified by lack of sureness about something. As a consequence, uncertainty is subjective and experienced differently by each individual, despite the same set of facts, objective reality, or risk. For example, one client may refuse to ride in a glass-enclosed elevator on the outside of a high-rise hotel, while another may be perfectly comfortable doing so. The risk—the possibility of loss in the form of bodily injury—is the same for both clients, but the uncertainty (doubt, worry, fear) differs greatly.

Uncertainty is often the result of risk. For example, a client may be highly uncertain because of the risk that his or her dependent parent may someday have to be confined to a nursing home for an extended period. On the other hand, uncertainty is also often unrelated to risk. One may be present while the other is absent, and one may be great while the other is small. A "fun-loving" client may be oblivious (no uncertainty) to the possibility (a very real risk) that a lewd remark to a colleague will lead to a suit for sexual harassment. Conversely, a more timid client may be terrified (highly uncertain) of flying commercially because of the possibility (but low risk) of a crash.

One important function of a financial planner in the field of insurance is to bring some balance between a client's risks and his or her uncertainties. As we will see later, there is much a planner can do to deal with the client's risks to reduce the client's uncertainty. Equally importantly, an effective financial planner can help develop in his or her client a healthy sense of uncertainty by pointing out the presence of risks that the client has not recognized or cannot realistically estimate.

Perils and Hazards

peril

In contrast to risk, the word *peril* is used to identify the cause of loss. Examples of perils are commonplace and include unemployment, illness, old age, death, forgery, theft, fire, earthquake, windstorm, flood, and hundreds of other causes of loss.

hazard

A *hazard* is an act or condition that increases the likelihood of the occurrence of a peril and/or increases the severity of a loss if a peril does occur. Ordinarily, any particular person or object is exposed to many separate hazards. The insurance business divides hazards into three major classifications:

- physical hazards
- moral hazards
- attitudinal hazards

Physical Hazards

physical hazard

The first category of hazards is *physical hazards*. These are physical conditions relating to location, structure, occupancy, exposure, and the like. Insurance underwriting requires an evaluation of all physical hazards. The following are a few examples of physical hazards: high blood pressure, a dangerous hobby, newspapers piled on a staircase, gasoline stored on the premises, weak construction that may fail in a heavy wind, unsafe brakes on a car, holes in a sidewalk, inadequate inventory checks in a store, and improper water drainage systems. Each of these conditions, as well as many others, increases the chance of a loss occurring, or perhaps the magnitude of the loss if one does occur, in regard to a specific peril such as death, accident, fire, windstorm, water, or theft.

Moral Hazards

moral hazard

The second category of hazards consists of moral hazards. *Moral hazards* are dishonest tendencies, often due to an insured's weakened financial condition, that are likely to increase loss frequency and/or severity. Examples include tendencies to cause deliberate damage in order to collect insurance proceeds and to intentionally inflate claims for insurance proceeds beyond the actual size of the sustained loss.

Appraisal of moral hazard requires studying the client's character and reputation. Evidence that an applicant ever defrauded another person, had a previous bankruptcy record, or has a poor credit reputation is an indication of possible moral hazard with regard to insurance. Investigators also scrutinize insurance applicants' reputations in trade, their ratings with banks, their standings with competitors, and the regard in which they are held by those with whom they transact business. Individuals who have a reputation for taking unfair advantage of legal technicalities or people who have repudiated contracts in the face of possible financial loss are generally regarded as likely prospects to resort to other unethical methods. Individuals known as *pyromaniacs*—people who act under an irresistible impulse to set fires—are also in the moral hazard category.

Attitudinal Hazards

attitudinal hazard

The third category of hazards consists of *attitudinal hazards*, evidenced by carelessness or indifference as to whether a loss occurs or the size of a loss if it does occur. For example, laziness, disorderliness, poor dental hygiene, and lack of concern for others are termed attitudinal hazards rather than moral hazards, which involve dishonesty. Leaving car doors unlocked increases automobile thefts; bad smoking habits increase fire losses; hurried, unthinking action can cause many personal injuries. Underwriting and rating of applicants based on apparent attitudinal hazards are important to the successful operation of the insurance mechanism, as is consideration of physical and moral hazards.

Example:	A client, Mr. Rich, owns a large yacht. He knows that some (1) hazards (contributing factors), such as the captain's negligence or structural faults of the ship, contribute to (2) the risk (possibility of loss) from (3) perils (causes of loss) such as fire, collision, or sinking. Consequently, Mr. Rich has (4) uncertainty (worry) about (5) financial loss (decrease in value) in the form of a repair bill for damage to the ship.

MEASUREMENT OF RISKS

In some cases, the probability of a loss can be measured, often precisely. In these cases, we can refer to the chance of loss, or the probability of loss, rather than merely to the possibility of loss. For example, if you enter a wager that, on the first draw from a fair deck of playing cards, you will not draw the ace of clubs, you know that the probability or chance of loss is one in 52.

In other cases, it is not possible to measure the probability of a loss. This is particularly true of unique or highly unusual risks. Consider the case of a healthy 42-year-old male client. Is it possible that he will die this year? Of course. Can we measure the probability? No. Although we may learn from statistical studies that the probability of death within one year for a 42-year-old male is, say, 1.8 in 1,000, that is no help in measuring this particular client's possibility of dying. He is one person, not a group of statistical persons. Therefore, either he will die or he won't die in the coming year, but certainly 1.8 one-thousandths of him will not die in the coming year. Statistical probabilities cannot be directly applied in this case.

In what ways can some risks be measured? Basically, there are two ways: through *deductive* reasoning, sometimes called *a priori* reasoning, and through *inductive* reasoning, which is reasoning based on statistical analysis.

Measurement of Risks

- Deductive (a priori) reasoning: risk is measured by physical examination before any losses occur.
- Inductive reasoning: risk is measured by statistical analysis of past loss experience.

In the a priori approach to risk measurement, we can physically examine in advance all the possible outcomes associated with a risk and calculate the chance of loss. For example, we can examine a fresh and shuffled deck of playing cards and note that it contains 52 different cards, of which only one is the ace of clubs. We can thus conclude that, in the absence of cheating, the probability of selecting the ace of clubs on the first draw from the deck is one in 52. Similarly, we can measure the odds of heads being the result in a coin flip, the odds of rolling a seven with a pair of dice, or the odds of losing in a "game" of Russian roulette.

It is important to remember that, in a small number of trials, the actual results may differ from the underlying probability. For example, 10 flips of a coin may produce seven heads and three tails. As the number of trials increases, however, the actual results will gradually come closer to the underlying 50-50 probability.

Of course, in the insurance business the probabilities of loss cannot be derived a priori, or deductively. For example, it would be fallacious to conclude that, because a 42-year-old male client will either die or not die in the coming year, the probability of death is 50 percent.

Insurers measure risk through inductive reasoning based on statistical analysis. To illustrate, assume that an insurance company observes the loss experience on 10,000 single-family brick homes in a particular city for one year. Assume that nine of these homes experience a fire during that period. The insurer could then conclude, at least tentatively, that the probability of fire loss for single-family brick homes in that city during a one-year period is nine per 10,000, or .9 per 1,000 homes. The insurer could then develop a premium for fire insurance based on, among other things, that probability of loss.[1] However, as with the coin-flipping example, in order for the insurer to measure the odds accurately and to achieve the expected results, certain practices must be observed. The group under analysis must have both mass and homogeneity.

Mass

First, the statistical group that is observed for purposes of measuring the probability must have *mass*—that is, the sample must be large enough to allow the true underlying probability to emerge. As with coin flipping, if there are only a few trials, we will not be able to discern the true probability. The *law of large numbers*, expressed simply, states that as the size of the sample or insured population (such as houses vulnerable to fire loss) increases, the actual loss experience will more and more closely approximate the true underlying probability. This means not only that the insurer's statistical group must be large enough to produce reliable results, but also that the group actually insured must be large enough to produce results that are consistent with the underlying probability.

law of large
numbers

Homogeneity

Second, the statistical group that is observed for purposes of measuring the probability must have *homogeneity*—that is, it must include exposure units that have similar characteristics in order for the true underlying probability to emerge. Note that the probability of .9 fire losses per 1,000 homes referred to earlier emerged from a fairly homogeneous group of exposure units: single-family brick homes in a particular city. A different probability would have emerged if apartment buildings, motels, frame-constructed homes, and homes in rural locations had been included.

Not only must the statistical group have homogeneity, but the group actually insured also must have homogeneous characteristics. Moreover, the characteristics of the homogeneous group actually insured must be similar to those of the homogeneous statistical group; otherwise, actual loss experience may depart substantially from expected experience. To take an extreme case, the loss probability derived from a statistical study of single-family brick homes in a particular city is unlikely to be the same as the loss probability for a homogeneous group of oil refineries in Texas.

CLASSIFICATIONS OF RISKS

There are several ways to classify risks. At least five of these classifications are all-inclusive and overlapping in the sense that any single risk fits into all five classifications. These classifications are as follows:

- financial versus nonfinancial
- particular versus fundamental
- static versus dynamic
- pure versus speculative
- insurable versus uninsurable

While some mention is made of ways to manage uninsurable risks, the overwhelming emphasis of this book is on insurance and therefore insurable risks. For the most part, these risks are financial, particular, static, and pure. Social insurance programs, which provide protection against fundamental risks, are also mentioned in this book.

Financial versus Nonfinancial Risks

financial risk

Risks can be *financial risks* in the sense that they involve financial loss, or they can be nonfinancial. Clearly, the possibility that a client may be faced with mountainous medical bills and lost earnings following a severe stroke is a financial risk. However, there may also be various *nonfinancial risks* which involve losses associated with a severe stroke: pain and suffering for the stroke victim, paralysis, loss of memory, loss of consortium for the victim and his or her spouse, worry and distress on the part of the stroke victim's loved ones, and so on.

nonfinancial risk

Insurance is primarily designed to treat financial risks through the payment of money as compensation in some way for monetary loss. However, insurance also frequently "compensates" for nonmonetary loss. For example, some policies cover an insured's responsibility arising out of a jury award of monetary damages to someone else for libel or invasion of privacy, even when the aggrieved party incurred no financial loss. From the insured's standpoint, the insurance policy is covering financial risk that arises out of legal liability. However, the aggrieved party is being compensated because a nonfinancial risk occurred.

Particular versus Fundamental Risks

particular risk

Risks can also be classified as particular or fundamental. *Particular risks* are loss possibilities that affect only individuals or small groups of individuals at the same time, rather than a large segment of society. Losses from events such as embezzlement, disability, lightning, and retirement are examples that fall into the category of particular risks.

fundamental risk

Fundamental risks, in contrast, are loss possibilities that can affect large segments of a society at the same time. Examples include possibilities of widespread unemployment in an economic downturn, lost purchasing power due to runaway inflation, and massive destruction due to a nuclear accident.

Dealing with particular risks is generally thought to be the responsibility of the individuals who are exposed to them. However, some social insurance programs also deal with particular risks. Fundamental risks, on the other hand, are not the fault of any specific individual, and dealing with them is generally thought to be the responsibility of society as a whole through government action.

Static versus Dynamic Risks

static risk

Another way in which risks may be categorized is to distinguish between static risks and dynamic risks. *Static risks* involve losses that would take place even in the absence of changes in society or the economy. Examples are losses arising from such events as the death of a family breadwinner or a court assessment of damages against a business that sold a defective product.

Static risks generally do not benefit society over the long run. Because static risks are usually fairly predictable, they are more suited to treatment by insurance and other risk management techniques than are dynamic risks.

dynamic risk

Dynamic risks are possibilities of loss resulting from changes in society or in the economy. For example, changes in consumer tastes can cause losses to some businesses, or changes in technology can cause losses to some individuals. Dynamic risks are not highly predictable, but they often benefit society over the long run as economic resources are reallocated to meet the new circumstances.

Pure versus Speculative Risks

Risks can be pure or speculative. Pure risks involve only the chance of loss or no loss, whereas speculative risks involve the chance of loss, no loss, or gain.

pure risk

Pure risks are "pure" in the sense that they do not mix both profits and losses. Insurance is concerned mainly with the economic problems created by pure risks. Risk aversion applies to pure risks, in which the prospect of loss only is the cause of concern. An example of a pure risk is that found in the ownership of property. In regard to a peril such as a windstorm, the owner may either suffer a loss or not suffer a loss. There cannot be a gain from having the loss as long as it is assumed that an insurance payment is not for more than the actual loss. On the other hand, risk seeking—for example, by businesspersons whose purpose is the realization of gain if the business venture is successful—applies to

speculative risk

speculative risks.

Pure vs. Speculative Risks

- Pure—Possibility of loss or no loss
- Speculative—Possibility of loss, no loss/gain, or gain

---

hedging

Because speculative risks involve an element of both profit and loss, they may sometimes be nullified by a process known as *hedging*. Hedging is a procedure by which two compensating or offsetting transactions are used to ensure at least "breaking even."

Example: Sam Farmer has a crop of corn that he will harvest and sell at the end of the season. He is concerned that the price of corn will decline and he will have difficulty recovering his cost of production. If his cost of production was $100, and at the time of harvest the market price if $140, he will have a $40 profit. If the market price at the time of harvest is $60, he will have a $40 loss. He currently has a *speculative* or *unhedged* position, where he has unlimited upside potential if the market price increases, but he also can lose up to his full investment if the market price declines.

He might hedge his position by selling a contract now that is binding on both sides, guaranteeing a sale price of $120. At the time of harvest, regardless of the market price, he must sell at the contract price of $120 and realize a $20 profit. Thus in a hedged position, both the upside potential and the downside loss are limited.

The hedging process is not always available because it depends on the existence of an active futures market. The futures market is well developed for some goods and financial instruments within certain time limits, but it does not exist for many others.

Subcontracting is another method of avoiding speculative risks. In subcontracting, for example, a general contractor obtains contracts at fixed prices for parts of the total job to be completed in the future.

gambling

Gambling, which is a special type of speculation, shares many of the attributes of insurance. Perhaps this is the reason so many uninformed persons think of insurance as gambling and sometimes even feel that they have "lost the bet" if they fail to have a loss equal to the cost of insurance. The distinction is not in the method of operation, which may appear similar, but in the fact that insurance is concerned with an existing risk. Risk as an existing condition is what removes insurance from the category of gambling. Insurance does not create risk, but it transfers and reduces a risk that already exists. Contrast this to a bet: No risk exists before, but one is created at the time of the gambling transaction, thereby putting values in jeopardy that were not in jeopardy before the bet.

Personal, Property, and Liability Risks

personal risk

The pure risks confronting individuals and businesses are ordinarily divided into three categories. The first of these categories of risks is ordinarily termed *personal risks* and is concerned with death, injury, illness, old age, and unemployment.

property risk

The second category of risks arises from the destruction or loss of property and is referred to as *property risks.* Direct losses from fire, lightning, windstorm, flood, and other forces of nature, and from man-made perils like vandalism, theft, and collision, offer a constant threat of loss to real estate, as well as to all kinds of personal property. Indirect losses also may occur, including the loss of profits, rents, or favorable leases.

liability risk

Finally, *liability risks* involve the operation of the law of liability. An individual may be legally liable for an injury to another—for instance, through an automobile accident where the driver is negligent and injures a pedestrian. Liability risks are termed "third-party" risks because, when insurance is used to shift the burden of responsibility, the insurer and the policyowner have agreed that a third party, the injured person, will be paid for injuries for which an insured is legally liable. The liability risk mainly includes both bodily injury and property damage and also includes various other types of risks. For example, the potential responsibility to pay personal injury damages for such offenses as libel, slander, trespass, invasion of privacy, or wrongful eviction is also a liability risk.

Insurable versus Uninsurable Risks

insurable risk

Not all risks are insurable. In order to be considered an *insurable risk*, a risk must substantially meet the five requirements outlined below:

- The amount of the loss must be important.
- The loss must be accidental in nature.
- Future losses must be calculable.
- The loss must be definite.
- The risk cannot be associated with an excessively catastrophic loss.

Many insured risks do not meet each of the requirements perfectly, but when considered as a whole, they must meet the requisites to the satisfaction of an insurer.

Importance

In the case of risks that involve a threat of no great consequence, the cost of handling the business would make the rate prohibitive. The rate would be prohibitive because the insurer's expense of selling and administering the insurance would be high relative to the small potential loss. For example, an inexpensive pen may be lost or eyeglasses may be broken. To make a risk insurable, the amount of future loss payments must be of such importance as to make them, rather than the insurer's expenses, the principal component in the premium charged.

Accidental Nature

Insurable risks normally must also be accidental in nature. Insurance is intended to cover fortuitous or unexpected losses. The loss need be accidental only from the insured's standpoint. The loss could, for example, be intentionally caused by someone else such as a thief or a vandal. Intentional losses caused by the insured are usually uninsurable because they cannot be reasonably predicted by the insurer, and payment for them would violate public policy by encouraging such actions as fraud or arson. Other losses are so common as to be expected rather than unexpected. Wear and tear and depreciation are examples of expected losses that normally are not insurable.

Calculability

A third requisite of an insurable risk is that the chance, size, and variability of future losses should be reasonably calculable. Losses may be unpredictable for any one individual, but an insurer should be able to obtain reasonable projections of future losses if it has a sufficiently large number of homogeneous (similar) loss exposures.

Insurers occasionally cover isolated loss exposures for which there is no previous experience. For example, aviation insurers must provide insurance that will keep pace with the rapid advances in the industry. The advent of rocket-propelled aircraft created a need for large amounts of insurance in a field where statistical data once were entirely lacking. Most insurance is written, however, to cover risks where losses may reasonably be expected and where mathematical treatment or judgment based on experience permits a sufficiently exact estimate of losses to project the aggregate probable cost. When experience extends over a period of years and the number of exposure units is great enough, a premium can be computed that will reasonably ensure a sum sufficient to pay losses, compensate the insurer, and provide stability and permanence in the business. When new insurance forms are instituted, such as long-term care insurance, it becomes necessary to make rates that are dependent on "underwriting judgment." In some instances this is nothing more than an approximation or guess that is adjusted with the accumulation of experience.

The need for large numbers applies not only to the total business an insurer accepts but also to each class of business. In addition, the exposures must be independent of one another so that reasonable estimates of loss can be made.

Definiteness of Loss

Losses should be definite; otherwise estimates of possible loss are difficult. Many insurance contract provisions have the objective of making the determination and measurement of insured losses as clear and definite as possible. The contract must clarify the perils as well as the losses. Whether or not the loss actually occurred and, if so, when, where, and why it occurred, as well as how many dollars of loss were involved, all usually must be discernible. A loss due to lightning meets the definiteness criterion rather well, whereas a loss due to sickness may not meet it as well.

Example:	Ted is a salesman of beachfront homes in Destin, Florida. His income is entirely in the form of commissions, almost all of which are earned during the spring and fall months. In December, Ted becomes ill with a case of the flu and is unable to work for 7 weeks. Ted's loss is not very definite. Was he really ill or just taking a vacation from work? Was he really laid up for the full 7 weeks? How much income would he have earned during the period of his illness?

No Excessively Catastrophic Loss

Ordinarily, no excessive catastrophic possibility of loss should be associated with an insurable risk. Accepting a few such loss possibilities together with smaller ones would make accurate predictions of loss impossible and could destroy an insurer's financial stability. A geographic concentration of many small loss possibilities can also produce a catastrophic potential for an insurer. Today many losses are called catastrophic if they exceed $5 million, but for most insurers losses are not excessively catastrophic unless many millions of dollars are involved. The size of loss deemed catastrophic depends on the financial resources available to the insurer. Flood and unemployment are examples of perils that can produce excessive catastrophic losses.

Summary

Note that the requirements for an insurable risk are not absolute. Insurability is best described as a relative matter in which the insurable quality of the risk is determined by appraisal of all the requirements together. The size and ability of the insurer are also important. Many common kinds of insurance do not meet each of the requirements perfectly. Consider, for example, the following: Is a theft loss definite (that is, was the item really stolen, or just lost)? Are all drivers similar in regard to the risk of automobile accidents? Obviously not, although they may be relatively similar within age, type of car, and other classifications. Is a fire caused by carelessness always accidental? Aren't windstorms such as hurricanes and tornadoes catastrophic in nature?

Careful analysis in applying each of the requirements for an insurable risk to a particular peril shows that few, if any, are perfect insurable risks. Most are only relatively good ones, and some are fine examples of bad ones. Many insurance contract and insurer underwriting restrictions deal with this problem, trying to improve the insurability of a risk by such methods as limitations on the amount of coverage and locations, prohibited types of activities, specific contract definitions, deductibles, and reinsurance. What is insurable may change over time and with the use of such limitations. Long-term care, for example, was considered uninsurable for many years, but it is now commonly written.

DIFFERENT REACTIONS TO RISK

Risk is sometimes desirable and at other times undesirable. Linus, in the famous *Peanuts* comic strip, enters the risky world reluctantly. He drags his security blanket around continuously in order to have the comfort of familiarity to buffer the unknown. His friend Charlie Brown deals with unpredictable risk as he attempts to kick off the new football season because he never knows whether Lucy will pull the ball away from him. This example illustrates the undesirable features of risk: unpredictability or not knowing, insecurity, and some resulting discomfort.

However, risk is desirable to those who believe "nothing ventured, nothing gained." Entrepreneurs invest time, effort, and money for the uncertain profits that may result. Businesspersons conduct their operations with the hope of profit and the threat of loss in mind. The skydiver, the astronaut, and the drag racer also are risk takers. Sir Walter Scott valued risk taking too when he said, "One hour of life . . . filled with noble risks, is worth whole years of paltry decorum."[2]

The influence of risk is apparent in the many attitudes toward it, varying from negative to positive reactions. It may result in substantial losses, worry, and inefficiency. It can also lead to great reward and satisfaction.

risk-tolerance level

The ways in which different people react to risks depend on what psychologists call their *risk-tolerance level*. Risk tolerance is extremely difficult to measure accurately, but it clearly differs widely from person to person, situation to situation, and risk to risk. It is critically important that the financial planner, including the insurance planner, be cognizant of the risk-tolerance level of each client in order to tailor an appropriate plan to fit each client.

To cite just a few of the findings of leading behavioral psychologists on the subject of risk tolerance of individuals:

- Most people are more risk averse than they are risk tolerant.
- Risk taking in physical or social activities (for example, race car driving or marital infidelity) is not correlated with financial risk taking.
- The way in which questions about a risk are worded or posed to a person can influence the person's attitude toward that risk.
- Emotions can severely limit a person's ability to make rational decisions about a risk.
- People tend to overestimate low-probability risks (for example, the risk of having one's child kidnapped) and to underestimate higher-probability risks (for example, disability).
- People tend to be risk averse if the major effect of a possible loss will fall on them or their loved ones, rather than mainly on strangers.
- Most people have a greater fear about risks with which they are unfamiliar (for example, skydiving) than about risks with which they are familiar (for example, driving on an interstate highway).

COSTS OF PURE RISKS

Because pure risks generally produce either losses or no losses, they represent a cost to society with little or no offsetting benefit. Actual losses may be serious, crippling a business or causing an individual or family great financial hardship. Direct physical loss, such as fire damage, results in several billion dollars of property loss each year in the United States. Indirect loss is also considerable such as lost profits following a direct loss. Billions of dollars are lost, too, because of the loss of human life values due to such perils as death and disability. It is no wonder that most people prefer to do something about pure risks, rather than merely to accept them.

In addition to the actual losses that take place, other undesirable results stem from pure risks. Even if no losses ever occur as anticipated, at least three factors add to the costs of risks: (1) fear and worry, (2) less-than-optimum use of resources, and (3) expenses of treating risks.

Fear and worry are very costly. The time spent thinking about real or imagined chances of loss is expensive. The opportunity cost of worry, time, and effort is probably staggering when we consider the many other things that we

---

Costs of Pure Risks

- Actual losses that occur
- Worry and fear about possible losses
- Inadequate preparation due to overestimation or underestimation of the likelihood of losses
- Costs of treating the risks

could do if there were no fear of loss. "If we only could work as hard as we worry" expresses the cost of lost peace of mind.

In addition, exposure to loss creates adverse effects on the behavior of individuals, organizations, and societies. Uncertainty arises from many situations where estimates of the probability of loss are necessary. Most people will not predict the chance of loss correctly. Some will be pessimistic and overestimate; others will be optimistic and underestimate. The result is either wasteful preparation for losses that are not as likely as expected or lack of preparation for unexpected losses that may have serious financial consequences.

Investments are frequently influenced by the exposures to loss with which they are associated. Sometimes activities or investments are completely avoided because the exposure to loss is high, in spite of excellent earnings potential. The amount of money "put away for a rainy day" may be put in very safe liquid investments to be readily available if and when it does rain, or some other peril causes loss. Without such risk and uncertainty, the money could be invested in a much more productive capacity, with potential for greater return. Returns in relation to true loss exposures are often less than optimum, and these reduced earnings are an additional cost of risk.

Because of loss exposures, there is also a tendency to concentrate planning on the near future rather than on the significant benefits of long-range planning. The cost of risk increases to the extent that exposures to loss cause this error in planning.

The third type of cost that society experiences because of the presence of pure risks is the cost of managing pure risks. There are numerous techniques available for treating pure risks. For example, a sprinkler system can be installed in a factory to minimize the size of a loss if a fire occurs. An alarm system can be installed in a jewelry store to reduce the likelihood of a burglary loss. An annual physical examination can help in the early detection of breast cancer. Insurance can be purchased to cover the possible legal liability for negligently driving an automobile. However, all of these techniques cost money, and these expenditures thus represent an added burden for society because pure risks are present.

INSURANCE AS A TECHNIQUE FOR TREATING PURE RISKS

In this section, we will examine the subject of insurance as a means of treating pure risks. For the time being, consideration is given only to what insurance is, the benefits it provides to society, the costs it entails for society, and the major categories of insurance.

We can develop a definition of insurance from several viewpoints: economic, legal, business, social, or mathematical. Regardless of the viewpoint, a full interpretation of insurance should include both a statement of its objective and a description of the technique by which the purpose is achieved.

There is no one brief definition that does justice to the many important viewpoints of insurance. Insurance may be an economic system for reducing financial risk through a transfer and combination (pooling) of losses, a legal method of transferring risk in a contract of indemnity, a business institution that provides many jobs in a free enterprise economy, a social device in which the losses of few are paid by many, or an actuarial system of applied mathematics. Insurance is all of these and more, depending on how we view its major purposes, methods, and results. Table 1-1 summarizes five viewpoints from which insurance can be defined.

TABLE 1-1
Viewpoints for Defining Insurance

Viewpoint	Objective	Technique
Economic	Reduction of risk	Transfer and combination
Legal	Transfer of risk	Payment of a premium by policyowner to insurer in a contract of indemnity
Business	Sharing of risk	Transfer from individuals and businesses to a financial institution specializing in risk
Social	Collective bearing of losses	Contributions by all members of a group to pay losses suffered by some group members
Mathematical	Prediction and distribution of losses	Actuarial estimates based on principles of probability

insurance

Probably the most widely used definition of insurance is the economic one. In this sense, *insurance* is a method that reduces financial risks when policyowners transfer risk to the insurer, who combines the potential losses. However, insurers sometimes write coverage for unique situations where there can be no combination of losses of similar policyowners. In addition, self-insurance often involves combination to accurately predict losses, but there is no transfer of risk to another party. Usually, however, the economic concept of insurance involves both transfer and combination.

From a legal standpoint, an insurance contract or policy is used to transfer financial risk for a premium (price) from one party known as the *insured* or *policyowner* to another party known as the *insurer*. By virtue of a legally binding contract, the possibility of an unknown large financial loss is exchanged for a comparatively small certain payment. This contract is not a guarantee against a loss occurring, but a method of ensuring that repayment, or indemnity, will be received for a loss that does occur as the result of risk.

Why is it important whether a plan is determined legally to be insurance? The legal aspect is significant because many types of regulation and taxation apply specifically to insurance. Product warranties, for example, are commonplace for new homes, automobiles, tires, and appliances. Warranties are not generally recognized by law as insurance and the companies offering the warranties need not organize an insurance company, hold reserves, or pay state insurance premium taxes. Variable annuity contracts, which are not defined by the courts as exclusively insurance contracts, are subject both to state insurance laws and to the federal securities legislation of the Securities and Exchange Commission. These legal decisions, and others in regard to contracts such as employee benefit plans and hospital and medical benefit plans, have become very important in insurance.

As a business institution, insurance has been defined as a technique that enables large numbers of people to transfer financial risks to a financial institution that specializes in the treatment of risks. Insurance can also be regarded as an important part of the financial world, where it serves as a basis for credit and a mechanism for savings and investments. Insurance is a major part of the free enterprise economy.

An adequate social definition giving recognition both to the objective of insurance and to the means for achieving it has been stated: "We should define insurance, then, as that social device for making accumulations to meet uncertain losses of capital which is carried out through the transfer of the risks of many individuals to one person or to a group of persons. Wherever there is accumulation for uncertain losses or wherever there is a transfer of risk, there is one element of insurance; only where these are joined with the combination of risks in a group is the insurance complete."[3]

With insurance, persons who are exposed to loss agree to contribute to indemnify or repay members of the group who suffer loss. All members contribute to a common fund, and payments are made out of this fund to those with a loss. Thus for the payment of a definite sum, the insurance premium, the financial consequences of a $250,000 total fire loss to a homeowner are eliminated by exchanging an uncertain large loss for a certain small cost. The sum total of these individual transactions makes insurance a social method by which those having losses are compensated by the rest of the group.

In the strictest interpretation of the term insurance, contributions to a fund are not essential. Private groups may rely entirely on assessments after losses to indemnify the sufferers, and in these instances no funds may be accumulated in advance. In the case of government functioning as the insurer, a fund may be accumulated, or the beneficiaries may depend for their insurance payments on the taxing power of the government.

In a mathematical sense, insurance is the application of certain actuarial principles, such as laws of probability and statistical techniques, in order to achieve predictable results.

BENEFITS AND COSTS OF INSURANCE

In a society without insurance, would banks loan money on homes or businesses if they were uncertain as to whether the collateral value could be lost due to fire, windstorm, or other perils? Would finance companies approve installment loans for automobiles or other household goods? Would anyone want to own an automobile if liability for losses caused to others could not be insured? Would anyone want to own a home that could be destroyed in a few hours without any way to recover the loss? Would workers choose hazardous but important occupations if they were uncertain whether employers would pay for work injuries? How would a young family man or woman provide an income for dependent children without life insurance? How would a person provide for payment of large medical bills? The business of insurance provides the protection factor regarded as essential throughout the economic and business environment.

Benefits of Insurance

We have already presented some examples of the wide scope and benefits of insurance. A summary of the most important benefits of insurance includes all the concepts discussed in the following paragraphs.

Encourages Peace of Mind

Almost everyone has a basic desire for some security or peace of mind. To the extent that insurance provides certainty or predictability, it improves the efficiency of individual or business decisions by reducing anxieties. This is a psychological factor that is difficult to measure in terms of specific benefits, but is nonetheless important in everyday life, regardless of whether losses actually occur.

Pays Losses

Insurance often supplies the financial resources that permit a family or organization to continue despite serious losses. The death or disability of a breadwinner can bring financial disaster to a family. With family income stopped, the spouse and/or children may have to give up their home and accept undesirable alternatives such as foster homes, living with relatives, or relief payments. A fire or a liability suit can cause the failure of an organization. These perils can be met through insurance, which provides indemnification or repayment at the time of need in order to keep the family or business intact. Insurers pay billions of dollars in benefits every year.

Increases Marginal Utility of Assets

From an economic standpoint, insurance serves as an intermediary between those who can give up a minor amount of capital or income (that is, the cost of insurance) and those who need the immediate use of large sums of money to meet losses they have suffered. Marginal utility refers to the use value of the last (marginal) unit. Basically, insurance takes the least useful "last" dollars of low marginal utility from all policyowners and repays the important "first" dollars of high marginal utility to the unfortunate persons who have suffered severe losses.[4]

Provides a Basis for Credit

Several kinds of insurance are invaluable as the foundation for credit transactions. Personal and business bank loans of many kinds use life insurance, either face values or cash values, to guarantee that the loan will be repaid despite contingencies such as the death or disability of the borrower. Fire insurance is invariably required by mortgagees who loan money with real or personal property as collateral. Creditors must know that their collateral will not disappear in a fire, windstorm, or other loss, and their security is accomplished by requiring debtors to purchase appropriate amounts of insurance for their homes or automobiles.

Stimulates Saving

Many kinds of insurance are important because they encourage thrift. An insurance premium, although small in relation to the possible loss it protects against, is basically a prepayment of a potential loss. All the payments are gathered together into a fund from which those few who do suffer losses are paid. In essence, the plan of insurance encourages all to save so that unfortunates can be repaid for their losses. In addition, life insurance has special advantages in stimulating savings. The long-term contracts, often over an insured's entire lifetime, build substantial loan, emergency, or retirement values. Policyowners treat their regular premium payments as an obligation to their families or beneficiaries, and greater savings result than in other well-intentioned but less regular savings programs.

Provides Investment Capital

The savings that insurers hold as assets provide a gigantic source of capital for the economy. Life insurers provide hundreds of billions of dollars of investable funds to governments and business organizations. A smaller amount, but very significant nonetheless, is invested by property and liability insurers.

Offers Advantages of Specialization

Certain efficiencies result when an organization specializes in risk bearing. When a business or organization transfers its financial risks to an insurer it says in effect: "Here, you take care of those bothersome, unpredictable risks, and we'll pay attention to the primary goals of our organization." The productive aspect of insurance thus emerges as an incentive to organizations or individuals, relieving them of accidental losses so that they can direct more effort, personnel, and capital toward the work for which they are best suited. For example, a department store is normally better off to shift its pure financial risks to an insurer and then to concentrate its efforts on greater sales or other merchandising services. Insurance also aids competition by permitting smaller organizations to transfer financial risks that they cannot safely retain themselves.

Fosters Loss Prevention

Insurance benefits society by fostering considerable effort to prevent losses. Loss prevention is a secondary goal for most kinds of insurance, but undoubtedly more loss prevention work occurs because of insurance than would occur without it. The net effect is advantageous, as lives are saved and property values preserved. Examples are fire prevention campaigns, motor vehicle safety research, education by health insurers, and elevator and boiler inspections. Also important in this work are associations such as Underwriters Laboratories Inc. and the Insurance Institute for Highway Safety.

Costs of Insurance

Insurance companies can only provide coverage when policyowners fund the insurers' costs. The costs of insurance include (1) operating costs, (2) profits, (3) opportunity costs, (4) possible increased losses, and (5) adverse selection. Policyowners fund costs by paying premiums.

Operating Costs

Insurers cannot in the long run pay out more dollars than they take in. Of the dollars paid out, not all are paid to the policyowners or beneficiaries of the insurance contracts. In fact, operating expenses that enable insurers to do business are approximately one-fourth of each dollar that insurers take in. The proportion varies by type of insurance. Operating expenses include agents' commissions, home office and field administrative expenses, loss adjustment expenses, and taxes. The costs of operating insurers, their agency systems, and other services must be balanced against the benefits of insurance enumerated earlier.

Profits

Insurers must earn profits to increase their surplus position and reward investors. The amounts are small, perhaps less than 5 percent on average, in relation to the total premium dollar. Profits are necessary, however, because otherwise no capital would be attracted to insurers in order for them to continue operating.

Opportunity Costs

From an economic viewpoint, the capital, personnel, and materials insurers require could be used elsewhere if they were not devoted to the insurance business. These alternative uses, or opportunities, could make other productive contributions to the economy and society. Therefore, the use of funds by insurers represents opportunity costs for foregone opportunities, in order to have insurance institutions. These opportunity costs must be considered one of the potential costs of insurance.

Increased Losses

Insurance occasionally has some direct adverse societal effects. Increased losses may sometimes result because insurance can stimulate moral hazards. Two examples are the encouragement of fraud to collect losses caused intentionally by insureds and the exaggeration of claims beyond actual losses. The greater carelessness that occurs when people feel completely insured is another cost of insurance. These effects tend to be relatively minor and rare; but some, such as fires caused by arson, are a major and growing problem. Although the costs are difficult to measure precisely, constant effort to control these possible costs is necessary.

Adverse Selection

adverse selection

Adverse selection is the tendency for those who know they are highly vulnerable to loss from specific pure risks to be most inclined to acquire and retain insurance to cover that loss. For example, a person who has just been diagnosed as a diabetic is likely to be highly desirous of obtaining and/or retaining medical expense insurance. A family with a 16-year-old son who has just acquired a driver's license will probably want full-coverage automobile insurance on the car. And a family living in southern California will be especially interested in obtaining earthquake coverage.

Occasionally, adverse selection is reflected in dishonesty on an insurance applicant's part—for example, false statements in the application for insurance. More often, adverse selection simply reflects a rational emphasis on the applicant's own self-interest. In any case, however, adverse selection produces poorer loss experience among those who are insured than among those who are not insured.

MAJOR CATEGORIES OF INSURANCE

Many types of insurance are available to households and organizations for the treatment of their pure risks. Several overlapping ways of grouping these types are as follows:

- life and health versus property and liability
- personal versus business
- private versus government
- individual versus group

Each of these groupings is described below.

Life and Health versus Property and Liability

The life and health category of insurance includes the various types of insurance dealing with losses arising out of death, medical care costs, disability, and old age. Examples in this category are life insurance, medical expense insurance, disability income insurance, and long-term care insurance.

The property and liability category of insurance includes those coverages that provide reimbursement for direct and indirect losses to property. It also includes those types of insurance that cover the possibility of being held legally responsible for damages to someone else. Examples in the property and liability category include automobile insurance, aviation insurance, marine insurance, and surety bonds.

Personal versus Business

Personal insurance is the category of insurance used by individuals and families. Examples in this category are homeowners insurance, personal automobile insurance, life insurance, and disability income insurance.

Business insurance is the category of insurance used by businesses and other organizations. Examples include key employee life insurance, commercial liability insurance, business overhead expense insurance, workers' compensation and employer's liability insurance, commercial automobile insurance, commercial property insurance, business income insurance, and disability income insurance to fund a disability buy-sell agreement.

Private versus Government

Private insurance includes all forms of insurance that are provided by privately owned insurers. Government insurance consists of various types of insurance programs operated by the state or federal governments. Government insurance programs can be divided into social insurance programs such as Medicare and other government insurance programs such as flood insurance and crop insurance. However, the distinction between social insurance programs and other government insurance programs is not always clear-cut.

social insurance

Social insurance consists of various government programs in which the elements of the insurance technique are present. These programs are designed to help solve the major social problems that affect a large portion of society. Social insurance programs are of several types: Social Security, Medicare, unemployment insurance, temporary disability insurance, and workers' compensation insurance. These major insurance programs are described in chapter 7.

Even though there are variations in social insurance programs, and exceptions to the rule always exist, social insurance programs tend to have the following distinguishing characteristics:

- compulsory employment-related coverage
- partial or total employer financing
- benefits prescribed by law
- benefits as a right
- emphasis on social adequacy

Compulsory Employment-Related Coverage

Most social insurance programs are compulsory and require that the persons covered be attached—either presently or by past service—to the labor force. If a social insurance program is to meet a social need through the redistribution of income, it must have widespread participation.

Partial or Total Employer Financing

While significant variations exist in social insurance programs, most require that the cost of the program be borne fully or at least partially by the employers of the covered persons. The remaining cost of most social insurance programs is paid primarily by the persons covered under the programs. With the exception of Medicare and certain unemployment benefits, the general revenues of the federal government and state governments finance only a small portion of social insurance benefits.

Benefits Prescribed by Law

Although benefit amounts and the eligibility requirements for social insurance benefits are prescribed by law, benefits are not necessarily uniform for everyone. Benefits may vary by such factors as wage level, length of covered employment, or family status. However, these factors are incorporated into the benefit formulas specified by law, and covered persons are cannot increase or decrease their prescribed level of benefits.

Benefits as a Right

Social insurance benefits are paid as a right under the presumption of need. This feature distinguishes social insurance programs from public assistance or welfare programs under which applicants, in order to qualify for benefits, must meet a needs test by demonstrating that their income or assets are below some specified level.

Emphasis on Social Adequacy

social adequacy

Benefits under social insurance programs are based more on social adequacy than on individual equity. Under the principle of *social adequacy*, benefits are designed to provide a minimum floor of income to all beneficiaries under the program, regardless of their economic status. Above this floor of benefits, persons are expected to provide additional resources from their own savings, employment, or private insurance programs. An emphasis on social adequacy also results in disproportionately large benefits in relation to contributions for some groups of beneficiaries. For some programs, high-income persons, single persons, small families, and the young are subsidizing low-income persons, large families, and the retired.

individual equity

If social insurance programs were based solely on *individual equity*, benefits would be actuarially related to contributions, as they are under private insurance programs. While this degree of individual equity does not exist, there is some relationship between benefits and income levels, and therefore contributions. Within certain maximum and minimum amounts, benefits are a function of a person's covered earnings under social insurance programs. The main emphasis, however, is on social adequacy.

Individual versus Group

Private insurance can be written on either a group or individual basis, and the likelihood of the method used varies by type of protection. For example, most automobile and homeowners insurance is individual insurance, whereas most medical expense insurance is group insurance provided through an employer. More persons have life insurance through group plans than under individual policies, but the premium volume and amount of coverage in force are greater for individual policies.

individual insurance

Individual insurance is usually owned by the person or entity who is the insured or who owns the insured property, but there are some cases where the policy may be owned by a third party. Examples include life and health insurance purchased by individuals on their family members and by businesses on key employees. The acceptability for coverage and the premium charged are usually determined by the characteristics of the person, entity, or property insured.

group insurance

master contract

In contrast to most individual insurance contracts, *group insurance* provides coverage to more than one person under a single contract issued to someone other than the persons insured. The contract, referred to as a *master contract*, provides benefits to a group of individuals who have a specific relationship to the policyowner. Group contracts usually cover full-time employees, and the policyowner is either their employer or a trust established to provide benefits for the employees. However, the policyowner can also be a union, association, fraternal group, or other organization.

Individual vs. Group Coverage

Individual	Group
• Mostly property and liability insurance	• Mainly life and health insurance
• Policyowner is usually the insured	• Policyowner is usually the sponsor of the group
• Only one or a few people are insured under one contract	• Many people are insured under one master contract
• Insured is usually the policyowner and receives the policy	• Insured is usually not the policyowner and receives a certificate of insurance
• Coverage begins at the inception of the policy	• Many people's coverage begins long after inception of the policy
• Individual evidence of insurability required	• Usually no individual evidence of insurability required
• Class rating often used to set rates	• Experience rating often used to set rates

certificate of insurance

Employees covered under the contract receive *certificates of insurance* as evidence of their coverage. A certificate is merely a description of the coverage provided and is not part of the master contract. In general, a certificate of insurance is not even considered to be a contract and usually contains a disclaimer to that effect. However, some courts have held the contrary to be true when the provisions of the certificate or even of the explanatory booklet of a group insurance plan vary materially from the master contract.

In individual insurance, the coverage of the insured normally begins with the inception of the insurance contract and ceases with its termination. However, in group insurance, individual members of the group may become eligible for coverage long after the inception of the group contract, or they may lose their eligibility status long before the contract terminates.

evidence of insurability

For group insurance, individual members of the group are usually not required to show *evidence of insurability* when initially eligible for coverage. Evidence of insurability is the documentation or other evidence submitted to the insurance company regarding the physical condition, financial condition, or other attributes of the applicant for insurance coverage. This evidence will be taken into account when the insurer determines whether to accept the risk.

This is not to say that group insurers neglect to underwrite group members, but rather that they focused on the characteristics of the group (such as its prior claims experience, size, composition, geographic location, and stability) instead of the insurability of individual members of the group. As with individual insurance, the underwriter must appraise the risk, decide on the conditions of the group's acceptability, and establish a rating basis. Underwriting is discussed in further detail in chapter 4.

A final distinguishing characteristic of group insurance is the use of experience rating. If a group is sufficiently large, the actual experience of that particular group will be a factor in determining the premium the policyowner will be charged.

OTHER INSURANCE TERMINOLOGY

Insurance is a large and diverse business, and its discussion requires the use of many terms that have specific insurance meanings. Some terms such as risk, hazard, peril, and loss exposure are defined earlier in this chapter. However, at this point we should mention a few additional terms that are used throughout this book.

applicant
policyowner

An *applicant* is a person or organization that applies for insurance coverage. If an insurance contract comes into effect, the applicant becomes a *policyowner* or policyholder. Traditionally, the common insurance usage was policyholder. However, over time and for many types of insurance, the term policyowner has become increasingly common, and, for the sake of consistency, this is the term the authors of this book have decided to use.

insured

An *insured* under a policy can be, but is not necessarily, the policyowner. In individual life insurance, for example, the person on whose life a policy is issued is always the insured and is often but not necessarily the policyowner. A policyowner may own a policy on the life of another person, the insured. Typically, the policyowner determines the beneficiary of the coverage for future death claims and has the rights to change, renew, or cancel the policy and the obligations to comply with policy conditions such as the payment of premiums.

In most types of individual insurance other than life insurance, the insured can best be defined as a party to whom, or on whose behalf, benefits may be payable. The policyowner (often referred to as the named insured) is usually an insured but so can many others be such as family members or employees of the policyowner.

In group insurance, the policyowner is usually a business or some other type of organization. The insureds are the persons who have coverage under the group, and, in most cases, the policyowner is not an insured. The definition of who is insured is discussed in later chapters for specific types of insurance.

line

In insurance terminology, a *line* usually means a type of insurance. Regulators are specific about what constitutes a line from a regulatory standpoint because detailed statistics must be reported by line. For example, some lines of insurance for property and liability insurance companies include homeowners, ocean marine, workers' compensation, private passenger automobile liability, and surety bonds. Lines of life and health insurance companies include ordinary life, credit life, individual annuities, and group accident and health. The functional operations of a specific insurer may or may not be broken down along these same regulatory lines, and an insurer may use the term line for nonregulatory purposes to describe its business from a functional standpoint. For example, all private passenger automobile insurance may be handled by one department and be referred to as a line, while regulators consider this insurance two lines—private passenger automobile liability and private passenger automobile physical damage. Types of insurance for individuals and businesses are often referred to as personal lines and commercial lines, respectively.

PLAN OF THIS BOOK

Chapter 2 of this book further examines pure risks, particularly the process for managing pure risks. The chapter describes various techniques for identifying these risks, as well as techniques, in addition to insurance, that can be used to treat them.

Thereafter, the focus of the book is on insurance. The insurance industry and its marketing and other functions are discussed, along with its regulation. Then the basic legal principles that underlie insurance contracts and insurance contract analysis are examined.

Chapter 7 deals with the principal social insurance programs noted earlier in this chapter. Individual life insurance and annuities for individuals, families, and businesses are the focus of chapters 8 to 11.

Health insurance—medical expense coverages, disability income insurance, and long-term care insurance—is discussed in chapters 12 to 15. Then attention is turned to several major personal property and liability coverages in chapters 16 to 19, including automobile and homeowners and concluding with a review of certain types of business property and liability coverages.

SOURCES FOR FURTHER IN-DEPTH STUDY

Many books include a bibliography of other material on the subjects covered. Unfortunately, many of these sources cover the material at a similar level and in similar detail. The authors of this book have instead decided to include a selected list of sources that go into more detail for those readers who desire further in-depth study. Each of the sources includes a phone number and/or Web site from which you can obtain ordering information.

•   •   •

- For more on the topic of client risk tolerance, Cordell, D. M., and Poole, Barbara S., *Readings in Financial Planning*, 7th ed., chapter 5 by Roszkowski, M. J., Bryn Mawr, PA: The American College, 2003. Phone 888-263-7265. Web site address www.amercoll.edu
- For a detailed discussion of group insurance, Beam, Burton T., Jr., *Group Benefits*: *Basic Concepts and Alternatives*, 9th ed., Bryn Mawr, PA: The American College, 2002. Phone 888-263-7265. Web site address www.amercoll.edu

CHAPTER REVIEW

Answers to review questions and self-test questions start on page 725.

Key Terms

risk	pure risk
loss exposure	speculative risk
direct loss	hedging
indirect (consequential) loss	gambling
uncertainty	personal risk
peril	property risk
hazard	liability risk
physical hazard	insurable risk
moral hazard	risk-tolerance level
attitudinal hazard	insurance
law of large numbers	adverse selection
financial risk	social insurance
nonfinancial risk	social adequacy
particular risk	individual equity
fundamental risk	individual insurance
static risk	group insurance
dynamic risk	master contract

certificate of insurance   policyowner
evidence of insurability   insured
applicant   line

Review Questions

1-1.   What is the difference between risk and uncertainty?

1-2.   Your client Jim owns a printing business but rents the premises where the business is conducted. What types of losses might a fire cause to Jim's business?

1-3.   Sally, a single working mother with two young children, recently learned that her stress at work is giving her high blood pressure. Sally is concerned that if she were to die, her children would no longer have her income to support them until they are grown. In this case, specify what the following factors represent for Sally:
   a.   risk
   b.   peril
   c.   hazard

1-4.   Alpha Market is applying for insurance to cover automobile exposure related to its catering service. For each of the following conditions identified in the underwriting process, indicate the type of hazard involved:
   a.   The principal driver of the delivery van is blind in one eye and has had two heart attacks recently.
   b.   The principal driver of the delivery van recently received two speeding tickets.
   c.   There have been several instances in the past where Alpha Market's management submitted inflated claims for property damage under its commercial property insurance coverage.

1-5.   Your client Janet Jones is 29 years old and works full-time to support her two small children and her husband, who was disabled in an auto accident last year. Although money is tight, you suggest that she consider the purchase of life insurance to provide support for the children and her disabled husband if she were to die. How would you respond to the following questions posed by Janet:
   a.   She first asks, "With the probability of death so small for a woman aged 29, there's very little chance that I'll die in the near future. So why do I really need to buy life insurance?"
   b.   After you respond, she asks, "If life insurance companies can use probabilities to determine the likelihood that a woman aged 29 will die, why can't I use them to determine the likelihood that I will die?"

1-6.   Distinguish between fundamental and particular risks with respect to
   a.   whom they affect
   b.   who is generally thought to be responsible for dealing with them

1-7. Give an example of how ownership of a home can provide a client with each of the following types of risk:
   a. pure risk
   b. speculative risk

1-8. Describe the types of risks with which insurance commonly deals.

1-9. Explain why insurance is not a form of gambling risk.

1-10. List the five requirements that must be met substantially in order for a risk to be considered insurable.

1-11. Explain why different people may react to risk differently.

1-12. What costs are experienced by society as a result of pure risks?

1-13. Define insurance from the following viewpoints:
   a. economic
   b. legal
   c. business
   d. social
   e. mathematical

1-14. Describe the benefits and costs of insurance.

1-15. Identify the distinguishing characteristics of social insurance programs.

1-16. Explain how group insurance differs from individual insurance.

Self-Test Questions

T F 1-1. Risk is the reason that insurance exists.

T F 1-2. Risk is the probability or chance of loss.

T F 1-3. The extra expense a client incurs by living in a hotel after a fire has damaged his home is an example of a direct loss.

T F 1-4. Because uncertainty is a state of mind, two clients facing the same risk situation can have varying degrees of uncertainty.

T F 1-5. Hazards are causes of loss such as death, fire, or legal liability.

T F 1-6. Moral hazards are evidenced by carelessness or indifference.

T F 1-7. Hazards are important in underwriting and rating applicants for insurance.

T F 1-8. An individual can use the probability of a loss to measure the risk he or she faces.

T F 1-9. If an insurer observes a large number of similar exposures in estimating the probability of loss, it is very likely that the actual loss experience for its own insureds will closely approximate the expected loss experience from its observations even though the number of its own insureds is very small.

T   F   1-10.   Because fundamental risks are not the fault of any specific individual and affect large segments of the population at the same time, they are generally thought to be the responsibility of society as a whole through government action.

T   F   1-11.   Because pure risks involve a possibility of gain as well as loss, they can be handled effectively with hedging.

T   F   1-12.   Insurance is essentially a form of gambling risk because the policyowner pays a relatively small premium to protect against a relatively large loss.

T   F   1-13.   To be insurable, a risk must substantially meet the requirements of importance, accidental nature, calculability, definiteness of loss, and no excessively catastrophic loss.

T   F   1-14.   The only cost associated with pure risk is the actual loss that takes place.

T   F   1-15.   One of the several ways in which insurance can be defined is as an economic system that reduces financial risk through a transfer and combination of losses.

T   F   1-16.   There are a variety of benefits as well as costs associated with insurance as a technique for handling risk.

T   F   1-17.   Depending on their characteristics, government insurance programs may or may not be social insurance.

T   F   1-18.   Unlike welfare programs, social insurance emphasizes individual equity rather than social adequacy.

T   F   1-19.   Employees covered under group insurance receive a certificate of insurance as evidence of their coverage.

NOTES

1. Among the other factors on which the premium would be based are the average size of the losses experienced, a margin for contingencies, a loading to cover the insurer's expenses, a margin for profit or addition to the insurer's surplus, and perhaps the investment earnings the insurer could realize from the time the premiums are collected until the losses must be paid.
2. Sir Walter Scott, *Count Robert of Paris*, chapter 25.
3. A. H. Willett, *The Economic Theory of Risk and Insurance*, Columbia University Studies in History, Economics, and Public Law, vol. 14 (New York: Columbia University Press, 1901), p. 388. See also reprinted edition published under the auspices of the S. S. Huebner Foundation for Insurance Education (Philadelphia: University of Pennsylvania Press, 1951), p. 72.
4. An exception to this statement is the use of insurance that contains deductibles, which may not pay the policyowner until after the loss has exceeded a specified minimum.

2

Managing Risks

Learning Objectives

An understanding of the material in this chapter should enable the student to

---

2-1. Describe the nature and scope of risk management.

2-2. Describe the objectives of risk management and the role of the risk manager.

2-3. Explain how insurance works.

2-4. List and describe the four steps in the risk management process.

Chapter Outline

risk management

Chapter 1 contains a description of the costs of pure risk to society. Those costs include (1) the actual losses that occur from various perils, (2) the fear and worry that people undergo because of possible losses from those perils, and (3) the less-than-optimum use of resources because of the difficulty of estimating the probability of loss. Because these costs are not accompanied by corresponding benefits, most people want to do something about the pure risks that confront them. *Risk management* is the term commonly used to describe a systematic process for dealing with these risks. The need for risk management, in turn, gives rise to a fourth cost of pure risks, the expenses that must be incurred in order to treat them.

Financial planners must identify risks for their clients and recommend alternatives for managing those risks. This chapter begins by looking at the nature, scope, and objectives of risk management as well as the role of the risk manager. Next, it describes the basic methods of treating risks because the major goal of risk management is the coordination of these various alternatives. Then it discusses the individual steps in the process of risk management in more detail. Finally, the entire risk management process is reviewed in two brief case studies that illustrate risk management decision making.

NATURE AND SCOPE OF RISK MANAGEMENT

The key steps in the risk management function are:

- identification. The process begins with the recognition and classification of various risks.
- measurement. The next step is the analysis and evaluation of risks in terms of frequency, severity, and variability.
- choice and use of methods to treat each identified risk. Some risks can be avoided, some retained under planned programs, and some transferred by a method such as insurance.
- administration. Once the methods of treatment are chosen, plans for administration of the program must be instituted. This last step includes both implementing the methods selected and monitoring the choices to see that they are effective.

The details involved in these steps are described later in this chapter.

Risk management can be applied to either a personal or an organizational situation, because both personal and organizational risks can be treated or managed. For example, every time a person locks his or her front door, buys insurance, fastens a seat belt, or gets an immunization, he or she is engaged in risk management. So far, most efforts and principles of formal risk management have centered on the risks of organizations, including those of business firms, nonprofit organizations, and government institutions. With increasing education in family finance, households can also use risk management techniques.

The term management refers to the process of planning, organizing, and controlling people and things. Risk management is a part of this process, which pertains to pure risks rather than speculative risks.[1] Risk management extends beyond insurance management, which is primarily limited to decisions regarding when, how much, how, and where to insure the insurable risks. Insurance is the principal method of treating the pure risks of many businesses and households. But without careful study of all the alternatives in risk management in a coordinated decision-making process, insurance may be used inappropriately, or not used where it is appropriate.

OBJECTIVES OF RISK MANAGEMENT

When business or personal risk managers are asked to describe the goal of risk management, the answers are likely to vary greatly. However, many risk managers might summarize by saying that the objective is to preserve the assets and income of the organization or household by providing protection against the possibility of accidental loss. Implicit is the idea that preservation includes all assets—those of physical property and of people. Also, the idea of protection encompasses many different methods of treating pure risks.

More specific risk management goals might be the following: (1) survival, (2) peace of mind, (3) lower costs or higher net income, (4) stable earnings, (5) minimal interruption of business operations or personal life, (6) continued growth, and (7) satisfaction of social responsibility with a good public image. Some of these are pre-loss objectives, meaningful before a loss has occurred. Some are post-loss objectives, and several are significant both before and after a loss.

ROLE OF THE RISK MANAGER

Many business firms and other institutions have created the position of risk manager as a specialist to carry out risk management decision making. Some of these specialists have this exact title, but many continue to be known as "insurance manager," "corporate insurance director," or "insurance buyer." Increasingly, the position is full-time, particularly in organizations with more than 1,000 employees.

The risk manager's responsibilities and authority in a large organization are quite broad and cut across many of the organization's activities. The risk manager often shares the responsibility for certain functions with other executives. The risk manager of a larger firm has, in a majority of cases, full responsibility in the property and liability area for (1) identifying and evaluating risks, (2) selecting insurers, (3) approving insurance renewals and amounts, (4) negotiating insurance rates, (5) seeking competitive insurance bids, (6) keeping insurance records, (7) choosing deductibles, and (8) handling insurance claims. The risk manager usually shares authority for (1) deciding whether to insure or retain (including self-insuring) financial risks, (2) selecting insurance agents and brokers, (3) instituting safety programs, and (4) reviewing contracts other than insurance. In some organizations, the risk manager also has some responsibility for life and health insurance programs, while in others these programs fall within the scope of the human resources or personnel department.

Sometimes, particularly in small- and medium-size firms, an insurance agent, broker, or consultant serves as the risk manager, because the organization has no one person assigned to these responsibilities. Larger agencies and brokerages, especially, offer to serve in this capacity. Care must be taken to see (1) that the services are much broader than mere insurance coverages and include loss prevention and other risk treatment alternatives and (2) that the insurance agency or brokerage representative or consultant knows the firm's special individual needs.

Risk management principles can also be applied to individuals and families. Like a large- or medium-size organization, an individual or household has only a limited amount of money to spend on protecting income and assets against loss. Also, like the organization, the individual or household has various techniques available that include, but are not limited to, insurance for treating its pure risks. The risk management process can help the individual or head of the family treat those risks in a cost-effective manner.

BASIC METHODS OF TREATING RISKS

Each individual method of treating risks is not a single and complete solution to a particular pure risk. In practice, usually all, or at least several, techniques are used together to provide the best answers for meeting the financial problems of risk. Two basic methods of treating risks are risk control in order to minimize losses, and risk financing in order to pay for those losses that do occur.

Risk Control Methods

risk control

Different ways of subdividing the major methods of *risk control* for clients are possible. The emphasis of each of the following four risk control methods is on minimizing losses that might occur to assets and income:

- risk avoidance
- segregation and diversification of items susceptible to loss
- loss prevention and reduction
- noninsurance transfers

Risk Avoidance

risk avoidance

One of the most obvious methods of handling risks is *risk avoidance*, or to avoid as many as possible. Some economic losses can be avoided by various decisions in which risks are either not created or are abandoned. For example, a family can decide to rent rather than buy a home, avoiding the possibility of losing the home's value through the peril of fire. A business may lease its automobiles and avoid the possibility of losing those values. However, the business may be accepting another risk in the lease—that of legal liability for returning the automobiles in good condition. A manufacturer may decide not to produce a chemical that has many potential product liability claims. People who worry about poisonous snakebites or heat exhaustion can live in the Arctic, or at least locate in an area with a minimum exposure to these perils. People who want to avoid the risk of airplane accidents, drownings, and sports injuries can do so largely by keeping away from airplanes, water, and sports activities, respectively.

Example:	Jack and Jean have recently relocated to Naples, Florida, with their three young children. They have instructed their realtor that they do not wish to consider any home that has a swimming pool. Thus, they wish to use avoidance to treat the liability risk of a child drowning in their pool.

Avoidance is not a practical solution to many risks inherent to normal activities. True, some unusual risks with a high chance of loss can be avoided, but realistically, risk avoidance is only an alternative for a limited number of risks. Some risks may be impossible to avoid; others may not be economically desirable to avoid because of the high costs of doing so or because avoiding one risk may create another. For unavoidable risks, other solutions must be considered.

Segregation and Diversification

segregation

Segregation and diversification are among the simplest but most important methods of risk control. *Segregation*, the separation or dispersion of items or lives susceptible to loss, is often an effective way of limiting the severity of loss

diversification

by reducing the concentration of these items or lives. *Diversification* is the duplication of assets or activities at different locations.

Some examples of segregation and diversification are

- physically separating buildings for business operations
- storing inventory in several locations and different types of buildings
- maintaining duplicate records of valuable personal papers such as wills and trust instruments, in separate locations
- transporting vacationing family members in separate vehicles instead of having both parents and all the children in a single vehicle

Loss Prevention and Reduction

Two methods of risk control, loss prevention and loss reduction, could be discussed separately, but they are combined in this section because they are closely related. Techniques that help prevent or reduce loss are both logical and important because losses are seldom completely handled by any other method of treating risks. The total effects of loss are usually much greater than the indemnification available through insurance or any other alternative. Therefore, preventing or reducing the loss is common sense if this can be done at reasonable cost relative to the potential benefits. In some cases, such as saving lives or preventing human injury and suffering, cost may be a secondary factor.

loss prevention
loss reduction

Loss prevention is directed at reducing the probability of loss. The goal of *loss reduction* is to reduce the severity of loss, and it includes steps taken either before or after the loss occurs.

Example: Marie's doctor has urged her to obtain a flu shot in November. He points out that the shot will reduce the likelihood that she will contract the flu in the ensuing months (loss prevention) and will speed up her recovery time if she does contract the flu (loss reduction).

Some loss-prevention and loss-reduction techniques available to families and organizations are as follows:

- building fire-resistant structures
- installing security devices in homes
- scheduling annual physical examinations and mammograms
- using automobile seatbelts
- introducing wellness programs into workplaces
- adding safety devices to guard against injuries from industrial machinery

- having firms such as Underwriters Laboratories Inc. inspect electrical appliances
- designing homes to reduce tornado, earthquake, and hurricane losses

Most of the techniques listed above take place before losses occur. Loss-reduction methods that are used after losses occur include the prompt investigation, reporting, and settlement of claims, the use of salvage companies to sell damaged goods, and reliance on rehabilitation programs to expedite injured persons' return to work.

Noninsurance Transfers

noninsurance transfer

The final method of risk control includes some *noninsurance transfers.* These transfers are effected by a contract other than an insurance contract, in which one party transfers legal responsibility for losses to another party. A later section of this chapter discusses other noninsurance transfers that are methods of risk financing rather than risk control. These methods transfer financial risk but not ultimate legal responsibility.

Subcontracting is one example of a noninsurance transfer as a means of risk control. To illustrate, a contractor may wish to transfer the possibility of injury to employees in a particularly dangerous part of a construction project to someone else. The contractor can do this by hiring subcontractors under contracts in which the subcontractors hire their own employees. The responsibility for these employees is, by contract, transferred to the subcontractors, who are then obligated to pay any workers' compensation losses. Subcontracting thus eliminates the original contractor's exposure to these losses.

Licensing by a manufacturer is another method of noninsurance transfer. If the manufacturer does not want to produce or sell certain goods, that manufacturer can transfer some of these responsibilities through licensing contracts. Under these arrangements, the manufacturer will receive only a royalty or fee for licensing others to do the work. The licensees will have the responsibility for injuries to their own employees.

Risk Financing Methods

risk financing

In most cases, the methods of risk control discussed previously reduce the possibility of losses. The one exception is risk avoidance, which eliminates the possibility of loss. However, eliminating all risk is not possible. Under the other risk control techniques, losses still occur—and some additional choices are necessary when deciding how to pay for them. These alternatives are the methods of *risk financing*, which may be divided into two major types:

- risk retention
- risk transfer

Within each of these major areas, there are several significant methods of risk financing.

Risk Retention

risk retention

If a risk has not been avoided, the exposed person or organization may assume the financial burden of any resulting losses by *risk retention*. This planned risk retention is the result of purposeful, conscious, intentional, and active behavior. For example, a household or firm may evaluate some of its risks as entailing high frequency and low severity and therefore deliberately decide to retain them. However, many pure risks are retained due to lack of planning or failure to recognize the risk rather than from a rational planning process. Some risks are retained because the existence or significance of the risks is not known. Lack of knowledge or inability to reach the right decision, even with adequate knowledge, may result in unplanned risk retention. Information may be available and not used, or perhaps the necessary information is unavailable. An illustration of retention due to lack of planning is the long-term care loss exposure. Retention here is often the result of (1) not knowing the probability or possibility of needing long-term care and the costs involved, or (2) not knowing that insurance can be obtained for such a loss exposure.

Unplanned risk retention can also result from unintentional or irrational action or from passive behavior due to lack of thought, laziness, or lack of interest in discovering possibilities of loss. Many young married people, for example, carry little or no life insurance because they view death as a problem for much later or a subject they wish to avoid discussing.

Some unimportant risks may be intentionally retained due to (1) necessity, when other alternatives are not possible, (2) control or convenience, or (3) cost of insuring. The first reason demands that risk retention be used; the second and third result from a conscious effort to analyze the benefits of retention in terms of control, convenience, or cost, and the ability of individuals or business firms to handle their own risks effectively.

Some pure risks must be retained because transferring them is not possible. For example, a self-employed person with a long history of heart disease is likely to be uninsurable for life and health insurance, so that retention of the loss possibilities associated with further heart disease may be the only available option. Uninsurable retained risks are relatively uncommon, however, because the transfer of most risks, at some price, even if very high, is usually possible. However, sometimes markets for insurance are temporarily unavailable, and retention is necessary until the competitive world markets make adjustments that permit risk transfer. For example, political risk insurance is sometimes unavailable to cover property loss exposures in certain foreign countries.

Organizations often practice risk retention because they wish to have the control or convenience of paying their own losses. Hospital expenses of employees, for example, may be paid directly by the employer to improve cash flow by paying expenses when they occur rather than paying a premium in advance. A manufacturer in a competitive technical field might decide to retain both property and product liability loss exposures in connection with a research laboratory's highly secret inventions.

The use of deductibles is a form of partial risk retention. Having the insured receive payment only for losses over a stated amount or duration has been accepted for many years in most types of medical expense, disability income, and property insurance. Deductibles are also found in some types of liability insurance policies. Deductibles lower insurance premiums by eliminating the relatively high claims costs associated with small losses. From the insurer's perspective, deductibles also minimize moral hazards by leaving an insured responsible for a portion of any loss.

Some insurance policies require the use of deductibles. However, in most cases, any required deductible is a relatively modest amount. Optionally higher deductibles are usually available, often at significant premium savings.

Example:	Tom Burton has a homeowners deductible of $1,000 rather than his insurer's standard amount of $250. The annual premium saving is $200. In other words, by decreasing his coverage by $750, he saves $200 per year. Inasmuch as the average policyowner has a homeowners loss only once every 15 to 20 years, the long-run savings could be substantial.

The appropriate deductible for a given situation varies, based on several factors. Among these factors are the nature of the perils, including the frequency and severity of loss patterns; the policyowner's financial ability to withstand losses; the existence of reserves or funds to help finance the deductible portion of losses; the desire for claims handling by the policyowner or the insurer; the need for loss-prevention services; and the policyowner's degree of risk aversion.

The economics of alternative risk treatment methods are a major consideration in most decisions to retain a risk. A comparison of the cost involved in each alternative method of financing losses is necessary. If insurance against earthquake damage is available, how much will it cost? If earthquake damage could be prevented by extra-strong building construction, how much would this cost? Would a self-insurance program with a reserve fund be feasible, and what would its cost be? In each of these comparisons, the need for complete evaluation is obvious. Not only must loss frequency and severity be considered, but all costs of the various alternatives, including indirect as well as direct costs, must be evaluated for fair comparisons. Another significant cost factor that must be evaluated is the cost of funds, which makes risk retention plans more desirable because assets are held until losses actually occur.

Risks that are retained by a family or business client must be financed in some way. The more common methods are described below.

Absorption in Current Operating Expenses. The most common method of risk financing for retained risk is to absorb losses out of regular operating expenses or family budgets. Large organizations often generate sufficient cash inflow to absorb costs, but smaller firms are less likely to be equipped to withstand ongoing losses. Some business perils that businesses might consider for absorption in current operating expenses are glass breakage, transportation shipment damage, and automobile physical damage. For individuals and families, the budget usually provides even less room for absorbing unexpected losses. However, dental bills, eyeglasses, and deductible amounts may be among the possible candidates for this type of treatment.

Funding and Reserves. Irregular drains of substantial funds are not desirable or practical for households or organizations. For an organization, a fund of actual segregated assets or a reserve, may be used to offset losses that are too large to absorb in current operating expenses but small enough that the entity can reasonably retain the risk.

The major disadvantage of many reserve accounts is that they do not guarantee that cash will be available to meet losses. Problems with segregated funds include (1) how large the fund should be, (2) how it can be accumulated with intervening losses that might be disastrous, and (3) how the fund can be maintained without raiding it for other emergencies or in the household's or organization's regular operations.

For households, reserves include savings and liquid investments. Within limits, these resources can enable a family to retain the financial consequences of a loss that is too large to assume out of the monthly budget. A good example of this type of loss is short-term disability or limited periods of unemployment.

self-insurance

Self-Insurance. While the term *self-insurance* is often used to apply to an assumption of financial risks, the proper use of the term applies to formal programs of risk retention. Self-insurance is generally appropriate only for a large business in which the business acts like an insurance company for its own risks. This involves having a large number of similar potential losses, the ability to predict overall losses with some degree of accuracy, and the establishment of a formal fund for future losses and their possible fluctuations.

Self-insurance renders many financial advantages to an organization by avoiding many of the costs associated with commercial insurance, but it also exposes the organization to the possibility of catastrophic losses. However, this exposure can be managed by purchasing various types of insurance products such as reinsurance, stop-loss coverage, or policies with very large deductibles. For example, an organization might self-insure all liability claims under $1 million but have insurance that pays the excess of any claim over $1 million.

The organization must also be able to properly administer its self-insurance program, but services can be purchased from various vendors, including third-party administrators.

captive insurer

Captive Insurers. Another risk financing method—the use of a *captive insurer*—is closely related to self-insurance. The captive insurer method has gained popularity as a way to achieve closer control of contract design and loss payment while obtaining some tax advantages. In this risk-financing method, a large organization establishes a separate subsidiary insurance company to write its own insurance. Today, many captive insurers also write insurance for unrelated outside firms as well as for their own parent companies or groups.

Risk Transfer

Some of the most important risks that individuals and organizations must finance cannot be retained. Often these risks entail low loss frequency but high loss severity. Then the sole risk financing method left for consideration is *risk transfer*, which involves shifting as much as possible of the financial consequence associated with the risk to someone else. The risk itself will still exist, but the financial consequences will be largely borne by the insurer. Three methods of risk transfers are possible: (1) credit arrangements, (2) other noninsurance transfers, and (3) insurance.

risk transfer

Credit Arrangements. The use of credit contracts to pay for losses may be considered a method of risk transfer. However, borrowing money usually has other primary purposes such as home financing or business expansion. Because credit is always limited, depending on the borrower's financial situation and capabilities ("All you have to do to get credit is to prove you don't need it"), it seems generally unwise to overly rely on credit for relatively unpredictable needs. Pure risks, especially for large and infrequent types of losses, are difficult to handle by borrowing after the need arises. Therefore, the household or organization should make prior arrangements to obtain these funds, such as establishing a line of credit, in case a loss occurs.

Other Noninsurance Transfers. Risks may also be shifted by several other types of noninsurance transfers. In a risk financing method, the financial burden of losses rather than the ultimate legal responsibility is transferred. For example, purchasing an extended warranty on an automobile or air conditioning system is a common noninsurance transfer method that can be used by individuals and households to handle pure risks. Likewise, businesses and organizations often use hold-harmless agreements to transfer the financial consequences of some of their pure risks.

hold-harmless agreement

Most noninsurance transfers to finance risk deal with liability risks. For example, in the *hold-harmless agreement,* the transferee agrees to hold the transferor harmless in case of legal liability to others. The transferee agrees to pay claimants or the defense costs of claims or lawsuits, or to repay these losses if they fall on the transferor. If the transferee is unable to pay the losses, the ultimate responsibility remains with the transferor.

Several types of legal contracts commonly include hold-harmless agreements. In lease contracts, a variety of legal responsibilities are transferred from one party to another in this manner. For example, a lease often states that property maintenance shall be the responsibility of the transferee (lessee) who rents the property from the owner. Homes, apartments, automobiles, and many other types of property are often leased subject to hold-harmless agreements.

Construction contracts often use hold-harmless agreements to transfer the financial burden of some, but seldom all, of the legal liability losses from the owner to the contractor. For example, in a supply contract, the supplier usually agrees to hold the manufacturer or distributor harmless for claims resulting from the supplier's negligence.

Bailees—persons holding property of others temporarily—often accept some risks from the property owners by bailment contract or common law. Responsibility for damage to goods is shifted from the owner to the bailee in hundreds of everyday situations involving truck shipments, laundries, warehouses, parking lots, and repair shops.

Example: Patrick boards his dog at a veterinarian's office while he takes a vacation for a few days. He has thus created a bailment, with himself as the bailor and the veterinarian as the bailee. Therefore, Patrick has used a noninsurance transfer of the financial impact of harm to the dog arising from negligence.

Most risk transfer methods are far from complete. In some circumstances, the financial risks in regard to certain perils may be transferred to others but only for a limited length of time and/or for a limited dollar amount. Nevertheless, the major financial risks of families and businesses remain with them unless the final method of risk transfer—insurance—is used.

Insurance. Among the methods of risk transfer, insurance is by far the most common. Chapter 1 describes the nature of this risk transfer method. The next section of this chapter describes briefly how insurance works.

HOW INSURANCE WORKS

How can any organization assume a large risk for a comparatively small premium and soon thereafter make a large loss payment? For example, life insurance pays some death claims on policies issued and in force for less than a year. Fire insurance on buildings may result in the payment of thousands of dollars in return for the payment of a few dollars in premiums. The following four concepts help explain how insurance works:

- the insurance equation
- probability and uncertainty
- the law of large numbers
- adequate statistical data

The Insurance Equation

insurance equation

The equality between the receipts taken in and amounts paid out constitutes the *insurance equation*. The receipts include (1) premium payments from policyowners, (2) investment earnings, and (3) other income. The cost factors that are paid out include: (1) the cost of losses, (2) the cost of doing business, or expenses, and (3) the cost of capital, or profits. Each of these cost factors is explained below.

Losses

Insurers deal primarily with groups. In the case of a life insurer, the company is not concerned with when one person will die but with how many will die each year out of a large group. Knowing this within reasonable limits, the life insurer sets its rates so that it will take in enough money to be able to pay all losses. In the case of other forms of insurance, the procedure is the same. The fire insurer is interested not in whether specific buildings will burn but in what the ratio of losses to premiums will be when a large group of buildings is insured.

The percentage of the premium paid in the form of losses varies with the line of insurance contract written. The losses per premium dollar may be 80 percent or more for group health insurance or less than 50 percent for lines such as surety bonds and boiler and machinery insurance, for which loss-prevention services are more feasible and important.

Margins are included in the rates that insurers charge. These margins are required by state law to cover specific loss reserves for some lines of insurance. Insurance rates also sometimes include margins to cover possible future catastrophic losses. For example, fires have destroyed large sections in major cities, windstorms have damaged wide areas, and accidents have caused the deaths of a large number of people at one time. Insurers must take catastrophes of this sort into consideration when computing premiums.

Expenses

In addition to securing sufficient funds to meet all losses, insurers must collect enough money to pay business expenses such as salaries, rents, supplies, taxes, and agents' commissions. Certain insurers also provide special services in engineering and loss prevention that are designed to save property and lives. The cost of doing business is affected greatly by the marketing system used and the services that insurers' agents render to policyowners.

Profits

Premiums must also be sufficient to generate profits. Profits are the amounts left after all losses and expenses have been paid out. In a stock company, some profits are usually retained by insurers to increase surplus, and the remainder is distributed to shareowners. Stockholders who invest funds in insurance companies do so for a return and, accordingly, in the computation of the premium there must be some provision to compensate the owners of the capital invested in the enterprise. Surplus and stockholders' capital also help to ensure financial solvency.

Other forms of insurers owned by their policyowners, such as mutual insurance companies, also make "profits" in the sense that revenue may exceed losses and expenses. Some of this profit is returned to policyowners as policy dividends, with the remainder contributed to surplus for purposes of growth and financial stability.

The insurance equation is an adaptation of the basic accounting concept that total income must equal total outgo plus profits. Total income in the insurance equation consists of premiums plus investment earnings and any miscellaneous income. This total income must equal the total outgo, which consists of incurred losses, expenses, and profits.

Probability and Uncertainty

Another explanation of how insurance works is based on the concepts of probability and uncertainty. Insurance assumes the burden of risks that individuals are unwilling to retain. The insurer can reduce the sum total of all the uncertainties to a reasonable degree of certainty. Within calculable limits, the insurer can foresee the normal losses and estimate losses from catastrophes in order to compute the premium necessary to pay all losses, as well as to cover expenses and profits.

The ability to use probabilities gives the insurer a different perspective than the policyowner. Without this ability, insurance would be nothing more than the accumulation of many small risks and accompanying uncertainties into one enormous risk and accompanying uncertainty. By using probabilities, even though the element of uncertainty is extreme in each individual case, the insurer can predict a reasonably definite loss in total. The uncertainty element is not entirely eliminated, because some insurers are more successful than others. Although every insurance company endeavors to achieve reasonable predictability, some companies will err and suffer losses and expenses beyond what they take in.

Insurance and Uncertainty

- The insurer virtually eliminates the insured's uncertainty.
- The insurer's uncertainty is far less, though not eliminated, than the sum of the former uncertainties of the insureds.

Probability measures the chance of occurrence of a particular event. In the field of insurance, the theory of probability has proved to be of great importance in predicting losses. The probability of loss is expressed algebraically in a fraction, with the numerator equaling the number of unfavorable outcomes and the denominator equaling the total number of all possible outcomes.

Variance of the chance of loss is a more difficult concept. Variance refers to the extent that actual losses deviate from expected losses over periods of time. Insurers must project variance of losses when they issue insurance contracts promising to pay future losses. A variety of statistical methods are helpful in measuring the variance of expected loss.

Law of Large Numbers

In addition to the concepts of probability and uncertainty, a principle referred to in chapter 1 is of great importance to insurance—the *law of large numbers*, or law of averages. This law states that as the number of independent events increases, the likelihood increases that the actual results will be close to the expected results.

Insurance is concerned with the number of times an event, or loss, can be expected to occur over a series of occasions. Certain events occur with surprising regularity when a large number of instances are observed. The regularity of the events increases as the observed instances become more numerous. The concept

credibility   is that of *credibility*, which indicates the degree of reliability placed on past experience to predict what will happen in the future.

Applying these conclusions to insurance in a hypothetical case, assume that we are considering the predictability of automobile accidents in a given city. We have gathered data on two different classes of drivers, under age 25 and age 25 or older, in the city over the past several years. The data are shown in table 2-1.

TABLE 2-1
Data on Two Different Classes of Drivers

	Under Age 25	Age 25 or Higher
Average annual number of drivers	2,000	25,000
Average annual percentage involved in an auto accident	20%	12%
Range of annual percentages involved in an auto accident during the period	9%–31%	8%–16%

It is perhaps not surprising that, on average, a higher percentage of young drivers were involved in automobile accidents during a year than older drivers. In addition, however, note that as a smaller group, the younger drivers showed a wider relative variation around their average from year to year than did the older, considerably larger group. If we were to use these data to predict future accident rates, we could only predict within a wide range of percentages for the younger drivers compared with the older group. As a result, there would be a rather low probability of actual experience equaling expected experience for the under-age-25 group. The relative variation in results for the 25-and-over group is smaller, so predictions for the future could be made more accurately. This is the "magic" of insurance—increasing predictability and reducing uncertainty through the use of the law of large numbers.

Adequate Statistical Data

Use of the mathematical laws of probability and large numbers requires adequate statistical data. Predictions in the form of probabilities must be based on accurate statistical information. In each of the lines of insurance, insurers carefully compiled statistics to accumulate experience as a basis for rate making. For example, the statistical data used in estimating the number of deaths for life insurance purposes are arranged in a mortality table that shows how many persons alive at different ages are expected to die during the coming year. In commercial property insurance, statistics are developed for such factors as construction, occupancy, fire protection, and location pertaining to different types of buildings. For automobile insurance, data for many classifications of type and use of car, territory, age of driver, and other factors are collected. Proper classifications help to achieve equity in the rates charged to many policyowners with different loss probabilities.

The insurer's goal is to reduce judgment factors to a minimum and to set rates scientifically, based on the use of statistical data in applying known laws of probability, variability, and large numbers. Insurance applies mathematical tools to statistical data on groups in order to achieve better predictions than individuals can make. Insurers' success in prediction explains why insurance, among the several alternatives discussed earlier in this chapter, has become the predominant method of treating pure risks.

STEPS IN RISK MANAGEMENT

The first part of this chapter presents the background of the basic methods of treating pure risks. The following pages explain the steps in risk management: (1) risk identification, (2) risk measurement, (3) choice and use of alternative methods of treatment, and (4) risk administration.

Risk Identification

risk identification

The process of risk management begins with *risk identification*, the careful and systematic discovery of all risks that confront a household or organization. Each identified risk is usually paired with a method of risk treatment that is available or in use. Often a risk and insurance survey form, sometimes called a loss exposure audit or fact finder, is used to organize this information. Several other effective methods of risk identification for households or small businesses are financial statement analysis, flowcharts, and personal inspections.

Survey Forms

Survey forms are most often used in business situations, but are also appropriate for nonprofit organizations, as well as for individuals and families. Elaborate survey forms have been designed to meet different types of business establishments' needs. Special survey forms have been prepared by insurers, insurance consultants, and insurance agencies. A sample survey form for a family is shown in table 2-2.[2]

State and city officials, guardians, executors, and trustees are subject to direct personal liability if, without verification, they decide that the current risk and insurance programs are sufficient. These individuals may be unaware of the risks that threaten the institutions or individuals under their care. Life and health and property and liability professionals can prepare and coordinate a risk and insurance program for these individuals.

In the business sector, businesses of all sizes need effective risk and insurance surveys. Smaller businesses are particularly vulnerable to financial ruin as the result of a mistake or omission in insurance protection. Alternatively, a small business might follow the rule, "When in doubt, insure," which may be less expensive than a program of risk management within the firm. However, all businesses must

TABLE 2-2
Identification of Household/Family Loss Exposures

Types of Loss Exposure	Consequences

Property
• Real property
  – Unimproved land
  – Residence premises
  – Other structures
  – Fixtures
• Personal property
  – Tangible
      At residence premises
      Elsewhere
  – Intangible
  – Property held as bailee
	Property
	• Reduction in value
	• Loss of use

Liability • Premises liability • Libel, slander, and other intentional torts • Employment of domestics • Automobiles • Recreational vehicles • Watercraft • Business-related liability • Personal activities (for example, hobbies, baby-sitting, serving alcohol, keeping pets)	Liability • Damage awards • Specific performance • Injunction • Fines • Costs of defense • Court costs
Illness and Injury • Related to employment • Not related to employment	Illness and Injury • Medical care expenses • Lost income • Extra expenses and loss of services • Long-term care
Death	Death • Costs associated with death (for example, funeral, taxes, estate administration fees) • Lost income for dependents • Lost employee benefits for dependents
Retirement	Retirement • Lost income
Unemployment	Unemployment • Lost income • Extra expenses (for example, relocation, job hunting)

Techniques for Risk Identification

- Survey forms
- Financial statements
- Flowcharts
- Personal inspections

---

take advantage of all insurance cost reductions that are economically advisable; otherwise, small profit margins can turn into business losses.

Risk and insurance survey forms involve risk detection, identification, and classification. Sometimes they also include estimates of the possible loss values, which are part of risk measurement. Survey forms may be brief or lengthy, depending upon whether they are for a household or business, and on complexity of the case under consideration.

Financial Statement Analysis

In financial statement analysis, each account on the balance sheet, the profit and loss statement, and other financial statements is listed and analyzed to determine the potential perils that might result in losses. For example, the cash item among the assets on a firm's balance sheet can be one of the listings. Opposite this item, the perils that could cause loss of cash can be enumerated such as fire, windstorm, explosion, water damage, vandalism, burglary, robbery, theft (including embezzlement by employees), and mysterious disappearance. Cash at different locations, such as in the office, retail stores, or in safes, should be separately analyzed to identify special perils to which cash is exposed in different circumstances. The items on the income statement and budget pinpoint the sources of income and profits subject to indirect loss when perils occur. A comprehensive analysis of a firm's financial statements thus becomes a very useful method for identifying both direct and indirect losses.

Flowcharts

Flowcharts are another systematic approach for identifying risks, particularly for an organization. Charts that show the entire operation in detail are constructed, and each step in the production and distribution of goods and services is analyzed to consider the potential losses that might occur at each point or location in the process.

For example, for a manufacturer, a flowchart shows how and where the raw materials are received and stored, the location of the separate steps in the production process, the inventory of finished goods, and the packaging and distribution process. Each of the steps is analyzed to identify the particular possibilities of loss to the various assets during each stage of the operation.

Personal Inspections

While many methods of risk identification are valuable as checks against possible sources of loss, none of them can replace the technical knowledge provided by insurance consultants or agents. Personal inspections of a business or a household remain a significant source of information about possible losses.

Risk Measurement

Risk measurement is the second step in risk management. Each risk must be measured in three basic ways: (1) loss frequency, (2) loss severity, and (3) variation. Risk managers need to estimate expected losses on the basis of past loss experience or judgment. Risk managers must also try to predict variations in future losses, in both frequency and severity.

Some losses can be so infrequent that it would be uneconomic to try to deal with them. Flood damage to property high on a mountain is an example of this type of loss probability. At the other extreme, some losses may be so frequent as to be regularly anticipated. If the losses are small relative to a family's or business firm's assets or income, retaining these risks by absorbing the losses in normal expenses or by reserving for the losses as they occur would be effective. For this sort of retention to work, however, not only must the frequency of loss be high and the severity low, but the variation of losses must also be regular and predictable within ranges that the household or firm can handle.

If complete data are lacking, or if the cost of making more precise estimates is too high, other methods of measuring risks may be advisable. For example, risk managers often divide potential losses into various categories according to the importance to their firm such as losses that are of high, moderate, or slight

maximum possible loss

importance. Estimates of *maximum possible loss*, the worst that could happen, and *maximum probable loss*, the worst that is likely to happen, can also be valuable.

maximum probable loss

The concept of maximum probable loss is most useful to the risk manager. By using some actual or hypothetical loss data, the risk manager can determine the probability that severe losses might occur. The risk manager can disregard some extreme probabilities that are possible, but unlikely, in the estimate of maximum probable loss. For example, a firm's risk manager might determine that there is only a .1 percent probability of being sued for more than $10 million. The risk manager can then concentrate on providing for the 99.9 percent of the losses that are more likely to occur.

Several dimensions of maximum probable loss are pertinent. To determine the effect of losses on a household or organization, it is worthwhile to estimate the maximum probable loss not only for a single item or life exposed to loss (such as one building or one person), but also for multiple losses that could occur together (such as a windstorm over a large area or the death or disability of both parents in an accident). In addition, the risk manager should evaluate the maximum probable loss per year in terms of its financial effect on the household's or organization's resources, budget planning, and taxes.

Choice and Use of Methods of Risk Treatment

The third step in risk management is to evaluate both the suitability and the cost of various methods of treating pure risks. Risk management synthesizes all methods of dealing with risks. Even considering one peril, such as fire, usually requires a risk manager to integrate the two basic methods of risk control and risk financing.

In order to choose among alternatives, the risk manager must understand each alternative, the conditions under which it should be considered, its advantages, and its limitations. Can the risk be avoided, or can it be controlled by other means such as loss prevention or reduction? Can some or all of the risk be financed by risk retention or risk transfer? More important, if several methods are feasible, which one method or combination of methods will provide the most desirable result?

Elaborate mathematical models have been designed for comparing the benefits and costs of the various methods, and combinations of methods, to treat various pure risks. However, these models are probably not very helpful when risk management is practiced at the level of the household or small business organization. At that level, the choice of the best technique or combination of techniques is likely to be determined by factors such as the following:[3]

- the maximum probable loss associated with a particular risk in comparison to the household's or firm's financial and other capacities for bearing risk
- the legal restrictions that may impose or preclude the use of one or more of the available techniques
- the extent to which the household or firm is able to exert control over the loss frequency or severity associated with the risk
- the loading fees (expense charges) associated with the available risk management techniques
- the value of ancillary services that may be provided as part of the risk treatment technique, especially the insurance technique
- the time value of investable funds that may be gained or lost by using certain of the available techniques
- the federal income tax treatment of losses under the various techniques
- the possible unavailability of certain techniques for dealing with some pure risks

Reviewing insurance priorities is one of the simplest approaches to choosing a technique or combination of techniques for a household or small business. Assume that insurance will be used, if available, for each of the pure risks that have been identified and measured in the risk management process. The most suitable policy and its cost are listed for each risk as a benchmark against which to evaluate other possible techniques. Listing insurance coverages also clarifies which risks must be treated by means other than insurance—that is, the risks for which no insurance is available.

Next, insurance coverages are grouped into priority categories such as

- essential (for example, insurance required by law or losses of possibly disastrous results for the household or business)
- desirable (for example, losses that would seriously impair but not totally wipe out the financial position of the household or business)
- available (all other types of insurance coverage)

Finally, each insurance coverage is compared with the other available techniques for treating the particular risk. For example, can some of the risks in the "essential" category be avoided? Reduced? Transferred? Can some of the risks in the "desirable" category be less expensively addressed through loss prevention and reduction? Can some of the risks in the "available" category be retained, at least partially?

A different approach to selecting the most appropriate technique, although it might lead to the same conclusion as the review of insurance priorities, is to group the most logical techniques based on the probable frequency and severity of the losses associated with each pure risk.

- For risks that involve both high loss frequency and high loss severity, the most suitable techniques are probably avoidance and, if possible, some form of segregation, diversification, loss prevention, loss reduction, or noninsurance transfer.
- For risks that involve low loss frequency and high loss severity, the most suitable techniques are probably insurance and, if possible, some form of segregation, diversification, loss prevention, loss reduction, or noninsurance transfer.
- For risks that involve high loss frequency and low loss severity, the most suitable techniques are probably retention and, if the benefits exceed the cost, loss prevention.
- For risks that involve both low loss frequency and low loss severity, the most suitable techniques are probably retention and, perhaps, loss prevention.

Risk Administration

The fourth step in the risk management process is risk administration. Actually, risk administration must be carried out in conjunction with each of the first three steps of risk management. New risks must be continually identified, and all risks

Appropriate Risk Management Techniques

Expected Frequency	Expected Loss Severity	
	High	Low
High	Avoidance, segregation, diversification, prevention, reduction, noninsurance transfer	Retention, prevention
Low	Insurance, segregation, diversification, prevention, reduction, noninsurance transfer	Retention, prevention

must be frequently remeasured. Treatment alternatives, too, must be reconsidered and reviewed for their effectiveness and their actual and potential costs.

Arranging for the actual issuance of the contracts of protection is an important part of risk administration. Sometimes insurers issue binders for temporary coverage, particularly in property and liability insurance. *Binders* make insurance effective immediately, even though the complete written contract may be delivered weeks later. The risk manager must have a clear understanding of when the protection is effective and what the scope of the coverage will be when the completed contract is written. Some binders can be given orally, but the best practice is to document these agreements in written form as soon as possible.

binder

Often the process of initiating and reviewing insurance coverages for a household or small business involves shopping around for the best coverage. Agents, brokers, or financial consultants are helpful in searching the available markets. Lowest costs are not the only factor to consider; the insurer's quality of service, financial strength, reputation, claims services, loss prevention, and other business are also important. Shopping around may be a useful way to compare markets periodically, but it is not practical to do so every year because there is value in continued services, and there are costs involved in shopping around.

The administration of existing insurance coverages is another part of risk management. Renewal and expiration records are essential to prevent any unplanned lapse in coverage. Amounts of coverage must be kept up to date through frequent appraisals. Rate classifications and costs must be checked.

If methods of risk treatment other than insurance have been chosen, risk administration includes additional procedures and review. For example, if loss prevention is significant, the risk manager must be certain that the household's or business's loss-control programs, as well as those provided by insurers, agents, or other loss and safety specialists, are performing well. The risk manager should analyze loss data and trends regularly to determine whether desired results are being achieved.

EXAMPLES OF RISK MANAGEMENT DECISION MAKING

Two brief case studies serve as a review of the steps in risk management and risk treatment techniques. The first case involves a small business firm, with emphasis on its property loss exposures. The second case involves a family, with emphasis on its life and health loss exposures.

Small Business Case

This case concerns a small manufacturer of specialty plastic goods. The risk manager or consultant for the firm might assemble a risk management package as described below.

Step 1—Risk Identification

Fire and explosion are relatively obvious as two major possible sources of loss. The risk manager or consultant also identifies and classifies other sources of loss by using a survey form covering perils or loss exposures and comparing these with financial statement accounts.

Step 2—Risk Measurement

Using past company records, the risk manager or consultant finds out that there has been extreme variation in both the number and amount of losses during the past 20 years. The degree of uncertainty and maximum probable loss are therefore high. Industry loss probability is also found to be higher than that for most manufacturers. Values of buildings, machinery, inventory, and other property are appraised.

Step 3—Choice and Use of Methods of Treatment

Risk control methods for this small manufacturer include

- avoiding some risks. In order to conserve working capital and avoid risks, the firm leases three trucks, with the rental company taking care of the fire, theft, and collision coverage. The manufacturer chooses the same risk management technique by leasing a new computer to replace an outdated one.
- segregating the storage of finished goods in a separate building, away from the more hazardous production facilities
- diversifying the product line, so that destruction of one type of specialized machine will not shut down production
- adopting an intensive loss-prevention and loss-reduction program against the perils of fire and explosion. The firm installs a sprinkler system,

hires night security guards, trains employees in fire prevention habits and the use of extinguishers, and conducts regular inspections.
- using noninsurance transfer of risk. The manufacturer subcontracts with another firm to produce one of the more toxic plastics necessary for the company's research department.

Risk financing methods include

- retaining some risks by:
  - setting up a reserve in the corporate accounts to cover small losses up to $1,000. Alternatively, these losses might simply be absorbed in the operating expense accounts.
  - selecting a deductible of $5,000 in connection with the fire insurance contract. Making the supervisors aware of the deductible may encourage loss prevention.
- transferring some risks by:
  - insuring the building and its contents, including fire and explosion coverage, for $1 million with a $5,000 deductible. Consultation with several insurers and agents will help determine the proper perils and the amount of coverage.
  - making a noninsurance transfer of risk through a hold-harmless agreement with the firm's major sales distributor. In the agreement, the distributor agrees to pay for any product liability losses caused by negligence in the distribution process.

Step 4—Risk Administration

The manufacturer implements the risk treatment alternatives in step 3 through the following procedures: communication and discussion with other departments of the firm, rental of the trucks through the purchasing department, segregation of finished goods by consultation with the inventory control section, diversification of its product line through the production department, establishment of reserve accounts with the accounting department and the treasurer's office, explanation of deductibles to the supervisors of various departments, coordination of the loss-prevention program with the safety and security department, and sale of the unneeded computer through the accounting and property departments. The manufacturer also purchases fire insurance through a carefully selected agent who will provide appraisal services for property values at stated time intervals.

Finally, the manufacturer schedules annual reviews of all risk management methods and property values, with the option to conduct more frequent reviews if necessary. The firm also hires a consultant to evaluate the risk management decisions and to arrange for the reevaluation of prices for the insurance at 5-year intervals.

Family Case

Now consider how the risk management process might be applied in a family situation—in this case, to the applicable life and health pure risks. Assume that Travis and Amy Jordan, a husband and wife, have two children: Edward and Penny. Edward is aged 17 and will begin college as a full-time student in a few months. Penny is aged 13 and in the eighth grade. Travis is 42, and he is an executive for a chain of grocery stores. He earns about $120,000 per year. Amy, aged 39, works part-time for an orthodontist and earns about $15,000 per year. Risk management as it relates to the family's life and health pure risks might be applied in this situation as shown below.

Step 1—Risk Identification

The following risks face the Jordan family:

- The death or disability of Travis might cause a major loss of earnings for the support of Amy, Edward, and Penny.
- Travis's death would result in some costs, perhaps significant, to clear his estate (funeral, probate, taxes, last illness, and so on).
- Travis's disability could cause extremely high medical bills and other costs (rehabilitation therapy, long-term care, and so on).
- Travis's unemployment could result in lost income for the support of Amy and the children, as well as some direct costs to obtain another job.
- Several years from now, Travis's retirement from his job will cause a significant loss of income for his and Amy's support.
- Amy's death, disability, unemployment, or retirement would cause the same types of losses as described for Travis. The size of the income losses (and some of the estate clearance costs) would be less than for Travis, but the out-of-pocket expenses if Amy becomes disabled could be fully as large as if Travis were disabled.
- The death of Edward or Penny would cause a loss of their future earning power, some of which might be needed eventually for the support of their parent(s). There would also be some out-of-pocket costs immediately if Edward or Penny were to die.
- The disability of Edward or Penny could lead to very high costs for medical and other types of care.

Step 2—Risk Measurement

Measurement of the death, disability, unemployment, and retirement risks for family members is extremely difficult. Except for short-term disabilities and periods of unemployment, loss frequency rates are meaningless for individuals. For example, although it is possible to calculate the odds of death, long-term disability, or long-term confinement in a nursing home within one year for a 42-year-old male, those odds mean nothing to Travis. The only safe assumption he can make is that, in fact, he will die, experience a long-term disability, or be confined in a nursing home within the next year—that is, that the odds are 100 percent against him. The risk of long-term unemployment may be slightly more measurable, although based only on Travis's informed judgment about the likelihood of being terminated by his employer. The retirement risk is reasonably measurable, because it is likely that Travis has a planned retirement date and desired income level if he survives to that date.

Measuring the loss severity of most risks to a family is more meaningful than measuring loss frequency. Therefore, the family's loss exposures can be subjectively grouped into three broad categories based on maximum possible or maximum probable loss, as follows:

- Calamitous losses include income loss due to Travis's death, medical bills and other expenses due to his or any other family member's serious disability, income loss due to his long-term disability or unemployment, and Travis's income loss due to his retirement.
- Serious losses include income loss due to Amy's death or long-term disability, income loss due to Travis's short-term unemployment, income loss due to Amy's retirement, estate clearance costs due to Travis's death, and medical bills due to routine accidents or illnesses of Travis, Amy, Edward, or Penny.
- Bearable losses include estate clearance costs due to the death of Amy, Edward, or Penny and lost income for possible support of Travis or Amy due to the death of Edward or Penny.

At this point, dollar values are not assigned to each of the potential losses in each category. Several later chapters, which deal with life insurance, annuities, medical expense insurance, disability income insurance, and long-term care insurance, offer guidance in assigning dollar values to all the Jordans' losses except the unemployment peril.

Step 3—Choice and Use of Methods of Treatment

The Jordan family can undertake some risk control techniques, particularly in the areas of loss prevention and loss reduction. For example, family members can schedule periodic medical checkups and take preventive measures to lower the likelihood of death or disability and so reduce the lost income and out-of-pocket costs associated with those two perils.

The family can also undertake some risk financing. For example, they can retain the losses listed in the "bearable" category, perhaps through the accumulation of an emergency fund and through absorption as part of normal operating expenses. The Jordans can partially retain some of the losses in the "serious" and "calamitous" categories through the use of deductibles and waiting periods in insurance policies. The household can also transfer some of these losses, perhaps through prearranged, guaranteed sources of credit in time of emergency (for example, a home equity line of credit from a bank). Of course, the best way for the Jordans to transfer the losses they cannot control or fully retain is through insurance. The family should give the highest priority to coverage of potentially calamitous losses through life insurance on Travis, major medical expense insurance on all four family members, long-term disability income coverage on Travis, and some type of retirement plan for Travis. The Jordans should also consider long-term care insurance, especially for Travis and Amy. Life insurance and, if available, disability income coverage for Amy are a somewhat lower priority, as is some type of retirement plan for her. The Jordans might also consider dental expense coverage for all family members.

Step 4—Risk Administration

For the Jordans to administer the risk treatment methods they have selected, they must adhere to a regular schedule of medical and dental examinations for all family members and systematically and rapidly build up a sizable emergency fund. They should also arrange a line of credit, perhaps secured by the equity in their home, but leave it untouched so it will be available in time of emergency.

Most of the Jordans' risk administration activities, of course, involve arranging and coordinating various forms of insurance coverage in proper amounts and with appropriate deductibles or waiting periods. They should consider three broad categories of insurance in this process: social insurance, employer-sponsored insurance, and individual insurance. These are the three building blocks that the Jordans can use to construct a program of economic security from the perils of death, disability, unemployment, and old age.

Social Insurance. The first building block for the Jordans is several social insurance programs, each of which is designed to provide a safety net of protection against certain perils. The benefits under these programs are discussed in detail in chapter 7. One of these programs is Social Security, which will provide a basic level of retirement income for Travis and Amy. Social Security will also replace a portion of the income lost following the death of Travis or Amy and, in certain cases, will replace some of the income lost should either of them become disabled.

Under certain circumstances, social insurance benefits may also be available under workers' compensation insurance, unemployment insurance, or temporary disability insurance programs.

Employer-Sponsored Insurance. The second building block for the Jordans is various insurance programs made available where Travis and Amy work—both

---

Building Blocks for Economic Security

- Social insurance
- Employer-sponsored insurance
- Individual insurance

---

group insurance plans and voluntary benefit plans. Because Amy is part-time, she may not be eligible for employee benefits. Group insurance programs—which may either be insured or self-funded by an employer—can provide specified types of coverage such as group life insurance, group medical expense insurance, and a pension plan. In some cases, coverage is automatically given to all employees at no cost; in other cases, an employee must elect coverage and pay a portion of the cost. However, the employer often pays a significant amount of the cost, and only in rare circumstances is the cost more than that of comparable coverage in the individual marketplace.

voluntary benefits

Employers are increasingly making *voluntary benefits* available to employees. Under these plans, which are referred to by various names such as worksite products or mass-marketed insurance plans, the employer makes the plan available but does not share in the premium cost. Voluntary benefit plans have some of the characteristics of group insurance and some of the characteristics of individual insurance. As in individual insurance, each employee decides whether to purchase the coverage, and individual underwriting of applicants is practiced, although sometimes the underwriting standards are less stringent than for individual insurance. Voluntary benefit products also have some of the convenience of group insurance, particularly premium payment by payroll deduction.

The most common products offered as voluntary benefits are various forms of life insurance, short-term and long-term disability income insurance, and more recently, long-term care insurance. Some insurers also offer automobile and homeowners insurance as voluntary benefits, although these are not a concern of the Jordan family in this case study. Employees should pay attention to the cost of voluntary products. In some cases, the cost of coverage may exceed the cost of comparable coverage in the individual marketplace, particularly if an employee is in good health.

cafeteria plan

Cafeteria plans, also referred to as flexible benefit plans, allow employees to choose among several different types of benefits options. In its purest sense, a cafeteria plan gives employees a specified amount of employer-provided dollars, and the employees can choose from among the available benefits, and possibly even cash. The plan generates no taxable income to the extent an employee chooses the types of benefits that are normally nontaxable. However, the choice of cash or normally taxable benefits, such as life insurance in excess of $50,000, will result

---

**Forms of Employer-Sponsored
Insurance**

- Group insurance plans
- Voluntary benefit plans
- Cafeteria plans

---

in taxable income. Cafeteria plans can also be designed so that employees can obtain additional benefits with optional payroll or salary deductions.

Various cafeteria plan options can enable employees to elect a before-tax salary reduction to pay for their contributions to any employer-sponsored health plan or certain other types of employee benefits. This option, called a *premium-conversion plan*, may be part of a broader cafeteria plan or may stand alone.

**premium-conversion
plan**

**flexible spending
account (FSA)**

In addition, a cafeteria plan may allow *flexible spending accounts (FSAs)*, under which an employee can fund certain types of expenses other than insurance premiums on a before-tax basis. FSAs are used almost exclusively for medical and dental expenses not covered by an employer's plan and for dependent care expenses.

Cafeteria plans are subject to very complex government rules, and an in-depth discussion is beyond the scope of this book. However, they do offer many employees a cost-effective way to meet some of their personal insurance needs.

Individual Insurance. After the Jordans have met their economic security needs to the greatest extent possible through the first two building blocks—social insurance and employer-sponsored benefit plans—they should turn to the third building block, individual insurance. Here, the Jordans should make purchases to fill in coverage gaps left by social insurance and employer-sponsored insurance and to increase total coverage amounts to the necessary levels.

Monitoring the Risk Program. Once the Jordans have implemented each of the risk treatment methods, including the insurance method, administration of the risk management process requires ongoing monitoring of the choices and coverages by the Jordans and their financial consultant. New risks must be identified as they arise. The Jordans' insurance coverages and other risk treatment methods must also be reviewed periodically in light of their costs and their effectiveness in meeting the Jordans' needs.

SOURCES FOR FURTHER IN-DEPTH STUDY

- For a detailed discussion of cafeteria plans:
  - Beam, Burton T., Jr., *Group Benefits: Basic Concepts and Alternatives*, 9th ed., chapter 19, Bryn Mawr, PA: The American College, 2002. Phone 888-263-7265. Web site address www.amercoll.edu

- Johnson, Richard E., *Flexible Benefits—A How-To-Guide*, 6th ed., Brookfield, WI: International Foundation of Employee Benefit Plans, 2002. Phone 888-334-3324 option 4. Web site address www.ifebp.org
- For a detailed discussion of voluntary benefit plans, Podgurski, Walter B., *From Worksite Marketing to Website Marketing*, 4th ed., Cincinnati, OH: National Underwriter Company, 2000. Phone 800-543-0874. Web site address www.nuco.com

CHAPTER REVIEW

Answers to review questions and self-test questions start on page 725.

Key Terms

risk management	risk transfer
risk control	hold-harmless agreement
risk avoidance	insurance equation
segregation	credibility
diversification	risk identification
loss prevention	maximum possible loss
loss reduction	maximum probable loss
noninsurance transfer	binder
risk financing	voluntary benefits
risk retention	cafeteria plan
self-insurance	premium-conversion plan
captive insurer	flexible spending account (FSA)

Review Questions

2-1. List the four steps in the risk management process.

2-2. List the objectives of risk management.

2-3. Explain how the risk manager's role is carried out differently in large organizations as opposed to small- and medium-sized firms.

2-4. Explain how the two basic methods of treating risk—risk control and risk financing—differ from one another.

2-5. Explain why risk avoidance is not a practical solution to many risks.

2-6. List the reasons pure risks may be retained.

2-7. What are the reasons for using deductibles?

2-8. Your client Sam Jones feels that if he is going to buy insurance, it should pay whenever he has a loss. As a result, his insurance program includes coverage for high-frequency, low-severity losses. For example, his health insurance program includes basic medical expense coverage that pays from the first dollar of expense when he or his family goes to the doctor or the hospital. What could you recommend to Sam that would treat his risks involving high-frequency, low-severity losses more efficiently than using insurance?

2-9. List the ways that risks retained by a family or business are commonly financed.

2-10. Four key concepts help explain how insurance works—(a) the insurance equation, (b) probability and uncertainty, (c) the law of large numbers, and (d) adequate statistical data. Explain each concept and how it is important to the operation of the insurance mechanism.

2-11. Describe four methods of risk identification that can be used with households or businesses.

2-12. What factors should be considered in choosing the best technique(s) for dealing with a risk situation, especially for a household or small business?

2-13. Describe two approaches that can be used in deciding which technique or combination of techniques would best handle the risks faced by households and small businesses.

2-14. Describe the three "building blocks" that can be used in forming an insurance program to protect a client from the perils of death, disability, unemployment, and old age.

Self-Test Questions

T F   2-1. Risk management is a systematic process for dealing with risks, usually pure risks.

T F   2-2. A weakness of using the risk management process is that only insurance products are considered for treating risks.

T F   2-3. While loss prevention involves a reduction of the probability of loss, loss reduction involves lessening its severity.

T F   2-4. Deductibles are a form of partial risk retention that can often be used to efficiently handle high-frequency, low-severity losses.

T F   2-5. Self-insurance is an especially appropriate technique for small businesses and families to use in dealing with risks.

T F   2-6. While there are a variety of noninsurance risk transfer methods, insurance is the only risk transfer technique that can be used to handle pure risks.

T F   2-7. For an insurance business to operate in the long run, premiums must equal losses, expenses, and profits.

T F   2-8. The law of large numbers states that as the number of independent events increases, there is a greater chance that the actual results will be close to the expected results. (For example, the more times a coin is flipped, the greater the chance that the ratio of heads to number of flips will be close to one-half.)

T F   2-9. The first step in the risk management process is risk measurement.

T F   2-10. In risk management, each risk should be measured in terms of frequency, severity, and variation.

T F   2-11. In measuring risk, the concept most useful to the risk manager is maximum possible loss.

T F   2-12. Risk management involves, among other things, a careful evaluation of the suitability and cost of various alternative methods of treating pure risks, and the choice of the method or combination of methods that provides the most desirable result.

NOTES

1. In a few business organizations in recent years, some speculative risks have been assigned to the risk manager for treatment. For example, some business risk managers have become responsible for the speculative risks associated with foreign exchange rate fluctuations.
2. Table 2-2 was created from materials in Hamilton, Karen L., and Malecki, Donald S., *Personal Insurance: Property and Liability*, 2nd ed., chapter 1. Malvern, PA: American Institute for CPCU, 1999.
3. For a fuller discussion of these factors, see Williams, C.A., Jr., Smith, M.L., and Young, P. C., *Risk Management and Insurance*, 8th ed., pages 280–286. New York: Irwin McGraw-Hill, 1998.

Types of Insurers and Their Marketing Systems

Learning Objectives

An understanding of the material in this chapter should enable the student to

---

3-1.   Compare and contrast stock, mutual, and other types of insurance companies.

3-2.   Describe the marketing process, the insurance market, the types of marketing representatives, and the key marketing systems used in insurance.

Chapter Outline

In the first two chapters, we discussed risk and the management of risk. The balance of this book deals primarily with the insurance technique for managing pure risks. To begin, this and the next two chapters examine the structure of the industry that produces and/or sells the insurance products that individuals, families, and businesses need. Financial planners must understand the industry in which they work in order to effectively serve their clients.

TYPES OF PRIVATE INSURERS

The following pages summarize the characteristics of each of the major types of private insurers that make up the United States insurance industry. Throughout this book, the terms "insurer," "insurance company," and "company" are used to identify the party or organization that issues insurance "contracts" or "policies." Although the first three terms and the last two terms are generally interchangeable, the terminology may vary depending on context. In addition, the authors believe that varying the terminology enhances the book's readability. Note that while the majority of insurance companies are corporations, as this chapter explains shortly, there are also other forms of insurers.

Private insurers might be classified according to the lines of insurance they write such as life and health insurers, property and liability insurers, or monoline specialty insurers. This system of categorizing insurers, however, is probably not as meaningful as it used to be because many of the largest insurers have formed groups of affiliated companies with a common field force that writes and sells all lines of insurance.

domestic insurer
foreign insurer
alien insurer

Private insurers can also be classified on the basis of where they are domiciled. Insurance companies operating in the United States are considered *domestic insurers* by the state in which they are organized, *foreign insurers* by all other states, and *alien insurers* if incorporated in another country. For example, New York Life Insurance Company is a domestic company regarding its operations in New York. Hartford Fire Insurance Company (domiciled in Connecticut) is a foreign company regarding its operations in New York. Munich Reinsurance Company (domiciled in Germany) is an alien company regarding its operations in New York.

Types of Private Insurers

- Corporate vs. unincorporated
- Life/health vs. property/liability vs. monoline
- Domestic vs. foreign vs. alien
- Stock vs. mutual vs. other
- Proprietary vs. cooperative

Private insurers can also be divided into three major groups according to their legal form of organization, as follows: (1) stock companies, (2) mutual companies, and (3) other insurers. "Other" insurers include reciprocal exchanges, Lloyd's associations, fraternal societies, banks, and health associations. These various legal types of insurers can also be separated into insurers that are commercial or proprietary in nature and those that are cooperative in nature. The former have profit-seeking owners other than policyowners such as are found in stock companies and Lloyd's associations. Cooperatives are organized for the benefit of the policyowners such as in mutual companies, reciprocal exchanges, and fraternals.

Another meaningful way of classifying insurers is based on their different insurance marketing systems. The second major section of this chapter examines these marketing systems.

Stock Companies

stock insurance company

A *stock insurance company* is an incorporated business organized as a profit-making venture owned by stockholders. The stockholders elect the members of the company's board of directors and vote on other major issues facing the company such as mergers or acquisitions. As with other types of insurers, insurance laws enacted by the various states govern the company's operation such as its reserve fund, asset, and investment activities. To be licensed, stock insurers must have at least a specified amount of capital and surplus that differs from the amount required for other types of insurers. The contracts stock companies issue are usually written for a definitely stated consideration or premium. As will be explained later, however, a significant portion of the company's business may be written on a flexible-premium basis. The policyowner usually receives no benefit in the form of dividends from the company's earnings, and policies are nonassessable. Nonassessable policies charge no additional premium if losses for a class of policies exceed income. Except for participating policies (those with dividends) issued by some stock life insurers, the policyowner's first cost is usually the final cost.[1]

Shareholder equity serves as an extra amount, in addition to premium payments and retained earnings, out of which losses can be paid. Stockholders are entitled to any of the residual profits declared by the board as dividends after losses and expenses have been paid and proper reserves established.

Stock insurance companies thus have the following basic legal characteristics:

- They are incorporated and owned by stockholders who supply capital funds that serve as part of the financial security for the firm's operations.
- Except for flexible-premium contracts, they issue contracts for a fixed cost. The contracts are usually nonparticipating and are nonassessable.
- They can pay residual profits to the stockholders.

Mutual Companies

mutual insurance company

A *mutual insurance company* is a corporation that is owned by its policyowners. The policyowners also participate in the operations of the company, at least through voting rights, and share in the company's financial successes and, sometimes, failure. The company is organized primarily for the purpose of providing insurance for its policyowners at low cost, rather than to seek a profit. Every policyowner is an owner of the company. There are no stockholders. The mutual policyowners elect the board of directors, and the board elects the executive officers who actually manage the company. The mutual corporation assumes the risks of its policyowners. When the premiums in a given period are more than adequate to meet losses and expenses, part or all of the excess is returned to the policyowners as a dividend. When premiums are inadequate, dividends may be omitted and, in a few cases, assessments can be levied on policyowners.

There are several different kinds of mutual insurers. These include (1) advance-premium mutuals, (2) assessment mutuals, and (3) special-purpose mutuals. These mutuals may differ greatly in some characteristics, but each is incorporated and is owned by policyowners who receive dividends if the company's operations are successful.

Advance-Premium Mutuals

advance-premium mutual

This type of company is by far the best known and most important of mutual insurers, writing all but a small percentage of total mutual insurance. The operations of *advance-premium mutuals* are very similar to those of stock companies. Legally, advance-premium mutuals are different because they are owned by the policyowners, have no stockholders, and usually pay policyowner dividends. However, like stock companies, advance-premium mutuals collect the cost of the insurance at the time the contract is written.

Advance-premium mutuals issue nonassessable contracts in which the maximum cost of the insurance is set when the policy begins. Legal requirements for writing nonassessable policies require these mutuals to possess specified amounts of surplus to ensure the company's financial solvency in case of temporary periods of heavier-than-normal losses or expenses.

Advance-premium mutuals issue dividends to policyowners. At the end of the policy period, a return may be made as a dividend for any amount beyond the company's losses, expenses, and reasonable contributions to reserves and surplus. The actual amount of the return is unknown to the policyowner until after the insurance contract expires, and depends on the company's experience for that policyowner classification. The actual net cost to the policyowner, which is the original premium less the dividend, is thus uncertain until the dividend is paid.

In most states, advance-premium mutuals must comply with the same reserve, investment, policy form, and regulatory laws as apply to stock companies. Organization requirements are somewhat different, in that a minimum number of policyowners is required to start a company, and the board of directors must be established in the charter and bylaws as subject to the control of policyowners, rather than stockholders.

Other Types of Mutuals

assessment mutual

Some small mutual companies are called *assessment mutuals*. Policyowners may or may not pay an advance premium, but they can be assessed for a portion of the company's losses and expenses at the end of the policy period. The policyowner's liability for the assessment may be limited or unlimited.

factory mutual

Factory mutuals are another type of specialized mutual company. Factory mutuals write property insurance on large, highly protected industrial loss exposures. These mutuals charge a high advance premium, and the insurer's emphasis is on providing loss-prevention services, including frequent inspections of the insured premises. Dividends from factory mutuals for favorable experience tend to produce low final premium costs.

fraternal insurer

The fraternal insurer is another type of mutual insuring organization. A fraternal is a special type of insurer providing insurance benefits, particularly life insurance, for its members. The operations of the fraternal are closely related to and controlled by the bylaws of a lodge or a nonprofit social organization. Many fraternals are church oriented.

Choosing between the Stock and Mutual Form

Stock companies are far more numerous in life and health insurance than are mutuals. Also, the bulk of life insurance is written by stock companies. Their share is increasing, due in part to the conversion of many mutual life insurers to the stock form of organization. In property and liability insurance, stock companies again are more numerous than mutuals, and stock companies write most of the business.

From the standpoint of the insurance consumer, which type of insurer is better—a stock company or a mutual company? The answer is that neither type is inherently superior. The stock form of organization may entail lower initial premiums than the mutual form, and a stock company may be better equipped to raise the capital needed for insuring, both initially and subsequently. The mutual form, on the other hand, may charge lower premiums net of dividends because of its nonprofit status. The real issue for the consumer of insurance, then, is which specific insurer to select, not which type of insurer to select. Chapter 5 deals with this issue.

From the standpoint of the insuring organization itself, which form is better—stock or mutual? Again, there is no definitive answer. For a new insurer about to be formed, the stock company mode of organization is a virtual necessity because it is very difficult to form a mutual by persuading would-be policyowners to put up capital before the insurer can come into existence.

For existing insurance companies, the choice between the stock or mutual form of organization is more complex. The choice depends on the company's objectives and the relative importance it places on the advantages of the stock

---

Reasons for Demutualizing

- Raising new capital
- Insurer diversification
- Noncash executive compensation
- Federal income savings

---

demutualization

and mutual forms. On balance, however, the number of mutual insurers in the United States is on the decline due to mergers, insolvencies, and intentional shifting of mutual companies to the stock form of organization—a process called *demutualization*. Probably the most important reason for demutualization is to enable the insurer to raise capital quickly. A stock company, of course, can raise new capital by issuing stock, bonds, warrants, and other types of debt instruments, as well as by earning profits. Mutual insurers have only their profits and borrowings to provide additional capital for expansion, acquisition, or other purposes.

A second and often related reason for demutualization is to enable the insurance company to diversify its activities by acquiring other insurers or other types of financial institutions through the issuance or exchange of stock. Mutual insurers, having no stock, are less able to diversify in this way. Also, stock insurers can create upstream holding companies to facilitate diversification. Until recently, this avenue was not open to mutual insurers, and in many states it still is not available.

A third reason for demutualization is to facilitate payment of certain types of noncash compensation to the insurance company's key executives and board members. Compensation through tax-advantaged stock options and stock-ownership plans is not available in a mutual company.

A fourth reason for demutualization is to gain federal income tax savings. The Internal Revenue Code, for example, limits the amount of dividends to policyowners that a mutual company may deduct for federal income tax purposes.

Nevertheless, the process of demutualization has certain significant disadvantages. The time, cost, and complexity may be enormous due to regulatory, tax, legal, and accounting requirements. Of particular importance is the regulatory requirement that the policyowners of the company seeking to demutualize be compensated adequately for loss of their ownership rights. A second disadvantage of demutualization is that, as a stock company, the insurer might become vulnerable to a hostile takeover. Third, as a stock insurer, the company would have to meet SEC and state rules relating to its equity securities. Fourth, demutualization represents a major change in corporate philosophy with the introduction of an explicit profit motive, a change that may be very difficult for senior executives and other long-standing employees of the former mutual company to accept.

**mutual holding
company**

Several states allow mutual insurers to create a hybrid form of organization—the *mutual holding company*—to overcome some of the disadvantages of either remaining a mutual or demutualizing. In this circumstance, the mutual insurer creates an upstream holding company controlled by the policyowners. The holding company then acquires at least 51 percent of the stock of a newly created stock insurance company that takes over the business of the former mutual insurer. The remaining stock can be sold to outsiders to raise new capital for the insurance company.

Other Types of Insuring Organizations

By far, the majority of the private insurance in the United States is written by stock companies and advance-premium mutual companies. There are, however, several other legal types of insurers that merit discussion because they represent the wide variety of insurers in the market or because they are relatively significant in particular types of insurance or in certain areas of the country.

Lloyd's Associations

Lloyd's association

In contrast to stock and mutual insurers, which are corporations, *Lloyd's associations* are groups of individual insurers. Although insurance written by Lloyd's associations accounts for only a small percentage of the total insurance sales in the United States, the concept of insurance written by individuals is important. Lloyd's organizations are also significant from a historical standpoint, and in the world market they are very important for reinsurance and for insuring unusual and difficult risks. There are two types of Lloyd's associations: Lloyd's of London, which is by far the more important, and the American Lloyd's, which are small and few in number.

Lloyd's of London is one of the most famous institutions for the insurance of loss exposures, and bears the name of the coffeehouse where it originated more than 300 years ago as a center of shipping news and financial information. Lloyd's itself does not directly issue insurance policies; rather, insurance is written by underwriting members who sign "each for himself and not for another." The insurer, then, is not Lloyd's but the underwriters at Lloyd's. A policyowner insures *at* Lloyd's but not *with* Lloyd's.

Underwriting members, also called *names*, from around the world supply capital but do not work at Lloyd's. These members are organized into syndicates, with membership varying from a few to more than 1,000 in each. Each syndicate is operated by an underwriting agent, who commits the members of that syndicate to the risks from the business written. There are firms consisting of authorized Lloyd's brokers. With an adequate description of the property, life, or activity to be insured, the broker offers the insurance to the underwriters. Each underwriter who wishes to signs a slip—underwriting his or her name to it, hence the term underwriter—indicating the amount of insurance accepted. When the broker has obtained enough signers so that the amounts the broker assumes total the required insurance, the Lloyd's Policy Signing Office draws up the policy and affixes its official seal. The document, however, is not signed by the corporation but by members, who must themselves pay their proportional share in the event of a loss. The function of the corporation of Lloyd's is purely to supervise transactions and to guard the institution's reputation.

The fame of Lloyd's of London is heightened by the unusual loss exposures that have been insured at Lloyd's. Practically any large loss in the world, such as a multimillion-dollar fire, the crash of a huge ship or airplane, or a major hurricane, involves Lloyd's of London as either an insurer or a reinsurer.

Lloyd's of London is licensed directly in only two states, Illinois and Kentucky, although Lloyd's brokers and agents operate throughout the United States and the rest of the world. In the United States, state excess and surplus line laws allow coverage to be placed at any nonadmitted insurer such as Lloyd's if the desired coverage is not available from licensed insurers. Although the usual household or small business would have little need for insuring at Lloyd's of London, businesses can insure at Lloyd's to obtain needed high liability limits, special coverages such as worldwide package policies, or difficult-to-obtain protection for unusual perils or very large amounts of insurance.

There are a few American Lloyd's associations, including several in Texas. These associations write primarily fire and allied lines and automobile physical damage insurance. In the American Lloyd's associations, each member is ordinarily liable for only a specified maximum, and the strict regulations of Lloyd's of London that govern membership, deposits, and audits are not present. Each American Lloyd's organization depends on the financial strength of its individual members within their limited liability. The American Lloyd's and the original London organization have no connection, and the American Lloyd's plays a relatively small role in United States insurance.

Reciprocal Exchanges

reciprocal exchange

In the property and liability insurance field, another type of insurer combines some characteristics of a mutual insurer, which is owned by its policyowners, and a Lloyd's association, in which individuals assume the risks. The *reciprocal exchange*, often called an interinsurance exchange, is an unincorporated association. In a reciprocal exchange's original and purest form, each policyowner is insured by all the others. Thus, each policyowner is also an insurer because contracts are exchanged on a reciprocal basis. In its now more popular modified form, a reciprocal exchange operates without individual accounts for its subscribers, and closely resembles a conventional mutual insurer.

The reciprocal exchange is not a mutual insurer in the legal sense because the individual subscribers assume liability as individuals, not as a responsibility of the group as a whole. Another basic difference from mutual insurers is that reciprocal exchanges are not incorporated but are formed under separate laws as associations under the direction of an attorney-in-fact. Reciprocal exchanges are contrasted with Lloyd's associations because Lloyd's associations are (1) proprietary or profit seeking, and (2) the Lloyd's insurer is not also a policyowner, whereas every policyowner in a reciprocal exchange is an insurer.

The funds held by a pure reciprocal exchange are the total of individual credits held for the accounts of individual subscribers. These subscribers are required to accumulate reserves representing a multiple ranging from two to five annual premiums before underwriting earnings, if any, are returned in cash. A separate account is maintained for each subscriber, and a proportional share of each loss and expense is paid out of each subscriber's account. Beyond that, the reciprocal exchange can usually levy an assessment of up to some multiple of premiums paid, such as 10 times, but each subscriber's liability is definitely limited.

Reciprocal exchanges are few in number and relatively unimportant in the total business of insurance, but in certain areas and for personal lines of insurance, they have some significance. Although usually small, a few reciprocal exchanges have grown to substantial size.

Banks

In recent years, the entry of banks into the business of insurance has been characterized by a considerable amount of publicity, controversy, and legal jousting. Note, however, that one particular type of bank—the mutual savings bank—has been active in the business of providing life insurance for many years in states including Connecticut, Massachusetts, and New York.

Laws in these states authorize mutual savings banks to write life insurance on residents of the state and on persons regularly employed there. The amounts that may be issued are limited, and the coverage is written without a commissioned agent as an intermediary. Consequently, premium rates for savings bank life insurance usually compare favorably with those charged by other insurers. Nevertheless, the amount of savings bank life insurance represents only a small percentage of the total amount of life insurance sold in the three states. Perhaps this is attributable to the absence of an aggressive, commission-based sales force in savings bank life insurance.

The past few years have also seen the gradual entry of other types of banks in other states into the insurance business, particularly in such lines as fixed and variable annuities, homeowners insurance, automobile insurance, and life insurance. Initially, the majority of these banks created entirely new insurance operations from scratch. Later entrants to the field, however, have tended to form alliances with existing insurers and their insurance agencies, thus becoming, rather than insurers, marketing channels for insurance "manufactured" by others.

Health Associations

In the field of medical expense insurance, Blue Cross and Blue Shield organizations and health maintenance organizations (HMOs) play a particularly important role. Detailed information about health maintenance organizations and other managed care organizations is contained in chapter 12. This chapter simply summarizes the basic characteristics of the "Blues."

Blue Cross organizations have historically provided coverage of hospital care costs in member hospitals on a service basis, rather than on a cash reimbursement basis. Blue Shield organizations have provided coverage of the costs of member physicians and surgeons, also on a service basis. Under the service-benefit concept, benefits are expressed in terms of the services that the hospitals or physicians participating in the plan will provide, rather than in terms of dollar maximums. For example, a Blue Cross plan might provide hospitalization in semiprivate accommodations. In contrast, an insurance company might provide reimbursement for hospital charges subject to a dollar limitation such as $400 per day.

While Blue Cross and Blue Shield plans have traditionally operated separately in limited geographic areas, most Blue Cross and Blue Shield plans in each area have now merged into a single entity. Blue Cross and Blue Shield plans must be members of the National Blue Cross and Blue Shield Association, which sets certain standards for the local organizations. Among these standards are requirements that the local organizations have boards of directors, the majority of whom are not health care providers, and that the organizations participate in national plans that offer portability of coverage and benefit availability for insureds outside their home service areas.

While the Blues and insurance companies were once quite different, they have evolved over the years so that they now probably have more similarities than differences. The Blues tend to exist under special enabling legislation, which gives them some advantages, such as favorable state taxation, but also limits their underwriting and rating flexibility. The majority of plans are structured as not-for-profit organizations, making them similar to mutual insurance companies. However, several have converted to the traditional forms of stock or mutual companies.

THE MARKETING PROCESS

With this background of the types of organizations that provide insurance to individuals, households, and businesses, we now turn to the process by which organizations market their insurance. Why do financial planners need to understand how the insurance business markets its contracts and services? First, financial planners are in many cases active participants in the marketing process, deriving some of their compensation from being participants. Second, working with consumers of insurance, financial planners may gain a better understanding about the choices among insurers and agents that clients must make in buying insurance. Finally, the marketing process is a key function in insurance operations, and the methods companies use to sell and service insurance contracts are significant in determining their costs and usefulness.

Marketing the Insurance Product

Figure 3-1 shows the relationship of marketing to the product design, underwriting, and loss payment functions as insurance is distributed from insurers to policyowners. A description of several of these other functions and of the regulation of insurance is contained in later chapters.

Marketing, or directing the flow of goods and services from the insurer to the consumer or user, is a particularly important business activity for insurance

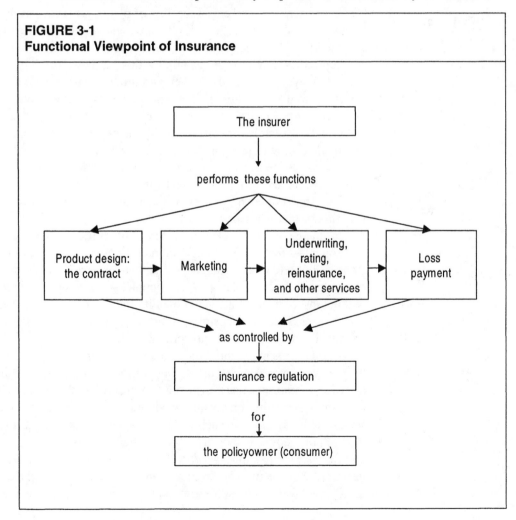

FIGURE 3-1
Functional Viewpoint of Insurance

companies. The insurance product consists of a written legal contract, plus a bundle of services. The educational, motivational, advisory, and other services prior to, at the time of, and after issuing the contract make the purchaser of insurance at least in some ways different from the purchaser of automobiles, restaurant meals, clothing, or other tangible goods.

The insurance agent is the primary basis of marketing for the typical insurer. The insurer must develop the marketing system that becomes the link between the insurer and the policyowner or consumer. Other types of businesses often can have small, yet profitable, operations. An insurer needs to have a reasonably large and diversified market to increase the predictability of losses. Thus, marketing insurance assumes a predominant place among functions that insurers perform.

The Insurance Market

In one sense, a market is a meeting of people who have as their purpose the transaction of business. The term can mean either the region in which a commodity is sold, the group of persons who might be expected to purchase it, or the place of purchase. As examples, there are, respectively, the West Coast market, the young marrieds market, and the local supermarket.

In insurance terminology, the term market is used to indicate both the area of distribution and the available sources of the different coverages. In the first instance, for example, persons in the middle salary brackets might be referred to as a market for retirement annuities, or small business organizations as a market for key employee life insurance or business overhead expense coverage. The second use of the term applies it to the place or source for the purchase of different forms of coverage such as the aviation, disability income, substandard life, fire, or marine insurance markets.

Insurance buyers or their agents have little difficulty in placing insurance for most clients—that is, in finding a market. Every company selects applicants on the basis of underwriting judgment, and there are many classes that one company or another will not write at all. For example, some commercial property insurers will not insure restaurants. In the liability field, some companies may not insure motorcycles. In life and health insurance, some insurers will not write insurance on sky divers, test pilots, or juvenile diabetics.

Local agents may limit their business to either life or property insurance, or they may embrace all forms of the insurance business. An all-lines agency represents companies that will afford facilities for all the classes of insurance that its customers require. Frequently, the limitations of local agents require that they seek outside facilities. In such instances, agents are said to "broker the line" or as much of the line as they are unable to handle themselves.

Because the risk manager for a household or organization selects agents and insurers, he or she must be familiar with the insurance market and its limits. The usual coverages, such as life, fire, and automobile insurance, are obtainable in every community through a local agency. For more hazardous lines that are not written in volume, the market is more limited. While almost every measurable risk is insurable, it does not necessarily follow that every agent has the facilities for placing every insurable risk. Ability to place unusual lines of insurance is evidence that the agent or broker is well informed and provides broad professional services.

Types of Marketing Representatives

The insurance buyer is often most concerned, and rightly so, with the representative of the insurance company with whom the buyer makes direct contact. The legal type of insurer or the marketing system used is often of secondary importance to the policyowner. The applicant for insurance makes contact with the insurer through one or more of the following: (1) agents, (2) brokers, (3) insurance consultants and financial planners, and (4) service representatives.

Agents

agent

The *agent*, often referred to as a producer, is a representative of the insurance company, also referred to as the principal. Agents are appointed by an insurance company to act on its behalf, with authority to solicit, negotiate, and in some cases put contracts of insurance into effect. Agents are normally compensated by a commission that is a percentage of a policy premium.

The agent's powers are governed by his or her agency contract with the insurer. The agency contract spells out the agent's express authority. The agent also has implied or incidental authority to carry out those acts needed to exercise his or her express authority. However, an agent's acts may bind the principal even if (1) those acts are outside the scope of the agent's express or implied authority, or (2) the acts are within the agent's apparent authority. This type of authority arises when the agent, without contrary action by the principal, performs an act that appears to a reasonable person to be within the agent's express or implied authority. For example, if a life insurance agent waives a policy provision for a policyowner relating to the grace period for payment of renewal premiums, the insurance company might, if silent on the matter, be bound by the apparent authority of the agent. To prevent this from happening, the insurer normally includes a provision in the policy stating that only specified home office personnel have the authority to waive or modify a policy provision.

A principal may even ratify an agent's actions that are outside the scope of the agent's authority, and as a result be bound by those actions. For example, if an insurance contract states that renewal premiums must be sent to the insurer's home office, but the company routinely accepts premiums sent to its local agent, in the event of a dispute, the insurer would probably be found to have ratified the agent's collection of renewal premiums.

An agent owes legal duties to his or her principal, including the duty to be loyal to the principal, the duty not to be negligent, and the duty to obey instructions given by the principal. Similarly, the principal owes certain duties to the agent, including the duty to give the agent an opportunity to work, to compensate the agent, to keep accounts of amounts owed to the agent, and to reimburse the agent for authorized payments the agent makes and liabilities he or she incurs while working for the principal.

Sources of Authority of an Agent

- Express authority
- Implied or incidental authority
- Apparent authority
- Authority arising from ratification

The terms general agent, local agent, and special agent, among others, are frequently used in the insurance business. All of these terms have a specialized significance within the business and may represent the nature of the agent's position with the company or the commission arrangement. Legally, regardless of terminology, an agent is either a general agent or a limited agent. A *general agent* can bind insurance for a client, making insurance effective immediately and prior to the actual issuance of the policy. A *limited agent's* powers are limited or restricted. The scope of the delegated authority determines what the agent may or may not do. Secret limitations, however, may not apply, and the principal may be bound if the action is within the limited agent's express, implied, or apparent authority.

general agent

limited agent

Life insurance companies customarily limit the authority to issue or modify life insurance contracts to salaried company officers. Life insurance agents, even those called general agents, are thus limited agents. Generally speaking, life insurance agents are authorized to solicit, receive, and forward applications for the contracts written by their companies. Agents are authorized to receive the first premiums due on applications but not subsequent premiums. The life insurance agent's authority is also limited in the ability to accept business or bind the coverage. The life insurer issues the contract after receiving the written, signed application and, often, a medical examination report. The agent may not cover the policyowner immediately, nor may contract modifications be made later without the insurance company's approval.

Agents appointed to represent property and liability insurers are often granted the powers of a general agent. The limitations on their authority are set forth in the agency agreement. General agents may bind their companies for a client's coverage in certain cases. This is done by an oral or written binder, which is temporary evidence of coverage until the full insurance policy is issued by the insurance company. Among their other responsibilities, these agents inspect and collect initial and sometimes renewal premiums. Some general agents even issue contracts in their own offices for automobile or homeowners policies. Contracts for other lines of insurance may have to be issued by the insurer in the home office or a branch office.

Brokers

broker

Brokers, who represent the policyowner rather than the insurer, can also be valuable in rendering service to the insurance purchaser. With widespread contacts and knowledge of many fields of insurance, brokers can offer significant advice and counsel to their clients. The larger insurance brokerage firms are especially well equipped to handle the problems of insurance for a buyer with individual and specialized requirements.

Unlike the agent, who legally represents the insurer, the broker acts on behalf of the applicant for insurance or the policyowner after the insurance goes into effect. Thus, the broker is an independent contractor. The broker assists the applicant for insurance by finding coverage, but the broker is paid by the insurer. By becoming knowledgeable about rates, forms, and markets, brokers are useful and recognized intermediaries between the insurer or the agent and the policyowner. The duties of a broker are similar to those of an agent as described earlier, except that the broker's duties pertain to the applicant or policyowner whom he or she represents.

Policyowners are sometimes confused because they do not differentiate between an insurance broker and an agent. As explained above, the insurance agent is acting under specific and delegated authority from the insurer and is sometimes authorized to bind coverage within specific limits. The broker, on the other hand, has no such authority. Because the broker represents the applicant or policyowner, the applicant or policyowner is bound by the broker's acts. For example, any misrepresentation, mistake, breach of warranty, or fraud perpetrated by the broker on a policyowner's behalf makes the policyowner responsible as if the policyowner had committed the act. Furthermore, a statement by an applicant to a broker is not presumed to be known to an insurance company, whereas a statement by an applicant to an agent is presumed to be known by the company.

It is important to understand that the broker cannot make insurance effective. The broker is not a party to the insurance contract. However, many insurance agents may be licensed as both agents and brokers. The simplest illustration is the case of an agent who commits the insurer for a part of a desired amount of coverage and acts as a broker in placing any excess coverage.

Example: Ripley is an agent for the XYZ Insurance Company, which specializes in substandard automobile insurance. Ripley also has a broker's license that includes automobile insurance. Ripley may have authority to bind coverage for an applicant in XYZ, but Ripley has no authority to bind coverage that he wishes to place in another insurer for which he acts a broker.

---

excess line broker

A special type of broker called an *excess line broker* or surplus line broker places coverage for which there is no available market in the state such as exposures that have a high loss frequency or severity. Examples of business that excess line brokers place are liability insurance for amusement parks and ski resorts and many product liability situations. Usually, the coverage is placed with companies that have not been licensed to do business in the particular state and are therefore known as *nonadmitted insurers*. The excess line broker may not always deal with the policyowner directly but may be sought out by the policyowner's broker. Many states require special licenses for excess line brokers.

nonadmitted insurer

While the major part of life insurance production is handled by company agents, life insurance brokers place business with the company that they believe can best handle and service the line. Because underwriting rules of companies differ so widely, applications to several companies may be necessary for group insurance, a fertile field for brokers. A significant volume of brokerage business also arises from life insurance agents who basically represent one life insurance company but place individual insurance business in another company because clients want the particular plan or price offered there. Substandard policies and policies in which the potential loss is extremely large, sometimes called jumbo risk policies, are often placed in this way. Estate planning and pension plans in which transactions are large and competition is keen are other fields where life insurance brokers play an important part.

Insurance Consultants and Financial Planners

In addition to agents and brokers, various types of insurance consultants and financial planners may serve as intermediaries between insurers and policyowners in the marketing process. Insurance consultants are usually compensated by the policyowner on a fee basis. Financial planners may be paid a fee by the policyowner, a commission from the insurer if they are also agents or brokers, or some combination of a fee and a commission. Because protecting a client's income and assets is fundamental to all financial plans, financial planners play a major role in the insurance marketing system.

Service Representatives

service representative

Many insurers and some large agencies employ salaried specialists to assist agents in writing the more complex lines of insurance. These *service representatives* may help an agent sell or service insurance. Company officers and managers of insurance companies employed on a salaried basis are not included in the category of service representatives. A license is not usually. required by the state to act as a service representative.

Examples of service representatives are common in both the life and property insurance fields. In life insurance, service representatives include advanced underwriting specialists who aid the life insurance agent in estate planning and pension or tax planning. General agents use salaried training specialists to recruit, supervise, and assist new life insurance agents. Most companies writing group life and health coverages have salaried company representatives who assist the life insurance agent with writing group contracts. In property insurance, many companies use special agents to initiate agency contracts, help the agent on special sales problems, and keep the agent informed of the insurer's new contracts and services. Engineering, appraisal, and loss-prevention services are often provided by company specialists in conjunction with local agents. In addition, company claims adjusters work in cooperation with agents on many losses involving large amounts or special problems.

Marketing Systems Used in Insurance

Agency versus Direct-Selling Systems

Insurance is distributed from insurers to policyowners in a variety of ways. The most important way is through an agency system of representatives who operate under the authority given to them by insurers to make legal transactions with consumers of insurance. The complex and intangible nature of insurance and its significance to the policyowner make personal contact through an intermediary essential to the sale of most insurance.

direct-selling system

Direct-selling systems are the exception to the general rule that insurance is sold through agents. Under these systems, the insurer deals directly with the applicant, without agents, through employees of the insurer. In specialized lines in certain market segments of insurance, these systems assume some importance. Dread disease insurers or hospital indemnity health insurers who use direct mail or television advertising are common examples. All correspondence circulates directly between the company and the prospect, and the insurance contract is written and serviced by mail or telephone without an agent.

As another example, some insurers are selling such coverages as annuities and life, health, automobile, homeowners, and long-term care insurance on a direct basis over the Internet. A few automobile insurers have applied the direct mail system successfully in writing automobile insurance. Some life insurance sales are also accomplished in this way.

In life and health insurance, the growth of group insurance with sales by salaried employees as a supplement to commissioned agents is evidence of a compromise between direct and agency systems of marketing. The idea of selling by employees also applies to more and more cases in the property and liability field, especially for automobile and homeowners insurance.

Life Insurance Agency Systems

general agency system

Agency systems for marketing life insurance differ from those for marketing property and liability insurance. Many life insurance companies use a *general agency system*, although as discussed earlier, an insurance general agent is not a general agent in the legal sense. Historically, a general insurance agent was an individual entrepreneur granted a franchise by an insurer to market the insurer's products in a specified geographic area. The general agent represented only that one insurer, and was responsible for hiring, training, motivating, and supervising agents. The general agent was compensated solely by commissions on business the agency produced and was fully responsible for all expenses of operating the agency. More recently, however, insurance companies typically provide some form of financial assistance to the general agent, perhaps paying some of the costs involved in hiring and training new agents and/or providing an allowance to cover some of the operating agency's expenses.

branch office system

In contrast with the general agency system, many life insurance companies use a *branch office system*, also referred to as a managerial system. Here, the insurer establishes branch offices in the areas where it writes business, with each branch headed by a manager who is a salaried employee of the insurance company. Again, the manager is responsible for hiring, training, motivating, and supervising agents for the company, but the insurer bears all costs of operating the branch. The branch manager may also receive a bonus as part of his or her compensation, depending on the quantity and quality of business the branch writes. Payment of bonuses to branch managers, together with coverage of some general agency operating expenses, has tended to blur somewhat the historical distinctions between the two agency systems.

Main Agency Systems in Insurance

- Life insurance
  - General agent system
  - Branch office system
  - PPGA system
- Property/liability insurance
  - Independent agent system
  - Exclusive agent system

---

personal producing general agent (PPGA)

A variation of the general agency system that has become significant in some life insurance companies is the *personal producing general agent (PPGA)* system. In this system, the insurer hires an experienced agent with a proven record of sales success as its general agent in a given territory. Unlike a traditional general agent, however, the PPGA's main responsibility is to sell the insurer's products, rather than to build an agency force for the company. The PPGA often receives higher commissions than other agents to help cover operating expenses. The PPGA may be expected to meet certain sales quotes for the company, but may also be allowed to represent other insurers.

Property and Liability Insurance Agency Systems

independent agency system

The two main agency systems that insurers use in the property and liability field are the independent agency system and the exclusive agency system sometimes referred to as the captive agent system. In the *independent agency system*, the insurance agency is an independent business organization that represents several insurance companies or groups of companies. The head of the agency pays all his or her own operating expenses and is compensated mainly through commissions on the business the agency writes. Independent agents may also receive contingent commissions from the insurer if the business they submit has favorable loss ratios. Some independent agencies are paid fees by the insurer for settling small claims or by the policyowner for providing risk management services.

The independent agent usually has some authority to bind the insurer for a client's coverage, to collect the initial premium and in some cases the renewal premiums, to submit the application to the insurer, and to deliver the policy to the policyowner. The policyowner is, by contract, the customer of the agent. The independent agent owns the policyowner's business and is free to place it with a different insurer when the policy comes up for renewal, unless the policyowner objects. One of the results of this ownership status is that commission rates tend to be the same for renewal policies as for new policies. If renewal commissions were lower, the independent agent may be inclined to place the business with a different insurer at each renewal date to earn the higher first-year commission. Another result of ownership of the customer's business is that when the independent agent elects to retire or leave the business, he or she can sell the book of business to another agent. The insurer may not interfere with the agent's ownership rights.

One of the main advantages of the independent agency system is the agent's ability to place business with the company that offers the best coverage at the best price for each applicant. On the other hand, one of the disadvantages is that a conflict of interest may exist when the agent is free to place business with any of several companies paying different commission rates.

exclusive agency system

In the *exclusive agency system*, the agent usually represents only one company or group of affiliated companies. Compensation comes mainly from commissions on the sale of new business, with lower commission rates on renewals. The insurer may cover some of the agent's operating expenses, particularly for new agents. The agency contract typically gives the agent either limited or no ownership, use, and control of policy and expiration data while the contract is in force. The agent has no control over what happens to the business when he or she retires or leaves the insurance field.

In the exclusive agency system, billing and collection of renewal premiums are almost always the insurer's responsibility, not the agent's. The agent may have the power, within limits, to bind the insurer on a client's coverage. The agent may also have the authority to settle small claims.

Comparing the market shares controlled by the two types of agency systems in property and liability insurance shows a rapid growth in the exclusive agency system share. This is particularly true in the personal rather than business lines of insurance, in which selling processes and coverage details are less complex.

Group Insurance Systems

Marketing to consumers in the group insurance system is usually done on a group basis through the employer. Payroll deductions are a convenient method of premium payment. Labor unions, credit unions, finance companies, professional associations, and other groups may also be used to obtain the desired result of lowering insurance costs to the members of the group.

In life insurance, the trend toward increased group insurance has been continuous since such plans began many years ago. Health insurance has used the group method of marketing even more extensively, especially in medical expense insurance. Annuities or insured pensions, too, have used the system widely.

Group plans in property and liability insurance are much less established and differ from group life and health insurance in some respects. Most of these plans have individual selection, rating, and contracts instead of group underwriting, master contracts, and certificates. However, employer participation is involved in the arrangements for the plans, premiums are collected through payroll deductions, and the objectives of the plans are similar to those of group life and health insurance. Automobile and homeowners policies are the principal fields in which mass merchandising of quasi-group property and liability insurance has been tried.

SOURCES FOR FURTHER IN-DEPTH STUDY

- For detailed information on banks in insurance:
  - American Bankers Insurance Association, 1120 Connecticut Ave. NW, Washington, DC 20036. Phone 202-663-5163, www.aba.com/
  - Bank Insurance and Securities Association, ABIA, 303 W. Lancaster Ave. Suite 1c, Wayne, PA 19087. Phone 610-989-9047, www.bisanet.org

- For a thorough treatment of the subject of agency law, especially in life insurance, Graves, Edward E., and Christensen, Burke A., editors, *McGill's Legal Aspects of Life Insurance,* 3d ed., chapter 16, Bryn Mawr, PA: The American College, 2002. Phone 888-263-7265. Web site address www.amercoll.edu

CHAPTER REVIEW

Answers to review questions and self-test questions start on page 725.

Key Terms

domestic insurer	general agent
foreign insurer	limited agent
alien insurer	broker
stock insurance company	excess line broker
mutual insurance company	nonadmitted insurer
advance-premium mutual	service representative
assessment mutual	direct-selling system
factory mutual	general agency system
fraternal insurer	branch office system
demutualization	personal producing general
mutual holding company	agent (PPGA)
Lloyds association	independent agency system
reciprocal exchange	exclusive agency system
agent	

Review Questions

3-1. Compare the features of stock and mutual insurance companies as to form of business, ownership, voters for the Board of Directors, and recipients of dividends.

3-2. In recent years, numerous mutual insurance companies have shifted to the stock form through the process of demutualization.
   a. Why do companies demutualize?
   b. What are the potential disadvantages associated with demutualizing?

3-3. Explain the following with regard to Lloyd's of London:
   a. Who provides the insurance (who is the insurer)?
   b. What function does the corporation of Lloyd's perform?
   c. How are underwriting members organized to do business?
   d. In what states is Lloyd's licensed directly?
   e. How is Lloyd's able to do business in states where it is not licensed?
   f. How do American Lloyd's associations differ from Lloyd's of London?

3-4. Explain how reciprocal exchanges differ from
   a. mutual insurers
   b. Lloyd's associations

3-5. Why does a financial planner need to understand how the insurance business markets its contracts and services?

3-6. Describe the three powers held by an agent and the legal duties an agent and principal owe each other.

3-7. Legally, an agent is either a general agent or a limited agent. Indicate which legal type each of the following insurance agents typically is and what authority is generally given to them by their insurers.
   a. life insurance agents
   b. property-liability insurance agents

3-8. At the advice of his financial planner, Tom Johnson meets with an agent at an all-lines agency to discuss obtaining coverage to meet his various protection needs. In each of the following cases, indicate whether or not Tom has coverage immediately and why:
   a. After gathering information about Tom's new home and its contents, the agent recommends a homeowners policy with XYZ Insurance Company. After getting satisfactory answers to questions regarding price and the claims service offered by the company, Tom tells the agent he wants the policy from XYZ. The agent tells Tom he's covered.
   b. After gathering information about the needs of Tom's family in the event of his death and about Tom's existing group life coverage at work, the agent recommends a $500,000 variable universal life policy from ABC Life to meet Tom's additional needs. The agent points out the flexibility of the policy both in terms of premium payments and investment choices. Tom fills out the application and gives the agent the minimum first premium. The agent tells Tom, "You're going to like the flexibility and performance of your new policy."

3-9. Explain the difference between an insurance agent and a broker in terms of
   a. who they represent
   b. their power to bind the insurance company

3-10. Describe the key features of the following agency systems used to market life insurance:
   a. general agent
   b. branch office or managerial system
   c. personal producing general agent (PPGA)

3-11. Compare the key features of the two main agency systems, the independent agency system and the exclusive agency system, used to market property-liability insurance:

a. How many companies or groups of companies are represented?
b. Who pays operating expenses?
c. How are agents compensated?
d. What is the relative size of renewal versus initial commissions?
e. Who generally has ownership, use, and control of policy and expiration data?
f. Who generally collects premiums and settles claims?

Self-Test Questions

T   F   3-1. On the basis of where they are domiciled, insurers are considered foreign if incorporated in another country.

T   F   3-2. Stock and mutual insurers are both owned by stockholders who elect the board of directors.

T   F   3-3. Stock and mutual insurers may both pay dividends—stock companies to their stockholders and mutual companies to their policyowners.

T   F   3-4. Because mutuals are owned by their policyowners, they are usually better than stocks from a consumer's standpoint.

T   F   3-5. In order to facilitate access to capital markets and diversification of activities, there is currently a trend for stock companies to convert to mutual companies.

T   F   3-6. In Lloyd's of London, insurance is written by the corporation of Lloyd's.

T   F   3-7. Because Lloyd's of London is not licensed directly in most states in the United States, the insurance coverage it writes in most states is the same as that permitted under state excess and surplus lines laws.

T   F   3-8. Because a reciprocal is an unincorporated association, each insured is also an insurer.

T   F   3-9. Although reciprocals are usually small, a few exchanges writing automobile insurance have grown to substantial size.

T   F   3-10. When representing an insurance company, an insurance agent has only the express authority spelled out in the agency contract.

T   F   3-11. From a legal standpoint, nearly all life insurance agents are granted the powers of a general agent.

T   F   3-12. A broker represents the policyowner, unlike an agent who is a legal representative of the insurance company.

T   F   3-13. Key life insurance marketing systems include general agents, branch offices managed by company employees, and personal producing general agents (PPGAs).

T   F   3-14.   In property and liability insurance, an independent agent can represent several insurers or groups of companies, whereas an exclusive agent normally represents only one company or group of affiliated companies.

T   F   3-15.   Exclusive agents generally receive the same commission rate for renewing a policy as for initially selling the policy, whereas independent agents have traditionally received renewal commissions that are considerably smaller than their initial commissions.

NOTE

1. In some commercial lines, such as workers' compensation insurance, the insured's first cost takes the form of a tentative deposit premium that is subject to adjustment after an audit at the end of the period of protection.

4

Insurance Company Operations

Learning Objectives

An understanding of the material in this chapter should enable the student to

---

4-1. Describe the purpose of underwriting and the selection of applicants.

4-2. Explain the purposes of reinsurance.

4-3. Explain the purpose of claims adjustment, the types of claims adjusters, and procedures for claims adjustment.

4-4. Describe factors involved in insurance rate making.

4-5. Explain the investment and other functions of an insurance company.

Chapter Outline

In the last chapter, we discussed types of private insurers and how they market their products to the public. Now we turn our attention to internal operations. The principal areas described are underwriting, reinsurance, claims adjusting, rate making, and investing. Understanding these areas can help financial planners improve their understanding and their clients' awareness of insurer operations as well as strengthen planners' relationship with the home office.

UNDERWRITING

Insurance is viewed in the law as a "business affected with a public interest."[1] While insurance provides a wide variety of coverages to almost everyone, the insurer is not usually required to write an insurance contract for each person who applies.[2] At first glance, there might appear to be something wrong with a business that can refuse to do business with persons most likely to have losses, who perhaps need the product most, while continually striving to accept as clients those persons who are least likely to have losses. However, in addition to the public interest, the insurer has an obligation to its insureds and owners to conduct business so that it remains financially solvent and obtains reasonable profits or contributions to surplus.

Purpose

underwriting

A general description of *underwriting* is simply the selection and classification of insurance applications that are offered to an insurer.[3] The basis for underwriting is that the insurer must accept only applicants who, on average, will have actual loss experience comparable to the expected loss experience for which the company has set its premium rates. Selection implies that there are some acceptances and some rejections, or that not all applicants will be accepted for insurance. Underwriting is an activity that is not found in most other businesses, where virtually all customers are accepted. However, in banks and other lending institutions, the credit selection process assumes a role that is similar to insurance underwriting.

Most insurance prices are based on an average rate for an entire class or group such as 30-year-old female nonsmokers or owners of 1999 Buick Park Avenues in Philadelphia with no youthful drivers. Some applicants within each class will be better than average and some worse than average. Which type of policyowners will an insurer that does no selection tend to have? Those persons who are better than average are most likely not to want or need the insurance at the price quoted for the class, and conversely, those persons who know they are worse than average will be most likely to desire the insurance contract at that price. This result is obvious: The bad applicants at the average rate would be getting a bargain.

Adverse selection is found throughout the field of insurance, and refers to the tendency for those who know they are highly vulnerable to specific pure risks to be most likely to acquire and retain insurance covering those risks. Whenever the applications result from free choice on the part of the individuals who wish to transfer their risks to an insurer, the choice will be against the insurer. Adverse selection can trigger financial disaster because the insurer can end up with poorer-than-average applicants but obtain only an average price for the protection it provides. The result will be the opposite of the stated purposes of insurance underwriting—to select a large, safely diversified, profitable group of applicants.

The major need for insurance underwriting stems from this tendency toward adverse selection that, without underwriting, would be ruinous to insurers. Even with selection by the insurer, some adverse selection always exists whenever a class or group rate is used. Profitable results can be achieved only by careful selection that reasonably offsets the adverse selection factors in insurance applications. The insurer also needs information about its applicants; only then can the company determine fair classifications and sufficient prices.

The process of underwriting is the means by which the insurer evaluates the applicants it has been asked to accept. A compromise is often necessary between two objectives: (1) to obtain a large number of individual insureds within each classification so that reasonable predictability of losses is possible and (2) to obtain a homogeneity of insureds within each classification so that reasonable equity between the better and poorer individual insureds is achieved. The care with which an insurer combines these objectives is vital to its underwriting success and thus to its entire operations.

Consequently, underwriters can be looked on as the backbone of the insurance business. They must decline applications many times, but they are also often able to help consumers become insurable and thereby have their applications accepted. Proper rate classes and prices, with good loss-prevention practices, can help make insurance available to all persons who need it.

Selection of Applicants

The selection of applicants and the pricing of the contracts are closely related. If an adequate price for a class of insureds has been established, the insurer must underwrite to secure at least an average group of insureds within that class. Otherwise, losses paid will exceed the premium income available for paying those losses. If the pricing for an insurance contract is inadequate, even reasonably careful selection can fail to produce a profitable group of applicants. The alternative in such a case is to underwrite strictly, accepting only the very best applicants in each rate class. Pricing, or rate making, is discussed later in this chapter.

The Agent and Insurer as Underwriters

field underwriting

For most insurers and most lines of insurance, the choice of applicants begins with the underwriting done by the agent, sometimes referred to as *field underwriting*. Each time an agent prepares a prospect list or, for example, telephones Mr. White instead of Mr. Green to sell insurance, the agent is performing the first step in underwriting. If an insurer appoints well-qualified agents, they will usually try to choose clients that meet the insurer's underwriting rules. Even though the agent does some underwriting for the insurer, most of the underwriting is an insurance company function, performed by salaried employees in the home office or branch office.

Types of Underwriting

- Field underwriting
- Initial home office underwriting
- Renewal underwriting

Underwriting is not just the technique of rejecting all difficult or doubtful applications. Both the agent and the insurer must frequently explain how an applicant can become acceptable through loss prevention or other methods. Good judgment and good information are needed in this process.

Generally, the insurer determines the underwriting rules to be carried out by its agents and its company personnel in the underwriting department. Agents receive instructions on what types of applicants are unacceptable, as well as encouragement through directives and sales contests that specify what types of contracts and what kinds of business the company particularly desires. Other types of applicants may be specified as insurable only after the insurer has detailed information.

The authority that many agents have to put the contract into effect immediately through the use of a binder, or temporary contract, is a good example of the importance of the underwriting services agents perform for their insurers. Many property insurance contracts, for example, go into effect immediately when the agent issues a binder for a period of about 20 days until the actual contract is written. The insurer can then decide not to write the contract or can cancel the contract written by the agent, but this would be unusual. Even in somewhat doubtful cases, the insurer is more likely to continue the protection and perhaps ask for additional information prior to renewing the contract.

Underwriting by the insurer and the agent takes place not only at the time of the original application but also at each expiration and renewal of the insurance contract. During post-selection underwriting, loss experience and other new information are considered in most insurance lines.

Sources of Underwriting Information

The sources of underwriting information on which insurers rely, depending on the line of insurance, include (1) the applicant, (2) the agent, (3) the insurer's own inspection or claims department, (4) insurer bureaus and associations, and (5) outside agencies. Some of these sources are internal, while several involve gathering external information from others.

The applicant for an insurance contract often makes both written and oral statements. Signed written statements are normal procedures in life and health insurance, and the application becomes a part of the contract. Automobile and business insurance applicants also frequently prepare written statements that give the insurer basic underwriting details. Agents in many kinds of insurance give their companies reports, opinions, and recommendations that are valuable aids in selecting or rejecting applications. Many insurers maintain separate inspection departments to provide the underwriters with physical inspection and engineering reports on applicants' properties. The insurer's claims department, too, can be a source of important underwriting data for renewal decisions.

Insurers also combine efforts to maintain bureau or association lists of insurance applicants. For example, the Medical Information Bureau (MIB) offers a centralized source of information about medical and other impairments of individual applicants for life insurance. Other bureaus that represent many insurers are maintained for regular inspection and rating services in regard to property insurance.

In many kinds of insurance, companies use outside agencies to supplement the information gathered from the applicants, agents, and other insurer representatives. For example, physicians supply life insurance companies with medical reports after physical examination of the applicants. Standard financial rating services such as Dun & Bradstreet (D&B) are used for many insurance applications from businesses. Life insurers have used credit investigations by outside firms for many years. Automobile insurers have used external agencies to check motor vehicle reports and court records of new applicants, especially for younger drivers. Credit-reporting agencies are becoming increasingly important sources of information in several other personal lines of property and liability insurance as well.

Inspection agencies are valuable not just for gathering factual data but also for identifying a prospect's poor habits or moral problems through such sources as employers, neighbors, or associates. The evaluation of moral hazard is crucial, yet difficult, for many kinds of insurance. The attitudes that cause increased losses are discussed in chapter 1. The aim of these investigations is not only to gather negative information but also to obtain positive character reports that will permit insurance to be written. The independent investigative companies must comply with federal legislation dealing with credit reporting and privacy. Insurers must also meet these requirements, as well as laws on the state level, such as the NAIC (National Association of Insurance Commissioners) Health Information Privacy Protection Model Act, adopted by many states.

REINSURING

reinsurance

The underwriting process is closely related to reinsurance, and the underwriter must know how his or her ability to accept applications is both broadened and limited by reinsurance available to the insurer. *Reinsurance* is insurance purchased by an insurer or sold to another insurer. In reinsurance, one insurer, the primary insurer or ceding company that issued the policy, transfers the risk to another insurer, the reinsurer.

Purposes

How can an insurer accept large loss exposures that sometimes exceed many millions of dollars in a single building, a ship, or an airplane? How can liability contracts for business firms be written that have policy limits of $100 million or more? How can a person obtain in excess of $10 million of life insurance? In loss exposures such as hurricanes that affect many policyowners at one time, how can insurers avoid the concentration of loss that occurs? Gigantic losses do not occur frequently, but when they do occur, they illustrate the real reason for insurance—protection against losses that perhaps only the insurance system can provide.

The occurrence of catastrophes illustrates the most important purpose of reinsurance: The spread or diversification of losses. One insurer can write large amounts of insurance on a single life or property or in a concentrated area; reinsurance then shifts part of the loss exposure to perhaps several other companies. Large losses are thus shared, and excessive losses in one occurrence are less likely to cause financial instability for individual insurers. Without reinsurance, each insurer would be limited to its own financial ability to pay losses. Reinsurance enhances financial strength by spreading losses throughout the insurance business.

Reinsurance also has other purposes. Reserve requirements drain surplus and restrict growth, a particularly severe problem for newer or smaller companies. These companies can achieve more rapid growth transferring part of the responsibility for maintaining reserves from the insurer to the reinsurer, permitting the insurer to increase its writing of new business. Reinsurers also offer many technical advisory services to new insurers or those expanding to new types of insurance or territories.

Significance to Financial Planners

Insurance companies usually obtain reinsurance from two basic types of organizations: (1) professional reinsurers, which do reinsurance business only, and (2) other insurance companies that write some reinsurance as a specialty line of business in addition to issuing policies directly to consumers. In either case, the financial planner should recognize that the policyowner is not a party to a reinsurance agreement. The policyowner or other claimant looks to the primary insurer that wrote the policy for claims payment. This primary insurer is responsible for paying the entire claim and is then reimbursed by the reinsurer.

Reinsurance agreements are often highly complex, and an understanding of the many types of such agreements probably is not needed by the typical financial planner. However, the planner should be aware of the difference between treaty, or automatic, reinsurance agreements and facultative agreements.

treaty (automatic) reinsurance

Treaty, or *automatic, reinsurance* exists when the primary insurer agrees in advance to transfer, or cede, some types of loss exposures and the reinsurer agrees to accept them. The reinsurer agrees to insure an amount or a proportionate part of a designated class of past or future business written by the primary insurer. The reinsurer is liable as soon as the primary insurer accepts the loss exposure. Automatic protection is thus ensured for the primary insurer because the reinsurer has agreed beforehand to accept all loss exposures with the terms of the treaty. Normally, the policyowner will not even be aware of the existence of this type of reinsurance.

facultative reinsurance

Facultative reinsurance, on the other hand, is optional for both the insurer and the reinsurer. Each facultative reinsurance contract is written on its own merits and is a matter of individual bargaining between the primary insurer and the reinsurer. The primary insurer may or may not offer part of a loss exposure to the reinsurer. The reinsurer is under no obligation through previous agreement or reciprocal arrangement to accept the loss exposure if it is offered. Each party thus retains the faculty or privilege of accepting or rejecting the reinsurance agreement. The availability of facultative reinsurance may be the deciding factor in the underwriting process as to whether an application for insurance is acceptable to the primary insurer. Delays in obtaining coverage for a client are often a result of the primary insurer's need to obtain a reinsurance commitment.

CLAIMS ADJUSTING

Payment of losses is certainly the most obvious of the important functions of insurance. Without claims that culminate in loss payments, there would be no insurance business. The purpose of this section is to provide a broad picture of insurance in action, explaining who pays insurance losses and how they do so.

claims adjusting

The basic function of loss payment is commonly referred to as *claims adjusting*. The term is not very satisfactory, but it has become well fixed in the business of insurance. "Adjustment" suggests a compromise or change before settlement is reached. This is not always true, so a better term might be claims payment, with the persons who do this work referred to as claims persons. However, because the more common reference is to adjusting and adjusters, these terms will be used here. Keep in mind, though, that a loss, a claim, and an adjustment can logically be three different amounts, although here the term adjustment is used to mean the final insurance payment by the insurer.

Claims adjustments are a daily routine of the insurance business. Thousands of loss checks are routinely delivered to claimants, either insureds or beneficiaries, every day. Sometimes, however, the routine becomes the spectacular. For example, losses from hurricanes can affect hundreds of thousands of persons. Even single-building fires can be devastating. Tornadoes, earthquakes, floods, explosions, and other natural catastrophes can destroy property values and cause deaths or injuries. Many large losses attributable to human failures can also result in multimillion-dollar liability lawsuits.

Often only when policyowners receive payment for values that have been lost do they realize why they purchased insurance contracts. Up to that time, they may have had a feeling that there were some vague reasons why they purchased the protection. When they actually receive a loss check that makes it possible for them to rebuild their homes or replace lost income, they fully realize the value of their insurance.

Purpose

Insureds and beneficiaries who have honestly suffered loss or damage need not approach the insurance company apologetically. The claim for which they seek payment is theirs by right of purchase. It should be the objective of both insurers and claimants to arrive at a fair and equitable measure of the loss. There are sometimes areas of disagreement, but if both parties resolve to reach an equitable adjustment, disagreements will usually be reconciled readily.

Insurance adjusters today are an important connection between the insurer and the policyowner. The adjusters deliver the goods that the agent has sold. The insurance business recognizes that years of insurance programming and planning will mean nothing if the policyowner faces difficulties following a loss. New adjusters are taught that their responsibility is to settle claims equitably and not, as is sometimes believed, to pay the least amount to which claimants will agree. Adjusters are also advised to give reasonable assistance to claimants during the traumatic days immediately following a serious loss—for example, helping the family relocate to temporary housing following a fire or providing names of reputable repair shops after an auto accident. Adjusters are further instructed, when claimants do not know what is due them under their contracts, to fully explain what amounts should be included in their claims. In the interest of equity, adjusters are also trained to recognize unethical practices and to resist padded claims or fraudulent demands. Fairness to uninformed claimants and resistance to wrongful claims benefit both the insurance business and the policyowners, who in the long run must pay premiums based on loss experience.

From the insurer's point of view, claims adjustments afford an attractive area of competition, especially in those types of insurance where premium rates are relatively similar. Although only a minority of all insureds have a loss in a given year, the reputation of the insurer rests not only on how satisfied the claimants are but also on how many other persons the claimants tell about their losses and payments. Dissatisfied policyowners will tell everyone why they believe they were unfairly treated, whereas satisfied claimants will take their payment as a matter of course. If the insurer fails to effect a prompt and equitable adjustment following a loss, it will have failed in the most crucial of all competitive areas.

Loss adjustments are set in motion when a notice of loss is filed with an insurer. The purpose of the adjustment process is to confirm the insurer's liability for a given loss and to reach an agreement on the amount of loss or damage payable under the insurance contract. In paying losses, adjusters have been advised to follow the "4F rules": Be fair, frank, friendly, and firm.

Insurance Adjusters: Types and Organization

There are four categories of adjusters:

- agents
- staff adjusters
- external adjusters
- public adjusters

Agents as Adjusters

It is common sense on the insurer's part to allow the agent, whenever possible, to pay the smaller losses to the policyowners. After all, the agent is usually closest to the client, is familiar with the policyowner's insurance contracts, and normally has the earliest facts on the occurrence of the loss. The agent also has a prime interest in seeing that the consumer receives prompt and fair treatment in the claims adjustment process. The policyowner's satisfaction is important to the agent in terms of goodwill and continued business with the policyowner and the policyowner's friends.

In property insurance, some agents have their companies' authority to settle a claim with the policyowner immediately. For smaller and uncomplicated losses, this is the most expedient way to pay claims. For large agencies and experienced agents, the authority can extend to actually issuing checks in the name of their company. The company, of course, must carefully control the custody of the checkbook. An abnormal number of losses would occasion a review by the insurer to be sure that the agent was not being overly liberal in paying claims. For agents, the authority to settle a claim with a policyowner immediately is a valuable right that enables the agents to render prompt service with a minimum of paperwork. This practice is common for fire, windstorm, and medical payments under homeowners and automobile insurance contracts. For larger losses or losses that involve more complex adjusting methods, such as in liability insurance, the insurer must provide specialized help to the agent and the insured. Staff or external adjusters are used in these cases.

In life insurance, the agent is often involved in loss payment as an intermediary but not as an adjuster. The claims procedure for smaller contracts is simple. Notice to the company and a death certificate are often all that is required before the policy's death benefit can be paid. The life insurance agent usually forwards the death notice and certificate to the insurer, and the check is issued by the company for delivery by the agent to the policyowner's beneficiary. Unlike property insurers, life insurers do not usually have the problem of determining the extent of loss payment because the contract itself states the amount to be paid upon loss. For larger policies, the agent may need to explain various installment payment options in place of a lump-sum cash payment. In health insurance loss payments, the agent can often use special personnel from the insurer's claims department.

One of the most rewarding feelings for an agent is the personal satisfaction he or she receives by actually seeing insurance in action. A disabled husband may thank the agent for having recommended disability income protection to provide the family with steady income during a long period in which he could not work. Or perhaps a dream home can be rebuilt on the ashes of a fire that otherwise would have caused the loss of a lifetime of savings. Many life insurance agents can point with quiet pride to families whose sons and daughters have grown up to attend college without financial hardship despite the unexpected early death of family breadwinners. Because agents see firsthand the value of insurance in such circumstances, it is easy to understand and appreciate their almost missionary zeal.

Staff Adjusters

staff adjuster

Many insurance claims are settled by *staff adjusters* who are employees of the insurer. Staff adjusters are the primary type of adjuster for life and health insurance claims. In property and liability insurance, the contact between the insurer's local agents and the home office is through special agents or state agents who sometimes, as part of their duties, help with claims adjustments. In automobile insurance, in particular, staff adjusters are usually employees who devote their entire time to loss settlements. Automobile claims lend themselves to the services of staff adjusters because the volume of claims is large enough that many companies find it advantageous to maintain claims offices staffed by specialists. Some automobile insurers in larger cities have drive-in claims locations where immediate estimates and payments for damages are made.

The use of staff adjusters depends on the volume and kinds of business written in the territory in which the loss occurs. To support a full-time staff adjuster in a given area, the insurer must have enough claims to be adjusted. Some companies use staff adjusters almost exclusively, while others are more apt to use the services of external adjusters or adjustment bureaus.

External Adjusters

Insurance companies often employ external adjusters to settle claims. External adjusters are experts who have made loss adjusting a business. Some have specialized in particular fields. Others have a general knowledge and understanding of adjustment procedures and handle losses whenever it is impossible or inconvenient for the staff or other types of adjusters to do so. *Independent adjusters*

independent adjuster
adjustment bureau

operate as individuals within a limited area. *Adjustment bureaus* have built sizable organizations and operate on a regional or national basis.

External adjusters work on a fee basis for the insurers who request their services. A typical use is in automobile insurance when the insurer has only a small volume of business in an area or when the policyowner has an accident while traveling. External adjusters are also used frequently to supplement staff adjusters when catastrophic events, such as a major hurricane, give rise to a large number of separate claims. External adjusters can also be used by insurers to settle claims in highly technical areas in which the staff adjusters lack the necessary skills or expertise. External adjusters often develop continuing working relationships with particular insurers, in addition to accepting infrequent adjusting assignments from a larger number of insurers.

Public Adjusters

public adjuster

As the name implies, *public adjusters* represent the public, in contrast to adjusters who represent insurers. The public adjuster is retained by the insured to negotiate the loss settlement. Policyowners may assume that a staff adjuster is biased and will make borderline decisions to the insurer's advantage. These situations are the exception, however; most insurers strive toward fair loss payments. Claimants who feel the need to have someone represent their interests can turn the claim over to a public adjuster. Sometimes claimants retain attorneys to perform a similar function.

Public adjusters offer their services, usually on a fee basis, using their expert insurance knowledge to estimate damages and effect loss settlements. In some states, public adjusters are required to obtain a license from that state's insurance department. This is important because public adjusters act as agents for the insureds within the scope of their employment. If a public adjuster perpetrates a fraud in an attempt to obtain a generous adjustment, the policy may be voided as if the fraud were perpetrated by the insured.

Claims Adjustment Procedures

The process by which claims are settled varies somewhat in different lines of insurance. The policy spells out the precise steps that the policyowner or other claimant must follow, as well as his or her responsibilities following a loss. Those steps and responsibilities are described in other chapters in this book as they relate to certain specific types of insurance. In general, however, there are four main steps in the claims adjustment process: (1) The policyowner furnishes a notice of loss to the insurer, (2) the insurer investigates the claim, (3) the policyowner files a proof of loss with the insurer, and (4) the insurer pays or denies the claim, sometimes compromising on the amount to be paid.

The notification to the insurer must be provided as spelled out in the policy. Often, the time frame is specified as "immediately," "promptly," or "as soon as practicable." A few types of policies may be more specific such as "within 30 days after the occurrence of a loss."

Claims investigation is designed to determine whether a loss occurred and, if so, whether it is covered by the policy. In life insurance, this process is usually quite simple, but complicating factors can arise in some cases. For example, what if the insured has mysteriously disappeared, so that at best it can only be presumed that he or she is dead? What if there is some evidence that the insured died by his or her own hand, in which case the policy's suicide clause may come into play? What if there was a material misrepresentation in the application for the coverage, in which case the incontestable clause may be applicable? Several of these and other clauses that may affect claims settlement in life insurance are discussed in chapter 9.

In other lines of insurance, the investigation phase can be more complex. Some of the questions that may have to be resolved include the following:

- Did a loss actually take place?
- Did the loss occur while the policy was in force?
- Did the loss occur at a location covered by the policy?

- Was the loss caused by a covered peril or activity?
- Are any policy exclusions applicable to the loss?
- Are any exceptions to policy exclusions applicable to the loss?
- Has the policyowner fulfilled all conditions that relate to coverage?
- Is there any evidence of fraud surrounding the loss?
- Is the claimant a person who is entitled to recover under the policy?
- Does the policy cover the particular type of loss consequence?

The third step in the process of adjusting a claim is filing a proof of loss. In life insurance, proof of loss may be in the form of a death certificate. In other lines, a written and sworn statement may be required that details all the specifics of the loss.

Finally, the amount to be paid must be determined in one of three ways: denial of the claim, payment of the claim in full, or payment of a lesser amount than the claimant seeks. Once again, life insurance claims are usually simpler because there are no partial losses. However, there can be some complicating factors that affect the amount to be paid, including an accidental death benefit provision, a misstatement-of-age-or-sex clause, or a settlement option selected by the policyowner or by the beneficiary. Various provisions that affect the amount to be paid are discussed, where appropriate, in later chapters.

In other lines of insurance, the amount to be paid, if any, can be a very troublesome issue. Numerous policy provisions may be applicable. These include provisions that

- deal with other insurance covering the same loss
- provide for a deductible
- specify that recovery will be affected by the amount of insurance carried relative to the value of the covered property
- give the insurer the choice of two or three methods of calculating the amount of the loss
- stipulate the use of appraisers to establish the amount of the loss
- impose a specific limit on the insurer's liability for certain types of losses

These types of policy provisions are described in later chapters that deal with specific lines of insurance.

RATE MAKING

Insurance rate making, or establishing the price to be charged for the insurance product, is based on the costs of providing the product, including a margin for profit. The task is complicated in insurance, however, because the insurer does not know the amount or timing of the largest cost element, the claims to be paid, in advance. Claims can only be estimated. Predicting future loss costs—and in long-term contracts such as life insurance, their timing—and adding to those predictions necessary margins for expenses and profit is called *rate making*. Rate making is carried out by actuaries, who are specialists in the mathematics of insurance.

rate making

Components of the Insurance Premium

rate

The insurance *rate* is the price charged for each unit of coverage, called an exposure unit, provided by the policy. Units of coverage are not the same for different lines of insurance. For example, in life insurance, the unit of coverage is $1,000 of face amount. For long-term disability income insurance, it is $100 of monthly income. For medical expense insurance, it is an individual or family. For most property insurance, it is $100 of value. For automobile liability insurance, it is one covered vehicle.

premium

The insurance *premium* is the price charged for the amount of coverage provided by the policy. The premium is found by multiplying the rate by the number of units of coverage. For example, in life insurance, the rate for a particular category of insureds might be $30 per $1,000 of face amount per year. The annual premium for a $50,000 policy, then, would be $30 x 50 units, or $1,500. In fire insurance, the annual rate might be $.25 per $100 of coverage. Therefore, the annual premium for coverage of a $200,000 building would be $.25 x 2,000 units of coverage, or $500.

How, then, is an insurance rate derived? Usually, the rate is developed by the pure premium method, which first requires an estimate of the future loss costs per unit of coverage during the policy period. That portion of the rate is called the *pure* or *net rate*. Then a factor, called a *loading*, is added to cover the insurer's anticipated expenses and to provide a margin for profit and contingencies. The sum of the pure or net rate and the loading is called the *gross rate*.

pure (net) rate
loading

gross rate

This leads to the next logical question: How is the pure or net rate derived? Most lines of insurance use a statistical analysis of past loss data for each class of insureds and a projection of that loss experience into the future time period during which the rate to be charged for each class will be in effect.

The rate-making task is complicated in some lines of insurance by a scarcity of data concerning past loss experience. This scarcity of data can exist either for all insureds, as in a new line of coverage such as long-term care insurance, or for particular classifications of insureds such as very elderly automobile drivers. In most lines of insurance, such as homeowners coverage or disability income insurance, loss data must also be sufficient to allow accurate predictions of both loss frequency and loss severity. An explanation of how actuaries deal with these and other rate-making complexities is well beyond the scope of this introductory text.

Property Insurance As an Example

advisory organization

As an example of insurance rate-making methods, the field of property insurance offers insight into the many factors involved. Here, insurance advisory organizations play a key role. An insurance *advisory organization,* also called a rating bureau, is an organization that assists insurers by collecting and furnishing loss statistics or by submitting recommendations but does not itself make rate filings. These advisory organizations, such as the Insurance Services Office (ISO), are permitted under state statutes in order to allow cooperation and limited price fixing for property insurance, subject to state regulation of their activities. Reasonable competition is achieved by permitting individual insurers to file separate rates or to add separate loadings to bureau-prepared pure or net rates.

A property insurance contract usually includes more than just the fire peril. Separate prices are developed by the advisory organization for such allied perils as windstorm, hail, smoke, explosion, riot, and others; business interruption loss of income, rents, and extra expenses; water damage and sprinkler leakage; and earthquake.

The price of property insurance also varies with the location or territory of the property, the construction of the building, the use or occupancy of the property, the loss-prevention or protection facilities, and the proximity or exposure to other properties from which a peril might spread. Standards for the classes are carefully defined by the advisory organizations, so a higher rate is charged for a frame building than for a brick or a fire-resistant building.

Two types of property insurance rates are set by the advisory organizations: (1) class rates, or tariff rates, for groups of similar properties and (2) specific rates, or schedule rates, for individual properties. Having some rates for groups of applicants with similar characteristics and separate individual rates for applicants that differ widely in their specific characteristics is common to many types of insurance.

Class Rates

class rate

As explained earlier, *class rates* are group rates with an average price that applies to each category or classification of similar insureds. A common example is class rating of separate dwellings or residential homes. Class-rated dwellings are subdivided into groups according to their construction, and a rate is assigned to such classes as frame or brick and to combustible or noncombustible roofs. The rate also varies as to the fire protection classification of the city or town and the number of families that occupy the property. In addition, many jurisdictions apply class rates to commercial buildings when the elements of construction and occupancy are similar enough to permit a ready grouping into rate classes. ISO filings expand class rating to most smaller buildings in general classes such as mercantile, churches, schools, warehouses, offices, and to habitational classes such as apartments, motels, and boardinghouses. Class rates must be used for properties to which the rates apply.

The purposes of class rates are not only economy and simplicity but also reasonable equity, in that the individual properties within a given class do not vary too much with regard to potential loss-causing characteristics. Thus, for example, all one-family brick dwellings in a midwestern town of 200,000 population and with fire hydrants within 1,000 feet might have a one-year fire rate of $.30 per $100 of insurance.

Specific or Schedule Rates

schedule rating

When class rates do not apply, the rate is said to be *specific*. Specific rates are set for larger mercantile and manufacturing properties, educational institutions, public buildings, and many types of business establishments. Specific rates are determined by applying a schedule that measures the relative quantity of fire hazard to the particular loss exposure, a system known as *schedule rating*. Most larger buildings use specific rates developed after a physical inspection of the individual property. These include manufacturing, hotel, restaurant, and other properties.

Schedule rating is a process that measures differences in hazards for different properties. This process takes into consideration the various items that contribute to the insured perils, including the construction of the building, its occupancy or use, its protection, and its exposure to nearby buildings. Credits and charges that represent departures from standard conditions for each of these items are incorporated into the schedules. Thus, a schedule rate is a basic rate plus the sum of all charges less the sum of all credits.

Rate Making Methods

- Class rating vs. schedule rating
- Pure premium vs. loss ratio

Life Insurance As Another Example

Life insurers collect voluminous amounts of data concerning mortality rates. The most important basis for classifying these data are the age and sex of insureds and whether they are smokers or nonsmokers.

net single premium

A large percentage of life insurance is sold on a level-premium basis. Death rates, on the other hand, rise with increasing age, so most claims on a block of policies occur long after the policies are issued. To deal with this imbalance of level premiums in traditional life insurance products and rising claim costs, life insurers first compute a *net single premium* per $1,000 of face amount for the policy. This net single premium is an amount that would be needed today from each insured in a classification, together with future investment earnings, to pay all claims within that class of insureds as those claims arise. The net single premium per $1,000 of face amount is then spread or leveled over the policy's premium-paying period on an actuarial basis to produce a *net level annual premium* per $1,000. Finally, a level annual amount of loading is added to cover such insurer expenses as commissions, premium taxes, general administrative expenses, and an allowance for contingencies and profit.

net level annual premium

The establishment of rates for nontraditional life insurance products, such as universal life insurance and variable life insurance (see chapter 8), is considerably more complex. A description of this is well beyond the scope of this book.

The Loss Ratio Method for Adjusting Rates

Up to this point, the pure premium method has been described, which entails development of a pure or net rate plus a loading. However, for many property and liability insurance lines in which rate changes upward or downward are frequent, the loss ratio method of rate making is used to adjust rates. The emphasis in the loss ratio method is not on calculating a new rate directly but on determining the necessary change in an existing rate.

loss ratio

Loss ratios can be calculated in various ways, but the most common way is to divide losses incurred and loss adjustment expenses incurred by earned premiums. The needed change in an existing insurance rate is found by comparing the actual loss ratio experienced with the expected or desired loss ratio. The difference is then divided by the expected or desired loss ratio.

Example: The present rate in a particular automobile liability insurance classification is $700 per year. The insurer's expected loss ratio in that classification is 65 percent. During the latest experience period that classification generated $4 million of incurred losses, $200,000 of expenses allocated to settle specific claims, and $7 million of earned premiums. The actual loss ratio was, therefore, 60 percent:

$$\left(\frac{\$4,000,000 + \$200,000}{\$7,000,000} \right) \times 100 = 60\%$$

The needed rate change, then, is a reduction of 7.7 percent, determined as follows:

$$\left(\frac{\text{Actual loss ratio} - \text{Expected loss ratio}}{\text{Expected loss ratio}} \right) \times 100 =$$

$$\left(\frac{60-65}{65}\right) \times 100 = \left(\frac{-5}{65}\right) \times 100 = -7.7\%$$

The new rate will therefore be $700 \times (1 - .077)$ = $700 \times .923$ = 646. Note, however, that because of expected inflation in the future, the rate might not be lowered by the full 7.7 percent.

Rate Classifications

The previous discussion implied that there are different rate classifications. Not all applicants for any type of insurance will be charged the same rate. Insurers must establish overall rates so that they have sufficient funds to pay losses and expenses. At the same time, they must provide reasonable equity among policyowners and charge rates that reflect quantifiable characteristics that affect losses. For example, because smokers on the average have shorter life expectancies than nonsmokers, most life insurers have both smoker and nonsmoker rates. Life insurance rates also vary by age and sex. At the opposite extreme is automobile insurance, where rate classifications reflect many factors, including age, sex, marital status, geographic location, miles driven, vehicle use, and driving record. In a given state, an insurance company may have several hundred classifications when all combinations of these factors are considered.

The degree to which rate classifications are refined depends on available and reliable statistics, the administrative costs of establishing classifications, and government regulations. For example, some states require the use of unisex rates for certain types of insurance even though loss statistics can justify sex-specific rates.

INVESTING

Insurers accumulate huge amounts of capital, most of it through premium payments by policyowners. Except for amounts needed for the insurer's operating expenses, those funds will be used primarily to pay claims, perhaps a few months or even many years into the future. In the interim, the funds are invested, both as a means of lowering the cost of insurance and as a source of profit for the insurer.

As explained in the next chapter, the ways an insurer can invest the funds it holds are closely regulated by state laws. The primary emphasis of the regulations and therefore the primary objective of an insurer's investment function is safety, both of principal and of income.[4] An additional objective is an adequate yield, or rate of return. Life insurers guarantee a minimum rate of return to policyowners in many of their products, so they must earn at least that much.

must be high enough to enable its insurance contracts to be priced at a competitive level. Even though in most states, property and liability insurers are not required by law to build investment income into their rate making, investment income still is essential. In many years and for lines of insurance in which loss experience is unfavorable, investment income is the insurer's only source of profit.

Life Insurer Investments

Most of life insurers' investable funds will not be paid out until well into the future. Consequently, life insurers tend to invest heavily in long-term securities, for which yields tend to be better, all other things being equal. Liquidity of the investments, or the ability to convert them into cash quickly without loss of value, is not a major consideration.

As shown in table 4-1, at the end of the year 2001, United States life insurers had $3.2 trillion of invested funds. About 53 percent was invested in government and corporate bonds. A much smaller percentage was invested in corporate stocks. Other investment assets took the form of cash equivalents, real estate mortgage loans, policy loans, and miscellaneous assets.[5]

TABLE 4-1 Insurance Company Investments—2001		
	Life Insurers	Non-life Insurers
Total amount of invested assets (in billions)	$3,224.6	$863.0
Distribution of invested assets		
Cash and cash equivalents	6.9%	5.0%
Bonds		
Government	11.4	37.1
Corporate	41.6	22.8
Stocks	26.5	20.2
Mortgages	7.5	0
Policy Loans	3.2	0
Other	2.9	14.9
All percentages rounded to nearest decimal place		

Non-Life-Insurer Investments

United States non-life insurers' invested assets show a somewhat different pattern. The aggregate amount invested, $863 billion, is much smaller than for life insurers because property and liability contracts are of short duration and do not build up a savings element. Moreover, in most property and liability policies, claims are settled not long after they arise.[6] As with life insurers, the invested assets of property and liability insurers heavily emphasize bonds and common stocks, vehicles that are attractive because of their usually generous yields.[7] Government bonds constitute a larger holding, percentagewise, for property and liability insurers than for life insurers.

OTHER FUNCTIONS OF INSURERS

Numerous other functions are performed by auxiliary departments of insurers. The word auxiliary does not mean that these functions are unimportant. In fact, many insurers' success can be traced to the excellent support these departments give to the primary operating functions of marketing, underwriting, reinsuring, adjusting claims, and investing.

The legal department, for example, often works closely with the property and liability insurers' underwriting and claims departments. The legal department is generally also responsible for meeting general incorporation, licensing, and taxation requirements of the many states in which insurers do business. Often, the legal department helps design insurance contracts, drafts agency agreements, and provides general legal counsel for the insurer. In life insurance, the department offers substantial aid to the sales and underwriting departments by reviewing cases that involve complex tax problems.

The actuarial department is most closely related to insurers' rating and underwriting departments. Life insurance companies need a separate actuarial staff to diagnose mortality trends, determine costs for various contracts, and provide research for many phases of their activities. Although separate research departments are not common for most insurers, companies are increasingly realizing the need for economic and social research. Many insurers also maintain public relations departments. Education and training is another important area for insurance companies.

Other functional areas within an insurance company are also critical to the organization's success. The accounting department prepares the insurer's financial statements, both for regulators and for the general public. Accountants also prepare various internal financial reports for managers and in preparation of the company's state and federal tax returns. The information systems department is responsible for automating many of the formerly manual tasks in policy issuance, premium billing, and claims payment, to mention just a few. Loss-control departments in property and liability insurance companies provide advice and inspection services in many areas of loss prevention and minimization. Finally, many general administrative functions are performed within an insurance company such as personnel management, purchasing, and word processing.

SOURCES FOR FURTHER IN-DEPTH STUDY

- For details of the underwriting process and the vesting function:
  - Graves, Edward E., editor, *McGill's Life Insurance*, 4th ed., chapters 17–19 (underwriting), Chapter 26 (investing), Bryn Mawr, PA: The American College, 2002. Phone 888-263-7265. Web site address www.amercoll.edu
  - Webb, Bernard L.; Launie, J. J.; and Dashzereg, B., *Insurance Operations*, (underwriting) Malvern, PA: American Institute for Chartered Property Casualty Underwriters, 2001. Phone 800-644-2101. Web site address www.aicpcu.org

CHAPTER REVIEW

Answers to review questions and self-test questions start on page 725.

Key Terms

underwriting	rate
field underwriting	premium
reinsurance	pure (net) rate
treaty (automatic) reinsurance	loading
facultative reinsurance	gross rate
claims adjusting	advisory organization
staff adjuster	class rate
independent adjuster	schedule rating
adjustment bureau	net single premium
public adjuster	net level annual premium
rate making	loss ratio

Review Questions

4-1. As a financial planner, you are working with a client, Bill Jackson, on meeting his various protection needs. Answer the following questions asked by Bill:
   a. Bill asks, "Why can't insurance companies insure every applicant since they seem to charge pretty high premiums?"
   b. After you answer that question, Bill asks, "Even if you qualify for insurance, sometimes companies charge a much higher rate than they charge other similar insureds. Why?"

4-2. Briefly explain the sources of underwriting information typically used by insurers.

4-3. What are the key purposes of reinsurance?

4-4. Explain the difference between facultative and treaty reinsurance.

4-5. What is the purpose of the claims (loss) adjustment process?

4-6. Compare the role of the agent in property insurance with that of the life insurance agent regarding the claims adjustment process.

4-7. List the four main steps in the claims adjustment process, and explain how their implementation differs in life insurance versus other lines of insurance.

4-8. During a discussion of insurance needs with a financial planning client, Sally Johnson, she asks the following questions:
   a. What's the difference between an insurance rate and an insurance premium?
   b. How is an insurance rate derived?

Self-Test Questions

T F 4-1. The general purpose of underwriting is to select only those insureds who are expected to have no losses.

T F 4-2. Among other things, reinsurance can help insurers spread large losses and reduce the surplus drain associated with writing new business.

T F 4-3. Under facultative reinsurance, the insurer agrees in advance to transfer some types of risks, and the reinsurer agrees to accept those risks.

T F 4-4. The purpose of the claims adjustment process is to determine the insurer's liability for a given loss and to reach agreement with respect to the amount of loss or damage payable under the insurance contract.

T F 4-5. Most life insurance agents have the authority of their companies to settle claims.

T F 4-6. Independent adjusters and adjustment bureaus usually represent the public, in contrast to staff adjusters, who represent insurers.

T F 4-7. In calculating the insurance premium, the pure (or net) rate is multiplied by the number of units of coverage.

T F 4-8. Under the loss ratio method of rate making, the actual loss ratio experienced is compared with the expected (or desired) loss ratio to determine the needed change in the existing insurance rate.

T F 4-9. Both life and property-liability insurers invest more heavily in bonds than in stocks.

NOTES

1. See *German Alliance Insurance Co. v. Lewis*, 233 U.S. 389 (1914).
2. A few exceptions apply. For example, some states may require insurers to accept all applications, as in automobile insurance for licensed drivers in a state with compulsory liability insurance laws. The insurance contracts, however, may be limited ones, assigned proportionally to all insurers in the state under a special plan.
3. In a few situations, there is no classifying of applicants because the application is so unusual that it does not fall neatly into a class of insureds. See the discussion of specific and scheduled rates in the later section of this chapter that covers insurance rate making.
4. These regulations apply to the insurer's general investment account. Life insurers also have substantial amounts of funds in separate accounts, where more aggressive investment goals are chosen by insureds. Examples of separate accounts are those that underlie a life insurer's variable life insurance business, variable annuities, and much of its pension business.
5. *Flow of Funds Accounts of the United States* (Board of Governors of the Federal Reserve System, 2002).
6. An important exception to this general rule exists in some liability lines, such as product liability insurance, where claims may not even arise until long after the period of coverage has expired and ensuing claim payments may be spread over many years.
7. *The Fact Book 2000 Property/Casualty Insurance Facts* (New York: Insurance Information Institute), pages 1.15 and 1.16.

Regulation and Evaluation of Insurers

Learning Objectives
An understanding of the material in this chapter should enable the student to

5-1. Explain why insurance regulation is needed.

5-2. Describe the methods of insurance regulation.

5-3. Describe the kinds of insurance regulation by the states, and explain the issue of state vs. federal regulation.

5-4. Discuss the criteria for selecting an insurer and agent or broker.

Chapter Outline

All forms of lawful private enterprise have some regulation of their activities, either by self-imposed rules and customs or by specific government regulations.

Sometimes the government provides extensive controls, including almost every phase of the operations from creation to liquidation. At other times, there is minimal government regulation, perhaps only for the purpose of obtaining necessary tax information. This chapter explains why and how the business of insurance is regulated as well as the evaluation and selection of insurers. Financial planners need to understand the regulatory environment in which they work. Further, they need to help their clients in their evaluation and selection of insurers.

WHY INSURANCE REGULATION IS NEEDED

The general purpose of insurance regulation is to protect the public against insolvency or unfair treatment by insurers. From the state's viewpoint, regulation is also important as a revenue producer through state taxes on insurance premiums.

The insurance business is among the types of private enterprise subject to much government regulation because it is generally considered to be "affected with a public interest." This characteristic explains why many types of government supervision of insurance are deemed necessary. Although competition is an effective regulator for some businesses, uncontrolled competition in insurance could impose a hardship on the buyers of insurance, most of whom do not understand insurance contracts. Also, much insurance is written to protect third parties who have not participated in making the contracts. The value of insurance contracts depends on the ability of the insurers to fulfill their promises to the public, sometimes many years after the issuance of a policy. Ability to carry out the provisions of contracts depends on many factors, including the efficient operation of the insurer, satisfactory underwriting, the use of proper premium rates, and the wise investment of adequate reserves. Consequently, the need for insurers to show integrity and long-range financial stability renders government regulation of insurance appropriate.

METHODS OF INSURANCE REGULATION

The state government is undoubtedly most important in the regulation of insurance. Before we consider this and other phases of government insurance regulation, however, we will begin with a summary of the self-regulation of insurance.

Self-Regulation of Insurance

To the extent that a business provides adequate self-regulation, government regulation is often unnecessary, or at least can be somewhat diminished. For insurance, it is not realistic to think that the entire job of regulation can be done by internal, as opposed to external, methods of supervision. However, cooperation by insurers to regulate themselves is permitted by law and is extensively practiced.

There are many insurers and trade association groups that exercise considerable control or provide advice with regard to each of the major functions of insurance. For example, forms and loss data for many property and liability types of insurance are filed by the Insurance Services Office (ISO) on behalf of individual insurers for approval by the state insurance departments, saving duplication of effort and reducing costs. In claims administration, adjustment bureaus handle many losses for insurers, so that several insurers involved in the same losses do not need to provide separate loss investigation and payment services. Many insurers cooperate with one another in coordinating loss prevention. Examples include the Insurance Institute for Highway Safety and the National Fire Protection Association. Information needed in life insurance and disability income insurance underwriting is gathered by the Medical Information Bureau. Marketing activities are regulated by rules applying to members of numerous organizations of insurance agents, brokers, and companies. Research is enhanced by insurers' joint efforts with LIMRA International and the Society of Insurance Research (SIR). Better public relations and legislation are promoted by the American Council of Life Insurance (ACLI), the Insurance Information Institute, and the Risk and Insurance Management Society (RIMS).[1] For improving insurance education and setting standards for professional courses and designations, the following organizations are important: the American Academy of Actuaries, The American College (and the related LUTC), the American Institute for CPCU (and the related Insurance Institute of America), and LOMA (Life Office Management Association). Professors of insurance and other industry personnel exchange much valuable information through conferences and publications of the American Risk and Insurance Association (ARIA). Many insurers and these types of organizations supply representatives directly to industry committees that work in conjunction with government regulatory bodies to draft legislation, coordinate programs, and improve both self-regulation and public regulation of insurance. For example, the National Association of Insurance and Financial Advisors (NAIFA) has encouraged much legislation for implementation in state legislative bodies.

Self-regulation, however, is no panacea. It works extremely well in some aspects of insurance, while in others it is disappointingly ineffective. Difficult areas for self-regulation include many aspects that involve competition such as production costs, commissions, advertising, selling practices, and rates.

In some foreign countries, such as England and the Netherlands, self-regulation has worked well. Cooperative action of insurers has succeeded in achieving high standards of financial solvency and fair treatment to policyowners. The reasons attributed to the excellent success of self-regulation in England include the philosophy, attitudes, and traditions of English insurers, as well as their smaller number and size. Other countries, such as Germany and the Scandinavian nations, follow the strictest patterns of governmental regulation of insurance, including approval procedures for most forms, commissions, and rates. The United States seems to fall between the extremes. Self-regulation is relied on much more in the United States than in Germany, but much less than in England.

As a review of this section on self-regulation and as an introduction to the next section on government regulation, see figure 5-1, which summarizes the methods of insurance regulation.

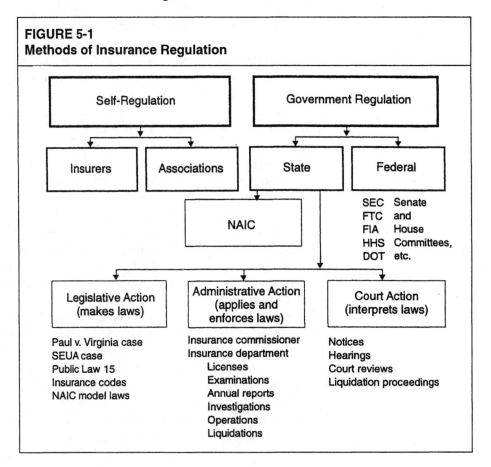

FIGURE 5-1
Methods of Insurance Regulation

Government Regulation of Insurance

Three basic methods of providing insurance regulation are available to government: (1) legislative action, (2) administrative action, and (3) court action. Corresponding to the three main branches of the government, each of these methods is significant in the supervision of insurance. Legislation is the foundation of insurance regulation because it creates the insurance laws. The insurance laws of each state are often combined in what is known as an insurance code,[2] and these codes are of primary importance. Administrative action is also very important because the application and enforcement of insurance laws are left in the hands of the insurance commissioner in each state. Court action has great value in regulation because of its effect in providing detailed interpretations of troublesome parts of the law.

Legislative Action

The regulation of the insurance business by the states was well established by the late 1800s and continues today as the predominant form of regulation. The practice is based on a series of court decisions, and has been continued despite some contention that, because of the number of jurisdictions, insurance might better be regulated by the federal government. In the classic 1868 case *Paul v. Virginia*, the Supreme Court decided that insurance "is not a transaction of commerce" and thus can be neither interstate commerce nor subject to federal regulation.[3] Until 1944, a period of about 75 years, the *Paul v. Virginia* decision was upheld by the Supreme Court.

In 1941, complaints were made to the Department of Justice that certain insurance company practices were in violation of the Sherman Antitrust Act. As a result, a momentous four-to-three decision was handed down in 1944 by the U.S. Supreme Court before one of its largest audiences in history. This case, *U.S. v. South-Eastern Underwriters Association (SEUA) et al,*[4] now known to the legal profession and to the insurance business as the *SEUA* case, held that insurance is commerce. Thus, because of its interstate nature, it would often be subject to federal regulation.

As a matter of practice, because of delegation of authority by Congress, the regulation of the business of insurance remains primarily a state function. The specific delegation to the states of the power to regulate insurance occurred with the passage of Public Law 15, also known as the McCarran-Ferguson Act or simply the McCarran Act, in 1945.[5] Congress made the Sherman Act, the Clayton Act, and the Federal Trade Commission Act applicable to the business of insurance after January 1, 1948, "to the extent that such business is not regulated by state law." In other words, the jurisdiction for regulating interstate insurance was left with the individual states as it had been for many years, but the important proviso was added permitting the federal government to take over insurance regulation whenever the state regulation became inadequate.

Most states increased their insurance regulation heavily in laws passed as a result of the SEUA decision and Public Law 15, and have continued in their efforts to retain the power to supervise insurance. Meanwhile, investigations totaling thousands of pages of testimony have been carried out by the Senate Antitrust and Monopoly Subcommittee. Alleged inadequacies in state insurance laws have been pointed out. Some of the targets of Senate and House investigations have been automobile insurance (particularly substandard or high-risk auto insurance), the credit life and health insurance field, and insurance activities of bank holding companies, insurer insolvency funds, product liability, and automobile no-fault plans.

Landmark Events in the History of Insurance Regulation

- U.S. Supreme Court decision in the case of *Paul v. Virginia*, 1868
- U.S. Supreme Court decision in the case of *U.S. v. South-Eastern Underwriters Association*, 1944
- Public Law 15 (McCarran-Ferguson Act), 1945

In summary, the regulation of insurance by governmental legislation has been found to be primarily a matter of insurance laws passed by the individual states. The state insurance codes have the distinct disadvantage of lacking uniformity. Critics of state regulation emphasize the duplication, complexity, and inefficiency that may result from nonuniformity. With increasing mobility, more uniformity of state laws is needed. The billions of dollars of taxes and fees, which are discussed in the later section on taxation, paid by insurers to the states each year are stark evidence of the stakes involved. Legal precedent to date has established that the individual states have the principal regulatory responsibility for insurance and its benefits in tax revenue. Nevertheless, the role of the federal government as an additional regulator of the insurance business has been growing steadily in recent decades, as will be noted later in this chapter.

Administrative Action

The broad powers that the insurance commissioner[6] of each state possesses are the key to the enforcement of insurance laws by the states. The administrative powers of the commissioners are derived from the statutes that created the office. Usually, these statutes are not very detailed in defining the authority and responsibility of the commissioner. The thousands of bills and laws that today concern insurance matters and the general increased reliance on administrative law have made the position of commissioner increasingly important in state government. The commissioner's wide authority extends from the licensing of insurers and agents to requiring annual reports from the insurers to approving forms and rates in some, but not all, lines of insurance and investigating complaints of many kinds.

In most states, the insurance commissioner is appointed by the governor and is a member of the governor's cabinet. The logic of this method of choosing the head insurance regulatory official is that the governor is ultimately responsible for the business success of his or her term of office and therefore should be able to appoint a person to carry out this responsibility. The prime disadvantage of this method is that political influence may be asserted on the commissioner's decisions. The short tenure of appointed commissioners, averaging 2 to 3 years, is also disadvantageous. In about 10 states, where the job of insurance commissioner is an elective office, the disadvantage of a short term in authority is also complicated by the vagaries of voter appeal. It is uncertain whether the electorate would choose a person of the necessary high caliber and integrity with any better measure of success than appointments of commissioners by the governors have produced. The dilemma of obtaining better commissioners and longer terms of office seems unavoidably tied to the political party system of government.

The insurance department within which insurance commissioners carry out their duties may vary from a few persons in some of the smaller states to several hundred employees in a state such as New York. Many departments have existed for a century or more. Some states have relied on New York as their guide for insurance legislation and administrative action. Also of importance is that some New York laws apply to all insurers licensed there, wherever they do business, **extraterritoriality** a provision called *extraterritoriality*. This is important in creating uniformity in regulations among many states.

The major powers of the insurance commissioner have been mentioned as licensing, examination, and investigation. In addition to following the required incorporation procedure for domestic organizations, each insurer wishing to do business in the state must be licensed for the lines of business it plans to write. The commissioner has broad interpretative powers in deciding whether an insurer is qualified, financially and otherwise, to operate in the state. After issuance, licenses are usually renewable on an annual basis. The insurance commissioner has considerable power to refuse to issue a renewal license, as well as the power of suspension or revocation. Tests are also administered that determine licensing of insurance agents or brokers.

The on-site examination of insurers once they have been licensed is also an important task of the commissioner. Insurers continued solvency is the major objective of detailed examinations that are conducted according to law, at intervals usually of from 3 to 5 years. The checking of assets, liabilities, and reserves is part of this procedure, as is the review of underwriting, investment, and claims practices of the insurer. A regional zone system is used in cooperation **National Association of Insurance Commissioners (NAIC)** with the *National Association of Insurance Commissioners (NAIC)* to avoid unnecessary redundant examination of multistate insurers by many states. In this way, the examination of insurers licensed in many states is standardized and simplified, and the results of the regular zone examination are accepted by all states in which the insurer does business. In the intervening years between complete examinations of insurers, every state requires the filing of an annual statement with the insurance commissioner. This filing reports current financial conditions and changes that have occurred during the year. A standard NAIC form is used that, for most details, provides uniformity of the information requested in the statement. These annual statements are available to the public in the state insurance department offices.

The NAIC is a voluntary nonprofit association of each state's top insurance administrators. The NAIC is important not only for the zone examination procedures but also for its influence through the commissioners on uniformity of insurance laws in the various states. Recommendations and model laws are studied by NAIC committees and discussed at semiannual meetings. The commissioners' support has aided to some extent in the adoption of suggestions by the states.

Criticism has been aimed at the NAIC for its inability to bring about greater uniformity in state insurance legislation. A highly controversial program under which the NAIC accredits state insurance regulatory bodies, based largely on the extent to which the state has adopted certain of the NAIC's model laws and regulations, has been developed to counter some of this criticism. Many model laws and regulations have been recommended for areas such as holding companies, variable contracts, guaranty funds, life insurance replacement, and unfair advertising. In addition, the NAIC has been instrumental in developing risk-based capital requirements. These requirements call for differing minimum amounts of capital that insurers must maintain, based on the riskiness of their insurance and investment operations. Other model laws or regulations of the NAIC deal with unfair claims practices, privacy protection, unfair sex discrimination, long-term care policies, and numerous other topics. Major research projects have been completed, covering topics such as automobile insurance, premium taxation, competitive rating, credit life and health insurance, and mass marketing. Statistical reporting systems both for testing company solidity and for measuring profitability have been operational for several years.

In most states, several investigative powers of the insurance commissioner help determine whether insurers and their representatives meet statutory requirements. Free access to records and books of insurers and hearings on matters such as rate violations or unfair trade practices are examples of this authority. As a result of such procedures, which are often informal, the commissioner may issue administrative rulings or advisory opinions with regard to the business conduct of insurers or their agents. In extreme cases, the commissioner can declare the insurer insolvent and order its liquidation. All these investigative powers have as their major goal the protection of insurance policyowners and claimants. Although these parties should not treat the functions of an insurance commissioner as a guarantee against any and all possible insolvencies and abuses, the commissioner's insurance regulatory powers do serve as an important means of preventing or reducing insolvencies and abuses.

Court Action

The extremely broad authority of insurance commissioners is subject to some measures of review and interpretation by the courts. The notice and hearing procedures that are conducted by commissioners in order to arrive at official rulings may be reviewed by the courts to determine whether the commissioner's duties conform with state statutes. Examples are actions to compel the commissioner to issue a license to an insurer or to prevent its cancellation, and court review of decisions to permit or refuse rate increases. Not only may the courts be used in private actions, or by the attorney general of the state against an insurance commissioner, but the commissioner may, for example, petition the courts to enforce compliance with laws or rulings. Courts are also occasionally called on to resolve disputes between insurers and policyowners or claimants.

KINDS OF INSURANCE REGULATION BY THE STATES

The insurance codes, as well as the general business laws, of each of the 50 jurisdictions vary too much to permit a complete treatment of the subject. For specific insurance laws, administrative practices, and court decisions, the lawyer and the student of insurance must refer to the regulatory activities in a particular state. However, a general picture of the kinds of insurance regulation in the states is also necessary. This section of the chapter summarizes the regulation usually found in the more important insurance jurisdictions such as New York state. Care must be taken to compare specific state laws and rulings with the general review presented here.

Insurance regulation by the states is largely aimed at the insurers that conduct an insurance business within their jurisdiction. Some regulation is also provided for agents, brokers, and other persons who are part of the marketing of insurance contracts and provide certain other services to insurance policyowners. The regulation of insurers falls into the following categories: (1) formation and licensing requirements, (2) supervision of operations, and (3) liquidation procedures. The second category includes a wide variety of regulatory controls, some extensive and some slight, over such activities as contract forms, rates, reserves, assets, and trade practices. Truly, the birth, life, and death of an insurer are in the hands of the state regulators.

Formation and Licensing of Insurers

Insurance companies are required to meet specific standards of organization that are often higher than those set for general business organizations. The rationale for such high standards is discussed earlier in this chapter. Standards that ensure the solvency, competence, and integrity of the insuring organization are necessary. The first step is incorporation,[7] an introductory process in which the state recognizes and approves the existence of a new legal identity.

The next step, licensing, is a check on the insurer's financial condition to ascertain that it has the required initial capital and surplus for the kinds of insurance permitted in the license. The statutory requirements for licensing must be met by domestic, foreign, and alien insurers that wish to become "admitted" insurers in the state. (The subject of nonadmitted insurers is referred to briefly in chapter 3.) The requirements to be admitted, or licensed, as an insurer sometimes vary among these three types of insurers, but the laws usually specify at least as high standards for foreign and alien insurers as for domestic insurers. Standards vary by legal type of insurer, with requirements for mutual insurers somewhat different from those for stock insurers. These standards also vary widely in the different states.

The licensing procedure is not dependent on financial requirements alone. Many states give the insurance commissioner leeway to apply considerable judgment in acting, or refusing to act, on a license application. The objective of licensing is to provide a preliminary method of lessening the chance of the insurer's financial insolvency, particularly during the difficult formative years. A license may be denied for many other reasons, including the bad faith or reputation of the proposed incorporators or management of an insurer. General managerial ability is undoubtedly as important as capital and surplus requirements in achieving sustained financial stability for an insurer. For that reason, the insurer's license is no more a guarantee against failure than an automobile driver's license is a guarantee against an accident.

Insurer Operations

As a protection against insolvency and unfair treatment of policyowners, insurance regulation continues after the formation and licensing of an insurer. The states exercise some control over many phases of the operations of insurers. Continual regulation is needed because most obligations of insurers extend years into the future, and the state should provide supervision so that the contractual promises are fulfilled. The ways in which insurer operations are supervised are strikingly different among the states and among the various kinds of insurance. Most states provide some regulation of the following types: contracts and forms, rates, reserves, asset and surplus values, investments, agents' licensing and trade practices, claims practices, and taxation.

Contracts and Forms

Because insurance policies are complex legal documents that are not often fully understood by consumers, they could be used to mislead or unfairly treat policyowners. Consequently, in many lines of insurance, policy forms must be approved by, or at least filed with, the insurance commissioner. The task of gaining approval is simplified if an insurer uses a standard policy form developed by an insurance advisory organization such as the ISO or the American Association of Insurance Services (AAIS). Independent insurers may have individualized contracts that vary significantly.

Life and health insurance contracts are not standard contracts in the sense that similar forms or benefits are required. Most states do, however, provide some uniformity by requiring standard provisions in life and health contracts pertaining to items such as the grace period and loan and surrender values. Examples of little regulation over contracts are found in the transportation insurance field. Except for a few required provisions, these contracts are among the most nonuniform of insurance contracts, and policyowners should review their benefits, conditions, and exclusions carefully.

Rates

The regulation of insurance pricing varies by line of business. In some lines of insurance, such as aviation insurance, practically no regulation exists in the states. In life insurance, regulation involves maintaining minimum reserves, rather than setting prices. Most other major kinds of insurance are subject to some direct rate regulation.

Statutory standards are set forth in insurance rating law. Basic standards recognized by rating laws usually require (1) that rates be adequate for the class of business to which they apply, (2) that no rate be unfairly discriminatory, and (3) that rates shall not be excessive. Rates are considered adequate when, along with investment income, they are expected to produce sufficient revenue to pay all losses and expenses of doing business along with a reasonable profit. Rates are considered not unfairly discriminatory if they reflect the expected loss costs and expenses of the homogeneous group of insureds for which they are applicable. Rates are considered nonexcessive if they do not generate an unreasonably high profit for the insurer.

Many of the states passed rating laws some 50 years ago that followed a model bill developed by the NAIC. In these states, the laws provide specifically that there is no intent to prohibit or discourage reasonable price competition, nor do the laws prohibit or discourage price uniformity. The laws permit, but do not require, concerted rate making. However, the state insurance department passes on the reasonableness of the rules and regulations of rating advisory organizations that furnish insurers with loss statistics and other material for rate making. An advisory organization may not exclude or withhold its facilities from any insurers, each of which has the statutory right to become a subscriber by paying reasonable fees.

Any rebate of the insurance premium to an insured, other than dividends to a class of policyowners, is considered discriminatory. A rebate is usually contrary to the law, whether it is made in the form of a direct payment or a credit against the premium or by means of any subterfuge. The statutes do not, however, prohibit the payment by one broker or agent of a part of his or her commission or other compensation to other licensed agents or brokers.

Proposed rates for personal lines of insurance are often based on loss data accumulated by advisory organizations, sometimes called *rating bureaus*. Subscribing insurers add loss data to margins for covering expenses, contingency reserves, and desired profits. Some large insurers do not subscribe to bureaus and instead base rates on their own independent loss and expense data. Individual insurer rate making has increased in recent decades and has become an important factor in automobile insurance and homeowners contracts.

Several different types of rating laws are used in different states and lines of insurance. The most common types are (1) prior approval laws, (2) file-and-use laws, (3) open competition laws, and (4) use-and-file laws.

prior approval law

Prior approval laws require that the proposed rates be filed with the insurance commissioner. The rates may not be used unless and until they are approved by the commissioner. With the desire of some for increased competition, potentially lower rates, and deregulation of insurance, the prior approval laws have come under heavy fire. Although some states have adopted other types, strict regulation through prior approval laws remains predominant.

Types of State Laws Affecting Insurance Rates

- Prior approval laws
- File-and-use laws
- Open competition laws
- Use-and-file laws
- Flex-rating laws
- Expense limitation laws

---

file-and-use law

Several states employ the *file-and-use law*, which permits the immediate use of filed rates without affirmative approval by the insurance commissioner. The commissioner, however, may disapprove the rates within a certain time limit such as 30 or 60 days. Some states use this method for one type of insurance while retaining the prior approval rule for other kinds of insurance.

open competition law

The *open competition law*, which was pioneered in California, has also been adopted by some states from time to time for some lines. Most open competition laws, which rely on competition to set rates, actually represent the absence of government regulation. These laws have been short lived in consumer lines of insurance, although some movement toward open rate competition for selected commercial insurers has begun in recent years.

use-and-file law

Numerous states have a *use-and-file law*. Rates are filed with the insurance commissioner within a specified time after they are first used. The rates may be disapproved if not in compliance with the law.

flex-rating law

A few states have enacted *flex-rating laws* for some lines of insurance. Under these laws, no prior approval is needed if a proposed new rate represents a change of less than 5–10 percent of the existing rate. Other rate changes require prior approval.

Instead of direct regulation of insurance prices by required rate approval, some state laws supervise the cost of life insurance by limiting the portion of the premium that can be used for expenses rather than claims. The New York law applicable to life insurance is most influential in this regard because, under the extraterritoriality provision, all insurers doing business in that state must conform to its regulations for all insurance contracts, regardless of where they are written.

Reserves

The states require insurers to maintain, as a liability, a minimum reserve considered adequate to meet policy obligations as they mature. In life insurance, the legal reserve is an amount that, augmented by premium payments under outstanding contracts and interest earnings, is sufficient to enable the life insurer to meet its expected policy obligations. These include death benefits and nonforfeiture benefits such as policy loans and surrender values. These minimum reserve requirements will also indirectly regulate life insurance rates, at least by reducing the likelihood of inadequate rates.

unearned premium reserve

In the field of property insurance, the *unearned premium reserve* must always be adequate to pay a return premium to policyowners if the policy is canceled prior to expiration. The unearned premium reserves the proportion of the written premium that has not been earned by the insurer through the provision of protection for the full policy period. The purpose of this reserve is to meet all liabilities under the contract and to pay expenses in the future. At the same time, it accounts for income received by the insurer but not yet fully earned.

Example: Assume that an insurer issues a one-year homeowners policy on November 1 of a particular year. On December 31 of that year, the insurer has a liability equal to five-sixths of the annual premium for the policy. This and the liabilities for other unexpired policies make up the unearned premium reserve shown on the insurer's balance sheet.

---

loss reserve

A second type of reserve required of property and liability insurers is the *loss reserve*. Because many contracts do not involve immediate payment of all incurred losses, a reserve must be set up to ensure their payment. For example, a workers' compensation or disability income claim may be made against the insurer today. In many cases, the loss payments may be made gradually over a long future period of disability. In automobile liability cases, several years may elapse after a loss before a court decides who is liable and for how much. In these cases, an estimate of the reserve that will be needed to pay the insurer's obligation is made and carried on its books as a loss reserve. In this way, losses and loss expenses for claims that are known but not yet paid are provided for by the insurer under the loss-reserve laws of the states.

Assets and Surplus Values

The value of assets appearing in the balance sheets of insurers must be correct and conservative in order for liabilities, reserves, and residual surplus items to be meaningful. Securities held by insurers are valued according to practices adopted by a committee of the NAIC. Stocks are usually given year-end market values, while most bonds are carried at amortized values. The valuations are only advisory to the states, but the result is a good example of voluntary and state regulation working together. For some insurers, such as mutual insurers, both surplus accumulation and distribution are subject to regulation aimed at providing equitable treatment for all policyowners.

nonadmitted asset

Some assets of insurance companies are not allowed to be carried on their balance sheets as assets. These assets, called *nonadmitted assets*, are thought to be of marginal quality or of little liquidity for policyowners if their insurers should get into financial difficulty. Examples of nonadmitted assets are most office furniture and supplies and premiums that are 90 days or more past due.

Investments

To protect the solvency of insurers, most states have laws governing the types of securities that may be purchased for investment. The strictest regulations apply to life insurers because they retain many billions of dollars of assets for many years for their policyowners.

Life insurers are subject to vigorous supervision of their investment portfolios. Each annual statement filed with the insurance department lists every individual investment with detailed information about its date of acquisition, costs, values, and earnings. As noted in chapter 4, bonds and common stocks are the prime investments in the portfolio of life insurers, involving a large majority of total assets. Most states grant some limited permission for certain investments. Stocks may be limited, for example, to a stated percent of assets or to 100 percent of surplus. Real estate holdings, especially commercial properties and housing projects, are also limited to a maximum in various states. The legality of all holdings of the insurer is checked carefully in periodic audits of the insurer's portfolio.

The investment of assets by property and liability insurers is also supervised, although the laws are more lenient and vary greatly among the states. The laws of each state must be consulted in order to determine the investment restrictions. The general practice aims at requiring the safest types of investments for all assets held as reserves, both for unearned premiums and losses, and other liabilities. Cash, high-grade bonds, and perhaps preferred stocks of proven quality may be permitted for such assets. The remainder of assets (representing capital and surplus) may be invested in a wider range of securities, including common stocks meeting certain standards. Limitations on real estate holdings, the size of single investments in relation to total assets or surplus, and investments in foreign companies, as well as many other restrictions, are also common.

Agents' Licensing and Trade Practices

An important control of insurer operations is maintained through laws in all states that require insurance agents and brokers to be licensed. The insurance departments usually administer these laws; the objective is insurer representation that is competent and trustworthy. The standards vary tremendously, from little more than payment of a license fee to a comprehensive written examination following mandatory attendance in insurance courses approved by the department. The examinations are often divided into separate tests for different lines of insurance. The examinations for insurance brokers are usually more difficult and extensive than those given to agents. Some adjusters and consultants also must be licensed in a few states. Almost all states now require continuing education as a condition for license renewal.

countersignature law   Special laws in many states, called *countersignature laws*, require that all property insurance contracts written in the state must be signed by an agent who is a resident of that state. These laws are often criticized because they may add to the cost of insurance without providing any real services to the consumer. Agents must also represent only insurers that are authorized and licensed in the state. An exception is made under surplus line laws that in some states permit a specially licensed agent to represent unauthorized insurers when licensed insurers within the state are unwilling to fully underwrite the risk.

Unfair trade practices in insurance are made illegal in all states under laws similar to the Federal Trade Commission Act. Under the provisions of Public Law 15, these laws aim at retaining jurisdiction for the states to prevent fraudulent and unethical acts of agents and brokers. They provide fines and, more important, suspension or revocation of licenses as penalties for violations. Examples of such unfair practices in insurance include the following:

rebating
- *rebating,* the return of any part of the premium, except in the form of dividends, to the policyowner by the insurer or agent as a price-cutting sales inducement[8]

twisting
- *twisting,* a special form of misrepresentation where an agent may induce the policyowner to cancel disadvantageously the contract of another insurer in order to take out a new contract

- misappropriation, when an agent unlawfully keeps funds belonging to others

- commingling of funds, prevented in some states by requiring a separate bank account for the agent's premium funds
- misleading advertising, restrained by many regulations requiring full and fair information in advertisements by insurance companies and agents

The insurance commissioner has broad powers to prevent unfair practices, and exercises this authority by investigating complaints as well as by initiating investigations of any questionable acts of insurance companies or their representatives.

Claims Practices

An insurer's practices in adjusting claims represent a major source of possible mistreatment of insureds and other claimants. The claimant may be unfamiliar with all of the technical details of his or her insurance contract. Moreover, the claimant may be emotionally very stressed and may, therefore, be an easy mark for an unscrupulous claims adjuster. Therefore, states impose regulations that are aimed at protecting insurance claimants from this possibility.

Most states now have enacted laws patterned after the NAIC's model acts and regulations pertaining to unfair claim settlement practices. Some of the practices that are regarded as unfair are the following:

- failing to investigate claims promptly
- failing to communicate with or acknowledge communications from clients on a timely basis
- failing to provide a reasonable explanation as to why a claim was denied
- failing to maintain procedures for complaint handling about claims
- misrepresenting pertinent policy provisions affecting claims
- failing to try to settle a claim once the insurer's liability becomes clear
- attempting to settle a claim for far less than a reasonable person would expect based on the insurer's advertising material

Other Areas of Consumer Protection

In some lines of insurance, insurers are required to use policies that meet specified readability standards. These standards relate not just to the size of the print used but to expressing policy provisions in terms that would be understandable by a typical high school graduate. Also, some states require that insurance consumers be given shopper's guide booklets for certain lines of insurance. These booklets help consumers make comparisons of the costs and benefits of different policies.

Taxation

Revenue for the states has become an important reason for insurance regulation. In addition to federal income taxes, insurers pay to the state what amounts to a sales tax on gross premiums received from all of their policyowners. This premium tax is usually about 2 percent of premiums. The tax is paid by insurers, but its cost, of course, is included in the price of insurance contracts and thus is paid by the policyowners.

The taxes are primarily for revenue purposes, rather than for the cost of insurance regulation. The state premium tax usually goes into the general revenue fund of the state, with insurance department expenses being based on separate appropriations from that fund. Only a small percent of the total tax revenue and fees is used for operation of the state insurance departments.

Rehabilitation and Liquidation of Insurers

The insurance commissioner of a state not only officiates at the birth and oversees the ongoing operation of an insurer but also presides over its demise if necessary. An insurer may be liquidated for numerous reasons, including financial insolvency. Some liquidations may be made voluntarily in order to effect a corporate reorganization or merger. Reinsurance of all outstanding liabilities and contracts may be achieved so that no loss results to policyowners.

rehabilitation
liquidation

The insurance commissioner acts under the insurance laws as the official in charge of supervising *rehabilitation* if the insurer can be restored to financial stability through reorganization, or *liquidation* if the insurer is dissolved. The purpose of both actions is to conserve as much of the insurer's assets as possible for fair distribution to claimants, policyowners, and investors. Sometimes the license of an insurer is suspended temporarily for not meeting financial solvency standards or for other noncompliance with department rulings on rates, advertising, and so on. This suspension may be a prelude to liquidation proceedings or may be a temporary action to force changes in the insurer's operations.

Some insurers suffer liquidation because of financial difficulty. In some cases in the 1980s and 1990s, the failed insurers were large and highly regarded companies. In other cases, insurers with serious financial problems were rescued from near insolvency by the infusion of major amounts of outside capital or by mergers. The result has been some support for a federal guaranty fund for insurers that would operate somewhat as the Federal Deposit Insurance Corporation (FDIC) does for banks. State deposit laws and several special state workers' compensation security funds are already in use that are similar in principle.

guaranty fund

In recent years, all 50 states have adopted insurance *guaranty fund* plans to at least partially protect consumers against the insolvency of insurers. Model legislation promulgated by the NAIC encouraged states to adopt these laws. The plans, administered on a state-by-state basis, usually assess solvent insurers in order to pay the unpaid claims of an insolvent company and to return unearned premiums to its policyowners. Insurers each pay a proportional share of the losses, based on their premium volume in the state.

The guaranty funds appear to be doing a reasonably good job of protecting the consumer, and some states have adopted several improvements. These improvements concern (1) giving the guaranty funds immediate access to assets of the insolvent insurer rather than waiting until liquidation proceedings are complete, (2) giving the guaranty funds priority over general creditors to obtain assets of the insolvent insurer, and (3) permitting a tax offset against premium taxes to solvent insurers for money paid into the guaranty funds. Even with these improvements, however, some problems remain, including lengthy delays before consumers receive their money and dollar limits on some types of claims.

Operating a system to pay for insolvencies does not completely protect the buyers of insurance against insurer insolvencies. Detecting troubled insurers in advance of insolvency proceedings is an important goal. The NAIC has developed an "early warning system" based on a series of financial ratio tests. These tests have dealt mainly with the adequacy of the insurer's reserves, changes in its surplus, its growth rate, and the adequacy of its prices. Other tools for the early detection of insurer financial difficulty include the risk-based capital standards and the on-site examination system developed by the NAIC, noted earlier in this chapter.

Federal versus State Regulation

This chapter emphasizes regulation of insurance by the states because most government legislation, administrative action, and court decisions pertaining to insurance have been at the state level. The McCarran-Ferguson Act reaffirmed the predominant role in insurance regulation by the states. This role still continues because the law conditionally exempts insurance from major federal statutes such as the Sherman Act (except for boycotts, coercion, or intimidation), Clayton Act, Robinson-Patman Act, and other laws. Federal laws apply only to the extent that state legislation is inadequate.

The federal government has increased its regulation of insurance in some specific and limited, but nonetheless important, areas of insurance. For example, federal agencies have regulated some aspects of interstate advertising and mergers through the Federal Trade Commission (FTC), variable life insurance and annuities through the Securities and Exchange Commission (SEC), occupational safety under various rules of the Occupational Safety and Health Administration (OSHA), and pensions and other employee benefits under the Employee Retirement Income Security Act (ERISA) administered mainly by the U.S. Department of Labor.

Why should regulation of insurance be performed mainly by the states? Advocates of state regulation have pointed out reasons such as (1) the local nature of many insurance transactions, for which any difficulties can best be resolved on a state basis; (2) the reasonable success of state regulation for many years, during which insurance has become an important and sound business; (3) the value of regulation on a state-by-state basis, which permits gradual changes and innovations in regulation without applying them to the entire country all at once; and (4) the help of the NAIC in recommending model legislation to the states in order to achieve some uniformity in insurance regulation. While supporters recognize that state regulation is not perfect, they claim that federal regulation would be much worse. It would be cumbersome, expensive, less effective, and fragmented among dozens of agencies.

Conversely, the proponents of federal regulation of insurance have criticized state regulation on many points, emphasizing (1) inconsistencies and lack of uniformity in regulation of insurers; (2) inadequate funding for the important tasks of the insurance commissioners, and the short-term and political aspects of their term of office; (3) greater standardization needed in insurance contracts to cover many interstate exposures; and (4) increased competition desired in order to ensure availability and lower and fairer prices for insurance. Although the federal government's assumption of the major role in insurance regulation is unlikely any time soon, its role is still growing. Also, the threat of federal regulation wherever the states fail to perform adequately is a constant impetus to improving state insurance regulation.

EVALUATING INSURERS

The second major topic in this chapter is the evaluation of insurers that have met the regulatory requirements for possible inclusion in a client's insurance program. That evaluation may be needed with respect to the insuring organization itself, the sales personnel who represent it, or both.

Criteria for Selecting an Insurer

A financial planner may assist the client in the selection of insurers. Because most insurance is written through the agency system, the choice of a competent and reliable insurance agent or broker is likely to be a part of this responsibility. Of course, the financial planner may himself or herself be the client's insurance agent or broker. If he or she represents only one insurer, the issue may be moot. Often, however, choices with respect to insurers must be made and the question is what criteria should be used in making these choices.

Probably the single most important criterion is the financial strength of the insurer. Because the basic function of an insurer is to pay claims, care must be taken to select only those insurers that are most likely to be able to do so if the need arises. In light of the number of insolvencies and near insolvencies among insurers in recent decades, and the limitations of state insurance guaranty funds noted earlier, an insurer's claims-paying ability cannot simply be taken for granted.

The size of an insurer is not always a controlling factor in its selection, as financial strength and size are not necessarily equivalents. Growth over a period of years is significant. The financial planner who limits recommended purchases to well-known and recognized companies will probably have made a good start on the task of choosing the best possible insurer. The state insurance departments can provide some current information about insurers, including records about consumer complaints against specific insurers, risk-based capital compliance, and early warning financial ratios noted earlier.

Several rating organizations publish the financial history, ratings, and analyses of individual insurers. These organizations include A.M. Best Company, Fitch Ratings (formed by a merger of Duff & Phelps and Fitch IBCA), Moody's Investors Service, Standard & Poor's, and Weiss Ratings. A few words of caution are in order with respect to reliance on ratings assigned by these organizations, however. First, the criteria and methodology differ among the rating organizations, so an insurer may receive different ratings from different organizations. Second, a rating of A, which many people associate with excellence, may not be particularly good. For example, Best's has two ratings higher than A, and Standard & Poor's has five ratings higher than A. Third, some rating agencies seem to be more generous in their ratings than others. Fourth, not all insurers are assigned ratings by all of the rating organizations. In light of all of these differences, it is probably wise advice to choose insurers that have very high ratings from at least two or three of the rating organizations.

Selecting an insurer should be based on willingness and ability to pay claims. Companies' attitudes toward claims may differ, and the applicant should be concerned with the company's attitude toward technicalities, as well as the reputation of the claims department for satisfactory dealings with insureds. Consumer complaint files maintained by state insurance departments can be helpful.

Service is another criterion that should be used in evaluating insurers. The insurer must be able to provide proper protection for the applicant. Does the insurer specialize in a few lines of insurance, or does it sell all coverages that the purchaser may need and want? Is the insurer experienced in offering all the contracts it will write? Will the insurer individualize contracts to meet the particular needs of the insurance buyer? Does it have capacity and adequate reinsurance for the amount of insurance the buyer may require? Is it licensed in all of the states in which the buyer needs coverage? In addition to indemnification for losses, can the insurer provide any engineering and loss-prevention services that the purchaser may need? And again, what is the insurer's general attitude and reputation with regard to prompt and fair settlement of all reasonable claims?

As part of the evaluation of an insurer's service, the applicant should be interested in knowing whether the insurer is liberal with respect to underwriting.

A company that is selective in underwriting may prove unsatisfactory when a consumer has a difficult situation such as poor health or extremely hazardous business activities. Conversely, a consumer with very favorable risk characteristics may benefit by dealing with a highly selective insurer. The insurer's facilities for loss-prevention recommendations that may reduce insurance costs are also important to the consumer.

Selecting an Insurance Company

- Financial strength
- Attitude concerning claims payment
- Lines of coverage offered
- Service before and after a claim
- Underwriting standards
- Cost of the coverage

Another important criterion in the evaluation of an insurer, of course, is the cost of the products. Cost should usually be considered and compared only after the above criteria are analyzed. Exorbitant rates are obviously undesirable. Lower rates are beneficial to the purchaser; however, rates that are too low could reflect an unduly strict attitude toward claims payment, inadequate financial reserves, restrictive policy provisions, or minimal services.

Initial costs are only part of the necessary analysis, for final costs over a longer period of protection must be considered, including possible rate changes, dividends, assessments, or premium adjustments under some types of rating plans. In life insurance, net cost comparisons over a period such as 20 or more years, considering dividends, cash values, and interest factors, may be appropriate. Also, all insurance costs should be analyzed along with other risk management costs such as those of loss prevention.

Criteria for Choosing an Agent or Broker

Because most insurance is written through the agency system, the choice of a competent and reliable insurance agent is often an important decision for the insurance buyer. If an exclusive agent who represents one insurer only is chosen, this selection also determines the insurer with which business is conducted. If an independent agent is chosen, the insurance buyer often leaves the selection of the insurer up to the agent, or at least relies heavily on the agent's recommendations.

A substantial part of the insurance premium represents commission or salary to the agent or broker. If no service or inadequate service is rendered for this part of the premium, the policyowner is paying for something not received. The purchaser of insurance must determine whether the agent or broker is only an order taker. If so, the policyowner is getting less than full value.

Some applicants place insurance with numerous agents. Frequently, this distribution is made on a reciprocity basis to create goodwill or on a patronage basis to distribute business among a number of friends. Sound practice suggests selecting one agent or broker, or as few as possible, to handle an entire insurance account. Both the insurance buyer and the agent should prefer this practice. Most agents would rather have fewer accounts for which they are fully responsible than to participate in many accounts to which they contribute little service. Sometimes an account may be split so that the property and liability lines are handled by one agent and the life, health, and annuity business by another agent. Regardless of the number of agents, the more information that an agent has about the client's total insurance account, the better he or she may be able to analyze the risks and recommend coordinated protection for the client's needs.

The insurance consumer or financial planner who allows friendship to govern the selection of an agent may receive inadequate protection or pay an exorbitant amount for excessive or duplicating coverages. Placing insurance only on the basis of personal friendship is as foolish as selecting a doctor, a lawyer, or an architect on that basis. Because of the complex nature of various risks, insurance coverages, and rates, the insurance agent or broker should be selected with the same care and discrimination used in choosing other professional advisers.

Choosing an agent or broker is an essential step toward a sound insurance and risk management program. Some of the criteria that might be used to evaluate insurance agents and brokers include knowledge and ability, willingness, integrity and character, and representation.

Knowledge and Ability

The agent or broker must learn about the client's insurance needs and help the client understand the value of the services rendered. The agent must have the background and experience necessary to identify, analyze, and treat risk properly. One method of evaluating the agent's knowledge and ability is to ask questions such as, "Are you a CFP®, ChFC, CLU, or CPCU?" "If not, are you working toward these or other educational objectives on a regular basis?" "Are you a full-time agent?" Some part-time agents and some agents who have not completed professional designations are still competent. However, agents who are fully committed to the insurance business are more likely to do a really successful job for their clients by keeping abreast of rapidly changing knowledge requirements.

The insurance consumer needs a technically competent agent who performs the wide variety of services essential to proper insurance protection. These services may include understanding needs, analyzing significant possibilities of loss, finding markets, comparing alternative coverages and contracts, arranging for credit or installment payments, checking on the accuracy of classifications and rates charged, providing loss prevention or engineering services, making evaluation appraisals, seeing that claims payments are made promptly, reviewing changing needs frequently, and many other important duties.

Willingness

Is the agent willing to take the time to conscientiously apply his or her knowledge and fully appraise all the client's needs and alternatives? If not, the client won't receive the benefit of that knowledge and ability. The agent must be able and willing to take the time to see that services, including those of agency staff and insurance companies, are performed as effectively as possible.

The agent should offer to recommend additional legal, accounting, or consulting services as needed. Loss-prevention suggestions and help with filing claims are also important services provided to the insurance buyer. The best qualified agent who is too busy is of no value to the client. The time and desire to perform these services regularly must be present when the client needs them.

Integrity and Character

Even willing and able agents or brokers lack an important requirement if they are unable to command the confidence and trust of the policyowner. An insurance purchaser who cannot trust recommendations is not receiving full value for the insurance dollar.

Because insurance is purchased in order to obtain certainty, agents or brokers must be able to give their clients both psychological and actual security. In other words, consumers need someone with whom they can identify closely in discussing their financial goals and needs. The values of agent and client, if similar, can help them establish a good rapport. The age of the agent in relation to that of the policyowner can be a factor in this regard, but differences in age are probably less important than differences in philosophy and lifestyle. Confidential information from the purchaser is often required in order to provide good insurance counseling services. Thus, the agent or broker must respect the buyer's trust with as complete honesty as would a doctor, a lawyer, or an accountant.

Representation

Good agents generally do not represent poor insurers. They must represent or have contacts with one or many insurers that can provide the required protection and services for the policyowner. All the necessary coverages, including even special or unusual ones, must be available through the agent(s) in a prompt and efficient manner at a reasonable cost. The insurer or insurers represented should be capable of writing many different kinds of insurance with a progressive attitude toward newer coverages and forms designed to meet the particular needs of individual buyers.

Insurance agencies and brokerage firms vary from the individual agent to organizations having a large staff and offering a wide range of specializations. Some agencies consist of one person, others have a half-dozen agents and office personnel, while still others have as many as 100 or more employees and operate much like a small insurance company. These organizations differ in the services they are able to offer, their methods of doing business, and the types and kinds of insurance they handle. Frequently, the members of an agency who handle the life business limit their activities to this field. Also, in a large agency certain persons become recognized experts in such lines as pensions, liability, workers' compensation, or surety coverages. When selecting the agent or broker, the insurance consumer should consider whether the particular agent and agency office have the needed experience and service facilities.

Some buyers solicit competitive bids on an annual basis for their property and liability insurance. Lower costs for insurance may come at the price of less satisfactory service from the agent, who may not regard the policyowner as a permanent client. Policyowners have found the competitive approach detrimental because in a period of unfavorable losses a business firm may have no assurance of continued coverage and competing insurers will be reluctant to participate. Thus, insurance buyers may seriously limit their market. This is less likely to occur if an insurer may expect to recoup over a period of years losses incurred in an unfavorable year. From the buyer's standpoint, as well as the agent's, a long-term relationship on a professional basis seems to work best in the long run.

CHAPTER REVIEW

Answers to review questions and self-test questions start on page 725.

Key Terms

extraterritoriality

National Association of Insurance
    Commissioners (NAIC)

prior approval law

file-and-use law

open competition law

use-and-file law

flex-rating law

unearned premium reserve

loss reserve

nonadmitted asset

countersignature law

rebating

twisting

rehabilitation

liquidation

guaranty fund

Review Questions

5-1. What is the general purpose of insurance regulation?

5-2. Describe the three basic approaches to insurance regulation.

5-3.   Briefly describe the three key categories of state regulation of insurance.

5-4.   Explain how each of the following aspects of insurer operations tends to be regulated, pointing out any differences between regulation applying to life insurers and that applying to property-liability insurers.
   a.   contracts and forms
   b.   rates
   c.   reserves
   d.   assets and surplus values
   e.   investments
   f.   agent's licensing and trade practices
   g.   claims practices

5-5.   Describe the ways in which insurance regulation seeks to protect buyers of insurance when insurer insolvencies occur.

5-6.   List the arguments for and against regulation of insurance by the states.

5-7.   What criteria can a financial planner use to help clients select insurers for their insurance programs?

5-8.   What criteria can a financial planner use to help clients choose reliable and competent agents or brokers for their insurance programs?

Self-Test Questions

T   F   5-1.   The general purpose of insurance regulation is to protect the public against insolvency or unfair treatment by insurers.

T   F   5-2.   At the state level, insurance is regulated by legislative, administrative, and court action.

T   F   5-3.   The insurance commissioner has the power to, among other things, enforce the laws passed by the legislature and interpreted by the courts, license insurers and agents, and investigate to determine whether insurers and agents are meeting the requirements of the statutes.

T   F   5-4.   Life insurance is subject to direct rate regulation under prior approval laws that require that rates be approved before they can be used.

T   F   5-5.   Insurers must comply with state laws governing the types of securities that may be purchased for investment.

T   F   5-6.   While unfair trade practices are illegal in all states, most states now permit rebating and twisting.

T   F   5-7.   Most premium taxes paid by insurers to the states are used to pay for the cost of insurance regulation.

T   F   5-8.   The key to assessing the financial strength of an insurer is the size of the insurer.

T   F   5-9.   In addition to financial strength, other important criteria for selecting an insurer are its willingness to pay claims, the service provided, and the cost of its products.

T   F   5-10.   The dominant factor in the selection of an agent is friendship.

NOTES

1. Some organizations function in several types of self-regulation activities. RIMS, for example, is active in education, research, public relations, and the promotion of legislation on behalf of its members.
2. The insurance code for an individual state can exceed several hundred pages.
3. Today it is difficult to rationalize such a decision, but in 1868 the now-famous decision stated: "Issuing a policy of insurance is not a transaction of commerce. They are not commodities to be shipped or forwarded from one state to another and then put up for sale. . . . Such contracts are not interstate transactions, though the parties may be domiciled in different states. They are, then, local transactions and are governed by local law." (*Paul v. Virginia*, 231 United States 495.)
4. 64 United States 1162.
5. C 20, 79th Cong., 1st sess.
6. Most of the states use this title of "commissioner of insurance," eight use "director of insurance," and three use "superintendent of insurance."
7. Reciprocal exchanges, Lloyd's associations, fraternals, and some health insurance associations do not legally become incorporated by this process. They do, however, file similar statements of their present status and proposed activities as stated in their charters and bylaws.
8. Rebating is allowed in two states, but only under very limited circumstances.

6

Basic Legal Principles and Contract Analysis

Learning Objectives

An understanding of the material in this chapter should enable the student to

6-1. Describe the unique aspects of an insurance contract that differentiate it from other goods and services.

6-2. Explain the general legal requirements of an insurance contract.

6-3. Describe the special legal characteristics of an insurance contract.

6-4. Explain how to analyze the various parts of an insurance contract.

Chapter Outline

Private insurance is usually created by a written contract or policy. Sometimes insurance begins with an oral agreement between the insurer, or its agent, and the policyowner, and is later completed by a written contract. The most tangible product resulting from the insurance system is the written contract that transfers financial risk from the insured to the insurer. Thus, insurance is fundamentally dependent on the legal principles of contracts.

Many persons think of the physical piece of paper on which the insurance contract is written as the whole of insurance. Because this document is what the insurance purchaser sees, he or she may unconsciously assume that this is all there is to it. There is a tendency to forget that there are many other parts of insurance. The risk transfer, the application of the law of large numbers, the freedom from worry, the inspections and the loss-prevention services, the advisory functions—all of these services tend to be forgotten by purchasers when only the contract of insurance is considered. Even the payment of losses is neglected in such thoughts by insurance purchasers, unless they happen to suffer losses for which reimbursement is paid! The contract is significant in insurance, but the service beyond the contract is also of tremendous importance to the consumer.

Before discussing more specific principles of insurance law, this chapter reviews other basic attributes of insurance. This background is essential for financial planners who assess risks and analyze insurance for clients.

INSURANCE: A FUTURE, CONTINGENT, SERVICE, RISK CONTRACT

Insurance is characterized as an intangible asset, in contrast to goods such as clothing or automobiles, which can be seen, felt, and used in everyday life.

Unlike these tangible assets that have value, intangible assets *represent* value. Besides insurance policies, other examples of intangible assets include stock certificates and savings bonds. The characterization as an intangible asset is not sufficient for describing how insurance differs from other economic products. Insurance has many tangible characteristics such as the physical contract or loss-payment check. Insurance, however, is more than a mere piece of paper; it is also a promise to pay money. The insurance contract is unique in that it is a future, contingent, service, risk contract.

Unlike most of the physical goods that are purchased for immediate enjoyment, insurance is usually thought of as providing future benefits when loss payments are made. The policyowner may not realize, however, that he or she is using the insurance by obtaining a significant benefit immediately and continually throughout the contract period of protection. The relief from anxiety and freedom from worry about financial losses are real benefits. The policyowner often forgets this and contemplates only the fact that the insurance is purchased to obtain a loss payment sometime well into the future. A hurricane, an automobile collision, a premature death, or a retirement are all future possibilities for the insurance purchaser.

More than that, policyowners buy insurance against many perils with the conviction that the perils will not really cause losses to them. They buy it "just in case" but at the same time think, "It will never happen to me." This quality of insurance emphasizes its contingent nature. The feeling of contingency is also supported by fact. Only the unfortunate minority who actually suffer loss see that benefit of insurance. Families may carry insurance for many years without a serious auto accident, or for a lifetime without a theft loss to their property. A business may continue through millions of worker hours without a disabling injury to any of its employees. The very nature of many kinds of insurance is based on contingencies that may or may not occur and that normally occur only infrequently.

The preceding comments have suggested considering insurance as a service contract, rather than simply an intangible product. It is, in fact, a bundle of services. Insurance becomes an unusual product because the policyowner needs help in understanding its varied benefits. That is why the personal service of an agent is so often necessary in marketing insurance. Even though it is the ultimate responsibility of the policyowner to understand the contract, agents can be most helpful. Through them, prospective insurance buyers learn about needs in regard to risks and how insurance prevents losses, transfers risks, and pays benefits in case of losses. They learn how liability insurance pays the legal costs of defense in lawsuits. They find out how life insurance serves as a basis for credit, creates a liquid estate, and offers alternatives for using capital in the form of life income guarantees. In return for the cost of the contract, the policyowner receives services, some at the inception of the policy, others during the term of the contract or at the time of a loss, and some at the end of the contract period.

Financial risk is a final characteristic that differentiates insurance from other goods and services. The basis of the insurance contract is uncertainty about many perils that may cause accidental loss. Insurance transfers the financial risk of losses to the insurer, a professional risk bearer. Other service contracts may be future and contingent, but they do not involve payment for the occurrence of unexpected perils such as fire, windstorm, disability, and death. The insurance contract is based on chance or fortuitous events and as a result is an *aleatory contract,* one in which unequal values are exchanged—that is, a small premium for a potentially large loss payment or many premiums with no corresponding loss payment.

aleatory contract

GENERAL LEGAL REQUIREMENTS

The rights and obligations of the parties to an insurance agreement are determined largely by reference to the general laws that govern contracts. The agreement by which insurance is effected is a contract in which the insurer, in consideration of the payment of a specified sum by the policyowner, agrees to make good the losses suffered through the occurrence of a designated unfavorable contingency. The insurance contract need not be in writing, but as a matter of business practice, these agreements are ordinarily written. Even social insurances, such as workers' compensation, are written, although the terms appear in a law rather than in a private agreement.

A contract has been defined as "an agreement enforceable by law." A more complete definition would include the following essentials required by law:

- offer and acceptance
- legal purpose
- competent parties
- consideration

A lack of any of the essential elements prevents enforcement of the contract. To be valid and enforceable, insurance contracts must meet these four general legal requirements.

Offer and Acceptance

A legally binding agreement, or contract, requires both an offer by one party and an acceptance by another party. In insurance, the offer is usually made in a request for coverage by the prospect, or applicant. The simplest method, used for many types of property and liability insurance, is an oral request to an agent either in person or by telephone. In life insurance and in many forms of health insurance, the offer must be made in a written application.

Before a contract is effective, acceptance of the offer is necessary. As has been noted earlier, in property and liability insurance, the agent often has authority to bind, or accept, the offer even without receiving any payment from the applicant. The protection may commence immediately, if desired, based entirely on the oral request of the applicant and the oral acceptance by the agent.

Example 1:	Shelley completed an application for $25,000 of nonmedical life insurance on her own life and gave it to the insurer's agent with a check for the first premium. Shelley died in an auto accident 2 days later. Three weeks later, the insurer reviewed the application and found that Shelley, at the time of the application, met the insurer's normal underwriting standards. The insurer will be obligated to pay $25,000 to Shelley's beneficiary.
Example 2:	Same facts as above, except that Shelley did not pay the premium. In this case, the insurer will not be obligated to pay anything because there was no acceptance of an offer.

In life insurance, the method and timing of legal acceptance are different. The written application and the first premium payment are usually submitted by the applicant as the offer to the insurer through the agent, who issues a conditional receipt. Acceptance is held by most courts to occur when the applicant meets the normal underwriting standards of the insurer, including a medical examination if required. Then coverage becomes effective as of the time of the application and premium payment. If the premium is not paid with the application, the offer to insure is made by the insurer. The insurance is accepted and becomes effective when the contract is delivered to the applicant while the applicant is in good health and the premium is paid. However, if the applicant does not meet the underwriting standards of the insurer, the insurer may make a counteroffer with a different contract, which the prospect may accept or reject upon delivery by the agent.

Legal Purpose

The second requirement of a legally binding contract is that it must have a legal purpose or object. The courts will not enforce an insurance contract if it has an illegal purpose or is contrary to public policy. Examples include a thief attempting to insure stolen property; an applicant contracting for life insurance with the proven intention of murdering the insured to collect payment; or a person purchasing fire insurance on a neighbor's house in the hope that it will burn. In these instances, there is no insurable interest, as discussed later in this chapter, which would be against public policy.

Competent Parties

Valid contracts require that the party making the offer and the one accepting the offer be legally competent to make the agreement. In insurance, the most common problem arises in connection with applicants who are under the age of legal majority, which differs by state. Minority applicants may have the option of repudiating contracts up to the time they reach legal adulthood, unless the contracts are for necessities such as food, shelter, or clothing. Some insurance contracts are thus voidable by applicants who are minors, and these applicants would receive a full return of the premiums paid if they later decide to make them void. Some states have made exceptions for life, health, and auto insurance contracts by establishing special age limits of 14 or 16; beyond this age, minors are considered to have the legal capacity to insure themselves, and a contract is binding on them.

A similar problem may occur in insurance purchased by legally insane or intoxicated persons. They cannot make legal contracts because they fail to understand the agreement.

Insurers, too, must be competent to enter into a legal contract by meeting charter and license requirements of the states. In cases where legal capacity is lacking, many courts have nevertheless held the contracts binding on the insurer, or on its corporate officers personally, rather than penalizing a good-faith purchaser of the coverage.

Consideration

The final requirement for a valid contract is some consideration exchanged by both parties to the agreement—a right or something of value given up, or an obligation assumed. In insurance, the applicant typically makes a premium payment, or the contract may become effective on the basis of the applicant's promise to pay and to meet other conditions of the contract. The insurer's consideration is its promise to pay for specified losses or to provide other services to the policyowner.

SPECIAL LEGAL CHARACTERISTICS

The next section of this chapter concerns special legal characteristics of the insurance contract. These are not necessarily unique to insurance contracts, but they help describe the fundamental ideas on which insurance contracts are based. A good understanding of these characteristics should aid the financial planner, insurance adviser, and consumer to read insurance contracts and comprehend the underlying legal concepts that are essential to most insurance contracts. Figure 6-1 summarizes the characteristics.

Unilateral Nature

unilateral contract

The insurance contract is a *unilateral contract* because only one party, the insurer, makes a legally enforceable promise. If the insurer fails to fulfill the promises it makes, such as to pay the specified benefits at the death of the insured, it may be held legally liable for breach of contract. The insured makes

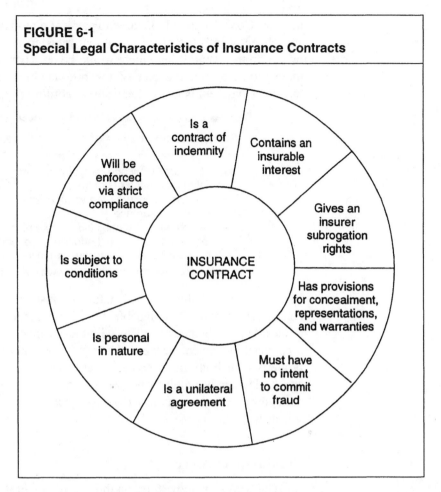

FIGURE 6-1
Special Legal Characteristics of Insurance Contracts

no promises after the contract comes into force, although, of course, failure to live up to policy conditions such as paying the premiums may release the insurer from the contract.

Unlike the insurance contract, most contracts are bilateral. When Able agrees to sell a car to Baker for $7,000, failure of either Able or Baker to live up to the contract's terms leaves him or her liable for damages to the other party on the basis of breach of contract.

Personal Nature

The insurance contract is personal and follows the person rather than the property concerned. We may speak of insuring property, but this is not technically the last. Insurance actually provides repayment of a loss arising out of an undesired happening. An insurer cannot guarantee that possessions will not be lost, or even guarantee replacement with items of like quality and kind. The insurer can, however, provide for indemnification of the person who has incurred the loss. Consider an individual who pays for a property insurance contract and subsequently sells the property without transferring the insurance to the new owner. In the event of loss, there would be no payment by the insurer because there is no loss on the part of the original insured. The determination of insurance payment is loss to the insured, not loss of specified property.

Some Characteristics of an Insurance Contract

- *Unilateral.* Only one party, the insurer, can be held liable for breach of contract.
- *Personal.* It insures a *person,* even if the policy is property insurance.
- *Conditional.* The obligation of one party, usually the insurer, depends on the fulfillment of certain conditions by the other party, usually the policyowner.

One result of the personal nature of insurance is that many insurance contracts are not freely assignable, or transferable, by the policyowner to other parties. Most insurance contracts, with the exception of life insurance, represent a personal agreement between the insurer and the policyowner. To permit a property or liability insurance contract to be assignable without the insurer's approval would be unfair to the insurer. Only by knowing and investigating each policyowner can the insurance company accurately appraise the potential losses it is insuring.

Conditional Nature

The obligation to perform on the part of one of the parties to an agreement may be conditioned on the performance of the second party. A clause in an insurance contract requiring performance is usually referred to as a condition.

conditional contract

Failure of one party to perform under such a *conditional contract* relieves the other party of his or her obligation.

Where an insurance contract is subject to a condition, the condition is usually regarded as either precedent (before) or subsequent (after) the time at which a promise becomes binding on the promisor. An illustration of a common condition precedent, which must take place before a promise becomes binding, is the requirement in many insurance contracts that an insurer must have proper notice and proof of loss before the claim is payable. Note that the policyowner does not have to file a claim, but the insurer is not obligated to pay unless the policyowner does so in the proper manner. An example of a condition subsequent is an insured's obligation to cooperate with the insurer in defending a liability claim. If the promise of the insured is not fulfilled, that failure subsequently relieves the insurer of its earlier obligation to pay.

Strict Compliance Nature

As a general principle, a contract will be enforced on the basis of strict compliance. However, applying this rather obvious principle is not always as simple as it may seem.

Contract of Adhesion

contract of
adhesion

The insurance contract is characterized as a *contract of adhesion* because the insurer ordinarily prepares all its details, and the policyowner has no part in drawing up its clauses or determining its wording. When applying for insurance, the applicant either accepts the policy as prepared by the insurer (adheres to it), or does not purchase the insurance. Insurers sometimes modify some types of contracts to meet the individual needs of large clients, but even when so modified, the contract with its amendments is prepared by the insurance company. In contrast, a *bargaining contract* is one in which both parties contribute to the terms and conditions.

The insurer does not always create the wording for the contract. Sometimes legislation requires that specific wording be used. Other times the policyowner may be a large corporation that may ask for and obtain special contract provisions. In these cases, the intent of the entire contract, and of both the insurer and the policyowner, would probably be considered in interpretations by the courts of contract ambiguities.

Benefit of Doubt to Policyowner

Because the insurer has the advantage in drawing up the agreement and is expected to clearly represent the intent of the parties when the terms of the policy are ambiguous, obscure, or susceptible to more than one interpretation, the construction most favorable to the policyowner generally prevails.[1] This rule is based on the assumption that the insurer is under a duty to make its meaning clear. When the insurer has failed to be clear, the benefit of the doubt goes to the policyowner. This benefit applies only when the court decides that the contract is unclear, not every time the policyowner misinterprets or does not understand a provision. Sometimes this principle may help policyowners, offsetting their lack of participation in drawing up the insurance contract.

Need for Policyowners to Read Contract

Where there is no ambiguity, the contract is to be enforced in accordance with its terms. If the contract is clear and understandable, few interpretations are necessary. Consideration must be given to the generally understood meaning of the terms used and to the entire context to determine the nature and extent of coverage.

A corollary to the strict compliance rule is that the law holds persons to be bound by the terms of a written contract that they sign or accept, regardless of whether they have acquainted themselves with all of its terms and conditions.[2] Many insurance contracts are complicated and difficult to understand. Regardless of the clarity or obscurity of the terminology, most people do not read their policies. Policyowners assume that a policy meets their needs and let it go at that. However, when a loss occurs, claiming ignorance of the terms of the policy because of failure to read the agreement is no defense. The policyowner's failure to read the contract does not change or extend the rights of the policyowner as stated in the written policy. The advice to insurance buyers should be: "To avoid problems (and uncertainties), know what is in your insurance policy by reading it, having it explained, or both."

Oral Evidence

parol evidence rule

In connection with the insurance contract, the rule of law applying to oral evidence, referred to in legal terminology as the *parol evidence rule,* has been expressed in a leading case. "It is a fundamental rule, in courts both of law and equity, that parol contemporaneous evidence is inadmissible to contradict or vary the terms of a valid written instrument."[3] Thus, for example, a policyowner may not usually contradict the written contract by saying that the agent promised that the policy covered a specific type of loss.

Although the written contract is not ordinarily subject to modification by oral evidence, the language of the policy is nevertheless not binding in clear cases of mutual mistake of fact or where there is a mistake on one side and fraud inducing it on the other. In these cases, the injured party has a right in equity to ask that the contract be reformed to the true agreement. An example might be a contract written on the wrong building based on incorrect oral information from an applicant.

Oral evidence also can be helpful to the policyowner. Usually, as noted in chapter 3, when information is given to the agent at the time of an application or loss, this knowledge is also assumed to be knowledge of the insurer.

Indemnity Nature

indemnity

Most property, liability, and health insurance contracts are contracts of *indemnity.* This common law principle, modified by state statute, means that a policyowner is entitled to payment only to the extent of financial loss or legal liability. In other words, the policyowner should remain in the same financial position that existed prior to a loss and should not be allowed to profit from the loss. Of course, indemnification only extends up to the policy limits and is subject to policy provisions and limitations such as deductibles.

For example, assume an insured has an individual major medical policy with a $1 million lifetime limit. Also assume that the policy limits hospital room and board benefits to the cost of semiprivate accommodations. Further, assume that the insured is hospitalized and incurs $25,000 in hospital bills, $1,200 of which is for the extra cost of a private room occupied at the insured's request. The policy would reimburse the insured for $23,800 of the hospital expenses, less policy deductibles and coinsurance. Therefore, the insured has been indemnified within policy limits and provisions.

Historically, the concept of indemnity limited property insurance settlements to the actual cash value of a loss. However, this basis of loss settlement has been modified over the years by (1) policy provisions that provide replacement cost coverage, (2) policies written for agreed values, and (3) valued policy laws. All of these concepts are covered in chapter 16.

Not all insurance policies are considered policies of indemnity under common law and state statutes. The major example of this exception is life insurance. The courts have determined that it is impossible to place a value on a human life, even though this is done by judges and juries in wrongful death suits. In addition, courts have held that most life insurance contracts are also investment contracts rather than solely insurance contracts. Therefore, the amount of the investment should be protected. The significance of life insurance not being a contract of indemnity is that the insurer must pay the death benefit if the insured dies. The insurer could not deny full payment under a $1 million policy, for example, by arguing that the insured's life was worth only $650,000.

Insurable Interest

insurable interest

All insurance contracts contain an element of *insurable interest*. An insurable interest is a right or relationship with regard to the subject matter of the insurance contract such that the policyowner would suffer financial loss from its damage, loss, or destruction.

The purposes of requiring an insurable interest in insurance contracts are to prevent gambling, to decrease moral hazard, and to help measure the actual loss. Without an insurable interest, a contract is a wager or gambling contract. The contract also could provide an undesirable incentive to purposely cause losses or injuries. When an insurable interest exists, no profit results because policyowners merely receive repayment for the loss they have suffered.

An example of insurable interest is the ownership of property, where a fire, windstorm, or other peril causes a financial loss. Mortgagees, bailees, and creditors may have insurable interests, and often several persons have an insurable interest in the same property. A homeowner may insure his or her interest in property, for example, while at the same time the policy insures the mortgagee's interest up to the value of the mortgage loan.

Liability creates many insurable interests. An automobile owner or driver may be held responsible for losses caused by the car; thus, each has an insurable interest. Employers may also be liable for employees' automobiles. Tenants often are liable for injuries caused to the public on the rented premises. Property owners may be held responsible for the actions of contractors, and contractors for the actions of subcontractors. All these losses may be the basis of an insurable interest.

The continuance of life and good health serves as the basis for many other examples of insurable interest. Death, injury, or sickness may result in financial losses to the persons insured, or to their families, creditors, business partners, or employers. The right of persons to insure their own lives, as well as the right of close family members to insure blood relatives, is based on a presumed insurable interest. Other insurable interests for life or health insurance are based on actual potential losses, either increased expenses or reduced income potential, resulting from the relationship to the insured. For example, a creditor may insure the life of a debtor, normally up to the amount of the loan, or a business person may insure a partner's life for the potential loss that his or her death would cause for the partnership.

The question of when an insurable interest is required also may be important. Generally, property insurance has the legal requirement that an insurable interest exists at the time of a loss. Of course, insurance company practice is also likely to require an insurable interest in the property at the time the policy is applied for. Life insurance requires an insurable interest only at the time the contract is purchased, and need not be present when the death occurs.

Subrogation Rights

subrogation

The common law doctrine of *subrogation* gives the insurer rights that the insured possessed against responsible third parties. Subrogation is basically a process of substitution, where the insurer takes over the legal rights of the insured that existed at the time of the loss. Therefore, from the time of the loss, the insured may not release any rights that might prove beneficial to the insurer.

In common law, a person who causes a loss or who is primarily liable should ultimately be made responsible for the damages sustained. In connection with insurance, as a matter of equity, on paying the insured the amount of the loss, the insurer has a right of action against any other person who may have caused the loss.

The right of the insurer against other negligent persons usually does not rest on any contractual relationship, but arises out of the indemnity nature of the insurance contract. If the insured is indemnified, it would be inequitable for him or her also to try to collect from the party responsible for the loss. If the insured were permitted to do this, a double collection of the loss from both the insurer and the party responsible might result in a profit to the insured. Additionally, subrogation holds wrongdoers responsible for the results of their wrongful actions, instead of permitting them not to pay only because an insurance contract bought by someone else was in force. The overall cost of the insurance to policyowners is also reduced in this manner.

Example:	Jesse Booth's home, which is insured by Bryn Mawr Fire Insurance Company, is damaged by fire caused by his negligent next-door neighbor, James Grey. The damage amounts to $11,000, and the insurance company pays Jesse that amount, minus the $250 deductible in Jesse's policy. Bryn Mawr Fire Insurance Company then brings action against James and is awarded $10,750 for itself and $250 for Jesse. Hence Jesse is indemnified but not over-indemnified, and James is held responsible for his negligence. Note that if James has liability insurance, his insurer may defend him and pay the judgment.

As a general rule, an insurer has this right of subrogation even when there is no subrogation clause in the indemnity contract. For the most part, this clause merely makes the policyowner aware of this common law doctrine. However, in some cases, the clause might also modify the insurer's subrogation rights.

The right of subrogation by the insurer is limited in amount to the loss payment made to the insured. The insurer may not make a profit by subrogating against the person who caused the loss. In fact, often subrogation rights are of little value to the insurance company. There may be no doubt that someone else was responsible for the loss, but in order to recoup its loss payments (1) the insurer must prove the liability of the wrongdoer and (2) the negligent party must have the financial ability to pay for the loss he or she caused. In many cases, the expense or difficulty of legal proof may prevent the insurer from using its subrogation rights. If it might cost $1,000 to collect a $600 claim, the subrogation right may be worthless.

The importance of subrogation varies greatly for various types of insurance. In life insurance, subrogation is not used at all because life insurance is not a contract of indemnity. Subrogation is commonly used in property insurance and, to a lesser extent, in health insurance. Tenants, for example, may be held liable when their carelessness causes a fire loss to rented property.

A more common illustration of subrogation is found in automobile insurance. If the insurer first pays under collision coverage for damage to the insured's car caused by the negligent driver of another car, then the insurer takes over the rights of the policyowner by subrogation and files a claim against the other driver involved in the accident to receive reimbursement. If the insured does not receive full payment from the insurer because of a deductible in the policy, the insured retains the right to file a claim against the other driver for that deductible. Sometimes the insurer files a joint suit for the loss on its own behalf and on behalf of the insured, but the insurer is not obligated to do so.

Two final points should be made about subrogation. First, insurers often waive their right to pursue a subrogation claim against anyone who is an insured under the policy. For example, assume a policyowner collects for collision damage to his car after it is wrecked by a friend to whom the car was loaned. The insurer will not subrogate because the friend fits the category of an insured under the policy. Second, the policy or court interpretations of subrogation specify the insurer's right to retain any subrogation proceeds if the insured has not been fully indemnified for a loss because of deductibles, copayments, exclusions, or inadequate limits. In some cases, the insurer and the insured will share the proceeds on a pro rata basis. In other cases, the insured must be fully indemnified before the insurer is entitled to any recovery.

Effect of Concealment, Representations, Warranties, and Fraud

Concealment

concealment

Because the contract of insurance is concerned with risk and uncertainty, a fundamental doctrine of insurance law is that neither party may practice *concealment*, or the failure of one party to the contract to affirmatively disclose all relevant information that is the party's exclusive knowledge. The contract is said to be one of utmost good faith, and both parties to the agreement must stand on an equal footing. For example, if there is knowledge on the part of the owner that the property insured was in grave danger of destruction at the inception of the agreement, and if this information was not disclosed to the insurer, an unbalanced agreement would result.

The concealment of a material fact need not be intentional or fraudulent in order to make a policy voidable, and pleading error or forgetfulness is no defense. If the insurer would have declined the application or issued the policy under different terms if it had possessed all the facts, the fact is material and the policy is voidable.

void contract

The terms *void* and *voidable* are sometimes used interchangeably, but this use is erroneous. A *void contract* is entirely without legal effect, and neither party may enforce it. The law makes certain requirements described earlier essential for the validity of a contract, and in the absence of these essentials, the contract is void. Thus, for example, a contract with an illegal objective may not be enforced legally by either party.

voidable contract

A *voidable contract* may be affirmed or rejected at the option of one of the parties, but it is binding on the other. For example, if the policyowner has failed to comply with a condition of the contract, the insurer may elect to fulfill its part of the agreement or may choose to treat the contract as voidable. Sometimes the insurer may have a technical right to claim a forfeiture but, in the interests of equity and good public relations, does not exercise that right. Only seldom does the policyowner have the right to treat a contract as voidable—perhaps where the insurer or its agent has grossly misrepresented the contract benefits.

The concealment doctrine had an early start in ocean marine insurance and, due to the nature of the business, a strict interpretation still applies today. A ship or cargo may be insured in London, yet the property may be located in some far corner of the globe. Because the property cannot be inspected by the insurer, full reliance and dependence must be placed on the applicant to disclose all pertinent facts.

In other types of insurance, the property or person insured is ordinarily readily available for inspection, so many of the material facts essential to appraise the risks are within the range of the insurer's observation. When a concealed matter is not made the subject of express inquiry by the insurer, the concealment must be intentional to make the policy voidable. The policyowner needs only to answer fully and in good faith all inquiries made by the insurer. One exception to the rule provides that when important facts bearing on the application for insurance are so unusual that they would not ordinarily be inquired about or readily discovered by the insurer, the obligation of affirmative disclosure is present, whether or not an express inquiry has been made.

Representations

representation

A *representation* is a statement made by an applicant to the insurer at the time of, or prior to, the formation of a contract. The insurer has the right to full knowledge of the subject of insurance and frequently must depend on statements of the applicant to ascertain the pertinent facts. A misrepresentation (false statement) on the applicant's part of any material (important) fact has the same effect as a concealment, and it affords a basis for making the contract voidable by the insurer. However, in some states, evidence of intent to defraud must be present to make the contract voidable.

The difference between concealment and misrepresentation is that the applicant conceals by maintaining silence when there is an obligation to speak; he or she misrepresents by making an untrue statement. The determination of what is material is based on the same ideas that apply in the cases of concealment explained earlier. Each set of facts must be evaluated in the given situation, by the courts if necessary. For example, a response of "no" by a businessperson applying for theft insurance to the question "Have you had any theft losses?" might be considered a material misrepresentation if, in fact, the applicant carelessly forgot a large loss that occurred 2 years earlier—but perhaps it would not be considered such if the only previous loss was a very small one that happened 5 years earlier.

Warranties

When the application for the insurance contract is made a part of the policy, the answers to specific questions on the application may be considered

warranty

warranties. If false, they make the policy voidable by the insurer regardless of their materiality. Some warranties may also be specifically added in the policy such as the promise of the policyowner in a burglary policy that an alarm system or security guard will be maintained.

The difference between a warranty and a representation is that a warranty is a part of the contract itself and must therefore be strictly complied with, whereas a representation is usually an incidental statement preceding the contract, although it may be an inducement to it. The difference, in effect, is that in order to make the contract voidable, a warranty need only be false, whereas a representation must be both false and material.

To constitute a warranty, a statement must not only be intended, but must also be definitely indicated as a warranty, either by its incorporation into the policy or by specific reference. Where there is any doubt as to whether a warranty was intended, the statement is to be regarded as a representation and must be shown to be material in order to defeat the policy.

Many states have modified by legislative act the strict application of the doctrine of warranties for most kinds of insurance, except ocean marine insurance. Where the doctrine has been thus modified, the insurance is sometimes voidable only if a loss occurs during a breach of warranty or is caused thereby, or if the breach materially increases the risk. In effect, this causes most warranties in insurance contracts today to be considered as representations. In some lines of insurance the application itself specifies that statements contained in it are representations, not warranties. Warranties incorporated into insurance policies should be complied with to the letter, for some courts still tend to enforce the original strict rule of declaring the policy voidable when a warranty is breached, regardless of how trivial or immaterial the loss.

Fraud

fraud

A false representation or the concealment of a material fact with the intent and result that it be acted on by another party may constitute *fraud*. A concealment may amount to fraud if active steps are taken to prevent discovery of the truth. To constitute fraud, a representation must be of past or existing facts. Therefore expressions of opinion, belief, expectation, or intention do not constitute fraudulent statements. Commendatory expressions of value or false representations made where the parties deal on an equal footing and have equal means of knowledge are not held to be fraudulent. For example, if an applicant for disability income insurance said, "I am in pretty decent health," there could be no fraud, as this was merely an expression of opinion. However, if an applicant said, "I have never had heart disease," when in fact the applicant had several recent heart ailments and was making the statement with the idea of obtaining a lower insurance cost, fraud might be provable.

In the case of fraud, an active intent to deceive or the intentional misleading by one person of another is usually present. The person making the statement must know that it is false or make the statement recklessly disregarding whether it is true or false. Finally, in order to constitute fraud, the misrepresentation must be relied on by and injure the other party. In these cases, a contract becomes voidable at the option of the injured party.

The requirements for proving fraud are difficult to meet. An insurer must prove intent to defraud. Intent involves premeditation, and it is difficult to show what a person thought before an action, unless intent is very clearly indicated by present or repeated past actions or statements. If proved, however, fraud is a serious matter and may enable the insurer to rescind the contract. For example, if in order to obtain a lower rate, the policyowner purposely misstated in an automobile insurance application that no young family members use the car, the coverage may be lost because of the policyowner's fraudulent action. A more common but perhaps equally serious example is the intentional exaggeration of any insurance claim for the purpose of receiving overpayment for a loss.

Summary

In order to review the concepts of concealment, representations, warranties, and fraud, the requirements for making an insurance contract voidable by the insurer are shown in table 6-1.

TABLE 6-1
Effects of Concealment, Representations, Warranties, and Fraud

Concept	Requirements for Voidability	Example
Concealment	Must be silence that is material (or important)	Applicant for fire insurance fails to tell agent that the property has been the target of recent arson attempts
Representations	Must be statement (oral or written) that is false and material (also fraudulent in some states)	Applicant for health insurance falsely states that no recent illnesses have been suffered, when in fact a mini-stroke was diagnosed a few months previously
Warranties	Must be false and incorporated and identified in the contract or application as a warranty	Applicant for marine insurance answers question in the application falsely by stating that the ship is used on inland rather than ocean waters
Fraud	Must be false and concern a fact, with an intent to deceive, and be relied on by and cause injury to the other party	Insured purposely overstates a car insurance claim in order to obtain a larger loss payment than is justified

ANALYZING AN INSURANCE CONTRACT

The legal characteristics of the insurance contract make it an exceedingly complex and intricate document. Without some system for analyzing the contract, the task of making sense of its many provisions might seem formidable. The remainder of this chapter is designed to provide a framework for the analysis. Many of the examples contained in this chapter are expanded on in the later chapters that cover specific types of insurance.

The provisions of the typical insurance contract can be grouped into the following categories, depending on the purposes they serve: declarations, definitions, insuring agreements, exclusions, conditions, and miscellaneous provisions. The contract also may be modified by adding endorsements or riders.

Declarations

declarations

Every insurance contract has a set of declarations, although they are not always labeled. *Declarations* are factual statements identifying the specific person, property, or activity being insured and the parties to the insurance transaction; they also provide descriptive information about the insurance being provided. They are usually grouped together in the initial section of the policy and are computer-printed for the individual contract, rather than preprinted for all contracts of the same type.

The declarations section of a life insurance policy typically shows the name of the insurer and agent, the name and age of the insured, the name of the policyowner if different from the insured, the type of policy, the amount of insurance, the policy number and effective date, the premium, and a listing of attachments to the policy showing items such as supplementary benefits and the beneficiary designation. In property and liability insurance contracts, the declarations section of the policy shows similar types of information as well as the address of the property or activity covered, a listing of endorsements attached to the policy, the names of additional persons or organizations that are insured (such as a mortgagee), the period of coverage, and any applicable deductibles.

Definitions

definitions

Because the insurance policy is a contract of adhesion, the insurer must define carefully what it wishes to cover or not cover. Otherwise, as mentioned earlier, ambiguities in the contract are likely to be construed against the insurer. The *definitions* section of the policy is an explanation of the key policy terms and is a major help in precisely defining the insured's intentions.

Often words or phrases that are included among the definitions appear in boldface type or quotation marks elsewhere in the policy. The definitions are usually grouped together in an early section of the policy or appear near the end of the policy, serving as a kind of glossary. Examples of a few terms that may appear in the definitions section of insurance contracts are as follows:

- life insurance—you, we, designated office (of the insurer), beneficiary, and new policy
- disability income insurance—monthly earnings, qualifying period, and total disability
- automobile insurance—bodily injury, family member, occupying (an auto), your covered auto, and trailer
- homeowners insurance—business, insured location, occurrence, and residence employee

One of the more important definitions in many policies defines who is insured. This definition is discussed in more detail in later chapters as it applies to specific lines of insurance. In homeowners policies, the insured means the person named in the declarations, his or her spouse and relatives if residents of the household, and persons under age 21 residing in the household and in the care of the named insured, spouse, or resident relatives. In the liability section of the personal auto policy, the definition of who is insured includes the named insured and his or her spouse if a resident of the household, and for up to 90 days after ceasing to be a member of the household. The definition also includes family members, also defined in the policy, who are residents of the household, anyone using a covered auto, and any person or organization that might be held vicariously liable for use of the auto.

Words and phrases that are not specifically defined in the contract are interpreted according to the following general principles:

- Everyday language is given its ordinary or normal meaning.
- Technical terms are assigned their technical definitions.
- Terms that have an established legal meaning are given that meaning.
- Where appropriate, meanings of words take into account local, cultural, and trade usage considerations.

Insuring Agreements

insuring agreement

The *insuring agreement* is the heart of any insurance policy. This agreement (or agreements, as many contracts contain several insuring agreements) spells out the basic promise of the insurance company. Examples of these promises are to pay the face amount of the policy in the event of the insured's death, to defend the insured in any suit alleging negligence associated with an auto accident, to pay the actual cash value of personal property damaged by a covered peril, and to pay up to $200 per day for loss of earnings because of the insured's attendance at a court hearing at the insurer's request.

The main insuring agreements in insurance policies are usually either of the open-perils type or the named-perils type. An *open-perils agreement*, also known as an *all-risks agreement* covers all losses except those that are specifically excluded by the policy. Even with the open-perils agreement, all policies have at least a few exclusions, and some have many. For example, a whole life insurance policy is an open-perils policy because it covers death from any cause except a few specified ones, such as death by suicide during the policy's first one or 2 years, and in some policies death by war or specifically excluded activities such as skydiving or crop dusting.

The *named-perils* or *specified-perils approach* to the insuring agreement is used in the personal property coverage of most homeowners policies. This agreement covers only losses that arise from one of the listed perils. If the peril is not listed, it is not covered. For example, one form of homeowners policy states that it covers direct physical loss caused by fire, lightning, windstorm, hail, explosion, riot, civil commotion, aircraft, vehicles, smoke, vandalism, malicious mischief, theft, falling objects, weight of ice, snow, or sleet, accidental discharge or overflow of water or steam from certain household systems, and a few other perils. Flood is not contained in the list, so loss to personal property and real property due to flood is not covered.

Exclusions

exclusions

As noted earlier, every insurance policy has *exclusions*—items that the insurer does not intend to cover. The exclusions usually apply either to certain perils, types of losses, types of property, or types of activities. For example, in major medical expense insurance, loss due to the peril of occupational injury or illness is usually excluded because the loss is covered under workers' compensation insurance. In long-term care insurance, costs of care for which the insured is reimbursed under a government program are excluded. In homeowners insurance, the property of boarders is excluded. And in automobile insurance, losses arising from use of the vehicle in a prearranged or organized racing contest in a facility designed for racing are excluded.

The following are the principal reasons for the presence of exclusions in insurance policies:

- Certain perils are uninsurable by private insurers.[4] Examples of such perils are wear-and-tear losses to automobiles and losses due to war.
- Certain conditions pose a major increase in risk not contemplated in the basic premium for the coverage. Examples of these conditions are, in auto insurance, the use of an automobile to carry persons for a fee other than in a simple carpooling arrangement and, in medical expense insurance, the cost of long-term custodial care.

- Certain losses are designed to be covered by other types of policies. For example, collision damage to an automobile is not covered by a homeowners policy, and losses due to occupational injury may be excluded by a disability income policy.
- Coverage of some losses would pose too great a potential moral hazard. For example, loss of more than $200 in cash is excluded by homeowners policies.
- Certain coverages are not needed by most policyowners, so they should not have to pay for them. For example, most individuals do not own large boats and, therefore, do not need liability insurance for these watercraft. As a result, liability arising from large watercraft is excluded from the homeowners policy. However, coverage can be added by endorsement for an extra premium.

A practical result of exclusions, if not a reason for their use by insurers, is to hold down the premium cost of coverage for policyowners.

Conditions

The insuring agreement is not an absolute promise by the company with "no strings attached." Instead, the promise is a qualified one, enforceable only if the policyowner fulfills the conditions that are spelled out in the policy. Those conditions may be grouped together in a section of the policy labeled "Conditions," or they may be scattered throughout the policy and its endorsements or riders.

Most of the conditions in an insurance policy must be fulfilled by the policyowner before the insurer may be held liable for a loss. An example of these conditions, called *conditions precedent*, is timely payment of premiums.

There are many conditions that relate to claims. Most policies, with the exception of life insurance, contain provisions pertaining to one or both of the following: the time period within which the insurer must be notified of a loss and the time period within which the insured must file a formal proof of loss. The information that must be included with the formal proof of loss may also be specified.

Other conditions, called *conditions subsequent*, must be fulfilled by the insured after the insurer has become liable in order to avoid releasing it from liability. All policies specify that the insured must cooperate with the insurer. Other examples in property and liability insurance include the condition that the insured must do nothing to jeopardize the insurer's right to recover from responsible third parties and the condition that the insured must cooperate with the insurer in legal proceedings against the insurer by a third-party claimant. Disability income insurance policies include the condition that the insurer can require the insured to submit to examinations by an insurer-selected physician at reasonable intervals during the continuation of a claim.

Miscellaneous Provisions

Some provisions found in insurance contracts do not fall into any of the preceding categories of declarations, definitions, insuring agreements, exclusions, or conditions. These provisions may deal with policy continuation, valuation of losses, or other administrative aspects of the policy.

Policy Continuation

One of the more important miscellaneous provisions in an insurance policy relates to the right of the policyowner to continue the coverage in force. Although policies can be issued for a specific term and terminate at the end of that term, many policies allow the policyowner to renew the policy and/or allow the insurer to refuse renewal. These policy renewal provisions fall into four categories: noncancelable, guaranteed renewable, nonrenewable for stated reasons only, and optionally renewable. In addition, some policies are cancelable.

noncancelable

Noncancelable. Some types of insurance policies are *noncancelable,* giving the policyowner the right to renew the coverage at each policy anniversary date, although possibly only to some stated age such as age 65. A noncancelable policy may not be terminated by the insurer during the period of coverage. Moreover, in a truly noncancelable policy, the future rates for the coverage are guaranteed in the contract itself. Examples of noncancelable policies are life insurance policies[5] and some disability income contracts. The term noncancelable may not be as broad as it first seems because the National Association of Insurance Commissioners (NAIC) allows the term to be used in a health insurance policy as long as the policy continues to at least age 50 or at least 5 years if issued to a person aged 44 or older.

Guaranteed Renewable. A guaranteed renewable policy provides a bit less certainty for the policyowner regarding the right to continue coverage. Guaranteed renewable policies are most often found in the health insurance area.

guaranteed renewable
Like a noncancelable policy, a *guaranteed renewable* policy gives the policyowner the right to renew the coverage at each policy anniversary date, but usually only to a stated age such as age 65. Also, the coverage may not be canceled by the insurer during the period of coverage. However, in a guaranteed renewable policy, the insurer does not guarantee future rates for the coverage. Instead, the insurer retains the right to raise the rates for broad classes of insureds, but not just for individual insureds with poor claims experience. Again, the NAIC allows the term to be used for policies that are guaranteed renewable only until age 50 or for at least 5 years if issued to persons aged 44 or older.

Nonrenewable for Stated Reasons Only. Some policies that are otherwise guaranteed renewable allow the insurer to refuse to renew the policy for conditions specifically listed in the policy. These reasons might include the attainment of a certain age. However, if this is the only condition, the policy still often qualifies as guaranteed renewable. Other conditions for nonrenewal include termination of the policyowner's employment in some disability income policies and the nonrenewal of all policies bearing the same form number as the policyowner's.

Optionally Renewable. This optionally renewable provision, found in most property and liability insurance policies, gives the insurer the unilateral right to refuse to renew a policy at the end of any period for which premiums have been paid. Even if the insurer agrees to renew the policy, it has the right to alter the policy's provisions. Some states have enacted legislation that allows an insurer to nonrenew only on annual anniversary dates. In addition, regulations may require the insurer to give specified periods of advance notice to policyowners whose coverage will not be renewed.

Cancelable. A few property and liability policies are cancelable during the period for which premiums have been paid. However, this provision is not allowed for automobile and homeowners policies in many states. When a policy can be canceled, the policy and/or state law determine the period of advance notice that must be given to the policyowner. In addition, a pro rata share of the premium must be returned.

Valuation of Losses

Another type of miscellaneous provision found in several types of insurance policies concerns a required sharing in the amount of the loss by the insured. For example, deductibles are common in homeowners insurance, auto physical damage insurance, and medical expense insurance. The most common form of deductible is an initial deductible, under which the insurer will pay claims to the extent that they exceed a specified amount. The amount, such as $100, may apply to each claim, as is common in property insurance policies, or to a period of time, such as a calendar year, as in medical expense policies. A similar provision in the form of a *waiting* or elimination period, during which no benefits are payable at the start of a disability, is found in workers' compensation coverage, disability income insurance, and long-term care insurance.

Other types of loss-sharing provisions are the coinsurance clause and copayment requirement found in major medical and other types of medical expense coverage. Under these types of provisions, the insured is required to assume a portion of certain covered expenses. For example, the insurer may pay 80 percent of certain medical expenses under a coinsurance clause, while the insured assumes 20 percent. Or the insured may pay a $5 or $10 copayment for each doctor's visit.

Several types of insurance contain a miscellaneous provision describing how the policy will respond if other insurance covers the same loss. For example, the property insurance portion of homeowners policies provides that the insurer will pay only that proportion of the loss that the limit of liability applicable in the homeowners policy bears to the total amount of insurance in all policies covering the loss. The liability section specifies that the homeowners coverage is excess over other valid and collectible insurance, except insurance written specifically to provide excess coverage over that of the homeowners policy. Group health insurance often contains a coordination-of-benefits provision to prevent duplication of benefits when an insured is covered by more than one group health insurance plan. For example, if a wife has coverage as an employee under her own plan and is a dependent under her husband's plan, her coverage as an employee is primary and her coverage as a dependent is excess.

Other Provisions

The following are a few illustrations of other miscellaneous policy provisions:

- Life insurance policies include a description of the optional modes of settlement under which the beneficiary may receive the death proceeds and a clause explaining the policyowner's right to assign the policy to another. There is also an incontestable clause stating that the insurer does not have the right to contest a death claim if the policy as been in force for at least 2 years during the insured's lifetime. In addition, policies contain an explanation of how the death proceeds will be calculated if the insured's age or sex has been misstated. If the policy is issued by a mutual insurer, the policyowner's right to vote for the company's board of directors is also described.
- In annuity contracts, a provision allows the annuitant to delay or accelerate the date when the annuity benefits are to begin; a description of how the beneficiary of any death proceeds may be changed is also included.
- Personal umbrella liability contracts contain a clause describing how the policy may be canceled by the policyowner or the insurer and a specification that the umbrella policy is excess over all other valid and collectible insurance.
- Disability income policies may include a clause specifying to whom the policy benefits will be paid and another clause stating that the policy and the application attached to it constitute the entire agreement between the parties.
- In major medical expense policies, a lengthy provision explains how coordination of benefits is achieved when more than one policy applies

to a loss; other provisions explain the application of the deductible, coinsurance, and stop-loss aspects of the coverage and the procedures for appealing the denial of benefits.

- In homeowners policies, several loss-settlement provisions describe losses that are covered on the basis of the cost to replace with new materials, called *replacement cost,* and losses where coverage includes a deduction for depreciation, referred to as *actual cash value,* as well as how a dispute between the insurer and insured over the amount of a loss may be resolved through an appraisal process.

- Personal automobile insurance policies contain a provision stating that bankruptcy or insolvency of the insured will not relieve the insurer of any of its obligations under the policy, a description of how coverage applies in a state other than the one where the auto is principally garaged, and an explanation of how disputes between the insured and insurer on matters of coverage may be resolved through arbitration.

- Several types of policies, including life, health, and annuity contracts, provide a grace period of 30 or 31 days. If a premium is paid after its due date but within the grace period, the coverage is still in effect. Note that property and liability insurance policies do not provide for a grace period.

Parts of an Insurance Contract

- Declaration—statements of fact that identify the parties to the insurance transaction, the amount of insurance, the property or activity being covered, the effective date of the coverage, etc.
- Definitions—precise meanings of terms used in the contract, like "family member," "disability," "covered auto," etc.
- Insuring Agreements—the promises made by the insurer such as to pay, to defend, to reimburse, etc.
- Exclusions—the perils, properties, types of losses, circumstances, etc. that the insurance does not cover.
- Conditions—the duties that (usually) the insured must fulfill before the other party is held to the terms of the contract.
- Miscellaneous Provisions—other clauses that don't fall into the above categories such as those concerning policy continuation, loss valuation, optional modes of settlement, etc.
- Endorsements or Riders—provisions added to the policy to modify or clarify the coverage, sometimes for an extra premium.

- Some types of policies allow for reinstatement of the coverage under certain conditions after the policy has lapsed. In life insurance, the right to reinstate usually is available only for 3 years following the lapse and only if the policy has not been surrendered for cash or the period of extended term insurance has not expired. Reinstatement requires submission of satisfactory evidence of insurability, the payment of all overdue premiums with interest, and the repayment or reinstatement of all policy indebtedness. In health insurance, payment of the overdue premiums reinstates the policy unless the insurer requires an application. If so, the policy is reinstated only if the application is approved. The reinstated policy is subject to a 10-day waiting period for sickness, but there is no waiting period for accident. No provision is made for reinstatement in the most common property and liability insurance policies.

Endorsements or Riders

endorsement (rider)

An *endorsement*, or in life insurance a *rider*, is a provision added to the policy, sometimes for an extra premium charge, by which the scope of its coverage is clarified, restricted, or enlarged. An endorsement may alter one of the declarations such as identifying an additional named insured in an auto policy. Endorsements also may add new definitions to the policy, such as the underinsured motorists endorsement to an auto policy, or modify exclusions in the policy such as removing earthquake from the list of excluded perils in a homeowners policy. Endorsements may even modify a policy condition, such as amending a 30-day notice of nonrenewal to conform with the statute of a particular state that requires a 60-day notice, or a miscellaneous provision such as limiting the insurer's right to cancel the policy to only specified reasons. Similarly, a rider may modify the insuring agreement—for example, adding a waiver-of-premium benefit to a life insurance policy.

As a general legal principle, whenever the wording in an endorsement or rider conflicts with the terms of the policy to which it is attached, the endorsement or rider takes precedence. This principle is based on the assumption that an alteration of the basic agreement between the policyowner and insurer more accurately reflects the true intent of the parties than does the basic agreement itself.

SOURCES FOR FURTHER IN-DEPTH STUDY

- For a detailed discussion of the legal aspects of life insurance policies:
  - Graves, Edward E., and Christensen, Burke A., editors, *McGill's Legal Aspects of Life Insurance*, 3d ed., Bryn Mawr, PA: The American College, 2002. Phone 888-263-7265. Web site address www.amercoll.edu

CHAPTER REVIEW

Answers to review questions and self-test questions start on page 725.

Key Terms

aleatory contract	representation
unilateral contract	warranty
conditional contract	fraud
contract of adhesion	declarations
parol evidence rule	definitions
indemnity	insuring agreement
insurable interest	exclusions
subrogation	noncancelable
concealment	guaranteed renewable
void contract	endorsement (rider)
voidable contract	

Review Questions

6-1.   What unique aspects of an insurance contract differentiate it from other goods and services?

6-2.   Define the following legal requirements of an enforceable contract:
a.   offer and acceptance
b.   legal purpose
c.   competent parties
d.   consideration

6-3.   Define the following legal characteristics of an insurance contract:
a.   unilateral nature
b.   personal nature
c.   conditional nature

6-4.   Your client, Sue Litigator, would like to know her legal rights concerning the following situations:
a.   Sue would like to amend several general provisions of the insurance contract.
b.   Sue claims that one of the provisions in the insurance contract is unclear.
c.   Sue wants to ignore a portion of the contract she did not read.
d.   Sue claims that the insurance agent told her something that contradicts the language of the contract.

6-5.   Explain the common law concept of indemnity as it relates to a client's property, liability, life, and health insurance contracts.

6-6.   Briefly describe three reasons for requiring an insurable interest in insurance contracts.

6-7. Explain whether your client has an insurable interest in the following situations:
   a. Your client loaned a large amount of money to a friend who is starting a business.
   b. Your client owns and drives a fancy red sports car.
   c. Your client owned a precious stone that was destroyed soon after he gambled it away.

6-8. Briefly describe how the doctrine of subrogation applies to insurance contracts.

6-9. Explain the difference between concealment and misrepresentation by an applicant for insurance.

6-10. Explain the purpose of each of these sections of a typical insurance contract:
   a. declarations
   b. definitions
   c. insuring agreements
   d. exclusions
   e. conditions

6-11. Explain the major distinction between a noncancelable policy and a guaranteed renewable policy.

6-12. Explain how each of the following provisions found in medical expense insurance operates:
   a. initial deductible
   b. coinsurance clause

6-13. The wording in an endorsement to your client's insurance policy conflicts with the terms of the policy itself. What is the significance of this conflict for your client?

Self-Test Questions

T F 6-1. There is no benefit to an insurance contract unless a claim for coverage is presented.

T F 6-2. Insurance transfers the financial risk of uncertain perils to the insurer.

T F 6-3. In life insurance, the offer can be orally transmitted.

T F 6-4. A 16-year-old client can always void his auto insurance policy because he is still a minor.

T F 6-5. An insurance contract is a bilateral contract.

T F 6-6. Property and liability insurance policies are freely assignable by policyowners without the insurer's approval.

T F 6-7. An example of a condition precedent in an insurance contract is that the insured is required to cooperate with the insurer in defending a liability claim.

T   F   6-8.   Most insurance contracts are contracts of adhesion.

T   F   6-9.   If there is an ambiguous clause in an insurance contract, the courts will typically interpret the clause in favor of the policyowner.

T   F   6-10. If a property is valued at $25,000 and insured for $50,000, the insurance company would pay $50,000 for a total loss under the general rule of indemnity.

T   F   6-11. Life insurance policies are considered contracts of indemnity.

T   F   6-12. Under the principle of subrogation, if the insurer indemnifies the insured for a loss, the insurer obtains whatever rights the insured possessed against responsible third parties.

T   F   6-13. The misrepresentation or concealment of a material fact by an applicant for insurance will void a contract that the insurer has issued to the applicant.

T   F   6-14. An innocent misrepresentation by an applicant for insurance constitutes fraud.

T   F   6-15. One reason exclusions are found in insurance policies is that the risks are covered by other insurance.

T   F   6-16. The requirement that the insured must cooperate with the insurer in legal proceedings against the insurer by a third-party claimant is an example of a condition subsequent.

T   F   6-17. Under an initial deductible, the insurer will pay for all losses up to a specified amount.

T   F   6-18. As a general legal principle, whenever the wording in an endorsement or rider conflicts with the terms of the policy to which it is attached, the endorsement or rider takes precedence.

NOTES

1. *Knouse v. Equitable Life Insurance Company of Ohio*, 181 Pac. (2d) 310.
2. This is the general rule. See *Grace v. Adams*, 100 Mass. 505. However, some cases seem to say that the policyowner does not have to read his or her policy. Special situations sometimes occur, such as those in which the policyowner has reasonably relied upon advice of a professional agent, but it is unwise for policyowners to assume that courts will be lenient in excusing them from a contract's written terms.
3. *Northern Assurance Co. v. Grand View Building Assn.*, 182 U.S. 380 (1902).
4. See the discussion of the requirements of insurable risks in chapter 1.
5. Term life insurance policies usually may be renewed only to a specified age, such as age 65 or 75, whereas whole life policies may be renewed for the insured's entire lifetime.

Social Security, Medicare, and Other Government Programs

Learning Objectives

An understanding of the material in this chapter should enable the student to

7-1. Describe the extent of coverage under the Social Security and Medicare programs, and explain how the programs are financed.

7-2. Explain the requirements for eligibility under Social Security, and identify the types and amounts of benefits available.

7-3. Explain the requirements for eligibility under Medicare, and describe the benefits available under Parts A and B.

7-4. Describe the option available to beneficiaries under Medicare+Choice.

7-5. Discuss the adequacy of Social Security and Medicare financing, and identify the ways in which long-term financial stability might be maintained.

7-6. Describe the federal income tax treatment of Social Security and Medicare contributions and benefits.

7-7. Describe the nature of unemployment insurance, temporary disability income insurance, and workers' compensation insurance.

Chapter Outline

Financial planners should understand social insurance because it lays a foundation of basic coverages on which employer-provided and private insurance are built.

Social insurance programs in the United States fall into several categories. The five that will be covered in this chapter are:

- Social Security
- Medicare
- unemployment insurance
- temporary disability insurance
- workers' compensation insurance

Two other programs, which are not covered, are established by the Railroad Retirement Act and the Railroad Unemployment Insurance Act. These acts provide benefits to railroad workers that are similar to the benefits provided to other persons by Social Security and state unemployment insurance programs.

The reasons for social insurance programs and their general characteristics are covered in chapter 1. This chapter is devoted to a discussion of specific programs. The major emphasis is on Social Security and Medicare, which are totally federal programs. The other three social insurance programs that are covered vary from state to state and are touched upon in a more general manner.

SOCIAL SECURITY AND MEDICARE

In a broad sense, the term *Social Security* can be used to refer to any of several programs resulting from the Social Security Act of 1935 and its frequent amendments over the years. The act established four programs aimed at providing economic security for the American society: (1) old-age insurance, (2) unemployment insurance, (3) federal grants for assistance to certain needy groups (the aged, the blind, and children), and (4) federal grants for maternal and child welfare, public health work, and vocational rehabilitation.

The main focus in this chapter is on the old-age insurance program and the benefits that have been added to that program over the years. These additional benefits include survivors insurance (1939), disability insurance (1956), hospital insurance (1965), and supplementary medical insurance (1965). Taken together, these programs constitute the old-age, survivors, disability, and health insurance (*OASDHI*) program of the federal government. This program is often separated into two broad parts. The first part is the old-age, survivors, and disability insurance (OASDI) program. Over the years OASDI has become commonly referred to as Social Security, and this is the terminology that will be used in this book. The remainder of the OASDHI program is called Medicare, with hospital insurance being called Part A and supplemental medical insurance being called Part B.

The following discussion of Social Security and Medicare begins with a description of the extent of coverage under the programs and the way the

OASDHI

programs are financed. It then focuses on the eligibility requirements and benefits under the various parts of the programs. Because of the many differences between Social Security and Medicare, the discussion largely treats each program separately. This is followed by a discussion of the adequacy of the funding of these programs. Finally, there is a description of the tax implications of Social Security and Medicare benefits and contributions.

Extent of Coverage

Over 90 percent of the workers in the United States are in covered employment under the Social Security program and over 95 percent under the Medicare program. This means that these workers have wages (if they are employees) or self-employment income (if they are self-employed) on which Social Security and Medicare taxes must be paid. The following are the major categories of workers who are not covered under the programs or who are covered only if they have met specific conditions:

- civilian employees of the federal government who were employed by the government prior to 1984 and who are covered under the Civil Service Retirement System or certain other federal retirement programs. This exclusion applies only to Social Security benefits. *All* federal employees have been covered for purposes of Medicare since 1983.
- railroad workers. Under the Railroad Retirement Act, employees of railroads have their own benefit system that is similar to Social Security. However, they are covered under Social Security for purposes of Medicare.
- some state and local government employees. Historically, employees covered under state and local government retirement plans have been covered under Social Security only if a state entered into a voluntary agreement with the Social Security Administration. Under such an agreement, the state may either require that employees of local governments be covered or allow the local governments to decide whether to include their employees. In addition, the state may elect to include all or only certain groups of employees. It is estimated that more than 80 percent of state and local government employees have Social Security and Medicare coverage as a result of such agreements. In addition, coverage under Medicare is compulsory for state and local employees hired after March 1986, and coverage under Social Security is compulsory for employees hired after July 1, 1991, if they do not participate in a public retirement system.
- American citizens working abroad for foreign affiliates of U.S. employers, unless the employer owns at least a 10 percent interest in

the foreign affiliate and has made arrangements with the Secretary of the Treasury for the payment of Social Security and Medicare taxes. However, Americans working abroad are covered under Social Security and Medicare if they are working directly for U.S. employers rather than for their foreign subsidiaries.

- ministers who elect out of coverage because of conscience or religious principles
- workers in certain jobs such as student nurses, newspaper carriers under age 18, and students working for the school at which they are regularly enrolled or doing domestic work for a local college club, fraternity, or sorority
- certain family employment. This includes the employment of a child under age 18 by a parent. This exclusion, however, does not apply if the employment is for a corporation owned by a family member.
- certain workers who must satisfy special earnings requirements. For example, self-employed persons are not covered unless they have net annual earnings of $400 or more.

Tax Rates and Wage Bases

Part B of Medicare is financed by a combination of monthly premiums paid by persons eligible for benefits and contributions from the federal government. Part A of Medicare and all the benefits of the Social Security program are financed through a system of payroll and self-employment taxes paid by all persons covered under the programs. In addition, employers of covered persons are also taxed. (These taxes are often referred to as FICA taxes because they are imposed under the Federal Insurance Contributions Act.)

In 2003, an employee and his or her employer pay a tax of 7.65 percent each on the first $87,000 of the employee's wages. Of this tax rate, 6.2 percent is for Social Security, and 1.45 percent is for the hospital insurance portion of Medicare. The Medicare tax rate of 1.45 percent is also levied on all wages in excess of $87,000. The tax rates are currently scheduled to remain the same after 2003, but the $87,000 wage base is adjusted annually for changes in the national level of wages. Therefore, if wage levels increase by 4 percent in a particular year, the wage base for the following year will also increase by 4 percent. The tax rate for the self-employed is 15.3 percent on the first $87,000 of self-employment income and 2.9 percent on the balance of any self-employment income. This is equal to the combined employee and employer rates.

Over the years, both the tax rates and wage bases have risen dramatically to finance increased benefit levels under Social Security and Medicare as

---

Paying for Social Security and Medicare

- Social Security—Employees pay 6.20 percent of the first $87,000 (2003) of earnings. Employers pay the same. Self-employed persons pay 12.40 percent of first $87,000 (2003) of self-employment income.
- Medicare Part A—Employees pay 1.45 percent of all earnings. Employers pay the same. Self-employed persons pay 2.9 percent of all self-employment income.
- Medicare Part B—Covered persons pay $58.70 (2003) monthly premium. General revenues of the federal government cover the remainder (about 75 percent) of the program's cost.

---

well as new benefits that have been added to the program. In 1950, a tax rate of 1.5 percent was levied on the first $3,000 of wages. These figures increased to 4.8 percent and $7,800 in 1970, and 7.65 percent and $51,300 in 1990. Starting in 1991, a two-tier program was introduced with a tax of 7.65 percent on the first $53,400 of wages and a Medicare tax of 1.45 percent on the next $71,500. By 1994, all wages were subject to the Medicare tax.

The adequacy of the current funding structure to pay for Social Security and Medicare benefits continues to be a source of public concern and political debate. This issue is addressed in more detail after the programs have been described.

SOCIAL SECURITY: ELIGIBILITY

To be eligible for benefits under Social Security, an individual must have credit for a minimum amount of work under the program. This credit is based on quarters of coverage. For 2003, a worker receives credit for one quarter of coverage for each $890 in annual earnings on which Social Security taxes were paid. However, credit for no more than 4 quarters of coverage may be earned in any one calendar year. As in the case of the wage base, the amount of earnings necessary for a quarter of coverage is adjusted annually for changes in the national level of wages.

Quarters of coverage are the basis for establishing an insured status under Social Security. The three types of insured status are fully insured, currently insured, and disability insured.

Fully Insured

A person is fully insured under Social Security if either of two tests is met. The first test requires credit for 40 quarters of coverage. Once a person

fully insured

acquires such credit, he or she is *fully insured* for life even if covered employment under Social Security ceases.

Under the second test, a person who has credit for a minimum of 6 quarters of coverage is fully insured if he or she has credit for at least as many quarters of coverage as there are years elapsing after 1950 (or after the year in which age 21 is reached, if later) and before the year in which he or she dies, becomes disabled, or reaches age 62, whichever occurs first. Therefore, a worker who reached age 21 in 1991 and who died in 2003 would need credit for only 11 quarters of coverage for his or her family to be eligible for survivors benefits.

Currently Insured

currently insured

If a worker is not fully insured, certain survivors benefits are still available if a *currently insured* status exists. To be currently insured, it is only necessary that a worker have credit for at least 6 quarters of coverage out of the 13-quarter period ending with the quarter in which his or her death occurs.

Disability Insured

disability insured

In order to receive disability benefits under Social Security, it is necessary to be *disability insured*. At a minimum, a disability-insured status requires that a worker (1) be fully insured and (2) have a minimum amount of work under Social Security within a recent time period. In connection with the latter requirement, workers aged 31 or older must have credit for at least 20 of the last 40 quarters ending with the quarter in which disability occurs; workers between the ages of 24 and 30, inclusively, must have credit for at least half the quarters of coverage from the time they turned 21 and the quarter in which disability begins; and workers under age 24 must have credit for 6 out of the last 12 quarters, ending with the quarter in which disability begins.

A special rule for the blind states that they are exempt from the recent-work rules and are considered disability insured as long as they are fully insured.

SOCIAL SECURITY: TYPES OF BENEFITS

As its name implies, the Social Security program provides three principal types of benefits: retirement (old-age) benefits, survivors benefits, and disability benefits.

Retirement Benefits

A worker who is fully insured under Social Security is eligible to receive monthly retirement benefits as early as age 62. However, the election to receive benefits prior to the full Social Security retirement age results in a permanently reduced benefit.

full retirement age

Full retirement age (sometimes referred to as *normal retirement age*), or the age at which nonreduced retirement benefits are paid, is 65 for workers born in 1937 or before. As shown in table 7-1, a gradually increasing full retirement age applies to workers born in 1938 and later.

TABLE 7-1 Retirement Age for Nonreduced Benefits	
Year of Birth	Full Retirement Age
1937 and before	65 years
1938	65 years, 2 months
1939	65 years, 4 months
1940	65 years, 6 months
1941	65 years, 8 months
1942	65 years, 10 months
1943–54	66 years
1955	66 years, 2 months
1956	66 years, 4 months
1957	66 years, 6 months
1958	66 years, 8 months
1959	66 years, 10 months
1960 and later	67 years

In addition to the retired worker, the following dependents of persons receiving retirement benefits are also eligible for monthly benefits:

- a spouse aged 62 or older. However, benefits are permanently reduced if this benefit is elected prior to the spouse's reaching full retirement age. This benefit is also available to a divorced spouse under certain circumstances if the marriage lasted at least 10 years.
- a spouse of any age if the spouse is caring for at least one child of the retired worker who is (1) under age 16 or (2) disabled and entitled to a child's benefit as described below. This benefit is commonly referred to as a *mother's* or *father's benefit.*
- dependent, unmarried children under 18. This child's benefit will continue until age 19 as long as a child is a full-time student in elementary or secondary school. In addition, disabled children of any age are eligible for benefits as long as they were disabled before reaching age 22.

It is important to note that retirement benefits, as well as all other benefits under Social Security and Medicare, are not automatically paid upon eligibility but must be applied for.

Survivors Benefits

All categories of survivors benefits are payable if a worker is fully insured at the time of death. However, three types of benefits are also payable if a worker is only currently insured. The first is a lump-sum death benefit of $255, payable if there is a surviving spouse or children.

Two categories of persons are eligible for income benefits as survivors if a deceased worker was either fully or currently insured at the time of death:

- dependent, unmarried children under the same conditions as previously described for retirement benefits
- a spouse (including a divorced spouse) caring for a child or children under the same conditions as described for retirement benefits

---

Social Security Blackout Period

No benefits are payable for the surviving spouse of a deceased covered worker from the time the youngest child reaches age 16 (or is no longer disabled in certain cases) until the surviving spouse is 60.

The following categories of persons are also eligible for benefits, but only if the deceased worker was fully insured:

- a widow or widower aged 60 or older. However, benefits are reduced if taken prior to full retirement age. This benefit is also payable to a divorced spouse if the marriage lasted at least 10 years. In addition, the widow's or widower's benefit is payable to a disabled spouse at age 50 as long as the disability commenced no more than 7 years after the (1) worker's death or (2) end of the year in which entitlement to a mother's or father's benefit ceased.
- a parent aged 62 or over who was a dependent of the deceased worker at the time of death

Disability Benefits

A disabled worker under full retirement age is eligible to receive benefits under Social Security as long as he or she is disability insured and meets the definition of disability under the law. The definition of disability is very rigid and requires a mental or physical impairment that prevents the worker from engaging in any substantial gainful employment. The disability must also have lasted (or be expected to last) at least 12 months or be expected to result in death. A more liberal definition of disability applies to blind workers who are aged 55 or older. They are considered disabled if they are unable to perform work that requires skills or abilities comparable to those required by the work they regularly performed before reaching age 55 or becoming blind, if later.

Disability benefits are subject to a waiting period and are payable beginning with the sixth full calendar month of disability. In addition to the benefit paid to a disabled worker, the other categories of benefits available are the same as those described under retirement benefits.

As previously mentioned, certain family members not otherwise eligible for Social Security benefits may be eligible if they are disabled. Disabled children are subject to the same definition of disability as workers. However, disabled widows or widowers must be unable to engage in any gainful (rather than substantial gainful) employment.

Eligibility for Dual Benefits

In many cases, a person is eligible for more than one type of Social Security benefit. Probably the most common situation occurs when a person is eligible for both a spouse's benefit and a worker's retirement or disability benefit based on his or her own Social Security record. In this and any other case when a person is eligible for dual benefits, only an amount equal to the higher benefit is paid.

Termination of Benefits

Monthly benefits to any Social Security recipient cease upon death. When a retired or disabled worker dies, the family members' benefits that are based on the worker's retirement or disability benefits also cease, but the family members are then eligible for survivors benefits.

Disability benefits for a worker technically terminate at full retirement age but are then replaced by comparable retirement benefits. In addition, any benefits payable because of disability cease if medical or other evidence shows that the definition of disability is no longer satisfied. However, the disability benefits continue during a readjustment period that consists of the month of recovery and 2 additional months. As an encouragement for them to return to work, disabled beneficiaries for whom there is no evidence that their disability has otherwise terminated are allowed a 9-month trial work period during which benefits are not affected regardless of how much the beneficiary earns. At the end of that period, a beneficiary's earnings are evaluated to determine if the earnings are substantial ($800 per month in 2003). If earnings then exceed this amount for 3 months, benefits are suspended but can be reinstated during the next 36 months without starting a new application process should the earnings fall below this level.

As long as children are not disabled, benefits will usually terminate at age 18 but may continue until age 19 if the child is a full-time student in elementary or secondary school.

The benefit of a surviving spouse terminates upon remarriage unless remarriage takes place at age 60 or later.

SOCIAL SECURITY: BENEFIT AMOUNTS

Calculating Benefits

With the exception of the $255 lump-sum death benefit, the amount of all Social Security benefits is based on a worker's primary insurance amount (PIA). The actual PIA calculation is complex and done by the Social Security Administration when a beneficiary is eligible for benefits. It involves indexing past wages on which taxes were paid to current wage levels, eliminating some years with the lowest or no earnings, and averaging the indexed wages for the remaining years. The result is then put into a formula that is weighted in favor of lower-income workers.

primary insurance amount (PIA)

The *primary insurance amount (PIA)* is the amount a worker receives if he or she retires at full retirement age or becomes disabled, and it is the amount on which benefits for family members are based. In 2003, the average PIA for a retired worker is almost $900. A worker who has continually earned the maximum income subject to Social Security taxes can expect to have a PIA for retirement purposes of about $1,750 if he or she retires at age 65 in 2003. The maximum PIA in 2003 for purposes of disability and survivors benefits ranges from approximately $1,750 to $2,000. The higher PIA results for workers who are disabled or who die at younger ages.

If a worker is retired or disabled, these benefits are paid to family members, as shown in table 7-2. If the worker dies, survivors benefits are as shown in table 7-3.

However, the full benefits described above may not be payable because of a limitation imposed on the total benefits that may be paid to a family. This family maximum is again determined by a formula and is usually reached if three or more family members (including a retired or disabled worker) are eligible for benefits.

TABLE 7-2 Benefits for Family Members of a Disabled or Retired Worker	
Family member	Percentage of Worker's PIA
Spouse at full retirement age	50%
Spouse caring for disabled child or child under 16	50%
Child under 18 or disabled	50% each

TABLE 7-3 Benefits for Survivors of a Deceased Worker	
Family member	Percentage of Worker's PIA
Spouse at full retirement age	100%
Spouse caring for disabled child or child under 16	75%
Child under 18 or disabled	75% each
Dependent parent	82.5% for one, 75% each for two

If the total amount of benefits payable to family members exceeds the family maximum, the worker's benefit (in the case of retirement and disability) is not affected, but the benefits of other family members are reduced proportionately.

Example: Sam Chen died, leaving a spouse under age 65 and three children who are each eligible for 75 percent of Sam's PIA of $1,200. If the family maximum is ignored, the benefits total $3,600 ($900 for each family member). However, the family maximum, using the prescribed formula for 2003 is $2,206.50. Therefore, each family member has his or her benefit reduced to $551 (rounded to the next lower dollar).

When the first child loses benefits at age 18, the other family members each have benefits increased to $735 (if any automatic benefit increases, including the family maximum, are ignored).

When a second family member loses eligibility, the remaining two family members each receive the full benefit of $900 because the total benefits received by the family are now less than the $2,206.50 calculated by the formula.

Other Factors Affecting Benefits

Benefits Taken Early

If a worker elects to receive retirement benefits prior to full retirement age, benefits are permanently reduced by 5/9 of one percent for each of the first 36 months that the early retirement precedes full retirement age and 5/12 of one percent for each month in excess of 36. For example, for a worker who retires 3 years before full retirement age, the monthly benefit is only 80 percent of that worker's PIA. A spouse who elects retirement benefits prior to full retirement age has benefits reduced by 25/36 of one percent per month, for each of the first 36 months and 5/12 of one percent for each month in excess of 36. A widow or widower has benefits reduced proportionately from 100 percent at full retirement ages to 71.5 percent at age 60. If the widow or widower elects benefits prior to age 60 because of disability, there is no further reduction.

Delayed Retirement

Workers who delay applying for benefits until after full retirement age are eligible for an increased benefit. Benefits are increased for each month of late retirement until age 70. For persons born from 1917 until 1924, the increase is 1/4 of one percent per month, which is equal to 3 percent for delaying application for benefits for one full year. To encourage later retirement, the monthly percentage gradually increases. Table 7-4 shows the percentage for each month of deferral as well as the maximum percentage increase that is available if retirement is postponed until age 70.

It should be pointed out that these increases apply to a worker's PIA as determined at the time he or she applies for retirement benefits. If a person continues to work during the period of delayed retirement and covered wages are sufficiently high, it is possible for a worker's PIA to be higher than it would have been at full retirement age. Therefore, the increased

TABLE 7-4
Increase for Delayed Retirement

Year of Birth	Monthly Percentage Increase	Maximum Percentage Increase
1917–24	1/4	15.00
1925–26	7/24	17.50
1927–28	1/3	20.00
1929–30	9/24	22.50
1931–32	5/12	25.00
1933–34	11/24	27.50
1935–36	1/2	30.00
1937	13/24	32.50
1938	13/24	31.42
1939	7/12	32.67
1940	7/12	31.50
1941	15/24	32.50
1942	15/24	31.25
1943–54	2/3	32.00
1955	2/3	30.67
1956	2/3	29.33
1957	2/3	28.00
1958	2/3	26.67
1959	2/3	25.33
1960 and later	2/3	24.00

monthly retirement benefit from working past full retirement age may be greater than the percentages in the table.

Earnings Test

earnings test

Through the 1999 tax year, benefits were reduced for Social Security beneficiaries under the age of 70 if they had wages that exceeded a specified level. For tax years beginning after 1999, Congress repealed this *earnings test* in and after the month in which a beneficiary attains the full retirement age. However, the earnings test still applies to beneficiaries under full retirement age. They are allowed earnings of up to $11,520 in 2003, and this figure is subject to annual indexing for later years. If a beneficiary earns more than this amount, his or her Social Security benefit is reduced by $1 for each $2 of excess earnings. There is one exception to the test: The reduction is $1 for every $3 of earnings in excess of $30,720 (in 2003) in the calendar year a worker attains the full retirement age, for earnings in months prior to such age attainment. Once the beneficiary reaches full retirement age, any amount can be earned without a Social Security reduction.

The reduction in a retired worker's benefits resulting from excess earnings is charged against the entire benefits that are paid to a family and

---

Social Security Earnings Test

- Beneficiaries who have reached full retirement age—no loss of benefits regardless of annual wages
- Beneficiaries who are under full retirement age—$1 of benefits lost for every $2 of annual wages in excess of $11,520 (2003). A more liberal test applies in the calendar year a worker attains the full retirement age.

---

based on the worker's Social Security record. If large enough, this reduction may totally eliminate all benefits otherwise payable to the worker and family members. In contrast, excess earnings of family members are charged against their individual benefits only. For example, a widowed mother who holds a job outside the home may lose her mother's benefit, but any benefits received by her children are unaffected.

Cost-of-Living Adjustments

Social Security benefits are increased automatically each January as long as there has been an increase in the Consumer Price Index (CPI) for the one-year period ending in the third quarter of the prior year. The increase is the same as the increase in the CPI since the last cost-of-living adjustment, rounded to the nearest 0.1 percent.

Offset for Other Benefits

Disabled workers under full retirement age who are also receiving workers' compensation benefits or disability benefits from certain other federal, state, or local disability programs will have their Social Security benefits reduced to the extent that the total benefits received (including family benefits) exceed 80 percent of their average current earnings at the time of disability. In addition, the monthly benefit of a spouse or surviving spouse is reduced by two-thirds of any federal, state, or local government pension that is based on earnings not covered under Social Security on the last day of employment.

SOCIAL SECURITY: REQUESTING BENEFIT INFORMATION

Social Security Statement

In 1995, the Social Security Administration began sending an annual Earnings and Benefit Estimate Statement to each worker aged 60 and older. This statement, renamed the *Social Security Statement*, is now provided annually to all persons aged 25 or older who have worked in employment covered by Social Security and who are not currently entitled to monthly benefits. The statement enables an employee to verify his or her contributions to the Social Security and Medicare programs. It also contains an estimate of benefits that will be available upon retirement, disability, or death, as well as a reminder of the right to request corrections of omissions or errors. As a general rule, such requests must be made within 3 years, 3 months, and 15 days following the year in which wages were paid or self-employment income was earned. However, clerical or fraudulent errors can be corrected after that time.

MEDICARE: ELIGIBILITY

Part A, the hospital portion of Medicare, is available to any person aged 65 or older as long as the person is entitled to monthly retirement benefits under Social Security or the railroad retirement program. Civilian employees of the federal government aged 65 or older are also eligible. It is not necessary for these workers to actually be receiving retirement benefits, but they must be fully insured for purposes of retirement benefits. The following persons are also eligible for Part A of Medicare at no monthly cost:

- persons aged 65 or older who are dependents of fully insured workers aged 62 or older
- survivors aged 65 or older who are eligible for Social Security survivors benefits
- disabled persons at any age who have been eligible to receive Social Security benefits for 2 years because of their disability. This includes workers under age 65, disabled widows and widowers aged 50 or over, and children 18 or older who were disabled prior to age 22.
- workers who are either fully or currently insured and their spouses and dependent children with end-stage renal (kidney) disease who require renal dialysis or kidney transplants. Coverage begins either the first day of the third month after dialysis begins or earlier for admission to a hospital for kidney-transplant surgery.

Most persons aged 65 or over who do not meet the previously discussed eligibility requirements may voluntarily enroll in Medicare. However, they must pay a monthly Part A premium and also enroll in Part B. The monthly Part A premium in 2003 is $316 for individuals with fewer than 30 quarters of Medicare-covered employment and $174 for individuals with 30 to 39 quarters. The premium is adjusted annually, and the $316 amount reflects the full cost of the benefits provided.

Any person eligible for Part A of Medicare is also eligible for Part B. However, a monthly premium must be paid for Part B. This premium ($58.70 in 2003) is adjusted annually and represents only about 25 percent of the cost of the benefits provided. The remaining cost of the program is financed from the general revenues of the federal government.

Persons receiving Social Security or railroad retirement benefits are automatically enrolled in Medicare if they are eligible. If they do not want Part B, they must reject it in writing. Other persons eligible for Medicare must apply for benefits. As a general rule, anyone who rejects Part B or who does not enroll when initially eligible may later apply for benefits during a general enrollment period that occurs between January 1 and March 31 of each year. However, the monthly premium is increased by 10 percent for each 12-month period during which the person was eligible but failed to enroll.

Medicare secondary rules make employer-provided medical expense coverage primary to Medicare for certain classes of individuals who are over 65, who are disabled, or who are suffering end-stage renal disease. These persons (and any other Medicare-eligible persons still covered as active employees under their employer's plans) may not wish to elect Medicare because it largely constitutes duplicate coverage. When their employer-provided coverage ends, these persons have a 7-month special enrollment period to elect Part B coverage, and the late enrollment penalty is waived.

Medicare is also secondary to benefits received by persons (1) entitled to veterans' or black lung benefits, (2) covered by workers' compensation laws, or (3) whose medical expenses are paid under no-fault insurance or liability insurance. Medicare secondary rules are covered in more detail in chapter 12.

MEDICARE: PART A BENEFITS

Part A of Medicare provides benefits for expenses incurred in hospitals, skilled-nursing facilities, and hospices. Some home health care benefits are also covered. In order for benefits to be paid, the facility or agency providing benefits must participate in the Medicare program. Virtually all hospitals are participants, as are most other facilities or agencies that meet the requirements of Medicare.

Part A of Medicare, along with Part B, provides a high level of benefits for medical expenses. However, as is described in the next few pages, deductibles and copayments may be higher than in prior group or individual coverage. In addition, certain benefits that were previously provided may be excluded or limited. For this reason, persons without supplemental retiree coverage from prior employment may wish to consider the purchase of a Medicare supplement (medigap) policy in the individual marketplace.

Hospital Benefits

Part A pays for inpatient hospital services for up to 90 days in each benefit period (also referred to as a spell of illness). A benefit period begins the first time a Medicare recipient is hospitalized and ends only after the recipient has been out of a hospital or skilled-nursing facility for 60 consecutive days. A subsequent hospitalization then begins a new benefit period.

In each benefit period, covered hospital expenses are paid in full for 60 days, subject to an initial deductible ($840 in 2003). This deductible is adjusted annually to reflect increasing hospital costs. Benefits for an additional 30 days of hospitalization are also provided in each benefit period, but the patient must pay a daily copayment ($210 in 2003) equal to 25 percent of the initial deductible amount. Each recipient also has a lifetime reserve of 60 additional days that may be used if the regular 90 days of benefits have been exhausted. However, once a reserve day is used, it cannot be restored for use in future benefit periods. When using reserve days, patients must pay a daily copayment ($420 in 2003) equal to 50 percent of the initial deductible amount.

There is no limit on the number of benefit periods a person may have during his or her lifetime. However, there is a lifetime limit of 190 days of benefits for treatment in psychiatric hospitals.

Covered inpatient expenses include the following:

- room and board in semiprivate accommodations. Private rooms are covered only if required for medical reasons.
- nursing services (except private-duty nurses)
- use of regular hospital equipment such as oxygen tents or wheelchairs
- drugs and biologicals ordinarily furnished by the hospital
- diagnostic or therapeutic items or services
- operating room costs
- blood transfusions after the first three pints of blood. Patients must pay for the first three pints of blood unless they get donors to replace the blood.

There is no coverage under Part A for the services of physicians or surgeons.

Skilled-Nursing Facility Benefits

In many cases, a patient may no longer require continuous hospital care but may not be well enough to go home. Consequently, Part A provides benefits for care in a skilled-nursing facility if a physician certifies that skilled-nursing care or rehabilitative services are needed for a condition that was treated in a hospital within the last 30 days. In addition, the prior hospitalization must have lasted at least 3 days. Benefits are paid in full for 20 days in each benefit period and for an additional 80 days with a daily copayment ($105 in 2003) that is equal to 12.5 percent of the initial hospital deductible. Covered expenses are the same as those described for hospital benefits.

A skilled-nursing facility may be a separate facility for providing such care or a separate section of a hospital or nursing home. The facility must have at least one full-time registered nurse, and nursing services must be provided at all times. Every patient must be under the supervision of a physician, and a physician must always be available for emergency care.

One very important point should be made about skilled-nursing facility benefits. Custodial care is not provided under any part of the Medicare program unless skilled-nursing or rehabilitative services are also needed and covered.

Home Health Care Benefits

If a patient can be treated at home for a medical condition, Medicare pays the full cost for an unlimited number of home visits by a home health agency. To receive these benefits, a person must be confined at home and be treated under a home health plan set up by a physician. The care needed must include skilled-nursing services, physical therapy, or speech therapy. In addition to these services, Medicare also pays for the cost of part-time home health aides, medical social services, occupational therapy, and medical supplies and equipment provided by the home health agency. There is no charge for these benefits other than a required 20 percent copayment for the cost of such durable medical equipment as oxygen tanks and hospital beds. Medicare does not cover home services that are furnished primarily to assist people in activities of daily living (ADLs) such as housecleaning, preparing meals, shopping, dressing, or bathing.

If a person has only Part A of Medicare, all home health care benefits are covered under Part A. If a person has both Parts A and B, the first 100 visits that commence within 14 days of a hospital stay of at least 3 days are covered under Part A. All other home health visits are covered under Part B.

Hospice Benefits

Hospice benefits are available under Part A of Medicare for beneficiaries who are certified as being terminally ill with a life expectancy of 6 months or less. While a hospice is thought of as a facility for treating the terminally ill, Medicare benefits are available primarily for benefits provided by a Medicare-approved hospice to patients in their own homes.

However, inpatient care can be provided if needed by the patient. In addition to including the types of benefits described for home health care, hospice benefits also include drugs, bereavement counseling, and inpatient respite care when family members need a break from caring for the ill person.

In order to qualify for hospice benefits, a Medicare recipient must elect such coverage in lieu of other Medicare benefits, except for the services of the attending physician or services and benefits that do not pertain to the terminal condition. There are modest copayments for some services. A beneficiary may cancel the hospice coverage at any time (for example, to pursue chemotherapy treatments) and return to regular Medicare coverage. The beneficiary can elect hospice benefits again but must be recertified as terminally ill.

Exclusions

There are some circumstances under which Part A of Medicare does not pay benefits. In addition, there are times when Medicare acts as the secondary payer of benefits. Exclusions under Part A include the following:

- services outside the United States and its territories or possessions. However, there are a few exceptions to this rule for qualified Mexican and Canadian hospitals. Benefits are paid if an emergency occurs in the United States and the closest hospital is in one of these countries. However, persons living closer to a hospital in one of these countries than to a hospital in the United States may use the foreign hospital even if an emergency does not exist. Finally, there is coverage for Canadian hospitals if a person needs hospitalization while traveling the most direct route between Alaska and another state in the United States. However, this latter provision does not apply to persons vacationing in Canada.
- elective luxury services such as private rooms or televisions
- hospitalization for services that are not necessary for the treatment of an illness or injury such as custodial care or elective cosmetic surgery
- services performed in a federal facility such as a veterans' hospital
- services covered under workers' compensation

Under these circumstances, Medicare is the secondary payer of benefits:

- when primary coverage under an employer-provided medical expense plan is elected by (1) an employee or spouse aged 65 or older or (2) a disabled beneficiary
- when medical care can be paid under any liability policy, including policies providing automobile no-fault benefits

- in the first 30 months for end-stage renal disease when an employer-provided medical expense plan provides coverage. By law, employer plans cannot specifically exclude this coverage during this period.

Medicare pays only if complete coverage is not available from these sources and then only to the extent that benefits are less than would otherwise be payable under Medicare.

MEDICARE: PART B BENEFITS

Benefits

Part B of Medicare provides benefits for most medical expenses not covered under Part A. These include

- physicians' and surgeons' fees. Under certain circumstances, benefits are also provided for the services of chiropractors, podiatrists, and optometrists.
- diagnostic tests
- physical therapy
- drugs and biologicals that cannot be self-administered
- radiation therapy
- medical supplies such as surgical dressings, splints, and casts
- rental of medical equipment such as oxygen tents, hospital beds, and wheelchairs
- prosthetic devices such as artificial heart valves or lenses after a cataract operation
- ambulance service if a patient's condition does not permit the use of other methods of transportation
- mammograms and Pap smears
- diabetes glucose monitoring and education
- colorectal cancer screening
- bone mass measurement
- prostate cancer screening
- pneumococcal vaccine and its administration
- dilated eye examinations for beneficiaries at high risk for glaucoma
- home health care services as described for Part A when a person does not have Part A coverage or when Part A benefits are not applicable

Over the last few years, there have been several bills introduced in Congress to add prescription drug coverage to Medicare. Even with maximum annual limits and copayments, the cost of such a benefit would be significant because of the high usage of expensive prescription drugs by the elderly. As a result, no political agreement was reached as to the precise nature of the benefit and how it would be financed. In the first half of the Bush administration, it finally looked as if some type of compromise was about to be reached, with at least a portion of the funding provided from projected budget surpluses over the next several years. Such legislation never materialized as a result of several factors, including partisan politics, projected surpluses that had been reduced or possibly eliminated by tax cuts, a deteriorating economy, and expenditures resulting from the September 11, 2001, terrorist attacks. However, as this book is being revised in early 2003, there is still considerable political support to add some type of prescription drug coverage to Medicare.

Exclusions

Although the preceding list may appear to be comprehensive, there are numerous medical products and services not covered by Part B, some of which represent significant expenses for the elderly. They include

- most drugs and biologicals that can be self-administered except drugs that are used for osteoporosis, oral cancer treatment, and immunosuppressive therapy under specified circumstances
- routine physical, eye, and hearing examinations except those previously mentioned
- routine foot care
- immunizations except pneumococcal vaccinations or immunization required because of an injury or immediate risk of infection
- cosmetic surgery unless it is needed because of an accidental injury or to improve the function of a malformed part of the body
- dental care unless it involves jaw or facial bone surgery or the setting of fractures
- custodial care
- eyeglasses, hearing aids, or orthopedic shoes

In addition, benefits are not provided to persons eligible for workers' compensation or to those treated in government hospitals. Benefits are provided only for services received in the United States, except for physicians' services and ambulance services rendered for a hospitalization that is covered in Mexico or Canada under Part A. Part B is also a secondary payer of benefits under the same circumstances described for Part A.

Amount of Benefits

The benefits available under Part B are subject to a number of different payment rules. A few charges are paid in full without any cost sharing.

These include (1) home health services, (2) pneumococcal vaccine and its administration, (3) certain surgical procedures that are performed on an outpatient basis in lieu of hospitalization, (4) diagnostic preadmission tests performed on an outpatient basis within 7 days prior to hospitalization, (5) mammograms, and (6) Pap smears.

For other charges, there is a $100 calendar-year deductible. When the deductible is satisfied, Part B pays 80 percent of approved charges for most covered medical expenses other than professional charges for mental health care and outpatient services of hospitals and mental health centers. Medicare pays only 50 percent of approved charges for the mental health services of physicians and other mental health professionals. There is a separate payment system under which Medicare determines a set payment for each type of service for outpatient services of hospitals and mental health centers. However, this amount varies across the country to reflect factors such as the level of hospital wages. For some services, Medicare patients are required to pay an amount equal to 20 percent of the set payment amount, with Part B paying 80 percent. For other services, there is a fixed copayment that may be more or less than 20 percent of the set payment amount. In no case can the amount paid by a Medicare patient for a single service exceed a dollar figure equal to the Part A hospital deductible ($840 in 2003).

The approved charge for doctors' services covered by Medicare is based on a fee schedule issued by the Center for Medicare & Medicaid Services, which administers Medicare. A patient will be reimbursed for only 80 percent of the approved charges above the deductible—regardless of the doctor's actual charge. Most doctors and other suppliers of medical services accept an assignment of Medicare benefits and therefore are prohibited from charging a patient in excess of the fee schedule. They can, however, bill the patient for any portion of the approved charges that were not paid by Medicare because of the annual deductible and/or coinsurance. They can also bill for any services that are not covered by Medicare.

Doctors who do not accept assignment of Medicare benefits cannot charge a Medicare patient more than 115 percent of the approved fee for nonparticipating doctors. Because the approved fee for nonparticipating doctors is set at 95 percent of the fee paid for participating doctors, a doctor who does not accept an assignment of Medicare benefits can charge a fee that is only 9.25 percent greater than if an assignment had been accepted (115 percent x 95 percent = 109.25 percent). As a result, some doctors either do not see Medicare participants or limit the number of such patients they treat.

The previous limitation on charges does not apply to providers of medical services other than doctors. Although a provider who does not accept assignment can charge any fee, Medicare pays only what it would have paid if the provider accepted assignment. For example, if the approved charge for medical equipment is $100 and the actual charge is $190. Medicare reimburses $80 (.80 x $100), and the balance is borne by the Medicare recipient.

MEDICARE+CHOICE

In 1985, Congress amended the Medicare program to allow a beneficiary to elect coverage under a health maintenance organization (HMO) as an alternative to the traditional Medicare program. At first, the number of persons electing this option was relatively small. Many of the elderly had not had HMO coverage during their working years and viewed such coverage with some skepticism. In addition, many HMOs continued to focus on expanding their traditional market of younger, healthier lives rather than entering a new and demographically different market. In addition, there were complex federal rules that had to be satisfied to enter the Medicare market.

The situation slowly changed as more HMOs got into the Medicare market and the public became more familiar with HMO coverage. In addition, as medical costs continued to rise, the election of an HMO option made more sense from a cost standpoint. As a result, HMO coverage for Medicare beneficiaries grew rapidly in the mid- to late 1990s, and approximately one out of six beneficiaries obtained such coverage.

Under the 1985 rules, an HMO is basically given 95 percent of what Medicare would expect to pay to provide benefits if a beneficiary electing HMO coverage had stayed in the traditional Medicare program. In turn, the HMO is expected to provide at least the same benefits that are available under Medicare. While an HMO can provide additional benefits and charge an extra premium, some HMOs have provided additional benefits, such as prescription drugs, without charging an additional premium. Such zero-premium plans have been very popular among Medicare beneficiaries. While they must continue to pay the Part B Medicare premium, these beneficiaries have been able to receive coverage that is broader than traditional Medicare and have no reason to purchase a Medicare supplement policy.

Medicare+Choice

In 1999, Part C of Medicare (called *Medicare+Choice*) went into effect. It expands the choices available to most Medicare beneficiaries by allowing them to elect health care benefits through one of several alternatives to the traditional Parts A and B as long as the providers of these alternatives enter into contracts with the Centers for Medicare & Medicaid Services.

The new Medicare+Choice plans include

- HMOs. (Most of the HMOs previously in the Medicare market became part of the Medicare+Choice program.)
- preferred-provider organizations (PPOs)

- provider-sponsor organizations (PSOs). These are similar to HMOs but established by doctors and hospitals that have formed their own health plans.
- private fee-for-service plans
- private contracts with physicians
- medical savings accounts

These plans must provide all benefits available under parts A and B. They may include additional benefits as part of the basic plan or for an additional fee.

Through 2004, beneficiaries are able to enroll in a Medicare+Choice plan or switch options (including reenrollment in parts A and B) at any time. Beginning in 2005, there will be a limited period each year during which beneficiaries can change their plans.

Unfortunately, the initial reaction to Medicare+Choice has been less than overwhelming. As of early 2003, few new providers of alternative coverage have entered the marketplace, and the enrollment in alternatives to traditional Medicare has decreased slightly after several years of growth. One reason for this is that the Medicare+Choice rules are extremely complex, and it is questionable if many of the potential providers can enter the market in a viable way. In addition, there has been a decrease in the number of HMOs offering coverage. While some HMOs continue to enter the Medicare market or expand their service areas for Medicare beneficiaries, a larger number of HMOs have either ceased providing Medicare coverage or reduced their service areas. While many of those who lose Medicare coverage have other HMOs available, a change to another HMO may also require the use of different physicians and hospitals. Other HMO participants have no choice but to return to the traditional Medicare program. Finally, some HMOs no longer offer zero-premium plans or have increased premiums and/or reduced benefits. These changes stem from two factors. First, HMO costs have increased significantly in recent years, partially because of substantial increases in the cost of prescription drugs, which are a major source of medical expenses for the elderly. Second, the rate of growth of Medicare payments to HMOs has been reduced so that many HMOs are receiving increases that fail to match their increases in expenses.

At the time this book is being revised, there is concern about the future of the Medicare+Choice program. The Bush administration and the Department of Health and Human Services are committed to reversing the decline in Medicare+Choice participation and stabilizing the program. As a result, some changes in reimbursement formulas and complex program rules are being made and other changes are being studied.

ADEQUACY OF FINANCING

partial advance funding

Social Security and Medicare are based on a system of funding that the Social Security Administration refers to as *partial advance funding*. Under this system, taxes are more than sufficient to pay current benefits and also provide some accumulation of assets for the payment of future benefits. Partial advance funding falls somewhere between pay-as-you-go financing, which was once the way Social Security and Medicare were financed, and full advance funding as used by private insurance and retirement plans. Under pay-as-you-go financing, taxes are set at a level to produce just enough income to pay current benefits; under full advance funding, taxes are set at a level to fund all promised benefits from current service for those making current contributions.

All payroll taxes and other sources of funds for Social Security and Medicare are deposited into four trust funds: an old-age and survivors fund, a disability fund, and two Medicare funds. Benefits and administrative expenses are paid out of the appropriate trust fund from contributions to that fund and any interest earnings on accumulated assets. The trust funds have limited reserves to serve as emergency funds in periods when benefits exceed contributions such as in times of high unemployment. However, current reserves are relatively small and could pay benefits for only a limited time if contributions to a fund ceased. In addition, the reserves consist primarily of IOUs from the Treasury since the contributions have been "borrowed" to finance the government's deficit.

In the early 1980s, considerable concern arose over the potential inability of payroll taxes to pay promised benefits in the future. Through a series of changes, the most significant being the 1983 amendments to the Social Security Act, these problems appeared to have been solved for the Social Security program—at least in the short run. The changes approached the problem from two directions. On one hand, payroll tax rates were increased; on the other hand, some benefits were eliminated and future increases in other benefits were scaled back. However, the solutions of 1983 have not worked. Without further adjustments, the trust funds will have inadequate resources to pay claims in the foreseeable future. The old-age and survivors fund will continue to grow and will be quite large by the time the current baby boomers retire. Benefits will then exceed income, and the fund will begin to decrease as the percentage of retirees grows rapidly. Current projections indicate that the assets of the combined old-age and survivors trust fund and the disability trust fund will run out in 2042.

Because of an increasing number of persons aged 65 or older and medical costs that continue to grow at an alarming rate, there is also concern about the Medicare portion of the program. Estimates are that its trust funds will be depleted by about 2026. The seriousness of this problem was made clear by the fact that one of the earliest actions of the second Clinton administration was the passage of legislation to help maintain the solvency of the Medicare trust funds for a few additional years, primarily through encouraging additional enrollment in managed care plans and trimming projected payments to HMOs, hospitals, and doctors.

It is obvious that changes must be made—either now or later—in the Social Security and Medicare programs. Probably the most important step in finding a solution is to convince the public that changes in this very popular entitlement program must be made. Changes, of course, have significant political implications. While most members of Congress realize the need for reform, neither political party has been willing to compromise and take the necessary initiative for fear of losing public support.

In the broadest sense, the solution lies in doing one or both of the following: increasing revenue into the trust funds or decreasing benefit costs. Changes that would increase revenue include the following:

- increasing the Social Security and/or Medicare tax rate
- increasing the wage base on which Social Security taxes are paid
- using more general tax revenue to fund the programs
- subjecting a greater portion of income benefits to taxation and depositing the increased tax revenue into the trust funds
- investing all or a portion of trust fund assets in higher-yielding investments than Treasury securities

Suggested changes that have been made for decreasing benefit costs include the following:

- raising full retirement age beyond the planned increase to age 67
- raising the early retirement age beyond 62
- lowering the benefit formula so that future retirees will get somewhat reduced benefits
- lowering cost-of-living increases
- imposing a means test for benefits
- shifting more of the inflation risk to workers through the use of separate accounts for all or part of each worker's contributions. This would give the worker some control over his or her account.
- increasing the Medicare eligibility age beyond 65
- increasing Medicare deductibles and copayments
- increasing the Medicare Part B premium for everyone or possibly only for higher-income retirees
- lowering or slowing the growth of payments to Medicare providers

- encouraging or requiring Medicare beneficiaries to enroll in managed care plans

In May 2001, President Bush announced the establishment of a bipartisan commission to study and report specific recommendations to preserve Social Security for seniors while building wealth for younger Americans. The commission was asked to make its recommendations using the following six guiding principles for modernizing the program:

- Modernization must not change Social Security benefits for retirees or near-retirees.
- The entire Social Security Surplus must be dedicated to Social Security only.
- Social Security payroll taxes must not be increased.
- Government must not invest Social Security funds in the stock market.
- Modernization must preserve Social Security's disability and survivors components.
- Modernization must include individually controlled, voluntary personal accounts, which will augment the Social Security safety net.

In late 2001, the commission issued a report. Rather than specifying one specific plan for reforming Social Security, it put forth three alternative proposals that contained the President's guiding principles. Two of the three proposals would also significantly increase benefits for low-income workers over what the current program pays. While the various proposals received some degree of support, there are also critics who argue for different changes. The details of the commission's proposals are lengthy, complex, and beyond the scope of this book. For readers desiring more details, the full commission report can be accessed at the commission's Web site: www.csss.gov.

Any single change to the Social Security program will clearly offend one important group of voters or another. As a result, the ultimate solution (which may or may not follow the commission's recommendations) will probably involve a combination of several of the previously mentioned suggestions for change so that everyone will bear a little of the pain.

TAXATION OF SOCIAL SECURITY AND MEDICARE

Deductibility of Premiums

Employer contributions to the Social Security and Medicare program are tax deductible for federal income tax purposes. Any employee contributions are paid with after-tax dollars. However, self-employed persons are able to deduct one-half of their Social Security and Medicare taxes as business expenses. In addition, Part B premiums are treated the same as other medical expense premiums for individual insurance and may be deductible as described in chapter 13.

Taxation of Benefits

Benefits received in the form of monthly income under Social Security are partially subject to income taxation for some Social Security recipients. To determine the amount of Social Security benefits subject to taxation, it is necessary to calculate modified adjusted gross income, which is the sum of following:

- the taxpayer's adjusted gross income (disregarding any foreign income and savings bond exclusions)
- the taxpayer's tax-exempt interest that is received or accrued during the year
- one-half of the Social Security benefits for the year

If the modified adjusted gross income is $25,000 or less for a single taxpayer ($32,000 or less for a married taxpayer filing jointly), Social Security benefits are not taxable. If the modified adjusted gross income is between this amount and $34,000 ($44,000 for a married taxpayer filing jointly), up to 50 percent of the Social Security benefit is includible in taxable income. If the modified adjusted gross income exceeds $34,000 ($44,000 for a married taxpayer filing jointly), up to 85 percent of the Social Security benefit is includible in taxable income. The exact amount of the taxable Social Security benefit is determined by complex formulas that are beyond the scope of this discussion.

Medicare benefits and any lump-sum Social Security benefits are received tax free.

OTHER SOCIAL INSURANCE PROGRAMS

The remainder of this chapter is devoted to social insurance programs other than Social Security and Medicare. Unemployment insurance is a joint federal and state program, and workers' compensation insurance and temporary disability laws are solely under state control. Because the programs of each state are unique, the discussion in this chapter is general in nature. Readers should familiarize themselves with the programs in their own state and not assume that these programs will always conform to the generalizations that follow. Detailed information on a specific state's program can be obtained from the state agency administering the program.

Unemployment Insurance

unemployment insurance

Prior to the passage of the Social Security Act in 1935, relatively few employees had any type of protection for income lost during periods of unemployment. The act stipulated that a payroll tax was to be levied on covered employers for the purpose of financing *unemployment insurance* programs that were to be established by the states under guidelines issued by the federal government. Essentially, the federal law levied a federal tax on certain employers in all states. If a state established an acceptable program of unemployment insurance, the taxes used to finance its program could be offset against up to 90 percent of the federal tax. If a state failed to establish a program, the federal tax would still be levied, but no monies collected from the employers in that state would be returned for purposes of providing benefits to the unemployed there. Needless to say, all states quickly established unemployment insurance programs. These programs (along with a federal program for railroad workers) now cover over 95 percent of all working persons, but major gaps in coverage exist for domestic workers, agricultural workers, and the self-employed.

There are several objectives to the current unemployment insurance program. The primary objective is to provide periodic cash income to workers during periods of involuntary unemployment. Benefits are generally paid as a matter of right, with no demonstration of need required. While federal legislation has extended benefits during times of high unemployment, the unemployment insurance program is basically designed for workers whose periods of unemployment are short-term; the long-term and hard-core unemployed must rely on other measures, such as public assistance and job-retraining programs, when unemployment insurance benefits are exhausted.

A second major objective of unemployment insurance is to help the unemployed find jobs. Workers must register at local unemployment offices, and unemployment benefits are received through these offices. Another important objective is to encourage employers to stabilize employment. As is described below, this is accomplished through the use of experience rating in determining an employer's tax rate. Finally, unemployment insurance contributes to a stable labor supply by providing benefits so that skilled and experienced workers are not forced to seek other jobs during short-term layoffs, thereby remaining available to return to work when called back.

Financing of Benefits

Unemployment insurance programs are financed primarily by unemployment taxes levied by both the federal and state governments. The federal tax is equal to 6.2 percent of the first $7,000 of wages for each worker, but this tax is reduced by up to 5.4 percentage points for taxes paid to state programs. The practical effect of this offset is that the federal tax is actually equal to 0.8 percent of covered payroll. A few states levy an unemployment payroll tax equal to only the maximum offset (5.4 percent on the first $7,000 of wages), but most states have a higher tax rate and/or levy their tax on a higher amount of earnings.

No state levies the same tax on all employers. Rather, they use a method of experience rating whereby all employers, except those that have been in business for a short time or those with a small number of employees, pay a tax rate that reflects their actual experience within limits. Thus, an employer who has laid off a large percentage of employees will have a higher tax rate than an employer whose employment record has been stable.

An employer who has good experience often has to pay a state tax of less than one percent of payroll and possibly even as little as 0.1 percent. On the other hand, some employers pay a state tax as high as 9 or 10 percent. Regardless of the amount of actual state tax paid, the employer still pays the 0.8 percent federal tax.

The major argument for experience rating is that it provides a financial incentive for employers to stabilize employment. However, those who are opposed to its use contend that many employers have little control over economic trends that affect employment. In addition, they argue that tax rates tend to escalate in bad economic times and thus may actually serve as an obstacle to economic recovery.

The entire unemployment insurance tax is collected by the individual states and deposited in the Federal Unemployment Insurance Trust Fund, which is administered by the Secretary of the Treasury. Each state has a separate account that is credited with its taxes and its share of investment earnings on assets in the fund. Unemployment benefits in the state are paid from this account. The federal share of the taxes received by the fund is deposited into separate accounts and is used for administering the federal portion of the program and for giving grants to the states to administer their individual programs. In addition, the federal funds are available for loans to states whose accounts have been depleted during times of high unemployment.

Eligibility for Benefits

The right to benefits depends on the worker's attachment to the labor force within a prior base period. In most states, this base period is the 52 weeks or 4 quarters prior to the time of unemployment. During this base period the worker must have earned a minimum amount of wages or worked a minimum period of time, or both.

The right to benefits is also contingent on an unemployed worker's being both physically and mentally capable of working. The worker must also be available for work. Benefits may be denied if suitable work is refused or if substantial restrictions are placed on the type of work that will be accepted. In addition to registering with a local unemployment office, most states require a worker to make a reasonable effort to seek work.

Most unemployment programs have a one-week waiting period before benefits commence. Benefits are not paid retroactively for that time of unemployment.

All states have provisions in their laws under which a worker may be disqualified from receiving benefits. This disqualification may take the form of (1) a total cancellation of benefit rights, (2) the postponement of benefits, or (3) a reduction in benefits. Common reasons for disqualification include the following: voluntarily leaving a job without good cause, discharge for misconduct, refusal to accept suitable work, involvement in a labor dispute, and receipt of disqualifying income such as dismissal wages, workers' compensation benefits, benefits from an employer's pension plan, or primary insurance benefits under Social Security.

Benefits

The majority of states pay "regular" unemployment insurance benefits for a maximum of 26 weeks; the remaining states pay benefits for slightly longer periods. In most states, the amount of the weekly benefit is equal to a specified fraction of a worker's average wages during the highest calendar quarter of the base period. The typical fraction is 1/26, which yields a benefit equal to 50 percent of average weekly earnings for that quarter. Other states determine benefits as a percentage of average weekly wages or annual wages during the base period. Some states also modify their benefit formulas to provide relatively higher benefits (as a percentage of past earnings) to lower-paid workers. Benefits in all states are subject to minimum and maximum amounts. Minimum weekly benefits typically fall within the range of $20 to $75, maximum benefits in the range of $200 to $400, and the average benefit in the range of $170 to $235. In addition, a few states currently provide additional benefits if there are dependents who receive regular support from the worker.

States also provide reduced benefits for partial unemployment. Such a condition occurs if a worker is employed less than full-time and has a weekly income less than his or her weekly benefit amount for total unemployment.

There is also a permanent federal-state program of "extended" unemployment benefits for workers whose regular benefits are exhausted during periods of high unemployment. The availability of these benefits is automatically triggered when a state's unemployment rate exceeds a specified level. The federal government and the states involved finance the benefits equally, and they can be paid for up to 13 weeks, as long as the total of regular and extended benefits does not exceed 39 weeks.

In 1988, Congress created a program for the payment of unemployment assistance to individuals whose unemployment is the direct result of a major disaster as declared by the President and who are not otherwise eligible for regular unemployment insurance benefits. In order to be eligible for benefits under this program, an individual must have worked or been scheduled to work in an area that was declared a federal disaster area, as were parts of New York after the terrorist attacks on September 11, 2001. In addition, benefits are paid only if the individual cannot work because of the disaster and the work he or she cannot perform is his or her primary source of income and livelihood. The benefits are administered by the state where a disaster occurred and the benefit amounts are the same as regular unemployment insurance benefits. The benefits are paid for up to 26 weeks but cease once the disaster assistance period (which is usually also 26 weeks) is over. The funds for these "disaster" benefits are provided by the federal government through the Federal Emergency Management Agency.

In periods of severe economic conditions on a national basis, the federal government often enacts legislation to provide additional benefits that are financed with federal revenue. The most recent such program went into effect in 2002.

Temporary Disability Laws

At their inception, state unemployment insurance programs were usually designed to cover only unemployed persons who were both willing and able to work. Benefits were denied to anyone who was unable to work for any reason, including disability. Some states amended their unemployment insurance laws to provide coverage to the unemployed who subsequently became disabled. However, five states—California, Hawaii, New Jersey, New York, and Rhode Island—and Puerto Rico went one step further by enacting *temporary disability laws* under which employees can collect disability income benefits regardless of whether their disability begins while they are employed or unemployed. While variations exist among the states,

temporary disability law

these laws (often referred to as nonoccupational disability laws since benefits are not provided for disabilities covered under workers' compensation laws) are generally patterned after the state unemployment insurance law and provide similar benefits.

Eligibility

Every jurisdiction requires that an employee must have worked for a specified time and/or have received a minimum amount of wages within some specific period prior to disability in order to qualify for disability income benefits. The usual waiting period for benefits is 7 days. However, in some jurisdictions the waiting period is waived if the employee is hospitalized.

Benefits

Benefits are a percentage, ranging from 50 percent to 66 2/3 percent, of the employee's average weekly wage for some period prior to disability, subject to maximum and minimum amounts. Benefits are generally paid up to 26 weeks if the employee remains disabled that long.

Workers' Compensation Laws

Prior to the passage of workers' compensation laws, it was difficult for employees to receive compensation for their work-related injuries or diseases. Group benefits were meager and the Social Security program had not yet been enacted. The only recourse for employees was to sue their employer for damages. In addition to the time and expense of such actions (as well as the possibility of the employee's being fired), the probability of a worker winning such a suit was small because of the three common-law defenses available to employers. Under the contributory negligence doctrine, a worker could not collect if his or her negligence had contributed in any way to the injury sustained. Under the fellow-servant doctrine, the worker could not collect if his or her injury had resulted from the negligence of a fellow worker. And finally, under the assumption-of-risk doctrine, a worker could not collect if he or she had knowingly assumed the risks inherent in the job.

workers' compensation law

To help solve the problem of uncompensated injuries, *workers' compensation laws*—a form of both social insurance and employers' liability insurance—were enacted to require employers to provide benefits to employees for losses resulting from work-related accidents or diseases. These laws are based on the principle of liability without fault. Essentially, an employer is absolutely liable for providing the benefits prescribed by the workers' compensation laws, regardless of whether the employer would be considered legally liable in the absence of these laws. However, benefits,

---

Common Law Defenses for Employers against Injured Workers

- Contributory negligence—The worker's own negligence contributed, even if only in a small way, to the injury.
- Fellow servant—The negligence of one of the other workers contributed to this worker's injury.
- Assumption of risk—The worker knew the risks inherent in the job, but he or she willingly accepted the job anyway.

---

with the possible exception of medical expense benefits, are subject to statutory maximums.

All states have workers' compensation laws. In addition, the federal government has enacted several similar laws. The Federal Employees Compensation Act provides benefits for the employees of the federal government and the District of Columbia. Other federal acts require benefits for various groups of persons who might be exempt from state workers' compensation laws.

Type of Law

Most workers' compensation laws are compulsory for all employers covered under the law. A few states have elective laws, but the majority of employers do elect coverage. If they do not, their employees are not entitled to workers' compensation benefits and must sue for damages resulting from occupational accidents or diseases. However, the employer loses the right to the three common-law defenses previously described.

Financing of Benefits

Most states allow employers to comply with the workers' compensation law by purchasing coverage from insurance companies. Several of these states also have competitive state funds from which coverage may be obtained, but these funds usually provide benefits for fewer employers than insurance companies. Five states have monopolistic state funds that are the only source for obtaining coverage under the law.

Almost all states, including some with monopolistic state funds, allow employers to self-insure their workers' compensation exposure. These employers must generally post a bond or other security and receive the approval of the agency administering the law. While the number of firms using self-insurance for workers' compensation is small, these firms account for approximately one-half the employees covered under such laws.

Ways of Complying with Workers' Compensation Laws

Depending on the state, the options include the following:

- Purchase insurance from a private insurance company
- Purchase insurance from a competitive state fund
- Purchase insurance from a monopolistic state fund
- Qualify as a self-insurer

In virtually all cases, the full cost of providing workers' compensation benefits is borne by the employer. Obviously if an employer self-insures benefits, the ultimate cost will include the benefits paid plus any administrative expenses.

Employers who purchase coverage pay a premium that is calculated as a rate per $100 of payroll, based on the occupations of their workers. For example, rates for office workers may be as low as $.10, and rates for workers in a few hazardous occupations may exceed $50. Most states also require that employers with total workers' compensation premiums above a specified amount be subject to experience rating. That is, the employer's premium is a function of benefits paid for past injuries to the employer's workers. To the extent that safety costs are offset or eliminated by savings in workers' compensation premiums, experience-rating laws encourage employers to take an active role in correcting conditions that may cause injuries.

Covered Occupations

Although it is estimated that about 90 percent of the workers in the United States are covered by workers' compensation laws, the percentage varies among the states from less than 70 percent to more than 95 percent. Many laws exclude certain agricultural, domestic, and casual employees. Some laws also exclude employers with a small number of employees. Furthermore, coverage for employees of state and local governments is not universal.

Eligibility

Before an employee can be eligible for benefits under a workers' compensation law, he or she must work in an occupation covered by that law and be disabled or killed by a covered injury or illness. The typical workers' compensation law provides coverage for accidental occupational injuries (including death) arising out of and in the course of employment. In all states, this includes injuries arising out of accidents, which are generally defined as sudden and unexpected events that are definite in time and place. Every state has some coverage for illnesses resulting from occupational diseases. While the trend is toward full coverage for occupational diseases, some states cover only those diseases that are specifically listed in the law.

Benefits

Workers' compensation laws typically provide four types of benefits: medical care, disability income, death benefits, and rehabilitation benefits.

Medical Care. Benefits for medical expenses are usually provided without any limitations on time or amount. They are not subject to a waiting period.

Disability Income. Disability income benefits are payable for both total and partial disabilities. In addition, it does not matter whether a disability is temporary or permanent.

Most workers' compensation laws have a waiting period for disability income benefits that varies from 2 to 7 days. However, benefits are frequently paid retroactively to the date of the injury if an employee is disabled for a specified period of time or is confined to a hospital.

Disability income benefits under workers' compensation laws are a function of an employee's average weekly wage over some time period, commonly the 13 weeks immediately preceding the disability. For total disabilities, benefits are a percentage (usually 66 2/3 percent) of the employee's average weekly wage, subject to maximum and minimum amounts that vary substantially by state. Benefits for temporary total disabilities continue until an employee returns to work; benefits for permanent total disabilities usually continue for life but have a limited duration (such as 10 years) in a few states.

Benefits for partial disabilities are calculated as a percentage of the difference between the employee's wages before and after the disability. In most states, the duration of these benefits is subject to a statutory maximum. Several states also provide lump-sum payments to employees whose permanent partial disabilities involve the loss (or loss of use) of an eye, an arm, or other body member. These benefits, determined by a schedule in the law, may be in lieu of or in addition to periodic disability income benefits.

Death Benefits. Most workers' compensation laws provide two types of death benefits: burial allowances and cash income payments to survivors.

Burial allowances are a flat amount in each state and vary from $300 to $5,000, with benefits of $1,000 and $1,500 common.

Cash income payments to survivors, like disability income benefits, are a function of the worker's average wage prior to the injury resulting in death.

Benefits are usually paid only to a surviving spouse and children under 18. Some states pay benefits until the spouse dies or remarries and all children reach 18. Other states pay benefits for a maximum time, such as 10 years, or until a maximum dollar amount has been paid, such as $50,000.

Rehabilitation Benefits. All states have provisions in their workers' compensation laws for rehabilitative services for disabled workers. Benefits are included for medical rehabilitation as well as for vocational rehabilitation, including training, counseling, and job placement.

Federal Taxation of Other Social Insurance Benefits

Unemployment insurance benefits are included in a recipient's gross income. However, workers' compensation benefits are received free of income taxation.

Benefits received under temporary disability laws must be included in gross income. However, disabled persons with gross incomes below a specified level may be eligible for a federal tax credit. In jurisdictions where unemployed persons can also receive benefits, any benefits paid to them are considered unemployment insurance benefits and are taxed accordingly.

SOURCES FOR FURTHER IN-DEPTH STUDY

- *Social Security Manual*, Cincinnati, OH: The National Underwriter Company (updated annually). Phone 800-543-0874. Web site address www.nuco.com
- Rejda, George E., *Social Insurance and Economic Security,* 6th ed., Englewood Cliffs, NJ: Prentice-Hall, Inc., 1999. Phone 800-282-0693. Web site address www.prenhall.com
- Social Security Administration. Web site address www.ssa.gov
- Centers for Medicare & Medicaid Services. Web site address www.cms.gov

CHAPTER REVIEW

Answers to review questions and self-test questions start on page 725.

Key Terms

OASDHI	disability insured
fully insured	full retirement age
currently insured	primary insurance amount (PIA)

earnings test   unemployment insurance
Social Security Statement   temporary disability law
Medicare+Choice   workers' compensation law
partial advance funding

Review Questions

7-1. How are the Social Security and Medicare programs financed?

7-2. As of this year, Evelyn Grey, aged 38, had 28 quarters of coverage under Social Security. Twenty-four of these quarters were earned prior to the birth of her first child 11 years ago. Four quarters have been earned since she reentered the labor force one year ago.
    a. Is Grey fully insured? Explain.
    b. Is Grey currently insured? Explain.
    c. Is Grey disability insured? Explain.

7-3. Describe the retirement benefits available under Social Security.

7-4. What categories of persons are eligible for Social Security survivors benefits?

7-5. a. What is the definition of disability under Social Security?
    b. What categories of persons may be eligible for disability benefits?

7-6. a. Explain the relationship between a worker's PIA and the benefits available for dependents and survivors.
    b. What happens if the total benefits for a family exceed the maximum family benefit?

7-7. Explain how a worker's retirement benefits under Social Security will be affected if that person elects early or delayed retirement.

7-8. Describe the earnings test applicable to the Social Security program.

7-9. Describe the automatic cost-of-living adjustment provision under Social Security as it relates to benefit amounts.

7-10. With respect to Part A of Medicare:
    a. Describe the types of benefits that are available.
    b. Explain the extent to which deductibles and copayments are required.
    c. Identify the major exclusions.

7-11. With respect to Part B of Medicare:
    a. Describe the types of benefits that are available.
    b. Explain the extent to which copayments are required.
    c. Identify the major exclusions.

7-12. Describe the managed care options available under Medicare.

7-13. a.   What is the purpose of the Social Security and Medicare trust funds?

b.   Identify possible actions that can better ensure the adequacy of these trust funds.

7-14. Explain the extent to which Social Security benefits are taxed to recipients.

7-15. a.   What are the objectives of unemployment insurance?

b.   How is the program financed?

c.   How is benefit eligibility determined?

7-16. What is the nature of temporary disability laws?

7-17. a.   What is the purpose of workers' compensation insurance?

b.   What types and amounts of benefits are available?

7-18. Explain the extent, if any, to which benefits from unemployment insurance, temporary disability insurance programs, and workers' compensation insurance are included in a recipient's gross income for federal income tax purposes.

Self-Test Questions

T   F   7-1.   A person is fully insured under Social Security if he or she has credit for 40 quarters of coverage.

T   F   7-2.   A person born in 1962 will be eligible to receive full Social Security retirement benefits when he or she reaches age 65.

T   F   7-3.   The definition of disability under Social Security is very rigid.

T   F   7-4.   The primary insurance amount is the amount a worker will receive if he or she retires at full retirement age or becomes disabled.

T   F   7-5.   The family maximum benefit will usually be reached if three or more family members are eligible for benefits.

T   F   7-6.   If a person continues to work during the period of delayed retirement, it is possible for a worker's primary insurance amount to be higher than it would have been at full retirement age.

T   F   7-7.   There is a reduction in Social Security benefits under the earnings test for a 72-year-old person who goes back to work and earns $40,000.

T   F   7-8.   Part A, the hospital portion of Medicare, is available to any person aged 65 or older who is entitled to monthly retirement benefits under Social Security.

T   F   7-9.   Part A of Medicare pays for inpatient hospital services for up to 365 days for an uninterrupted stay in a hospital.

T   F   7-10.   Your client, who was released last week from the hospital but is going back after 7 days, will start a new benefit period for Medicare Part A purposes.

T   F   7-11.   Part A of Medicare provides benefits for home health care.

T   F   7-12.   Part B of Medicare will pay for prostate cancer screening.

T   F   7-13.   Social Security and Medicare are based on a system of funding that the Social Security Administration refers to as partial advance funding.

T   F   7-14.   Unemployment insurance is intended to provide short-term benefits (typically 26 weeks) to workers who lose their jobs.

T   F   7-15.   Workers' compensation laws are based on the principle of liability without fault.

T   F   7-16.   In virtually all cases, the full cost of providing workers' compensation benefits must be borne by employees.

T   F   7-17.   Workers' compensation benefits are included in a recipient's gross income for income tax purposes.

8

Introduction to Life Insurance

Learning Objectives

An understanding of the material in this chapter should enable the student to

8-1. Identify the family and business purposes of life insurance.

8-2. Explain the methods of providing life insurance protection.

8-3. Describe the three traditional types of life insurance.

8-4. Describe variations on the traditional types of life insurance.

8-5. Describe the life insurance provided by employers and other types of groups.

Chapter Outline

A human life possesses many values, most of them irreplaceable and not conducive to measurement. These values are founded on religious, relational, and societal bases. From a religious standpoint, for example, human life is regarded as immortal and endowed with a value beyond the comprehension of mortal man. In a person's relationship with other human beings, a set of emotional and sentimental attachments is created that cannot be measured in monetary terms or supplanted by material things. A human life may be capable of artistic achievements that contribute in a unique way to the culture of a society.

human life value

These values, however, are not the foundation of life insurance. Although not oblivious to these values—in fact, the life insurance transaction has strong moral and social overtones—life insurance is concerned with the economic value of a human life, or, more briefly, a person's *human life value*. An individual's human life value is derived from earning capacity and the financial dependence of other lives on that earning capacity. More precisely, a person's human life value is the present value of that portion of estimated future earnings which, if he or she lives long enough to achieve all of the earnings, will be used to support dependents. Financial planners must be able to apply the concept of human life value in order to identify appropriate ways to meet their clients' insurance needs.

Because the human life value may arise out of either a family or a business relationship, we will begin the discussion of life insurance by looking at its purposes for families and businesses. The chapter continues with an analysis of the basic methods of providing life insurance protection. The focus of the chapter then turns to the types of individual life insurance policies. First, the three traditional types of life insurance (term insurance, whole life insurance, and endowment policies) are discussed. Then the chapter looks at some of the newer variations of life insurance policies: current assumption whole life insurance, variable life insurance, universal life insurance, variable universal life insurance, and joint-life insurance. The final section of the chapter is devoted to group insurance, a marketing variation of some types of life insurance previously mentioned.

PURPOSES OF LIFE INSURANCE

In terms of earning capacity, a human life may be worth millions of dollars. Yet earning power alone does not create an economic value that can logically serve as the basis of life insurance. A human life has an economic value only if some other person or organization can expect to derive pecuniary advantage through its existence. If an individual is without dependents and no other person or organization stands to profit through his or her living, either now or in the future, then that life, for all practical purposes, has no monetary value that needs to be perpetuated. Such an individual is rare. Most income producers either have dependents or can expect to acquire them in the normal course of events. Even those income earners with no family dependents often provide financial support to charitable organizations. In either case, a basis exists for insurance.

Preservation of a Family's Economic Security

In many cases, an income producer's family is completely dependent on his or her personal earnings for subsistence and the amenities of life. In other words, the "potential" estate is far more substantial than the existing estate—the savings that the family accumulated. If the income earner lives and stays in good health, the total income potential will eventually be realized, to the benefit of the family and others who derive financial gain from his or her efforts. When an income earner dies, the unrealized portion of his or her total earnings potential is lost, and in the absence of other measures, the family might soon find itself destitute or reduced to a lower standard of living.

Life insurance contracts can create a fund at death to partially or fully offset the lost income of the insured. By means of life insurance, an individual can provide the family with the monetary value of those income-producing qualities that lie within his or her physical being, regardless of when death occurs. Life insurance enables the income earner to leave the family in the same economic position that they would have enjoyed had the decedent lived.

Obligation to Provide Protection

Most people assume major responsibility for the support and maintenance of their dependents during their lifetimes. In fact, they consider providing for their families to be one of the rewarding experiences of life. Additionally, the law attaches a legal obligation to the support of a spouse and children. Thus, if there is a divorce or legal separation, the court will normally decree support payments for dependent children and possibly alimony for the dependent spouse. In some cases, these payments, including alimony, continue beyond the provider's death if the children are still dependent or if the alimony recipient has not remarried.[1] Nevertheless, it takes a high order of responsibility for a parent to voluntarily provide for continuation of income to dependents after his or her own death. It virtually always involves a reduction in the individual's own standard of living. Yet most would agree that any person with a dependent spouse, children, or parents has a moral obligation to provide them with the protection afforded by life insurance, to the extent that his or her financial means permit.

Business Purposes of Life Insurance

Life insurance also serves a wide variety of purposes in the business world. The primary purposes of life insurance in business are key person indemnification, business continuation, and protection for employees and executives. Business applications are discussed in chapter 10. Group life insurance coverage for employees is discussed later in this chapter.

METHODS OF PROVIDING LIFE INSURANCE PROTECTION

An insurance company can use two approaches to provide life insurance protection: term insurance, which is temporary, or cash value insurance, which is permanent protection that builds up a reserve or savings component. An understanding of these two approaches is essential to understanding some of the fundamental aspects of life insurance such as the reason term insurance must be only temporary, the methods by which an insurer can provide permanent life insurance protection, and the source of life insurance policy reserves. As an alternative to the term versus cash value distinction, life insurance can be looked at from the perspective of whether there are guaranteed premiums throughout the premium-paying period or whether the policyowner or the insurer has some flexibility as to the premium to be paid. Several of the newer, nontraditional types of policies that are described later in this chapter have this type of flexibility.

The Term Insurance Approach

yearly renewable term insurance

Term insurance is the simplest form of insurance offered by life insurance companies. *Yearly renewable term insurance* provides protection for a period of one year only but permits the policyowner to renew the policy for successive periods of one year without the necessity of furnishing evidence of insurability. Term insurance can also be written for longer periods such as 5 or 10 years. In all cases, however, the right to renew is usually limited to a specified period or to a specified age. If the insured dies while the term policy is in force, the face amount is paid to the designated beneficiary. If the insured does not die during the period of protection, no benefits are payable at the expiration of the policy or on the insured's subsequent death.

To better understand the term insurance approach, the following discussion deals only with the net premium and does not include the insurer's operating expenses. The net premium for term insurance is determined by the death rate for the attained age of the individual involved. Subject to minor exceptions, the death rate increases with age, so the term insurance policy's net premium needed to pay death claims increases at the start of each new term. Moreover, because death rates rise at an increasing rate as ages increase, the net premium also rises at an increasing rate, much like a flight of steps with successively higher risers.

If the surviving members of the insured group continue to renew their term insurance, the steadily rising premiums necessary to cover death claims become increasingly unaffordable. As premiums increase, healthy individuals will tend to give up their protection, while those in poor health may sacrifice to renew their policies regardless of cost. This is a type of adverse selection, a term that was previously discussed. The withdrawal of the healthy members accelerates the increase in the death rate among the continuing members, and can produce death claims in excess of premiums unless ample margins are provided in the insurance company's net premium rates. In this event, the loss is borne by the insurance company, as the rates at which the policy can be renewed are usually guaranteed for the entire period of renewability. For this reason, companies offering term insurance on an individual basis limit the time during which the insurance can be renewed such as up to age 65. At these older ages, the premium rates are extremely high. However, many individuals need coverage that extends throughout their lifetime. This need led to the development of cash value or permanent life insurance as premiums become prohibitively expensive as age increases.

The Cash Value Approach

cash value life insurance

Cash value life insurance is just what the name implies—an approach of insurance under which premiums are sufficient not only to pay the insurer's mortality costs (death claims) and expenses but also to build a savings fund (or cash value) within the policy. That savings fund's growth depends in part on the premiums paid and is designed to result in the fund equaling the face amount of the policy by the last age shown in the mortality table such as age 100.

In many cash value policies, the annual premium does not increase from year to year but remains level throughout the premium-paying period. This does not mean that the policyowner must pay premiums as long as insurance protection is in force, but only that all required premiums will be of equal size.

As previously mentioned, net premiums tend to rise as a result of increasing death rates. If those premiums are leveled out, those paid in the early years of the contract must be more than sufficient to meet current death claims, while those paid in the later years generally will be less than adequate to meet incurred claims. This is a simple but significant concept for the practice of insurance.

In cash value life insurance, the net premiums beyond those needed for death claims in the early years of the contract create an accumulation that is held in trust[2] by the insurance company for the benefit of, and to the credit of, the policyowners. This accumulation is called a *reserve*, which is not merely a restriction on surplus in the accounting sense, but an amount that must be accumulated and maintained by the insurance company in order to meet definite future obligations. The manner in which the fund is to be accumulated and invested is strictly regulated by law, and the fund is usually referred to as *the legal reserve*. Technically, the reserve is a liability account of the insurance company, and not allocated to individual policies, but it may be viewed as an aggregate of individual savings accounts established for the benefit of the policyowners.[3]

A comparison of the net level premium for a type of cash value policy known as whole life with the net premium that would be required for a yearly renewable term policy is presented in figure 8-1. The age of issue in both cases is 25.

Assume that an annual net level premium of $6.09 per $1,000 of insurance is paid for the whole life policy as long as the insured lives. This premium is the actuarial equivalent of a series of increasing net premiums on the yearly renewable term basis, ranging from $1.16 per $1,000 of insurance at age 25 to $956.94 at age 99.

The mortality table used in this example assumes that everyone who survives to age 99 will die during the following year, producing a net premium at age 99 on the yearly renewable term basis equal to the face of the policy, less the interest earned on the premium during the year.

In figure 8-1, line CD, the net level premium for the whole life policy, bisects the curve AB, the rising net premiums for the term policy, between the ages of 53 and 54. The disparity between the areas bounded by AXC and BXD shows that excess net premiums (AXC) in the early years of a whole life contract (or, for that matter, any type of insurance contract except term) will offset the deficiency in the net premiums of the later years when the term insurance net premium is in the hundreds of dollars. In addition, with the aid of compound interest, the excess premium will accumulate a reserve equal to the face of the policy by the time the insured reaches the terminal age in the mortality table. In contrast, the yearly renewable term contract will have no reserve at the expiration of the contract. The risk (possibility of death) under a contract that provides protection for the whole of life is one "converging into a certainty," while the risk under a yearly renewable term policy (except for the final year in the mortality table) is a mere contingency—one that may or may not occur. Under a permanent or cash value life insurance contract, provision must be made for a death claim that is certain to occur, the only uncertainty being the time of its occurrence.

Under a cash value contract, the accumulated reserve becomes part of the face amount payable at the death of the insured. From the standpoint of the

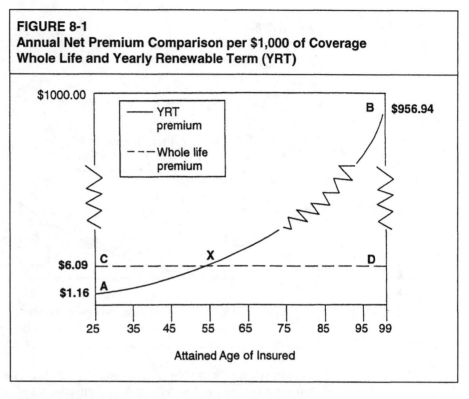

FIGURE 8-1
Annual Net Premium Comparison per $1,000 of Coverage
Whole Life and Yearly Renewable Term (YRT)

net amount at risk

insurance company, the effective amount of insurance is the difference between the face amount of the policy and the reserve. This amount is called the *net amount at risk*. As the reserve increases, the net amount at risk decreases if the face amount remains constant.

Because of the accumulated reserve, a $1,000 permanent life insurance policy does not provide $1,000 of insurance and the company is not "at risk" for the face amount of the policy. The amount of actual insurance is always the face amount, less the policyowner's total excess net premium payments, plus interest. From the insurance company's perspective, the accumulation is the reserve and, from the policyowner's perspective, it is the cash value, which is slightly less than the reserve in the early years. Because the excess net premium payments in the form of the cash value can be withdrawn by the policyowner at virtually any time, these excess net premium payments can be regarded as a savings or accumulation account. Thus, a cash value life insurance policy does not provide pure insurance but a combination of protection and cash values, the sum of which is always equal to the face amount of the policy. This is illustrated in figure 8-2 for a level-premium whole life policy of $1,000 issued at age 25.

The area below the curve represents the reserve under the contract or, as mentioned above, the policyowner's equity in the contract. The area above the

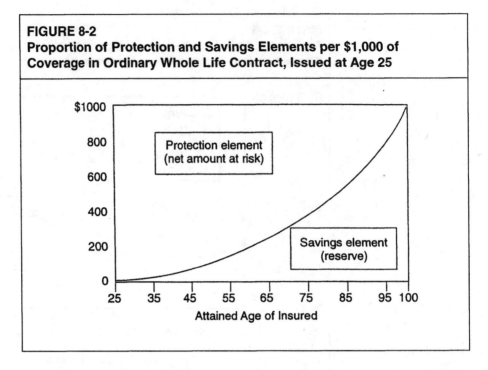

FIGURE 8-2
Proportion of Protection and Savings Elements per $1,000 of Coverage in Ordinary Whole Life Contract, Issued at Age 25

curve represents the company's net amount at risk and the policyowner's amount of protection. As the reserve increases, the amount of protection decreases. At any given age, the two combined will equal the face amount of the policy. By age 95, the protection element of the contract has become relatively minor, and by age 100—frequently, the end of the contract—it has completely disappeared. At age 100, the policyowner will receive $1,000, composed entirely of the policy's cash value element.

This combination of protection and accumulated cash values is characteristic of all permanent life insurance. Fundamentally, one contract differs from another only by the proportions in which the two elements are combined.

Yearly renewable term insurance is all protection with no cash value, while single premium life insurance is at the other end of the spectrum, with the highest cash values and the lowest net amount at risk. Accumulated cash values should be thought of as a degree of prefunding. Single premium policies are fully prefunded, and lower premium policies that develop cash values are only partially prefunded. The shorter the premium-paying period, the higher the relative proportion of cash value to death benefit.

The effect of the cash value or permanent life insurance plan is felt in nearly all operations of a life insurance company. The reserve accounts for a major portion of the aggregate assets of life insurance companies. The need to invest funds presents the life insurance institution with a challenge, but also enables the institution to materially contribute to economic expansion. The cash value makes the life insurance contract one of the most flexible and valuable contracts in existence, and one of the most acceptable forms of collateral for credit purposes. The cash value or permanent life insurance plan is most significant because it is the only practical arrangement to provide insurance protection for the entire life span, without the possibility that the cost will become prohibitive.

Effect of the Cash Value

- Serves as a major source of an insurer's investable funds
- Adds to the flexibility of the life insurance policy
- Is useful as collateral for credit purposes
- Makes permanent death protection possible

Guaranteed Premiums

In most types of life insurance policies, the periodic premiums paid throughout the premium-paying period of coverage are known in advance and guaranteed by the insurance company. However, these premiums are not necessarily level over time. For example, in a yearly renewable term policy, the annual premium increases are usually guaranteed by the insurer at the issue of the contract. A similar guarantee is provided with respect to the renewal premiums for 5-year, 10-year, and other renewable term policies. Even in cash value policies, the annual premiums can be both nonlevel and guaranteed. For example, *modified whole life insurance* guarantees a level premium for the first few policy years, with a higher guaranteed level premium thereafter.

modified whole life insurance

Flexible Premiums

In several newer types of life insurance policies, some of which are described later in this chapter, the premium is flexible, either at the option of the policyowner or of the insurance company. For example, in *reentry term insurance*, the insurer uses one schedule of renewal premiums if the insured can periodically prove his or her continuing insurability, and a higher schedule of renewal premiums if the insured's health has declined so that he or she no longer qualifies for the lower rate. In universal life insurance—a cash value, permanent type of policy—the policyowner can elect to pay, within limits, more or less than the target premium established at the issue of the contract. In current assumption whole life insurance, the insurer redetermines the premium periodically based on experience and assumptions for mortality, expenses, and interest. The growth of the policy's savings element is influenced by the modified premium of the universal life policy or the redetermined premium rates of the current assumption whole life insurance.

reentry term insurance

TRADITIONAL TYPES OF LIFE INSURANCE

There are three traditional types of life insurance:

- term insurance
- whole life insurance
- endowments

Term Insurance

As described earlier, term insurance provides life insurance protection for a limited period only. The face amount of the policy is payable if the insured dies during the specified period, and nothing is paid if the insured survives.

Term insurance may be regarded as temporary insurance and, in principle, is more nearly comparable to property and liability insurance contracts than any other life insurance contract. If a person insures his or her life under a 5-year term contract, no obligation is incurred by the insurance company unless the death of the insured occurs within the term. All premiums paid for the term protection are considered to be fully earned by the company by the end of the term, whether or not a loss has occurred, and the policy has no further value.

The premium for term insurance is initially relatively low, even though it includes a relatively high expense loading and an allowance for adverse selection. Premiums can be low because most term contracts do not cover the period of old age when death is most probable and when the cost of insurance is high.

Renewability

Many term insurance contracts contain an option to renew for a limited number of additional periods of term insurance, usually of the same length. The simplest policy of this type is the yearly renewable term policy, which is a one-year term contract renewable for successive periods of one year each. Longer term contracts, such as 10-year term, may also be renewable.

renewability

Renewability refers to the right to renew the contract without a medical examination or other evidence of insurability. When the term policy contains no renewal privilege, or when it can be renewed only upon evidence of insurability satisfactory to the company, the insured may find that coverage cannot be continued as long as needed. Because of poor health, a hazardous occupation, or some other reason, the insured might be unable to secure a renewal of the contract or to obtain any other form of life insurance. The renewal feature protects the insurability of the insured.

Under a term insurance policy, the premium increases with each renewal and is based on the insured's attained age at the time of the renewal. Within each contract period, however, the premium is level. The schedule of renewal rates is included in the original contract, and the company cannot change these rates while the contract remains in force. As a safeguard against adverse selection, companies historically did not permit renewals to carry the coverage beyond a specified age such as 65. However, renewals that continue the coverage to later ages are now commonly available.

Convertibility

convertibility

A term policy might be convertible, permitting the policyowner to convert, or exchange, the term contract for permanent insurance within a specified time frame, without evidence of insurability. This *convertibility* feature serves the needs of those who want permanent insurance but are temporarily unable to afford the higher premiums required for whole life and other types of cash value life insurance. Convertibility is also useful when the policyowner desires to postpone the final decision as to the type of permanent insurance until a later date when, for some reason, it may be possible to make a more informed choice. Thus, convertible term insurance provides a way to obtain temporary insurance with the option to purchase permanent insurance.

The conversion from term to permanent insurance may be effective as of the date of the conversion or as of the original date of the term policy. If the term policy is converted as of the current date, conversion is usually referred to as the *attained age method* because the current age determines the premium rate. A conversion using the original date of the term policy is referred to as the *original age method* or a *retroactive conversion*. When the conversion is effective as of the original date, the premium rate for the permanent contract is that which would have been paid had the new contract been taken out originally, and the policy form is that which would have been issued originally. The advantage of the lower premium is obvious, but in many cases, the contract issued at the original date contains actuarial assumptions or other features that are more favorable than those incorporated in current policies.

Attained Age vs. Retroactive Conversion

- Attained age method: new premium is based on insured's age at time of conversion; policy form is one that the insurer issues at that time.
- Retroactive (original age) method: new premium is based on the insured's age when the term insurance was first taken out; policyowner must make a lump-sum payment equal to the difference in the reserves or premiums plus interest on the old and new policies; policy form is one that the insurer issued when the term insurance was first taken out.

Offsetting the advantages of the original age method, however, is the financial adjustment—a payment by the policyowner to the company—which may be quite substantial if the term policy has been in force for several years. The financial adjustment can be computed on a variety of bases, but many companies specify that the payment will be the larger of (1) the difference in the reserves under the policies being exchanged or (2) the difference in the premiums paid on the term policy and those that would have been paid on the permanent plan, with interest on the difference at a stipulated rate. The purpose of the financial adjustment, regardless of how it is computed, is to place the insurance company in the same financial position as it would have been in had the permanent contract been originally issued.

Nonlevel Term Insurance

The preceding discussion has presumed that the amount of insurance is level or uniform throughout the term of the policy. However, the amount of insurance may increase or decrease throughout the period of protection. As a matter of fact, a substantial—if not predominant—portion of term insurance provides systematic decreases in the amount of insurance from year to year. This type of term insurance, appropriately called *decreasing term insurance*, may be written as a separate contract, a rider to a new or existing contract, or as an integral part of a combination contract. Decreasing term insurance is often used to provide the funds necessary to pay off a mortgage loan.

decreasing term insurance

Increasing term insurance can be provided on a year-to-year basis through the operation of a common provision in cash value life insurance policies, referred to as the *fifth dividend option*. Increasing term insurance can help meet families' needs for the death benefit to increase with inflation or salary increases and also has business applications that will be discussed in chapter 10.

fifth dividend option

Areas of Usefulness

Term insurance is suitable when either (1) the need for protection is purely temporary, or (2) the need for protection is permanent, but the policyowner temporarily cannot afford the premiums for permanent insurance. In the first case, term insurance is the complete answer, but it should be renewable in the event that the temporary need extends over a longer period than was originally anticipated. The second case requires that the policy be convertible. The conversion privilege spans the gap between the need for permanent insurance and the financial ability to meet the need. Thus, the renewable and convertible features serve quite different functions and, ideally, should be incorporated in all term policies.

Whole Life Insurance

In contrast with term insurance, which pays benefits only if the insured dies during a specified period of years, *whole life insurance* provides for the payment

whole life insurance

of the policy's face amount at the death of the insured, regardless of when death occurs. This characteristic—protection for the whole of life—gives the insurance its name. The expression has no reference to the manner in which the premiums are paid, only to the duration of the protection. If the premiums are to be paid throughout the insured's lifetime, the insurance is known as *ordinary life*; if premiums are to be paid only during a specified period, the insurance is designated as *limited-payment life*.

Characteristics of Whole Life Insurance

Whole life insurance offers permanent protection and cash values, and it can be either participating or nonparticipating.

Permanent Protection. The protection afforded by the whole life contract is permanent—the term never expires, and the policy never has to be renewed or converted. If policyowners continue to pay premiums or pay up their policies, they have protection for as long as they live, regardless of their health; eventually, the face amount of the policy will be paid. This is a valuable right because virtually all people need some insurance as long as they live, if only to pay last-illness and funeral expenses. In most cases, the need is much greater than that.

In one sense, whole life can be regarded as an endowment. As discussed later in this chapter, an endowment insurance contract pays the face amount of the policy, whether the insured dies prior to the endowment maturity date or survives to the end of the period. If age 100 is considered to be the end of the endowment period—as well as the terminal age in the mortality table—then a whole life policy is equivalent to an endowment contract that pays the face amount as a death claim if the insured dies before age 100 or as a matured endowment if he or she survives to age 100.

Cash Value or Accumulation Element. As level premium permanent insurance, whole life insurance accumulates a reserve that gradually reaches a substantial level and eventually equals the face amount of the policy. The contract emphasizes protection, but it also accumulates a cash value that can be used to accomplish a variety of purposes.

Cash values are not generally available during the first year or two of the insurance contract because of the insurer's cost of putting the business on the books. Common exceptions are single-premium policies and some durations of limited-payment whole life policies where initial premiums exceed all first-year expenses incurred to create the policy and maintain policy reserves. The cash values that accumulate under whole life insurance can be utilized as cash surrender values, paid-up insurance, or extended term insurance. These *nonforfeiture options* are discussed in chapter 9 along with options available for borrowing cash values.

Participating versus Nonparticipating. Whole life policies can be issued as *nonparticipating or non-dividend-paying policies.* Historically, nonparticipating policies were associated with stock life insurance companies. The insurance company retains all gains from favorable experience for its shareholders.

Whole life policies issued as *participating policies* anticipate charging a small extra margin in the fixed premium with the intention of returning part of the premium in the form of policyowner dividends. This approach allows the insurance company to maintain a stronger contingency margin and still adjust the cost downward after periods of coverage have been evaluated. Policyowner dividends are based on favorable experience such as higher-than-expected investment returns or lower-than-expected mortality and/or expenses for operations.

Although participating policies were originally offered by mutual life insurers, the appeal of policyowner dividends prompted stock life insurance companies to offer participating policies. Many stock life insurance companies offer a choice of both participating and nonparticipating policies. Almost all policies sold by mutual companies are participating policies. Current assumption whole life policies, described later, are nonparticipating policies sold by many stock companies. In these policies, periodic redeterminations of premiums allow the policyowner to share in the insurer's favorable mortality, expense, and investment results.

Policyowner dividends are generally declared annually, based on the insurance company's experience. Investment results usually account for the largest portion of dividends. The amount of dividends cannot be guaranteed, and it is illegal for an agent to present projections of future dividends as if they were guaranteed or certain. If insurance company experience turns unfavorable, policyowner dividends may decline, or they may cease altogether. The policyowner chooses among the dividend options, which are discussed in the next chapter.

Types of Whole Life Insurance

There are two types of whole life insurance: ordinary life insurance and limited-payment life insurance.

Ordinary Life Insurance. *Ordinary life insurance* (also called continuous premium whole life) is a type of whole life insurance with premiums that are assumed to be paid until the insured's death. It is desirable to define ordinary life insurance in this way because, in an increasing number of cases, policyowners purchase life insurance without the intention of paying premiums for the life of the insured. In many cases, the insurance is purchased with the intention of using dividends to pay up the insurance prior to the life expectancy of the insured. In other cases, the plan may be to eventually surrender the insurance for an annuity or for a reduced amount of paid-up insurance. Ordinary life should not be envisioned as insurance on which the policyowner must pay premiums for a lifetime, or even into the insured's extreme old age. Rather, it should be viewed as a contract that provides permanent protection for the lowest total premium outlay and some flexibility to meet changing needs and circumstances for both long-lived persons and those with average-duration lifetimes. Ordinary life is the most basic lifelong coverage any life insurance company offers.

Because the premium rate for an ordinary life contract is calculated assuming that premiums will be payable throughout the insured's life, the lowest premium rate for any type of whole life policy is produced. Naturally, the longer the period over which the premium payment is spread, the lower each periodic premium will be. However, lower premiums also result in lower cash values than other types of whole life policies. Nevertheless, many financial advisers believe that the ordinary life contract offers the optimal combination of protection and savings.

Limited-payment insurance contracts provide benefits that justify the higher premium rates. If, however, the policyowner's objective is to secure the maximum amount of permanent insurance protection per dollar of premium outlay, then his or her purposes will be best served by the ordinary life contract. Its moderate cost can bring the policy within reach of most purchasers except those in the older age brackets.

limited-payment life insurance

Limited-Payment Life Insurance. *Limited-payment life insurance* is a type of whole life insurance for which premiums are limited by contract to a specified number of years. The extreme end of the limited-payment policies spectrum is the single-premium whole life policy. However, few people can afford the premium or are willing to pay that much in advance.

The limitation in limited-payment policies can be expressed in terms of the number of annual premiums or of the age beyond which premiums will not be required. Policies with premiums limited by number usually stipulate one, 5, 7, 10, 15, 20, 25, or 30 annual payments. These policies are usually referred to as, for example, 20-pay life. The greater the number of premiums payable, naturally, the more closely the contract approaches the ordinary life design. For those who prefer to limit their premium payments to a period measured by a terminal age, companies make policies available that are paid up at a specified age—typically, 60, 65, or 70. These policies are often referred to, for example, as life paid up at 65 or more simply, life at 65. The objective of these age-related premium horizons is to confine premium payment to the insured's working years.

Because the value of a limited-payment whole life contract at the date of issue is precisely the same as that of a contract purchased on the ordinary life basis, and it is presumed that there will be fewer premium payments under the limited-payment policy, it follows that each premium must be larger than the comparable premium under an ordinary life contract. Moreover, the fewer the premiums specified or the shorter the premium-paying period, the higher each premium will be. However, the higher premiums are offset by greater cash and other surrender values. Thus, the limited-payment policy will provide a larger fund for use in an emergency and will accumulate a larger fund for retirement purposes than will an ordinary life contract issued at the same age. On the other hand, if death takes place within the first several years after issuance of the contract, the total premiums paid under the limited-payment policy will exceed those payable under an ordinary life policy. The comparatively long-lived policyowner, however, will pay considerably less in premiums under the limited-payment plan than on the ordinary life basis.

The limited-payment policy contains the same surrender options, dividend options, settlement options, and other features of ordinary life policies.

It is important to differentiate between a limited-payment policy, which guarantees paid-up status at the end of the premium-paying period, and a vanishing premium approach, which uses policyowner dividends to pay all of the premiums as soon as they are adequate to do so. Vanishing premium approaches have been sold much more frequently than limited-payment policies over the last decade. Dividends are not guaranteed and may decline in the future, and if dividends are inadequate to pay the premiums under the vanishing premium approach, the policyowner will have to resume actual premium payments out of pocket or let the policy lapse. There is no guarantee that so-called vanishing premiums will actually vanish or, if they do vanish, that they will never reappear.

Endowment Policies

endowment life insurance

Endowment life insurance policies are a variation of cash value life insurance. They not only provide level death benefits and cash values that increase with duration so that a policy's cash value equals its death benefit at maturity, but they also allow the purchaser to specify the policy's maturity date. Among the wide variety of endowments available are 10-, 15-, 20-, 25-, 30-, 35-, and 40-year endowments (or longer), or the maturity date can be a specific age of the insured such as 55, 65, 70, or older. As mentioned earlier, whole life insurance is identical in design to an endowment at age 100, when the cash value equals the death beneift.

The endowment contract was designed to provide a death benefit during an accumulation period that is equal to the target accumulation amount. Purchasing an endowment policy with a face amount equal to the desired accumulation amount ensures that the funds will be available regardless of whether the insured survives to the target date. In the past, the policy was popular for policyowners who were beyond the chronological midpoint of their careers and sought accumulation for retirement or other objectives. During the late 1970s and early 1980s, when inflation was in double digits, consumer demand shifted from long-term fixed-dollar contracts, including nearly all forms of life insurance, particularly endowment policies.

Although endowment contracts were readily available, sales were declining in the United States even before the 1984 federal income tax law change eliminated the tax-advantaged buildup of most endowment policies' cash values. Congress was concerned that life insurance policies (especially endowments) with high cash values relative to their death benefit amounts were being used as tax-advantaged accumulation vehicles by the wealthy.

Since 1984, sales of new endowment contracts have been very limited. While contracts are still available from a few insurers, most new sales are for policies used in tax-qualified plans where the tax treatment is controlled by other factors.

Outside of the United States, especially in countries with high savings rates, the endowment policy is still quite successful and widely purchased to accumulate funds for a variety of purposes including to fund retirement or children's higher education.

VARIATIONS OF TRADITIONAL POLICIES

Numerous variations of traditional life insurance policies have been developed in recent years. Some of these are

- current assumption whole life insurance
- variable life insurance
- universal life insurance
- variable universal life insurance
- joint-life insurance

Current Assumption Whole Life Insurance

current assumption whole life insurance

A *current assumption whole life insurance* (CAWL) policy is a whole life policy with a premium charge that varies with changes in the insurer's actual or anticipated mortality, expense, and interest earnings experience. Whatever the premium charge is at a given time, that premium is a fixed obligation for the policyowner. If the premium is not paid, the policy will lapse after the grace period. CAWL policies are usually issued on a nonparticipating basis.

As each premium is paid, it is added to the policyowner's accumulation account. An expense charge and a mortality charge to cover the policy's share of current death claims are deducted. Also, an interest credit is added to the account. These charges and the credit are based on current mortality, expense, and interest assumptions, subject to a guaranteed maximum charge for mortality and expenses and a guaranteed minimum interest rate credit. The cash surrender value of the policy at any point is equal to the value of the accumulation account minus a surrender charge that gradually reduces to zero after a specified time such as after the first 15 or 20 years of the policy's life.

CAWL policies have been marketed in low-premium and high-premium designs. However, both reflect the general features described above. With the low-premium design, sometimes called interest-sensitive or indeterminate premium whole life, the policyowner initially pays a low-level premium in comparison to that paid for a traditional nonparticipating whole life policy. This premium is guaranteed for the first few (generally 3 or 5) policy years. At the end of the guarantee period, the insurer redetermines the premium required to keep the CAWL policy in force under then-current assumptions, given the amount already available in the accumulation account. Redetermination of the required premium will again occur on specified policy anniversary dates or at specified intervals such as every 5 years.

If on a particular redetermination date, the premium charge increases because anticipated experience assumptions have worsened, the policyowner has the option of paying the new, higher premium and keeping the policy's death benefit unchanged. Alternatively, he or she may continue to pay the old, lower premium and accept a reduction in the death benefit. If the premium charge is reduced because assumptions have improved, the policyowner may pay the new, lower premium with no change to the death benefit. Alternatively, he or she may elect to continue paying the old, higher premium with the same death benefit as formerly but with a more rapid buildup of the accumulation account. The policyowner may even have the option, if he or she can provide satisfactory evidence of insurability, of continuing to pay the old, higher premium and increasing the policy's death benefit. Therefore, with a low-premium CAWL policy, changes in current mortality, expense, and, especially, interest assumptions can affect the policy's premium, cash value, and death benefit.

With the high-premium design of CAWL insurance, sometimes called vanishing premium whole life insurance, the policyowner pays a relatively high level premium compared to that of traditional whole life insurance. The high premium charge causes a much more rapid buildup of the accumulation account

---

**Distinctive Features of
Current Assumption Whole Life Insurance**

- Usually nonparticipating, but favorable experience may reduce or eliminate premium charges
- Guaranteed maximum premium based on maximum mortality and expense charges and minimum interest rate credit
- Premiums must be paid when due or policy lapses
- Low-premium design—premiums redetermined periodically as current conditions warrant
- High premium design—policy may reach paid-up status for a time, perhaps even permanently

than would occur in the low-premium design. If the insurer's mortality, expense, and interest results are favorable enough, the accumulation account will grow to an amount that eventually equals or exceeds the net single premium needed to pay up the policy under then-current assumptions. At that time, the policyowner can elect to stop paying premiums. However, unlike a traditional paid-up whole life policy, which guarantees that premiums will never have to be paid again, the CAWL does not guarantee that premiums will not have to be resumed if experience and assumptions worsen sufficiently. Indeed, the CAWL policy does not guarantee that premiums will ever completely vanish.

Variable Life Insurance

variable life insurance

Variable life insurance was the first life insurance policy designed to shift the uncertainty of investment gains or losses to policyowners. This product had a long and expensive gestation period. It not only had to run the gauntlet of state insurance department approvals but it also needed, and finally acquired after many years of negotiations, approval by the Securities and Exchange Commission (SEC).

A variable life insurance policy provides no guarantee of either interest rate or minimum cash value. Theoretically, the cash value can go down to zero, and if so, the policy will terminate. As the SEC pointed out, in order for policyowners to gain the additional benefit of better-than-expected investment returns, they also must assume all the risk of investment losses. Consequently, the SEC required that variable life policies be registered and that all sales be subject to the requirements imposed on other registered securities. In other words, policy sales may be made only after the prospective purchaser has read the policy prospectus. The SEC also required that the insurance company be registered as an investment company and that all sales agents be registered with the SEC for the specific purpose of variable life insurance policy sales. Agents who sell variable life insurance policies must be licensed as both life insurance agents and securities agents.

Investment Choices

Variable life insurance policies give the policyowner several investment options into which the cash value can be directed. The policyowner is free to put all of the funds into one of these choices or to distribute the funds among the options in whatever proportions he or she desires. Some insurance companies have more than a dozen funds to choose from. There are usually a variety of stock funds, including growth stock funds, income stock funds, balanced stock funds, and international stock funds. Bond fund offerings include different durations and different types of issuers (large corporations, small corporations, state governments, and the federal government) as well as Government National Mortgage Association (GNMAs) funds and collateralized mortgage obligations (CMOs).

In addition, many insurance companies offer a managed fund as one of the portfolio choices. The policyowner can put all of the policy funds in a managed portfolio fund and have the investment allocation decisions made by a professional money manager working for the insurance company. This option appeals to policyowners who do not want to spend a lot of time learning about the market and making investment decisions.

Some insurance companies have allied with large mutual fund groups that make their entire range of mutual funds available. These agreements enable smaller life insurance companies to gain access to the administrative services already in place in these large mutual fund family groups.

By allowing the policyowner to direct the policy cash value, the policyowner becomes the portfolio director, within limits. Obviously, the policyowner has no control over the selection of assets and the timing of trades. Those investment decisions are made by the insurance company's portfolio management team. With variable life insurance, the policyowner participates in portfolio investment and, consequently, benefits directly from better-than-expected results and bears the risk of poor investment performance. The results of the investment performance are credited directly to the policy's cash values.

Ability to Tolerate Investment Fluctuations. Individuals who are already experienced in equity investments are quite comfortable with the variable life insurance policy. However, this policy is subject to daily portfolio fluctuations and can provoke great anxiety in individuals who are not accustomed to or risk tolerant enough to be comfortable with market value fluctuations.

Market volatility is part of the challenge of marketing variable life policies. Many life insurance agents are reluctant to sell a policy that depends on the policyowner's investment decisions for its success. Agents are afraid that some purchasers will expect the life insurance agent to offer investment advice.

A variable life policy is a market-driven product, and its popularity, to some extent, is influenced by general investment market conditions. This type of policy becomes more acceptable to consumers after a long period of market increases and falls out of favor when the market experiences a general price decline.

Insurance Charges

If favorable investment choices are made, variable life insurance enables the policyowner's money to work harder. But variable life insurance contracts are not exclusively investments. They are, in fact, life insurance contracts, and they include mortality charges for the death benefits. Consequently, the return on the invested funds within a variable life insurance contract will never be equal to the return on a separate investment fund that invests in assets of a similar type and quality but that does not provide a death benefit.

Variable life insurance is not a short-term investment vehicle. The combination of sales load, mortality charges, and surrender charges will significantly reduce any potential gains in the policy's early years.

Linkage of Death Benefits with Investment Performance

Because the primary objective of life insurance is to provide death benefits, it makes sense to link superior investment performance with increases in the death benefit level. Theoretically, this is a way of keeping up with inflation. In fact, studies indicate that such a linkage would more than keep pace with inflation. However, there is an important caveat. Although investment performance in equities tends to equal or exceed inflation in the economy over the long term, the correlation is as strong in the short term. In other words, it is possible for inflation to exceed increases in the investment performance for short durations of time such as 2 or 3 years. This is another reason to regard life insurance as a long-term financial security purchase and not as a short-term investment.

There are two ways to link the policy's death benefit to the associated portfolio's investment performance, the level additions method and the constant ratio method, discussed later. Regardless of the linkage design, all of the contracts provide a minimum guaranteed death benefit. Also, all have the purchaser select a target level of investment performance as a benchmark against which actual investment performance will be measured. Performance in excess of the target level will fund incremental increases in the death benefit; performance below the target amount requires downward adjustments in the death benefits to make up for the deficit.

Usually, variable life policies have positive excess investment earnings in the early years of the contract, and provide incremental increases in the death benefit before the investment earnings drop below the target rate. Most variable life

---

Distinctive Features of Variable Life Insurance

- Policyowner selects the types of investments into which the savings element will be directed
- No minimum guaranteed crediting rate or minimum cash value
- Can be sold only with a prospectus
- Guaranteed minimum death benefit equal to the policy's original face amount
- Above that minimum, the death benefit depends on the investment performance of the policyowner-selected separate account(s)
- Policy loans allowed, but to a smaller percentage of the cash value than in traditional contracts
- Contains usual range of nonforfeiture options

---

insurance policies issued since 1976 have experienced investment earnings over the target rate more frequently and for longer durations than they have experienced investment earnings below the target rate. There is no guarantee that this will always be true, but the expectation is that overall investment earnings will exceed the target amount over the bulk of the policy duration.

Level Additions Model. The level additions model uses investment returns in excess of the target rate to purchase paid-up insurance added to the base policy. The face amount or death benefit will rise as long as investment performance equals or exceeds the target rate. This model does not cause as rapid an increase or decrease as the constant ratio method of linking the policy's death benefit to investment performance. The strength of the level addition design is that it does not require an ever-increasing investment return to support incremental increases in death benefits. Additional coverage is added more slowly, but it is more easily supported once it is added. Similarly, downward adjustments in death benefits are less rapid, and they are less likely to accelerate downward in future years. Furthermore, policies that use the level additions design provide a minimum face value guarantee equal to the amount of coverage when the policy was first purchased.

Constant Ratio Method. The constant ratio method also uses the excess investment earnings as a net single premium to purchase a paid-up additional amount of coverage. Under this method, the paid-up additional coverage is not a level amount, but rather a decreasing benefit amount. The policy is designed to maintain a ratio between the death benefit and the policy reserve that prevents the investment element of the contract from becoming excessive relative to the protection element. Under this policy design, more volatile increments are added to or subtracted from the contract as investment performance differs from the target amount. Like the level additions model, this design has a minimum death benefit guarantee equal to the initial face amount of the policy.

Policy Cash Values

Policy premiums paid under variable life insurance contracts are often subject to an administrative charge. The balance of the premium payment goes into the cash value account, from which mortality charges are deducted. The actual value of the cash component is determined by the net asset value of the separate account funds that make up the policy portfolio. The cash value of a variable life policy fluctuates daily. Each day's net asset value is based on the closing price for the investments in the portfolio on that trading day.

As with traditional life insurance contracts, the policyowner has access to the cash value via policy loans. Variable life insurance policies usually limit maximum policy loans to a slightly smaller percentage of the total cash value than is traditionally available in whole life policies. Policy loans may be repaid at any time in part or in full, but there is no requirement that policy loans be repaid in cash at any time during the existence of the life insurance contract. Interest accrues on any unpaid loan balance. As in any other form of whole life policy, outstanding policy loans under a variable life insurance policy reduce the death benefit payable. The policy loan is always fully secured by the remaining cash value in the policy. Whenever the outstanding loans plus accrued interest equal the remaining cash value, the net cash value becomes zero and the policy terminates.

The net cash value in the contract is also closely related to the nonforfeiture options available under the policy. Variable life insurance contracts provide the same range of nonforfeiture options as do traditional whole life policies. The net cash surrender value may be obtained by surrendering the contract to the insurance company, or the net cash value may be applied as a single premium to purchase either a reduced amount of paid-up insurance or the same amount of extended term insurance. The duration of the extended term insurance will be the longest period of coverage for the same death benefit amount that can be obtained from the insurance company for the policy's net cash value.

Prospectus

Variable life insurance policies must be sold with an accompanying prospectus. The prospectus mandated by the SEC is similar in many respects to the prospectus required for new stock issues. This prospectus is a full and accurate disclosure of all the contract provisions, including expenses, surrender charges, and investment options. While the prospectus is a lengthy and detailed document that most purchasers are reluctant to read, it is an important source of information not available elsewhere.

Expense Information. The prospectus has very detailed information about all of the expense charges levied by the insurance company against variable life insurance contracts. These charges include commissions paid to soliciting agents, state premium taxes, administrative charges, collection charges, and any fees for specific future transactions.

In addition, the prospectus sets forth the manner in which charges are made against the asset account to cover the cost of insurance under the contract. This is usually referred to in the prospectus as the cost-of-insurance charge. The prospectus specifies exactly what rate will be used to determine cost-of-insurance charges and explicitly specifies if there is any maximum rate above the intended rate. The prospectus also explains the manner in which charges are levied against the separate account itself—essentially the fees associated with managing the various investment accounts from which the policyowner may choose. Part of that charge is always some specified percentage (usually less than one percent) of the assets in the separate accounts themselves. There also may be specific charges to establish and maintain the trusts necessary for managing those assets.

Surrender Charges. The charge applicable to policy surrenders is clearly spelled out in the prospectus. In most cases, this information is set forth in a schedule, listing each policy year with its applicable percentage surrender charge. Surrender charges are applicable only if the policy is surrendered for its cash value, allowed to lapse, or (under some contracts) adjusted to provide a lower death benefit. Surrender charges are commonly levied during the first 10 to 15 years of the contract.

Investment Portfolio Information. The prospectus sets forth the objectives of each of the available investment funds and a record of their historical performance. There is detailed information on the current holdings of each of the available portfolios, usually supplemented by information about trades of equities or debt instruments over the previous 12 months. Further information is given about earnings during that same period of time and usually for longer intervals of prior performance if those portfolio funds have been in existence long enough to give investment results for trades over 5 or 10 years. Any investment restrictions applicable to these portfolios as indicated in the trust instruments themselves are fully disclosed.

The prospectus also includes projections of future performance under the contract if portfolio funds generate an assumed level of investment earnings over the projected interval. Under SEC regulations, the permissible rates of return that can be projected are the gross annual rates after tax charges but before any other deductions at 0, 4, 6, 8, 10, or 12 percent. The insurer decides which of those permissible rates to project.

Universal Life Insurance

universal life insurance

Universal life insurance was the first variation of whole life insurance to offer truly flexible premiums. These policies shift some of the possibility of investment fluctuations to the policyowner because the premium is based on interest rates in excess of the guaranteed interest rate, but they do not allow the policyowner to direct the investment portfolio. Two other features of universal life insurance policies are: (1) the policyowner's ability to withdraw part of the cash value without having the withdrawal treated as a policy loan and (2) the choice of either a level death benefit design or an increasing death benefit design.

Flexible Premiums

Universal life insurance has the unusual feature of completely flexible premiums after the first year—the only time a minimum level of premium payments for a universal life policy is rigidly required. As usual, the first year's premium can be arranged on a monthly, quarterly, semiannual, or annual basis. The insurance company requires only that a minimum specified level of first-year premium payments be equaled or exceeded. After the first policy year, the policyowner can determine how much premium to pay and even whether or not to pay premiums with one constraint.

The one constraint regarding premium payments is that the aggregate premiums paid, regardless of their timing, must be adequate to cover the costs of maintaining the policy. Consider the analogy of an automobile's gas tank, where premium payments are synonymous with filling the tank. Premium payments (tank refills) can be made frequently to keep the tank nearly full at all times. With that approach, the automobile is never likely to run out of gas. The same automobile, however, can operate on a just-in-time philosophy, where premium payments (or additional fuel) of minimal amounts are made only as frequently as necessary to keep the policy (the car) from running out of gas.

Under a universal life insurance policy, if the policy's cash value is allowed to drop too low (the cash value is inadequate to cover the next 60 days of expense and mortality charges), the policy will lapse. If an additional premium payment is made soon enough, the policy may be restarted without a formal reinstatement process. However, if an injection of additional funds comes after the end of the grace period, the insurance company may force the policyowner to request a formal reinstatement before accepting any further premium payments.

Prefunding

The higher the amount or proportion of prefunding through premium payments, the more investment earnings will be credited to the policy and utilized to cover mortality and administrative costs. All premium suggestions are based on some assumed level of investment earnings, and the policyowner assumes the possibility that actual investment earnings will be less than necessary to support the suggested premium. Even though investment earnings cannot go below the guaranteed rate, a long-term shortfall may necessitate either an increase in premiums or a reduction in coverage at some future point.

Under traditional contracts with cash values, the only mechanism for returning policy overfunding in the early years is policyowner dividends. With universal life policies, however, the accumulations from prefunding are credited to the policy's cash value and are quite visible to the policyowner. The earnings rates applied to those accumulations are also clearly visible as they fluctuate with current economic conditions. This open disclosure for universal life policies eliminates some of the doubts about fair treatment often directed at whole life insurance.

Withdrawal Feature

As previously noted, another feature of universal life policies is the policyowner's ability to make partial withdrawals from the policy's cash value without incurring any indebtedness. In other words, money can be taken out of the policy's cash value just like a withdrawal from a savings account. There is no obligation to repay those funds, nor is there interest incurred on the amount withdrawn. Withdrawals do affect the policy's future earnings because the fund still intact to earn interest for future crediting periods is reduced by the amount of the withdrawal. The effect of the withdrawal on the death benefit depends on the type of death benefit in force, as explained below.

Target Premium Amount

Nearly every universal life policy is issued with a target premium amount. The target amount is the suggested premium to be paid on a level basis throughout the contract's duration or for a shorter period of time if a limited-payment approach was originally intended to fund the policy. The target premium amount is merely a suggestion and carries no liability if it is inadequate to maintain the contract to any duration, much less to the end of life.

In some insurance companies, the target premium is actually sufficient to keep the policy in force (under relatively conservative investment return assumptions) through age 95 or 100 and to pay the cash value equivalent to the death benefit amount if the insured survives either to age 95 or 100. On the other hand, some companies with a more aggressive marketing stance have chosen lower target premiums, which may not be adequate to carry the policy in force to advanced ages even under more generous (if questionable) assumptions of higher investment returns over future policy years. If, in fact, the investment return credited to the policy's cash value falls short of the amount assumed in deriving the target premium, the policy may essentially run out of gas before age 95 or 100. In these cases, the policyowner will be faced with two options: (1) to increase the premium level or (2) to reduce the death benefit amount. Neither one of these options is necessarily desirable, but they are the only acceptable ways under the contract's provisions to correct for unfulfilled optimistic assumptions about investment returns in the contract's early years.

Some insurance companies have introduced a secondary guarantee associated with their target premium. These companies have pledged contractually to keep the policy in force for, say, 15 to 20 years and to pay the full death benefit as long as the premium has been paid in an amount equal to or greater than the target premium amount at each suggested premium-payment interval. Even these guarantees do not extend to age 95 or 100, but they ensure that the premium suggested as a target will be adequate to provide the coverage for at least as long as the guarantee period.

The flexible features of universal life premiums allow policyowners to make additional premium payments above any target premium amount at any time and without prior negotiation or agreement with the insurance company. The only limitation on paying excess premiums is associated with the income tax definition of life insurance, which is discussed in chapter 10. However, the insurance company reserves the right to refuse additional premium payments under a universal life policy if the policy's cash value is large enough to encroach on the legal upper limit allowed for cash values relative to the level of death benefit granted in the policy.

The premium flexibility also allows the policyowner to skip premium payments, again without any prior negotiation or notification, or to pay premium amounts lower than the target premium suggested at the time of purchase. The lower limitations on premium payments have two constraints. The first is that nearly every company specifies a minimum acceptable amount for any single payment. The second is that there must be enough cash value in the contract to meet the mortality and administrative charges for the next 60 days. In other words, if the tank is running on empty, more premium is required.

Death Benefit Type

Universal life insurance gives policyowners a choice between level death benefits and increasing death benefits. The level death benefit design is much like the traditional whole life design. When the death benefit stays constant and the cash value increases over the duration of the contract, the net amount at risk, or the protection element, decreases. The one new aspect of a level death benefit design under universal life policies is not really a function of universal life itself but a function of the tax law definition of life insurance requiring that a specified proportion of the death benefit is derived from the net amount at risk. Whenever the cash value in the contract gets high enough that this proportion is no longer satisfied, the universal life policy starts increasing the death benefit, even though the contract is called a level death benefit contract. This phenomenon does not occur until ages beyond normal retirement, and it is not a significant aspect of this design.

The increasing death benefit design is a modification that was introduced with universal life policies. Under this approach, there is always a constant net amount at risk that is superimposed over the policy's cash value, whatever it may be. As the cash value increases, so does the total death benefit payable under the contract. A reduction in the cash value will reduce the death benefit. This design

---

Distinctive Features of Universal Life Insurance

- Premium flexibility
- Market rates of interest credited
- Unbundling of cost elements
- Partial withdrawals allowed
- Differential interest crediting rates if policy loans are outstanding
- "Back-end" expense loads in case of surrender
- Choice of death benefit designs (level or increasing)

pays the policy's stated face amount plus its cash value at the insured's death. Policies with an increasing death benefit design overcome the criticism of whole life policies that the death benefit consists partially of the contract's cash value. By selecting the increasing death benefit option under a universal life policy, the policyowner is ensuring that the death benefit will be composed of the cash value and an at-risk portion equal to the original face value of the contract.

Effect of Policy Loans

Another aspect of policy design in universal life policies is the differential crediting rate on the cash value, depending on whether there are policy loans outstanding. Most insurance companies credit current interest rates on the cash value as long as there are no policy loans outstanding. Once the policyowner borrows funds from the cash value, the insurance company usually credits a lower interest rate or earnings rate to the portion of the cash value associated with the policy loan.

Internal Funds Flow

Although universal life insurance policies are still relatively young in the overall realm of life insurance products, some companies' policies are already in their fifth or sixth series. As with all products, the individual policy designs constantly evolve in response to the economy, competitive pressures, and market demand.

Most of the first generation of universal life policies were heavily front-end loaded products. They took a significant proportion of each premium dollar as administrative expenses, and the remaining portion was then credited to the policy's cash value account. In most insurance companies, the mortality rate then charged against the cash value for the amount at risk was often about 50 percent of the guaranteed maximum mortality rate set forth in the policy contract for the insured's attained age.

The difference in the mortality rate actually being charged and the maximum permitted mortality rate published in the policy represents the safety margin the life insurance company holds in reserve. If the future mortality costs for the block of policies turn out to be more expensive than initially assumed, the insurance company can increase the mortality charge, as long as it does not exceed the guaranteed maximum rates specified in the contract.

As noted, from each premium dollar paid for universal life insurance, deductions are made for expenses and mortality. In addition, the universal life cash value account is increased at the current crediting rate to reflect investment earnings on that cash value. These dollars help to reduce the policyowner's current and future out-of-pocket premium expenses. The actual rate credited is a discretionary decision on the part of the insurance company, and it tends to fluctuate freely, reflecting current market conditions.

Interest crediting rates have been the focal point of most of the competition among companies selling universal life policies. There has been very little emphasis on the mortality rates charged or the expense charges levied against incoming premiums. In reality, all three factors constitute the total cost of insurance. Interest rates can be (and have been) intentionally elevated to a level above what the investment portfolio actually supports, but they are still viable because of compensating higher levels of mortality charges and expense deductions. When consumers choose to focus on only one of the three elements, it is not surprising that marketing efforts zero in on that element. Assessment of overall policy efficiency requires that all factors be considered in concert.

Many universal life insurance policies are now based on a back-end loading design. In other words, they lower or eliminate up-front charges levied against incoming premium amounts and, instead, impose new or increased surrender charges applicable to the cash value of a policy surrendered during the contract's first 7 to 15 years. Surrender charges are usually highest during the first policy year and decrease on a straight-line basis over the remaining years until the year in which the insurance company expects to have amortized all excess first-year expenses. At that point, the surrender charges is reduced to zero and is not applicable at later policy durations.

Competitive pressures have caused many insurance companies to minimize front-end loading in order to emphasize that nearly all premium dollars go directly into the cash value account. The actual expenses are still being exacted internally, but the manner in which they are handled is not easily discernible by the consumer. For example, expenses can be embedded in the spread between actual mortality costs and actual mortality charges or in the spread between investment earnings and the interest rate credited to the cash value account.

Cash Value Account for a Universal Life Policy

Ending account balance, previous period
+   Flexible premium paid
   –   Current expense charge (guaranteed maximum)
   –   Current mortality charge (guaranteed maximum)
+   Interest credit at current rate (guaranteed minimum)
   –   Partial withdrawal (if any)
=   Ending account balance, current period

Variable Universal Life Insurance

variable universal life insurance

Variable universal life insurance is one of the more recently developed variations of whole life. This policy incorporates all of the premium flexibility features of the universal life policy with the policyowner-directed investment aspects of variable life insurance.

One of the most interesting aspects of variable universal life insurance is that it eliminates the direct connection between investment performance above or below some stated target level and the corresponding formula-directed adjustment in death benefits. Instead, variable universal life insurance adopts the death benefit designs applicable to universal life policies—either a level death benefit or an increasing death benefit design where a constant fixed amount of protection is paid in addition to the cash accumulation account. Under the first option, the death benefit usually does not change, regardless of how positive or negative the investment performance under the contract. If the policyowner wants to vary the death benefit with the performance of the investments under the contract, he or she must choose the increasing death benefit design. Any increase or decrease is a direct result of the accumulation balance.

Variable universal life policies offer the policyowner a choice among a specified group of separate investment accounts that are usually created and maintained by the insurance company itself. Some insurance companies have made arrangements with other investment companies to utilize separate account portfolios created and maintained by those investment management firms.

Like variable life insurance, variable universal life insurance policies are technically classified as securities and are subject to regulation by the SEC. The SEC requires registration of the agents who market the product, the separate accounts that support the contracts, and the contracts themselves. In addition, policies must conform with the SEC requirements that the investment funds be in separate accounts that are segregated from the insurance company's general investment portfolio and are therefore not subject to creditors' claims on the insurer's general portfolio should the company face financial difficulty. As with all insurance, variable universal life contracts are also subject to regulation by state insurance commissioners.

Because variable universal life is a registered investment product, policies must be accompanied by a prospectus, which is governed by the same rules that are applicable to prospectuses for variable life insurance policies. The prospectus provides the necessary information for a meaningful evaluation and comparison of policies.

Variable universal life insurance is similar to universal life insurance, but with the added feature that the policyowner chooses the investments, as under fixed-premium variable life insurance contracts. Variable universal life offers the policyowner both flexibility and the potential for investment gain or loss. There are no interest rate or cash value guarantees and very limited guarantees on the applicable maximum mortality rates. Policyowners have wide-open premium flexibility under this contract and can choose to fund it at whatever level they

---

**Distinctive Features of Variable Universal
Life Insurance**

- Premium flexibility of universal life
- Death benefit design flexibility of universal life
- Investment flexibility of variable life

---

desire, as long as it is at least high enough to create coverage similar to yearly renewable term insurance and not in excess of the amount that would drive the cash accumulation account above the maximum threshold set forth in the Internal Revenue Code. Policyowners do not need to negotiate with or inform the insurer in advance of any premium modification or cessation.

These variable universal life contracts permit partial withdrawals that work like those under universal life policies. Early partial withdrawals may be subject to surrender charges, which apply to surrenders during the policy's early years, when the insurance company is still recovering excess first-year acquisition costs. The surrender charges vanish at a specified policy duration.

Variable universal life insurance can be aggressively prefunded so that later the policy can completely support itself from its cash value. If large premiums are contributed to the contract, this self-support can be accomplished in a relatively short period. As with universal life insurance, variable universal life policies have no guarantee that once the cash value is large enough to carry the policy, it will always be able to do so. The policyowner assumes the uncertainty of investment return and, to a limited extent, some of the uncertainty of mortality rate charges. Consequently, the policyowner may either pay more premiums or reduce the death benefit at some future time if, in fact, the cash value subsequently dips below the level needed to totally prefund the remaining contract years.

By choosing the increasing death benefit option under the variable universal life contract, policyowners are afforded an automatic hedge against inflation. This inflation protection is general in nature and subject to a timing mismatch in that investment experience may not keep pace with short-term bursts of inflation. Over the long haul, however, the investment-induced increases in coverage should equal, if not exceed, general increases in price levels.

As with variable life, the policyowner is able to switch investment funds from one of the available choices to any other single fund or combination whenever desired. Some insurance companies limit the number of fund changes permitted before charging the policyowner for additional changes. Switching investment funds is accomplished without any internal or external taxation of inherent gains in the funds. The internal buildup of the cash value is tax deferred at least as long as the policy stays in force and will be tax exempt if the policy matures as a death claim.

Joint-Life Insurance

joint-life (first-to-die) policy

The typical life insurance contract is written on the life of one person and is technically known as *single-life insurance*. A contract written on more than one life is known as a *joint-life policy*, also called a *first-to-die policy*. Strictly speaking, a joint-life contract is one written on the lives of two or more persons and payable upon the death of the first person to die. If the face amount is payable upon the death of the last of two or more lives insured under a single contract, the policy is called either a *survivorship* or a *second-to-die policy*. These policies have become quite popular as a means of funding federal estate taxes of wealthy couples whose wills make maximum use of tax deferral at the first death. Joint-life policies are fairly common for funding business buy-sell agreements.

survivorship (second-to-die) policy

Joint-life policies are usually some form of cash value insurance. A term insurance rider may be used to increase the overall amount of protection in the cash value policy. Some joint-life policies consist solely of term insurance.

GROUP LIFE INSURANCE

The discussion of life insurance up to this point has focused on individual insurance. However, for many people, group insurance is their principal, or perhaps only, source of life insurance protection. One indication of the important role of group life insurance is that, of the total life insurance in force in the United States in 2000, about 40 percent was group coverage.[4] Group purchases also represent the fastest growing portion of life insurance sales.

By far the most common type of coverage issued under group life plans is term insurance, accounting for over 90 percent of the total. The remainder consists mainly of universal life insurance or variable universal life insurance. In 2001, variable universal life was the largest selling type of permanent contract sold to individuals.

The groups that are eligible for group life insurance are established by state law. In general, the minimum size required is 10 lives. Five types of groups are usually eligible: individual employer groups, negotiated trusteeships (also known as Taft-Hartley trusts), trade associations, creditor-debtor groups, and labor union groups. Of these, the most common eligible group is the employees of a common employer.

In a typical group term life insurance plan covering employees, a benefit schedule is included to define the classes of employees that are eligible for coverage and to specify the amount of life insurance that will be provided to the members of each class. The employee also is given a conversion privilege, and certain supplemental benefits may be provided as well.

Eligibility

To be eligible, an employee must be in a covered classification of workers, work on a full-time basis, and be actively at work. He or she may be required to fulfill a probationary period and, in some cases, to show insurability and meet premium contribution requirements.

The employer defines the classes of workers that will be eligible for the group life insurance; eligibility is usually restricted to full-time workers such as those who work at least 30 hours per week. Many group life insurance master contracts also contain an actively-at-work requirement, meaning that the employee is not eligible for coverage if absent from work due to sickness, injury, or other reasons on the otherwise effective date of coverage. Coverage commences when the employee returns to work.

probationary period

The master contract may also specify a *probationary period* of employment with the employer, such as 6 months, that must be satisfied before an employee is eligible for coverage. After the employee fulfills the required probationary period, he or she then becomes eligible for coverage.

Most group life coverage is provided without individual evidence of insurability. However, this evidence is required in some cases such as when an employee decides after the expiration of the eligibility period that he or she wants the coverage.

If the group plan is contributory, meaning that covered employees pay a portion of the premium, the coverage will not take effect until the employee properly authorizes payroll deduction. Usually, a 31-day eligibility period is provided during which the employee may make the decision on this matter without having to show evidence of insurability.

Benefit Amounts

The amount of group life insurance on each covered worker is normally set according to a schedule, rather than a choice for the employee. The most common schedules are based on earnings or position. In an earnings schedule, the amount of insurance is often equal to some multiple of earnings, such as two times the employee's annual earnings, rounded up to the next $1,000 and subject to a maximum benefit of, for example, $100,000. In a position schedule, differing benefit amounts are provided based on each employee's position within the firm. For example, the president and vice presidents might have $100,000 of coverage, managers $60,000, salespersons $40,000, and other employees $20,000.

Convertibility

Any employee whose group life insurance ceases has the right according to the master contract to convert to an individual insurance policy. For example, an individual who terminates his or her employment or ceases to be a member of an eligible classification of employees has the right to convert. Conversion does not require proof of insurability and must occur within the first 31 days of eligibility to convert. The individual policy may be any type the insurer offers *except term insurance*, and the face amount may not exceed the amount of group life insurance being terminated. The premium for the individual policy is based on the employee's attained age as of the time of conversion.

Supplemental Benefits

Certain supplemental benefits may be provided as part of a group life insurance plan. For example, additional amounts of insurance may be made available to some or all classes of employees. Proof of insurability is usually required to obtain the additional amount, except when the amount of coverage is small and the employer does not usually pay any part of the premium for it. For employees who need additional protection, premiums for supplemental coverage can be paid by payroll deduction. However, the premium is not necessarily any less expensive than coverage that an employee might be able to purchase in the individual marketplace.

Dependent life insurance may also be available as supplemental benefit. Coverage is usually optional, with the employee paying the entire cost. The amount of insurance is usually modest such as $5,000 on the employee's spouse and $1,000 on each dependent child over 14 days of age and under age 21. The employee usually is not allowed to select which of his or her eligible dependents will be covered but must decide on an all-or-none basis.

SOURCES FOR FURTHER IN-DEPTH STUDY

- Black, Kenneth, Jr., and Skipper, Harold D., Jr., *Life and Health Insurance*, 13th ed., Englewood Cliffs, NJ: Prentice-Hall, Inc., 2000. Phone 800-282-0693. Web site address www.prenhall.com
- Graves, Edward E., editor, *McGill's Life Insurance*, 4th ed., Bryn Mawr, PA: The American College, 2002. Phone 888-263-7265. Web site address www.amercoll.edu

CHAPTER REVIEW

Answers to review questions and self-test questions start on page 725.

Key Terms

human life value	reserve
yearly renewable term insurance	net amount at risk
cash value life insurance	modified whole life insurance

reentry term insurance
renewability
convertibility
decreasing term insurance
fifth dividend option
whole life insurance
nonparticipating policy
participating policy
ordinary life insurance
limited-payment life insurance

endowment life insurance
current assumption whole life
    insurance
variable life insurance
universal life insurance
variable universal life insurance
joint-life (first-to-die) policy
survivorship (second-to-die)
    policy
probationary period

Review Questions

8-1.   Briefly explain the family purposes of life insurance.

8-2.   Explain the differences between yearly renewable term insurance and level premium cash value insurance. (Ignore the loading to cover expenses, profit, and contingencies.)

8-3.   Your financial planning client requires some life insurance to meet various needs. You begin discussing some products available to meet those needs. How would you answer the following questions?
   a.   What is the difference between term and whole life insurance regarding
      (1) the permanence of death protection provided?
      (2) their benefit promises if I live until the end of the policy?
      (3) their use of premiums to save money as well as provide death protection?
   b.   If I buy a 10-year term policy, can I extend it at the end of 10 years to satisfy new needs?
   c.   If I buy a 10-year term policy and then need a more permanent form of insurance, can I switch the policy to whole life insurance?
   d.   Is there a policy that would pay the balance of my mortgage when I die so my family would be relieved of that burden?
   e.   What is the difference between ordinary life and limited-payment whole life in terms of the
      (1) permanence of protection?
      (2) amount of premium outlay per year?
      (3) relative size of their cash values?

8-4.   Your financial planning client says she's heard that some life insurance policies pay dividends and others don't. She asks you to explain.

8-5.   Your financial planning client tells you that his grandmother bought a $50,000 20-year endowment policy 30 years ago that paid her even though she didn't die. The client asks you
   a.   how that type of policy works
   b.   whether it would make sense for him to buy one today

8-6. Describe the following features of variable life insurance:
    a. guarantees with respect to interest rate or minimum cash value
    b. SEC requirements
    c. investment choices
    d. insurance charges
    e. linkage of death benefits with investment performance
    f. policy cash values
    g. contents of the prospectus

8-7. Describe the following features of universal life insurance:
    a. flexible premiums
    b. prefunding
    c. withdrawal
    d. target premium amount
    e. death benefit type
        (1) level death benefit design
        (2) increasing death benefit design
    f. effect of policy loans
    g. internal funds flow

8-8. Explain to your client how a universal life policy with a level death benefit design can take on an array of different forms (depending on how much premium is paid to the insurance company) ranging from those comparable to yearly renewable term insurance to those comparable to limited-payment whole life insurance.

8-9. Explain why a universal life policy with
    a. the level death benefit design may not always provide a level death benefit
    b. the increasing death benefit design may not always provide an increasing death benefit

8-10. Explain how variable universal life insurance is similar to
    a. variable life insurance
    b. universal life insurance

8-11. Briefly describe the operation and primary use of each of the following life insurance policies:
    a. joint-life or first-to-die policy
    b. survivorship or second-to-die policy

8-12. Explain the following features of a typical group life insurance plan covering employees:
    a. employee eligibility requirements
    b. evidence of insurability requirements
    c. benefit amounts
    d. convertibility
    e. supplemental benefits

Self-Test Questions

T   F   8-1.   No individuals are ever legally obligated after their deaths to provide for family support.

T   F   8-2.   With yearly renewable term insurance, no benefits are paid if the insured does not die during the period of protection.

T   F   8-3.   Yearly renewable term insurance premiums increase each year because of increases in the death rate.

T   F   8-4.   With a level premium policy, level premiums in excess of the policy's share of death claims in the early years of the contract are accumulated at interest in a reserve.

T   F   8-5.   To safeguard against adverse selection, insurers offering term insurance on an individual basis typically allow it to be renewed regardless of the insured's age at the time of renewal.

T   F   8-6.   With a whole life policy, the policyowner receives a combination of increasing cash values and decreasing (pure insurance) protection.

T   F   8-7.   Even with renewable term insurance, the policyowner/insured would not be permitted to renew the policy if he or she had contracted a terminal disease prior to a renewal date.

T   F   8-8.   Decreasing term insurance no longer has much use for financial planning purposes.

T   F   8-9.   Term insurance tends to be suitable when the need for protection either is purely temporary or is permanent but the insured temporarily cannot afford the premiums for permanent insurance.

T   F   8-10.   Ordinary life insurance provides protection for a longer period of time than does limited-payment whole life insurance.

T   F   8-11.   Life insurance policies that provide for the payment of policyowner dividends are participating policies.

T   F   8-12.   Because of federal income tax reform in 1984, endowment policies play a major role in financial planning in the United States today.

T   F   8-13.   In exchange for investment flexibility, variable life insurance shifts the investment risk to the policyowner and provides no guarantee of either interest rate or minimum cash value.

T   F   8-14.   With variable life insurance, cash values reflect investment performance, but death benefit amounts do not.

T   F   8-15.   Variable life insurance policies must not be sold without an accompanying prospectus.

T   F   8-16.   With universal life insurance, the policyowner can skip premium payments (after the first one) and the policy will stay in force as long as there is enough money in the policy's cash value account to cover current mortality and expense charges.

T   F   8-17.   With universal life insurance, death benefits are always level unless the cash value gets too close to the death benefit to comply with federal income tax law.

T   F   8-18.   Variable universal life insurance incorporates the premium flexibility features of the universal life policy with the policyowner-directed investment aspects of variable life products.

T   F   8-19.   A joint-life policy is payable upon the death of the last of two or more lives insured under the single contract.

T   F   8-20.   Most group life coverage is provided without individual evidence of insurability.

NOTES

1. In such an event, the parent and ex-spouse are required to provide life insurance or to set funds aside in trust.
2. This is not a trust fund in the legal sense, which would require the insurance company to establish separate investment accounts for each policyowner and render periodic accountings.
3. In practice, each policy is credited with a cash value or surrender value, which is not the same as the reserve but also has its basis in the redundant premiums of the early years.
4. Data concerning the amount, growth, and types of group life insurance in force are taken from *Life Insurance Fact Book 2001*, published by the American Council of Life Insurance.

Life Insurance Policy Provisions

Learning Objectives

An understanding of the material in this chapter should enable the student to

9-1.   Describe the policy declarations page and the standard policy provisions laws.

9-2.   Describe the provisions that are required in life insurance policies.

9-3.   Indicate the provisions that are prohibited in life insurance policies.

9-4.   Identify the optional provisions that may be found in life insurance policies.

9-5.   Describe three types of riders that policyowners often add to their life insurance policies.

9-6.   List the typical state requirements for policy filing and approval.

Chapter Outline

The previous chapter introduced the types of life insurance. This chapter looks more closely at the life insurance contract. We will review provisions and riders associated with life insurance so that financial planners can understand them and therefore help their clients make use of the contract privileges available to them.

Recall from chapter 1 that the insured is the person on whose life a policy is issued. The policyowner or policyholder is the individual or entity that owns the insurance contract, and that generally has the rights to change, renew, or cancel a policy and the obligations to comply with policy conditions such as premium payment.

Chapter 6 noted that most insurance contracts, including life insurance contracts, are contracts of adhesion, which means that the policyowner and the insurer do not negotiate the contract's terms. In the creation of a life insurance contract, the prospective policyowner:

- Applies for the policy (the contract) by filling out the application and supplying medical information required by the insurer. This is not a negotiation. The applicant is merely specifying what type and amount of insurance he or she would like to purchase. Based on this information, the insurer will decide whether it wishes to issue a policy.

- Accepts or rejects the contract offered by the insurer. The applicant accepts the contract by paying the initial premium. If a partial premium is paid and a premium receipt is issued by the insurer's agent, only temporary coverage under the terms of the receipt is in effect. The contract is accepted by the applicant and binding on the insurer under the particular terms of the receipt and the policy. The applicant rejects the contract by refusing delivery of the policy. Even after he or she accepts the coverage and a contract is binding on the insurer, the policyowner may, in effect, reject the contract and obtain a full refund based on the 10-day free-look provision (explained later in this chapter). Many states require this provision.

Because the prospective policyowner can only accept or reject the contract issued by the insurer, the contract of adhesion rule provides that all ambiguities in the contract of insurance will be resolved in favor of the policyowner and against the insurer. This rule of law is not entirely fair to insurance companies because there are substantial limitations on the insurer's freedom to draft the insurance contract as it wishes. Insurers are required by law to include many types of provisions and in some cases are required to use or not use certain words. Thus, it is not entirely correct to state that, because the insurers are free to select the contract language, they have to give the benefit of ambiguity to the applicant.

Many states require that the contract avoid complex sentences and arcane legal terminology in order to make the contracts easier for the consumer to read and understand. While laudable, this requirement for simplicity can conflict with the lawyers' need to be certain that a contract will be interpreted exactly as the drafter intended. Over many years, courts have given certain legal terms specific meanings on which lawyers have come to rely in drafting contracts. This legalese may be difficult for the uninitiated to understand, but offers a certainty that lawyers prefer. The practice in the United States is to prefer less technical language over the certainty of interpretation. Lawyers will have to rely on current and future cases to develop that certainty as the simplified language of modern contracts is interpreted by the courts.

There are a variety of required, prohibited, and optional life insurance policy provisions that are controlled by state law. Before a policy can be sold in a particular jurisdiction, its provisions must be filed with that state's insurance department for approval.

POLICY DECLARATIONS PAGE

Although the placement of the provisions may vary from company to company, the declarations page of most life insurance contracts is quite similar, and has the following information:

- the name of the insurance company
- specific details for the policy. These include the name of the insured and the name of the policyowner, the face amount of the policy, the policy number, and the policy date or issue date (some declarations pages include both dates).
- a general description of the type of insurance provided by the policy contract. For example, the declarations page of a traditional participating whole life policy might read as follows:

> Whole Life—Level Face Amount Plan. Insurance payable upon death. Premiums payable for life. Policy participates in dividends.

Dividends, dividend credits, and policy loans may be used to help pay premiums.

- a statement about the policy's free-look provision. This is a provision that gives the policyowner a period of time, usually 10 days, to return the policy after acceptance. The following is an example of such a provision:

  You may return this contract no later than 10 days after you receive it. All you have to do is take it or mail it to one of our offices or to the agent who sold it to you. The contract will be canceled from the start, and a full premium refund will be made promptly.

- the insurer's promise to pay. This is the heart of the insurance contract. Three different but typical statements read as follows:

  We will pay the beneficiary the sum insured under this contract promptly if we receive due proof that the insured died while this policy was in force. We make this promise subject to all of the provisions of this contract.

  We will pay the benefits of this policy in accordance with its provisions.

  We agree to pay the death benefits of this policy to the beneficiary upon receiving proof of the insured's death, and to provide you with the other rights and benefits of this policy.

The remainder of the required and optional provisions are not usually included on the declarations page.

STANDARD POLICY PROVISIONS

standard policy provisions laws

The *standard policy provisions laws* of the various states require that life and health insurance policies include certain provisions but allow the insurance companies to select the actual wording as long as it is at least as favorable to the policyowner as the statutory language. However, the wording must be submitted to and approved by the state insurance department. For some insurance contracts, such as term, single premium, and nonparticipating policies, some of the standard provisions may not be applicable. To that extent, those contracts are excused from compliance with the law.

REQUIRED PROVISIONS

Grace Period

grace period

The *grace period* provision grants the policyowner an additional period of time to pay any premium after it has become due. While the provision is now required by law, acceptance of a slightly overdue premium was a common practice among insurers before laws compelled the inclusion of the provision in the contract. Because of the provision, a policy that would have lapsed for nonpayment of premiums continues in force during the grace period. The premium remains due, however, and if the insured dies during the grace period, the insurer may deduct one month's premium from the death benefit.

Note that although insurers could charge interest on the unpaid premium for the late period, they do not normally do so. If the insured survives the grace period but the premium remains unpaid, the policy lapses. However, cash value life insurance policies are required to include a nonforfeiture provision, discussed in a later section, that may enable the policyowner to continue coverage.

As with all renewal premiums, the policyowner has no obligation to pay the premium for the insurance coverage provided under the grace period clause. Thus it might be said that the policyowner has received "free" insurance during that time, but only when the insured does not die within the grace period.

The standard length of the grace period is 30 or 31 days in fixed-premium policies. In flexible-premium policies, such as universal life insurance, a grace period of 60 or 61 days is common. If the last day of the grace period falls on a nonbusiness day, the period is normally extended to the next business day.

Late Remittance Offers

It is important to make a distinction between the grace period rules and a late remittance offer that is made by the insurer after the grace period expires. They are not the same, and there is usually no provision in the contract concerning a late remittance offer. Such an offer is made solely at the insurer's option. It is not a right of the policyowner or an obligation of the insurer included in the insurance contract under the requirements of the law.

Some insurers will make a late remittance offer to a policyowner whose coverage has lapsed after the grace period has expired. This is not an extension of the grace period, and coverage is not continued as a result of the offer. A late remittance offer is intended to encourage the policyowner to reinstate the policy; it does not extend coverage. The inducement from the insurer is that coverage may be reinstated without providing evidence of insurability. The policyowner accepts a late remittance offer by paying the premiums due and meeting any other conditions imposed by the insurer. The most common condition is that the insured must have been alive when the late premium payment was made.

Policy Loans

policy loan

The law requires that the insurance contract permit policy loans if the policy generates a cash value. *Policy loans* give the policyowner access to the cash value that accumulates inside the policy without having to terminate the policy. The policyowner merely requests a loan and the life insurer lends the funds confidentially. The loan provisions in the policy specify what portion of the cash value is available for loans and how interest will be determined. In most policies, over 90 percent of the cash value is available for loans—some policies may restrict the amount of loanable funds to 90 percent of the cash value in recognition of an 8 percent policy loan interest rate—and any portion of the cash value may be borrowed. Policyowners indicate in their request the amount desired. More than one policy loan can be taken as long as the aggregate amount of all outstanding loans plus accrued interest does not exceed the policy's cash value available for loan.

Policy loans accrue interest on the borrowed funds. At the time of application, the policyowner selects one of two different approaches to setting the policy loan interest. The policy will contain either (1) a fixed rate as specified in the policy (now commonly 8 percent) or (2) a variable interest tied by formula to some specified index. One variable approach is to use Moody's composite yield on seasoned corporate bonds or some other index that is regularly published in the financial press such as *The Wall Street Journal* or *The Journal of Commerce*. Another index may be the interest rate being credited to the cash value plus a specified spread.

The Policy Loan Provision

- No credit questions
- May borrow up to 90 percent to 100 percent of cash value
- Technically, insurer can delay lending for up to 6 months
- Fixed or variable interest rates charged
- Unpaid interest is added to the loan balance
- No repayment schedule or requirement
- Indebtedness is repaid when policy is surrendered or matures as a claim
- May include automatic premium loan feature

The policyowner has the option of paying loan interest in cash or adding unpaid interest charge to the balance of the outstanding loan. The policyowner can choose to pay any part of the loan and interest he or she desires, as there is no repayment schedule or requirement. If any repayments are made, they are totally at the discretion of the policyowner as to both timing and amount. If the policy loan and accrued interest are not paid in cash, the life insurer recovers the outstanding balance of the loan and accrued interest either from (1) the death benefits if the insured dies or (2) the cash surrender value if the policy is terminated. In fact, the policy automatically terminates if the policy loan balance plus unpaid interest ever exceeds the policy's cash value.

Some whole life policies give policyowners an automatic premium loan option. When this option is selected, a delinquent premium is paid automatically by a new policy loan. This keeps the policy in force as long as there is adequate cash value to cover each delinquent premium. However, the policy will terminate if the cash value is exhausted.

The creation of a policy loan has negative consequences on benefits and can reduce the amount credited to the cash value and/or the level of policyowner dividends. The death benefit payable to the beneficiary is reduced by the full amount of outstanding policy loans and accrued interest under most types of policies. Outstanding policy loans also reduce nonforfeiture benefits.

Policy loans result in the life insurer's release of funds that would otherwise have been invested. If investment return on the insurer's portfolio exceeds the rate paid on the policy loan, the insurer experiences a reduction in earnings. Therefore, the insurance company usually takes steps to offset such loan-induced losses to preserve an approximate equity between policyowners who leave their cash values invested and those who preclude the insurer from reaping the higher yield. In traditional participating whole life policies, policyowner dividends were not affected by policy loans, but most participating whole life policies sold today use *direct recognition* to reduce dividends on policies with outstanding loans. This not only adjusts for the differential in earnings but also discourages policy loans.

State statutes allow life insurers to delay lending funds for up to 6 months after requested. Although this right is almost never exercised, it serves as a form of emergency protection in case policyowners' demands for loans accelerate to the point that the insurer must liquidate other assets at significant losses to satisfy the loan demands.

Incontestable Clause

incontestable clause

Brief mention is made in chapter 6 of a life insurance policy provision called the *incontestable clause*. This clause is a provision that makes the life insurance policy incontestable by the insurer after it has been in force for a certain time period. State laws differ as to the form of the clause prescribed, but no state permits a clause that would make the policy contestable for more than 2 years.

The following is a sample incontestable clause:

> Except for nonpayment of premium, we will not contest this contract after it has been in force during the lifetime of the insured for 2 years from the date of issue.

After a policy has been in effect for the period of time prescribed by the incontestable clause (normally 2 years), the insurance company cannot have the policy declared invalid. The courts have generally recognized three exceptions to this rule, deeming that the incontestable clause does not apply because the contract was void from its inception. These three exceptions are:

- There was no insurable interest at the inception of the policy.
- The policy was purchased with the intent to murder the insured.
- There was a fraudulent impersonation of the insured by another person (for example, for purposes of taking the medical exam).

The incontestable clause exists due to a belief that a life insurance policy's beneficiaries should not suffer for mistakes made in the application. The beneficiary is protected by the incontestable clause even if the error in the application is based on a fraudulent or material misrepresentation by the applicant or by a failure to meet a condition precedent to the existence of the contract.

After the insured's death, it would be extremely difficult, if not impossible, for the beneficiary to disprove the allegations of the insurance company that there were irregularities in procuring the policy. If there were no time limit on the insurance company's right to question the accuracy of the information provided in the application, there would be no certainty during the life of the policy that the benefits promised would be payable at maturity. Honest policyowners need assurance that at the insured's death, the beneficiary will be the recipient of a check. The incontestable clause gives policyowners that assurance. The clause is based on the theory that, after the insurance company has had a reasonable opportunity to investigate the circumstances surrounding issuance of a life insurance policy, it should thereafter relinquish the right to question the validity of the contract.

The typical incontestable clause makes the policy incontestable after it has been in force during the lifetime of the insured for a specified period. This means that, if the insured dies during that period, the policy never becomes incontestable. As a result, if the insured dies a few days before the contestable period expires, the policy remains contestable by the insurer even if it is not notified of the death claim until after that period expires.

Example: Donald took out a life insurance policy on June 16, 2000, naming his wife as the beneficiary. The policy contained the typical 2-year incontestable clause. Donald died on June 9, 2002. Knowing that Donald had lied about his health on the insurance application, Donald's wife waited till June 17, 2002, before filing the claim. Will she collect the proceeds? Probably not.

> Because the life insurance policy wasn't in force for
> 2 years *during Donald's lifetime*, it never became
> incontestable.

Other points are worth noting. First, refusal to pay a claim because of nonpayment of the premium is not governed by the incontestable clause. Second, some insurers specify in their incontestable clause that it does not apply to disability benefits or accidental death benefits that may be provided as part of the life insurance policy. Third, the policy provision relating to misstatement of the insured's age or sex, described later in this chapter, takes precedence over the incontestable clause.

Divisible Surplus

divisible surplus   An insurer's *divisible surplus* is that portion of an insurer's surplus declared as a dividend to be distributed to policyholders and/or stockholders of the insurer. The divisible surplus provision appears only in participating policies. The provision requires the insurer to determine and apportion any divisible surplus among the insurer's participating policies at frequent intervals.

A typical divisible surplus provision reads as follows:

> While this policy is in force, except as extended term insurance, it is
> entitled to the share, if any, of the divisible surplus that we shall
> annually determine and apportion to it. This share is payable as a
> dividend on the policy anniversary.

In addition, some contracts provide that payment of a dividend is conditional on payment of all premiums then due. The provision in most contracts notes that a dividend is not likely to be paid before the second anniversary of the policy.

Dividend Options

dividend options   Participating life insurance policies offer the policyowner several *dividend options* for the use of his or her dividends. The application for the policy has a section in which the applicant is asked to select the desired dividend option.

The most commonly offered dividend options, in addition to the cash option, are to reduce premiums, to accumulate at interest, to purchase paid-up additions, or to buy term insurance.

- *reduction of premiums*. With this option, the policyowner simply subtracts the amount of the dividend from the premium currently due and remits the difference to the insurer.

- *accumulation at interest.* With this option, the dividends are maintained in the equivalent of an interest-bearing savings account for the policyowner. A minimum rate of interest is guaranteed, but a higher rate of interest may be credited if conditions warrant. The accumulated dividends may be withdrawn at any time. If not withdrawn, they are added to the death proceeds or to the nonforfeiture value if the policy is surrendered.
- *purchase of paid-up additions.* With this option, each dividend is used to purchase on an attained-age basis a small amount of additional, fully paid-up whole life insurance. The purchase is made at rates that do not contain a loading for expenses, and no evidence of insurability is required.
- *purchase of term insurance.* Some insurers that offer this "fifth dividend" option use a portion of the dividend to buy one-year term insurance equal to the policy's then cash value, with the remainder used to buy paid-up additions or to accumulate at interest. Other insurers use the entire dividend to buy one-year term insurance. In either case, the term insurance is purchased on the basis of the insured's attained age.

Other dividend options that may be available enable the policyowner to shorten the premium-paying period or to cause the policy to mature as an endowment. In the former case, the policy becomes paid up when its reserve, together with the reserve value of the dividends, equals the net single premium for a paid-up policy that could be issued to the insured on the basis of his or her attained age. In the latter case, the face amount of the policy is paid when the reserve, together with the reserve value of the dividends, equals the policy's face amount.

Entire Contract

Ordinarily, one would expect that a contract of any type includes all the provisions that are binding on the parties. However, this is not always the case. Sometimes one contract includes the terms of another document without actually including that second document in the contract. This is done by referring to the other document and incorporating it into the contract by that reference, a practice known as incorporation by reference. Entire contract statutes grew out of an attempt to prohibit insurers' use of incorporation by reference and to make life insurance contracts more understandable for consumers. One goal was to ensure that the policyowner was given a copy of all documents that constitute the contract. Another was to preclude any changes in the contract after it had been issued.

entire contract provision

The various states impose different requirements concerning the entire contract. Some states require an *entire contract provision* disclosing that the policy and the application constitute the entire contract; other states simply provide that the policy and the application are the contract, regardless of what the policy may say.

A sample provision is as follows:

> This policy and any attached copy of an application form the entire contract. We assume that all statements in an application are made to the best of the knowledge and belief of the person who makes them; in the absence of fraud, they are deemed to be representations and not warranties. We rely on those statements when we issue the contract. We will not use any statement, unless made in an application, to try to void the contract, to contest a change, or to deny a claim.

Reinstatement

reinstatement provision

Reinstatement provisions allow a policyowner to reacquire coverage under a policy that has lapsed. This right is valuable to both the policyowner and the insurer. The various state laws and the insurance contracts impose certain requirements that the policyowner must meet to reinstate the policy.

A typical reinstatement clause might provide the following:

> This policy may be reinstated within 3 years after the due date of the first unpaid premium, unless the policy has been surrendered for its cash value. The conditions for reinstatement are that (1) the insured must provide evidence of insurability satisfactory to us, (2) the policyowner must pay all overdue premiums plus interest at 6 percent per year, and (3) the policyowner must repay or reinstate any policy loan outstanding when the policy lapsed, plus interest.

Normally, insurers do not permit reinstatement of a policy that has been surrendered for its cash value, and this prohibition is often included in the contractual definition of the requirements for reinstatement.

Misstatement of Age or Sex

misstatement of age or sex clause

The age and sex of the insured are fundamentally important factors in the evaluation of the risk the life insurance company assumes. Inaccurate statements about the insured's age or sex are material misrepresentations. Rather than voiding the contract based on such misrepresentations, the practice is to adjust the policy's premium or benefits to reflect the truth. Adjustments in the policy's premiums or benefits based on misstatements of age or sex are not precluded by the incontestable clause, because incontestable clauses preclude contests of the validity of the policy. Also, because a *misstatement of age or sex clause* appears in the contract, an adjustment based on that clause would be an attempt to enforce the terms of the contract, not to invalidate it.

A sample provision in an individual life insurance policy might read as follows:

> If the age or sex of the insured has been misstated, we will adjust all benefits payable under this policy to that which the premium paid would have purchased at the correct age or sex.

Example:	Jim took out a life insurance policy for an annual premium of $1,300. He stated that his age was 41, when in fact he was 46. When he died, the misstatement of age was discovered. The insurer will pay an amount less than the face of the policy to Jim's beneficiary, namely, the amount of insurance that an annual premium of $1,300 would have bought for a 46-year-old male.

However, if the insured is still alive when the age or sex misrepresentation is discovered, the parties typically will agree to adjust the premium to the correct amount, rather than to adjust the benefits. An adjustment of premium is also the method used in group life insurance, whether the insured is living or not. A majority of states require a provision that adjusts for misstatements of age, but fewer than half require a provision that applies to misstatement of sex.

Nonforfeiture Provisions

When insurers developed the concept of insurance policies with level premiums over the insured's lifetime, the goal was to make life insurance more affordable to older policyowners. As explained in chapter 8, in the early years of the policy, the level premium was higher than necessary to cover the mortality costs. The excess portion of the premium in the policy's early years, and the interest it earned, built up a cash reserve that was used to pay the mortality costs at older ages, which then exceeded the attained age level premium. A question soon arose concerning who was entitled to those reserves when a policy lapsed in the early years. Initially, these reserves were forfeited by the policyowner, but this was clearly inequitable, and the practice was soon modified. Today that question has been answered by the nonforfeiture laws.

The states require that insurers assure policyowners who voluntarily terminate their contracts a fair return of the value, if any, built up inside their policies. These laws are known as *nonforfeiture laws*. As late as the middle of the nineteenth century, insurance policies in the United States made no provision for refunds of excess premiums paid on cash value policies upon the policyowner's termination of the policy before maturity. However, in 1861, Massachusetts recognized that the policyowner had a right to at least a portion of those funds, and the first nonforfeiture law was enacted in that state. By 1948, that idea had evolved into the Standard Nonforfeiture Law, and subsequent versions of the law have become effective in all jurisdictions. Policies issued since that date have provided at least the minimum surrender values prescribed by the version of the law in effect when the policy was issued.

The NAIC Standard Nonforfeiture Law for Life Insurance, which has been widely adopted by the states, does not require specific surrender values. The only requirement is that surrender values are at least as large as those that would be produced by the method the law prescribes. In addition, each policy must contain a statement of the method used to determine the surrender values and benefits provided under the policy at durations not specifically shown.

nonforfeiture options

Nonforfeiture laws require that after a traditional cash value policy has been in effect for a minimum number of years—usually 3—the insurer must use part of the reserved excess premium to create a guaranteed minimum cash value. In addition, the insurer must make that value available to the policyowner in cash as a surrender value and must give the policyowner a choice of two other *nonforfeiture options*: (1) paid-up insurance at a reduced death benefit amount or (2) extended term insurance for the net face amount of the policy. If the policyowner has not elected a nonforfeiture option, the policy must provide that one of these two options will be effective automatically if the policy lapses. Under most plans and issue ages, nonforfeiture values are made available by the end of the second policy year.

Nonforfeiture Options

- Surrender for cash
- Buy a reduced amount of paid-up permanent insurance
- Buy the same amount of extended term insurance
- Insurer may allow purchase of an annuity

As for the cash option, the policy may be surrendered at any time for its cash value, less any policy indebtedness, and plus accumulated dividends. In that event, the protection terminates and the company has no further obligation under the policy. As with policy loans, a 6-month delay clause applies to cash surrenders, though it is very rare for an insurer to make use of this right to delay payment.

The next option permits the insured to take a reduced amount of paid-up whole life insurance, payable upon the same conditions as the original policy. The amount of the paid-up insurance is the amount that can be purchased at the insured's attained age with the net cash value (cash value, less any policy indebtedness, plus any dividend accumulations) applied as a net single premium.

Note that the paid-up insurance is purchased at net rates, meaning they contain no expense loading, which may constitute a sizable savings to the policyowner.

The extended term option provides term insurance in an amount equal to the original face amount of the policy, increased by any dividend additions or deposits, and decreased by any policy indebtedness. The length of the term is that which can be purchased at the insured's attained age with the net cash value applied as a single premium. If the insured fails to elect an option within a specified period after default of premiums, this option usually automatically goes into effect.

Surrender values may also be used to purchase an annuity for retirement income. If the life insurance policy does not specifically give the policyowner the right to take the cash value in the form of a life income, purchased at net rates, the insurer will usually grant the privilege on request. More and more policyowners are purchasing ordinary life insurance to protect their families during the child-raising period with the objective of eventually using the cash values for their own retirements. The cash value, supplemented by Social Security benefits, private retirement plan benefits, and income from other savings, could provide a policyowner with an adequate retirement income.

Nonforfeiture options in universal and variable life insurance policies have special characteristics that differentiate them from traditional whole life policies. First, variable life policies provide no guarantees as to the minimum nonforfeiture values available under any of the three options. Second, universal and variable life policies in force under the reduced paid-up option or the extended term option may require further adjustments of the coverage if investment earnings or interest crediting rates fall significantly.

Settlement Options

settlement options

The standard policy provisions of the various states require that a life insurance policy include certain settlement option tables for the policy's death proceeds if the *settlement options* include installment payments or annuities. These tables must show the minimum amounts of the applicable installment or annuity payments.

The types of settlement options, other than the lump-sum or cash option, most commonly found in life insurance policies are the interest option, the fixed-period option, the fixed-amount option, and one or more life income options.

Interest Option

Under the interest option, the death proceeds are retained temporarily by the insurer, and only the interest is paid to the beneficiary periodically such as monthly or annually. A minimum rate of interest is guaranteed in the policy, although insurers frequently pay a higher rate if investment earnings warrant it. The death proceeds are paid at a specified later date at the request of the beneficiary, or on the occurrence of a specified event such as the beneficiary's death.

Fixed-Period Option

Under the fixed-period option, installment payments consisting of both the death proceeds and interest are made to the beneficiary over a specified period of time such as 10 years following the insured's death. Again, a minimum interest rate is guaranteed. If the insurer pays a higher rate than the guaranteed rate, the amount of the installment payment is increased accordingly.

Fixed-Amount Option

Under the fixed-amount option, level periodic installments of a specified amount are paid to the beneficiary. The payments consist of a portion of the death proceeds and interest earnings and continue for as long as the funds held by the insurer last. Unlike the fixed-period option, excess interest earnings under the fixed-amount option do not increase the size of the periodic payments. Rather, they extend the length of time during which the payments will continue.

Life Income Options

Under the life income options, the death proceeds are used as a single premium to purchase an annuity for the beneficiary. Various forms of annuities may be available, but the most common ones are a straight life income, a life income with a period certain, a life income with some type of refund feature, and a joint-and-survivor life income. Details concerning these life income options are contained in chapter 11.

PROHIBITED PROVISIONS

Although the state laws are not uniform, most states prohibit insurers from including certain provisions in their policies. For various reasons, courts or state legislatures have determined that these prohibited contract provisions violate public policy.

There are five generally prohibited provisions:

- The insurance producer, who is the agent of the insurance company, may not be made the agent of the policyowner for purposes of filling out the application for insurance. If the producer could be made the policyowner's agent, rather than the company's agent, then the insurance company could not be charged with knowing facts that were presented to the agent but not communicated to the insurance company by the agent.
- Nonpayment of a loan cannot cause a forfeiture. The state laws generally provide that as long as the cash value of the insurance policy exceeds the

total indebtedness on the policy, the policyowner's failure to repay the loan or to pay interest on the loan may not cause a forfeiture of the policy.

- An insurer cannot promise something on the declarations of the policy and take it away in the "fine print." This is spelled out in laws called *less value statutes* because the insurer is prohibited from providing a settlement option that is of less value than the death benefit of the policy.

- The insurance codes of several states prohibit use of a policy provision that gives the policyowner too short a time in which to bring suit against the insurer. Statutes of limitations place an upper limit on the time during which legal action can be brought for alleged wrongs of various types, but sometimes parties to a contract can agree on a shorter period. Some states allow insurers to include a shorter time period in their policies; the permissible periods vary from one to 6 years. Other states do not allow insurers to reduce the time specified in the statute of limitations. These laws protect the interests of the insurers and the public. Insurers are protected because the laws allow them to impose shorter limitation periods than otherwise permitted in the state. This benefits insurers because it requires plaintiffs to sue while information relevant to the insurance policy is still easy to obtain. The public is protected because the statutes do not allow insurers to shorten the limitation period so much that the public does not have sufficient time to determine whether a lawsuit is worthwhile.

- Although not directly related to a policy provision, state laws typically include a limitation concerning the effective date of the policy as specified on the declarations page of the policy. The limitation involves the practice of *backdating*, which means to issue the policy as if it had been purchased when the insured was younger. The consumer advantage is that the policyowner pays lower periodic premiums for the policy because the premium is based on the younger age. The consumer disadvantage is that the policyowner must pay the premium for the backdated period, during which no coverage existed. Statutes generally limit backdating to no more than 6 months.

OPTIONAL PROVISIONS

In addition to the required provisions and the prohibited provisions, there are numerous other provisions that are neither required nor prohibited. Some of these relate to the beneficiary designation.

Beneficiary Provisions

Several provisions in a life insurance policy relate to designation of the beneficiary of the policy proceeds at maturity. The first reference to the beneficiary appears on the policy's declarations page. There the policyowner names the primary, and perhaps a contingent, beneficiary.

primary beneficiary

The *primary beneficiary* is the person or organization that is to receive the proceeds if he, she, or it survives the insured. The policyowner may even name the estate of the insured as the primary beneficiary, although naming the estate is usually unwise because it subjects the proceeds to transfer taxes and costs that can be avoided. Naming the estate as primary beneficiary may be acceptable, however, if the proceeds are small and/or are designed only to pay last-illness costs, funeral expenses, estate debts, and taxes. Among the parties who are often named as primary beneficiaries are the policyowner (if different from the insured), the heirs of the insured, other donee beneficiaries (such as charitable organizations), and creditors of the insured.

contingent beneficiary

A *contingent beneficiary* is a person or organization that is to receive the proceeds only if the primary beneficiary predeceases the insured or loses entitlement to any of the proceeds for some other reason (for example, if a charity named as primary beneficiary goes out of existence or if the primary beneficiary murders the insured). If the primary beneficiary is eligible to receive the policy proceeds, the rights of the contingent beneficiary are extinguished.

When life insurance proceeds are payable under a settlement option (other than the lump-sum cash option), a contingent payee, as contrasted with a contingent beneficiary, may have a claim on the proceeds. For example, assume that the primary beneficiary begins receiving the policy's death proceeds under the life income with a 10-year period certain. If he or she dies after, say, 7 years, the remaining 3 years of income would go to the named contingent payee, who may or may not be the same person or organization as the contingent beneficiary.

Whether primary or contingent, beneficiaries may be named specifically (for example, my wife, Anne J. Kirby) or as a class (for example, the children born to my wife, Anne J. Kirby, and me). In either case, every effort should be made to be clear in spelling out who is to receive the proceeds. For example, simply designating "my husband" is unclear, as the policyowner may have more than one husband during her lifetime. Or simply designating "my grandchildren" is unclear because the policyowner's children may have children of their own from different marriages or from outside the state of marriage. Class designations present many possible problems identifying who is a member of the class; therefore, insurers often limit the use of such designations.

Example: Dolores named her husband to receive the death proceeds of her life insurance policy. She also specified that, if her husband predeceased her, the proceeds would be paid to her brother. The settlement option Dolores selected was the 10-year fixed period option. Dolores died in 2004, her husband in 2003, and her brother in 2007.

Who gets what?

- The husband was the *primary beneficiary* but he gets nothing because Dolores outlived him.
- The brother was the *contingent beneficiary* but became the primary beneficiary when the husband died. The brother gets 3 years of death benefit payments.
- The brother's heirs or his estate are the *contingent payees* and get 7 years of death benefit payments.

The declarations page of the life insurance policy, in addition to requiring identification of the beneficiaries, may also ask whether they are named revocably or irrevocably. If a beneficiary is named revocably, the policyowner can change the designation at any time prior to the insured's death without the beneficiary's consent. If the beneficiary is named irrevocably, however, the policyowner must obtain the beneficiary's consent before making a beneficiary change. Normally, an irrevocable designation also requires that the beneficiary consent to the policyowner's exercise of other ownership rights in the policy such as surrendering it for cash or borrowing against the cash value.

Provisions in the body of the life insurance policy concerning the beneficiaries are not standardized. Policies often contain provisions specifying the conditions under which a policyowner can change the beneficiary designation. Also, the policy may describe the right of the beneficiary to name or change the contingent payee, who will receive the remaining proceeds if the beneficiary dies before all the death proceeds have been distributed. The policy can also specify that, if the beneficiary predeceases the insured, and if no contingent beneficiary has been named or is alive when the insured dies, the proceeds will be paid to the policyowner or to his or her estate.

Other Optional Provisions

Life insurance policies usually contain optional provisions concerning suicide, ownership, assignment, and changes of plan. Increasingly, a provision concerning accelerated benefits is also included.

suicide provision

- *suicide provision.* An insurer can elect to cover suicide from the day the policy is issued. However, this is not normally the case, and most insurance contracts do not provide coverage for a death by suicide within the first one or 2 years after the policy issue date. If the policy does not contain a suicide exclusion provision, then a death by suicide is covered by the policy, and the death benefit is payable to the beneficiary regardless of when the suicide occurs.

The following is a typical insurance contract suicide provision:

> Suicide of the insured, while sane or insane, within 2 years of the issue date, is not covered by this policy. In that event, we will pay only the premiums paid to us, less any unpaid policy loans.

ownership provision

- *ownership provision.* Ordinarily the insured is the applicant and owner of the policy. The ownership provision in the life insurance contract describes the rights of the owner. The typical ownership provision stipulates that the owner of the policy is the insured unless the application states otherwise. The provision usually states that the policyowner may change the beneficiary, assign the policy to another party, and exercise other ownership rights. If these powers are described, the provision will also define how such powers are to be exercised in order to be recognized by the insurance company.

assignment provision

- *assignment provision.* In contract law, assignment is the act of transferring a property right. As with most contracts and most interests in property, the policyowner has, as a matter of law, the right to assign some or all of his or her rights to another person. The right to assign an ownership interest in a life insurance policy exists even without an assignment provision in the contract. However, most contracts include an assignment clause clearly specifying the conditions under which an assignment may be made. If the policy contains a prohibition against an assignment, any attempted assignment by the policyowner will not be binding on the insurer. If the policy sets conditions for an assignment, the policyowner must comply with these restrictions. A sample assignment clause might provide the following:

> You may assign this policy if we agree. We will not be bound by an assignment unless it has been received by us in writing at our home office. Your rights and the rights of any other person referred to in this policy will be subject to the assignment. We assume no responsibility for the validity of an assignment. An absolute assignment will be the same as a change of ownership to the assignee.

plan change provision

- *plan change provision.* This provision asserts that the parties may agree to change the terms of the contract, but does not add anything that does not already exist under the law. A sample plan change provision might read as follows:

> Subject to our rules at the time of a change, you may change this policy to another plan of insurance, you may add riders to this policy, or you may make other changes if we agree.

accelerated benefits provision

- *accelerated benefits provision.* Some insurers have added a provision that permits the policyowner to withdraw a portion of death benefits under certain circumstances. These accelerated benefits or living benefits provisions state that if the insured becomes terminally ill, then the policyowner may withdraw a portion of the policy's death benefit. According to the NAIC Accelerated Benefits Model Regulation, the condition that permits the payment of the accelerated benefits must be a medical condition that drastically limits the insured's normal life span expectation (for example, to 2 years or less). The regulation also lists several examples of a qualifying medical condition: acute coronary artery disease, a permanent neurological deficit resulting from a cerebral vascular accident, end-stage renal failure, AIDS, or other such medical condition as the commissioner may approve. To qualify as accelerated benefits, the lifetime payments must reduce the death benefit otherwise payable under the contract. About half of the states have adopted regulations or statutes similar to the NAIC model.

RIDERS TO LIFE INSURANCE POLICIES

Common riders that policyowners can add to their life insurance policies include those concerning accidental death benefits, the guaranteed purchase option (also known as the guaranteed insurability option), and waiver of premium in the event of the insured's disability.

Accidental Death Benefits

accidental death benefits

Accidental death benefits are added to some insurance contracts in the form of a rider, or amendment, to the policy. The rider is also known as the *double indemnity provision* because it normally doubles the standard death benefit if the insured dies accidentally.

In the absence of a specific definition of accidental death, *accident* means an unintentional event that is sudden and unexpected. An accidental death is one that is caused by an accident. This statement seems quite clear, but it is not always easy to apply. An insured may have been mortally injured in an accident, but died from a disease. The accidental death benefit is payable only if the accident was the cause of death. If the insured is in an automobile accident but dies from a heart attack, the accidental death benefit is payable only if the accident is proven to have triggered the heart attack.

The problems caused by cases where there may be more than one cause of death are mitigated somewhat by the standard practice of including a time limit in the accidental death benefit provision. In the most common type of provision, the death must occur within 90 days of the accident said to have caused the injury.

These basic definitions preclude coverage for any death that is the natural and probable result of a voluntary act. An unchallenged principle of law is that people are presumed to expect and intend the probable or foreseeable consequences of their actions. This concept is sometimes described by the term *assumption of risk*. If an individual plays Russian roulette, jumps off buildings, or runs with the bulls in Pamplona, Spain, his or her death as a result of those activities cannot be described as accidental.

A sample accidental death benefit provision is as follows:

> We will pay this benefit to the beneficiary when we have proof that the Insured's death was the result, directly and apart from any other cause, of accidental bodily injury, and that death occurred within one year after that injury and while this rider was in effect.

Some life insurance agents routinely include an accidental death benefit rider in virtually every life insurance contract they sell. The cost of the rider is small because a small percentage of all deaths occur as a result of accident. On the other hand, there is little reason for an individual to carry more insurance for an accidental death than for any other type of death, except perhaps as an appeal to the policyowner's gambling instinct.

Guaranteed Purchase Option

guaranteed purchase (insurability) option

Another popular policy provision is the *guaranteed purchase option*, also called the *guaranteed insurability option*. This provision helps policyowners protect themselves against the possibility that the insured might become uninsurable. Under the typical provision, the policyowner may purchase the right to acquire additional insurance in specified amounts at specified times or ages. Typically, this provision allows additional purchases every 3 years, upon marriage, and after the birth of a child, provided the events occur before the insured reaches a specified maximum age, often age 45. This right to purchase additional insurance can be very valuable because the insured need not provide evidence of insurability in order to exercise the option. Another benefit of the guaranteed purchase option is that the new coverage is normally not subject to a new suicide provision or a new incontestable clause.

There is a ceiling on the maximum amount of insurance available under the guaranteed purchase option and a maximum age at which the option may be

---

Guaranteed Purchase Option

- Allows purchase of specified additional amounts of insurance at specified times and ages
- No need to show evidence of insurability
- No new suicide exclusion or incontestable period
- Options are not cumulative

exercised. Once the insured passes an age or event that triggers the right to purchase additional insurance and does not exercise the option, that option lapses, but future options are not affected.

Waiver of Premium

A *waiver-of-premium provision* in the event of the insured's disability is another commonly available rider. According to a typical waiver-of-premium rider, if the insured becomes totally disabled as defined in the rider or policy, the insurance company will waive payment of premiums on the policy during the continuance of the insured's disability.

The disability waiver of premium has some limitations. For example, the waiver will not be granted if the insured's disability begins after a specified age. In addition, the provision usually will not waive premiums if the disability is self-inflicted or the result of an act of war.

As in any contract, it is important to pay close attention to the wording of the waiver-of-premium rider. For example, these riders usually require that the disability last for at least 6 months before premiums will be waived. Some riders specify that only premiums due thereafter will be waived, while others provide that premiums that were paid during the 6 months will be refunded, as well as waiving premiums due thereafter.

Care should be taken to examine the definition of total disability used in the rider. A common definition of *total disability* is the inability to perform the essential duties of the insured's own job or of any job for which he or she is suited by reason of training or experience. However, definitions that are less liberal to the insured also can be found in some riders.

POLICY FILING AND APPROVAL

If a policy is sold in a state but does not include a required provision or has not been filed with the state for approval, the courts will treat the policy as if it did include all of the required provisions under the law of that jurisdiction. The policyowner or beneficiary will be permitted to enforce the policy against the insurer as if it complied in all respects with the applicable state law. The state insurance commissioner is responsible for the compliance of insurance companies doing business in his or her state with that state's laws regarding the permitted and prohibited policy provisions. A policy may not be issued or delivered in a state until it has been approved by the state insurance department. In some states, the insurer can assume that the policy has been approved if it has not been advised otherwise within a fixed period of time, such as 30 days, after submission to the state insurance department. In other states, the insurer may not issue the policy until it has received notice of approval from the department.

If an insurer issues a policy that has not been approved by the insurance department, the policyowner can seek a refund of premiums or seek enforcement of the policy. If suit is brought, the courts will enforce the unapproved contract against the insurer on behalf of the beneficiary. If the unapproved policy does not include a provision that would have been required for approval, the policy will be treated by the courts as if it did contain such a provision. Furthermore, if a required provision is more favorable to the policyowner than one actually included in the contract, the courts will treat the contract as if it included the more favorable provision. The insurer that violates the laws requiring filing of the policy and approval of its provisions by the state is also subject to fines or other penalties such as revocation of the insurer's right to do business in that state.

SOURCES FOR FURTHER IN-DEPTH STUDY

- Graves, Edward E., and Christensen, Burke A., *McGill's Legal Aspects of Life Insurance*, 3d ed., Bryn Mawr, PA: The American College, 2002. Phone 888-263-7265. Web site address www.amercoll.edu

CHAPTER REVIEW

Answers to review questions and self-test questions start on page 725.

Key Terms

standard policy provisions laws	primary beneficiary
grace period	contingent beneficiary
policy loan	suicide provision
incontestable clause	ownership provision
divisible surplus	assignment provision
dividend options	plan change provision
entire contract provision	accelerated benefits provision
reinstatement provision	accidental death benefits
misstatement of age or sex clause	guaranteed purchase (insurability)
nonforfeiture options	option
settlement options	waiver-of-premium provision

Review Questions

9-1.   What information is usually found on the declarations page of most life insurance policies?

9-2.   Frank purchased a participating whole life policy many years ago, and over time, several questions have arisen regarding his coverage. Which policy provision should be reviewed to clarify each of the following questions, and what would that provision typically suggest?

a. Frank just discovered that his premium was due 2 weeks ago. Is the coverage still in force?

b. Frank is facing a liquidity crunch. He needs some cash but does not want to exercise a nonforfeiture option. Can his life insurance policy help?

c. When Frank purchased the policy, he lied about his family's health history. Will this prevent his beneficiary from collecting the face amount of the coverage?

d. Frank has been using his dividends to help pay premiums. Are other options available to him?

e. When he applied for his policy, Frank understated his age to get a lower premium. What effect, if any, will this have on the benefits payable to his beneficiary when Frank dies?

9-3. Describe the two options in addition to cash surrender values that life insurance companies are required to provide under the Standard Nonforfeiture Law.

9-4. Describe the settlement options most commonly provided by life insurance policies.

9-5. What is the difference between
a. a primary beneficiary and a contingent beneficiary?
b. the rights of the policyowner when the beneficiary is named revocably versus irrevocably?

9-6. Bill purchased a $500,000 whole life policy 10 years ago. When his marriage and business recently failed, he became distraught and committed suicide. Would Bill's beneficiary receive the $500,000 policy death benefit?

9-7. Harold has the AIDS virus. His prognosis is not good, and he has exhausted all of his financial resources on treatment. His life insurance contract includes an accelerated benefits (living benefits) provision. How can this provision benefit Harold?

9-8. When Rita purchased a whole life policy, she added a double indemnity rider and was surprised to learn that adding the rider did not double her premium. Rita believes that she "slipped one past" the insurance company. Is Rita overlooking something?

9-9. How does a guaranteed purchase option protect an insured policyowner who may need additional life insurance protection in the future?

Self-Test Questions

T   F   9-1. Standard policy provisions laws require that life insurance policies include certain provisions and stipulate that they be worded precisely as contained in the statute.

T   F   9-2.   If the insured dies 2 weeks after the premium was due but not paid, the life insurance company must pay the beneficiary only an amount equal to the premiums paid in the past plus interest.

T   F   9-3.   If the insured dies or surrenders the policy while a loan is outstanding, the loan and accrued interest are deducted from the amount otherwise payable.

T   F   9-4.   After John's policy has been in force for 2 years during John's lifetime, the insurer can no longer contest the policy based on a false answer about John's health made in the application.

T   F   9-5.   The use of dividends to purchase paid-up additions may be advantageous because the purchase is made at rates that do not contain a loading for expenses, and no evidence of insurability is required of the insured.

T   F   9-6.   If Bill died 20 years after purchasing his whole life policy and it was discovered that he had understated his age in the application, the company would have to pay the face amount to the beneficiary because the policy is no longer contestable after 2 years.

T   F   9-7.   If the premium for a whole life insurance policy is not paid by the end of the grace period, the policy will lapse and automatically pay the cash surrender value to the policyowner.

T   F   9-8.   If Sarah named her husband as primary beneficiary and her children as contingent beneficiaries of her life insurance policy, and her husband predeceases her, the death proceeds from Sarah's policy will be paid to her husband's estate if she has not changed the beneficiary designation.

T   F   9-9.   If Janet committed suicide 5 years after purchasing her whole life policy, the face amount would be paid to the beneficiary.

T   F   9-10. The person who has the power to exercise the rights in a life insurance policy is called the insured.

T   F   9-11. While accidental death benefit riders typically exclude death by suicide, they do pay for most deaths caused by disease.

T   F   9-12. If a person purchases a life insurance policy that has not been approved by the state insurance department, the policyowner can seek a refund of premiums paid or seek to enforce the policy.

Life Insurance Planning and Purchasing Decisions

Learning Objectives

An understanding of the material in this chapter should enable the student to

---

10-1. Explain the key approaches to determining the amount and type of life insurance appropriate for a client.

10-2. Explain the key methods for measuring the cost of life insurance.

10-3. Describe the issues involved in the replacement of a life insurance policy.

10-4. Explain the reason for and methods used to treat substandard risks.

10-5. Explain the regulation, ethics, taxation, and planning considerations of policy viatication.

10-6. List and explain business uses of life insurance.

10-7. Describe the taxation of life insurance benefits and premiums.

10-8. Describe the uses of life insurance in estate planning.

Chapter Outline

As the preceding chapters have shown, there is a wide array of life insurance coverages available and many different features of each available type. Therefore, clients who are considering the purchase of life insurance must make a variety of decisions with which the financial planner should be able to provide assistance. The present chapter provides guidance for financial planners regarding making life insurance recommendations, along with the implications of those recommendations.

LIFE INSURANCE PLANNING

Life insurance planning includes determining both how much and what type of insurance is needed. The first of these tasks is usually completed based on an analysis of the client's needs. The second task begins with a decision between temporary versus permanent coverage and proceeds to the selection of a particular type of policy.

This chapter assumes that clients are serious about their financial futures and that the financial services professional has established enough trust for the information-gathering and analysis process to proceed. Problem solving in this arena requires complete and accurate information about the client's finances. In addition, the planner must understand the client's priorities and goals or objectives. The planner must gather this information prior to making any recommendations.

This chapter begins with a discussion on determining the appropriate amount and type of life insurance to provide future income for persons who are dependent on the insured for support. Then other uses of life insurance are discussed. The discussion of this use is at the end of the chapter, following an overview of estate and gift taxation. An understanding of these tax rules is necessary to appreciate the role life insurance can play.

The Appropriate Amount of Life Insurance

There are many different approaches to determine the amount of life insurance appropriate for any given client. Some of these approaches include the following:

- multiple of income approach
- financial needs analysis approach
- capital needs analysis approach

Multiple of Income Approach

Financial journalists tend to prefer a simplistic approach, expressed as a multiple of annual income, because it is short and easy to explain. However, this approach ignores information about how much the client has already accumulated and any external sources of funds such as trusts and inheritances. This approach can err in either direction—that is, it can either overinsure or underinsure the client.

The more sophisticated approaches to determine needs are described below. These approaches translate the client's into estimated costs, then evaluate assets and existing coverage to determine how much of the funding is already in place. Any deficit between the intended goals and objectives and current financial sources is usually a candidate for additional coverage. Life insurance provides a means of completing the financing of the goals and objectives that families work toward during their lifetimes.

Financial Needs Analysis Approach

financial needs analysis

The *financial needs analysis* approach is commonly used to determine how much life insurance a person should carry. However, every family is different, anticipating every need is not possible, and needs change over time. This section will identify general categories of needs likely to be found in any family situation. The financial needs approach begins with estimates of the family's financial needs if the client were to die today. The two main categories of financial needs approaches are lump-sum needs at death and ongoing income needs.

Lump-Sum Needs at Death. The usual cash needs at death include such items as final illness costs not covered by insurance; repayment of outstanding debt, perhaps including the home mortgage loan that becomes due and payable upon death; estate taxes, if applicable; the expenses of the funeral, burial, or cremation, as applicable; the costs of probate court to prove the validity of the will; attorneys' fees; and operational expenses to cover the ongoing short-term costs of the survivors' household. Examples of short-term costs include the mortgage or rent payment, utility bills, property insurance premiums, property taxes, food, clothing, transportation costs, and costs of child care and/or education.

The lump-sum needs at death should also include an emergency fund. This safety net or shock absorber will help the survivors cope with unexpected costs that could otherwise devastate an already strained cash-flow budget. An emergency fund provides for emergencies without sacrificing funds needed for ongoing expenses.

An important factor in setting the level of the emergency fund is whether the family has other liquid or near-liquid assets that could easily be used to cover such emergencies. Money market accounts and listed security holdings can be acceptable sources of funds to cover all or part of any potential emergency, thus reducing or eliminating the amount of funds from life insurance death proceeds that would be needed.

Many financial planners suggest that prefunding of children's educational needs should be classified under the lump-sum category, rather than being funded from income. Obviously, the amount needed to prefund children's education is a function of the number and current ages of those children, the costs associated with the intended educational institutions, the number of years for which educational support is intended to be provided, and the proportion of financing for education that the parents intend to prefund. For some families, the intent is to provide a public school education through high school, while other families may provide full funding for private preparatory schools and an Ivy League education up to the completion of a professional degree such as a JD or MD, or even a PhD program.

Ongoing Income Needs. The ongoing income needs of the surviving dependent family members continue until those dependents can become self-supporting. In some families, that can be a relatively short time, and in others it can take decades. In some families, the dependent spouse never becomes self-sufficient, and there is no intention for the spouse to do so. At the other end of the spectrum is the family in which all members are expected to become self-sufficient shortly after the head of the household dies. In some cases, such an extreme expectation can be unrealistic and even constitute neglect on the part of the deceased. In many families, there is both a desire and the financial ability to prefund the survivors' income needs at least until the youngest child becomes self-sufficient, often when he or she completes formal education. This type of evaluation becomes more difficult when there are children with special needs that will keep them from ever becoming self-sufficient. These special children can actually have ongoing income needs for many years beyond the death of the surviving parent.

Survivors' ongoing income needs are commonly classified into four objectives:

- readjustment income for the period immediately after death
- adjusted income starting after the initial transition period, continuing until the youngest child becomes self-sufficient
- income for the surviving spouse, if any, after the children have become self-sufficient and before the spouse is again eligible for Social Security benefits (the blackout period)
- surviving spouse's income after renewed eligibility for Social Security benefits and initial eligibility for private pension benefits

Because the purpose of life insurance is to fund the unfunded portion of these objectives, all existing funds that can provide part or all of these needs should be considered. For simplicity and efficiency, most planners suggest the use of a percentage of the insured's current income as the target income level, rather than calculating a composite of each separate anticipated need. That the survivors will need about 70 percent of the predeath income to carry on after the insured's death is often assumed, but a higher or lower percentage may be needed depending on a particular family's circumstances.

Social Security benefits are the most commonly available source of income for survivors. These benefits are discussed in chapter 7. Other potential sources of income include employer-provided plan benefits such as deferred compensation, group life insurance, any qualified plan participation funds that are not forfeited or terminated upon the employee's death, and perhaps the surviving spouse's earnings.

Once the desired income goal has been set, the deficits in each future period can be estimated by deducting the existing sources at their anticipated benefit or income levels. The next step is to find the present value of all of the future additional income needs. This calculation can be done in many different ways and with many different levels of specificity. Often, it is broken into component segments so that the income deficit is the same throughout that particular component period. If the calculation is done that way, the final calculation of the total income need is the sum of the present values of each of the separate, individually calculated segments.

Most financial advisers suggest that the number of these components be kept at a minimum and that simplifying assumptions be made whenever possible or appropriate. This approach keeps the estimation process from becoming too cumbersome and time consuming. The financial planner should remember that this is still an estimation process intended to simulate unknown future occurrences. For example, the estimates are made without the benefit of knowing future inflation rates and investment returns. Financial advisers and insurance agents are no more omniscient than economists when it comes to estimating future investment income and inflation rates. In fact, some advisers suggest that all values should be done in current dollar amounts with no discounting applied to future income periods. These advisers maintain that the discounting merely complicates an imprecise estimation process and that ignoring inflation as well will probably make the estimates somewhere near what will ultimately happen.

After future additional income needs have been estimated and combined into a total, another important step must be completed to translate this need into a stated funding objective. Future income payments can be comprised solely of investment earnings on a capital sum, or they can be a combination of investment earnings and liquidation of part of the capital sum. The fund's eventual dissipation is a serious shortcoming of the liquidating approach. The strategy requires the estimation of the insured's likely age at death and the plan for liquidation at that date or later. Any liquidation planning predicated on the beneficiary's death at an early age runs a high probability of using all of the proceeds while the beneficiary is still dependent on them.

Example:	Based on a 7 percent interest assumption, a $1 million capital sum will provide a monthly income of approximately $11,500 for 120 months under the liquidating approach. Under the nonliquidating approach, a $1 million capital sum will provide a monthly income of only approximately $5,800, but the income will continue indefinitely. To provide a monthly income of $11,500 under the nonliquidating approach would require a capital sum of almost $2 million.

capital needs analysis

Two approaches can eliminate the potential problem associated with liquidating the principal sum over the beneficiary's lifetime. The financial needs analysis uses policy proceeds at death, or at a later time, to provide a life income through policy settlement options or separate annuity contracts. These arrangements guarantee lifelong income payments regardless of how long the recipient lives. The *capital needs analysis* does not liquidate the principal, and capitalizes at a high enough level that all the income benefits can be provided from the investment income only. The following sections describe both approaches.

A Case Example of Financial Needs Analysis

To illustrate the use of the financial needs analysis method of determining the amount of life insurance needed, a simplified case situation will be considered. Based on the ages and income levels of the people in the case, no preservation of capital is assumed.

Ted and Amy Stringer are a young married couple with a 4-year-old daughter, Laura. Ted is age 31 and is a bank executive earning $48,000 per year. Amy, age 27, is an elementary school teacher earning $28,000 per year.

Following a series of conversations with Ted and Amy, their financial planner has summarized their objectives or needs in today's dollars, if Ted were to die today, as follows:

- Lump-sum needs at Ted's death

Estate clearance fund	$ 10,000
Mortgage retirement fund	140,000
Emergency fund	15,000
Education fund for Laura	100,000
Total	$265,000

- Income needs after Ted's death

Readjustment period income for one year	$ 65,000
Dependency period income per year for 17 years	$ 50,000
Life income per year for Amy after Laura finishes college	$ 40,000

The financial planner next gathers information about the sources of funds Ted and Amy already have for meeting the above needs. Their principal resources are as follows:

- Group term life insurance on Ted provided by the bank (face amount) — $96,000
- Individual universal life insurance on Ted (face amount) — $50,000
- Investments (mutual funds and 401(k) plan, market value) — $20,000
- Checking account (average balance) — $ 2,045
- Social Security lump-sum death benefit — $ 255
- Social Security survivorship benefits (Laura until she finishes high school at age 18) — $ 6,000/yr.
- Amy's income — $28,000/yr.
- Amy's combined Social Security retirement benefits and miscellaneous income at age 65 for life — $15,000/yr.

Notice that no specific amount of Social Security survivorship benefits is identified for Amy. Instead, Amy's earned income is assumed to cause her to forfeit these benefits as long as she is working. A further assumption for purposes of simplicity is that Amy's income is shown as an annual average, rather than an estimated amount year by year. Also, notice that a combined income of $15,000 per year is assumed for Amy beginning at her projected retirement age of 65 from her pension, Social Security benefits, and miscellaneous sources. Note that Amy would not have been eligible for full Social Security retirement benefits until age 67.

As noted earlier, a total of $265,000 is needed as a lump sum at Ted's death. The present sources of funds with which to meet this need total only $166,000, consisting of group insurance of $96,000, individual insurance of $50,000, and investments of $20,000. The checking account and Social Security lump-sum death benefit are ignored. Thus, a first need is for an additional $99,000 to meet the lump-sum needs (the difference between $265,000 and $166,000).

A time line, as shown in figure 10-1, is useful for planning the income needs of the family. The uppermost set of lines shows the desired income level of $65,000 for the readjustment period of one year, followed by $50,000 per year for the dependency period of 17 years until Laura's age 22, followed by $40,000 per year as the income needs of Amy beginning at her age 45 and continuing for the rest of her life. Below the lines are the various sources of income available to provide the desired income, consisting of a Social Security benefit for Laura until her age 18, an unspecified mix of Social Security benefits and earned income of Amy until her age 65, and Amy's pension, Social Security benefits, and miscellaneous income beginning at her age 65 and continuing for life.

The income gap, or the difference between the desired or needed income during each period and the available income at that time, is shown in figure 10-1. This gap amounts to

$65,000 minus $34,000, or $31,000, for one year; followed by
$50,000 minus $34,000, or $16,000, for 13 years; followed by
$50,000 minus $28,000, or $22,000, for 4 years; followed by
$40,000 minus $28,000, or $12,000, for 20 years; followed by
$40,000 minus $15,000, or $25,000, for the rest of Amy's life

The amount of life insurance proceeds needed today to fill the income gap is the present value of each of the separate gaps. If discounted at an assumed after-tax rate of return of 6 percent per year, the total present value can be found with a financial calculator's net present value (NPV) function as approximately $293,000.

Thus, the total additional life insurance that should be written on Ted's life is $99,000 for the lump-sum needs and $293,000 for the survivors' income needs, or approximately $392,000. There are two difficulties with this amount of insurance:

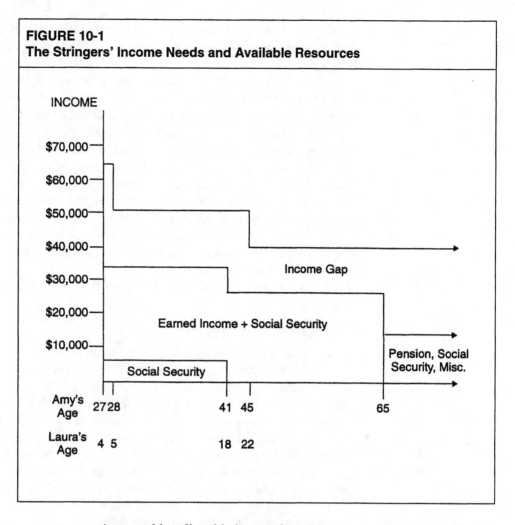

FIGURE 10-1
The Stringers' Income Needs and Available Resources

- Amy could outlive this income because an assumption was made that she would live for no more than 20 years, or to age 85, after she retired. The insurance needs would increase by approximately $8,000 if a life expectancy of age 100 were used. Note how little additional insurance is required to guarantee income for a longer time, if that time is far in the future.
- No inflationary increase in the annual income is provided to the survivors.

As to the first point, a partial solution can be provided through additional life insurance on Ted at a later date, if he does not die soon, or through election of a life income settlement option for a portion of the life insurance death proceeds. Alternatively, at some point Amy could use the then unliquidated capital sum from the life insurance proceeds to purchase an annuity. Annuities, which are discussed in chapter 11, can provide an income for Amy's lifetime. Then, too, if all else fails, perhaps Laura will be able and willing to help support her mother in Amy's later years.

As for the latter point regarding inflation, several approaches can alleviate the problem. For example, Social Security benefits for survivors and retirees are automatically adjusted annually for inflation. Also, a rate of interest lower than 6 percent could be used in calculating the present value of the income. The lower discount rate would create a larger amount of additional life insurance needed but would allow for modest periodic increases in the income it provides. Alternatively, Ted's life insurance could be increased later by including a guaranteed insurability option in the policy and/or by using policy dividends to buy additional insurance. Another possible approach is for Ted to buy a variable or variable universal type of life insurance policy. The premium cost, however, may be prohibitive at this point in light of the Stringers' present income and the large amount of life insurance needed.

A similar approach can be used to determine Amy's life insurance needs.

Capital Needs Analysis Approach

If capital is to be retained, determination of the amount of life insurance to own based on needs proceeds as in the capital liquidation approach. Then a personal balance sheet of the client is prepared. All the liabilities, immediate cash needs, and all assets that do not produce income, such as the residence, are subtracted from the total assets. The remainder is the client's present income-producing capital. The last step is to compute the amount of additional capital needed to achieve the desired income objective net of all other income sources.

The amount of additional capital needed to meet the desired objective is found by dividing the amount of additional income needed by the applicable interest rate that represents the after-tax rate of investment return anticipated on the capital sum. For example, if $100,000 per year of additional income is desired, and the capital sum generating those income payments can realistically be expected to generate a 5 percent return after taxes, a $2 million fund is sufficient ($100,000 divided by .05 equals $2 million).

Obviously, the lower the after-tax investment return rate, the higher the capital fund needed to produce the same amount of income. Similarly, higher marginal tax rates will lower the after-tax return rate and increase the size of the fund needed to generate the income.

The choice between capital liquidation and capital retention is not necessarily an all-or-nothing decision. A planner may use a combination of the two approaches, liquidating some of the client's capital and retaining some of it, as a compromise approach to filling the gap between the income needs of the survivors and the other available sources of income.

Retirement Needs

Retirement needs do not fall within the income categories previously described. On the contrary, the need arises only if the others do not. Yet retirement planning is a contingency that the financial planner must anticipate and one that must be considered to arrive at the amount of insurance a family head should carry. To be more precise, this contingency determines the type of insurance the family providers should purchase because, if the family needs are met with permanent insurance and there are adequate funds for premiums, the cash values under this insurance are usually sufficient to take care of at least a large part of the postretirement needs of the insured and the spouse, if still living.

The Appropriate Type of Life Insurance

After the needed amount of life insurance has been determined, there is a question about the most appropriate types of life insurance for the client. Too often, this question resolves itself into the highly debatable and often emotional matter of term life insurance versus permanent life insurance. In fact, each of these types has a legitimate role in life insurance planning for a client.

Chapter 8 describes the characteristics of term insurance, including

- the temporary nature of the coverage. Even the right to renew or to convert expires at some point.
- the low initial premium cost per $1,000 of coverage because of the absence of a savings element
- the rising premium, at an increasing rate, at the expiration of each period of coverage
- the inclusion in the rate of a margin to offset the adverse selection among term insurance purchasers
- the availability of a death benefit that can be level over time, decreasing, or in some cases increasing

Needs that can and should be met through term insurance are encountered daily. One of the most obvious is to hedge a loan. A term policy in the amount of the loan payable to the lender not only protects the lender against possible loss but also relieves the insured's estate of the burden of repaying the loan if the insured dies. An entrepreneur who has invested heavily in a speculative business venture should protect his or her estate and family by obtaining term insurance in the amount of the investment. A parent with young children is likely to need more insurance while the children are dependent than he or she will need when they are grown and self-sufficient. Additional insurance during the child-raising period can be provided through term insurance, frequently through decreasing term insurance superimposed on a permanent policy.

On the other hand, some needs for life insurance are permanent, or at least extend over a very long period. For example, a client's need for funds with which to provide a life income for his or her spouse may not arise in the next few years, or even by age 65. A wealthy client's need for a substantial sum with which to meet estate clearance costs at his or her death or that of his or her spouse is likely to extend for several decades. Permanent life insurance is an efficient, cost-effective way to partially fill these needs.

Nonetheless, some financial planners find virtually no legitimate role for permanent insurance in life insurance planning for their clients. They argue that clients are best served by providing for their death protection needs initially through low-premium term coverage and by meeting their other needs through investing the premium dollars saved in a separate fund. Buying term and investing the difference, or separating the savings and protection elements of the life insurance contract, is based on the assumption that an individual can invest his or her surplus funds more wisely and with a greater return than can the life insurance company. This argument should be analyzed in terms of the objectives of any investment program: safety of principal, yield, and liquidity.

Regarding safety of principal, the life insurance industry has compiled a solvency record over the years that is unmatched by any other type of business organization. Losses to policyowners have been relatively rare despite periods of war, depression, and inflation. Even the few insurance companies seized by regulators in recent years have been able to honor most of their policyowners' contracts.

Life insurance companies unquestionably obtain the highest possible yield commensurate with the standard of safety they have set for themselves and the regulatory constraints within which they operate. Precise measurement of their yield is complicated by several aspects of life insurance accounting. Comparisons of the returns earned by life insurers depend on which invested assets are being considered, and whether they are total invested assets or various separate blocks of assets supporting variable insurance and annuity products.

At certain times, many individuals may be able to secure a higher yield than that provided by a life insurance company by investing in common stocks or other equity investments, and some exceptional investors will be able to do it under virtually any circumstances. The typical life insurance policyowner is unlikely, over a long period, to earn a consistently higher yield than a life insurance company without taking on a greater degree of speculative investment risk. As described later, annual increases in cash values are not subject to federal income taxes as they accrue, while the earnings from a separate investment program are often taxed as ordinary income.

With respect to the third objective of an investment program, the liquidity of a life insurance contract is unsurpassed. The policyowner's cash value can be taken out at any time with no loss of principal. This can be accomplished through surrender for cash, policy loans, or in many newer life insurance products, partial withdrawals. In traditional products, the policyowner virtually never faces the possibility of liquidating his or her assets in an unfavorable market, and policy loans cannot be called because of inadequate collateral.

More important perhaps than any of the preceding factors is the question of whether savings under a separate investment program will actually take place. Fixed-premium life insurance that develops cash values is a form of "forced" saving. Periodic premiums provide a simple and systematic mechanism for saving, and when the savings feature is combined with the protection feature, there is also far more incentive for the policyowner to save consistently than otherwise might be present. An individual who voluntarily buys a bond a month, who purchases a flexible-premium form of life insurance, or who sets a certain amount per month in another type of savings program might skip a month or two if some other use of money is more appealing. If, however, failure to set aside the predetermined contribution to a savings program would result in loss of highly prized insurance protection that might be irreplaceable, he or she will be far more likely to make the savings effort.

Buy Term and Invest the Difference?

- Safety of principal and income
- Rate of return
- Liquidity
- Assurance that saving will be done

The foregoing is not to disparage other forms of investment. All have their place in an individual's financial program. Permanent life insurance, however, should be the foundation for funding lifelong financial needs.

If permanent life insurance is to play a role in financial planning for a client, each of the types of such insurance should be considered. The characteristics of several types of permanent life insurance are described in chapter 8. Among the distinguishing characteristics that may make one type preferable over another for a particular client are the following:

- length of the planned premium-paying period. The shorter this period, the higher the periodic premium. Consider limited-payment whole life to confine premium payments to the client's years of earned income. Alternatively, use ordinary life but use dividends or a nonforfeiture option to avoid the need for lifelong premium payments.
- emphasis on saving versus protection. Again, limited-payment life builds up the savings component more rapidly than ordinary life. If very heavy emphasis is to be placed on the savings element, consider a very short premium-paying period, perhaps even single-premium whole life, or an

endowment, although some of the advantage of the tax-deferred buildup of the savings element can be lost.

- time when death benefits are needed. If the principal need for funds is at the death of the main income-earner, a single-life policy is appropriate. However, if the principal need for funds is to provide estate liquidity when the surviving spouse dies, consider a joint or survivorship life (second-to-die) policy.

- desire for inflation protection. Variable life, universal life, or variable universal life insurance can provide increasing amounts of death benefit protection. In these and other types of insurance, the use of dividends to buy additional insurance or the use of a guaranteed insurability option is also helpful.

- importance of yield versus safety in the savings component. If the client's risk-tolerance permits, variable, universal, or variable universal life may be appropriate as a way to achieve a higher yield.

- unbundling of cost components. If the client wants to know where his or her premium dollars go, consider variable, universal, or variable universal life insurance.

- premium-payment flexibility. Universal life or variable universal life can be appropriate if premium flexibility is important to the client.

MEASURING THE COST OF LIFE INSURANCE

Of course, one of the important factors in a rational life insurance purchasing decision is the cost. If all other factors are equal, low-cost insurance obviously is preferable. If the other factors are unequal, the prospective purchaser needs to weigh price differentials against the differences in other factors that are important to him or her. Therefore, meaningful cost information is an essential element in intelligent decision-making.

At one time, it was common for insurers and their agents to show the net cost of a policy as equal to the sum of the premiums to be paid during the first, for example, 20 years of the policy, minus the sum of the dividends anticipated during that period, and minus the cash value available at the end of that period. The rather ludicrous result of this traditional net cost method was often a net cost of less than zero. Purchasers were asked to believe not only that their insurance for the 20 years would be free but also that the insurer would pay them for the privilege of giving them the coverage!

The weakness of the traditional net cost method was the disregard for the time value of money. Specifically, the method ignored that premiums must be paid out by purchasers every year, whereas most of the dividends and cash values are not available until much later. Also, dividend growth patterns, and perhaps those of cash values, can differ significantly for different insurance companies.

Example:	Under the traditional 20-year net cost method, if the annual premium for a $100,000 policy is $1,600, the 20th-year cash value is $28,000, and the projected dividends total $7,200, the annual net cost per $1,000 of coverage would be shown as

Premiums ($1,600 x 20)	$32,000
Minus dividends	7,200
Minus cash value	28,000
Net cost	–$ 3,200
Net cost per $1,000 (–$3,200 ÷ 100)	–$ 32.00

The NAIC has developed a model regulation to improve the quality of the cost information offered to prospective life insurance buyers. The regulation requires insurers to give the prospective purchaser a buyer's guide that contains a clear explanation of products and how to shop for them, and a policy summary that contains essential information pertaining to the particular policy under consideration. The policy summary is required to disclose two interest-adjusted cost indexes for the policy. These indexes reflect the time value of money by recognizing that money is paid and received at different times and that costs can be better compared by using a specified interest assumption.

surrender cost index

The *surrender cost index* is useful when the main concern is the level of cash values. This index indicates the cost of surrendering the policy for the cash value at some future point in time such as 20 years. The result is the average amount of each annual premium that is not returned if the policy is surrendered for its cash value.

To compute the surrender cost index, the usual steps are:

1. Assume that each annual premium, paid at the beginning of the year, is placed in an account to accumulate at 5 percent interest until the end of a 20-year period.
2. Assume that each annual dividend, paid at the end of the year, is placed in an account to accumulate at 5 percent interest until the end of the 20-year period.
3. Subtract the 20th year cash value and the result of step (2) from the result of step (1).
4. Using the result of step 3 as the future value, solve for the beginning of year annuity, discounted for 20 years at 5 percent. The result represents the estimated level annual cost of the policy.
5. Divide the result of step (4) by the number of thousands of dollars in the policy's death benefit. The result is the estimated level annual cost per $1,000 of coverage.

net payment cost index

  The other interest-adjusted cost index is the *net payment cost index,* useful when the main concern is with the death benefit to be paid at the end of the 20th year, rather than the cash value. The procedure for calculating this index is identical to that for the surrender cost index, except that in step (3) there is no subtraction of the 20th year cash value.

  Although the use of these cost indexes is subject to caveats, including that the indexes do not reflect actual net costs to the individual policyowner, the prospective cost estimates can be valuable in giving the applicant a relative sense of which similar policies are high or low in cost. Note, however, the actual cost of a life insurance policy to an individual depends on his or her own circumstances and the actual cash flows experienced under the policy. This actual cost cannot be ascertained until the contract expires by death, maturity, or surrender, and when assumptions are made as to the time value of money for the individual.

Example: Assume that a policy has a $100,000 death benefit. Assume also that the level annual premiums, if accumulated at 5 percent compound interest from the time of payment until the end of the 20th policy year, would amount to $75,931. Further, assume that the 20th year cash value is $35,900. Last, assume that the anticipated dividends, if accumulated at 5 percent compound interest from the time of receipt until the end of the 20th policy year, would amount to $14,119. The 20-year surrender cost index would be

Accumulated premiums	$75,931.00
Minus cash value	35,900.00
	$40,031.00
Minus accumulated dividends	14,119.00
Cost	$25,912.00

Discounted over 20 years at 5 percent, to a beginning of year annuity	= $	746.33
Divided by 100 units of coverage	= $	7.46

The net payment cost index would not entail subtraction of the cash value. It would therefore be

Accumulated premiums	$75,931.00
Minus accumulated dividends	14,119.00
Cost	$61,812.00

Discounted over 20 years at 5 percent, to a beginning of year annuity	= $	1,780.34
Divided by 100 units of coverage	= $	17.80

LIFE INSURANCE POLICY REPLACEMENT

replacement

Life insurance purchasing decisions may involve the *replacement* of an old policy with a new one. An existing insurance policy may be replaced by another policy from the same insurer or by a policy issued by a different insurer. Twisting takes place when a policyowner is induced to discontinue and replace a policy through agent or insurer distortion or misrepresentation of the facts. However, replacement is broader than twisting, because it can occur in the absence of any distortion or misrepresentation.

The replacing agent's motives may or may not be laudable. If an agent accurately discloses the facts and the replacement works to the policyowner's benefit, replacement does not present a social problem. However, because of high first-year commissions on new policies, agents have financial incentives not only to take business away from another insurer but also to replace a policy in their own company to generate another first-year commission. Furthermore, insurers who seek new business may not be averse to taking it away from a competitor, even though doing so may not benefit the policyowner.

Traditionally, most replacements were considered detrimental to the policyowner because he or she had already incurred the high first-year expenses, because the premiums under the new policy might be higher because of the insured's increased age, and because the suicide and incontestable provisions might expire sooner, if they have not already done so, under the existing policy. Recently, however, with sometimes higher interest rates and improved mortality experience, policyowners may be able to substantially improve their situations by replacing an existing policy with either the same or a different company.

To protect policyowners' interests, the NAIC developed the Unfair Trade Practices Act, which contains prohibitions against misrepresentation, including misrepresentations to induce the lapse, forfeiture, exchange, conversion, or surrender of any life insurance policy. The NAIC has also adopted what is now called the Life Insurance and Annuities Replacement Model Regulation, which focuses on providing the buyer with full disclosure of information in a fair and accurate manner and provides ample time to review the information before making a final decision.

When an agent submits an application for life insurance or an annuity to the insurer, he or she must include a statement about whether the policy is a replacement. If a replacement is involved, the agent must give the applicant a prescribed notice alerting the applicant to the need to compare the existing and the proposed benefits carefully and to seek information from the agent or insurer from whom he or she purchased the original policy. The replacing insurer must advise the other insurer of the proposed replacement and provide information on the new policy. The replacing insurer must also give the applicant at least a

---

Some Issues in Policy Replacement

- Pay high first-year expenses again?
- Higher premium?
- New suicide clause?
- New incontestable clause?
- More or less favorable policy terms?

20-day free look at the new policy, during which time he or she has an unconditional right to a full refund of all premiums paid if he or she decides not to retain the policy. The existing insurer or agent has 20 days to furnish the policyowner with information on the existing policy, including the premium, cash values, death benefits, and dividends. Both insurers and agents are responsible for the accuracy of the information submitted to the existing policyowner.

SUBSTANDARD COVERAGE

An insurance company may be willing to write the policy applied for, but only on a substandard basis. This situation occurs in about 6 percent to 7 percent of all new policies issued, and introduces some additional complexities into the life insurance purchasing decision.

A group or classification that is rated as substandard by an insurer, such as male applicants who have elevated blood pressure readings, is expected to produce a higher mortality rate than a group of normal lives. The group concept must be emphasized because, as with insuring standard applicants, there is no certainty about any individual's longevity expectations. All assumptions therefore are based on the anticipated average experience of a large number of individuals.

The law of large numbers should be reiterated in any consideration of substandard insurance, involving, as it does, extra cost or restricted benefits for the policyowner or beneficiary. Some believe that if an individual is placed in a substandard classification and subsequently lives to a ripe old age, the company erred in its treatment of the case. However, if 1,000 persons, each of whom is suffering from a particular physical impairment, are granted insurance, the death rate among them will be greater than the death rate among a group of people the same age who are free of any discernible impairments. To allow for the higher death rates or extra mortality that will certainly occur within the substandard group, the company must collect an extra premium from or impose special terms on all who are subject to the extra mortality. The insurer does not expect that every member of the group will survive for a shorter period than the normal life expectancy, just that a larger proportion of the people in a standard group will attain normal life expectancy.

Incidence of Extra Mortality

If a group of substandard applicants is to be fairly treated, the degree of extra mortality represented by the group and the approximate period in life when the extra mortality is likely to occur must both be known within reasonable limits. The timing of claims makes a great deal of difference financially to the insurer, whether the extra claims are expected to occur primarily in early life, middle age, old age, or at a level rate throughout the individuals' lifetimes. If the extra mortality occurs during the early years of the policies, when the net amount at risk is relatively large, the burden on the insurance company will be greater than if it occurs later, when the net amount at risk is relatively small. Therefore, between two substandard groups representing the same aggregate amount of extra mortality, the group whose extra mortality is concentrated later in life should pay a smaller extra premium than the group whose extra mortality occurs earlier.

The majority of companies assume that each substandard applicant falls into one of three broad groups. In the first group, the additional hazard increases with age; in the second group, the hazard remains approximately constant at all ages; in the third, the hazard decreases with age. Examples of each type of hazard are easy to find. High blood pressure presents an increasing hazard. Occupational hazards represent a fairly constant hazard, as do certain types of physical defects. Impairments attributable to past illnesses and surgical operations are usually hazards that decrease with time.

Treatment of Substandard Applicants

Several methods have been devised to provide insurance protection to people with impaired health. In general, companies make an effort to adapt the method to the type of hazard represented by the substandard applicant.

Increase in Age

rate-up age method

One method of treatment is to *rate up* the age of the applicant. Under this *rate-up age method*, the applicant is assumed to be a number of years older than his or her real age, and the policy is written accordingly. For example, if a male applicant, aged 25, is placed in a classification that is expected to produce an extra mortality equivalent to the rate for a male aged 33, the applicant would be rated up 8 years and thereafter treated in all respects as if he were 33 years of age. His policy would contain the same surrender and loan values and would be entitled to the same dividends, if any, as any other similar contract issued at age 33. This method of dealing with substandard applicants is often used when the extra mortality is decidedly increasing and will continue to increase indefinitely.

The chief appeal of this method for the insurance company is its simplicity. Policies can be dealt with for all purposes as standard policies issued at the assumed age. No separate set of records is required; no special calculations of premium rates, cash and other surrender values, reserves, and dividends are involved. For the applicant, the method is attractive because the higher premium is accompanied by correspondingly higher surrender values and dividends, if the policy is participating.

Extra Percentage Tables

extra percentage tables

Extra percentage tables are the most common method of dealing with applicants who present an increasing hazard. These tables classify applicants into groups based on the expected percentage of standard mortality and charge premiums that reflect the appropriate increase in mortality. The number of substandard classifications can vary from three to 12, depending to some extent on the degree of extra mortality the company is willing to underwrite. For example, a company might establish three acceptable substandard classifications with expected average mortalities of 150, 175, and 200 percent of standard, respectively. In effect, a special mortality table that reflects the appropriate degree of extra mortality is prepared for each substandard classification, and a complete set of gross premium rates is computed for each classification. Depending on company practice and state law, surrender values may be based on the special mortality table or may be the same as surrender values under policies issued to standard applicants.

Flat Extra Premium

flat extra premium

A third method of underwriting substandard applicants is to assess a *flat extra premium*. Under this method, the standard premium for the policy in question is increased by a specified number of dollars per $1,000 of insurance. Assessed as a measure of the extra mortality involved, the flat extra premium does not vary with the age of the applicant. The extra premium may be paid throughout the premium-paying period of the policy, or may be terminated after a period of years when the extra hazard has presumably disappeared.

The flat extra premium method is normally used when the hazard is thought to be constant, for example, deafness or partial blindness, or decreasing, as with a family history of tuberculosis or the aftermath of a serious illness or surgical operation, in which case the flat extra premium is usually temporary. The flat extra premium is widely used to cover the extra mortality associated with certain occupations and avocations.

The flat extra premium is not reflected in policy values and dividends. It is assumed that the entire amount of the extra premium is needed each year to pay additional claims and expenses. The dividends and guaranteed values are identical to those of a comparable policy without the flat extra premium.

Liens

lien

When the extra mortality to be expected from an impairment is of a distinctly decreasing and temporary nature, such as that associated with convalescence from a serious illness, an insurer may create a *lien* against the policy for a number of years, with the amount and term of the lien depending on the extent of the impairment. If this method is utilized, the policy is issued at standard rates and is standard in all respects except that, should death occur before the end of the period specified, the amount of the lien is deducted from the proceeds otherwise payable.

The lien method has a psychological appeal in that few persons who are refused insurance at standard rates believe themselves to be substandard applicants and tend to resent the company's action in classifying them that way. If the only penalty involved is a temporary reduction in the amount of protection, most applicants are willing to go along with the company's decision, confident that they will survive the period of the lien and thus prove the company wrong.

A practical and serious disadvantage of the method is that the reduction in coverage occurs in the early years of the policy, when the need for protection is presumably the greatest. Frequently, the beneficiary has no knowledge of the lien, and the company's failure to pay the face amount of the policy can be the source of great disappointment and resentment, to the detriment of the company's reputation in the community. There is also a possibility that the lien is in conflict with laws in certain states that prohibit any provision that permits the company to settle a death claim with a payment smaller than the face amount.

Other Methods

When the degree of extra mortality is small or when its nature is not well known, the insurer may make no extra charge but, if the policy is participating, place all of the members of the group in a special class for dividend purposes, adjusting the dividends in accordance with the actual experience. Alternatively, the insurer may simply limit the plan of insurance to one with a high savings component.

TABLE 10-1
Ways of Dealing with Substandard Applicants

Hazard Increases with Age	Hazard Remains Constant	Hazard Decreases with Time or is Temporary
• Age rate-up • Extra percentage table	• Flat extra premium	• Flat extra premium • Liens • Special dividend class • Limit policy type to one with high savings component

Removal of a Substandard Rating

Frequently, a person who is classified as substandard and insured on that basis by one company subsequently may apply for insurance with another company, or even the same company, and is found to be standard in all respects. Under these circumstances, the person's natural reaction is to request the removal of the substandard rating. The insurer must determine whether to remove the rating.

Theoretically, the rating should not be removed unless the impairment on which it was based was known to be temporary or was due to occupation or residence. At the time the policy was originally issued, the insured was placed in a special classification whose members were presumably impaired to approximately the same degree. The company knew that some of the members of the group would die within a short period, while others would survive far beyond their normal expectancy. If the company reduces the premiums for those whose health has improved, the insurer should also be permitted to increase the premiums of those whose health has deteriorated. However, the premiums of those in the latter category cannot be adjusted upward, and therefore the premiums of those in the former category should not be reduced.

As a practical matter, however, the company is virtually forced to remove the substandard rating of a person who can demonstrate current insurability at standard rates. If the insurer does not do so, the policyowner will almost surely surrender the substandard insurance and replace it with insurance at standard rates with another company. Thus, the common practice is to remove the extra premium upon proof that the insured is no longer substandard.

Value of Substandard Insurance

Substandard insurance is of great social importance because it makes insurance protection available to millions of American families that would otherwise be without it. It is perhaps fair to conclude that life insurance is now available to all except those subject to such excessive rates of mortality as to entail premiums beyond their ability or willingness to pay.

VIATICAL AGREEMENTS

Part of insurance planning pertains to alternative uses of the life insurance policy. At certain times, the benefits payable at the insured's death may become less important than the cash that may be available from the policy during the insured's last months. The policyowner may need access to funds during the insured's final months for funding experimental treatments or other treatments not covered by insurance, for keeping the insured comfortable at home rather than in an institution, or simply for financing enjoyable final experiences. These needs may be satisfied by entering into a viatical agreement.

Numerous alternatives may be available if the policyowner needs funds prior to the dying insured's death. First, the policyowner can access the cash value in the form of a loan. Alternatively, the policyowner may use the cash value as collateral for a loan from a bank or from a family member, possibly from the beneficiary against the future death benefit. In both of these cases, the policy will remain in force and premiums will continue to be due, which may be prohibitive for the policyowner. Another alternative to accessing additional funds is to utilize the policy's accelerated benefits provision. This provision was discussed in chapter 9. The policyowner should check with the insurance company to see whether this alternative is available, as some insurers will allow payment of an accelerated death benefit even when the provision is not included in the policy.

viator
viatical settlement
provider

Finally, the policyowner may enter into a viatical settlement purchase agreement. The agreement is a contract for the policyowner, or *viator,* to sell the life insurance policy to a third party, the *viatical settlement provider,* who purchases the policy. The settlement provider becomes the new policyowner, is responsible for future premium payments, and is entitled to receive the death benefit at the insured's death.

viatical settlement
purchase agreement

In the *viatical settlement purchase agreement,* in exchange for the rights to the insurance policy, the viator receives a lump-sum cash settlement from the settlement provider. This lump sum is a percentage of the death benefit, based on various factors, such as the insured's life expectancy, the premiums that will be required to keep the policy in force, the insurer's financial strength, and the settlement provider's required rate of return. Settlements generally are paid in the range of 40–80 percent of the death benefit.

The policyowner may engage a viatical settlement broker to comparison shop for the best offer and negotiate the agreement between the viator and the viatical settlement provider. The broker will usually charge a fee of 5–7 percent of the policy's face amount. Alternatively, policyowners can comparison shop on their own to find the best offer. Most life insurance policies can be viaticated, including (under some circumstances) term insurance and group policies. Any policy must have been in force for at least 2 years so that the contestability period is past.

Regulation and Ethics

Viaticals for Viators

Viatical settlements became available in the mid-1980s in response to a new demand created by the AIDS epidemic. AIDS patients, as well as patients with other terminal illnesses such as cancer, rely on viatical settlements to help with expenses during the insured's final months. Regulation of these transactions did not follow until years after their introduction and, as discussed in this section, remain inadequate to protect the public.

Whether the sale of the life insurance policy in the viatical contract constitutes a security sale was not settled until the mid-1990s. In 1994, the Securities and Exchange Commission (SEC) sued the largest viatical settlement provider, Life Partners, on the grounds that viaticals are securities transactions subject to the Securities Act of 1933. This act required that securities issuers register their securities with the federal government and provide a prospectus to any potential investor. The federal district court for the District of Columbia ruled in favor of the SEC, but this decision was reversed on appeal in 1996. As a result, viatical settlements are not considered securities and are not subject to SEC regulation.

Regulation of viaticals is left to the states. The National Association of Insurance Commissioners (NAIC) developed the 1993 Viatical Settlement Model Regulation Act, which provides guidelines to help state insurance commissioners protect viators. The act mandated full disclosure to consumers and established fair payment guidelines based on the estimated life expectancy of the insured. The act requires that the viatical settlement provider grant a 15-day cooling off period during which the viator can rescind the viatical agreement. Nearly half of the states have adopted the act. Additionally, some, but not all, states require licensing of viatical settlement brokers and viatical settlement providers.

Due to the lack of disclosure requirements, the provider's financial strength may not be known. Because there is little financial protection to the viator, consumer groups recommend that the viator insist that an independent escrow agent hold funds in order to ensure that the funds will be available to pay the viator.

Viaticals for Investors

After the settlement is complete, viatical settlement providers may retain the insurance as an asset in their investment portfolios. Alternatively, the settlement provider may offer the insurance contract to a third-party investor, who will pay the settlement provider cash in exchange for the ownership rights to the policy. Depending on the conditions of sale, remaining premiums may be paid by the investor or, more commonly, by the settlement provider.

Investment in insurance policies as the result of viatication is not well regulated, and fraudulent practices have tainted the industry. Viatical salespeople have promised investors high returns with no risk, and have misrepresented the life expectancy of the insured. Further, dishonest practices such as the sale of nonexistent policies to investors have made front page news in the past few years. Additionally, the fraudulent practice of clean sheeting, or inducing terminally ill individuals to apply for life insurance and then selling those policies to investors, has been identified.

The current inadequacy of regulation has created a climate with potential for abuse of both the viator and the investor. The viator is not assured of a fair and adequate payment at a time of physical, emotional, and financial vulnerability. The morality of investing in a viatication contract may be difficult for some investors because, the earlier the insured dies, the higher the return to the investor.

When a life insurance policy is viaticated, the new policyowner has no insurable interest in the life of the insured. Insurance laws require that insurable interest exists only at the time of application, not throughout the life of the policy. However, the ownership of the policy by a complete stranger could create an incentive for the investor to encourage the death of the insured. Although there has been no evidence in the United States of homicide of an insured by an investor, some experts caution that the contract can encourage murder for profit.

Taxation

The Health Insurance Portability and Accountability Act of 1996 (HIPAA) defined situations under which viatical and accelerated death benefits are tax exempt on the federal level. The insured must be terminally ill, having been certified by a physician as having a life expectancy of 24 months or less or chronically ill, defined as permanently and severely disabled. Also, if the viator's state requires licensing, the viatical settlement provider must be licensed with the state. If the state does not require licensing, the settlement provider must meet selected requirements of the NAIC Model Act. Most, but not all, states also exempt these settlements from taxation if these conditions are met. Even in states where viatical settlements are tax exempt, capital gains taxes may be imposed on the difference between the settlement received and the total premiums paid.

Planning Considerations

A major weakness in using the viatical settlement is that at the death of the insured, the policy will not provide death benefits to the surviving family but rather to the investor. Thus the income and burial protection will not be provided to the survivors. However, needs may have changed since the policy was purchased, with the death benefit no longer necessary for the surviving family, if any.

Other weaknesses of the viatical approach are less obvious. First, the proceeds may make the viator ineligible for assistance for which he or she otherwise would be eligible. This assistance may include Medicaid, Supplemental Social Security Income, Aid for Families with Dependent Children, food stamps, and state prescription programs. The proceeds may also be subject to creditors' claims.

Another weakness of the viatical settlement is that personal and medical information may be passed along to the investor. This information may include the insured's identifying information, life expectancy, and other medical information. With no privacy regulation, the policyowner has no control over who may have access to this information. A contractual agreement regarding privacy should be a consideration to a potential viator who is comparison shopping for a settlement provider.

Viatication can provide much needed financial relief to a dying client. The financial planner should help the client explore all other options available, and consider both the benefits and the shortcomings of viatication. The client should compare provider offers as to the amount of cash offered, as well as other factors such as reputation, financial strength, state licensure, and privacy provisions. A thorough review of the client's tax situation should also be undertaken to ensure that the settlement will be tax exempt. The financial planner should help the client reach the solution that will best serve the client's needs and provide for the client's wishes as to the financial security of the surviving family.

BUSINESS USES OF LIFE INSURANCE

All of the discussion of life insurance in this and the preceding chapters has explicitly or implicitly assumed its use for family purposes. However, life insurance also serves a number of functions in the business world, and for these purposes, additional factors bear on the purchase decision. In this text, only a few of the many ways in which life insurance can be used in a small business situation are described, namely, indemnifying a small business for death of a key employee; funding a business buy-sell agreement; serving as a group employee benefit plan; and furnishing an executive compensation benefit under a split-dollar plan. Other uses and the sometimes intricate tax aspects of business life insurance are described in more advanced texts.

Key Person Indemnification

The success of a closely held business often depends on the personal services of a key employee. The loss of a key employee's services due to death or disability will probably result in a loss of income, at least temporarily, to the closely held business. In addition, the business could incur increased expenses if a replacement employee has to be recruited at a higher salary and requires extensive training.

What makes someone a key employee? He or she might have a specialized skill critical to the success of the particular closely held business. Potential replacements may possess this same skill, but replacement employees might have to be recruited at higher salary levels. Or perhaps the employee has a significant customer or client base and is responsible for attracting significant amounts of business. As another example, the employee might be a source of capital if his or her loss would damage the closely held business's credit rating.

Valuing the Key Employee

Determining the key employee's value to the closely held business is very speculative. The actual valuation method depends on the characteristic of the employee that creates the key employee status. Determining the value of the key employee who attracts substantial business might be relatively easy. The net income resulting from the business he or she produces in excess of the amount of net income that could be expected from a similarly situated but less effective employee could be capitalized in some manner. In other cases, the firm may have to consider various subjective factors to arrive at a proxy for the key employee's value. For example, the firm should consider replacement salaries and the training required for a replacement employee to become effective.

Key Employee Life Insurance

key employee insurance

A business can purchase *key employee insurance* on the life of the key employee to cover the possibility of an income loss and/or increase in expenses resulting from the key employee's death. Key employee insurance as a result of disability is discussed in chapter 14. Term insurance can be purchased if the primary concern is the key employee's dollar value to the business. Decreasing term might be appropriate because the key employee loss exposure decreases as the insured approaches retirement. Key employee life insurance, however, is usually coupled with some other purpose such as providing a retirement benefit for the key employee. Permanent life insurance is typically purchased to meet this objective. The life insurance death benefit is received by the business as indemnification for the income loss and/or increase in expenses resulting from the key employee's death. If the insured survives to retirement, the corporation can use the cash surrender value to fund a retirement benefit. Another approach is for the business to transfer the policy to the employee at retirement.

The business should be the owner and beneficiary of key employee life insurance. The premiums for key employee life insurance are nondeductible, while death benefits are received tax free.

Funding Buy-Sell Agreements

The death or disability of an owner of a closely held business is typically disruptive for the business and often leads to its failure. When a business owner dies, the executor of his or her estate must collect, preserve, and distribute the decedent's assets. Of course, these assets include both the business and personal assets owned by the decedent at the time of his or her death. The closely held business presents many difficulties for the executor unless the decedent has appropriately planned for business continuation.

buy-sell agreement

A properly designed buy-sell agreement ensures that the estate can sell its interest in the closely held business for a reasonable price. A *buy-sell agreement* is a contract binding the owner of a business interest to sell at his or her death, and a designated buyer to buy at that time, the business interest for a specified or determinable price. The purchasers of the business interest, perhaps the surviving co-owners of the business, will obtain the business interest and avoid the difficulties associated with passing it through probate. Without an appropriate continuation plan, the executor may be compelled to sell the business interest to pay the estate's settlement costs and federal estate taxes and/or state inheritance taxes. The settlement costs must be paid in cash promptly after the business owner's death. Under these circumstances, the executor has a tenuous bargaining position, and a forced sale of the business interest may yield far less than its full fair market value. The surviving co-owners also face a great deal of uncertainty. The survivors may be pressured to provide distributions of business income to the decedent's heirs. They may also face the prospect that the executor or the heirs will choose to sell the business interest to outsiders.

Benefits of the Buy-Sell Agreement

Proper estate planning with a buy-sell agreement offers several advantages, which include:

- a guarantee that there will be a market for the closely held business interest
- liquidity for the payment of death taxes and other estate settlement costs
- establishment of the estate tax value of the decedent's business interest, making the estate planning process more reliable for the owner
- continuation of the business in the hands of the surviving owners and/or employees
- improved credit risk because the probability of continuation of the business is enhanced

Basic Structure of a Buy-Sell Agreement

A properly designed buy-sell agreement has several provisions that are generally included. Among these are the following:

- purpose of the agreement. A buy-sell agreement should contain a statement indicating its purpose. One advantage of including a statement of purpose is to document the intent of the agreement should a dispute arise later.
- commitment of the parties. The obligation of all parties to the agreement should be clearly stated. For example, it should be clear that the estate of the deceased business owner will sell the business interest to the parties who become purchasers under the terms of the agreement.

- lifetime transfer restrictions. Most buy-sell agreements contain a first-offer provision preventing the parties to the agreement from disposing of the business interest to outsiders while all the parties are living.
- purchase price. The buy-sell agreement should specify a purchase price or, in the alternative, a method for determining the purchase price at which the business interest will be bought and sold.
- funding provisions. The terms of the agreement should specify how the purchase price will be funded. For example, if the agreement is funded with life insurance, the agreement should indicate how such life insurance will be structured and paid for.

Continuation Agreements for Partnerships and Corporations

entity agreement

In the case of a partnership or closely held corporation, the agreement may be structured under an entity or a cross-purchase approach. Under an *entity agreement*, the firm itself enters into an agreement with each owner specifying that, on the death of an owner, the firm will buy and the deceased's estate will sell the business interest of the deceased. Technically, the firm liquidates the interest of the deceased partner or redeems the stock of the deceased stockholder. The firm carries life insurance on each owner, with the firm as beneficiary, to provide the money to fund the agreement.

cross-purchase agreement

Under a *cross-purchase agreement*, each partner or stockholder is both a seller and a purchaser. The agreement provides that, on the death of one owner, his or her estate will sell, and the other owners will buy, the deceased's interest. To fund this type of agreement, each owner should carry and be the beneficiary of insurance on the lives of the other owners. For example, if there were three equal partners, the two surviving partners would each purchase one-half, or another agreed-upon share, of a deceased partner's interest.

Continuation Agreements for Sole Proprietorship

The sole proprietorship is by far the most common form of business organization. By definition, there is only one owner of the firm, so on his or her death there are no surviving co-owners to serve as purchasers of the deceased's business interest. Nevertheless, the advantages of having a binding buy-sell agreement are as important for a sole proprietorship as they are for a closely held corporation or a partnership. The new issue in a proprietorship is to find the appropriate purchaser.

Often the sole proprietor has no family successors who are capable and/or willing to step in at the sole proprietor's death. However, there may be a key employee or group of employees who would like to be purchasers of the business. Such individuals, if available, are logical choices for two reasons. First, the key employee or employees of the sole proprietorship are familiar with the business.

This is particularly important if the business requires unique skills to perform its function. Second, the key employees may be willing to enter into a buy-sell agreement to protect their own future employment. Without a buy-sell agreement, the sole proprietorship is often liquidated or sold to outsiders at the death of the proprietor. This could leave the key employees unemployed and without a future in the proprietorship. If there are no key employees or natural successors to the sole proprietor, the sole proprietor could seek a buyer from competitors who might want to take over the proprietor's business at some point in the future.

The life insurance arrangements for a sole proprietorship buy-sell agreement are relatively simple. The purchasing party is obligated to provide sale proceeds to the deceased proprietor's estate. Accordingly, the owner and beneficiary of the life insurance should be the purchasing party. The purchaser should obtain sufficient coverage on the life of the sole proprietor to make the required payments to the estate.

Group Term Life Insurance Plans

Group term life insurance is a benefit plan provided by an employer to a group of participating employees. Such plans are also known as *Sec. 79 plans,* referring to the section of the Internal Revenue Code that applies to them. These plans allow the employer a tax deduction for premium payments on behalf of a participant unless the premium amounts exceed the tax code's reasonable compensation test, which is unlikely.

If the coverage provided by the plan is nondiscriminatory, the first $50,000 of coverage is provided tax free to all plan participants. The taxable amounts of coverage, that is, amounts above $50,000, are taxed according to a rate schedule, referred to as Table I, provided by IRS regulations. These rates are as shown in table 10-2.

TABLE 10-2
Uniform Premium Table I

Age	Cost per Month per $1,000 of Coverage
24 and under	$.05
25–29	.06
30–34	.08
35–39	.09
40–44	.10
45–49	.15
50–54	.23
55–59	.43
60–64	.66
65–69	1.27
70 and over	2.06

If the plan discriminates in favor of key employees with respect to coverage or benefits, the actual premiums paid on behalf of these key employees for their entire amount of coverage are taxable as ordinary income to them, but other employees still receive the previously mentioned favorable tax treatment. A key employee generally includes the shareholder-employees and officers of a closely held corporation. The actual nondiscrimination rules are complex and beyond the scope of this book. However, a plan is generally nondiscriminatory if (1) it covers at least 70 percent of a firm's employees, (2) key employees make up fewer than 15 percent of plan participants, and (3) benefits are either a flat amount or a uniform percentage of salary.

Split-Dollar Life Insurance Plans

split-dollar life insurance

Split-dollar life insurance is a form of permanent life insurance frequently used prior to 2003 as an executive compensation benefit. In a traditional split-dollar plan, a corporation and an employee split a life insurance policy covering the life of the employee. The corporation contributes an amount equal to the annual increase in the cash surrender value, while the executive pays the remainder of the annual premium. In the past, the executive was only taxed for the PS 58 cost of one-year term insurance funded by the employer.

Under split-dollar, the death benefit is split between the participating executive and the corporation as follows:

- The corporation receives a return of its contributions, which equals the cash surrender value.
- The beneficiary named by the insured receives a death benefit equal to the net amount at risk.

The Sarbanes-Oxley Act, enacted in 2002 to bar insider loan transactions, has caused a rethinking of the advantages of split-dollar life insurance. The law prohibits publicly traded companies from using corporate funds to personally finance its directors or officers. The insurance industry views the split-dollar arrangement as compensation rather than a loan and is seeking further clarification. In the meantime, however, public companies are determining whether to terminate existing plans, skip premium payments, pay premiums by policy loan, or treat employer premium payments as compensation to the employee. No new split-dollar arrangements are expected to be executed until final clarification is obtained.

TAXATION OF LIFE INSURANCE

Quite often, especially for affluent clients, how the life purchase can legitimately serve to reduce the client's federal tax burden is a key consideration.

The subject of federal income, estate, and gift taxes is sufficiently broad and deep to fill an entire textbook, and many authors have done so. In this chapter, only a thumbnail sketch of some of the most common tax aspects of individual life insurance is included. The major aspects of the taxation of annuities are explained in chapter 11.

Income Taxation of Death Proceeds

In general, and subject to some exceptions, proceeds paid under a life insurance contract by reason of the insured's death are excludible from gross income for federal income tax purposes. The basic requirement for the income tax exclusion for life insurance proceeds is that they be paid by reason of the death of the insured. Current law also extends the exclusion to certain viatical settlements and accelerated death benefits made on behalf of an insured who is terminally ill and expected to die within 24 months.

Transfer-for-Value Rule

transfer-for-value rule

The most important exception to the general rule of exclusion of life insurance death proceeds from federal income taxation is the *transfer-for-value rule*. This rule provides that if a policy is transferred from one owner to another for valuable consideration, the income tax exclusion is lost. When the insured dies in these cases, only the amount the transferee-owner paid for the policy, plus any premiums subsequently paid will be recovered income-tax-free by the policy beneficiary. The transfer-for-value rule is not limited to an outright sale of a policy. This rule can also apply when a noncash consideration for a policy transfer can be inferred.

Thus, the transfer-for-value rule is an exception to the general rule of exclusion for policy proceeds. There are also exceptions to the exception (a common phenomenon in tax law). Policy transfers that are not jeopardized by the transfer-for-value rule are as follows:

- transfers in which the transferee-owner is the insured
- transfers to a partner of the insured
- transfers to a partnership in which the insured is a partner
- transfers to a corporation of which the insured is a shareholder or officer
- transfers in which the transferee's tax basis of the policy is determined by reference to its basis to the transferor

Income Tax Definition of Life Insurance

The full exclusion for life insurance death proceeds depends in part on whether the policy itself meets the definition of life insurance under the Internal Revenue Code. There are two alternative tests under this definition. A policy qualifies as life insurance for income tax purposes if it satisfies either of these two tests. The determination whether a policy qualifies is not performed by the consumer or agent, but rather by the insurance company that makes this information available.

cash value accumulation test

The first test, the *cash value accumulation test,* generally applies to more traditional cash value policies such as whole life policies. Under this test, the cash value is generally limited to the net single premium that would be needed to fund the policy's death benefit. The net single premium is calculated by the insurance company using an assumed interest rate and certain mortality charges.

guideline premium and corridor test

The second two-pronged test is the *guideline premium and corridor test.* Policies that are designed to pass the second test must meet both of the requirements. The guideline premium requirement limits the total premium that may be paid into the policy at any given time. This limit varies with each life insurance company based on its own expenses and its own mortality experience. The limit also varies with the insurer's own interest assumptions, subject to specified IRS limits. The corridor or death benefit requirement, the second prong of the test, is met if the contract's death benefit exceeds a specified multiple of its cash value at all times. This multiple varies according to the insured's attained age. Generally, universal life and other similar types of policies are tested under this second, two-pronged test.

Settlement Options

Death proceeds distributed as a series of payments under a settlement option generally include an element of interest earned, which is taxable. However, the portion of a settlement option payment that represents principal (the policy's face amount) still qualifies for the income tax exclusion.

The portion that represents the death benefit is calculated by prorating the face amount over the option's payment period. This is the excludible portion. Any excess amount of each payment represents interest. If the interest-only option is used, all interest paid or accrued is taxable. If the fixed-amount option is used, the payment period is calculated by determining the number of fixed payments needed to exhaust the policy's face amount at its guaranteed interest rate. If a life-income option is used, the present value of any refund or period-certain feature is subtracted from the excludible amount to be prorated.

Income Taxation of Living Proceeds

Amounts paid under a life insurance contract while the insured is still living can take several forms. The most common of these are policy dividends, withdrawals from the policy's cash value or investment fund, policy loans, and proceeds from the cash surrender of a policy.

To determine the income tax effect of most of these transactions, the policyowner's tax basis in the policy must first be known. A policyowner's basis is initially determined by adding the total premiums paid into the policy and subtracting the dividends, if any, that have been paid by the insurer. If nontaxable withdrawals have previously been made from the policy, such amounts also reduce the policyowner's basis. Policy loans generally have no effect on basis unless the policy is a modified endowment contract, which is discussed below. However, it is important to remember that if a policy is surrendered, the principal amount of any loan outstanding against the policy is includible in the surrender value of the policy for tax purposes.

Policy dividends are treated as a nontaxable return of premium and reduce the policyowner's basis. If total dividends paid exceed total premiums, dividends are taxable to that extent. If dividends are used to reduce premiums or otherwise paid back into the policy (for example, to buy paid-up additions), the basis reduction caused by the payment of the dividend is offset by a corresponding basis increase when the dividend is reinvested in the policy because it is then treated as an additional premium payment.

If a policy is surrendered for cash, the taxable amount is the total surrender value minus the policyowner's current basis in the policy. Dividends left with the insurer to accumulate at interest are not included in the surrender value for tax purposes because they have already reduced the policyowner's basis in the contract.

Example:	Aaron Sloan, age 40, owns a level premium whole life policy. He has paid $25,000 in premiums and has received $4,000 in dividends from the policy. The face amount of the policy is $100,000. The total cash value of the policy is $29,000. The policy is also subject to an outstanding loan of $15,000. Aaron decides to surrender his policy for cash. The tax effects of Aaron's surrender of his policy are as follows:

Surrender Value	
Policy loan	$15,000
Plus net cash value ($29,000 total value less $15,000 policy loan)	14,000
Total surrender value	$29,000

Basis	
Premium paid	$25,000
Less dividends	4,000
Total basis	$21,000

Taxable Gain	
Surrender value	$29,000
Less basis	21,000
Taxable gain	$ 8,000

inside buildup

The *inside buildup,* or increase in the cash value or investment fund of a permanent life insurance policy, is not subject to taxation as long as it is left inside the policy. Loans from a policy are not taxable unless the policy is a modified endowment contract. If a policyowner withdraws funds from a policy's cash value, the general rule is that the withdrawal is first treated as a nontaxable return of basis. The excess, if any, of the amount of the withdrawal over the policyowner's current basis is taxable in the year of withdrawal. However, there are important exceptions to this general rule. These exceptions include certain withdrawals from universal life policies and withdrawals from policies classified as modified endowment contracts.

If a withdrawal is made from a policy that results in a reduction in the policy's death benefit during the first 15 years of the policy, the withdrawal may first be taxed as income to the extent of income earned within the contract. A death benefit reduction resulting from a cash value withdrawal typically occurs in a universal life contract. This income first or LIFO (last in, first out) method of taxation is the reverse of the general rule of basis first or FIFO (first in, first out) taxation that life insurance typically enjoys.

modified endowment contract (MEC)

A policy is treated as a *modified endowment contract (MEC)* if it fails a test called the *7-pay test.* This test is applied at the inception of the policy and again if the policy experiences a material change. A material change generally includes most increases and certain decreases in future benefits under a policy. A common example of a material change is an increase in death benefits under the policy resulting from a flexible premium payment.

The 7-pay test is designed to impose MEC status on policies that take in too much premium during the first 7 policy years, or in the 7 years after a material change. For each policy, a net level premium is calculated. If the total premium actually paid into the policy at any time during the 7-year testing period is more than the sum of the net level premiums that would be needed to result in a paid-up policy after 7 years, the policy is an MEC. Simply stated, the 7-pay test is designed to discourage a premium schedule that would result in a paid-up policy before the end of a 7-year period.

Any life insurance policy that falls under the definition of an MEC is also subject to an income first or LIFO tax treatment with respect to loans and most distributions from the policy. A 10 percent penalty tax also generally applies to the taxable portion of any loan or withdrawal from an MEC unless the taxpayer has reached age 59½. With respect to loans (not withdrawals) from an MEC, the policyowner does receive an increase in basis in the policy equal to the amount of the loan that is taxable. However, as shown in the example, the nontaxable portion of a loan from an MEC will not affect the policyowner's basis. A nontaxable portion of a withdrawal, on the other hand, will reduce the basis.

Example: Assume that Aaron Sloan's policy in the previous example is an MEC and that the $15,000 loan from the policy is taken out this year. Prior to the loan, Aaron has a total of $8,000 in untaxed gain in the policy. However, the withdrawal of any untaxed gain from the policy triggers a taxable event. Therefore, the loan will first be treated as a taxable event to the extent of $8,000. The remaining $7,000 of the loan is not taxable to Aaron. The $8,000 taxable portion of the loan will also be subject to the 10 percent penalty tax because Aaron is under age 59½. Aaron's basis in the policy will be increased by $8,000 (the taxable portion of the loan). Therefore, Aaron's basis is now $29,000 ($21,000 + $8,000).

Deductibility of Premium Payments

As a general rule, premium payments for individual life insurance policies are not deductible for federal income tax purposes. This rule applies regardless of who owns the policy and whether it is used for personal or business purposes. However, in certain situations, life insurance premiums can be deductible because they also fit the definition of some other type of deductible expense, not because they are premium payments. For example, a premium payment for a policy on behalf of a charitable organization is deductible by the payor if the charity owns the policy outright. The premium is deductible because it is treated as a charitable contribution, not because it is a life insurance premium. Similarly, in cases where a corporation pays the premium on a policy covering an employee and the death benefit is payable to the employee's beneficiary, the premium can be deductible as compensation paid to the employee. Another situation in which premium payments can fit the definition of a particular deductible expense is where premium payments constitute alimony, made on behalf of an ex-spouse.

Transfer Taxation of Life Insurance

In addition to income taxation, the federal transfer tax system also can apply to life insurance. The following pages provide a brief overview of the transfer tax system and the general transfer tax treatment of life insurance products.

The Federal Transfer Tax System

The federal tax system consists of three components—gift taxes, estate taxes, and generation-skipping taxes. The federal estate and gift taxes are separate tax systems imposed on different types of transfers and although these systems have been unified in the past, the 2001 Economic Growth and Tax Relief Reconciliation Act separated the treatment of estates from gifts. The generation-skipping transfer taxes are separate taxes applied under different rules in addition to any applicable estate or gift taxes. This component of the transfer tax system is not addressed in this book.

The Federal Gift Tax

gift tax

The federal *gift tax* is a tax imposed on transfers of property by gift during the donor's lifetime. This tax applies only if both of the following two elements of a *gift* are present:

gift

- a completed transfer and acceptance of property
- a transfer for less than full and adequate consideration

The essential elements of a taxable gift reveal some noteworthy facts. First, only property transfers are subject to gift taxation. Thus, the transfer of services by an individual is not a taxable gift. Second, the taxation of a transfer does not require an element of donative intent; simply, the transfer must be made for less than full consideration.

The 2001 Economic Growth and Tax Relief Reconciliation Act increased the lifetime amount that a person can gift on a tax-exempt basis to $1 million. The act provides for this amount to remain constant through 2010, then increase with inflation thereafter. There is no sunset provision on this part of the act.

annual exclusion

The Annual Exclusion. Much of the planning and complexity associated with gift tax planning involves the *annual exclusion*. In 2003, qualifying gifts of $11,000 or less may be made annually by a donor to any number of donees without gift tax. The exempt amount can be increased to $22,000 if the donor is married and the donor's spouse elects to split gifts on a timely filed gift tax return. The annual exclusion amount is indexed to inflation, and will increase in $1,000 increments. The annual exclusion is in addition to the tax-exempt amount described in the previous paragraph.

To qualify for an annual exclusion, the gift must provide the donee with a present interest. Outright interests or current income interests in a trust provide the beneficiary with a present interest. Trust provisions that provide the beneficiaries with current withdrawal powers can be used to qualify gifts to a trust for an annual exclusion even if the trust provides for deferred benefits. Use of the annual exclusion in the transfer of life insurance products is discussed later in the chapter.

Deductions from the Gift Tax Base. Two types of gifts are fully deductible from the transfer tax base. First, the marital deduction provides that unlimited qualifying transfers made by a donor to his or her spouse are fully deductible from the gift tax base. The marital deduction proves quite useful if it is necessary to rearrange ownership of marital assets in the implementation of one's estate plan. This deduction is similar to the marital deduction against federal estate taxes discussed later. Second, qualifying gifts to a legitimate charity are deductible.

The Federal Estate Tax

estate tax

The federal *estate tax* is a tax imposed on the transfer of property at death. The most difficult task in calculating the estate tax is often the determination of the assets included in the decedent's estate tax base. Some of the included assets are obvious such as individually owned property, but the estate tax rules often cause the inclusion of property in surprising circumstances. For example, property previously transferred by a decedent can be brought back to the estate tax base by provisions in the statute.

gross estate

The Gross Estate. The starting point in the federal estate tax calculation is determining the property included in the decedent's *gross estate*. It includes the property in the probate estate, which is all property that passes under the deceased's will or, in the absence of a valid will, under the state intestacy law, but it also includes property transferable by the decedent at death by other means. The gross estate of the decedent includes, among other things, the following:

- property individually owned by the decedent at the time of death
- (some portion of) property held jointly by the decedent at the time of death
- insurance on the decedent's life if either (1) incidents of ownership were held by the decedent or transferred by gift within 3 years of death or (2) the proceeds are deemed payable to the estate
- property transferred by the decedent during his or her lifetime if the decedent retained (1) a life interest in the property, (2) a reversionary interest valued at greater than 5 percent of the property at the time of death, or (3) a right to revoke or amend the transfer at the time of death

Items Deductible from the Gross Estate. Certain items are deductible from the gross estate for estate tax calculation purposes: legitimate debts of the decedent, reasonable funeral and other death costs of the decedent, and the reasonable cost of estate settlement such as the executor's commission and attorney fees. As with the gift tax, qualifying transfers to a surviving spouse are deductible under the marital-deduction rules. Because the marital deduction is unlimited, the usual dispositive scheme (100 percent to the surviving spouse) for married individuals results in no federal death taxes for a married couple until the death of the survivor of the two spouses. As a client's wealth increases, sophisticated planning is needed to make optimal use of the marital deduction. (Planning for the marital deduction for life insurance proceeds is discussed later in this chapter.) Moreover, the federal estate tax charitable deduction provides that transfers at death to qualifying charities are fully deductible from the estate tax base.

Credits against the Estate Tax. The state death tax credit provides a dollar-for-dollar reduction, with certain limits, against the federal estate tax for any state death taxes paid by the estate. The state death tax credit is limited, and the maximum state death tax credit available to a particular estate is provided for by a progressive rate schedule in the federal tax code. The size of the credit against the federal estate tax is equal to the lesser of the state death tax actually paid or the maximum state death tax allowable under the progressive credit schedule. State death taxes are often greater than the maximum allowable under the federal estate tax rules.

The Taxable Estate. The 2001 Economic Growth and Tax Relief Reconciliation Act significantly revised federal estate taxation. The act increased the exclusion amount, which can pass by death on a tax-exempt basis, to the levels indicated in table 10-3. The act also reduced the marginal tax rates, which are based on the amount in excess of the exclusion amount. Further, the exclusion amount increases and the marginal tax rate decreases for larger estates periodically through 2009, and in 2010 the exclusion amount will be unlimited. However, the estate portion of the act will sunset at the end of 2010, and in 2011, estate taxation will revert back to the law that was in effect in 2001.

TABLE 10-3
Exclusion Amounts for Estate Taxation

Year of Death	Exclusion Amount
2003	$1,000,000
2004–2005	1,500,000
2006–2008	2,000,000
2009	3,500,000
2010	Unlimited
2011	1,000,000

Federal Gift Taxation of Life Insurance

Gifts of life insurance are treated in the same manner as gifts of any other assets as far as the $11,000 annual exclusion for 2003 is concerned. That is, the outright gift of a policy is a transfer of property that provides a present interest. The system used for determining the value of the gifted policy is beyond the scope of this introductory discussion.

Sometimes there is an inadvertent gift of life insurance policy proceeds. This can happen when a policy owned by one individual on another's life matures by reason of the insured's death and a person other than the policyowner has been named as beneficiary. For example, if a wife purchases a policy on her husband's life and names her children as beneficiaries, the proceeds that otherwise would have been payable to her are payable instead to her children at her husband's death. The transaction is treated as if the policyowner, the wife, had received the proceeds and made a gift in that amount to her children. Moreover, gift splitting will not be allowed because there is no longer a spouse with whom to split the gift.

Federal Estate Taxation of Life Insurance

As explained earlier, estate taxes are payable on property included in a decedent's gross estate if the decedent's estate exceeds the available deductions and credits. Frequently, life insurance is the single largest asset or group of assets in the gross estate. Including life insurance can often mean the difference between a federal estate tax liability and no tax liability. For this reason, it is important to look at the factors that determine when life insurance is included in the decedent-insured's gross estate for federal estate tax purposes:

- Life insurance proceeds payable to the executor, that is, to or for the benefit of the insured's estate, are includible in the estate, regardless of who owned the contract or who paid the premium.
- Life insurance proceeds are included in the estate of an insured if he or she possessed an incident of ownership in the policy at the time of his or her death.
- Life insurance proceeds are included in the gross estate of an insured who transferred incidents of ownership in the policy by gift within 3 years of his or her death.

Life Insurance Payable to the Executor. In general, life insurance should not be made payable to a decedent's estate. There are many reasons in addition to avoiding federal estate taxation why estate planners seldom recommend such a beneficiary designation. These reasons include:

- Insurance payable to a decedent's estate subjects the proceeds to the claims of the estate's creditors.
- Insurance payable to a decedent's estate subjects the proceeds to costs of probate administration, such as executor's fees, but provides no corresponding advantages.

incident of ownership

Possession of Incidents of Ownership. When insurance proceeds are paid to a named beneficiary other than the insured's estate, *incidents of ownership* in the policy at the time of death are the key criteria for determining inclusion. If the insured held an incident of ownership at the time of his or her death, the policy is included in his or her gross estate. An incident of ownership is broadly defined for this purpose as any right to the economic benefits of the policy. Incidents of ownership include, but are not limited to, the power to

- change the beneficiary
- assign the policy
- borrow on the policy
- surrender the policy
- exercise any of the other essential contract rights or privileges

Like any other property, the insurance policy is an asset that can be freely assigned by a policyowner in a gift or sale. Thus, the policyowner may transfer limited interests to others while retaining some of the privileges and rights in the policy. However, to remove the proceeds from the scope of the federal estate tax, the insured must divest himself or herself of all significant rights and privileges under the contract.

Transfers of Policies within 3 Years of Death. Policies are often transferred to others so that policy proceeds will not be in the insured's gross estate when he or she dies. Inclusion will still result, however, if the insured dies within 3 years of a gratuitous transfer. Under this 3-year rule, life insurance transferred to a third party for less than full consideration within 3 years of the insured's death is automatically includible in the insured's gross estate. Transfers made more than 3 years before the insured's death are not normally includible in the insured's estate if the insured has retained no incidents of ownership. In addition, a sale to a third party for the full fair market value of the policy will not be included even if the sale occurs within 3 years of the insured's death.

Life Insurance and the Federal Estate Tax Marital Deduction. Life insurance proceeds payable at the insured's death to his or her surviving spouse can qualify for the federal estate tax marital deduction. Because the marital deduction is unlimited, the full value of life insurance proceeds payable in a qualifying manner to the surviving spouse is deductible from the insured's gross estate.

USES OF LIFE INSURANCE IN ESTATE PLANNING

The goal of life insurance in the estate plan depends on many factors specific to the client. However, the goals for life insurance in general can be divided into two categories: life insurance can serve either as an estate enhancement or as an estate liquidity/wealth replacement device. The goals of a specific client for his or her life insurance planning depend on his or her age, family circumstances, and financial status.

Estate Enhancement Purposes

In many cases, a client's estate at death will not be sufficient to provide for the basic needs of his or her heirs. This is particularly true for (1) young clients,

(2) clients with family members dependent on their income, and/or (3) clients with small to moderate-sized estates. These clients generally have estate enhancement as the primary goal for their life insurance coverage. They may still have their peak earning years in front of them. The basic support needs of their family, such as educational, medical, and retirement savings programs, depend on this income. It is essential for these clients to investigate their life insurance coverage needs and secure sufficient insurance to enhance their estates to a size that is, at the very least, adequate to handle their dependent family members' basic needs. Life insurance is the perfect estate enhancement device to replace the financial loss created by premature death. The methods for determining the amount of life insurance a client needs for this purpose are discussed earlier in this chapter.

Estate Liquidity/Wealth Replacement Purposes

For older clients or clients with large estates, estate liquidity/wealth replacement is the primary goal of life insurance coverage. Their children's support and educational expense needs are usually things of the past. In addition, these older clients are nearing the end of their income-producing years and should, presumably, have less future income to replace. Their needs for estate enhancement from life insurance should have diminished in importance relative to their estate liquidity/wealth replacement needs.

A prospective insured may need coverage for estate liquidity/wealth replacement for the following purposes:

- probate expenses. Estate settlement costs usually increase with the size of the estate. The cost for professionals such as executors, attorneys, accountants, and appraisers to settle an estate is often based on a percentage of the total size of the probate estate. Generally, the larger the estate, the greater the complexity and need for costly professional help. One advantage of life insurance is that it avoids probate if paid to a named beneficiary.
- death taxes. As discussed above, federal estate taxes, as well as other taxes, also increase with the size of the estate. Federal estate taxes, and state death taxes in many states, are based on a progressive rate schedule. Thus, wealthy individuals often desire life insurance to replace the wealth lost to death taxes.
- liquidity needs. Wealthy clients often face an additional problem. Frequently, their accumulated wealth contains assets that are not liquid. For example, wealthy individuals often own closely held businesses that may be unmarketable to outsiders. Death taxes and other estate settlement costs are based on the full value of such assets owned by the estate and must be paid in cash. The liquidity problems faced by an estate often result in the forced sale of estate assets on undesirable terms.

Estate Planning Techniques with Life Insurance

There are many practical uses for life insurance in the estate planning context. Three are described briefly here:

- gifts of policies to family members
- providing estate liquidity
- the second-to-die policy

Gifts of Policies to Family Members

Although the 3-year rule causes estate tax inclusion if the insured transfers incidents of ownership within 3 years of his or her death, transferring or assigning the policy to family members might still be an appropriate planning step. The insured simply has to live more than 3 years following the transfer to avoid inclusion of the proceeds in his or her estate. And even if the insured dies within 3 years, he or she will be no worse off from an estate tax standpoint since the policy would have been included in any event had the transfer or assignment not occurred.

There are many reasons why estate planners recommend a life insurance policy gifting program. Some of the reasons include:

- The donee feels no richer after the gift of the life insurance policy and will seldom dispose of it foolishly.
- The donor-insured's financial position is not markedly affected by making a gift of life insurance.
- The gift tax cost to transfer a policy is usually nominal compared to the potential estate tax savings. Through efficient use of the donor-insured's annual exclusion, the gift of the policy and subsequent premiums can actually avoid gift taxes entirely.
- The gift of a life insurance policy is particularly advantageous for older donors whose estate planning concerns have risen in priority in relation to their other financial planning goals. Usually, older insureds can select appropriate beneficiaries with more certainty, and they are less concerned about a policy's cash surrender value. If a life insurance policy is gifted more than 3 years before the donor's death, the transfer tax savings is substantial.

Providing Estate Liquidity

Unless the executor of an estate wishes to go through a series of complex and burdensome requests for an extension, the estate tax due must be paid within 9 months of the date of death. If the gross estate is composed of liquid assets, the executor or administrator faces no problem in meeting the 9-month deadline successfully. For example, if the estate is composed of sufficient cash, marketable securities, or life insurance proceeds, there will be ample liquidity to ensure that the tax can be paid within the required time. Conversely, if the federal estate tax liability exceeds the amount of liquid assets available, there will be an estate liquidity deficit. To meet the 9-month deadline, a forced liquidation of assets, possibly at a loss, will be necessary.

Life insurance is the most effective way to supply needed dollars to meet federal estate tax obligations. First, the dollars, in the form of death proceeds, are free of federal income taxation. Second, if the life insurance is owned by someone or some entity other than the insured, the policy's face amount will not be included as part of the decedent's gross estate. Finally, a sizable death benefit may be purchased for pennies on the dollar in the form of premium payments.

The Second-to-Die Policy

The federal estate tax marital deduction is now unlimited in nature and scope. Consequently, there is a propensity by estate owners to leave their entire estates to their surviving spouses, which ensures no estate tax liability at the first death. There is, unfortunately, a serious flaw in this approach.

The concept of the federal estate tax marital deduction is based on deferral rather than complete avoidance of estate tax liability. Although the deduction is unlimited, to use the deduction to its fullest extent creates a stacking of estate taxes at the second death. The estate tax liability from the first to die is added to that of the second to die. The result is a higher estate tax liability overall.

The unlimited marital deduction has created a need for greater planning for the death of the second spouse. That is why the second-to-die policy, described in chapter 8, was instituted. At the death of the first spouse, no death benefit is paid; at the death of the second spouse, the policy proceeds are paid to the named beneficiary.

Second-to-die coverage is often a perfect fit in a married couple's estate plan. The most common use of second-to-die coverage is in an estate plan in which taking the unlimited marital deduction after the death of the first spouse

---

Survivorship Life Insurance
(Second-to-Die Coverage)

- Pays the death benefit only at the death of the surviving spouse
- The federal estate tax system allows an unlimited marital deduction
- Problem: the estate tax bill at the death of the surviving spouse
- Solution: death benefit payable at the second death on a far less costly basis than two separate policies

will result in more substantial death taxes at the death of the second spouse. With second-to-die coverage, policy benefits will be paid when the insured married unit incurs these more substantial taxes—at the second death of the two spouses.

CHECKLIST FOR EVALUATING AND COMPARING LIFE INSURANCE POLICIES

☐ What are the provisions concerning premium payments?

___ Are they level or rising at each renewal date?
___ Are they flexible at the policyowner's option at each renewal date?
___ Are they payable for life or for a specified number of years?

☐ What is the initial policy premium?

___ What is the 20-year surrender cost index?
___ What is the 20-year net payment cost index?

☐ Is the duration of death benefit protection for a limited number of years? If yes,

___ Is the policy renewable for additional periods? If yes, until when?
___ Is the policy convertible to permanent coverage? If yes, until when?

☐ What is the initial amount of death benefit protection?

☐ How does the amount of death protection change thereafter?

☐ Does the policy contain a savings element? If yes,

___ Is there a minimum guaranteed amount?
___ Is there a minimum guaranteed interest rate?
___ In what year is it first available?
___ Will it grow with inflation?
___ What nonforfeiture options are available?
___ Are withdrawals permitted?
___ Are policy loans allowed?
___ What is the interest rate for policy loans?
___ Is an automatic premium loan option available?
___ Is the inside buildup tax deferred?
___ Are policyowner-directed types of investments available?

☐ Is the policy participating? If yes,

___ When are dividends likely to be available for the first time?
___ Are dividends useable to buy additional term or permanent insurance?
___ Are dividends affected by policy loans?
___ What is the interest rate if dividends are left to accumulate?
___ What is the insurer's track record of meeting dividend projections?

☐ What settlement options does the policy contain?

☐ How soon can the policy be made to mature as an endowment?

☐ What is length of the contestable period?

☐ What is length of the suicide exclusion?

☐ What is length of time available to reinstate?

☐ Are accelerated benefits available?

☐ Is an accidental death benefit rider available?

☐ Is a guaranteed purchase (insurability) rider available?

___ What is the amount that may be bought?
___ What is the frequency of purchase dates?

☐ Is a waiver-of-premium rider available?

___ What is the definition of disability?
___ What is the length of the waiting period?
___ Are premiums waived retroactively to the start of disability?
___ Is there an age before which disability must occur?

SOURCES FOR FURTHER IN-DEPTH STUDY

- For more on life insurance planning and company operations:
  - Black, Kenneth, Jr., and Skipper, Harold D., Jr., *Life and Health Insurance*, 13th ed., Englewood Cliffs, NJ: Prentice-Hall, Inc., 1999. Phone 800-282-0693. Web site address www.prenhall.com
  - Graves, Edward E., editor, *McGill's Life Insurance*, 4th ed., Bryn Mawr, PA: The American College, 2002. Phone 888-263-7265. Web site address www.amercoll.edu
  - *Life Insurance Fact Book* (published annually), Washington, DC: American Council of Life Insurance. Phone 202-624-2000.

- For highly detailed information on the determination of the cost of life insurance, various issues of Belth, Joseph M., editor, *The Insurance Forum* (a monthly publication), Elletsville, IN: Insurance Forum, Inc. Phone 812-876-6502.
- For a thorough treatment of the complex subject of many of the business uses of life insurance, Kurlowicz, Ted; Ivers, James F. III; and McFadden, John J., *Planning for Business Owners and Professionals*, 8th ed., Bryn Mawr, PA: The American College, 2002. Phone 888-263-7265. Web site address www.amercoll.edu
- For the answer to virtually any question one might have on the federal taxation of life insurance, *Tax Facts 1* (published annually), Cincinnati, OH: The National Underwriter Company, Phone 800-543-0874. Web site address www.nuco.com

CHAPTER REVIEW

Answers to review questions and self-test questions start on page 725.

Key Terms

financial needs analysis	cross-purchase agreement
capital needs analysis	split-dollar life insurance
surrender cost index	transfer-for-value rule
net payment cost index	cash value accumulation test
replacement	guideline premium and corridor
rate-up age method	test
extra percentage tables	inside buildup
flat extra premium	modified endowment contract
lien	(MEC)
viator	gift tax
viatical settlement provider	gift
viatical settlement purchase	annual exclusion
agreement	estate tax
key employee insurance	gross estate
buy-sell agreement	incident of ownership
entity agreement	

Review Questions

10-1.   What two basic tasks are involved in life insurance planning?

10-2.   Before gathering the information required for determining the amount of additional life insurance your client needs, explain to your client the key steps involved and types of information required in the financial needs analysis approach.

10-3.   Janet Jones, a single mother and corporate manager on the "fast track," needs help in determining the amount of additional life insurance she needs to provide support for her children if she should die before they finish college. After gathering information regarding the family's needs in the event of Janet's death, you find that support for the children including college educations would require $300,000 to meet lump-sum needs. Also, taking into account reasonable assumptions regarding inflation, after-tax investment returns, and Social Security benefits for the children, you calculate that a present value of $200,000 would be required to meet the children's income support needs if Janet were to die today. Fact-finding indicates that Janet already has $200,000 of group term life insurance and $50,000 in savings. How much additional life insurance would Janet need if the principal will be liquidated to help meet the family's needs?

10-4.   Describe the steps in the capital needs analysis approach for determining the amount of additional life insurance your client needs. Explain how that approach differs from the financial needs analysis approach.

10-5.   The "buy term and invest the difference" argument against the use of permanent life insurance is based on the assumption that an individual can invest his or her surplus funds more wisely and with greater returns than a life insurance company can. Analyze this argument in terms of the following objectives of an investment program: safety of principal, yield, and liquidity.

10-6.   Discuss the distinguishing characteristics that may make one type of permanent life insurance preferable over another type for a particular client.

10-7.   A financial planning client of yours received a buyer's guide and policy summary from an agent trying to sell him some additional life insurance. Your client asked the agent several questions, but the agent said, "Don't worry about that detail. We're just required by law to give it to you. Our policy is a good buy." Answer the following questions asked by your client:

     a.   The summary says the policy has a surrender cost index of $7.35 per $1,000 of coverage. What does that number indicate, and generally how was it calculated?

     b.   How does the net payment cost index shown in the summary differ from the surrender cost index?

     c.   Why is there so much concern with taking interest into account in these calculations? Why can't you just calculate the cost of a life insurance policy by adding the premiums for 20 years and subtracting the sum of the illustrated dividends for 20 years and the 20th year cash value?

10-8.   You suggested to a financial planning client that she might want to consider replacing a life insurance policy she already owns with a new one. She quickly replied, "An agent told me at a cocktail party last week that you should never replace a life insurance policy. In fact, it's against the law." Advise her by answering the following questions:

    a.   Why might replacement of an existing policy be advantageous to a client?

    b.   If replacement itself is not illegal, what type of replacement is illegal?

    c.   What requirements are typically imposed on the replacing agent, the replacing insurer, and the existing insurer or agent by state law?

10-9. A client of yours applies for life insurance, and he is placed in a substandard classification. He says, "So my job is hazardous. I'm in great health as the underwriting showed. Besides, no one has ever died on a job site where I've worked except from bad health. What's the deal?" Explain to your client the rationale for substandard insurance.

10-10. Briefly describe several methods used by life insurers for handling substandard risks. Be sure to indicate the type(s) of substandard risk for which each is most commonly used.

10-11. Describe the benefits and pitfalls of a policyowner viaticating an insurance policy.

10-12. Suzie Pomeranz, a financial planning client, owns her own rapidly growing business with two minority stockholders. As CEO, she asks for advice in dealing with the following:

    a.   The firm has a number of salespersons, but one, Betty, is the superstar in terms of generating and closing deals. Suzie is concerned with the loss of income, the extra expenses, and the potential effect on the corporate credit rating if Betty were to die. What can you suggest as a solution, and how might it be funded?

    b.   The two minority stockholders who own a total of 40 percent of the voting stock are also corporate vice presidents. They have expressed concern to Suzie about their futures because, if she were to die, her majority shares would currently pass to her playboy son Lance, who has already indicated he would change operations significantly to focus on current return to the owners rather than on long-term growth. What could you suggest as a means to financially protect the interests of both Suzie's estate and the two minority stockholders in the event of Suzie's death? How might your recommended solution be funded?

    c.   Suzie feels that because the business is growing rapidly due to the very productive contributions of her employees, as an employee benefit they should all be provided with life insurance protection equal to 2 times their salary. What would you suggest as a cost-effective way to accomplish this objective?

    d.   Suzie also would like the firm to provide each executive with additional life insurance beyond that provided to all employees. She feels that this should be permanent life insurance and that the company should contribute part of the premium but not all of it. What can you suggest?

10-13. Describe the general rules and key exceptions with regard to the federal income tax treatment of the following aspects of life insurance:

  a. death proceeds distributed in a lump sum

  b. death proceeds distributed under a settlement option

  c. policy dividends

  d. inside buildup of a policy's cash value

  e. withdrawal of funds from a policy's cash value

  f. policy loans

  g. loans and most other distributions from a policy that falls under the definition of an MEC

  h. premium payments

10-14. Describe the following aspects of the federal gift tax system:

  a. the essential elements of a taxable gift

  b. the annual exclusion

  c. deductions from the gift tax base

10-15. List and explain briefly the key factors taken into account in calculating the federal estate tax.

10-16. In each of the following situations, indicate whether the proceeds of the life insurance policy would be included in your client John's estate for federal estate tax purposes upon his death and if so, why:

  a. John's wife purchased a policy on John's life. She was the policyowner and paid all the premiums. She named John's estate as primary beneficiary so there would be sufficient liquidity to pay estate taxes and she would not be required to sell the family home upon his death.

  b. John purchased a policy on his own life and named his children as beneficiaries. Although he was initially the policyowner, he transferred all the rights in the policy to his wife 5 years ago except the right to change the beneficiary.

  c. John purchased a policy on his own life and named his children as beneficiaries. Although he was initially the policyowner, he gave all the rights in the policy to his wife 2 years before his death.

10-17. Discuss some key uses of life insurance in estate planning.

Self-Test Questions

T F 10-1. Using a simple multiple of earnings method to determine the amount of life insurance needed ignores key information about how much a client has already accumulated.

T F 10-2. The financial needs analysis approach considers both lump-sum needs at death and ongoing income needs.

T F 10-3. With the financial needs analysis approach, the amount of additional life insurance needed is determined by subtracting the resources already available from the resources needed by the surviving dependents if the client should die today, assuming all future income payments are comprised solely of investment earnings on a capital sum.

T   F   10-4.   A major advantage of the financial needs analysis approach is that it does not take into account factors that may be difficult to forecast such as Social Security benefits and future earnings by a spouse.

T   F   10-5.   While term insurance is available in the marketplace, virtually all client life insurance needs are best met with whole life insurance.

T   F   10-6.   The basic fallacy of the traditional net cost method for measuring the cost of life insurance is that it ignores the time value of money.

T   F   10-7.   The surrender cost index indicates the cost of surrendering the policy for the cash value at some future point in time.

T   F   10-8.   All life insurance policy replacements involve twisting and thus are detrimental to the policyowner.

T   F   10-9.   If a group of substandard risks is to be treated fairly, the degree of extra mortality represented by the group and the approximate period in life when the extra mortality is likely to occur must both be known within reasonable limits.

T   F   10-10.   The most common method of dealing with risks that present an increasing hazard is to assess a flat extra premium.

T   F   10-11.   It is common practice to remove the extra premium upon proof that the insured is no longer substandard.

T   F   10-12.   Viatication, or the selling of a life insurance policy to a viatical settlement provider, is a securities transaction subject to SEC regulation.

T   F   10-13.   Federal privacy laws regarding viaticals protect insureds from being identified and their medical information from being provided to third-party investors.

T   F   10-14.   One of the common uses of life insurance in business is to serve as an alternative to having a properly designed buy-sell agreement.

T   F   10-15.   In a traditional split-dollar plan, the executive contributes an amount equal to the annual increase in the policy's cash surrender value, while the corporation pays the remainder of the annual premium.

T   F   10-16.   In nearly all cases, the beneficiary of a life insurance policy must include the proceeds paid by reason of the insured's death in his or her gross income for federal income tax purposes.

T   F   10-17.   If Jim withdraws $2,000 from the $15,000 cash value of his (non-MEC) universal life policy for which he has already paid $12,000 in premiums, he would not have to pay income tax on any portion of the $2,000 withdrawal.

T   F   10-18. Federal gift taxes do not apply if there is a completed transfer and acceptance of property for less than full and adequate consideration.

T   F   10-19. The unified credit is applicable to both the federal gift tax due on taxable lifetime transfers and transfers occurring at death.

T   F   10-20. If Sally transfers all incidents of ownership in a life insurance policy on her life to her grown son through a gift and she dies a year later, the life insurance is automatically included in her estate.

T   F   10-21. The primary goal of life insurance coverage for young clients is estate liquidity, whereas for older clients it tends to be estate enhancement.

11

Annuities

Learning Objectives

An understanding of the material in this chapter should enable the student to

11-1.   Explain the nature of annuities, and compare and contrast them with life insurance.

11-2.   Explain the key features of single-life annuities.

11-3.   Explain the key features of joint annuities.

11-4.   Explain the key features of variable annuities.

11-5.   Explain the key features of equity-indexed annuities.

11-6.   Describe actuarial considerations regarding annuities.

11-7.   Describe the taxation of annuities during the accumulation and liquidation periods.

11-8.   Explain uses of annuities, including structured settlements.

Chapter Outline

annuity

This chapter discusses the annuity product of the life insurance company. An *annuity* is a periodic payment that will begin at a specified or contingent date and that will continue throughout a fixed period or for the duration of a designated life or lives. The person on whose life the duration of the payments is based is

annuitant

called the *annuitant*. The annuitant is usually but not always the person who receives the periodic payments. The payments under the annuity contract may be on an annual, semiannual, quarterly, or monthly basis, depending on the conditions of the agreement. Normally the payments are made monthly.

If the payments are to be made for a definite period of time without being linked to the duration of a specified human life, the agreement is known as an

annuity certain

annuity certain. If the payments are to be made for the duration of a designated

life annuity

life, the agreement is called a *life annuity* or, more accurately, a *single-life annuity*. This annuity is also referred to as a *whole life annuity* to distinguish it

temporary life annuity

from a *temporary life annuity*, under which payments are made during a specified period of time, but only for as long as a designated person is alive. In other words, a temporary life annuity terminates with the death of the designated individual or at the expiration of the specified period of time, whichever occurs earlier. The word *life* in the title of an annuity indicates that the payments are based on life contingencies or continue only as long as a designated person is alive. This chapter is concerned primarily with life annuities created by insurance companies. Financial planners need an understanding of annuities to help their clients make decisions about creating and liquidating a principal sum.

NATURE OF ANNUITIES

Comparison with Life Insurance

The primary function of life insurance is to create an estate or principal sum; the primary function of an annuity is to liquidate a principal sum, regardless of how it was created. Despite this basic dissimilarity in function, both life insurance and annuities are based on the same fundamental pooling, mortality, and investment principles.

Both life insurance and annuities can protect against loss of income. Life insurance furnishes protection against loss of income arising out of premature death; an annuity provides protection against loss of income arising out of excessive longevity. While life insurance can provide a financial hedge against dying too soon, an annuity can provide a hedge against living too long. From a financial standpoint, both contingencies are undesirable.

A second common feature shared by life insurance and annuities is the pooling technique. Insurance is a pooling arrangement where all members contribute so that the dependents of those who die prematurely are partially compensated for loss of income. An annuity is a pooling arrangement where those who die prematurely contribute so that those who live beyond their life expectancy will not outlive their income.

A third common feature shared by life insurance and annuities is that contributions are based on probabilities of death and survival derived from a mortality table. For reasons that will be apparent later, the same mortality table is not used for both sets of calculations. Finally, for both life insurance and annuities, premiums (often referred to as deposits) are discounted for the compound interest that the insurance company will earn on them.

The Annuity Principle

The annuity concept is founded on the unpredictability of human life. A person may have accumulated a principal sum to be liquidated for old-age support over the person's remaining years. However, the individual must accurately predict the number of years remaining. With average health and vitality for his or her age, the individual could expect to live exactly the calculated life expectancy, based on a mortality table. But because survival beyond this predicted life expectancy is unsure, to be conservative, the accumulated principal would have to be adequate to fund a longer period than the annuitant is likely to live. Even then there is some danger of surviving the assumed life expectancy and finding the assets and income totally consumed prior to death. On the other hand, the annuitant might die after only a few years, leaving funds to the estate that could have been used to provide more comforts during the decedent's lifetime. If the annuitant is willing to pool savings with those of other people in the same situation, the administering agency, relying on the laws of probability and large numbers, can provide all the participants with an income of a specified amount as long as they live—regardless of longevity. In this way none of the participants could outlive their income. This arrangement relies on participants' willingness to have all or a portion of their unliquidated principal at the time of death used to supplement the principal of those who live beyond their life expectancy. Therefore, each payment under an annuity is composed partly of the annuitant's principal, the unliquidated principal of other annuitants who die early, and investment income on these funds.

Classifications of Annuities

As can be seen in figure 11-1, annuities can be classified in many different ways, depending on the point of emphasis.

The distribution of benefits may extend only for the life of the annuitant or may include some minimum guaranteed total payout. The annuity may cover only one life or it may depend on the longevity of two (or more) persons. The benefit payments may begin immediately or at some future date. The annuity may be purchased through a single premium or through installment premiums. Lastly, the amount of each annuity payment may be fixed or variable. The discussion that follows provides details on the types and characteristics of annuities.

Number of Lives Covered

joint (joint-life) annuity
**joint-and-last-
   survivor annuity**

The annuity may cover a single life or more than one life. The conventional form is the single-life annuity. A contract that covers two or more lives may be a joint annuity or a joint-and-last-survivor annuity. The seldom-issued *joint* or *joint-life annuity* provides that the income ceases at the first death among the lives covered. A *joint-and-last-survivor annuity*, on the other hand, provides that the income ceases only at the last death among the lives covered. In other words, payments under a joint-and-last-survivor annuity continue for as long as either of two or more specified persons lives. This annuity contract is very useful, and widely marketed, especially for husband and wife couples. Annuity contracts that involve more than two lives are uncommon.

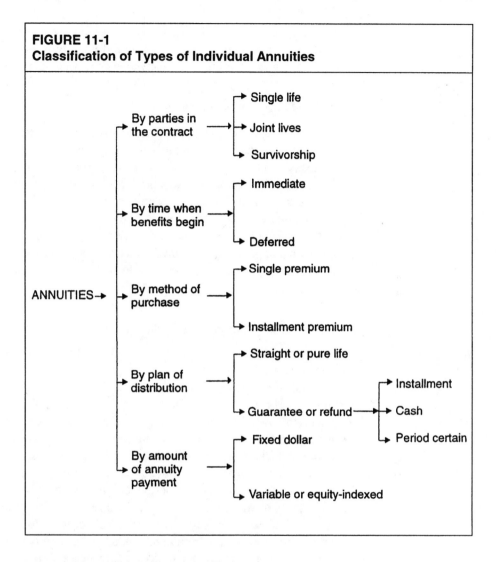

FIGURE 11-1
Classification of Types of Individual Annuities

Time When Benefit Payments Commence

immediate annuity

Annuities can also be classified as immediate or deferred. An *immediate annuity* makes the first benefit payment one payment interval after the date of purchase. If the contract provides for monthly payments, the first benefit payment is due one month after the date of purchase; if annual payments are called for, the first payment is due one year after the date of purchase. An immediate annuity is always purchased with a single premium; the annuitant exchanges a principal sum for a lifetime income or some other payment promise.

deferred annuity

Under the *deferred annuity*, a period longer than one payment interval must elapse after purchase before the first benefit payment is due. As a matter of fact, normally at least several years elapse between the date of purchase and the time when payments commence. The deferred annuity is suitable for many people, including those of ordinary means who want to accumulate a sum for their old age.

Method of Premium Payment

Deferred annuities can be purchased with either single premiums or periodic premiums. Originally, an annuity was developed as a contract purchased with a lump sum, perhaps accumulated from a successful business venture or an inheritance. The lump sum was paid in exchange for an immediate income of a stipulated amount. Immediate annuities are still purchased with a lump sum, but most annuities today are purchased on an installment basis. Periodic payments may be scheduled level deposits or may be flexible deposits with the amount and timing at the purchaser's discretion. The deferred annuity provides an attractive and convenient method of accumulating the necessary funds for an adequate old-age income.

Nature of the Insurer's Obligation

pure (straight life) annuity

A *pure annuity*, frequently referred to as a *straight life annuity,* provides periodic—usually monthly—income payments that continue as long as the annuitant lives and terminate at that person's death. The annuity is considered fully liquidated upon the death of the annuitant, regardless of how soon that may occur after purchase. No refund is payable to the deceased annuitant's estate, and there is no guarantee that any particular number of monthly payments will be made. This nonrefund feature applies to both an immediate and a deferred annuity. So under a pure annuity, no part of the purchase price will be refunded even if the annuitant dies during the accumulation period, before the income commences.

The pure annuity may provide for a refund of all premiums paid, with or without interest, in the event of the insured's death before commencement of the annuity income, with no refund feature after the annuity begins. Therefore, in the description of a deferred annuity, it is necessary to distinguish between the accumulation and liquidation periods in labeling the contract as pure or refund.

refund annuity

A *refund annuity* is any type that promises to return, in some manner, a portion or all of the purchase price of the annuity. These refund annuity contracts take several forms, which are discussed in the following section. As might be expected, refund annuities are far more popular than pure annuities.

Fixed or Variable Benefit Amounts

fixed annuity

Annuities may provide a fixed number of dollars for each benefit payment or may provide a varying payment based on the investment performance of the assets underlying the annuity. The conventional *fixed annuity* provides payments of a fixed amount over a specified period or throughout the lifetime of one or more

variable annuity

persons. Significant inflation during past decades, however, focused attention on the need to protect the purchasing power of benefits. In response to this need, *variable annuity* contracts were developed to provide benefits that vary with changes in investment performance, a proxy for changes in purchasing power.

SINGLE-LIFE ANNUITIES

Liquidation Period

liquidation period

This section discusses the payment period, or liquidation period, of annuity benefits, whether under an immediate or a deferred annuity. During the *liquidation period,* the principal sum is paid out on the basis of life contingencies. The principles involved also apply under the structured settlement to the life-income options of life insurance contracts funded by the death benefit.

Pure Annuities

As stated previously, a pure annuity provides periodic benefit payments for the lifetime of the annuitant. The consideration paid for the annuity is regarded as fully earned by the insurance company when the benefit payments begin. The payments can be made monthly, quarterly, semiannually, or annually. The more frequent the periodic payments, the more costly the annuity for the owner due to the greater expense of writing frequent checks, the loss of interest earnings by the insurance company, and the greater probability that the annuitant will live to receive at least some of the payments. For example, if the annuitant dies 6 months and one day after purchasing the annuity, he or she would have received six monthly payments if the benefit payment is monthly, but no benefit payments if the benefit is payable annually.

Occasionally, annuities are made apportionable—that is, they provide for a pro rata payment covering the period from the date of the last regular payment to the date of death. This feature necessitates an increase in the purchase price because premiums for the usual type of annuity are calculated on the assumption that there will be no such pro rata payment.

The pure annuity provides the maximum income per dollar of outlay and for that reason is perhaps most suitable for people with only a limited amount of capital. According to typical actuarial assumptions, $1,000 of capital will provide monthly income between $7 and $10 for males age 65 and between $6 and $9 for females age 65 under a straight life annuity (see table 11-2 later in this chapter). If payments are guaranteed for 10 years, whether the annuitant lives or dies, the monthly income will be reduced approximately $.50 for each $1,000 increment. On an investment of $100,000, the difference in monthly income will be $50, which might be the difference between dependency and self-sufficiency for an elderly person. For a person aged 70, the difference in monthly income from $100,000 will be $100, and at 75 the difference will be $175—too large to ignore.

At younger ages, because of the high probability of survival, the difference in income between an annuity without a refund feature and one with a refund feature is extremely small. A person aged 35 can obtain an annuity with a 5-year guarantee for the same cost as a pure annuity and an annuity with a 10-year guarantee at the sacrifice of only a few cents of monthly income per $1,000 of outlay. Even someone aged 55 can obtain a 10-year guarantee at a reduction in monthly income of less than $.50. In general, the chances for males under 60 and females under 65 to survive the typical periods of guaranteed payments are so high that little in monthly income is gained by giving up the refund feature. Even so, if a particular younger-aged annuitant does die early during the liquidation period and he or she has not opted for a refund feature, the financial loss to the heirs can be substantial.

Refund Annuities

Most people have strong objections to placing a substantial sum of money into a contract that promises little or no refund to their heirs if the annuitant dies at an early age. Therefore, to make annuities marketable, insurance companies have found it necessary to add a refund feature. The refund feature can take two general forms: a promise to provide at least a certain number of annuity payments whether the annuitant lives or dies, or a promise to refund all or a portion of the purchase price in the event of the annuitant's early death.

life annuity certain

Life Annuity Certain. One type of contract goes under various names, including *life annuity certain*, life annuity certain and continuous, life annuity with installments certain, life annuity with a period certain guarantee, and life annuity with minimum guaranteed return. This annuity pays a guaranteed number of monthly payments regardless whether the annuitant lives or dies, and payments continue for the whole of the annuitant's life if he or she lives beyond the guaranteed period. Contracts can be written with payments guaranteed for 5, 10, 15, 20, or even 25 years, although not all insurers offer such a wide range of choices.

The life certain annuity can be viewed as a combination of two components: an annuity certain and a pure deferred life annuity. The *annuity certain* covers the period of guaranteed payments and provides the payments regardless of whether the annuitant is living. The pure deferred life annuity becomes effective if the annuitant is still alive at the end of the period of guaranteed payments, and provides continuing lifetime benefits. If the annuitant does not survive the period of guaranteed payments, no payments are made under the deferred life annuity, and no refund is forthcoming.

All other things being equal, an annuity with a period certain is always more expensive per dollar of income than a straight life annuity because it is not based solely on life contingencies. Some of the payments are a certainty; the only cost-reducing factor is the compound interest earned on the unliquidated portion of the purchase price. Therefore, the longer the term of the period certain—or to put it more specifically, the longer the period of guaranteed payments—the more costly this type of refund annuity is or the lower the yield on the purchase price. Because the annuity certain is not based solely on life contingencies, the cost of an annuity certain does not depend on the age of the annuitant; it varies directly with the length of the term. At any particular age, however, the longer the period of guaranteed payments, the less expensive the deferred life annuity will be because the higher the age at which the deferred life annuity commences, the smaller the probability that the annuitant will survive to that age. This means that the larger the number of guaranteed payments, the smaller the portion of the purchase price going into the deferred life annuity.

installment refund annuity

    Installment Refund Annuity. Under an *installment refund annuity,* if the annuitant dies before receiving monthly payments equal to the purchase price of the annuity, the payments will continue to a designated beneficiary or beneficiaries until the full cost is recovered. Of course, payments to the annuitant continue as long as he or she lives, even though the purchase price may long since have been recovered in full.

> ***Example:***   Assume that an immediate annuity is purchased by a male age 65 for $100,000. This annuity will provide a monthly life income of about $750 on an installment refund basis. If the annuitant dies after receiving 100 payments ($75,000), the payments will be continued to a designated beneficiary until an additional $25,000 is paid out, for a total of $100,000. If the annuitant dies after 13 years, there will be no further payments because the entire purchase price already will have been recovered.

---

cash refund annuity

    Cash Refund Annuity. The *cash refund annuity* promises, at the death of the annuitant, to pay to the annuitant's estate or to a designated beneficiary a lump sum amounting to the difference, if any, between the purchase price of the annuity and the sum of the monthly payments. The only difference between the cash refund and installment refund annuities is that in the former, the unrecovered portion of the purchase price is refunded in a lump sum at the time of the annuitant's death; in the latter, the monthly installments are continued until the purchase price has been completely recovered. The cash refund annuity is naturally somewhat more expensive because the insurance company loses the interest it would have earned while liquidating the remaining portion of the purchase price on an installment basis. Under the cash refund annuity, the insurer uses the interest earnings on the unliquidated portion of the premiums of all

TABLE 11-1		
Refund Features During Liquidation		
	Annuitant dies:	Then
Pure annuity	During liquidation	No further payments
Life annuity with period certain	During period certain	Payments to contingent payee for remainder of period certain
	After period certain	No further payments
Installment refund	When total payments < purchase price	Payments to contingent payee until purchase price is recovered
	When total payments ≥ purchase price	No further payments
Cash refund annuity	When total payments < purchase price	Lump sum paid to contingent payee equal to purchase price minus total payments
	When total payments ≥ purchase price	No further payments
50% refund annuity	When total payments < 50% x purchase price	Payments on lump sum paid to contingent payee equal to (50% x purchase price) minus total payments
	When total payments ≥ 50% x purchase price	No further payments
Modified cash refund annuity	When payments < accumulated contributions	Lump sum paid to contingent payee equal to accumulated contribution minus total payments
	When payments ≥ accumulated contributions	No further payments

annuitants receiving benefits to fund for benefit payments in excess of any particular annuitant's purchase price.

50 percent refund annuity

50 Percent Refund Annuity. A *50 percent refund annuity* contract guarantees a minimum return of one-half of the purchase price, a compromise between the straight life annuity and the 100 percent refund annuity. Under this contract, if the annuitant dies before receiving benefits equal to half of the cost of the annuity, monthly installments are continued until the combined payments to both the annuitant and a designated beneficiary equal half of the cost of the annuity. Usually, if the beneficiary so elects, he or she can receive the present value of the remaining payments in a lump sum. Because the guarantee under this contract is smaller than that under the 100 percent refund annuity, the cost is lower, or restated, the income per dollar of purchase price is larger.

Another form of annuity sometimes provides that, regardless of the number of payments received prior to the annuitant's death, 50 percent of the cost of the contract will be returned in the form of a death benefit. This contract is not a refund annuity in the strict sense. Instead, one-half of the premium is used by the company to provide a straight life annuity, and the other half is held on deposit. Earnings from the half held on deposit are used to supplement the annuity benefits provided by the other half of the premium. At the annuitant's death, the premium deposit is returned to the annuitant's estate or to a designated beneficiary in the form of a death benefit.

modified cash refund annuity

Modified Cash Refund Annuity. Finally, the *modified cash refund annuity* is found in contributory pension plans. This contract promises that if the employee dies before receiving retirement benefits equal to the accumulated value of his or her contributions, with or without interest, the difference between the employee's benefits and contributions will be refunded in a lump sum to the employee's estate or to a designated beneficiary. In other words, the refund feature is based on the employee's contributions and not on the portion of the total cost of the annuity paid by the employer.

Comparisons. Monthly income amounts provided by a typical insurer under various forms of annuities per $1,000 of premium accumulations are shown in table 11-2. This table illustrates the small cost of a refund feature at age 60 or 65 and the high cost at more advanced ages. Note that at the highest age shown, the refund form is least expensive—or, conversely, purchases more monthly benefit than a life annuity with a 10-year guarantee. Remember, however, that the benefits under each of the forms are the actuarial equivalent of those under all the other forms, and the annuitant must choose the form that is most appropriate to his or her financial and family circumstances.

Insurance companies can design annuity contracts with any period certain or with a refund guarantee for any specified percent from 0 to 100 percent of the purchase price. In practice, however, each insurer is likely to offer only a few options, primarily due to the costs of getting regulatory approval for each type of contract.

Accumulation Period

accumulation period

The preceding discussion of annuities related entirely to their liquidation phase, with no discussion concerning how the funds for payout had been accumulated. With deferred annuities, during an *accumulation period* funds are invested at the insurance company to grow to the amount necessary to fund benefits promised at a specified future date.

Annuity contracts that allow flexible premium payments during the accumulation phase cannot specify in advance the level of benefit payments that will be paid during the liquidation phase. Instead, these annuities specify the amount of benefit for each $1,000 of fund balance when the annuity switches over to the liquidation phase.

TABLE 11-2
Typical Monthly Annuity Benefits Available per $1,000 of Purchase Price (Immediate Annuities)

Type	Male Age				
	60	65	70	75	80
Life	$6.30	$6.99	$7.96	$9.30	$11.19
10-year certain + life	6.15	6.71	7.38	8.14	8.90
Refund	6.04	6.56	7.23	8.09	9.16
Type	Female Age				
	60	65	70	75	80
Life	$5.78	$6.30	$7.04	$8.14	$9.78
10-year certain + life	5.71	6.18	6.79	7.56	8.44
Refund	5.65	6.08	6.66	7.44	8.47

Almost without exception, deferred annuities sold to individuals promise to return all premiums, with or without interest, if the annuitant dies during the accumulation period. The usual contract provides for a return of either gross premiums without interest or the cash value, whichever is larger. This contract is a type of refund annuity with respect to the period of accumulation.

Under private pension plans, employer contributions are almost invariably used to purchase pure deferred annuities with respect to the accumulation period. If the purchaser dies prior to the date the income is scheduled to commence, there is no refund of premiums. If the employee terminates employment before retirement, the employer recovers the employer's contributions, plus interest, but if the employee dies, employer contributions on his or her behalf remain with the insurance company to provide benefits to employees who remain with the employer until retirement. This annuity can be purchased at a much lower premium than one that promises to return contributions, with the result that the employer can either finance the pension plan at the lowest possible outlay or can provide larger retirement benefits than he or she could otherwise afford.

Structuring the Annuity Contract

The premiums for an annuity contract bought with periodic premiums can be quoted in units of $100 of annual premium or in terms of the annual premium needed to provide a monthly life income of $10 at a designated age. In the first case, the premium will be an even amount, and the benefit amount will vary with the age of issue and the age at which the benefit payments will commence. In the second case, the benefit payments will be fixed, and the premium will vary.

In every deferred annuity except a variable annuity, which is described later, a minimum rate of interest on the cash value is guaranteed throughout the accumulation period. Many annuities, however, also provide a secondary guaranteed rate that is higher than the minimum floor rate. The secondary guaranteed rate usually applies only for the first several years of the accumulation period, with a higher rate for short periods than for long periods. At the conclusion of the initial guarantee period, a lower or unspecified secondary guaranteed rate, perhaps zero, will be applicable.

The effect of cash withdrawals should also be considered when evaluating a secondary guaranteed rate during the accumulation period. Some insurers reduce this secondary rate, sometimes even retroactively, if funds are withdrawn from the cash value rather than left to eventually be taken in annuity benefits.

Evaluating a Secondary Guaranteed Interest Rate

- At what rate will funds accumulate?
- For how long does the rate apply?
- After the rate expires, is a subsequent rate guaranteed ?
- What will be the effect of withdrawals on the rate?
- After the rate expires, can the contract be terminated without a surrender charge?

After the secondary guaranteed rate expires, some contracts contain a bail-out provision that allows the contract to be terminated without a surrender charge. The bail out may be allowed if the interest rate falls below a stipulated rate, often 2 percentage points below the secondary guaranteed rate. The bail-out provision may seem much more attractive than it really is for two reasons: (1) competitors are unlikely to be able to pay higher rates if and when the release is triggered, and (2) interest on a cash-out will be subject to income taxes and possibly a 10 percent penalty tax. In the event of the annuitant's death before age 65 or other scheduled start of the liquidation period, the company will return the accumulated gross premiums without interest or the cash value, whichever is larger. The cash value is equal to the gross premiums plus interest at a guaranteed rate, after deducting an expense charge. After about 10 years, the cash value exceeds the accumulated value of premiums paid without interest, and becomes the effective death benefit. Note that, although this is an annuity contract, there is an insurance element during the accumulation period in that the death benefit exceeds the cash value.

The annuitant can withdraw the full cash value at any time during the deferral period, whereupon the contract terminates and the company has no further obligation. Under some contracts, the annuitant can borrow against the cash value, which would not bring about a termination of the contract.

Liquidation Options

At the maturity date, the annuitant can elect to have the accumulation applied under any of the annuity forms offered by the company. Depending on the option elected at maturity, the actual monthly income might be more or less than the amount originally anticipated, based on the owner's payout option selection at the time of issue. Moreover, the annuitant usually has a cash option of taking a lump sum in lieu of an annuity. The *cash option* exposes the company to serious adverse selection. Persons in poor health tend to withdraw their accumulations in cash, while those in excellent health usually choose an annuity. To offset this selection, if the annuitant selects the cash option, some companies provide a retroactive reduction in the investment earnings rate applied to accumulations under a deferred annuity. The resultant penalty can be a substantial dollar amount.

cash option

Under most contracts, the annuitant can choose to have the benefit payments commence at an earlier or a later date than the one originally specified in the contract, with a subsequent adjustment in the amount of monthly benefits. Beginning the income at an earlier age than the age specified in the contract amounts to converting the cash value to an immediate annuity. There is usually no age limit below which the benefit payments must not begin, although the option is subject to the general requirement that the periodic income payments equal or exceed a stipulated minimum amount.

There is usually an upper age limit, sometimes as high as age 80 or as low as age 70, beyond which commencement of the income benefits cannot be postponed. The option to postpone the commencement of benefit payments can be particularly attractive if the annuitant is still in good health at the original maturity date and plans to work for a few more years. The life income payable at any particular age, whether the maturity date is moved ahead or set back, is the same amount that would have been provided had the substituted maturity date been the one originally selected and funded with the actual amount accumulated.

JOINT ANNUITIES

There are basically two types of joint annuities. One, the joint-life annuity, provides income benefits only until the death of the first of two or more annuitants. The other, the joint-and-last-survivor annuity, continues benefit payments until the last of the named annuitants dies.

Joint-Life Annuity

A joint-life annuity provides an income as long as the two or more persons named in the contract live. Because the income ceases at the first death among the covered lives, the coverage is relatively inexpensive. This contract is always sold as a single premium immediate annuity.

This contract has a very limited market. It might be appropriate for two persons—elderly sisters, for example, who have an income from a stable source large enough to support one but not both of the sisters. If they can purchase a joint-life annuity in an amount adequate to support one sister without disturbing the other income, the combined income will be adequate for their needs while both sisters are alive. Upon the death of one of the sisters, the income from the original source will meet the survivor's needs.

Joint-and-Last-Survivor Annuity

A joint-and-last-survivor annuity is a far more marketable contract than the joint-life annuity because the income under this form of annuity continues as long as any of two or more persons live. This arrangement is ideal for a husband and wife or for families in which there is a permanently disabled dependent child.

For most combinations of ages, the joint-and-last-survivor annuity is the most expensive of all annuity forms. According to a typical insurer, an accumulation of $18,350 is required to provide an income of $100 per month on the joint-and-last-survivor basis to a man and woman both aged 65. If the man is 65 and the woman 60, a sum of $19,827 is needed to provide $100 per month on the joint-and-last-survivor basis. Compare those figures to the approximate amount of $14,306 that is required, according to the $6.99 rate shown in table 11-2, to provide a life income of $100 per month with no refund feature only to a man aged 65.

The joint-and-last-survivor annuity can be purchased as a single-premium immediate annuity at a cost somewhat higher than the accumulation figures quoted above, as an optional form under an annual-premium deferred annuity, or in conjunction with the settlement of life insurance or endowment proceeds.

Although a typical joint-and-last-survivor contract does not contain a refund feature, most insurance companies offer a contract under which 120 monthly installments are guaranteed, and a few offer 240 guaranteed installments. Under these contracts, if the last survivor dies before the minimum number of payments has been made, the remaining installments continue to a designated beneficiary. As with single-life annuities, the designated beneficiary may be permitted to take the present value of the remaining installments as a lump sum. When both husband and wife are 65, a life income of $100 per month with 120 guaranteed installments requires an accumulation of $18,560—only $120 more than a similar annuity without a refund feature.

The conventional joint-and-last-survivor annuity continues the same income to the survivor as was paid while both annuitants were alive. A common modification, which reduces the cost, decreases the income to the survivor to two-thirds of the original amount. This contract, the joint-and-two-thirds annuity, is based on the assumption that the survivor does not require as much income as the two annuitants. This contract written in an original amount of $100 per month on the lives of a husband and wife, both aged 65, requires an accumulation of slightly more than $15,960.

In a *joint-and-one-half annuity*, the income to the survivor is reduced to one-half of the original amount. This form has not had the popular appeal of the joint-and-two-thirds annuity. Many insurers have introduced more than the one-half and two-thirds options for continuation at the death of the first annuitant.

The joint-and-last-survivor form is widely used by private pension plans to pay retirement benefits to married plan participants. When the joint-and-two-thirds annuity has been elected by the employee, often the income is reduced only if the employee dies first. If the employee's spouse dies first, the employee continues to receive the full income. Federal law requires written consent of the nonemployee spouse in order to drop the survivorship benefit.

VARIABLE ANNUITIES

For a contract to provide benefits with stable purchasing power, the contract should provide more dollars when prices rise and fewer dollars when prices decline. Theoretically, benefits could be adjusted as the appropriate price index, such as the consumer price index, changes. From the standpoint of insurance companies, however, there is no mechanism by which the value of the assets backing the annuity can be adjusted automatically to reflect changes in the dollar value of the annuity promises. As a practical solution, variable annuity contracts have been developed that provide benefits adjusted to changes in the market value of the assets—typically common stocks—in which the annuity reserves are invested. The tie to common stock is based on the theory that over a long period of time, the market value of a representative group of common stocks tends to conform rather faithfully to changes in the consumer price level. Moreover, inasmuch as the insurance company's liabilities to its annuitants are expressed in terms of the market value of the assets offsetting the liabilities, funds for the payment of annuity benefits are available in the appropriate proportions at all times.

Proponents of the variable annuity believe that annuitants need protection against inflation and that a common stock investment program administered by a life insurance company is the best approach yet developed. Critics of the variable annuity approach question whether continuing inflation is inevitable, and even if it is, whether common stock investments provide an effective hedge against rising prices in the short run. These critics also cite the absence of any guaranteed minimum interest rate credit as an important disadvantage of the variable annuity.

Accumulation Units

At present, variable annuities are most often issued on a deferred basis. During the accumulation period, premium payments—or deposits, as they are

accumulation unit

frequently called—are applied to the purchase of accumulation units. The *accumulation unit* is assigned an arbitrary value, such as $10, at the inception of the plan, and the initial premiums purchase accumulation units at that price. Thereafter, the units are revalued each month to reflect changes in the market value of the common stock that makes up the company's variable annuity portfolio. On any valuation date, the value of each accumulation unit is determined by dividing the market value of the common stock underlying the accumulation units by the aggregate number of units. Dividends are usually allocated periodically to the participants and applied to the purchase of additional accumulation units, although they may simply be reinvested without allocation and permitted to increase the value of each existing accumulation unit. Capital appreciation or depreciation is always reflected in the value of the accumulation units, rather than in the number of units. (In other words, both realized and unrealized gains and losses are reflected for individual participants through an increase or decrease in the value of their accumulation units.) A portion of each premium payment is deducted for expenses, and the remainder is invested in accumulation units at their current market value.

A hypothetical accumulation is shown in table 11-3. In this example, the initial purchase is made at age 35 with a premium high enough to cover a $200 purchase of units each month after paying insurer expenses. The assumptions behind the table 11-3 numbers are that the accumulation units change value once each year and that a full $200 is available each month to acquire more units. The units in this example grow at approximately 7.5 percent in most years but fluctuate more or less than that in some years as stock prices are prone to do over short intervals. In this case, there is an accumulation of $258,459.62 at the end of the 30th year (end of age 64 or beginning of age 65) consisting of 31,751.80 accumulation units.

Annuity Units

annuity unit

At the beginning of the liquidation period, the accumulation units are exchanged for *annuity units*. The number of annuity units acquired by the annuitant depends on the company's assumptions as to mortality, dividend rates, and expenses, and on the market value of the assets underlying the annuity units. In essence, the number of annuity units is determined by dividing the dollar value of the accumulation units ($258,459.62 in the example) by an actuarial factor (assumed to be $35 in this case) designed to provide a benefit of $1 per year for the annuitant's remaining lifetime. While the owner's number of accumulation units increases with each premium payment and each allocation of dividends during the accumulation period, the number of annuity units remains constant throughout the liquidation period (7,384.6 annuity units in this case). However, the units are revalued each year, to reflect the current market price of the common stock and the mortality, investment, and expense experience for the preceding year.[1] The dollar

TABLE 11-3
Variable Annuity Accumulation Units
Deferred Annuity Purchased at Age 35 at $200 per Month

Year	Age	Unit Value	New Units	Total Units	Total Value
1	35	$1.00	2,400.00	2,400.00	$ 2,400.00
2	36	1.08	2,232.56	4,632.56	4,980.00
3	37	1.16	2,076.80	6,709.36	7,753.50
4	38	1.24	1,931.91	8,641.26	10,735.01
5	39	1.34	1,797.12	10,438.38	13,940.14
6	40	1.07	2,242.99	12,681.37	13,569.07
7	41	1.15	2,086.50	14,767.88	16,986.75
8	42	1.24	1,940.93	16,708.81	20,660.76
9	43	1.88	1,276.60	17,985.41	33,812.56
10	44	2.12	1,132.08	19,117.48	40,529.06
11	45	2.28	1,053.09	20,170.57	45,968.74
12	46	2.45	979.62	21,150.20	51,816.39
13	47	2.63	911.28	22,061.47	58,102.62
14	48	2.83	847.70	22,909.17	64,860.32
15	49	3.04	788.56	23,697.73	72,124.84
16	50	3.27	733.54	24,431.27	79,934.21
17	51	3.52	682.36	25,113.63	88,329.27
18	52	3.78	634.76	25,748.39	97,353.97
19	53	3.50	685.71	26,434.10	92,519.37
20	54	3.25	738.46	27,172.57	88,310.84
21	55	3.00	800.00	27,972.56	83,917.70
22	56	3.60	666.67	28,639.23	103,101.24
23	57	4.01	598.50	29,237.74	117,243.32
24	58	4.97	482.90	29,720.63	147,711.55
25	59	5.76	416.67	30,137.70	173,590.85
26	60	6.25	384.00	30,521.30	190,758.13
27	61	7.16	335.20	30,856.50	220,932.51
28	62	7.90	303.80	31,160.29	246,166.32
29	63	8.09	296.66	31,456.96	254,486.78
30	64	8.14	294.84	31,751.80	258,459.62

income payable to the annuitant each month is determined by multiplying the number of annuity units owned by the annuitant by the current value of one unit. During the liquidation period, the higher the market price of the stock and the greater the dividends, the greater will be the dollar income of the annuitant. During the accumulation period, however, it is to the annuitant's advantage for stock prices to be relatively low, because he or she will thus be able to acquire a larger number of accumulation units for each premium payment.

Some of the more recent variable annuity contracts differ from the above by using only one unit throughout the contract period, by discounting for mortality before as well as after retirement, and by limiting variations in the unit value to investment experience only.

Accumulation Units vs. Annuity Units in a Variable Annuity

- Accumulation units: the number of units bought, and the value of each unit, vary depending on when the purchases are made
- Annuity units: the number of annuity units distributed periodically is constant, but their value varies depending on when the distributions are made

---

Surrender Provisions

When the variable annuity is sold as an individual contract, surrender privileges are made available but on a much more restricted basis than in connection with ordinary annuities. When the variable annuity is used as part of a pension plan, surrender values are not generally made available. Under all plans, the current value of the accumulation units is payable to a designated beneficiary, if any, or to the estate, usually as a continuing income. However, a lump-sum settlement is possible at the death of the participant during the accumulation period.

Regulation

In a landmark decision,[2] the United States Supreme Court held that an individual variable annuity contract is a security within the meaning of the Securities Act of 1933 and that any organization offering such a contract is an investment company subject to the Investment Company Act of 1940. Any company that offers individual variable annuity contracts is subject to dual supervision by the Securities and Exchange Commission and the various state insurance departments. Persons selling variable annuities must pass the Series 6 licensing exam of the National Association of Securities Dealers (NASD).

EQUITY-INDEXED ANNUITIES

equity-indexed annuity

Equity-indexed annuities are a variation of fixed-interest, traditional deferred-annuity products. These annuities were introduced in the mid-1990s to enhance the appeal of fixed-interest annuities. Fixed-interest annuities were very attractive during the high-interest-rate era of the 1980s and early 1990s. However, their appeal waned as interest rates dropped and stock market yields significantly surpassed the yields in traditional fixed-interest annuities.

An equity-indexed annuity offers guaranteed minimum interest rates and at the same time pays a higher return if a specified stock index increases enough to provide a higher yield. They are designed to appeal to persons who want to participate in high-equity investment yields without bearing the full downside investment risk assumed through the purchase of a variable annuity.

The equity-indexed annuity provides only a portion of the capital gain of the stocks making up the applicable index, commonly the Standard & Poor's Composite Index of 500 Stocks. Variable annuities are still the only annuity products that provide most of the full yield of the equity investments to the owner/annuitant.

Participation Rate Formula

Prospective purchasers of equity-indexed annuities should understand that their potential return based on increases in the value of the index is determined by the formula approach set forth in the contract. Generally, this formula includes a participation rate as well as the increase in the index from the beginning of the term to the verified anniversary-date value of the index. The participation rate is a percentage (always less than 100 percent) of the defined increase that will be used to calculate the crediting amount. This participation rate is set by the insurer and is subject to change. Some companies do not even specify the current participation rate in their promotional materials. Often the participation rate is guaranteed for a specified term such as the first 5 or 7 years. The insurance company reserves the right to change the participation rate at the expiration of each term, but the company usually guarantees the then-current rate for the subsequent term.

Most contracts anticipate a series of terms of uniform length, much like renewals of 5-year term life insurance. However, some contracts reserve the insurer's right to modify the term period available for continuation at the expiration of any existing term. In most designs, a higher increase from the index calculation is available only at the end of the applicable term unless the owner dies or the contract is converted to benefit-payout status (annuitized) before the end of the term. The higher value based on the index will not apply if the contract is terminated before the end of the term.

The participation rate restricts the amount of the index gain, if any, that can be applied to produce more than the guaranteed yield. The participation rate and the guaranteed interest rate are linked. Higher participation rates may be available from some insurers if the purchaser accepts a lower guaranteed interest rate. One company guarantees that the participation rate will never be lower than 25 percent. Illustrations are often based on 80 percent or 90 percent participation rates. The participation rate cannot be changed more than once per year under most contracts.

Another aspect of the indexed benefit is that some contracts include a cap on the crediting rate that is applied to the accumulated value of the contract. This cap prevents full formula participation in times of very rapid index increases.

As downside protection, most contracts specify a floor of zero percent as the minimum extra interest crediting rate applicable to the accumulated value. This prevents the application of a negative percentage in the formula to reflect plunges in the index value. The intent is that the fixed-interest-rate guarantee is the worst possible outcome, and if the equity index does better, the accumulation can be even better than the guaranteed accumulation.

No Securities and Exchange Commission Regulation

Equity-indexed annuities are classified as fixed annuities and may be sold by agents who are not licensed to sell variable products. Thus, the agent has a product that offers a minimum accumulation guarantee but is partly influenced by equity performance. The agent is allowed to sell the product without having to acquire the training and licensing necessary to enter the variable-annuity market.

The Securities and Exchange Commission (SEC), which is currently examining insurance products could decide that equity-indexed annuities really are a variable product rather than a fixed product. Many experts argue that the current definitions of terms adhered to by the SEC are broad enough for such an interpretation without changing any existing authorizations or guidelines. Others believe equity-indexed annuities cannot be classified as variable products without some action to change the SEC definitions.

The Guarantees

The minimum guarantees under equity-indexed annuities are lower than those for traditional fixed-interest annuities. In fact, the rates actually guaranteed apply to less than the full amount paid as a premium. The guaranteed rate is usually applied to 90 percent of the amount paid to purchase the annuity. The percentage (10 percent in this example) not included in the guarantees can be used to cover insurer expenses. With this approach, usually 3 or 4 years elapse before the guaranteed amount equals or exceeds the original purchase amount. The contract indicates the specified interest rate applied each year to the contract value. This rate remains fixed unless a negotiated change is later agreed to by both the contract owner and the insurance company. Many of the existing equity-indexed annuities have guaranteed rates in the range of 2 percent to 3.5 percent.

Value of the Contract at End of Term

At the end of each term or participation period, the value of the annuity is the greatest of the following three amounts:

- the contract value based on the minimum interest rate guarantees
- the accumulated value derived by applying the participation rate to the increase in the index on the applicable anniversary. This amount is

subject to any cap on the maximum crediting rate and to any floor on the minimum crediting rate.

- the premiums paid through the end of the term, minus any withdrawals

In many contracts, the same procedures are used to calculate the death benefit payable if the owner dies during the deferral phase of the contract.

Terminating an equity-indexed annuity before the end of a specified term usually results in loss of the index-crediting option. The termination is usually the greater of the following two amounts:

- the guaranteed-interest contract value
- the aggregate purchase amount minus adjustments for any partial withdrawals previously taken

Indexes

Although the most commonly used index is the Standard & Poor's Composite Index of 500 Stocks, some insurers use another index specified in the contract. These are generally established indexes that regularly appear in financial publications such as the *Wall Street Journal*. However, some insurers use international indexes or a composite of two or more established indexes. The definition of the index is under the insurance company's control. Theoretically the company could change the definition of the index after the contract is created, leaving open the possibility of intentional manipulation of the index in the future.

Asset Match

All financial products involve risks to the issuer, and the equity-indexed annuity is no exception. The issuer needs to invest in assets that will provide an adequate return to honor the contractual promises.

Because the index participation promises some results that are above those of bond returns when the stock index outperforms the bond market, how can a company invest assets to produce the higher return? The closest match is achieved by investing the funds in the same stocks that make up the index. However, some insurers have chosen to invest in derivatives and other financial assets that they believe will track well with the index, even though these choices are not a composite of the items that make up the index. Over the long run, there could be a significant difference between investment results and contractual obligations. If the investment results exceed the contractual obligations, there will be no problem honoring the annuity contract terms. Conversely, underperformance of asset returns relative to obligations could threaten the insurer's financial viability. Purchasers should feel more comfortable with issuing companies whose investments closely resemble the index to which the benefits are related.

ACTUARIAL CONSIDERATIONS FOR ANNUITIES

The insurance company's cost of providing annuity benefits is based on the probability of survival, rather than the probability of death. In itself, this fact would seem to have no greater significance than that the insurance company actuaries, in computing premiums for annuities, have to refer to the actuarial probabilities of survival rather than probabilities of death. As a matter of fact, however, writing annuities poses a unique set of actuarial problems.

First, insurance companies have found that the mortality, or probability of death, among annuity purchasers tends to be lower, age for age, than that of persons who purchase life insurance, due mainly to adverse selection against the company. Individuals who know that they have serious health impairments rarely, if ever, purchase annuities. In fact, many persons contemplating the purchase of immediate annuities subject themselves to a thorough medical examination to make sure that they have no serious impairments before committing their capital to annuities. On the other hand, people who know or suspect that they have an impairment usually seek life insurance. Whatever its origin, the mortality difference between life insurance insureds and annuitants is so substantial that special annuity mortality tables must be used for the calculation of annuity premiums.

Second, the trend toward lower mortality, resulting in longer lifespans, has been a favorable development for insurers with respect to life insurance but an unfavorable development with respect to annuities. Many annuity contracts, including the accumulation period, run for 60 to 75 years, and rates that were adequate at the time of issue can, with the continued increase in longevity, prove inadequate over the years. All mortality tables, of course, contain a safety margin—which, for life insurance mortality tables, means higher death rates than those likely to be experienced, and for annuity mortality tables, lower rates of mortality than anticipated. While a long-run decline in mortality rates increases the safety margin in life insurance mortality tables, this decline shrinks the margin in annuity mortality tables, sometimes to the point of extinction. Therefore, an annuity mortality table that accurately reflects the mortality among annuitants at the time it was compiled gradually becomes obsolete and eventually overstates the expected mortality.

Annuitants Never Die—Well, Hardly Ever

- Purchasers of annuities have generally lower mortality rates than others (adverse selection).
- Mortality rates for most people, including annuitants, have been declining.
- A high percentage of annuitants are women, who have greater average longevity than men.

Finally, a high percentage of annuitants are women, who as a group enjoy greater longevity than men. This gender difference in longevity forced companies to use a rate differential between male and female annuitants long before a rate differential based on sex was applied to the sale of life insurance policies. However, court decisions have required insurers to base some group annuity contracts on unisex mortality rates.

Revised Mortality Tables

Life insurance companies cope with these mortality differences in various ways. First, the insurers can compute annuity premiums on the basis of mortality tables that reflect annuitants' lower mortality.

For many years, companies used age setbacks for rates. The setbacks were used to recognize mortality differences between annuity and life insurance purchases. For example, the rate for an age 65 applicant may have been based on a 2-year age setback, thereby increasing the premium for a given amount of income to that based on the mortality of an age 63 individual. Ages for females were usually set back 4 or 5 years in addition to the setback for males, in recognition of the gender differential in mortality.

The 2000 Annuity Mortality Table enables insurers, by means of projection factors, to make long-range adjustments for future reductions in mortality rates. Modern annuity tables all contain a set of projection factors that can be used to adjust the mortality assumptions for all ages from year to year or, instead, to project the basic rates of mortality to some future date. The projections make allowances for anticipated future improvements in mortality.

Lower Interest Assumptions

Historically, insurance companies attempted to hedge future improvement in annuitant mortality by using an unrealistically low interest assumption in the premium formula. The rates were substantially lower than those used in the calculation of life insurance premiums. This technique can be quite effective because an interest margin of 25 basis points can absorb a general reduction in mortality of 6 or 7 percent. Intensified competition among insurance companies and between insurance companies and investment media, however, has now caused companies to adopt interest assumptions much closer to the level of their actual investment earnings.

Use of a Participating Basis

A third approach to adjusting annuity prices for anticipated future increases in life expectancy is to compute the premiums and/or benefits on a participating basis, which permits conservative assumptions with respect to all factors in the premium calculations. Annual-premium annuities issued by mutual companies are almost invariably participating during the liquidation period. Some stock companies also issue annuities that are participating during the accumulation period. Single-premium immediate annuities, whether written by mutual or stock companies, are usually not participating.

FEDERAL INCOME TAXATION

Annuities enjoy a significant federal income tax advantage of accumulating on a tax-deferred basis, with the investment income credited to the contract not taxable until it is received by the annuitant or beneficiary.

Amounts Received during the Accumulation Period

Amounts received as loans and withdrawals during an annuity's accumulation period are taxable to the extent of income earned on the contract. This represents a kind of LIFO (last in, first out) tax treatment.[3] Also, a 10 percent penalty tax generally applies to the taxable portion of these amounts unless they are made after the taxpayer's age 59½ or are made by reason of the taxpayer's death or disability.

Amounts Received during the Liquidation Period

The portion of benefit payments taxable during the liquidation period depends on the applicable exclusion ratio. This ratio is calculated by dividing the amount invested in the annuity by the total amount expected to be received. The exclusion ratio is then multiplied by the amount of each payment to the annuitant to determine the excluded amount, which is presumed to be a return of the investment in the contract. The balance of each payment is taxable.

The amount invested in the contract is generally the premiums paid, minus any previous nontaxable distributions and minus the actuarial value of any period certain or other guarantee feature. The amount expected to be received depends on the type of payout option selected. If the annuity provides payments for a fixed period of time, the total payments to be received constitute the expected amount to be received. If the annuity provides a life income, the expected amount to be received is based on life expectancy tables from the U.S. Treasury Department.[4]

After the annuitant has received excludible amounts equal to the investment in the contract, the basis in the annuity has been fully recovered. Thereafter, under current tax law any remaining benefit payments are fully taxable to the annuitant. If he or she dies before the basis is fully recovered, a deduction is applicable for the unrecovered amount in the taxpayer's final return.

USES OF THE ANNUITY

The market for annuities is composed of two broad categories of individuals: those who have already accumulated an estate, either through inheritance or by their own personal efforts, and those who are seeking to accumulate an estate.

Wealthy individuals purchase annuities as a hedge against adverse financial developments. Large estates can be destroyed through business reverses, unwise investments, and reckless spending. Insurance company records abound with cases of individuals who at one time were wealthy but whose fortunes melted away, leaving payments from annuities purchased in their more affluent days as their sole source of income. There are also numerous cases of individuals who are dependent on relatives for whom they had purchased annuities during a more solvent period. Wealthy people, then, purchase annuities in a search for security, with yield a secondary consideration.

Yield is a primary consideration for those individuals, often middle-aged or elderly, who have accumulated a modest estate and envision this estate as the source of financial security during the remaining years of their lives. The life annuity, or the joint-and-last-survivor form for couples, promises a continuation of the benefit payments and some deferral of income taxes as long as the annuitant or annuitants live. While some people are reluctant to invest their capital in an annuity because they want to leave an estate to their children or other close relatives, others feel that a greater responsibility is providing for their own old-age maintenance, relieving the children of that burden.

The entire capital accumulation may not be needed to provide for the parents' old-age support and an appropriate annuity may be purchased with the remainder of the estate to be distributed either during the parents' lifetime or after their deaths. Annuities can be used in a similar manner to provide living bequests to charitable, educational, and religious organizations.

Finally, the annuity is also an attractive savings medium for the person who has not yet accumulated an estate but wants to achieve financial independence in old age. Premium deposits can be made on a flexible schedule and the accumulation grows on a tax-deferred basis.

STRUCTURED SETTLEMENTS

Over the past decade, the courts have been involved in at least 5,000 cases involving personal injury or wrongful death in which the negligent party was required to pay at least $1 million in damages. More than 95 percent of these cases were settled prior to the rendering of a verdict, although the settlement is still enforceable by the court. Most of these cases were settled on a lump-sum basis.

Quite frequently, the courts seek lifetime financial support for the injured party or throughout the minority of dependent heirs. Consequently, it is usually

structured settlement

acceptable to the court for the award to be paid as *structured settlements*, which are periodic payments instead of, or in addition to, a single lump-sum payment. Insurance companies issue immediate annuity contracts that guarantee the payments over the required lifetime or over the mandated support period. These contracts are specifically tailored to the needs of the claimants, who are the injured or wronged parties.

While making periodic payments over time for claimant damages can be traced to the 1950s, independent full-time structured settlement specialists were not common until the 1970s. Since then, the number of cases using structured settlement contracts to satisfy plaintiffs' claims has grown substantially. The most frequent cases in which a structured settlement can be appropriate involve general liability, medical malpractice, defective products, automobile accidents, or workers' compensation injuries.

Personal injury claims adjusters and/or defense attorneys work together with a structured settlement specialist in order to arrange appropriate settlements. Suitable structured settlements provide an adequate amount of immediate cash for liquidity needs, as well as reimbursement for past expenses, legal fees, and other cash needs. If the recipient is unable to work, an income stream can be designed to fund his or her normal living expenses, custodial and medical services, rehabilitation costs, and where appropriate, tuition for educational programs.

Annuities Utilized in Structured Settlements

The customary structured settlement uses an annuity to provide periodic payments that meet the recipient's financial needs as much as possible. The periodic payments of income are received tax free by the claimant during his or her life and by the claimant's beneficiaries thereafter for the balance of any guarantee period. Two of the requirements for the claimant's income-tax-free treatment are the absence of any evidence of ownership by the annuitant of the annuity funding the structured settlement and the absence of constructive receipt or economic benefit in the annuity itself. Therefore, all timing decisions, as well as the exact amount of money, are predetermined by the defendant, who is the legal owner of the annuity, and the insurer.

If the claimant has no reduction in life expectancy from the injuries that caused the claim, standard rates are applied for life annuities. Likewise, standard rates are used for fixed-period annuities because there is no life contingency. An example of a fixed-period annuity is payment of $1,000 per month for 5 years and $2,000 per month during years 6 through 10. This is also referred to as a

step-rate annuity

step-rate annuity. Annuity benefit payments can generally be increased on a compound annual rate, ranging from 3 percent to 6 percent. In addition to life income guarantees, period-certain and joint-life guarantees can be used, depending on the circumstances involved. The insurer may issue a rated age or substandard life annuity if the claimant's life expectancy has been reduced.

In a catastrophic injury case, the structured settlement broker submits the medical data to different insurance companies for evaluation. Each company makes its own judgment as to the claimant's life expectancy and bases its annuity quotes on that opinion. Life expectancy estimates vary among companies, just as substandard life insurance varies among insurers. The lower the life expectancy, the lower the annuity cost. Then the broker presents the bids to the defendant and his or her legal counsel to make an informed selection.

Generally, this kind of annuity can be purchased only by defendants or their insurers in personal injury and wrongful death cases, and the number of insurance companies that issue such contracts is rather small.

Advantages of Structured Settlements

The advantages of a structured settlement for each of the individual entities involved are explained below.

For the Injured Party

Financial Security. The major advantage of a structured settlement for the injured party is financial security. A lifetime income is especially practical and desirable when a minor or someone acknowledged to be incompetent is involved or whenever there is reason to be concerned about protecting the injured party's, or the surviving family's, future finances.

Benefits that Match Needs. An injured party needs regular income to meet living expenses and medical care costs. On occasion, when future medical costs are estimated to be substantial but the timing of these costs is unknown, a medical trust, similar to an emergency fund, can be created with the defendant as grantor under the trust agreement.

Management of Benefits. Claimants and their families or guardians are usually not trained to manage large sums of money. The risk of dissipation of funds through mismanagement, imprudent investment, unwise expenditures, misuse, or even neglect is significantly reduced through the use of periodic payments in a structured settlement.

Guaranteed Payment. Because the income payments are guaranteed for life or for a fixed period, the settlement can never be prematurely exhausted.

Income-Tax-Free Payments. Whether payments are in a lump sum or periodic, they represent personal injury damages, which are excluded from income tax.[5]

For the Plaintiff Attorney

Attorneys are assured that their client's settlement is guaranteed and will not be subject to the potential dissipation of a lump-sum settlement. Some attorneys even believe that recommending a structured settlement insulates them from exposure to legal malpractice because they are not taking a sizable portion of the total value of the entire benefit payable as a lump sum right in the beginning.

For the Judge

Under the structured settlement, guaranteed periodic payments for life ensure the plaintiff's ongoing financial security for a lifetime. The judge or jury simply identifies the amount of monthly need rather than the actuarially equivalent lump sum present value of payments over an uncertain number of years.

For the Public

The public benefits from the structured settlement because the injured party does not become a ward of the state and is assured a guaranteed income and proper care. In addition, the delay of prolonged litigation is avoided, reducing court costs and placing fewer burdens on the already overloaded judicial system.

Disadvantages of Structured Settlements

If the life insurance company becomes insolvent, the annuitant may have a delay of benefit payments. Also, the annuitant will absorb all of the losses in excess of any state guaranty fund limitations. Further, the benefit payments may be reduced with the new insurer. Therefore, structured settlement specialists should select only the most secure and well-managed insurance companies.

The periodic payment schedule cannot be changed, so problems can occur if more immediate cash is needed than the stream of payments provides. This may be due to an unprecedented financial reversal, a medical necessity, an educational need, or greater than expected inflation. The original design of the structured settlement should therefore anticipate increasing payments annually (or at least periodically), build in periodic deferred lump sums, or include a medical trust for future medical and custodial needs.

CHECKLIST FOR EVALUATING AND COMPARING ANNUITIES

Accumulation Period

☐ Is the annuity funded with a single premium? If yes, how much?

☐ Is the annuity funded with periodic premiums? If yes,

___ Are premiums fixed or flexible?
___ What is the annual premium?
___ What is the premium frequency?
___ For how many years are premiums payable?

☐ Is there a minimum interest rate guaranteed for the length of the accumulation period?

☐ Is there a secondary interest rate guaranteed? If yes,

___ What is the rate?
___ How long is it guaranteed?
___ What happens after it expires?
___ Is a bail-out option provided?

☐ What is the benefit amount for death or surrender of the contract?

___ If there is a return of premiums, is it with interest?
___ When will the cash value exceed premiums paid?
___ Are there surrender charges? If yes, describe.

Liquidation Period

☐ When does the liquidation period begin?

___ Is there an option to accelerate the starting date?
___ Is there an option to delay the starting date? If yes, how long?
___ Is a cash option available at the start of the liquidation period?

☐ How much is the periodic benefit payment?

☐ Is the periodic benefit amount guaranteed or variable?

☐ Is the benefit payment based on the insurer's investment results?

☐ Is the benefit payment based on a stock market index? If yes,

___ What is the participation rate?
___ What is the index?
___ Is there a cap on participation?
___ Is there a guaranteed minimum?

☐ How frequently is the periodic benefit paid?

☐ Do the benefit amounts continue for only a specified number of years? If yes, how many?

☐ Do the benefit payments continue for only one lifetime? If yes,

___ Is there any period certain? If yes, how long?
___ Are there any installment or cash refund features? If yes, how much?

☐ Do the benefit payments continue for two lifetimes? If yes,

___ Are the benefit payments reduced after the first death? If yes, by how much?
___ Is there any guaranteed minimum amount of the total benefit payments? If yes, what is the amount?

SOURCES FOR FURTHER IN-DEPTH STUDY

- Chandler, Darlene K., *The Annuity Handbook: A Guide to Nonqualified Annuities*, 2d ed., Cincinnati, OH: The National Underwriter Company, 1998. Phone 800-543-0874. Web site address www.nuco.com
- For further information about structured settlements, the National Structured Settlement Trade Association. Web site address www.nssta.com/general

CHAPTER REVIEW

Answers to review questions and self-test questions start on page 725.

Key Terms

annuity	liquidation period
annuitant	life annuity certain
annuity certain	installment refund annuity
life annuity	cash refund annuity
temporary life annuity	50 percent refund annuity
joint (joint-life) annuity	modified cash refund annuity
joint-and-last-survivor annuity	accumulation period
immediate annuity	cash option
deferred annuity	accumulation unit
pure (straight life) annuity	annuity unit
refund annuity	equity-indexed annuity
fixed annuity	structured settlement
variable annuity	step-rate annuity

Review Questions

11-1. Explain how annuities and life insurance are
   a. dissimilar in function
   b. based on the same principles

11-2. Explain how an annuity can guarantee a lifetime income to an individual.

11-3. Indicate how annuities can be classified by
   a. plan of distribution
   b. parties in the contract
   c. time when benefits begin
   d. method of purchase
   e. amount of annuity payment

11-4. Explain how immediate and deferred annuities differ with regard to
   a. the method of premium payment possible
   b. the existence of accumulation and/or liquidation periods

11-5. Your client, Jim Smith, wishes to supplement over time the funds being accumulated in his corporate pension so that he will be able to more adequately meet the anticipated needs for him and his wife after he retires in 20 years. Jim has indicated in his discussions with you that he is willing to take sufficient investment risk in an attempt to protect his retirement savings and benefits from inflation. What features would you have Jim consider in purchasing an annuity to accomplish his goal?

11-6. Ann Peterson purchased an immediate annuity for $300,000 at retirement, received two monthly payments, and died. What would happen after Ann died if her annuity was
   a. a pure annuity
   b. a life annuity with 20-years certain
   c. an installment refund annuity

11-7. Describe the operation of a variable annuity issued on a deferred basis in terms of the role of accumulation units and annuity units.

11-8. Describe the key features of equity-indexed annuities.

11-9. Explain the three approaches for adjusting annuity prices for anticipated future increases in life expectancy.

11-10. Explain how an annuity is used in a typical structured settlement.

11-11. Discuss the advantages and disadvantages of structured settlements.

Self-Test Questions

T F 11-1. The person whose life governs the duration of payments in an annuity is called the annuitant.

T F 11-2. Annuities serve essentially the same function as life insurance.

T F 11-3. If Jack would like to accumulate money for his planned retirement in 20 years, he should purchase an immediate annuity with periodic premiums.

T F 11-4. If Rachel purchased a life annuity with 20-years certain to liquidate her retirement savings and was still alive at the end of 20 years, her annuity benefit payments would cease.

T F 11-5. An installment refund annuity promises to keep paying installment benefits to the annuitant and/or beneficiary until the total equals the purchase price of the annuity plus interest at a guaranteed rate.

T F 11-6. A joint-and-last-survivor annuity continues to pay benefits as long as any of the annuitants are alive.

T F 11-7. During the liquidation period, a variable annuity promises to pay a variable number of annuity units of fixed value in each payment period.

T F 11-8. Equity-indexed annuities offer no minimum guaranteed interest rate.

T F 11-9. Annuity considerations are generally calculated using the same mortality rates as are used in calculating life insurance premiums.

T F 11-10. If properly designed, a structured settlement can provide periodic payments of income that are received tax free by the claimant during his or her life and by the claimant's beneficiaries thereafter for the balance of any guaranteed period.

NOTES

1. More precisely, the value of an annuity unit at the end of each fiscal year is obtained by dividing the current market value of the funds supporting the annuity units by the total number of annuity units expected to be paid over the future lifetimes of all participants then receiving annuity payments, in accordance with the assumptions as to mortality, investment earnings, and expense rates for the future.
2. *Securities and Exchange Commission v. Valic*, 359 U.S. 65 (1959).
3. Different treatment is applicable for amounts invested in the annuity before August 14, 1982.
4. Special rules apply to the calculation of the exclusion ratio for equity-based annuity contracts.
5. IRC Sec. 104(a)(2). Also see Rev. Ruls. 79-220, 79-313, and 77-230.

Medical Expense Insurance As an Employee Benefit

Learning Objectives
An understanding of the material in this chapter should enable the student to

12-1. Describe the development of medical expense coverage.

12-2. Describe traditional major medical expense coverage and explain how this approach has incorporated managed care provisions.

12-3. Identify the reasons for the use of managed care and describe the recent developments that pertain to the quality of care.

12-4. Describe the various types of managed care plans.

12-5. Describe the nature and purpose of defined-contribution medical expense plans.

12-6. Explain why benefit carve-outs are used with managed care plans and describe the carve-outs used for prescription drugs, vision benefits, and behavioral health.

12-7. Describe the provisions found in medical expense plans that pertain to eligibility, coordination of benefits, Medicare, and claims.

12-8. Describe the nature of dental insurance plans.

12-9. Explain the rationale for supplemental medical expense plans for executives and describe the nature of such plans.

Chapter Outline

health insurance

medical expense insurance

The next four chapters of this book are devoted to various aspects of health insurance. Although the term *health insurance* is often used in a narrow sense to mean protection against financial loss resulting from medical bills, the term actually has a much broader meaning. In this book, health insurance refers to protection against the financial consequences of poor health. These financial consequences can result from incurring medical bills as the result of an accident or illness (including dental expenses) for which *medical expense insurance* provides protection. Poor health can also result in lost income and additional expenses. Protection against lost income is provided by disability income insurance, and long-term care insurance covers one significant expense that can be a result of poor health. This and chapter 13 focus on medical expense insurance; chapters 14 and 15 cover disability income insurance and long-term care insurance, respectively. Chapter 7 describes health insurance provided by the Social Security and Medicare programs.

Medical expense insurance is arguably the most important type of insurance protection to most Americans and the type of protection that causes the most anxiety if it is lost or unaffordable. It is also the type of personal insurance for which the greatest dollar outlay is made. However, approximately 90 percent of the persons who have medical expense insurance obtain it as an employee benefit, and a major portion of the cost of coverage for most working persons is paid by their employers. Employer-provided coverage is the focus of this chapter. It is important for the financial planner to understand a client's coverage to determine whether it is adequate. If it is not, sometimes the client can obtain supplemental coverage. It is equally important to know when supplemental coverages, such as dread disease policies, may be inappropriate because they only duplicate employer-provided coverage or provide poor or inadequate protection for the client's actual needs.

It is also important for financial planners to know what alternatives are available when a client's employment or insurance coverage terminates. The next chapter covers various forms of individual coverage. These coverages can also be used for clients who are self-employed or work for employers that do not have a group insurance plan.

Medical expense insurance is the most significant type of employee benefit in terms of both the number of persons covered and the dollar outlay. With the exception of employers with a small number of employees, virtually all employers offer some type of medical expense plan. In almost all cases, coverage identical to that offered for employees is also available for eligible dependents. In the absence of employee contributions, the cost of providing medical coverage for employees will be several times greater for most employers than the combined cost of providing life insurance and disability income insurance.

Group medical expense coverage is not as standardized as other types of employer-provided coverage such as group life insurance and group disability income insurance. Coverage may be provided through Blue Cross and Blue Shield plans, health maintenance organizations (HMOs), and preferred-provider organizations (PPOs) as well as insurance companies. In addition, a large and increasing percentage of the benefits is provided under plans that are partially or totally self-funded (self-insured). An overall medical expense plan may be limited to specific types of medical expenses, or it may be broad enough to cover almost all medical expenses. Even when broad coverage is available, benefits may be provided either under a single contract or under a combination of contracts. Furthermore, in contrast to other types of group insurance, benefits may be in the form of services rather than cash payments.

Finally, the skyrocketing cost of providing medical expense benefits over a long period of time has led to changes in coverage and plan design aimed at controlling these costs. Many of these changes have resulted in more similarities among providers of medical expense coverage than existed in the past.

Over the last decade, two major issues—affordability and accessibility of medical care—have led to profound changes in the health care industry. Not only has there been a continued shift to managed care plans, but the entire character of the health care industry has also changed. Where once there was a distinction among the providers of care (such as doctors and hospitals) and the organizations that financed the care (such as insurers, the Blues, and HMOs), this distinction is now blurred. For example, physicians and hospitals have established HMOs and PPOs, and physicians may be employees of managed care plans. There are those who feel that in the not-too-distant future most Americans will receive their medical expense coverage from one of a small number of large organizations that both provide medical care and finance the cost of that care.

The issues surrounding medical care have also become a concern of government. Many states have enacted programs to make coverage available to the uninsured, including those who work for employers with a small number of employees. At the federal level, lively debate over health care has occurred and is likely to continue.

HISTORY OF MEDICAL EXPENSE INSURANCE

Development of Medical Expense Coverage

Until the 1930s, medical expense coverage was borne primarily by ill or injured persons and their families. Blue Cross and Blue Shield Plans, as well as HMOs, were developed during the Great Depression, and the Blues were the predominant providers of medical expense coverage through the 1940s. HMOs remained only a small player in the marketplace for medical expense coverage until the last two decades.

Insurance companies were only modestly successful in competing with the Blues until a new product was introduced in 1949—major medical insurance. By the mid-1950s, insurance companies surpassed the Blues in premium volume and number of persons covered.

The number of persons with medical expense insurance plans grew rapidly during the 1950s and 1960s. For the first time, the federal government became a major player in providing medical expense coverage by creating national health insurance programs for the elderly and the poor. Medicare provides benefits for persons aged 65 and older. The second program—Medicaid—provides medical benefits for certain classes of low-income individuals and families.

By 1970, expenditures for health care equaled 7.3 percent of GNP, and the country saw the first large-scale debate over national health insurance. The result was legislation to encourage HMOs. The Employee Retirement Income Security Act (ERISA) also freed self-funded plans from state regulation and hastened the growth of this financing technique.

Attempts to rein in the cost of medical care in the 1970s seemed to have little effect, and health care expenditures now account for about 14 percent of GNP. In addition, over 40 million Americans, including many employed persons and their families, remain uninsured.

The many efforts by employers to contain these rising health care costs include the following:

- increased use of self-funding
- cost-shifting to employees. It has become increasingly common for employers to raise deductibles and require employees to pay a larger portion of their medical expense coverage.
- increased use of managed care plans that are alternatives to HMOs, such as PPOs and point-of-service (POS) plans
- requiring or encouraging managed care plans. Many employers have dropped traditional medical expense plans, and they offer managed care alternatives only. However, another prevalent approach is for employers to offer employees a financial incentive to join managed care plans.
- introduction of defined-contribution medical expense plans

Data collected by the Kaiser Family Foundation[1] show that enrollment in medical expense plans that can be characterized as traditional indemnity plans dropped from over 70 percent to 5 percent since the early 1990s. During the same period, the number of enrollees in plans that use PPOs increased significantly to 52 percent. Point-of-service plans and HMOs grew more slowly and now account for about 18 percent and 26 percent, respectively, of the number of enrollees.

One important change is hidden in these statistics—the increasing trend toward self-funding of medical expenses by employers. It is estimated that over 50 percent of all workers are covered under plans that are totally or substantially self-funded. It should be noted that the way benefits are provided under a self-funded plan can vary—the employer may design the plan to provide benefits on an indemnity basis or as an HMO or PPO.

A Look at the Future

As in past decades, the health care system will continue to evolve in the first decade of this millennium. What the changes will be is only speculation, but a few observations can be made about the current environment:

- Renewal rates for employer-provided medical expense plans are increasing at the highest percentage since the early 1990s; these high percentage increases are predicted to continue in the foreseeable future.
- Surveys indicate that a large majority of Americans, including those with HMO coverage and other forms of managed care, are satisfied with their own health care plan. The relatively low degree of dissatisfaction, however, is higher among plans with the greatest degree of managed care.
- Surveys also indicate that despite satisfaction with their own coverage, Americans are becoming less satisfied with and less confident about the health care system.
- There is a growing backlash against managed care, particularly HMOs. Two observations can be made about this trend. First, many persons appear to have based their opinions on media reports and stories from friends, not on their own experiences. Second, this backlash has attracted the attention of Congress and the states. Some legislation has resulted at the state level. However, managed care plans are also becoming increasingly flexible and consumer friendly, possibly to prevent further legislation aimed at managed care reform. (Managed care reform is discussed later in this chapter.)
- There has been little federal health care legislation during the last few years. Although there has been bipartisan agreement that many problems exist with the current system, there has also been bipartisan disagreement about what should be done.

TRADITIONAL PLANS

Prior to the mid-1970s, most employees were covered by what are commonly referred to as traditional, or indemnity, plans. However, these plans have evolved. Although they are still far from what might be called managed care plans, these plans increasingly contain provisions designed to control costs and influence the behavior of persons needing medical care.

Historically, medical expense coverage consisted of separate basic benefits for hospital expenses, surgical expenses, and physicians' visits. Coverage was limited, and many types of medical expenses were not covered. However, the available coverage was "first dollar" in that covered expenses were paid in full without deductibles and coinsurance. Over time, employers began to offer more extensive benefits to employees. Although this broader coverage is usually provided through a single major medical contract, some employees are still covered under medical expense plans that consist of selected basic coverages typically provided by Blue Cross and/or Blue Shield. In most cases, these basic coverages are supplemented by a major medical contract so that the effect is essentially the same as if a single major medical contract was used.

Before proceeding further, two comments need to be made about the importance of this section of the chapter. First, interest in traditional plans will undoubtedly vary by the state in which a reader resides. It was pointed out earlier that only about 14 percent of employees and their families are covered under traditional plans. However, this percentage varies significantly by state. For example, HMO enrollments are small (10 percent or less) in about 20 percent of the states—mostly states with small and heavily rural populations. In these states, most employees and their families are covered by traditional plans or PPOs, which can be viewed as traditional major medical plans that have adopted a wide range of managed care characteristics. In another 20 percent of the states—typically populous and urban states—40 to 55 percent of employees and their families are covered by HMOs and almost all of the remaining employees and families are covered by other forms of managed care.

Second, the discussion of traditional medical expense plans largely follows their historical development. Much of the terminology and coverage of legislation introduced here also applies to the managed care approaches to medical care that are discussed later.

Major Medical Coverage

major medical insurance

Major medical insurance protects against catastrophic medical expenses, with few exclusions or limitations. The distinguishing features of major medical expense plans include a broad range of covered expenses, deductibles, coinsurance, and high overall maximum benefits.

Basic Characteristics of Major Medical Expense Insurance

- Wide range of covered expenses
- Use of deductibles
- Use of coinsurance
- High maximum benefits

Covered Expenses

Major medical plans give broad coverage for necessary expenses incurred for medical services and supplies that a physician has ordered or prescribed. These services and supplies, which are specified in the contract, generally include the following:

- hospital room and board. Traditionally, coverage has not been provided either for confinements in extended care facilities or for home health care. However, major medical plans now often include such coverage. Some plans also provide benefits for room and board in alternative facilities such as birthing centers.
- other hospital charges
- charges of outpatient surgical centers
- anesthetics and their administration
- services of doctors of medicine or osteopathy. Coverage for the services of other medical practitioners (such as chiropractors or podiatrists) may also be included.
- professional services of registered nurses. The services of other nurses (such as nurse midwives) may also be covered.
- prescription drugs
- physical and speech therapy
- diagnostic X-ray and laboratory services
- radiation therapy
- blood and blood plasma
- artificial limbs and organs
- pacemakers
- casts, splints, trusses, braces, and crutches
- rental of wheelchairs, hospital beds, and iron lungs
- ambulance services

Even though coverage is broad, major medical contracts contain certain exclusions and limitations.

Exclusions. The list varies, but exclusions in most major medical contracts include charges arising from the following:

- occupational injuries or diseases to the extent that benefits are provided by workers' compensation laws or similar legislation
- care provided by family members or when no charge would be made for the care received in the absence of the insurance contract
- cosmetic surgery, except as required by the Women's Health and Cancer Rights Act, unless such surgery is to correct a condition

resulting from either an accidental injury or a birth defect (if the parent has dependent coverage when the child is born)

- most physical examinations, unless such examinations are necessary for the treatment of an injury or illness. However, plans are increasingly providing preventive medicine that might involve specific types of physical examinations.
- convalescent, custodial, or rest care
- dental care except for (1) treatment required because of injury to natural teeth and (2) hospital and surgical charges associated with hospital confinement for dental surgery
- eye refraction, or the purchase or fitting of eyeglasses or hearing aids
- expenses either paid or eligible for payment under Medicare or other federal, state, or local medical expense programs
- experimental services

preexisting-conditions provision

Most major medical plans also contain an exclusion for preexisting conditions. However, such a *preexisting-conditions provision* applies only for a limited time, after which the condition is no longer considered preexisting and covered in full, subject to any other contract limitations or exclusions.

A *preexisting condition* is typically defined as any illness or injury for which a covered person received medical care during the 3-month period prior to the person's effective date of coverage. Usually, the condition is no longer considered preexisting after the earlier of (1) a period of 3 consecutive months during which no medical care is received for the condition or (2) 12 months of coverage under the contract by the individual.

It is also not unusual, particularly with large employers, for the preexisting-conditions clause to be waived for persons who are eligible for coverage on the date a master contract becomes effective. However, future employees will be subject to the provision. In addition, the Health Insurance Portability and Accountability Act (HIPAA) limits the use of preexisting-conditions provisions with respect to newborn or adopted children. Preexisting-conditions provisions also cannot apply to pregnancy.

The exclusion for cosmetic surgery is subject to the Women's Health and Cancer Rights Act, which amended ERISA and applies to all types of group health plans as well as individual medical expense insurance. Under the provisions of the federal act, any benefit plan or policy that provides medical and surgical benefits for mastectomy must also provide coverage for the following: (1) reconstruction of the breast on which the mastectomy has been performed; (2) surgery and reconstruction of the other breast to produce a symmetrical appearance, and (3) prostheses and physical complications of all stages of mastectomy, including lymphedemas.

Until the passage of the Pregnancy Discrimination Act, it was not unusual to exclude benefits for maternity-related expenses. However, the act requires that benefit plans of employers with 15 or more employees treat pregnancy, childbirth, and related conditions the same as any other medical condition. In the absence of a state law to the contrary, pregnancy may be and is sometimes excluded under group insurance contracts written for employers with fewer than 15 employees.

Limitations. Major medical plans also contain "internal limits" for certain types of medical expenses. Although the expenses are covered, the amounts paid under the contract are limited. For example, benefits are rarely paid for charges that exceed what is reasonable and customary, room-and-board benefits are generally limited to the charge for semiprivate accommodations unless other accommodations are medically necessary, and benefits for infertility treatments might be subject to 50 percent coinsurance or a maximum dollar limitation.

Treatment of Mental Illness, Alcoholism, and Drug Addiction. It is common for major medical plans to provide limited benefits for treatment for mental and nervous disorders, alcoholism, and drug addiction. Unless state laws require that these conditions be treated like any other medical condition, inpatient coverage is often limited to a specific number of days each year (commonly 30 or 60). Outpatient benefits, which are even more limited, are often subject to 50 percent coinsurance and to a specific dollar limit per visit.

It has been common for major medical plans to impose an annual maximum (such as $1,000) and/or an overall maximum lifetime limit (such as $25,000) on benefits for mental and nervous disorders, alcoholism, and drug addiction. However, the provisions of the Mental Health Parity Act, which apply only to employers with more than 50 employees, prohibit a group health plan, insurance company, or HMO from setting annual or lifetime *dollar* limits on mental health benefits that are less than the limits applying to other medical and surgical benefits. Besides imposing no limitations on benefits for alcoholism or drug addiction, the act is noteworthy for other things it does not do. It does not require employers to make any benefits available for mental illness, and it does not impose any other restrictions on mental health benefits. Employers can still impose limitations such as an annual maximum on number of visits or days of coverage and different cost-sharing provisions for mental health benefits than those that apply to other medical and surgical benefits.

Also note that some states require more comprehensive coverage than the federal act and/or mandate benefits for employers with a smaller number of employees.

Deductibles

deductible

A *deductible* is the initial amount of covered medical expenses an individual must pay before he or she receives benefits under a major medical plan. For example, if a plan has an annual deductible of $200, the covered person is responsible for the first $200 of medical expenses incurred each year. The major medical plan then pays covered expenses in excess of $200, subject to any limitations or coinsurance.

The simplest and most common form of deductible is the *initial deductible*. Essentially, a covered person must satisfy this deductible before the plan will pay any insurance benefits. However, the deductible can vary with respect to (1) the amounts of the deductible, (2) the frequency with which it must be satisfied, and (3) the expenses to which it applies.

Deductible Amounts. Deductible amounts for any covered person tend to be relatively small. Most deductibles are fixed-dollar amounts that apply separately to each person and usually fall within the range of $100 to $250. In most major medical expense plans, the deductible must be satisfied only once during any given time period (usually a calendar year), regardless of the number of causes from which medical expenses arise.

Deductibles apply to each covered individual, including an employee's dependents. To minimize the family's burden of satisfying several deductibles, however, most major medical expense plans contain a family deductible. Once the family deductible is satisfied, future covered medical expenses of all family members are paid just as if every member of the family had satisfied his or her individual deductible.

The most common type of family deductible waives any future deductible requirements for other family members once a certain number of family members (generally two or three) have satisfied their individual deductibles.

Example: A family deductible might specify that the first $100 per year for each covered family member is the deductible. However, if three of five covered members of the family have each satisfied the deductible in a given year, no further deductibles need be met for that year. Thus when Mom, Dad, and child #1 each incur $100 or more of covered expenses during the year, no further deductible applies to the expenses of child #2 and child #3 incurred after the family deductible is satisfied.

Most major medical expense contracts also contain a *common accident provision,* whereby if two or more members of the same family are injured in the same accident, the covered medical expenses for all family members are at most subject to a single deductible, usually equal to the individual deductible amount.

Deductible Frequency. A deductible usually applies to medical expenses incurred within a specified 12-month period, typically a calendar year (January 1 to December 31). Under such a *calendar-year deductible,* expenses incurred from January 1 apply toward the deductible. Once the deductible has been satisfied, the balance of any covered expenses incurred during the year are then paid by the major medical plan, subject to limitations and coinsurance.

Many plans with a calendar-year deductible also have a carryover provision that allows any expenses (1) applied to the deductible and (2) incurred during the last 3 months of the year to also be applied to the deductible for the following year.

Expenses to Which the Deductible Applies. Most major medical plans have a single deductible that applies to all medical expenses. However, some plans have two (or more) deductibles that apply separately to different categories of medical expenses. In some major medical plans, the deductible does not apply to certain expenses, in effect giving the covered person first-dollar coverage for these charges.

Coinsurance

coinsurance (medical expense insurance)

Major medical expense plans contain a coinsurance provision whereby the plan pays only a specified percentage (in most cases, 80 percent) of the covered expenses that exceed the deductible. For purposes of medical expense insurance, the term *coinsurance* as used in this book refers to the percentage of covered expenses paid by a medical expense plan. Thus, a plan with 80 percent coinsurance, sometimes referred to as an 80/20 plan, pays 80 percent of covered expenses while a person who receives benefits under the plan must pay the remaining 20 percent. In some plans, a percentage participation, such as 20 percent, is specified. As commonly used, a *percentage participation* refers to the percentage of covered medical expenses that a medical expense plan does not pay and that a person receiving benefits must pay. Note that percentage participation is sometimes referred to as a *copayment,* but that terminology usually implies a fixed-dollar amount that an insured must pay for a covered service. To make the matter even more confusing, some insurers refer to the percentage participation, rather than their portion of the benefit payment, as coinsurance.

Example: If a comprehensive major medical expense plan has a $200 calendar-year deductible and an 80 percent coinsurance provision that applies to all expenses, an individual who incurs $1,200 of covered medical expenses during the year (assuming no limitations) will receive an $800 reimbursement, calculated as follows:

Covered expenses	$1,200
Less deductible	200
	$1,000
Multiplied by coinsurance percentage	.80
	$ 800

Just as deductibles vary, so do coinsurance provisions. Sometimes different coinsurance percentages apply to different categories of medical expenses. For example, outpatient psychiatric charges may be subject to 50 percent coinsurance, while other covered medical expenses are subject to 80 percent coinsurance. In addition, certain medical expenses may be subject to 100 percent coinsurance (and usually no deductible), which in effect means that the expenses are paid in full, subject to any limitations. Such full coverage is most likely to exist (1) for those expenses over which an individual has little control, (2) when there is a desire to provide first-dollar coverage for certain expenses, or (3) when there is a desire to encourage the use of the most cost-effective treatment (such as outpatient surgery, preadmission testing, or birthing centers).

stop-loss limit

In the case of catastrophic medical expenses, the coinsurance provision could result in an individual's having to assume a large dollar amount of his or her own medical expenses. Consequently, many major medical expense plans place a limit, often called a *stop-loss* (or *coinsurance*) *limit* or *cap,* on the amount of out-of-pocket expenses that a covered person must bear during any time period. For example, the plan may have a $200 deductible, an 80 percent coinsurance provision that applies to the next $3,000 of covered expenses, and full coverage for any remaining covered expenses. Therefore, the most an individual will have to pay out of pocket in any year is the $200 deductible and 20 percent of $3,000 (for a total of $800).

Maximum Benefits

Many major medical contracts contain a lifetime maximum that applies to all medical expenses paid (after the application of deductibles and coinsurance) during the entire period an individual is covered under the contract. Most benefit maximums fall within the range of $1 million to $2 million. In some instances, the benefit amount is unlimited.

In addition to the overall lifetime maximum, major medical contracts sometimes have *internal maximums*. For example, a plan may have a $1 million overall lifetime maximum but a $10,000 lifetime maximum for benefits relating to alcoholism and drug addiction.

Managed Care Provisions in Traditional Plans

Historically, traditional medical expense plans contained few provisions aimed at managing the care of covered persons, but this situation continues to evolve. Provisions such as hospital precertification and second opinions have existed for many years. It is also common for benefits to be provided for treatment in facilities other than hospitals. Other managed care provisions and practices that traditional plans may contain include the following:

- preapproval of visits to specialists
- increased benefits for preventive care
- carve-outs of benefits that can be provided cost effectively under arrangements that employ various degrees of managed care. Examples include prescription drugs, treatment of mental illness, and substance abuse treatment. These types of carve-outs are discussed as part of managed care plans.

Some traditional major medical plans actually make wide use of managed care techniques; the primary factor that prevents them from being called managed care plans is that there are few restrictions on access to providers.

Hospital Precertification

As a method of controlling costs, medical expense plans have adopted utilization review programs. One aspect of these programs is preadmission certification. Such a program requires that a covered person, or his or her physician, obtain prior authorization for any nonemergency hospitalization. Authorization usually must also be obtained within 24 to 48 hours of admissions for emergencies.

Most plans reduce benefits if the preadmission certification procedure is not followed. If a patient enters the hospital after a preadmission certification has been denied, many plans do not pay for any hospital expenses, whereas other plans provide a reduced level of benefits.

Second Surgical Opinions

second surgical opinion

Most major medical expense policies provide benefits for *second surgical opinions* in an attempt to control medical costs by eliminating unnecessary surgery. A voluntary approach for obtaining second surgical opinions is often used. If a physician or surgeon recommends surgery, a covered person can seek a second opinion and the medical expense plan bears the cost. Some plans also pay for a third opinion if the first two opinions disagree. When there are divergent opinions, the final choice is up to the patient, and the plan's regular benefits are usually paid for any resulting surgery.

Some medical expense plans require mandatory second opinions, which may apply to any elective and nonemergency surgery but frequently apply only to a specified list of procedures. In most cases, a surgeon selected by the insurance company or other provider of benefits must give the second opinion. If conflicting opinions arise, a third opinion may be obtained. The costs of the second and third opinions are paid in full. In contrast to voluntary provisions, mandatory provisions generally specify that benefits are paid at a reduced level if surgery is performed either without a second opinion or contrary to the final opinion.

Alternative Facilities for Treatment

Many traditional medical expense plans provide coverage for treatment in facilities that are alternatives to hospitals. Initially, this coverage was provided primarily to the extent that it reduced hospital benefits that were otherwise covered. Although this is still the primary effect of this coverage, it is often an integral part of medical expense plans, and benefits are provided even if they might not have been covered under a plan limited solely to treatment received in hospitals.

extended care facility

Extended Care Facility Benefits. Many hospital patients recover to a point where they no longer need the full level of care a hospital provides but still require a medically supervised period of convalescence. *Extended care facilities* (often called convalescent nursing homes or skilled-nursing facilities) have been established in many areas to provide this type of care. Treatment in these facilities, which are often adjacent to hospitals, can reduce daily room-and-board charges—often substantially. As a result, a small but increasing number of contracts include benefits for situations where extended care facilities are used in lieu of hospitalization to contain medical care costs.

Extended care facility coverage provides benefits to inpatients in an extended care facility, which is typically defined as an institution that furnishes room and board and 24-hour-a-day skilled-nursing care under the supervision of a physician or a registered professional nurse. It does not include facilities that are designed as a place for rest or domiciliary care for the aged. In addition, facilities for the treatment of drug abuse and alcoholism are often excluded from the definition.

The maximum length of time for which extended care benefits will be paid is usually limited to a specific number of days; 60 days is fairly common.

home health care

Home Health Care Benefits. *Home health care* coverage is similar to extended care facility benefits but designed for when the necessary part-time nursing care ordered by a physician following hospitalization can be provided in the patient's home. Coverage is for (1) nursing care (usually limited to a maximum of 2 hours per day) under the supervision of a registered nurse, (2) physical, occupational, and speech therapy, and (3) medical supplies and equipment such as wheelchairs and hospital beds.

In most cases, the benefits payable are equal to a percentage, frequently 80 percent, of reasonable-and-customary charges. Benefit payments are limited to either a maximum number of visits (such as 60 per calendar year) or to a period of time (such as 90 days after benefits commence).

hospice care

Hospice Benefits. Hospices for the treatment of terminally ill persons are a recent development in the area of medical care. *Hospice care* does not attempt to cure medical conditions but is devoted to easing the physical and psychological pain associated with death. In addition to providing services for the dying patient, a hospice may also offer counseling to family members. Although a hospice may be a separate facility, this type of care is frequently provided on an outpatient basis in the dying person's home.

Hospice benefits may be subject to a maximum, such as $5,000.

birthing center

Birthing Centers. Another recent development in medical care is *birthing centers*, which are designed to provide a homelike facility for the delivery of babies. Nurse-midwives perform deliveries in a facility separate from a hospital, and mothers and babies are released shortly after birth.

Preapproval of Visits to Specialists

Many persons elect to bypass their primary care physicians, such as family physicians and pediatricians, and use specialists as their main access to medical care. This practice results in additional costs but, in the opinion of much of the medical community, does not improve medical outcomes. To counter this practice, some medical expense plans require that a visit to a specialist be preceded by a visit to a primary care physician. It is not necessary for the primary care physician to actually certify that a trip to a specialist is needed, only that he or she has been told that the patient plans to make such a visit. The rationale for this procedure is that the primary care physician may convince the patient that he or she is able to treat the condition and that a specialist is unnecessary, at least at that time. If a specialist is needed, the primary care physician is also in a better position to recommend the right type of specialist and to coordinate health care for persons seeing multiple specialists.

The patient's failure to use the primary care physician as a quasi-gatekeeper will result in a reduction in benefits. Usually, benefits will still be paid but at a lower level.

Benefits for Preventive Care

Most traditional medical expense plans provide at least a few benefits for preventive care. Probably the most frequent benefits, because of state mandates for group insurance contracts, are well-baby care, childhood immunizations, and mammograms. Plans may also go as far as to provide routine physicals for children at specified ages and, perhaps, for all covered persons, typically subject to an annual maximum benefit such as $150 or $200. Coverage for routine adult physicals, however, is much more likely under managed care plans.

MANAGED CARE PLANS

Over the last few years, the number of persons having medical expense coverage from managed care plans has grown rapidly. Slightly over 50 percent of managed care participants are enrolled in PPOs, and the remaining participants are split between traditional HMOs and point-of-service (POS) plans. Although managed care plans have evolved over the last few years, it is generally felt that a true *managed care* plan should have five basic characteristics:

managed care

- *controlled access to providers.* It is difficult to control costs if participants have unrestricted access to physicians and hospitals. Managed care plans attempt to encourage or force participants to use predetermined providers. Because a major portion of medical expenses results from referrals to specialists, managed care plans tend to use primary care physicians as gatekeepers to determine the necessity and appropriateness of specialty care. By limiting the number of providers, managed care plans are better able to control costs by negotiating provider fees.

- *comprehensive case management.* Successful plans perform utilization review at all levels. This involves reviewing a case to determine the type of treatment necessary, monitoring ongoing care, and assessing the appropriateness and success of treatment after it has been given.

- *preventive care.* Managed care plans encourage preventive care and the attainment of healthier lifestyles.
- *risk sharing.* Managed care plans are most successful if providers share in the financial consequences of medical decisions. Newer managed care plans have contractual guarantees to encourage cost-effective care. For example, a physician who minimizes diagnostic tests may receive a bonus. Ideally, such an arrangement will eliminate unnecessary tests, not discourage tests that should be performed.
- *high-quality care.* A managed care plan will not be well received and selected by participants if there is a perception of inferior or inconvenient medical care. In the past, too little attention was paid to this aspect of cost containment. Newer managed care plans not only select providers more carefully but also monitor the quality of care on a continuing basis.

Basic Characteristics of Managed Care Plans

- Controlled access to specialists and hospitals
- Emphasis on case management, including utilization review
- Encouragement of preventive care and healthy lifestyles
- Sharing by medical care providers in the financial consequences of medical decisions
- Careful selection and monitoring of medical providers

This section on managed care first looks at the issue of quality of care and discusses some recent developments. It then describes the types of managed care plans.

Quality of Care

A difficult question to answer is whether persons covered by managed care plans receive the same quality of care as persons covered under traditional medical expense plans. If the sole objective of a managed care plan is to offer coverage at the lowest possible cost, there may be a decline in the quality of care. However, some type of quality assurance program is one aspect of any managed care plan.

The results of numerous surveys and studies on the quality of medical care plans have been mixed. Some studies show that persons in managed care plans are less likely than persons in traditional medical expense plans to receive treatment for a serious medical condition from specialists, and they are also likely to have fewer diagnostic tests. There are those who argue that family physicians can treat a wide variety of illnesses and avoid unnecessary diagnostic tests and referrals to specialists. An opposing argument contends that the decline in the use of diagnostic tests indicates a corresponding decline in the level of medical care. Other studies show that persons in managed care plans are much more likely than the rest of the population to receive preventive care and early diagnosis and treatment of potentially serious conditions such as high blood pressure and diabetes. In addition, managed care plans are viewed as having been successful in coordinating care when it is necessary for a person to see several different types of specialists. There is no doubt that there are some small provider networks with a limited choice of specialists, but most networks are relatively large or allow persons to select treatment outside the network. There are also many managed care plans that do refer patients to highly regarded physicians and hospitals or include these providers in their network.

As managed care matures and becomes more widespread, there is an increasing focus by some employers on quality. This has led many employers, particularly large employers, to require that managed care organizations for their employees meet some type of accreditation standards. Several not-for-profit organizations set these standards and provide the accreditation.

Recent Developments

As previously mentioned, the majority of employers and employees are reasonably satisfied with managed care plans but have increasing concerns. However, the satisfaction of physicians and other providers is much more negative, primarily because of decreased control over medical decisions for their patients and a loss of income. As a result, there has been what the media describe as a "backlash against managed care." In some ways, this terminology is inaccurate. First, some of the public's concerns, such as lack of complete mental health parity and inadequate coverage for certain preventive medical screenings, apply to the entire health care system, not just to manage care. Second, although some dissatisfactions are aimed at all types of managed care plans, many are targeted solely at practices of HMOs.

This backlash has had several results:

- States continue to enact legislation to address many of the concerns.
- Managed care organizations voluntarily modify their practices in light of legislative activity and competitive forces.
- The federal government continues to grapple with consumer legislation.

State Reform

State legislatures in recent years have passed several types of laws aimed at managed care reform. Some of these changes bring managed care plans closer to traditional indemnity plans in both coverage and cost. Some of these laws, passed by anywhere from 12 to 15 to almost all states, include

- antigag-clause rules that prevent managed care organizations from including provisions in their contracts that prevent doctors from discussing with patients treatment options that may not be covered under their health plans or from referring patients who are very ill for specialized care by providers outside the plan
- grievance, review, and appeal procedures
- mandatory point-of-service options that require managed care organizations to permit enrollees to seek treatment from nonnetwork providers by paying a portion, but not all, of the expenses incurred with these providers. In effect, such legislation transforms a traditional HMO into a point-of-service plan.
- emergency room coverage that requires a plan to pay emergency room charges whenever a prudent layperson considers a situation to be an emergency
- mental health parity laws that require either complete parity for benefits arising from physical illnesses and mental illnesses or complete parity for physical illnesses and certain severe mental illnesses, such as schizophrenia, depression, or bipolar disorder
- minimum stays for certain procedures such as maternity or breast cancer surgery
- plastic surgery mandates that require all health insurance contracts or health plans to provide coverage for certain types of reconstructive surgery. This legislation may apply to the repair of birth defects only, or it may apply to a broader list of situations in which reconstruction might be needed as a result of mastectomies, trauma, infections, tumors, or disease.
- legislation that allows women covered under managed care plans to have direct access to obstetricians/gynecologists without obtaining approval or a referral from their health plan. A few states require direct access to other types of providers such as dermatologists.

Voluntary Reform by Managed Care Organizations

Many managed care organizations have voluntarily initiated reforms. Some reforms are probably a result of the natural evolution of a new form of financing and providing health care; other changes have occurred because of competition among managed care organizations for market share. Most reforms are reactions to legislation that is proposed or passed by the states. After a few states enact a certain type of managed care legislation, managed care organizations nationwide often revise their plans to address the concerns that resulted in the legislation.

Just as it is for other types of businesses, the threat of legislation, at either the state or federal level, is also a major impetus for voluntary changes by managed care plans. Such voluntary reform may forestall more restrictive government regulation.

Federal Reform

Congress has addressed some health care concerns with the passage of such legislation as the following acts, which are mentioned in this chapter: the Health Insurance Portability and Accountability Act, the Mental Health Parity Act, and the Women's Health and Cancer Rights Act.

At the time this book is being revised, there are bills in Congress that would add significant federal legislation to the health care environment. Sometimes referred to as a patient's bill of rights, this type of legislation seems to have bipartisan support. However, there are differences of opinion as to what should be done, and these often vary by political party. Readers should monitor legislative developments and their potential effect on health care plans.

Health Maintenance Organizations

health maintenance organization (HMO)

Health maintenance organizations (HMOs) are generally regarded as organized systems of health care that provide a comprehensive array of medical services on a prepaid basis to voluntarily enrolled persons living within a specified geographic region. HMOs act like insurance companies and the Blues in that they finance health care. Unlike insurance companies and the Blues, however, they also deliver medical services. HMOs can be either profit or not-for-profit organizations. They may be sponsored or owned by insurance companies, the Blues, consumer groups, physicians, hospitals, labor unions, or private investors.

Even though the term health maintenance organization is a relatively modern term, the concept of the HMO is not. For many years prepaid group practice plans (as they were called) have operated successfully in many parts of the country. However, growth was relatively slow until the passage of the Health Maintenance Organization Act of 1973. This act resulted from a belief on the federal government's part that HMOs were a viable alternative method of financing and delivering health care and thus should be encouraged with grants for feasibility studies and development and loans (or loan guarantees) to assist them in covering initial operating deficits. Many HMOs were formed as the result of these grants and loans.

The act introduced the concept of the federal-qualified HMO. To become federally qualified, an HMO must meet certain requirements (set forth in the act) to the satisfaction of the secretary of health and human services. In return for a periodic prepaid fee, an HMO must provide a broad array of benefits to its subscribers at no cost or with nominal copayments.

In addition, the HMO must meet the following other requirements regarding its operations:

- a fiscally sound operation, including provisions against the possibility of insolvency
- annual open enrollment periods
- an ongoing quality assurance program

The need now for a federal HMO law is debatable. Most states already have similar legislation. Although newer HMOs may forgo federal qualification, the majority of older HMOs still retain that status and the majority of HMO subscribers are covered under federally qualified plans. It is felt that this grants them a "seal of approval" from the federal government. In addition, many employers will deal only with federally qualified HMOs.

Characteristics of HMOs

HMOs have several characteristics that distinguish them from traditional medical expense contracts that are offered by insurance companies and the Blues.

Comprehensive Care. HMOs offer their subscribers a comprehensive package of health care services, generally including benefits for outpatient services as well as for hospitalization. Subscribers usually get these services at no cost except the periodically required premium. However, in some cases a copayment, such as $5 or $10 per physician's visit, may be imposed for certain services. HMOs emphasize preventive care and provide such services as routine physicals and immunizations.

Delivery of Medical Services. HMOs provide for the delivery of medical services, which in some cases are performed by salaried physicians and other personnel employed by the HMO. Although this approach is in contrast to the usual fee-for-service delivery system of medical care, some HMOs do contract with providers on a fee-for-service basis.

Subscribers are required to obtain their care from providers of medical services who are affiliated with the HMO. Because HMOs may operate in a geographic region no larger than a single metropolitan area, this requirement may result in limited coverage for subscribers if treatment is received elsewhere. Most HMOs do have out-of-area coverage but only in the case of medical emergencies.

HMOs emphasize treatment by primary care physicians to the greatest extent possible. These practitioners fulfill a gatekeeper function and historically have controlled access to specialists. The traditional HMO covers benefits provided by a specialist only if the primary care physician recommends the specialist, who may be a fellow employee in a group-practice plan or a physician who has a contract with the HMO. The subscriber has little or no say regarding the specialist selected, which has been one of the more controversial aspects of HMOs and one that has discouraged larger enrollment. In response to consumer concerns, many HMOs now make the process of seeing a specialist easier. Referrals can often be made by nurses in physicians' offices or by HMO staff members whom subscribers can contact by telephone. Some HMOs, referred to as direct-access or self-referral HMOs, allow subscribers to see network specialists without going through a gatekeeper. However, the specialist may have to contact the HMO for authorization before proceeding with tests or treatment. A variation of an HMO, called a point-of-service plan, allows even more choice.

Cost Control. HMOs emphasize control of medical expenses. By providing and encouraging preventive care, HMOs attempt to detect and treat medical conditions at an early stage, thereby avoiding expensive medical treatment in the future.

The use of salaried employees by many HMOs may also result in lower costs because the physician or other care provider has no financial incentive to prescribe additional, and possibly unnecessary, treatment. In fact, the physicians and other medical professionals in some HMOs may receive bonuses if the HMO operates efficiently and has a surplus.

Types of HMOs

There are several types of HMOs: closed-panel, individual practice associations, and mixed model.

Closed-Panel. The earliest HMOs can best be described as closed-panel plans under which subscribers must use physicians employed by the plan or by an organization with which it contracts. Because most closed-panel plans have several general practitioners, subscribers can usually select their physician from among those accepting new patients and make medical appointments just as if the physician was in private practice. However, there is frequently little choice among specialists because a plan may have a contract with only one physician or a limited number of physicians in a given specialty.

The number of closed-panel plans is relatively small, but they account for almost 20 percent of all HMO subscribers. These HMOs may operate in a variety of ways with respect to providing physicians' services. They may own their own facilities and hire their own physicians, who are paid a salary and possibly an incentive bonus. They are more likely, however, to enter into contracts with one or more groups of physicians to provide services. In many cases, these groups are paid on a capitation basis, which means that they receive a predetermined fee per year for each subscriber and must provide any and all covered services for this fee.

Closed-panel plans may own their own hospitals, laboratories, or pharmacies or contract with other entities to provide their services.

Individual Practice Associations. Many newer HMOs have been formed as individual practice associations (IPAs). This type of plan has more flexibility with respect to subscribers' ability to choose physicians and physicians' ability to participate in the plan. About 45 percent of HMO subscribers are in individual practice associations.

In IPAs, participating physicians practice individually or in small groups at their own offices. In most cases, these physicians accept both nonmanaged care patients (on a traditional fee-for-service basis) and HMO subscribers. IPAs are often referred to as open-panel plans, because subscribers choose from a list of participating physicians. The number of physicians participating in this type of HMO is frequently larger than the number participating in group practice plans and may include several physicians within a given specialty. Because most of the newer HMOs are IPAs, the percentage of HMO subscribers served by these plans continues to grow.

Several methods may be used to compensate physicians participating in an IPA. The most common is a fee schedule based on the services provided to subscribers. To encourage physicians to be cost effective, it is common for plans to have a provision for reducing payments to physicians if the experience of the plan is worse than expected. On the other hand, the physicians may receive a bonus if the experience of the plan is better than expected. Particularly with respect to general practitioners, some individual practice association plans pay each physician a flat annual capitation for each subscriber who has elected to use him or her. For this annual payment the physician must see these subscribers as often as necessary during the year.

It is unusual for IPAs to own their own hospitals or other medical facilities. Rather, they enter into contracts with local hospitals or other organizations to provide the necessary services for their subscribers.

Mixed-Model HMOs. About 35 percent of HMO subscribers are covered by mixed-model plans. This means that the organization of the plan is a combination of the approaches previously described. Such a combination generally occurs as a plan continues to grow. For example, a plan might have been established as a closed HMO but at a later time decided to expand its capacity or geographic region by adding physicians under an IPA arrangement. Some mixed models have also resulted from the merger of two plans that each used a different organizational form.

Types of HMOs

- Closed-panel
- Individual practice association
- Mixed-model

Preferred-Provider Organizations

A concept that continues to receive considerable attention from employers and insurance companies is the preferred-provider organization (PPO). A few PPOs have existed on a small scale for many years, but since the early 1980s, PPOs have grown steadily in number and in membership. Today, PPOs provide coverage for medical expenses to more Americans than do HMOs, primarily because of covered persons' flexibility to choose their own medical providers.

Insurance companies own the majority of PPOs. Some are owned by HMOs to diversify their health plan portfolios. Still others have a variety of ownership forms, including third-party administrators, private investors, and groups of physicians and/or hospitals.

PPOs are regulated by the states but somewhat less strictly than HMOs. Note that most PPO contracts also meet the definition of insurance and are subject to the same regulation by state insurance departments as traditional insurance contracts with respect to contract provisions and benefit mandates.

What Is a PPO?

preferred-provider organization (PPO)

The term *preferred-provider organization (PPO)* tends to be used in two ways. One way is to apply it to health care providers that contract with employers, insurance companies, union trust funds, third-party administrators, or others to provide medical care services at a reduced fee. Using this definition, a PPO may be organized by the providers themselves or by other organizations such as insurance companies, the Blues, HMOs, or employers. Like HMOs, they may take the form of group practices or separate individual practices. They may provide a broad array of medical services, including physicians' services, hospital care, laboratory costs, and home health care, or they may be limited only to hospitalization or physicians' services. Some of these types of organizations are very specialized and provide specific services such as dental care, mental health benefits, substance abuse services, maternity care, or prescription drugs. In this book, these providers are referred to not as *PPOs* but as *preferred providers* or *network providers.*

The second use of the term *PPO,* and the one generally assumed when the term is used throughout this book, is to apply it to benefit plans that contract with preferred providers to obtain lower-cost care for plan members. PPOs typically differ from HMOs in several respects. First, the preferred providers are generally paid on a fee-for-service basis as their services are used. However, fees are usually subject to a schedule that is the same for all similar providers within the PPO contracts, and providers may have an incentive to control utilization through bonus arrangements. Second, employees and their dependents are not required to use the practitioners or facilities that contract with the PPO; rather, a choice can be made each time medical care is needed, and benefits are also paid for care provided by nonnetwork providers. Employees are offered incentives to use network providers; they include lower or reduced deductibles and copayments as well as increased benefits such as preventive health care. Third, most PPOs do not use a primary care physician as a gatekeeper; employees do not need referrals to see specialists.

Characteristics of a Typical PPO

- Network of medical care providers contracts to offer medical services to plan participants at reduced rate.
- Medical care providers are paid on a fee-for-service basis.
- Insureds have a choice of using network or nonnetwork providers.
- Insureds who opt to use a network provider pay lower deductibles or copayments or receive broader types of covered care.

Variations. Over time, PPOs have continued to evolve. Some PPOs compensate providers on a capitation basis, while others perform a gatekeeper function. If a subscriber's primary care physician does not recommend a specialist, benefits may be reduced. With these changes, it is sometimes difficult to determine the exact form of a managed care organization. However, those that operate as traditional HMOs generally provide medical expense coverage at a slightly lower cost than those that operate as traditional PPOs, but there are wide variations among HMOs as well as among PPOs. Therefore, a careful analysis of quality of care, cost, and financial stability is necessary before selecting a particular HMO or PPO.

**exclusive-provider
organization (EPO)**

Another variation of the PPO is the *exclusive-provider organization (EPO)*. The primary difference is that an EPO does not provide coverage outside the preferred-provider network, except in those infrequent cases when the network does not contain an appropriate specialist. This aspect of an EPO makes it very similar to an HMO. The number of EPOs is small.

Benefit Structure

The basic benefit structure of a PPO is similar to that of the traditional major medical contract, which is discussed earlier in this chapter. The most significant difference is that PPOs include a higher level of benefits for care received from network providers than for care received from nonnetwork providers. Many PPOs have extensive networks of preferred providers, particularly in the geographic areas in which they operate; hence, there is little reason to seek care outside the network. However, other PPOs have more limited networks, so their subscribers' need for treatment from nonnetwork providers is greater.

The level of benefits under PPOs may vary because of differences in deductibles, coinsurance, maximum lifetime benefits, and precertification rules. There may also be a few additional benefits that are available only if care is received from a network provider. Finally, procedures for filing claims also differ. The major purpose of these differences is to encourage an employee or dependent to receive care from preferred providers who have agreed to charge the plan a discounted fee.

Deductibles. A PPO may have annual deductibles that apply separately to network and nonnetwork charges—for example, $100 and $250, respectively. However, many PPOs have no deductible for network charges or waive this deductible for certain medical services such as emergency or preventive care.

Coinsurance. Most PPOs use coinsurance percentages that are 20 percent (and occasionally 30 percent) lower when care is received from nonnetwork providers. The most frequently found provision applies 90 percent coinsurance to network charges and 70 percent coinsurance to nonnetwork charges. Coinsurance provisions of 100/80, 90/80, and 100/70 are also frequently used. As with deductibles, the percentage participation may be waived for certain medical services. In addition, different stop-loss limits or coinsurance caps, such as $1,000 and $3,000, may apply to network and nonnetwork charges.

Although PPOs typically have higher coinsurance percentages for network charges than do traditional major medical plans, a covered person may be responsible for modest copayments in some circumstance. For example, there might be a copayment of $5, $10, or $15 for each visit to a primary care physician.

Maximum Benefits. Although there are variations, most PPOs have a lifetime maximum of $1 million for nonnetwork benefits. The lifetime maximum for network benefits is seldom less that $2 million and may even be unlimited.

Precertification Rules. PPOs often have precertification requirements for many types of hospitalizations, outpatient procedures, and medical supplies. For network benefits, the person responsible for obtaining the needed precertification is the network provider, and the covered person is not penalized if the network provider fails to obtain the proper precertification. However, this responsibility shifts to the employee or family member for nonnetwork services. If precertification is not obtained when required, there usually is a reduction in benefits.

Additional Network Benefits. For the most part, PPOs pay benefits for the same medical procedures, whether they are performed by a network or nonnetwork provider. A few procedures, however, may be covered only if they are received from network providers. For example, routine physical exams may be covered only in the network. In addition, there might be coverage for more outpatient psychiatric visits if a network provider is used.

Claims. There are no claim forms required for network services. The covered person merely pays any required copayment, and the provider of medical services does the paperwork needed to receive the additional amounts payable by the plan.

Point-of-Service (POS) Plans

point-of-service
(POS) plan

A newer and fast-growing type of managed care arrangement is the *point-of-service (POS) plan*. A *POS plan* is a hybrid arrangement that combines aspects of a traditional HMO and a PPO. With a POS plan, participants in the plan elect, at the time medical treatment is needed, whether to receive treatment within the plan's tightly managed network, usually an HMO, or outside the network. Expenses received outside the network are reimbursed in the same manner as described earlier for nonnetwork services under PPO plans.

There are two basic types of POS plans: the open-ended HMO and the gatekeeper PPO. An open-ended HMO is by far the most common form and is the HMO industry's response to the demand for more consumer flexibility in the choice of providers, even though it increases costs somewhat. It essentially consists of traditional HMO coverage with an endorsement for nonnetwork coverage. It can take the basic form of any of the HMOs previously described. However, at any time a subscriber can elect to go outside the HMO network of medical care providers.

It can be argued that any PPO is actually a POS plan. However, the normal usage of the term POS implies a higher degree of managed care than is found in most PPOs. A gatekeeper PPO requires the PPO participant to elect a primary care physician in the manner of an HMO participant. This physician acts as a gatekeeper to control utilization and refer members to specialists within the PPO network. At any time care is needed, however, a covered person can elect to go outside the network.

Under some POS plans, a covered person can go outside the plan's network without informing the plan. In other POS plans, the person must notify the gatekeeper that he or she is seeking such treatment.

COMPARISON OF TYPICAL MEDICAL EXPENSE PLANS

This chapter has discussed the various types of medical expense plans and how they differ. Although variations within each type of plan exist, some generalizations, which are summarized in table 12-1, can be made. The degree of managed care increases as one moves from left to right in the table. However, the cost of the plans, on the average, decreases as the degree of managed care increases. In addition, a higher degree of managed care is generally associated with lower annual premium increases by a plan.

DEFINED-CONTRIBUTION PLANS

defined-contribution medical expense plan

Since the beginning of the new decade, there has been considerable interest in the concept of the *defined-contribution medical expense plan*. Under such plans, the employee has increased choices and responsibilities with the selection of his or her own medical expense coverage.

A definition of a defined-contribution plan is difficult because the term has been used in many different ways. However, the common thread is that the employer makes a fixed contribution, which the employee can use to "purchase" his or her own coverage. In theory, this practice enables an employer to control costs because the amount of the contribution can remain level from year to year or increase at any rate an employer chooses. In practice, however, many employers who have used this approach have increased their contributions to match some or all of the increases in the cost of medical expense coverage.

TABLE 12-1
Comparison of Health Insurance Plans

	Traditional Major Medical Contracts	PPOs	POS Plans	HMOs
Provider Choice	Unlimited	Unlimited in network, but benefits are greater if network provider is used	Unlimited in network, but benefits are greater if network provider is used	Network of providers must be used; care from nonnetwork providers covered only in emergencies
Use of Gatekeeper	None	None	Used for care of network specialists	Used for access to specialists
Out-of-pocket Costs	Deductibles and percentage participation	Deductibles and percentage participation, which are lower if network providers are used; may have small copayment for network services	Small copayments for network services; deductibles and percentage participation for non-network services	Small copayments for some services
Utilization Review	Traditionally little, but a few techniques are likely to be used now	More than traditional plans, but less than HMOs; network provider may be subject to some controls	Like HMOs for network services; like PPOs for non-network services	Highest degree of review, including financial incentives and disincentives for providers
Preventive Care	Little covered other than that required by law	Usually more coverage than traditional major medical plan but less coverage than HMOs and POS plans	Covered	Covered
Responsibility for Claims Filings	Covered person	Plan providers for network services; covered person for non-network services	Plan providers for network services; covered person for non-network services	Plan providers

Even though some defined-contribution approaches for medical expense plans are in their infancy or still in the proposal stage, defined-contribution medical expense plans have actually been used for some time. For example, many employers make several medical expense plans available to their employees such as an HMO, a PPO, and a traditional major medical plan. The employer contribution to the cost of coverage for each plan may be a dollar amount that is pegged to a fixed percentage of the cost of the HMO plan. Therefore, an employee who elects a more expensive PPO or major medical plan will need to make a greater out-of-pocket contribution for his or her coverage than if he or she had selected the HMO.

Newer types of defined-contribution medical expense plans, often referred to as *consumer-directed health care*, have features other than just fixed employer contributions. At a minimum, these approaches force employees to make financial decisions involving their health care. For example, an employer might provide employees with a health plan that has a very high deductible, such as $5,000 per year. The employer might also contribute a lower amount, such as $2,500 per year, to an account (often called a *health reimbursement account*, or HRA) from which the employee can make withdrawals to pay medical expenses that are not covered because of the deductible. The employee can carry forward any unused amount in the account and add it to the next year's employer contribution. Such a plan gives the employee an immediate incentive to purchase medical care wisely because, if the amount in the account is exceeded, the employee will have to pay medical expenses out of his or her own pocket until the deductible is satisfied. The plan may incorporate one or more preferred-provider-type networks to give employees choices in how their account balances are spent. In addition, members of the preferred-provider network may be required to meet certain standards and to disclose information to employees so that they can make more informed decisions. Medical savings accounts, which are discussed in chapter 13, fall into this type of defined-contribution plan.

Defined-contribution plans have been designed to eliminate, or at least minimize, employer decisions about specific benefit plans. Under such a plan, an employee can use an employer contribution (along with any additionally needed employee contribution) to shop at some type of "health care supermarket," where many different types of medical expense plans are available. An insurer or some type of Internet provider may offer these plans, and the employer may or may not be involved in the selection of the supermarket that an employee uses.

There are still legal, regulatory, and tax issues that need to be addressed for many defined-contribution models. Whether employers will embrace these newer defined-contribution approaches on a large scale is still open to conjecture. So far, there seems to be more interest in the approach than in the implementation, but that is often the way with new concepts.

BENEFIT CARVE-OUTS

The use of benefit carve-outs by medical expense plans has grown in recent years, often as a method of cost containment via managed care techniques. In addition, many medical expense plans have come to realize that they cannot always provide as high a quality of care as a well-managed specialty provider. Carve-outs for prescription drugs, vision care, dental care, and behavioral health have been common for a number of years. Increasingly, carve-outs are being used to better manage a wide variety of medical conditions such as pregnancy, asthma, and diabetes.

carve-out (medical expense insurance)

A benefit *carve-out* can best be defined as coverage under a medical expense plan for a health care service that has been singled out for individual management by a party other than the employer or the employer's primary health plan provider. Some types of carve-outs predate managed care as it is now known. For example, many employees have long been covered under separate prescription drug plans. The early emphasis under these plans, however, was on discounts with preferred providers of prescription drugs. Today, prescription drug plans and other types of carve-outs use a wider variety of managed care techniques.

An employer can purchase a medical expense plan to provide benefits to its employees for most types of medical care and then enter into a separate contract with another provider for the carved-out benefit. However, in many cases, it is the insurance company, Blue Cross–Blue Shield plan, HMO, or PPO that enters into the carve-out arrangement with a "subcontractor" that manages the benefits. From the standpoint of employers and employees, the benefit is part of the provider's plan.

It should be pointed out that the vendors who provide carve-outs often act as managed care plans for a single medical expense benefit and take on characteristics of HMOs or PPOs. They also have learned over time that their type of specialty care should sometimes be accompanied by a unique benefit structure. This is one reason why mental health and prescription drug benefits are often subject to different deductibles, copayments, or benefit limitations than those used for most types of medical expenses.

There are numerous types of benefit carve-outs. The three discussed in this chapter are prescription drugs, vision benefits, and behavioral health.

Prescription Drugs

Although separate prescription drug plans have existed for many years, the initial focus was on obtaining lower costs through discounts with participating pharmacies and mail-order suppliers of drugs. The situation changed significantly in the early 1980s when pharmacy benefit managers (PBMs) appeared in the marketplace. It is estimated that over 75 percent of prescription drugs are provided through PBMs, and that fewer than 10 large PBMs cover over 80 percent of the health plan participants who receive drugs in this manner. PBMs may be affiliated with pharmaceutical companies or health care providers such as insurance companies. They may also be independently owned.

PBMs administer prescription drug plans on behalf of self-funded employers, HMOs, PPOs, insurance companies, Blue Cross–Blue Shield plans, and third-party administrators. PBMs' on-line capabilities enable them to offer considerable flexibility in designing a prescription drug program for a specific employer or benefit plan provider. PBMs have been leaders in the integration of formularies into prescription drug plans. A formulary is a list, developed by a committee of pharmacists and physicians, of preferred medications for a specific medical condition.

The typical prescription drug plan covers the cost of drugs (except those dispensed in a hospital or in an extended care facility) that are required by law to be dispensed by prescription. Drugs for which prescriptions are not required by law are usually not covered even if a physician orders them on a prescription form. One frequent exception to this general rule is injectable insulin, which is generally covered despite the fact that in many states it is a nonprescription drug. No coverage is provided for charges to administer drugs or the cost of the therapeutic devices or appliances such as bandages or hypodermic needles. It is also common to exclude benefits for a quantity of drugs in excess of a specified amount.

Contraceptive drugs are usually covered but may be excluded. Some prescription drug plans take a middle approach by covering these drugs only when they are prescribed for treating some medical condition rather than for preventing conception. (Note that recent court decisions and the position of the Equal Employment Opportunity Commission seem to indicate that an employer will have a more difficult time defending a legal challenge by female employees over the failure to provide less-than-complete coverage for prescription contraceptives.) Drugs for treatment of infertility or sexual dysfunction, such as Viagra, may or may not be covered.

Drug plans are increasingly requiring precertification for the use of certain expensive drugs.

Most prescription drug plans have a copayment that a covered person pays for any prescriptions filled; in some cases, it is a flat amount that usually varies from $5 to $10 per prescription. Other plans have one copayment amount for generic drugs and a higher one for brand-name drugs. A three-tier structure, such as a $10 copayment for brand-name generic drugs, $15 for brand-name formulary drugs, and $25 for nonformulary drugs, is becoming increasingly common as well. Some plans provide financial incentives for prescriptions filled by mail-order pharmacies or on the Internet. A few plans have quarterly, semiannual, or annual spending caps.

For example, benefits might be limited to $500 per person per quarter or $3,000 per year per family.

Two basic methods are used to provide prescription drug coverage: a reimbursement approach and a service approach. Under plans using a reimbursement approach, a covered individual personally pays the cost of prescription drugs and files a claim for reimbursement.

The majority of prescription drug plans use a service approach. Under this approach, participating pharmacies provide drugs to covered persons upon receipt of prescriptions, proper identification (usually a card issued by the plan), and any required copayments. The pharmacy then bills the provider of coverage (usually electronically) for the remaining cost of any prescription filled. Prescriptions filled at nonparticipating pharmacies are often covered but on a reimbursement basis.

Vision Benefits

Carve-out vision benefits may be provided by insurance companies, Blue Cross-Blue Shield plans, plans of state optometric associations patterned after Blue Shield, closed-panel HMO-type plans established by local providers of vision services, vision care PPOs, or third-party administrators.

Over half of the persons covered under employer-provided medical expense plans have some type of vision coverage, and the majority of this coverage is provided under a carve-out arrangement. Normally, a benefit schedule is used that specifies the types and amounts of certain benefits and the frequency with which they will be provided. Table 12-2 is an example of one such schedule. If a provider of vision services writes the plan, it is

---

TABLE 12-2
Example of Benefit Schedule

Type of Benefit	Maximum Amount
Any 12-month Period	
Eye examination	$ 45
Lenses, pair	
single vision	45
bifocal	75
trifocal	125
lenticular	200
contact (when medically necessary)	300
contact (when not medically necessary)	125
Any 24-month Period	
Frames	60

common for a discount, such as 20 percent, to be available for costs incurred with the provider that are not covered by the schedule of benefits. Under some plans, most benefits are provided on a service basis rather than being subject to a maximum benefit. These plans usually cover only the cost of basic frames, which the covered persons can upgrade at an additional expense.

Exclusions commonly exist for any extra charge for plastic lenses or the cost of safety lenses or prescription sunglasses. Benefits are generally provided for eye examinations by either an optometrist or an ophthalmologist, and larger benefits are sometimes provided if the latter is used. Vision care plans do not pay benefits for necessary eye surgery or treatment of eye diseases because these services are covered under a medical expense plan's regular coverage. However, many vision plans make benefits available for elective procedures to improve vision such as LASIK surgery. This benefit is usually in the form of a discounted fee from a provider who has a relationship with the plan.

Behavioral Health

Providing behavioral health benefits has always been a difficult area for medical expense plans. There is less uniformity in treatment standards for mental health, alcoholism, and drug addiction than for most other medical conditions. This, and the difficulty of monitoring treatment, has often led to unnecessary, expensive, and dangerous treatment by less-than-scrupulous providers of behavioral health care. Historically, benefit plans addressed these problems by having very limited benefit levels. But even these benefit levels had a tendency to encourage more expensive inpatient care over outpatient treatment, which in most cases appears to be as clinically effective. Moreover, there was little follow-up care after treatment. With rapidly increasing costs for behavioral health, employers and providers of benefit plans are increasingly carving out this benefit by contracting with vendors that use managed care techniques. Even with the use of carve-outs, benefit plans continue to limit behavioral health benefits to a level significantly below that for other medical conditions.

Characteristics of a successful behavioral health program, whether or not it is a carve-out arrangement, include the following:

- the use of case management to design and coordinate treatment plans and to monitor the need for follow-up care
- a mechanism for referring a patient to the program. In many cases, this is through a primary care physician gatekeeper.
- the development of a provider network that specializes in behavioral health. In addition to physicians, the network will include psychologists and therapists. It will also include alternatives to

hospital treatment such as residential centers, halfway houses, and structured outpatient programs. Benefits may or may not be provided if patients seek nonnetwork treatment. If it is covered, there is usually a lower benefit level than for network treatment.

- 24-hour patient access to care. Persons who have behavioral health problems often need immediate crisis intervention. Of course, the availability of such care needs to be well communicated to patients.

PLAN PROVISIONS

Medical expense plans have numerous provisions that concern financial planners. This section discusses provisions that pertain to eligibility, coordination of benefits, the relationship with Medicare, and claims. The next chapter covers other provisions that pertain to persons whose active employment has ceased.

Eligibility

The eligibility requirements for medical expense coverage are essentially the same as those for other types of group insurance—an employee must usually be in a covered classification, must satisfy any probationary period, and must be employed full-time.

Eligibility requirements may vary somewhat if an employer changes insurance companies. Eligible employees who were covered under the old plan are automatically covered under the new plan and are exempt from any probationary periods.

Dependent Eligibility

Typically, the same medical expense benefits that are provided for an eligible employee are also available for that employee's dependents. If coverage under a contributory plan is not elected within 31 days after dependents are eligible, future coverage is available only during an open enrollment period or when satisfactory evidence of insurability is provided. However, if an employee was previously without dependents (and therefore had no dependent coverage), any newly acquired dependents (by birth, marriage, or adoption) are eligible for coverage as of the date that they gain dependent status.

The term *dependents* most commonly refers to an employee's spouse who is not legally separated from the employee and any unmarried dependent children (including stepchildren, adopted children, and children born out of wedlock) under the age of 19. However, coverage is usually provided for children to age 23 or 26 if they are full-time students. In addition, coverage may also continue (and is required to be continued in some states) for children who are incapable of earning their own living because of a physical or mental infirmity. Such children are considered dependents as long as this condition exists, but periodic proof of the condition may be required. If an employee has dependent coverage, all of the employee's newly acquired dependents (by birth, marriage, or adoption) are automatically covered.

Portability

The Health Insurance Portability and Accountability Act also affects eligibility for medical expense coverage. HIPAA's provisions do not allow an employee to take specific insurance from one job to another. Rather, they put limitations on preexisting-conditions exclusions and allow an employee to use evidence of prior insurance coverage to reduce or eliminate the length of any preexisting-conditions exclusion when the employee moves to another employer-provided medical expense plan. The act's provisions on portability generally override state laws. However, state laws that provide more liberal portability are not overridden.

Restrictions for preexisting conditions are limited to a maximum of 12 months (18 months for late enrollees). In addition, the period for preexisting conditions must be reduced by the length of coverage under a prior medical expense plan as long as there has not been a break in coverage of 63 days or more. The prior coverage can have been under an individual policy, an employer-provided group plan (either insured or self-funded), an HMO, Medicare, or Medicaid.

The act requires an employer to give persons losing group coverage a certificate that specifies the period of coverage under the plan they are leaving, including any period of COBRA coverage.

Benefits for Domestic Partners

In the mid-1980s, the plans of a few employers began to define the term *dependent* broadly enough to include unmarried domestic partners. For example, one plan covers unmarried couples as long as they live together, show financial interdependence and joint responsibility for each other's common welfare, and consider themselves life partners. This type of requirement is fairly typical, as is the additional requirement that the employee's relationship must have lasted some specified minimum period of time such as 6 or 12 months. The employee must usually give the employer an affidavit that these requirements have been satisfied.

An estimated 15 percent of employers now provide medical expense benefits to domestic partners. Most plans provide benefits to domestic partners engaged in either heterosexual or homosexual relationships. Some plans provide benefits only to persons of the opposite sex of the employee, while a small number of plans limit benefits only to persons of the same sex. The rationale for the latter is that persons of opposite sexes can obtain benefits by marrying, whereas this option is not available to persons of the same sex.

Coordination of Benefits

In recent years, the percentage of individuals who have duplicate group medical expense coverage has increased substantially and is estimated to be about 10 percent. Probably the most common situation is the one in which a husband and wife both work and have coverage under their respective employers' noncontributory plans. If the employer of either spouse also provides dependent coverage on a noncontributory basis, the other spouse (and other dependents if both employers provide such coverage) is covered under both plans. If dependent coverage is contributory, it is necessary for a couple with children to elect such coverage under one of their plans. Because a spouse is considered a dependent, he or she also has duplicate coverage when the election is made. Duplicate coverage may also arise when an employee has two jobs, or children are covered under both a parent's and a stepparent's plans.

coordination-of-benefits (COB) provision

In the absence of any provisions to the contrary, group medical expense plans are obligated to provide benefits in cases of duplicate coverage as if no other coverage exists. To prevent individuals from receiving benefits that exceed their actual expenses, most group medical expense plans contain a *coordination-of-benefits (COB) provision*, under which priorities are established for the payment of benefits by each plan covering an individual.

Most COB provisions are based on the NAIC Group Coordination of Benefits Model Regulation. This regulation is periodically revised, and almost all states have adopted all or portions of one of the versions. As with all NAIC model legislation and regulations, some states have adopted the COB provisions with variations.

Although some flexibility is allowed, virtually all COB provisions apply when other coverage exists through another employer's group insurance plans or group benefit arrangements (such as the Blues, HMOs, or self-funded plans). They may also apply to no-fault automobile insurance benefits and to student coverage that is either sponsored or provided by educational institutions. However, these provisions virtually never apply (and cannot in most states) to any other coverages provided under contracts purchased on an individual basis outside of the employment relationship.

As a general rule, coverage under multiple policies will allow a person to receive benefits equal to 100 percent of his or her medical expenses. The coverage determined to be primary will pay as if no other coverage exists. If some expenses are not reimbursed (because, for example, of deductibles, copayments, or policy limitations), the secondary coverage will pick up the balance as long as it is less than what that coverage would have paid if it were the only coverage in existence.

Determination of Primary Coverage

The usual COB provision stipulates that any other plan without the COB provision is primary and that any plan with it is secondary. If more than one plan has a COB provision, the following priorities are established:

- Coverage as an employee is usually primary to coverage as a dependent. The exception occurs if a retired person is covered (1) by Medicare, (2) under a retiree plan of a former employer, and (3) as a dependent of a spouse who is an active employee. In this case, coverage as a dependent is primary, Medicare is secondary, and the retiree plan pays last.
- Coverage as an active employee (or as that person's dependent) is primary to coverage as a retired or laid-off employee (or as that person's dependent).
- Coverage as an active employee (or that person's dependent) is primary to a plan that provides COBRA continuation benefits.
- If the specific rules of a court decree state that one parent must assume responsibility for his or her child's health care expenses, and the plan of that parent has actual knowledge of the terms of the court decree, then that plan is primary.
- If the parents of dependent children are married or are not separated (regardless of whether they have ever been married) or if a court awards joint custody without specifying that one parent has the responsibility to provide health care coverage, the plan of the parent whose birthday falls earlier in the calendar year is primary and the plan of the parent with the later birthday is secondary.
- If the parents of dependent children are not married, are separated (regardless of whether they have ever been married), or are divorced and if there is no court decree allocating responsibility for the child's health care expenses, the following priorities apply:

- The plan of the parent with custody is primary.
- The plan of the stepparent who is the spouse of the parent with custody is secondary.
- The plan of the parent without custody is tertiary.
- The plan of the stepparent who is the spouse of the parent without custody pays last.

- If none of the previous rules establishes a priority, the plan covering the person for the longest period of time is primary. However, if this rule also fails to determine the primary plan, then benefit payments are shared equally among the plans.

Relationship with Medicare

Because most employees and their dependents are eligible for Medicare upon reaching age 65 (and possibly under other circumstances), a provision that eliminates any possible duplication of coverage is necessary. The simplest solution is to exclude any person eligible for Medicare from eligibility under the group contract. In most cases, however, this approach conflicts with the Age Discrimination in Employment Act, which prohibits discrimination in benefit plans for active employees.

Medicare Secondary Rules

Employers with 20 or more employees must make coverage available under their medical expense plans to active employees aged 65 or older and to active employees' spouses who are eligible for Medicare. Unless an employee elects otherwise, the employer's plan is primary and Medicare is secondary. Except in plans that require large employee contributions, it is doubtful that employees will elect Medicare to be primary because employers are prohibited from offering active employees or their spouses a Medicare carve-out, a Medicare supplement, or some other incentive not to enroll in the employer's plan.

Medicare is the secondary payer of benefits in two other situations. The first situation involves persons who are eligible for Medicare benefits to treat end-stage renal disease with dialysis or kidney transplants. Medicare provides these benefits to any insured workers (either active or retired) and to their spouses and dependent children, but the employer's plan is primary during the first 30 months of treatment only; after that time Medicare is primary and the employer's plan is secondary.

Medicare is also the secondary payer of benefits to disabled employees (or disabled dependents of employees) under age 65 who are eligible for Medicare and covered under the medical expense plan of large employers (defined as plans with 100 or more employees). Medicare, however, does not pay anything until a person has been eligible for Social Security disability income benefits for 2 years. The rule applies only if an employer continues medical expense coverage for disabled persons; there is no requirement for such a continuation.

Medicare Carve-Outs and Supplements

An employer's plan may cover certain persons aged 65 or older who are not covered by the provisions of the Age Discrimination in Employment Act—specifically, retirees and active employees of firms with fewer than 20 employees. Although there is nothing to prevent an employer from terminating coverage for these persons, many employers provide them with either a Medicare carve-out or Medicare supplement.

Medicare carve-out

Medicare supplement

With a *Medicare carve-out*, plan benefits are reduced to the extent that benefits are payable under Medicare for the same expenses. As an alternative, some employers use a *Medicare supplement* that provides benefits for certain specific expenses not covered under Medicare. These include (1) the portion of expenses Medicare does not pay because of deductibles, coinsurance, or copayments and (2) certain expenses that Medicare excludes such as prescription drugs. Such a supplement may or may not provide benefits similar to those available under a carve-out plan.

Claims

Medical expense contracts that provide benefits on a service basis (such as HMOs and the Blues) or that use preferred providers generally do not require covered persons to file claim forms. Rather, the providers of services perform any necessary paperwork and are then reimbursed directly.

Medical expense contracts that provide benefits on an indemnity basis typically require that the insurance company (or other provider) be given a written proof of loss (that is, a claim form) concerning the occurrence, character, and extent of the loss for which a claim is made. This form usually contains portions that must be completed and signed by the employee, a representative of the employer, and the provider of medical services.

The period during which an employee must file a claim depends on the provider of coverage and any applicable state requirements. An employee generally has at least 90 days (or as soon as is reasonably possible) after medical expenses are incurred to file. Some insurance companies require that they be notified within a shorter time (such as 20 days) about any illness or injury on which a claim may be based, even though they give a longer time period for the actual filing of the form itself.

Individuals have the right under medical expense plans to assign their benefits to the providers of medical services. Such an assignment, which authorizes the insurance company to make the benefit payment directly to the provider, may generally be made by completing the appropriate portion of the claim form. In addition, the insurance company has the right to examine any person for whom a claim is filed at its own expense and with the physician of its own choice.

DENTAL INSURANCE

Since the early 1970s, dental insurance has been one of the fastest-growing employee benefits. It has been estimated that in the last 30 years the percentage of employees who have dental coverage has grown from about 10 percent to over 70 percent. Dental benefits may be offered by insurance companies, dental service plans (often called Delta Dental plans), the Blues, and managed care plans such as dental HMOs (called DHMOs). Like medical expense coverage, a significant portion of dental coverage is also self-funded.

Although group dental insurance contracts have been patterned after group medical expense contracts, some of their provisions are different while others are unique to dental coverage. These provisions pertain to benefits, exclusions, and benefit limitations.

Benefits

Most dental insurance plans pay for almost all types of dental expenses, but a particular plan may provide more limited coverage. One characteristic of dental insurance that is seldom found in medical expense plans is the inclusion of benefits for both routine diagnostic procedures (including oral examinations and X rays) and preventive dental treatment (including teeth cleaning and fluoride treatment). In fact, a few dental plans actually require periodic oral examinations as a condition for continuing eligibility. There is clear evidence that the cost of providing these benefits will be more than offset by the avoidance of the expensive dental procedures required when a condition is not discovered early or when a preventive treatment has not been given.

In addition to benefits for diagnostic and preventive treatment, benefits for dental expenses may be provided for the following categories of dental treatment:

- restoration (including fillings, crowns, and other procedures used to restore the functional use of natural teeth)
- oral surgery (including the extraction of teeth, as well as other surgical treatment of diseases, injuries, and defects of the jaw)
- endodontics (treatment for diseases of the dental pulp within teeth such as root canals)
- periodontics (treatment of diseases of the surrounding and supporting tissues of the teeth)

- prosthodontics (replacement of missing teeth and structures by artificial devices such as bridgework and dentures)
- orthodontics (prevention and correction of dental and oral anomalies through the use of corrective devices such as braces and retainers)

Most dental plans usually cover any expenses that arise from the first five categories listed above, and they may include benefits for orthodontics. Whatever benefits are provided may be on a scheduled basis, a nonscheduled basis, or some combination of the two.

Scheduled Plans

A scheduled dental plan pays benefits up to the amount specified in a fee schedule. Most scheduled dental plans provide benefits on a first-dollar basis and contain no deductibles or specified coinsurance percentage.

Nonscheduled Plans

Nonscheduled dental plans, often called *comprehensive dental plans*, are the most common type of dental coverage. They resemble major medical expense contracts because covered dental expenses are paid on a reasonable-and-customary basis, subject to any exclusions, limitations, or copayments in the contract.

Nonscheduled dental plans usually have both deductibles and coinsurance provisions. Although a single deductible and a single coinsurance percentage may apply to all dental services, the more common practice is to treat different classes of dental services in different ways. The typical nonscheduled dental plan breaks dental services into three broad categories: diagnostic and preventive services, basic services (such as fillings, oral surgery, periodontics, and endodontics), and major services (such as inlays, crowns, dentures, and orthodontics).

Diagnostic and preventive services are typically covered in full and not subject to a deductible or coinsurance. (They are subject to any other contract limitations.) The other two categories, however, are generally subject to an annual deductible (usually between $50 and $100 per person). In addition to the deductible, the cost of basic services may be reimbursed at a higher percentage (most often 80 percent), while major services are subject to a lower percentage (most often 50 percent).

Combination Plans

Combination plans contain features of both scheduled and nonscheduled plans. The typical combination plan covers diagnostic and preventive services on a usual-and-customary basis but uses a fee schedule for other dental services.

Exclusions

All dental plans contain exclusions, but the number and type vary. Some of the more common exclusions are charges for the following:

- services that are purely cosmetic, unless necessitated by an accidental bodily injury while a person is covered under the plan. (Orthodontics, although they are often used for cosmetic reasons, can usually also be justified as necessary to correct abnormal dental conditions.)
- replacement of lost, missing, or stolen dentures, or other prosthetic devices
- duplicate dentures or other prosthetic devices
- services that do not have uniform professional endorsement

Limitations

Dental insurance plans also contain numerous limitations that are designed to control claim costs and to eliminate unnecessary dental care. In addition to deductibles and coinsurance, virtually all dental plans have overall benefit maximums. Except for DHMOs, which usually do not have a calendar-year limit, most plans contain a calendar-year maximum (varying from $500 to $2,000) but no lifetime maximum. However, some plans have only a lifetime maximum (such as $1,000 or $5,000), and a few plans contain both a calendar-year maximum and a large lifetime maximum. These maximums may apply to all dental expenses, or they may be limited to all expenses except those that arise from orthodontics (and occasionally periodontics). In the latter case, benefits for orthodontics will be subject to a separate, lower lifetime maximum, which is typically between $500 and $2,000.

Most dental plans limit the frequency with which some benefits will be paid. Routine oral examinations and teeth cleaning are usually limited to once every 6 months, and full mouth X rays to once every 24 or 36 months. The replacement of dentures may also be limited to one time in some specified period (such as 5 years).

The typical dental plan also limits benefits to the least expensive type of accepted dental treatment for a given dental condition. For example, if either a gold or silver filling can be used, benefit payments will be limited to the cost of a silver filling, even if a gold filling is inserted.

ADDITIONAL BENEFITS FOR EXECUTIVES

Some employers have plans that provide additional medical and dental benefits for executives. Although this group of employees is most likely to be able to pay for the expenses covered by such plans, these supplemental benefits are frequently viewed as a way to attract and retain key employees.

From a purely administrative standpoint, it would be relatively easy to self-fund these benefits, but the benefits, as explained later under the section on federal taxation, would most likely represent taxable income to employees. As a result, these additional executive benefits are usually insured as either separate coverage or as a rider to the plan covering other employees.

This type of plan usually covers the executives and their dependents. Benefits almost always include coverage to provide reimbursement for deductibles and coinsurance under the employer's plan that apply to all covered employees. It is also common to find coverage for annual physicals and the extra cost of private hospital rooms. In addition, there frequently is extra coverage, although possibly limited to an annual maximum, such as $10,000, for expenses such as mental or emotional treatment, hearing care, vision care, and dental work.

FEDERAL TAXATION

In many respects, the federal tax treatment of employer-provided medical and dental expense premiums and benefits parallels that of other group coverage if they are provided through an insurance company, a Blue Cross–Blue Shield plan, an HMO, or a PPO. Contributions by the employer for an employee's coverage or coverage of the employee's dependents are tax deductible to the employer as long as the employee's overall compensation is reasonable. Employer contributions do not create any income tax liability for an employee. Moreover, benefits are not taxable to an employee except when they exceed any medical expenses incurred. The value of any employer-provided coverage for an employee's domestic partner, minus any employee contributions, represents taxable income to the employee unless the partner qualifies under IRS rules as the employee's dependent.

One major difference between group medical expense coverage and other forms of group insurance is that a portion of an employee's contribution for coverage may be tax deductible as a medical expense if that individual itemizes his or her income tax deductions. Under the Internal Revenue Code, individuals are allowed to deduct certain medical care expenses (including dental expenses) for which no reimbursement was received. This deduction is limited to expenses (including amounts paid for insurance) that exceed 7.5 percent of the person's adjusted gross income.

Self-employed persons (for example, sole proprietors), partners, and persons who own more than 2 percent of the stock of an S corporation are not considered employees. If a sole proprietorship, partnership, or S corporation pays the cost of medical expense coverage for those persons or their family members, this amount constitutes taxable income to the proprietor, partner, or 2 percent owner. However, the proprietor, partner, or S corporation may be entitled to an income tax deduction for this amount. The deduction cannot exceed the individual's earned income from the proprietorship, partnership, or S corporation that provides the medical expense plan. In addition, the deduction is available only if the person is not eligible to participate in any subsidized medical expense plan of another employer for whom the person or his or her spouse works. The remainder of the cost of the medical expense coverage can be deducted as an itemized expense to the extent that it and other medical expenses exceed the 7.5 percent threshold that was previously described.

The tax situation may be different if an employer provides medical expense benefits through a self-funded plan (referred to in the Internal Revenue Code as a self-insured medical reimbursement plan), under which employers either (1) pay the providers of medical care directly or (2) reimburse employees for their medical expenses. If a self-funded plan meets certain nondiscrimination requirements for highly compensated employees, the employer can deduct benefit payments as they are made, and the employee will have no taxable income. If a plan is discriminatory, the employer will still receive an income tax deduction. However, all or a portion of the benefits received by highly compensated employees, but not by other employees, will be treated as taxable income.

SOURCES FOR FURTHER IN-DEPTH STUDY

- Beam, Burton T., Jr., *Group Benefits: Basic Concepts and Alternatives,* 9th ed., Bryn Mawr, PA: The American College, 2002. Phone 888-263-7265. Web site address www.amercoll.edu
- Rosenbloom, Jerry S., editor, *The Handbook of Employee Benefits*, 5th ed., New York: McGraw-Hill, 2001. Phone 800-262-4729. Web site address www.books.mcgraw-hill.com
- *Managed Care: Integrating the Delivery and Financing of Health Care. Part A* (1996), *Part B* (1996), *Part C* (1998), Washington, DC: Health Insurance Association of America. Phone 202-824-1600. Web site address www.hiaa.org
- *Kongstvedt, Peter R., Managed Care: What It is and How It Works,* 2d ed., Gaithersburg, MD: Aspen Publishers, Inc., 2002. Phone 800-638-8437. Web site address www.aspenpublishers.com

CHAPTER REVIEW

Answers to the review questions and self-test questions start on page 725.

Key Terms

health insurance
medical expense insurance
major medical insurance
preexisting-conditions provision
deductible
coinsurance (medical expense
    insurance)
stop-loss limit
second surgical opinion
extended care facility
home health care
hospice care
birthing center
managed care

health maintenance organization
    (HMO)
preferred-provider organization
    (PPO)
exclusive-provider organization
    (EPO)
point-of-service (POS) plan
defined-contribution medical
    expense plan
carve-out (medical expense
    insurance)
coordination-of-benefits (COB)
    provision
Medicare carve-out
Medicare supplement

Review Questions

12-1.   What observations can be made about the future of the health care system?

12-2.   Your client, Sue, is covered by an employer-provided major medical policy. Which of the following medical expenditures that Sue incurred is covered under the policy?

   a.   She required hospitalization in a semiprivate room for a period of 20 days following an operation on her heart.
   b.   She had cosmetic surgery on her nose in order to improve her looks for a career in modeling.
   c.   She required care as an inpatient at an extended care facility after release from a 4-day stay in the hospital following a serious operation.
   d.   She received custodial or rest care for 5 days at her home after release from an overnight stay in the hospital following minor surgery.
   e.   She required a prescription drug for her arthritis that costs $500 per month.

12-3.   Most major medical plans contain an exclusion for preexisting conditions. How does this exclusion differ from the other exclusions found in major medical plans?

12-4. Your client is concerned about the types of deductibles that apply to her medical expense plan. Explain to her how the following deductibles operate:
a. initial deductible
b. family deductible

12-5. Peggy is covered under a comprehensive major medical plan that has a $250 calendar-year deductible and an 80 percent coinsurance provision. If Peggy incurs $1,500 of covered medical expenses during the year (assuming no limitations), how much of this will she have to pay out of pocket?

12-6. What are the basic characteristics of a managed care plan?

12-7. What are the characteristics of HMOs that distinguish them from insurance companies and/or the Blues?

12-8. How do preferred-provider organizations (PPOs) differ from traditional major medical contracts?

12-9. Briefly describe how a point-of-service (POS) plan is a modification of a traditional HMO arrangement.

12-10. What is the value of benefit carve-outs?

12-11. Briefly describe the following types of benefit carve-outs.
a. prescription drugs
b. vision benefits
c. behavioral health

12-12. What other person may be eligible for coverage under an employee's medical expense plan?

12-13. How does the Health Insurance Portability and Accountability Act (HIPAA) affect eligibility under medical expense plans?

12-14. A child in the custody of her mother is covered as a dependent under the major medical coverage of both her father and her stepfather. Which coverage is primary if both coverages are subject to the usual coordination-of-benefits provision?

12-15. Explain when Medicare is the primary and secondary payer of benefits for individuals who are also covered under an employer medical expense plan.

12-16. Explain whether each of the following dental expenses is typically covered under a group dental plan:
a. X rays
b. root canal
c. replacement of lost dentures
d. teeth whitening
e. braces

12-17. What types of additional medical expense benefits may be available to executives?

12-18. To what extent are employee contributions for medical expense coverage deductible for federal income tax purposes?

Self-Test Questions

T   F   12-1. Medical expense insurance is the most significant type of employee benefit in terms of both the number of persons covered and the dollar outlay.

T   F   12-2. Maternity-related expenses are usually excluded from basic hospital expense benefits.

T   F   12-3. Major medical plans contain "internal limits" for certain types of medical expenses.

T   F   12-4. Many major medical plans with a calendar-year deductible also have a carryover provision that allows any expenses applied to the deductible and incurred during the last 3 months of the year to also be applied to the deductible for the following year.

T   F   12-5. Many major medical expense plans place a limit on the amount of out-of-pocket expenses that a covered person must bear during any time period.

T   F   12-6. Extended care facility benefits cover rest or domiciliary care for the aged.

T   F   12-7. Basic hospice care benefits cover treatments that attempt to cure seriously ill patients.

T   F   12-8. Managed care plans typically encourage preventive care and the attainment of healthier lifestyles.

T   F   12-9. HMOs typically provide out-of-area coverage for all medical services because their scope is national.

T   F   12-10. Cost controls of HMOs tend to discourage preventive care.

T   F   12-11. An exclusive-provider organization is so named because it allows subscribers to pay an additional premium for the right to see the most prominent specialist in a medical field.

T   F.   12-12. A PPO often has different deductibles and coinsurance that apply to network and nonnetwork charges.

T   F   12-13. PPOs typically provide benefits for a much wider array of medical procedures if nonnetwork providers are used.

T   F   12-14. A point-of-service plan allows subscribers to be reimbursed for treatment received outside the HMO network.

T F 12-15. Benefit carve-outs are often used as a method of cost containment through the use of managed care techniques.

T F 12-16. Most prescription drug plans cover nonprescription drugs as long as a physician orders them on a prescription form.

T F 12-17. A successful behavioral health program should permit patient access on a 24-hour basis.

T F 12-18. For purposes of group medical expense benefits, a 27-year-old woman is fully covered as a dependent child under her father's coverage if she is living at home and is a full-time student.

T F 12-19. Most group medical expense plans contain a coordination-of-benefits (COB) provision under which coverage as an employee is primary to coverage as a dependent.

T F 12-20. If an employee who is eligible for Medicare works full-time for a large employer, Medicare is the primary medical expense coverage while the employer's plan is secondary.

T F 12-21. The typical dental plan limits benefits to the least expensive type of accepted dental treatment for a given dental condition.

T F 12-22. Premium contributions by an employer to group medical and dental coverage for an employee are considered taxable income to the employee.

NOTE

1. The Henry J. Kaiser Family Foundation and Health Research and Educational Trust, *Employer Health Benefits, 2002.*

13

Individual Medical Expense Insurance

Learning Objectives

An understanding of the material in this chapter should enable the student to

13-1. Explain COBRA and the various other alternatives for continuing employer-provided medical expense coverage.

13-2. Describe the various types of medical expense coverages available in the individual marketplace.

13-3. Explain how the market has evolved to make it easier for the unhealthy to obtain medical expense insurance.

13-4. Explain what medical savings accounts are and how they operate.

13-5. Describe the premium and renewability provisions found in medical expense contracts.

13-6. Explain the federal income tax rules that apply to individual medical expense insurance.

Chapter Outline

CONTINUATION OF EMPLOYER-PROVIDED
        COVERAGE 417
    Continuation of Coverage under COBRA 418
    Continuation of Coverage in Addition to COBRA 421
    Extension of Benefits 423
    Conversion 423
    Group-to-Individual Portability 424
TYPES OF POLICIES AVAILABLE 425
    Individual Major Medical Policies 426
    HMO Coverage 427

415

The previous chapter was devoted to a discussion of employer-provided medical expense insurance to active employees and their dependents. This coverage is the source of medical-expense protection for almost two-thirds of all Americans under age 65. The majority of this chapter is devoted to the private insurance protection available to persons in this age group who do not qualify for this employer-provided coverage. While the chapter title uses the word *individual,* some of the insurance available is a continuation of prior employer-provided coverage.

Numerous circumstances account for the need for individual medical expense insurance. These include

- the lack of employer-provided coverage for some employees, usually those who work for small employers
- the termination of employment for reasons such as voluntarily quitting, being fired or laid off, becoming disabled, or retiring
- the termination of dependent coverage, even when employee coverage continues. This can occur because of divorce, separation, or a child becoming too old.
- not being in the labor market. Some people have the resources to forego employment. Others, for many reasons, are unable to find or hold jobs.
- self-employment

It is important to point out that fewer than 10 percent of the population under age 65 obtain private individual medical insurance for themselves and their families. An estimated 15 percent of the population have no medical expense insurance and almost as many are covered by Medicaid. One reason for this lack of individual coverage is its significant cost. While legislation has made coverage potentially available for more persons in recent years, there is still a severe affordability problem. For example, the premium for a person in his or her late 50s can be several thousand dollars per year.

Another segment of the population that often obtains individual coverage consists of those persons eligible for Medicare. As mentioned in chapter 7, Medicare has some limitation, including no out-of-country coverage, extremely limited coverage for prescription drugs, and higher copayments than many major medical policies. Over 60 percent of individuals over the age of 65 have some type of coverage to supplement Medicare.

Several topics are covered in this chapter. These include the ways in which employer-provided coverage can be continued, types of individual coverage for those under age 65, Medicare supplements, policy provisions, and the tax treatment of premiums and benefits. Finally, there is a checklist for evaluating and comparing policies. Financial planners can use this information to help their clients assess and choose needed coverage.

CONTINUATION OF EMPLOYER-PROVIDED COVERAGE

In the absence of any provisions for continuation or conversion, employer-provided coverage on an employee generally ceases on the earliest of the following:

- the date on which employment terminates. In some plans, coverage ceases on the last day of the month in which employment terminates.
- the date on which the employee ceases to be eligible
- the date on which the master contract for the employer-provided coverage terminates
- the date on which the overall maximum benefit of major medical coverage is received
- the end of the last period for which the employee has made any required contribution

Coverage on any dependent usually ceases on the earliest of the following:

- the date on which he or she ceases to meet the definition of dependent
- the date on which the coverage of the employee ceases for any reason except the employee's receipt of the overall maximum benefit

- the date on which the dependent receives the overall maximum benefit of major medical coverage
- the end of the last period for which the employee has made any required contribution for dependent coverage

However, insurance coverage often is available past these dates because of federal legislation or employer practices. In some cases, the former coverage can be continued, at least for a period of time; in other cases, the prior employment results in the availability of individual coverage without evidence of insurability.

Continuation of Coverage under COBRA

COBRA

The Consolidated Omnibus Budget Reconciliation Act of 1985 (*COBRA*) requires that group health plans allow employees and certain beneficiaries to elect to have their current health insurance coverage extended at group rates for up to 36 months following a "qualifying event" that results in the loss of coverage for a "qualified beneficiary." The term *group health plan* as used in the act is broad enough to include medical expense plans, dental plans, vision care plans, and prescription drug plans, regardless of whether benefits are self-funded or provided through other entities such as insurance companies or managed care organizations. Long-term care coverage is not subject to COBRA rules. COBRA applies to group health plans even if employees pay the full cost of coverage as long as the plan would not be available at the same cost to an employee if he or she were not employed. However, there is one exception to this rule: voluntary benefit plans under which the employer's only involvement is to process payroll deductions are not subject to COBRA.

The act applies only to employers who had the equivalent of 20 or more full-time employees on a typical business day during the preceding calendar year; however, certain church-related plans and plans of the federal government are exempt from the act. Failure to comply with the act will result in an excise tax of up to $100 per day for each person denied coverage. The tax can be levied on the employer as well as on the entity (such as an insurer or HMO) that provides or administers the benefits.

qualified beneficiary

A *qualified beneficiary* is defined as any employee, or the spouse or dependent child of the employee, who on the day before a qualifying event was covered under the employee's group health plan. In addition, the definition includes any child who is born to or placed for adoption with the employee during the period of COBRA coverage. This change gives automatic eligibility for COBRA coverage to the child as well as the right to

qualifying event

have his or her own election rights if a second *qualifying event* occurs.

Under the act, each of the following is a qualifying event if it results in the loss of coverage by a qualified beneficiary:

- the death of the covered employee
- the termination of the employee for any reason except gross misconduct. This includes quitting, retiring, or being fired for anything other than gross misconduct.
- a reduction of the employee's hours so that the employee or dependent is ineligible for coverage
- the divorce or legal separation of the covered employee and his or her spouse
- for spouses and children, the employee's eligibility for Medicare
- a child's ceasing to be an eligible dependent under the plan

The act specifies that a qualified beneficiary is entitled to elect continued coverage without providing evidence of insurability. The beneficiary must be allowed to continue coverage identical to that available to employees and dependents to whom a qualifying event has not occurred. Coverage for persons electing COBRA continuation can be changed when changes are made to the plan covering active employees and their dependents.

Each qualified beneficiary must be allowed to continue coverage from the qualifying event until the earliest of the following:

- 18 months for employees and dependents when the employee's employment has terminated or coverage has been terminated because of a reduction in hours. This period is extended to 29 months for a qualified beneficiary if the Social Security Administration determines that the beneficiary was or became totally disabled at any time during the first 60 days of COBRA coverage.
- 36 months for other qualifying events
- the date the plan terminates for all employees
- the date the coverage ceases because of a failure to make a timely payment of premium for the qualified beneficiary's coverage
- the date the qualified beneficiary subsequently becomes entitled to Medicare or becomes covered (as either an employee or dependent) under another group health plan, provided the group health plan does not contain an exclusion or limitation with respect to any preexisting condition. If the new plan does not cover a preexisting condition, the COBRA coverage can be continued until the earlier of (1) the remainder of the 18- or 36-month period or (2) the time when the preexisting-conditions provision no longer applies.

If a second qualifying event (such as the death or divorce of a terminated employee) occurs during the period of continued coverage, the maximum period of continuation is 36 months.

Example:	When Peter Gonzalez terminated employment, he and his family were eligible for 18 months of COBRA coverage. When he died 15 months after electing the coverage, a second qualifying event occurred for his spouse and dependent children. The normal period of COBRA continuation resulting from the death of an employee is 36 months. However, because the spouse and children had already had COBRA coverage for 15 months, the second qualifying event extended the potential period of coverage for an additional 21 months.

At the termination of continued coverage, a qualified beneficiary must be offered the right to convert to an individual insurance policy if a conversion privilege is generally available to employees under the employer's plan.

When a qualifying event occurs, the employer must notify the benefit plan administrator, who then must notify all qualified beneficiaries within 14 days. In general, the employer has 30 days to notify the plan administrator. However, an employer may not know of a qualifying event if it involves divorce, legal separation, or a child's ceasing to be eligible for coverage. In these circumstances, the employee or family member must notify the employer within 60 days of the event, or the right to elect COBRA coverage will be lost. The time period for the employer to notify the plan administrator begins when the employer is informed of the qualifying event as long as this occurs within the 60-day period.

The continuation of coverage is not automatic; a qualified beneficiary must elect it. The election period starts on the date of the qualifying event and may end not earlier than 60 days after actual notice of the event to the qualified beneficiary by the plan administrator. Once coverage is elected, the beneficiary has 45 days to pay the premium for the period of coverage prior to the election.

Under COBRA, the cost of the continued coverage may be passed on to the qualified beneficiary, but the cost cannot exceed 102 percent of the cost to the plan for the period of coverage for a similarly situated active employee to whom a qualifying event has not occurred. The extra 2 percent is supposed to cover the employer's extra administrative costs. The one exception to this rule occurs for months 19 through 29 if an employee is disabled, in which case the premium can then be as high as 150 percent. Qualified beneficiaries must have the option of paying the premium in monthly installments. In addition, there must be a grace period of at least 30 days for each installment.

Because of cost economies associated with employer-provided coverage, COBRA is more often than not the most cost-effective way to obtain medical expense coverage. However, with significant cost variations in both the group and individual insurance markets, it is wise to shop around. For example, a young, healthy person might find the purchase of individual coverage to be significantly less expensive.

Continuation of Coverage in Addition to COBRA

Even before the passage of COBRA it was becoming increasingly common for employers (particularly large employers) to continue group insurance coverage for certain employees—and sometimes their dependents—beyond the usual termination dates. Obviously when coverage is continued now, at a minimum an employer must comply with COBRA. However, an employer can be more liberal than COBRA by paying all or a portion of the cost, providing continued coverage for additional categories of persons, or continuing coverage for a longer period of time. Some states have continuation laws for insured medical expense plans that might require coverage to be made available in situations not covered by COBRA. One example is coverage for employees of firms with fewer than 20 employees; another is coverage for periods longer than those required by COBRA.

Retired Employees

Many employers continue coverage on retired employees. Although coverage can also be continued for retirees' dependents, it is often limited only to spouses. Retired employees under age 65 usually have the same coverage as the active employees have. However, coverage for employees aged 65 or older (if included under the same plan) may be provided under a Medicare carve-out or a Medicare supplement. The lifetime maximum for persons eligible for Medicare is often much lower (such as $5,000 or $10,000) than for active employees.

Because of changes in accounting rules for retiree medical expense coverage and increasing benefit costs, many employers have lowered or eliminated retiree benefits or are considering such a change. However, there are legal uncertainties as to whether benefits that have been promised to retirees can be eliminated or reduced. Many employers also feel that there is a moral obligation to continue these benefits. As a result most employers are not altering plans for current retirees or active employees who are eligible to retire. Rather, the changes apply to future retirees only. These changes, which seem to be running the gamut, include the following:

- the elimination of benefits for future retirees
- the shifting of more of the cost burden to future retirees by reducing benefits. Such a reduction may be accomplished by providing lower benefit maximums, covering fewer types of expenses, or increasing copayments.
- adding or increasing retiree sharing of premium costs after retirement
- shifting to a defined-contribution approach to funding retiree benefits. For example, an employer might agree to pay $5 per month toward the cost of coverage after retirement for each year of service by an employee. Many plans of this nature have been designed so that the employer's contribution increases with changes in the consumer price index, subject to maximum increases such as 5 percent per year.
- encouraging retirees to elect benefits from managed care plans. With this approach, retirees are required to pay a significant portion of the cost if coverage is continued through a traditional indemnity plan.

Surviving Dependents

Coverage may also continue for the survivors of deceased active employees and/or deceased retired employees. However, coverage for the survivors of active employees does not commonly continue beyond the period required by COBRA, and coverage for the survivors of retired employees may be limited to surviving spouses. In both instances the continued coverage is usually identical to what was provided prior to the employee's death. It is also common for the employer to continue the same premium contribution level.

Laid-off Employees

Medical expense coverage can be continued for laid-off workers, and large employers frequently provide such coverage for a limited period. Few employers provide coverage beyond the period required by COBRA, but some employers continue to make the same premium contribution, at least for a limited period of time.

Disabled Employees

Medical expense coverage can be continued for an employee (and dependents) when he or she has a temporary interruption of employment, including one arising from illness or injury. Many employers also cover employees who have long-term disabilities or who have retired because of a disability. In most cases, this continuation of coverage is contingent upon satisfaction of some definition of total (and possibly permanent) disability. When coverage is continued for disabled employees, an employer must determine the extent of employer contributions. For example, the employer may continue the same premium contribution as for active employees. However, there is nothing to prevent a different contribution rate—either lower or higher.

Extension of Benefits

extension of benefits

When coverage is terminated rather than continued, most employer-purchased medical expense contracts have an *extension of benefits* for any covered employee or dependent who is totally disabled at the time of termination. However, the disability must have resulted from an illness or injury that occurred while the person was covered under the contract. Generally, the same level of benefits is available as before termination. Although some contracts cover only expenses associated with the same cause of disability, other contracts cover any expenses that would have been paid under the terminated coverage, regardless of cause. The extension of benefits generally ceases after 12 months, or when the individual is no longer totally or continuously disabled, whichever comes first.

Conversion

Except when termination results from the failure to pay any required premiums, medical expense contracts usually contain (and are often required to contain) a conversion provision, whereby most covered persons whose group coverage terminates are allowed to purchase individual medical expense coverage without evidence of insurability and without any limitation of benefits for preexisting conditions. Covered persons commonly have 31 days from the date of termination of the group coverage to exercise this conversion privilege, and coverage is then effective retroactively to the date of termination.

This conversion privilege is typically given to any employee who has been insured for at least 3 months, and it permits the employee to convert his or her own coverage as well as any dependent coverage. In addition, a spouse or child whose dependent coverage ceases for any other reason may also be eligible for conversion (for example, a spouse who divorces or separates, and children who reach age 19).

A person who is eligible for both the conversion privilege and the right to continue the group insurance coverage under COBRA has two choices when eligibility for coverage terminates. He or she can either elect to convert under the provisions of the policy or elect to continue the group coverage. If the latter choice is made, the COBRA rules specify that the person must again be eligible to convert to an individual policy within the usual conversion period (31 days) after the maximum continuation-of-coverage

---

The Conversion Privilege

- No evidence of insurability required
- Full coverage of preexisting conditions
- 31 days allowed for conversion
- Coverage retroactive to start of 31-day period
- Includes right to convert dependents' coverage
- May not be available to anyone covered by Medicare
- May not be available if conversion would result in overinsurance

---

period ceases. Policy provisions may also make the conversion privilege available to persons whose coverage terminates prior to the end of the maximum continuation period.

The insurance company or other provider of the medical expense coverage has the right to refuse the issue of a conversion policy to anyone (1) who is covered by Medicare or (2) whose benefits under the converted policy, together with similar benefits from other sources, would result in overinsurance according to the insurance company's standards. These similar benefits may be found in other coverages that the individual has (either group or individual coverage) or for which the individual is eligible under any group arrangement.

The use of the word *conversion* is often a misnomer. In actuality, a person whose coverage terminates is only given the right to purchase a contract on an individual basis at individual rates. Most Blue Cross and Blue Shield plans and some HMO plans offer a conversion policy that is similar or identical to the terminated group coverage. However, insurance companies may offer a conversion policy (or a choice of policies) that contains a lower level of benefits than existed under the former employer-provided coverage.

Some plans offer a conversion policy that is written by another entity. For example, an HMO might enter into a contractual arrangement with an insurance company. In some cases, the HMO and insurance company are commonly owned or have a parent-subsidiary relationship.

Self-funded plans, which are exempt from state laws that mandate a conversion policy, may still provide such a benefit. Rather than providing coverage directly to the terminated employee, an agreement is made with an insurance company or other provider of medical expense coverage to make a policy available.

Group-to-Individual Portability

The Health Insurance Portability and Accountability Act (HIPAA) makes it easier for individuals who lose employer-provided medical expense coverage to find alternative coverage in the individual marketplace. The purpose of the federal legislation is to encourage states to adopt their own mechanisms to achieve this goal and most states have complied. The federal rules apply in a state only if the state does not have its own plan. The state alternative must do all the following:

- provide a choice of health insurance coverage to all eligible individuals
- impose no preexisting-conditions restrictions
- include at least one policy form of coverage that is either comparable to comprehensive health coverage offered in the individual marketplace or comparable to, or a standard option of, coverage available under the group or individual laws of the state

If a state fails to adopt an alternative to federal regulation, then insurance companies, HMOs, and other health plan providers in the individual marketplace are required to make coverage available on a guaranteed-issue basis to individuals with 18 or more months of creditable coverage and whose most recent coverage was under a group health plan. However, coverage does not have to be provided to an individual who has other health insurance or who is eligible for COBRA coverage, Medicare, or Medicaid. No preexisting-conditions exclusions can be imposed. Health insurers have three options for providing coverage to eligible individuals:

- They may offer every health insurance policy they offer in the state.
- They may offer their two most popular policies in the state, based on premium volume.
- They may offer a low-level and a high-level coverage as long as they contain benefits that are similar to other coverage offered by the insurer in the state.

Rules similar to those described in chapter 12 for group health insurance coverage require the renewal of individual coverage.

TYPES OF POLICIES AVAILABLE

A variety of medical expense policies are available in the individual marketplace. These can be purchased from insurance companies and, in some cases, from managed care organizations. Some of these policies provide broad coverage; other policies provide more limited coverage. It should also be pointed out that many associations, such as AARP and professional societies, have programs through which their members can obtain coverage.

Individual Major Medical Policies

Many companies offer major medical insurance in the individual marketplace. In some cases, these are traditional indemnity policies with covered persons having complete freedom to choose any medical provider and have the same level of benefits paid. In other cases, the policies are actually individual PPO coverage, with a lower level of benefits if services are received from providers outside the PPO network. With a few exceptions, such as those mentioned below, the coverage available is very similar to what is found under employer-provided medical expense plans.

Unlike employer-provided coverage, for which an employee must accept the plan limits as determined by the employer, the purchaser of individual coverage has some choices to make. The most frequent choice is the selection of the annual deductible. The number and dollar amount of options vary by company, but a set of choices ranging from $150 to $2,500 is quite common. Most policies are sold with deductibles of $250, $500, or $1,000. A few insurers offer major medical contracts with very high deductibles, ranging from a low of $10,000 or $20,000 to a high of $1 million. These policies also have very high lifetime maximums. While underlying medical expense coverage is not required, such "catastrophic" insurance is often used as an umbrella or excess major medical policy to fill gaps after an underlying medical expense plan reaches its maximum limits. Some insureds also use catastrophic insurance as supplementary coverage when their managed care plan excludes or limits nonnetwork benefits.

Some policies have a maximum lifetime benefit of $1 million or $2 million; other policies have several options, which might vary from $250,000 to $5 million or more. With today's health care costs, it is questionable if a limit below $1 million would qualify as adequate coverage. A similar situation might exist with respect to a policy's coinsurance percentage. The policies of some companies have the same limit for all contracts; other companies allow a choice. For example, one company lets the purchaser of a policy select whether the policy will pay 50, 80, 90, or 100 percent of covered expenses. The latter option is available only if a high deductible is also selected.

Some major medical policies cover prescription drugs like any other medical expenses; other policies impose limitations such as separate copayments, maximum annual benefits, or different coinsurance percentages. Still other policies make prescription drug coverage an optional benefit that must be added by the purchase of a policy rider.

Maternity coverage frequently requires the purchase of a separate rider for coverage. Benefits are often subject to a waiting period of 10 or 12 months for a normal pregnancy. Benefits may also be paid at something less than their full level during the first year or two of coverage.

Individual policies are likely to have slightly less generous benefits than employer-provided coverage. For example, there may be more limited coverage for mental and nervous disorders. However, because of state-mandated benefits, individual policies might provide broader coverage than major medical coverage that would exist under a self-funded, employer-provided plan. Examples in some states are coverage for acupuncture treatment or mammograms. It is such state mandates that encourage many employers to self-fund benefits because ERISA exempts noninsured plans from state insurance mandates.

HMO Coverage

Many HMOs sell individual coverage, which usually is identical to coverage offered to employers for their benefit plans. However, the emphasis on first-dollar coverage and preventive medicine often makes the HMO coverage more expensive than the coverage available under major medical policies. Some HMOs offer coverage only to persons who have lost employer-provided coverage from the same HMO. Other HMOs market their coverage to everyone, with the premium sometimes being lower for persons who converted from employer-provided coverage. While the situation is changing somewhat, HMOs have historically emphasized the marketing of coverage through employer plans and have marketed individual coverage less aggressively than insurance companies.

Medicare Supplement (Medigap) Policies

Chapter 7 is partially devoted to a discussion of the benefits available under Medicare. While it is a program that provides significant benefits to many Americans, Medicare has many limitations that can lead to large out-of-pocket costs for many beneficiaries. Some of the reasons for these costs are the following:

- a significant Part A deductible for each spell of illness
- unlimited coinsurance for many Part B expenses
- very limited coverage for treatment outside the United States
- very limited coverage for prescription drugs outside a hospital or skilled-nursing facility

Estimates indicate that about two-thirds of Medicare recipients have some type of coverage to supplement Medicare, with this group being split about equally between those with coverage provided by a former employer and those who purchase coverage in the individual marketplace. As mentioned in the previous chapter, employer-provided coverage for retirees may take the form of either a Medicare carve-out or a Medicare supplement.

Medicare supplement insurance in the individual marketplace is frequently referred to as *medigap insurance*. As the name implies, the objective is to fill some of the gaps left after Medicare benefits have been exhausted. When originally developed, medigap plans were as diverse as the companies that sold them. This led to confusion in the marketplace and to questionable sales practices and duplications of coverage. As a result, the federal government began to take a greater interest in what was going on, and eventually enacted legislation to deal with the structure and marketing of medigap plans.

In 1990, the medigap market became directly subject to federal regulation when Congress directed the National Association of Insurance Commissioners (NAIC) to develop a group of standardized medigap policies. Congress mandated several other features, including a 6-month open enrollment period, limited preexisting-conditions exclusions, prohibition of the sale of duplicate coverage, increased individual loss ratios, and guaranteed renewability.

Basic Benefits

The NAIC adopted 10 standard medigap plans, with all 10 requiring the inclusion of a core of specified basic benefits. States may approve, and insurers may offer, fewer than the 10 standard plans, but all states must permit the core benefits to be sold. Most states now permit the sale of all 10 plans, but a few limit the types sold, and a few states are not affected by the mandate because alternative standardized programs were already in place prior to the federal legislation.

The basic benefits that must be included in all plans consist of the following:

- hospitalization. This is the copayment or cost sharing of Part A benefits for the 61st through the 90th day of hospitalization and the 60-day lifetime reserve. In addition, coverage is extended for 365 additional days after Medicare benefits end.
- medical expenses. This is the Part B percentage participation for Medicare-approved charges for physicians' and medical services.
- blood. This is the payment for the first 3 pints of blood each year.

Other Types of Benefits

Medigap plans that can be sold include, in addition to the basic benefits, an array of benefits that provide additional coverage for benefits included in Medicare or that add coverage for benefits not included in Medicare. These benefits include

- paying the Part A copayment for the 21st through the 100th day of skilled-nursing facility care
- paying the hospital inpatient Part A deductible for each benefit period
- paying the Part B deductible
- paying charges for physicians' and medical services that exceed the Medicare-approved amount (either 80 or 100 percent of these charges)
- paying 80 percent of the charges for emergency care in a foreign country (with several limitations)
- paying for an at-home provider to give assistance with activities of daily living (ADLs) while a beneficiary qualifies for Medicare home health care benefits (with certain limitations)
- paying limited annual amounts for preventative care (flu shots, physicals, screening tests, and so forth)
- paying 50 percent of outpatient prescription drug charges after a $250 deductible with either a $1,250 or $3,000 calendar-year limit

The 10 medigap plans are illustrated in table 13-1. The policies available in the individual marketplace must be identified by the letters A through J, and, with two exceptions, insurance companies cannot offer policies that provide benefits that differ from these available options. The first exception is that the companies can offer two high-deductible medigap standard policies for use with medical savings accounts. These policies are identical to plans F and J except that they can have a deductible of $1,530 in 2000. The deductible amount is subject to annual changes based on the consumer price index.

Medicare SELECT policy

The second exception is for policies issued under the Medicare SELECT program, which has been in existence since 1994. A *Medicare SELECT policy* is one of the 10 standard medigap policies, but it can exclude or limit benefits (except in emergencies) for medical services if they are not received from network providers. Medicare SELECT policies are issued by insurance companies as PPO products and by some HMOs. As a general rule, the cost of a Medicare SELECT policy is 15 to 25 percent less than the cost of a comparable medigap policy that does not use such preferred-provider networks. An insured who has a Medicare SELECT policy has the right to switch to a regular medigap policy sold by the same company as long as the new policy has equal or less coverage than the Medicare SELECT policy.

It should be pointed out that the rules for standardized policies apply to the individual marketplace. Group Medicare supplements offered by employers to their retirees are not considered medigap policies and may differ. In addition, three states—Massachusetts, Minnesota, and Wisconsin—had medigap

TABLE 13-1
Medicare Supplement (Medigap) Policies

Benefits	A	B	C	D	E	F	G	H	I	J
Basic	X	X	X	X	X	X	X	X	X	X
Skilled-nursing facility (days 21–100)			X	X	X	X	X	X	X	X
Part A deductible		X	X	X	X	X	X	X	X	X
Part B deductible			X			X				X
Part B excess charges						100%	80%		100%	100%
Foreign travel emergency			X	X	X	X	X	X	X	X
At-home recovery				X			X		X	X
Preventive medical care					X					X
Prescription drugs								$1,250	$1,250	$3,000

programs prior to the NAIC standards. These programs were allowed to continue, and the policies issued are somewhat different than those previously described. However, they are required to contain the basic medigap benefits available in all other states.

Eligibility

Persons aged 65 or older may buy any available Medicare supplement policy, regardless of health status, at any time during the 6-month period after initial enrollment for Medicare Part B benefits. Insurance companies are allowed to exclude benefits for no more than 6 months because of preexisting conditions. However, some policies immediately provide benefits for preexisting conditions or have an exclusion period shorter than 6 months. If a person initially elects a managed care option in lieu of regular Medicare benefits, the person will be eligible to purchase a Medicare supplement policy, without evidence of insurability, if he or she leaves the managed care option during the first 12 months of coverage and returns to regular Medicare benefits. Similarly, a person who drops Medicare supplement coverage and elects a managed care option can regain Medicare supplement coverage if he or she decides to drop the managed care option during the first 12 months of coverage.

In addition, a person can obtain a medigap policy on a guaranteed-issue basis because of the termination of an employer-provided plan that supplements Medicare, or because a Medicare+Choice plan no longer provides coverage or the person loses eligibility by moving out of the plan's service area.

Other Individual Health Insurance Coverages

Several other forms of health insurance coverage are relevant to the discussion of individual medical expense insurance. This section focuses on dental, temporary medical, international travel medical, hospital-surgical, hospital indemnity, and specified disease policies available in the individual insurance market.

Dental Insurance

Most dental coverages are offered through group contracts under employer-provided plans. However, individual policies are available, though not widely purchased because of their relatively high cost in relation to the maximum benefits available. Individual dental coverages are similar in most aspects to the employer-provided benefits described in the previous chapter. However, they are more likely to provide the following:

- lower maximum benefits per calendar year for all services with lower internal benefit limits for specified services, such as orthodontia, if offered
- higher patient copayments
- longer waiting periods for specified basic and major dental services

Coverage is sometimes made available for an additional premium under individual major medical policies.

Temporary Medical Insurance

temporary medical insurance

Temporary medical insurance (sometimes called short-term medical insurance) generally provides coverage for periods between 30 days and one year to under-age-65 individuals and their dependents who are between permanent medical plans. This market includes people who are

- between jobs
- graduating from college
- waiting for group coverage to become effective
- dependents no longer eligible under a parent's plan
- temporary or seasonal employees

These plans are quite similar to individual major medical policies, with applicants usually having a choice of deductibles and coinsurance percentages. These plans are nonrenewable, but an individual may purchase an additional policy beyond the original policy period if he or she is insurable, and any condition that occurred during prior coverage will be considered a preexisting condition under subsequent coverage periods. Some companies do not limit the number of additional periods for which coverage is available; other companies impose a maximum period of total coverage such as one year.

International Travel Medical Insurance

international travel medical insurance

International travel medical insurance is also available for international travelers. U.S. citizens traveling abroad, foreign nationals traveling anywhere internationally (such as Canadians who winter in the United States), and recent immigrants to the United States may purchase some form of this coverage. In addition to vacation travelers, this market includes employees of domestic, international, and multinational corporations that require their employees to travel abroad, missionary groups, and intercultural and student exchange programs.

The period of coverage can range from a minimum of 15 days to a maximum of one year with optional renewal of some policies for up to 5 years. Benefits cover the expenses of inpatient and outpatient hospitalizations as well as medical and related services. Deductibles may be selected from a range of $100 to $2,500. Coinsurance levels are frequently available at 80 percent up to a specific dollar amount—$5,000, for example—with a benefit payment of 100 percent thereafter to the policy maximum. Such maximums may range from $50,000 to as high as $1 million. The expense of repatriating mortal remains in the event of death and medical evacuation to a person's home country for more suitable treatment or after an extended hospitalization are usually covered. Coverage typically ceases when a person returns to his or her home country.

Generally, the health-related benefits are folded into a broader policy covering many non-health-related travel contingencies and may also provide assistance in making arrangements to obtain covered services.

Hospital-Surgical Policies

Hospital-surgical policies in the individual marketplace are similar to the basic medical expense coverages that are sometimes found in employer-provided medical expense plans. Hospital-surgical policies typically provide coverage for a limited number of days of hospitalization, and the daily benefit can be less than the cost of semiprivate accommodations. Surgical benefits are usually paid on a fee-schedule basis. Depending on the policy, benefits may be available for expenses associated with physician's visits, maternity, and extended care facilities.

The basic group coverages are almost always supplemented by major medical coverage. However, this is not the case with hospital-surgical policies. As a result, such policies are typically inadequate for prolonged sicknesses, serious accidents, or the significant medical expenses that can arise outside a hospital setting. While this type of medical policy is obviously better than no medical expense coverage, it is no substitute for a major medical policy. The purchasers of hospital-surgical policies are generally lower-income individuals and families who are unlikely to be financial planning clients.

Hospital Indemnity, Specific Disease, and Critical Illness Insurance

There are three types of medical expense insurance that are designed to supplement the benefits that are available under principal policies of medical expense insurance such as major medical insurance. These policies—hospital indemnity insurance, specified disease insurance, and critical illness insurance—share certain characteristics. The insured is assisted with the significant additional financial consequences of a serious episode of illness or injury by receiving direct cash payments, usually made without regard to other coverages. These payments may be used for

- out-of-pocket expenses of medical treatment left uncovered by even a comprehensive medical plan
- associated nonmedical expenses such as travel, lodging, meals, child care, and loss of income

Hospital indemnity insurance, specified disease insurance, and critical illness insurance are no substitute for adequate medical expense and disability income insurance. And if medical expense and disability income coverages are adequate, there are many financial planners who question whether such supplemental policies are necessary, particularly if a person has appropriate financial reserves for emergencies.

hospital indemnity insurance

Hospital Indemnity Insurance. *Hospital indemnity insurance* provides the insured with a fixed daily cash benefit during a covered hospitalization. A spouse or dependent child is usually eligible for coverage, although benefits may be reduced.

The policy provides daily benefits in the event of hospital confinement in a specified dollar amount (such as $150 per day) for a defined period (such as 90 days). These additional benefits are available as a standard feature or as a rider:

- a lump-sum payment on the first day of hospital confinement
- an intensive care benefit such as $100 for a specified number of days in addition to the standard daily payment
- payment for emergency room and related physician services due to an illness or accident, with limitations on duration or expense per event or per year
- daily payment for recovery after a qualified hospital stay
- an accidental death benefit

specified disease insurance

Specified Disease Insurance. *Specified disease insurance* (also referred to as dread disease insurance) provides benefits to insured individuals and covered family members upon the diagnosis of, or medical events related to the treatment of, a disease named in the policy. It does not cover accidents or injuries. Specified disease insurance for cancer only has been the most prevalent form of this insurance. Today, however, most policies cover cancer in addition to other diseases that might include many or all of the following:

- Addison's disease
- amyotrophic lateral sclerosis
- botulism
- Budd-Chiari syndrome
- cystic fibrosis
- diphtheria
- encephalitis
- histoplasmosis
- Legionnaires' disease
- lupus erythematosus
- malaria
- meningitis
- multiple sclerosis
- muscular dystrophy
- myasthenia gravis
- osteomyelitis
- poliomyelitis
- Q fever
- rabies
- Reye's syndrome
- rheumatic fever
- Rocky Mountain spotted fever
- sickle-cell anemia
- Tay-Sachs disease
- tetanus
- toxic shock syndrome
- trichinosis
- tuberculosis
- tularemia
- typhoid fever
- undulant fever
- whooping cough

Specified disease policy benefits vary widely. Benefit provisions may utilize a combination of three payment structures: per-day or per-service, expense-incurred, or a lump-sum payment. Benefits are contingent on a diagnosis of the specified disease, but payments will cover the first day of care or confinement even though the diagnosis is made at some later date. This retroactive application of benefits usually applies to relevant services received within 90 days prior to the diagnosis. Table 13-2 presents a summary of illustrative benefits.

Specified disease policies frequently offer a first-occurrence benefit that pays a one-time amount for each covered person who receives a diagnosis of internal cancer. The amount may range from $1,000 to as high as $50,000 or more.

critical illness insurance

Critical Illness Insurance. *Critical illness insurance* (sometimes referred to as serious illness insurance) is a relatively new form of supplemental medical insurance that provides a substantial one-time lump-sum cash benefit for listed critical illness. Some of these conditions result from injury as well as disease and include specified major surgeries.

TABLE 13-2
Specified Disease Insurance: Summary of Selected Benefits

Service	Benefit
Hospital confinement	$300 daily for up to 90 days; $600 daily in coronary or intensive care unit up to 30 days
Surgery	Up to $7,500 per fee schedule
Anesthesia	Up to 25 percent of the surgical benefit
Physician's attendance	Actual charges up to $35 per day for in-hospital visits
Chemotherapy, radiation, immunotherapy, or radio-active isotopes therapy	50 percent of the first $50,000 of charges and 100 percent of the next $100,000 limited to $125,000 per calendar year
Experimental treatment	Up to $25,000 for experimental bone marrow transplant and $2,500 for donor-related expenses plus transportation
Transportation and lodging	Up to $50 per day for lodging, mileage, or coach airfare for travel for insured and companion (each)
Ambulance	Actual charges for an ambulance to the hospital and up to $5,000 for air ambulance
Artificial limbs and prostheses	Actual charges with lifetime maximum of $2,000 per insured person
Equipment	Up to $1,000 per calendar year for rental or purchase

The applicant selects a maximum benefit amount, which can range from $10,000 to several hundred thousand dollars. The maximum benefit is payable only once—upon the first diagnosis of a condition or specified surgical treatment that it is covered. Each covered condition and surgical treatment is explicitly defined in the policy. Typically, the maximum benefit is payable for the following medical conditions or major surgery:

- Alzheimer's disease
- blindness
- life-threatening cancer
- deafness
- heart attack
- major organ transplant
- multiple sclerosis
- paralysis
- renal failure
- stroke

The policy may also provide a lesser benefit, such as 25 percent of the maximum benefit, for each of the following:

- initial coronary angioplasty (surgical treatment)
- initial coronary artery bypass (surgical treatment)
- initial diagnosis of cancer in its original site (other than skin cancer)

The percentage payment of the maximum benefits for the above conditions is payable only once; the maximum benefit is reduced by the amount paid, and the premium is also reduced accordingly. The policyowner is notified of the new maximum amount and the new premium. The policy terminates on the date the maximum benefit amount is paid under the terms of the policy.

INSURING THE UNHEALTHY

Historically, persons with a preexisting medical condition had a difficult time obtaining individual medical expense coverage. If the medical condition was severe, insurers would often decline coverage. If the medical condition was less severe, insurers might write coverage on a nonstandard basis by doing one or more of the following: charging an additional premium, excluding the condition, or imposing a waiting period before benefits would be payable for the condition.

Over time, the ability of the unhealthy to obtain coverage has improved significantly. If there is prior employer-provided coverage, federal legislation like COBRA and HIPAA eliminates the availability, but not necessarily the affordability, problem for many persons. States have also increasingly addressed the issue of access to individual medical expense coverage. Some of these state actions, such as the mandate of a conversion provision in group medical expense contracts, date back many years. In addition, some Blue Cross and Blue Shield plans, in return for preferential regulatory and tax status, offer periodic enrollment periods when normal medical underwriting requirements are reduced or waived.

In more recent years, more than half of the states have established some type of high-risk pool, whereby anyone turned down for medical expense coverage in the normal marketplace can obtain coverage through the pool. While these pools vary among the states, basic major medical coverage is usually available, but benefits for preexisting conditions are often subject to waiting periods. Premiums tend to be higher than regular medical expense insurance, but state subsidies keep premiums below the level needed to fully cover expenses and claims costs.

The best way to find out about the options for insuring an unhealthy person is to contact the insurance department of the state where that person resides.

ARCHER MEDICAL SAVINGS ACCOUNTS

medical savings account (MSA)

A *medical savings account (MSA)* is a personal savings account from which unreimbursed medical expenses, including deductibles and copayments, can be paid. MSAs have been touted as one way of financing medical expenses and a viable alternative in reforming the health care system. It is argued that MSAs will result in significant cost savings for two primary reasons. First, the expensive cost of administering small claims is largely eliminated. Second, covered persons will have a direct financial incentive to avoid unnecessary care and seek out the most cost-effective treatment.

The Health Insurance Portability and Accountability Act provides favorable tax treatment for MSAs established in the years 1997 through 2003 if certain criteria are satisfied. In 2001, these MSAs were given the name Archer MSAs. Fewer than 100,000 have been established—far below original expectations. Studies by the Treasury Department and the General Accounting Office will aid Congress in determining whether to extend the favorable tax treatment to MSAs established after 2003. (At the time this book was revised in early 2003, there was proposed legislation to make permanent the favorable tax treatment as well as to liberalize many of the rules applying to MSAs.) However, existing Archer MSAs can generally continue under the current rules even if Congress decides not to extend the favorable tax treatment for newly established MSAs.

Coverage under an Archer MSA can be limited to an individual or include dependents. The Archer MSA must be in the form of a tax-exempt trust or custodial account established in conjunction with a high-deductible health (that is, medical expense) plan. An Archer MSA is established with a qualified trustee or custodian in much the same way that an IRA is established.

Even though employers can sponsor Archer MSAs, these accounts are established for the benefit of individuals and are portable. If an employee changes employers or leaves the workforce, the Archer MSA remains with the individual.

Eligibility

Two types of individuals are eligible to establish Archer MSAs:

- an employee (or spouse) of a small employer (generally one with fewer than 50 employees) that maintains an individual or family *high-deductible health plan* covering that individual. These persons will establish their Archer MSAs under an employer-sponsored plan.
- a self-employed person (or spouse) maintaining an individual or family high-deductible health plan covering that individual. These persons will need to find a custodian or trustee for their Archer MSAs.

A *high-deductible health plan,* for purposes of Archer MSA participation, is a plan that has the following deductibles and annual out-of-pocket limitations, all of which are adjusted for inflation. The figures below are for 2003:

- In the case of individual coverage, the deductible must be at least $1,700 and cannot exceed $2,500. The maximum annual out-of-pocket expenses cannot exceed $3,350.
- In the case of family coverage, the deductible must be at least $3,350 and cannot exceed $5,050. The maximum annual out-of-pocket expenses cannot exceed $6,150.

A high-deductible plan can be written by an insurance company or a managed care organization such as an HMO. Currently, the high-deductible plans are being written primarily by insurance companies in the form of traditional major medical products but possibly with the requirement that covered persons use preferred-provider networks. No HMOs have yet established high-deductible plans.

A high-deductible plan can be part of a cafeteria plan, but the Archer MSA must be established outside the cafeteria plan.

With some exceptions, a person who is covered under a high-deductible health plan is denied eligibility for an Archer MSA if he or she is covered under another health plan that does not meet the definition of a high-deductible plan but that provides any benefits that are covered under the high-deductible health plan. The exceptions include coverage for accident, disability, dental care, vision care, and long-term care as well as Medicare supplement insurance, liability insurance, insurance for a specific disease or illness, and insurance paying a fixed amount per period of hospitalization.

Contributions

Either the account holder of an Archer MSA or the account holder's employer, but not both, may make a contribution to an Archer MSA. If the employer makes a contribution, even one below the allowable limit, the account holder may not make a contribution. Contributions must be in the form of cash.

Contributions by an employer are tax deductible to the employer and are not included in an employee's gross income or subject to Social Security and other employment taxes. Employee contributions are deductible in computing adjusted gross income. As with IRAs, individuals' contributions must generally be made by April 15 of the year following the year for which the contributions are made.

The amount of the annual deductible contribution to an employee's account is limited to 65 percent of the deductible for the health coverage if the Archer MSA is for an individual. The figure is 75 percent if an Archer MSA covers a family. If each person in a married couple has an Archer MSA and if one or both of the Archer MSAs provide family coverage, the aggregate deductible contribution is equal to 75 percent of the deductible for the family coverage with the lowest deductible. The deductible contribution is split equally between the two persons in the couple unless they agree to a different division.

Growth

Unused Archer MSA balances carry over from year to year, and there is no prescribed period in which they must be withdrawn. Earnings on amounts in an Archer MSA are not subject to taxation as they accrue.

Distributions

An individual can take distributions from an Archer MSA at any time. The amount of the distribution can be any part or all of the account balance. Subject to some exceptions, distributions of both contributions and earnings are excludible from an account holder's gross income if used to pay medical expenses of the account holder and the account holder's family as long as these expenses are not paid by other sources of insurance. For the most part, the eligible medical expenses are the same ones that would be deductible, ignoring the 7.5 percent of adjusted gross income limitation, if the account holder itemized his or her tax deductions. However, tax-free withdrawals are not permitted for the purchase of insurance other than long-term care insurance, COBRA continuation coverage, or premiums for health coverage while an individual receives unemployment compensation. In addition, in any year a contribution is made to an Archer MSA, tax-free withdrawals can be made to pay the medical expenses of only those persons who were eligible for coverage under an Archer MSA at the time the expenses were incurred. For example, Archer MSA contributions could not be withdrawn tax free to pay the unreimbursed medical expenses of an account holder's spouse if the employer's health plan under which the spouse was covered was not a high-deductible plan.

Distributions for reasons other than paying eligible medical expenses are included in an account holder's gross income and are subject to a 15 percent penalty tax unless certain circumstances exist. The penalty tax is not levied if the distribution is made after the account holder turns 65 or because of the account holder's death or disability.

Estate Tax Treatment

Upon death, the remaining balance in an Archer MSA is includible in the account holder's gross estate for estate tax purposes. If the beneficiary of the account is a surviving spouse, the Archer MSA belongs to the spouse and he or she can deduct the account balance in determining the account holder's gross estate. The surviving spouse can then use the Archer MSA for his or her medical expenses. If the beneficiary is anyone else, or if no beneficiary is named, the Archer MSA ceases to exist.

POLICY PROVISIONS

Premiums

Premiums for individual health insurance policies can be paid annually, semiannually, quarterly, or possibly monthly. However, the total premiums for a year will be higher than the annual premium if paid in installments. Several factors may affect the level of premiums. These include age, sex, occupation, and whether the insured has certain avocations, or is a smoker.

As long as a premium is paid at least monthly, most policies have a 30-day grace period. If the premium is paid during this period, the policy will continue in force with no lapse in coverage. If a premium is not paid within the grace period, the policy will lapse at the beginning of the grace period.

Most policies contain a provision whereby a lapsed policy can be reinstated for some period of time after it lapses. Some insurers will automatically reinstate a policy if a premium is received within a short period of time following the grace period. Otherwise, the insurer may wish to reunderwrite the policy. No benefits are paid for losses that occur between the period of lapse and a policy's reinstatement. Accidental injuries sustained after the date of reinstatement are covered from the date of reinstatement. However, there is usually a 10-day waiting period before losses from sickness are covered.

Renewability

It is important to look at the provision in a medical expense policy regarding renewability. Because of the uncertain nature and cost of future medical claims, it is rare to find noncancelable policies, unless they provide very limited benefits. Many policies are guaranteed renewable to at least age 65 when a person qualifies for Medicare. Many policies also limit their obligation to continue coverage if the insurer decides to stop writing that particular type of insurance contract. Insurers that issue optionally renewable policies are required to give the policyowner advance notice of any intention to not renew, usually at least 30 days.

FEDERAL TAXATION

The tax situation for self-employed individuals is discussed in the previous chapter. Other individuals who itemize deductions are allowed to deduct most unreimbursed medical care expenses (including dental expenses) to the extent the total of these expenses exceeds 7.5 percent of adjusted gross income. Premiums paid for medical expense and dental insurance are included as an expense for purposes of this deduction. However, premiums for policies that pay a stated periodic payment to a person while hospitalized, regardless of benefits from other sources, are considered premiums for disability income insurance and are not deductible.

As a result of trade legislation passed in 2002, a tax credit is available to certain taxpayers. These include (1) individuals who are certified as having lost their jobs because of trade-related reasons such as competition from foreign imports, and (2) individuals who are at least age 55 and receiving benefits from the Pension Benefit Guaranty Corporation. The credit is equal to 65 percent of the cost of the premium for continuing coverage under COBRA (and possibly for the purchase of certain other medical expense coverage) for an individual and his or her eligible family members. The credit, however, is not available to a taxpayer who has medical expense coverage under Medicare, Medicaid, or an employer-sponsored plan for which the employer pays at least 50 percent of the cost of the coverage.

As a general rule, benefits received from individually paid medical expense and dental insurance are not subject to income tax, even if they exceed expenses actually incurred. One exception includes benefits received for expenses that were deducted in prior years.

CHECKLIST FOR EVALUATING AND COMPARING MEDICAL EXPENSE INSURANCE

☐ What is the type of coverage?

___ Major medical
___ HMO
___ PPO
___ Point-of-service
___ Other

☐ What is the annual policy premium?

☐ Are there any discounts for good health or healthy behaviors such as not smoking?

☐ Are there any preexisting conditions that are not covered? If so, for how long?

☐ To what extent is each of the following services covered? Identify any exclusions or limitations that apply to each service that will affect the client or family.

___ Inpatient hospital services
___ Outpatient surgery
___ Physician visits (in the hospital)
___ Office visits
___ Skilled-nursing care
___ Medical tests and X rays
___ Prescription drugs
___ Mental health care
___ Drug and alcohol abuse treatment
___ Home health care visits

  ___ Rehabilitation facility care
  ___ Physical therapy
  ___ Speech therapy
  ___ Hospice care
  ___ Maternity care
  ___ Chiropractic visits
  ___ Preventive care and checkups
  ___ Well-baby care
  ___ Dental care

☐ Are there any lifetime maximum limits? If so, what are they?

☐ What is the annual deductible?

  ___ Per person
  ___ Per family

☐ What coinsurance or copayments apply?

  ___ After meeting deductible
  ___ Per office visit
  ___ For inpatient hospital care

☐ What preauthorization or certification procedures must be met?

☐ If coverage is individually purchased, what are the provisions for renewal?

SOURCES FOR FURTHER IN-DEPTH STUDY

- For a discussion of continuing coverage after termination of employment, Beam, Burton T., Jr., *Group Benefits: Basic Concepts and Alternatives*, 9th ed., chapter 12, Bryn Mawr, PA: The American College, 2002. Phone 888-263-7265. Web site address www.amercoll.edu
- For a discussion of individual medical expense coverages:
  - Thomas P. O'Hare, *Individual Medical Expense Insurance*, 2d ed., Bryn Mawr, PA: The American College, 2002. Phone 888-263-7265. Web site address www.amercoll.edu
  - *Supplemental Health Insurance*, Washington, DC: Health Insurance Association of America, 1998. Phone 202-824-1600. Web site address www.hiaa.org

CHAPTER REVIEW

Answers to review questions and self-test questions start on page 725.

Key Terms

COBRA	international travel medical
qualified beneficiary	insurance
qualifying event	hospital-surgical policy
extension of benefits	hospital indemnity insurance
medigap insurance	specified disease insurance
Medicare SELECT policy	critical illness insurance
temporary medical insurance	medical savings account (MSA)

Review Questions

13-1. COBRA requires that group health plans allow employees and certain beneficiaries to elect to have their current health coverage extended following a "qualifying event." Briefly describe
   a. the types of plans covered by COBRA
   b. the various qualifying events
   c. the categories of qualified beneficiaries

13-2. Explain how the Health Insurance Portability and Accountability Act makes it easier for individuals who lose employer-provided medical expense coverage to find alternative coverage in the individual marketplace.

13-3. What are the basic benefits that must be included in all medigap insurance plans?

13-4. What are the eligibility criteria for medigap insurance?

13-5. Describe the following types of individual health insurance coverages:
   a. temporary medical insurance
   b. international travel medical insurance
   c. hospital-surgical policies
   d. hospital indemnity insurance
   e. specified disease insurance
   f. critical illness insurance

13-6. Explain who is eligible to establish Archer MSAs.

13-7. Explain the rules that apply to Archer MSAs with respect to
   a. contributions
   b. distributions

13-8.   Explain why insurers rarely issue medical expense policies on a noncancelable basis.

Self-Test Questions

T   F   13-1.   The term group health plan as used for COBRA purposes is broad enough to also include dental plans, vision care plans, and long-term care plans.

T   F   13-2.   A qualified beneficiary can obtain COBRA coverage after a qualifying event without having to provide evidence of insurability.

T   F   13-3.   COBRA coverage is automatic for qualified beneficiaries who lose their group health coverage because of a qualifying event.

T   F   13-4.   The insurance company has the right to refuse conversion of group coverage for anyone who is covered under Medicare.

T   F   13-5.   The HIPAA rules apply in a state only if the state does not have its own plan.

T   F   13-6.   AARP and many professional societies have programs through which their members can obtain medical expense coverage.

T   F   13-7.   The purchaser of an individual major medical policy has to select the annual deductible and lifetime maximum limit he or she wants in the policy.

T   F   13-8.   ERISA requires that self-funded, employer-provided medical expense plans include state-mandated benefits.

T   F   13-9.   HMO coverage for individuals is typically less expensive than an individual major medical policy.

T   F   13-10.   Only 10 percent of Medicare recipients have some type of coverage to supplement Medicare.

T   F   13-11.   Group Medicare supplements offered by employers to their retirees are not considered medigap policies and may differ.

T   F   13-12.   Insurance companies are allowed to permanently exclude benefits for preexisting conditions from their medigap policies.

T   F   13-13.   Cancer insurance is the most prevalent form of specified disease insurance in the marketplace today.

T   F   13-14.   More than half of the states have established some type of high-risk pool, whereby anyone turned down for medical expense coverage in the normal marketplace can obtain coverage through the pool.

T   F   13-15.   Coverage under an Archer MSA can be limited to an individual or include dependents.

T F 13-16. Both the account holder of an Archer MSA and the account holder's employer may make a contribution to the account.

T F 13-17. Individuals who itemize deductions for income tax purposes are allowed to deduct all unreimbursed medical expenses regardless of their amount.

Disability Income Insurance

Learning Objectives

An understanding of the material in this chapter should enable the student to

14-1.   Explain the need for and sources of disability income protection.

14-2.   Briefly describe how sick leave plans work.

14-3.   Describe in detail the characteristics of group disability income plans.

14-4.   Explain the income tax treatment of employer-provided disability income benefits.

14-5.   Describe in detail the characteristics of individual disability income policies.

14-6.   Describe the business uses of disability insurance.

Chapter Outline

In terms of its financial effect on the family, long-term disability is more severe than death. In both cases, income ceases. In the case of long-term disability, however, family expenses—instead of decreasing because the family has one less member—may actually increase due to the cost of providing care for the disabled person. Financial planners need to understand the disability risk and the methods for managing this risk.

The purpose of disability income insurance is to partially (and sometimes totally) replace the income of persons who are unable to work because of sickness or accident. Any employee may miss a few days of work from time to time; however, there is a tendency to underestimate both the frequency and severity of disabilities that last for longer periods. At all working ages, the probability of being disabled for at least 90 consecutive days is much greater than the chance of dying. About half of all employees will have a disability that lasts at least 90 days during his or her working years, and one out of every 10 persons can expect to be permanently disabled prior to age 65.

SOURCES OF COVERAGE

Disability income protection can come from several sources: social insurance programs, employer-provided benefits, and individually purchased policies.

Social Insurance Programs

Several types of disability coverage under social insurance programs are discussed in chapter 7. For example, persons suffering injury or illness in the workplace will be covered under workers' compensation programs. Although benefits may be payable for life for total disabilities and may be as high as two-thirds of predisability income, benefits are subject to maximum amounts that make them inadequate for all but lower-paid workers. Benefits of limited duration are also available in a few states under temporary disability laws.

Possible Sources of Disability Income Coverage

- Workers' compensation programs
- State temporary disability laws
- Social Security
- Employer-provided sick leave plans
- Employer-provided short-term disability income insurance plans
- Employer-provided long-term disability income insurance plans
- Individual disability income insurance policies

Most employed persons are potentially eligible for disability benefits under the Social Security program if they are disabled longer than 5 months. However, the definition of disability is more restrictive than that found in most individual or group insurance policies. In addition, benefits are likely to be inadequate for many workers, particularly those with annual earnings over $30,000. In spite of these limitations, the Social Security program is the major source of disability income coverage, with approximately 5 million disabled workers and over 1.5 million dependents annually collecting in excess of $60 billion in benefits.

Employer-Provided Benefits

Employers are less likely to provide employees with disability income benefits than with either life insurance or medical expense benefits, but the disability coverage available to many employees is significant. It is estimated that at least three-quarters of all employees have some form of employer-provided short-term protection, either in the form of self-funded plans or insured short-term disability income insurance plans. However, only about one-third of employees have any type of employer-provided long-term protection other than Social Security.

Employer-provided income protection consists of two distinct types of plans:

short-term disability income plan

- *short-term disability income plans*, which provide benefits for a limited period of time, usually 6 months or less. Benefits may be provided under sick-leave plans, which are often uninsured, or under insured plans.

long-term disability income insurance

- *long-term disability income insurance*, which provides extended benefits (possibly for life) after an employee has been disabled for a period of time, frequently 6 months

The types of employer-provided coverage are discussed in a later section of this chapter.

Individual Disability Income Insurance

Many individuals have a need for disability insurance that is not met by social insurance and employer-provided coverage. However, insurance companies that offer disability income policies are very concerned about overinsurance and the accompanying moral hazard, and, consequently, limit the amount of benefits relative to the individual's income. As a result, many individuals with coverage through other sources are ineligible for additional disability income protection.

Anyone who earns at least $20,000 per year from gainful employment and is not already covered by private disability insurance has a significant need for disability income protection. Obviously, this includes the self-employed, business owners and partners, individual workers, and anyone who would have an inadequate income if he or she were to become disabled and be unable to continue working for compensation.

Unfortunately, disability insurance is not available for every occupation from every insurance company. Therefore, it is important for persons in many occupations and their financial planners to be aware of variations in the marketplace. For example, some companies do not insure persons in certain hazardous or unstable occupations for disability income; other insurers offer a special disability policy for these occupations; still other insurers offer their regular policy at higher-than-standard premium rates.

Furthermore, many corporate events can alter employer-provided disability income protection and therefore increase the need for individual protection. First, corporate mergers or acquisitions may result in a change in management and management philosophy, which may result in the termination of previously provided benefits. Second, bankruptcy or severe financial problems may prompt management to cut back on such employee benefits as disability income insurance. Third, the insurance company that provides disability income protection through the employer could terminate the policy; if the employer is unable to find another insurance company willing to write the coverage, disability protection ceases. Even if coverage could be obtained from another insurer, management may decide not to seek replacement coverage.

Since most employers do not provide long-term disability income insurance, it is quite possible that an employee who leaves a job in which he or she had disability income protection may not be provided with that protection by a new employer. Such job changes create a definite need for individual disability income protection. One advantage of relying on individual protection rather than on employer-provided group protection is that the individual is not subject to termination at the whim of corporate decision makers. Also, individual coverage is portable and can go with the insured to new geographic locations and down new career paths.

Disability income coverages are also important for partnerships and closely held corporations. Such coverages can provide the financial means for healthy partners or stockholders to purchase the ownership interest of the disabled partner or stockholder. Disability income policies can also be used by the business enterprise to pay business overhead and to replace lost income or revenue that results from a key person's disability.

Individual disability income policies are discussed following the sections on employer-provided coverage.

SICK-LEAVE PLANS

sick-leave plan

Employers provide short-term disability benefits to employees through two approaches: sick-leave plans and short-term disability income insurance plans. *Sick-leave plans* (often called salary continuation plans) are usually uninsured and generally fully replace lost income for a limited period of time, starting on the first day of disability. In contrast, short-term disability income insurance plans (which are covered in the next section of this chapter) usually provide benefits that replace only a portion of an employee's lost income and often contain a waiting period before benefits start, particularly for sickness.

Eligibility

Almost all sick-leave plans are limited to permanent full-time employees. Most plans also require an employee to satisfy a short probationary period (commonly 1 to 3 months) before being eligible for benefits. Sick-leave plans may also be limited to certain classes of employees such as top management or nonunion employees.

Benefits

Most sick-leave plans are designed to provide benefits equal to 100 percent of an employee's regular pay. Most plans, however, provide a reduced level of benefits after an initial period of full pay.

Several approaches are used in determining the duration of benefits. The most traditional approach credits eligible employees with a certain amount of sick leave each year such as 10 days. Most plans with this approach allow employees to accumulate unused sick leave up to a maximum amount, which rarely exceeds 6 months (sometimes specified as 180 days or 26 weeks).

Another approach bases the duration of benefits on an employee's length of service. For example, an employee with less than 3 months of service may get no sick days. After this limited period, the employee may get 5 days during the next year, with the number of days increasing to 30 with 10 years of service.

An alternative to this approach provides benefits for a uniform length of time (such as 26 weeks) to all employees, except possibly those with short periods of service. However, benefits are reduced to less than full pay after some period of time that is related to an employee's length of service. For example, an employee with 2 years of service might get 4 weeks of sick leave at full pay and 22 additional weeks at half pay. After each additional year of service, the number of weeks at full pay increases by 4, until all 26 weeks would be available at full pay after 6 years of service.

Most sick-leave plans are coordinated with social insurance programs. For example, if an employee is entitled to 100 percent of pay and receives 60 percent of pay as a workers' compensation benefit, the sick-leave plan pays the remaining 40 percent.

INSURED GROUP DISABILITY INCOME PLANS

As previously mentioned, insured group disability income plans consist of two distinct products: short-term coverage and long-term coverage. In many respects, the contractual provisions of both short-term and long-term disability income contracts are the same or very similar. In other respects—notably, the eligibility requirements, the definition of disability, and the amount and duration of benefits—they differ significantly.

Eligibility

Many of the eligibility requirements in group disability income insurance plans are similar to those found in other types of group insurance contracts. In addition to being in a covered classification, an employee must usually work full-time and be actively at work before coverage commences. Any requirements concerning probationary periods, insurability, and premium contributions must also be satisfied.

Disability income insurance plans frequently differ in both the classes of employees who are eligible for coverage and the length of the probationary period. Employers are more likely to provide short-term benefits to a wider range of employees, and it is not unusual for short-term plans to cover all full-time employees.

Long-term disability plans often limit benefits to salaried employees because claims experience has traditionally been less favorable for hourly paid employees. Some long-term plans also exclude employees below a certain salary level since this category of employees, like hourly paid employees, is considered to have a reasonable level of benefits under Social Security.

Long-term disability income plans tend to have longer probationary periods than short-term disability income plans. While the majority of short-term disability plans either have no probationary period or have a

---

Eligibility for Group Disability Income Insurance

- Member of a covered class of employees
- Full-time employee
- Actively at work
- Satisfy any probationary period
- Show any required evidence of insurability
- Authorize withholding of any required employee contributions

probationary period of 3 months or less, it is common for long-term disability plans to have probationary periods ranging from 3 months to one year. Whereas short-term plans only require that an employee be actively at work on the date he or she is otherwise eligible for coverage, long-term plans sometimes require that the employee be on the job for an extended period (such as 30 days) without illness or injury before coverage becomes effective.

Definition of Disability

Benefits are paid under disability income insurance contracts only if the employee meets the definition of disability as specified in the contract. Virtually all short-term disability income insurance contracts define disability as *the total inability of the employee to perform each and every duty of his or her regular occupation.* A small minority of contracts uses a more restrictive definition, requiring that an employee be unable to engage in any occupation for compensation. Partial disabilities are usually not covered, but a few newer plans do provide benefits. In addition, the majority of short-term contracts limit coverage to nonoccupational disabilities because employees have workers' compensation benefits for occupational disabilities.

A few long-term disability income contracts use the same liberal definition of disability that is commonly used in short-term contracts, but the term *material duties* often replaces the term *each and every duty.* These are

own-occupation

referred to as *own-occupation* definitions of disability. However, the majority of long-term disability contracts use a dual definition under which benefits are paid for some period of time (usually 24 or 36 months) as long as an employee is unable to perform his or her regular occupation. After that time, benefits are paid only if the employee is unable to engage in any occupation for which he or she is qualified by reason of training, education, or experience. The purpose of this combined definition is to require and encourage a disabled employee who becomes able after a period of time to adjust his or her lifestyle and earn a livelihood in another occupation.

A more recent definition of disability found in some long-term contracts contains an occupation test and an earnings test. Under the occupation test, a person is totally disabled if he or she meets the definition of disability as described in the previous paragraph. However, if the occupation test is not satisfied, a person is still considered disabled as long as an earnings test is satisfied; that is, the person's income has dropped by a stated percentage, such as 20 percent, because of injury or sickness. This newer definition makes a group insurance contract similar to an individual disability income policy that provides residual benefits.

The definition of disability in long-term contracts may differ from that found in short-term contracts in several other respects. Long-term contracts are somewhat more likely to provide benefits for partial disabilities. However, the amount and duration of such benefits may be limited when compared with those for total disabilities, and the receipt of benefits is usually contingent upon a previous period of total disability. In addition, most long-term contracts provide coverage for both occupational and nonoccupational disabilities. Finally, short-term contracts usually have the same definition of disability for all classes of employees. Some long-term contracts use different definitions for different classes of employees—one definition for most employees, and a more liberal definition for executives or salaried employees.

Exclusions

Under certain circumstances, disability income benefits are not paid even if an employee satisfies the definition of disability. Common exclusions under both short-term and long-term disability income contracts specify that no benefits will be paid

- for any period during which the employee is not under the care of a physician
- for any disability caused by an intentionally self-inflicted injury
- unless the period of disability commenced while the employee was covered under the contract

It was once common for disabilities resulting from pregnancy to be excluded. Such an exclusion is now illegal under federal law if an employer has 15 or more employees. Employers with fewer than 15 employees may still exclude pregnancy disabilities unless they are subject to state laws to the contrary.

Additional exclusions are often found in long-term contracts. These commonly deny benefits for disabilities resulting from

- war, whether declared or undeclared
- participation in an assault or felony. Some insurers have recently expanded this exclusion to include the commission of any crime.
- mental illness, alcoholism, or drug addiction. However, most contracts provide benefits for an employee who is confined in a hospital or institution that specializes in the care and treatment of such disorders; other contracts provide employees with benefits but limit their duration (such as for 24 months per disability).
- preexisting conditions

The exclusion for preexisting conditions is designed to counter the adverse selection and potentially large claims that could occur if an employer established a group disability income plan or if an employee elected to participate in the plan because of some known condition that is likely to result in disability. While variations exist, a common provision for preexisting conditions excludes coverage for any disability that commences during the first 12 months an employee is covered under the contract if the employee received treatment or medical advice for the disabling condition both (1) prior to the date the employee became eligible for coverage and (2) within 90 consecutive days prior to the commencement of the disability.

When coverage is transferred from one insurance company to another, it is not unusual, particularly in the case of large employers, for the new insurance company to waive the limitation for preexisting conditions for those employees who were insured under the previous contract.

Benefits

Group disability income contracts contain benefit schedules that classify employees and specify the amount of disability income to be provided. They also include provisions pertaining to the length of time that benefits are paid and the coordination of benefits with other available types of disability income.

Benefit Schedules

There are a variety of benefit schedules found in group disability income contracts. Benefits may be available to all employees or limited to specific groups of employees. In addition, benefits may be expressed as either flat-dollar amounts, varying dollar amounts by classification, or a percentage of earnings.

Absenteeism is encouraged and the incentive to return to work is diminished if a disabled employee is given a level of income that is comparable to his or her regular earnings. In general, disability income plans are designed to provide a level of benefits that replaces between 50 and 70 percent of an employee's gross income. Although this may appear to represent a substantial reduction of regular earnings, it should be remembered that a disabled employee does not have the usual expenses associated with working such as transportation costs. In addition, disability income benefits financed with after-tax employee contributions are not subject to Social Security and Medicare taxes, and employer-financed benefits are subject to Social Security and Medicare taxes only during the last calendar month in which an employee worked and during the 6 months that follow.

Many short-term disability income plans and the majority of long-term plans base benefits on a single percentage of regular earnings (excluding

---

Reasons for Limited Benefits

- Return to work is encouraged.
- Work-related expenses are reduced.
- Benefits may not be subject to Social Security taxation.

---

bonuses and overtime). This percentage varies widely for short-term plans, and benefits as low as 50 percent or as high as 100 percent are not unusual. However, many insurers are reluctant to underwrite plans that provide benefits higher than 70 percent of earnings. In some instances, short-term plans may use different percentages such as 100 percent of earnings for 4 weeks and 70 percent of earnings for the remaining benefit period. The length of time for which the higher level of benefits is provided may also be a function of the length of an employee's service.

Long-term plans typically provide benefits that range from 50 to 70 percent of earnings, with 60 and 66 2/3 being the most prevalent percentages. Some plans also use a sliding scale such as 66 2/3 percent of the first $4,000 of monthly earnings and 40 percent of earnings in excess of $4,000.

Plans that determine benefits as a percentage of earnings also commonly place a maximum dollar amount on the benefit that will be provided, regardless of earnings. For example, a long-term plan might be subject to a monthly maximum that varies from $1,000 for some small groups to $4,000 or $5,000 (and sometimes higher) for large groups. The purpose of such a maximum is to prevent the absolute benefit from being so high that an employee, by adjusting his or her lifestyle, could live comfortably on the disability income benefit and thus have no financial incentive to return to work.

Period of Benefits

To determine the period for which benefits are paid, it is necessary to determine when benefits begin and how long they are paid. In both respects, there are differences between short-term and long-term plans.

waiting period

Short-term Plans. Short-term disability income contracts commonly contain a *waiting period* (often referred to in such contracts as an elimination period). The waiting period is the length of time for which an employee covered under the contract must be disabled before benefits begin. The typical short-term contract has no waiting period for disabilities resulting from accidents, but a waiting period of 1 to 7 days is used for disabilities resulting from sicknesses. However, some plans have a single waiting period that applies to disabilities from either accidents or sicknesses; a few plans have no waiting periods for either. Waiting periods longer than 7 days are occasionally used, particularly when there is a sick-leave plan to provide benefits during the initial portion of a disability. In a few cases, benefits are paid retroactively to the date of disability if the disability lasts for a predetermined period of time, but it is generally felt that retroactive benefits cause employees to prolong their return to work in order to receive benefits for the full period of their disability.

Once an employee begins receiving benefit payments under a short-term disability contract, the benefits continue until the end of the benefit period specified in the contract, if the employee remains disabled for that long. Although short-term contracts may provide benefits up to 2 years (with long-term contracts providing benefits for periods over 2 years), benefits rarely continue for more than one year. In fact, the majority of short-term contracts stipulate that benefits are paid for either 13 or 26 weeks, with the latter period being most prevalent.

Typical Benefit Periods

- Short-term plans—13 weeks or 26 weeks subject to a 1- to 7-day waiting period for sickness
- Long-term plans—2 years to life, subject to a 3-month or 6-month waiting period

---

In a few cases, the maximum period of benefits applies to a specified duration of time (such as any consecutive 12 months) regardless of the number of separate disabilities. However, in most plans, both the maximum benefit period and the elimination period apply to each separate disability. Moreover, successive periods of disability caused by the same accident or the same or related sickness are generally considered to be a single disability, unless they are separated by a period of continuous resumption of active employment.

Although reducing short-term disability income benefits for older employees may be justifiable on a cost basis, few plans do so.

Long-term Plans. Long-term disability income plans have elimination periods of 3 to 6 months, with 6 months most common. The length of the waiting period often corresponds to the length of time benefits are paid under a firm's short-term disability income plan or salary continuation plan. Unlike short-term plans, the waiting periods for sicknesses and accidents are the same.

Long-term disability income benefits may be paid for as short a period as 2 years or as long as the lifetime of the disabled employee. At one time it was common for long-term disability income benefits to stop at age 65, but this is no longer permissible under the Age Discrimination in Employment Act. Several different approaches are now used for older employees. In a few cases, benefits are paid until age 70 for any disability that occurred before that age. For disabilities occurring at age 70 or later, benefits are paid for a reduced duration. A more common approach is to use a graded benefit period and give benefits to age 65 for employees who are disabled before a specified age. Employees disabled after the specified age get benefits for a limited duration, as shown in table 14-1.

TABLE 14-1 **Duration of Disability Income Benefits**	
Age at Commencement of Disability	Benefit Duration
59 and younger	To age 65
60–64	5 years
65–69	To age 70
70–74	1 year
75 and older	6 months

As in short-term disability income plans, provisions are made in long-term plans for successive disabilities. The majority of contracts stipulate that successive periods of disability that are separated by less than some period (usually varying from 3 to 6 months) of continuous, active full-time employment are considered a single disability, unless the subsequent disability (1) arises from an unrelated cause and (2) begins after the employee has returned to work.

Coordination with Other Benefits

To minimize the possibility of an employee receiving total benefits higher than his or her predisability earnings, disability income plans commonly stipulate that benefits are coordinated with other sources of disability income. In general, the insurance laws or regulations of most states allow such reductions to be made as a result of benefits from social insurance programs and group insurance or retirement plans provided by the employer, but not as a result of benefits from individual disability income contracts unless they were purchased by the employer.

Benefits under short-term plans are generally integrated with (1) workers' compensation benefits, if the plan covers occupational disabilities; (2) temporary disability laws, if they are applicable; and (3) Social Security benefits, if the maximum benefit period is longer than 5 months.

Long-term disability income benefits are usually integrated with benefits provided under the following:

- Social Security
- workers' compensation laws
- temporary disability laws
- other insurance plans for which the employer makes a contribution or payroll deduction
- pension plans for which the employer has made a contribution or payroll deduction to the extent that the employee elects to receive retirement benefits because of disability
- sick-leave plans
- earnings from employment, either with the employer or from other sources

It is possible for the integration with other benefits to totally eliminate a long-term disability benefit. To prevent this from happening, many plans provide (and some states require) that a minimum benefit, such as $50 or $100 per month, be paid. Most plans also contain a provision freezing the amount of any Social Security reduction at. the initial level that was established when the claim began.

As a general rule, both the insured and the insurer profit if the insured is able to collect Social Security benefits for a disability; the insured has an increased overall benefit, and the insurer has a substantially lower claim to pay. Consequently, insurers are often willing to provide assistance to claimants by helping them file Social Security claims and appeal decisions denying claims.

Supplemental Benefits

It is becoming increasingly common to find group long-term disability income plans that provide employees with a base of employer-paid benefits and that allow each covered employee to purchase additional coverage at his or her own expense. For example, a plan may provide basic benefits of 50 percent of earnings and an option for an employee to increase this amount to

buy-up plan

55, 66 2/3, or 70 percent of earnings. These *buy-up* (or supplemental) *plans* are becoming more popular because employers feel the need to control the costs of benefits by shifting a greater burden of the cost to employees.

carve-out (benefit plan)

Some plans are also designed as *carve-out* plans to provide benefits for certain employees, typically key executives. For example, an employer might design one plan to cover most of its employees, but top executives might be covered with another group plan that provides enhanced benefits in the form of a larger percentage of earnings and a more liberal definition of disability. Another variation of a carve-out plan would provide the executives with a lower benefit percentage than other employees receive, but it could include supplemental benefits in the form of individual disability income policies. In addition to more favorable policy provisions, a carve-out plan might offer better rate guarantees and an overall higher benefit than a group plan could offer. Furthermore, the portability of the individual policy might be attractive to executives but might not necessarily appeal to the employer.

Catastrophic Benefits Rider

A few disability insurers that also sell long-term care insurance have recently started to make available additional benefits if the insured suffers a severe disability that includes cognitive impairment or the inability to perform two or more of six activities of daily living (ADLs). These are the same criteria that trigger benefits in long-term care policies, which are discussed in chapter 15.

The employer can typically purchase benefits that range from an additional 10 to 40 percent of earnings as long as total disability benefits do not exceed a specified limit that may be as high as 100 percent of earnings. The length of time the catastrophic benefits are paid is also selected by the employer and can vary from one year to the duration of the regular disability benefits provided by the policy. (Note that at least one insurer offers a 10 percent benefit for one year as part of its standard disability income policies, with the employer having the option of selecting larger benefits or a longer benefit duration.) In addition, an employer may have the option of adding a flat monthly benefit that is payable if an employee's spouse suffers a cognitive impairment or is unable to perform two or more ADLs.

Other Contract Provisions

Many provisions in group disability income contracts are similar to those in other types of insurance contracts previously discussed and, therefore, are not discussed further in this chapter. These provisions pertain to incontestability, a grace period, the entire contract, and the payment of premiums. The provisions discussed here either are unique to group disability income benefit contracts or differ in certain respects from similar provisions found in other types of group insurance contracts.

Claims

The provisions concerning claims under both short-term and long-term disability income contracts are essentially the same. The insurance company must be notified within a relatively short time period—20 or 30 days (or as soon as is reasonably possible)—after the disability for which benefits are being claimed begins. A formal proof of loss must then be filed with the insurance company, usually within 90 days after the commencement of the disability or after the end of the week, month, or other time period for which benefits are payable. The proof of loss normally consists of a statement by the employee concerning the disability, a statement by the attending physician, and a statement by the employer indicating the date and reason that active employment ceased. Provisions also require periodic reports from the attending physician or permit the insurance company to request such reports at reasonable intervals. The insurance company also has the right to have the employee examined by a physician of its own choice (and at its own expense) at reasonable time periods during the duration of the claim.

Rehabilitation

As an incentive to encourage disabled employees to return to active employment as soon as possible, but perhaps at a lower-paying job, most insurance companies include a rehabilitation provision in their long-term disability income contracts. This provision permits the employee to enter a trial work period of one or 2 years in rehabilitative employment. During this time, disability benefits continue but are reduced by some percentage (varying from 50 to 80 percent) of the earnings from rehabilitative employment. If the trial work period indicates that the employee is unable to perform the rehabilitative employment, the original long-term benefit is continued and the employee is not required to satisfy a new waiting period.

While there are seldom other provisions in long-term disability income contracts that require the insurance company to aid in the rehabilitation of disabled employees, it has become increasingly common for insurance companies to provide benefits for rehabilitation when it is felt that the cost of these benefits will be offset by shortening an employee's disability period. These benefits may be in the form of physical therapy, job training, or adaptive aids to enable a disabled person to perform job functions.

In the past, the decision to seek rehabilitation was left to the disabled person. Some insurers now require the person to undertake rehabilitation or have benefits reduced or stopped.

The rehabilitation of disabled persons is continuing to grow in importance among companies. More and more companies are taking a proactive role in managing disability claims by employing more skilled professionals and by intervening earlier in the claims process. Because early intervention is undoubtedly a key factor in getting disabled employees back to work sooner, many benefit consultants think it advantageous for an employer to use the same company for its short-term and long-term disability income plans. This approach enables the insurer's rehabilitation staff to become involved when a claim is filed under the short-term plan rather than waiting until the elimination period for long-term benefits has been met.

Termination

For the most part, the provisions in disability income contracts concerning the termination of either the master contract or an employee's coverage are the same as those found in other types of group insurance. There is one notable exception: a conversion privilege is rarely included.

Additional Benefits

Several types of additional benefits are occasionally found under long-term disability income contracts. The most common are a cost-of-living adjustment (COLA), a pension supplement, and a survivors' benefit.

Some disability income plans have COLAs to prevent inflation from eroding the purchasing power of disability income benefits being received. Under the typical COLA formula, benefits increase annually along with changes in the consumer price index.

Many firms make provisions in their pension plan for treating disabled employees as if they were still working and accruing pension benefits. Such a provision requires that contributions on behalf of disabled employees be made to the pension plan, usually from the employer's current revenues. However, some disability income contracts stipulate that the contributions necessary to fund a disabled employee's accruing pension benefits will be paid from the disability income contract.

It should also be noted that some pension plans provide disability income benefits by allowing disabled employees to begin receiving retirement benefits when they are totally and permanently disabled. It is common, however, to limit these early retirement benefits to employees who have satisfied some minimum period of service or who have reached some minimum age. Recently, employee benefit consultants seem to feel that separate retirement and disability income plans are preferable.

Additional Benefits Sometimes Provided

- Cost-of-living adjustments
- Continued growth of pension benefits
- Income benefit to survivors
- Payments for child care
- Benefits for disability of employee's spouse
- Payment of medical expense insurance premiums

Some long-term contracts provide a benefit to survivors in the form of continued payments after the death of a disabled employee. In effect, the disability income payments are continued, possibly at a reduced amount, for periods ranging up to 24 months, but with 3 to 6 months being more common. Payments are generally made only to eligible survivors, who commonly are the spouse and unmarried children under age 21.

While even less common, other types of additional benefits may also be found. Examples include child-care payments for disabled employees who can work on a part-time basis, spousal disability benefits payable to the employee, and benefits to pay premiums for medical expense coverage.

FEDERAL INCOME TAXATION OF EMPLOYER-PROVIDED BENEFITS

Deductibility of Contributions

Employer contributions for an employee's disability income insurance are fully deductible to the employer as an ordinary and necessary business expense. Contributions by an individual employee are considered payments for personal disability income insurance and are not tax deductible.

Federal Income Tax Liability of Employees

Employer contributions for disability income insurance result in no taxable income to an employee. However, the payment of benefits under an insured plan or sick-leave plan may or may not result in the receipt of taxable income. In order to make this determination, it is necessary to look at whether the plan is fully contributory, noncontributory, or partially contributory.

Fully Contributory Plan

Under a fully contributory plan, the entire cost of an employee's coverage is paid by after-tax employee contributions and benefits are received free of income taxation.

Noncontributory Plan

Under a noncontributory plan, the employer pays the entire cost and benefits are included in an employee's gross income. Some persons who are permanently and totally disabled may be eligible for a tax credit, but this credit is relatively modest. For example, the maximum credit for a married person filing jointly is $1,125, and this figure is reduced if adjusted gross income (including the disability benefit) exceeds $10,000. For purposes of this tax credit, the IRS uses the stringent Social Security definition of disability.

Partially Contributory Plan

Under a partially contributory plan, benefits attributable to employee contributions are received free of income taxation. Benefits attributable to employer contributions are includible in gross income, but employees may be eligible for the tax credit described previously.

The portion of the benefits attributable to employer contributions (and thus subject to income taxation) is based on the ratio of the employer's contributions to the total employer-employee contributions for an employee who has been under the plan for some period of time. For example, if the employer paid 75 percent of the cost of the plan, 75 percent of the benefits would be considered attributable to employer contributions and 25 percent to employee contributions.

Example: Harry is covered under a long-term disability income insurance plan of his employer. Harry and the employer pay 25 percent and 75 percent of the premium cost, respectively. The income tax treatment is as follows:

- The employer's contributions are deductible as a normal business expense and are not taxable as income to Harry.
- Harry's contributions are not tax-deductible.
- 25 percent of any disability income benefit payments are tax free to Harry; 75 percent of such payments are taxable as income, but Harry may be eligible for a tax credit if his adjusted gross income is low enough.

INDIVIDUAL DISABILITY INCOME INSURANCE POLICIES

Individual disability income coverages and related disability policies vary widely. Many variations involve such factors as the definition of disability itself, the duration of benefits, the elimination period, whether and how partial-disability benefits are provided, waiver-of-premium protection, how recurring disability is handled, and COLAs.

Definition of Disability

A few private insurance company contracts use a definition of disability that is as restrictive as the Social Security definition, but these products should not be considered high-quality ones. These definitions are commonly referred to in the insurance industry as *any-occupation* definitions of disability, which means that benefits are payable only if the individual is disabled severely enough that he or she cannot engage in any occupation.

Most individual disability income contracts use definitions of disability that are similar to those for group plans discussed earlier in this chapter. It should be noted that most companies, because of adverse claims experience, no longer issue contracts of long benefit duration that have own-occupation definitions of disability for the contract duration. Such policies, many of which are still in force, were once common. The dual definition of disability is the norm, with insureds sometimes having a choice regarding how long the own-occupation definition of disability remains in force. When such a choice is available, there are typically two options ranging from 2 to 5 years. A common modification of the own-occupation definition is to continue benefits as long as an insured is not working in some other occupation.

To this point, the definitions discussed have dealt primarily with total disability. Currently, many individual disability policies also provide benefits for either partial disability or residual disability. Both of these types of benefits are intended to encourage insureds to return to the workforce prior to total recovery. Some experts argue that the absence of these benefits encourages disabled insureds to malinger so that they can collect total-disability benefits. It should be emphasized that partial-disability benefits and, in many policies, residual-disability benefits are payable only following a period for which total-disability benefits have been paid.

Partial-Disability Benefits

partial disability

Partial disability is usually defined as the inability to perform some stated percentage of the duties of the insured's occupation or to perform at such a speed that completion of those duties takes a longer-than-normal amount of time; the more severe the limitations, the higher the benefit paid. Theoretically, under such a contract, an individual could return to work on a full-time basis at full salary, and he or she would still be eligible for partial-disability benefits.

Residual-Disability Benefits

residual-disability
benefits

Residual-disability benefits provide for a replacement of lost earnings due to less-than-total disability. Here the focus is on how much income reduction has occurred as a result of the disability rather than on the physical dimensions of the disability itself. Residual-disability benefits are particularly well suited for self-employed professionals whose caseloads often determine their income such as accountants, attorneys, and physicians. A disability that reduces their capacity for work would automatically lead to a reduction in income.

Policies providing residual-disability benefits usually specify a fraction (representing the proportion of lost income) that is multiplied by the stated monthly benefit for total disability to derive the residual benefit payable. The numerator of that fraction is usually income prior to disability minus earned income during disability; the denominator of the fraction is income prior to disability. The contract specifies a definition of each form of income. The definitions differ from one insurance company to another, and these differences become extremely important for individuals whose income fluctuates widely. Some contracts may specify predisability income as the average monthly income during the 6 months immediately preceding the onset of disability; others may specify predisability income as the greater of the average monthly income during the 12 months preceding the onset of disability or the highest 12 months of consecutive earnings during the 3 years preceding the onset of disability. There are many variations, but the important concept here is that persons subject to income fluctuation should insist on a definition allowing the *greater* of two different base periods so that they are not unduly penalized as a result of a single base period applied during a slump in income. Most of the definitions either explicitly or implicitly include not only income earned from work activities but also pension or profit-sharing contributions made on behalf of the individual.

The income received during residual disability that is used to calculate the income loss is usually defined to include all money received during the period being evaluated even if the money represents payment for services rendered prior to the disability. However, a few insurance company definitions exclude payments made for services rendered prior to the disability.

Example: Barbara Graves had a $66,000 annual predisability income and a policy providing $3,500 per month for total disability. She was able to return to work following a total disability and is earning $2,500 per month during the current period of residual disability. Subtracting $2,500 in residual earnings from the predisability income of $5,500 per month results in a lost income of $3,000 per month. The lost-income ratio ($3,000 ÷ $5,500) is then multiplied by the stated monthly benefit for total disability ($3,500) to determine her residual-disability benefit of $1,909 (rounded to the nearest dollar). Most residual-disability benefits cease whenever the income loss drops below 20 percent of the predisability income. If this were the case, residual benefits would cease when Barbara's monthly income exceeds $4,400.

A clause common within residual-disability-benefit provisions specifies that the minimum benefit payable for residual-disability periods is at least 50 percent of that payable for total disability. At least one insurance company provides 100 percent of the total-disability benefit during residual disability if the lost income exceeds 75 percent of the predisability income. Under most policies, residual-disability benefits are payable to the end of the benefit period, but some policies impose an 18- or 24-month limitation on residual benefits for partial disabilities beginning after a specified age such as 54.

Ability to Keep the Coverage in Force

Top-quality contracts are at least guaranteed renewable to some specified age, such as 65, or even for the insured's lifetime; better still are noncancelable contracts. Guaranteed renewable means that the policyowner has the right to continue the coverage in force by paying the premium due. The premium itself may be increased on a class basis for all guaranteed-renewable policies in the classification, but the premium cannot be increased on an individual basis. The important point is that the insurance company does not have the option to refuse renewal of these contracts before the end of the guaranteed-renewal period. Noncancelable disability contracts guarantee that the policyowner can keep the policy in force by paying the premium and that the premium will not increase beyond the scheduled amount specified in the policy.

Cancelable disability insurance contracts have less generous renewability provisions than guaranteed-renewable or noncancelable ones. These cancelable policies offer very questionable protection for the insured because the insurance company is allowed to refuse renewal of the contract in some circumstances or to increase the premium.

When Benefits Start

Disability income policies generally have an elimination period before benefit payments begin. Most insurance companies give the purchaser an option to select the duration of this period. Since benefits are paid on a monthly basis at the end of the month, the first benefit payment is made 30 days after the end of the elimination period. Common elimination periods are 30, 60, 90, and 120 days. A few policies are available with a zero-day elimination period but only for disability due to accident; the premium increase to get rid of the elimination period is significant, because benefits are payable for many short-term disabilities.

Many factors should be considered when selecting the elimination period for a disability income policy. The ability of the insured to pay living costs and other expenses during the elimination period is of utmost importance. Another pertinent factor is whether or not the insured has other sources of funds available during short-term disabilities.

Insurance companies differ as to whether they require the elimination period to be satisfied with consecutive days or allow the accumulation of nonconsecutive disability days to satisfy the elimination period. Some policies explicitly spell out that the elimination period can be satisfied with nonconsecutive days. In other policies, the language is silent on this point, and the company's claims-handling philosophy determines the answer.

Residual-disability benefits provided in many policies have what is commonly known as a qualification period, which specifies the number of days of total disability that must be sustained before residual-disability benefits are payable. The most generous residual-disability policies have a zero-day qualification period and therefore require no total-disability period prior to eligibility for residual- or partial-disability benefit. Under that type of contract, residual benefits could begin at the end of the elimination period to replace lost income such as the income lost by a surgeon suffering from severe arthritis. A policy that has residual benefits with a qualifying period equal to the elimination period could also start paying residual benefits at the end of the elimination period if the individual had been totally disabled for the entire elimination period and recovered enough to return to work with a reduced income immediately after the end of the elimination period. It is quite common for the qualification period associated with residual benefits to actually exceed the elimination period, but there is not necessarily a connection between the elimination period and the qualification period.

Recurring Disability

Most disability policies have provisions setting forth a specified period of recovery (usually measured by return to work) that automatically separates one disability from another. For example, suppose an individual became disabled as a result of an automobile accident and was totally disabled for 6 months. The individual then returned to work for 8 months before having a relapse and becoming totally disabled again from causes associated with the automobile accident. The new disability is treated as a separate disability because the recovery and return to work exceeded 6 months, which is the specified period separating recurring disabilities in most disability income policies. If the return to work lasted fewer than 6 months, the second period of disability would be treated as a continuation of the initial disability, and no new elimination period would be applicable.

For disability policies with a limited benefit period, it can be advantageous to have each relapse classified as a new disability, which then starts with a full benefit period.

Duration of Benefit Period

Just as disability income policies differ according to definitions of disability and length of elimination period, they also differ according to the duration of benefits that they provide once the individual becomes disabled. Disability contracts often provide choices such as 2 years, 3 years, 5 years, to age 65, or even for the insured's lifetime. Some disability coverages are automatically renewable to age 65 and conditionally renewable to age 70 or 75 if the individual continues to work at his or her occupation. Obviously, the longer the potential benefit period, the higher the premium necessary to support such benefits.

Most companies do not differentiate between disabilities caused by injury and disabilities caused by illness. However, some policies do make such a differentiation. It is not uncommon for these policies to provide lifetime benefits if the disability results from injury but to limit benefits to age 65 if the disability stems from illness. Other companies offer a total range of options or the selection of the maximum benefit period for both injury and illness. For example, an individual could select injury to age 65 and illness to age 65, injury for the insured's lifetime and illness to 65, or the maximum of lifetime for both injury and illness. Companies that differentiate between injury and illness as a source of disability do not usually allow the maximum benefit period for illness to exceed the maximum benefit period for injury.

Policies with short benefit durations do not provide comprehensive protection against disability, but their main appeal is the premium savings associated with the relatively short maximum benefit period. The premium for a 2-year benefit period can be as low as 40 to 50 percent of the premium required to extend benefits to age 65.

In recent years, the predominant maximum benefit period for disability income policies is to age 65. Such coverage ensures a source of replacement income until the normal retirement age for most individuals. The availability of Medicare, Social Security, pensions, and other benefits makes it less important to rely on disability income benefits beyond age 65.

Even those policies purporting to provide lifetime benefits for disability include limitations on disabilities occurring after specified ages such as 50, 55, or 60. Disabilities with their first onset after the specified age are often limited to benefit periods of 2 or 5 years or may terminate at a specified age such as 65, 68, or 70. In other words, lifetime benefit payments are only available for disabilities that initially occurred before the specified age limitation and remained continuous and uninterrupted for the remainder of the insured's life.

Policies with long benefit durations are being issued to high-income individuals for significant amounts of coverage such as $10,000 to $20,000 in benefits per month. These policies present a potential liability of millions of dollars to the insurance company. With such potential liabilities, it is understandable that insurance companies are more restrictive in writing these policies than they are in writing policies of short benefit duration. Fewer occupations qualify for policies with long benefit durations than for policies of short benefit durations. Policies with long benefit durations are rarely available to any occupation that involves physical labor or direct involvement in dangerous processes.

Disability benefits continue for as long as the insured individual is disabled according to the contract provisions. Insurance companies often require repeated verification that the disability still satisfies the qualifications for benefit eligibility. Benefits for total disability cease when the individual has recovered enough that the disability no longer satisfies the criteria of total disability. In policies providing residual benefits, benefit payments may continue at a reduced amount when the individual has recovered enough to return to work but still sustains more than a 20 percent reduction in income.

Level of Benefits Payable

Disability income policies specify the amount of monthly benefits payable during periods of total disability after the elimination period has been satisfied. At the time of policy issuance, the stated monthly benefit amount should be in line with the insured's income and provide fairly complete protection. However, over time, the stated benefit amount is likely to become inadequate as the insured's income increases because of both inflation and job promotions. Disability income policies are available with provisions to counteract such erosion in benefit levels. These provisions fall into two different categories. The first category consists of provisions that provide increases in the benefit payments during periods of disability when benefits are being distributed. The second consists of provisions aimed at increasing the benefit level while the coverage is in force but the insured is not disabled.

Cost-of-Living (COLA) Riders

Provisions dealing with increasing benefits during periods of disability are often referred to as either *cost-of-living-adjustment (COLA) riders* or inflation-protection provisions. They tend to provide either a fixed-percentage increase per year or a floating-percentage increase where the floating amount is determined by some external index such as a consumer price index. These benefits are almost always provided as an optional rider for an additional premium over and above the base policy. Many companies that do provide COLA riders offer purchasers a choice about the percentage increase ceilings on the rider, with increases of up to 7 percent often allowed. However, the higher the percentage, the higher the cost of the rider.

In addition to these annual increase limitations, COLA riders usually contain an aggregate limit on benefit increases such as two times the original monthly benefit amount. For example, an insured may purchase a fixed 5 percent COLA rider to a policy originally providing $2,000 per month in benefits and may subsequently become disabled for a continuous period of 20 years. After the individual has been disabled for one year, the benefit amount increases to $2,100 per month, reflecting the 5 percent increase. After 2 years, the benefit increases to $2,205 if the increases are based on a compound-interest adjustment, or to $2,200 if the increases are based on a simple-interest adjustment. If the COLA rider contains an aggregate limit of twice the original benefit amount, no additional increases are allowed once the benefit amount reaches $4,000.

Increased Predisability Benefits

There are basically three approaches to keeping disability income benefits in step with increased income for insured individuals who are not disabled. The oldest and least attractive method is to purchase new policies to supplement the in-force policies incrementally as income increases. The drawback to this approach is that it requires evidence of insurability every time incremental amounts of coverage are obtained. If the individual's health deteriorates, additional coverage may not be available at any price.

The second approach to adjusting disability benefit levels is through a rider that guarantees the right to purchase additional coverage at specified future intervals up to some specified maximum age such as 45, 50, or 55. This approach is similar to the first one in that additional coverage must be purchased every time an adjustment is needed, but the additional amounts can be acquired at the specified intervals regardless of the health of the insured. However, these incremental purchases are subject to underwriting requirements regarding the individual's current income. In other words, the insurance company will not issue new coverage if the incremental addition would increase aggregate disability income benefits above the underwriting guidelines for that individual's current income on the option date.

The third and most attractive way to adjust benefits upward for inflation while the insured is not disabled is to use riders that automatically increase the base benefit amount on a formula basis such as a stated flat-percentage amount at each policy anniversary. Even this approach requires purchasing additional coverage, and the premium will be increased appropriately. As with the second approach, the additional increment of coverage is purchased at premium rates based on the insured's attained age at the time it is added to the policy. The real advantage to this approach is that the changes are automatic unless they are refused by the policyowner.

Ways of Keeping Up with Inflation Before Becoming Disabled

- Purchase new policies periodically (requires evidence of insurability)
- Purchase a guaranteed insurability (guaranteed purchase) option
- Purchase a rider that automatically increases the benefit amount periodically

---

Insurance companies are not required to provide any inflation adjustments, and some insurance companies selling disability income policies choose not to make such riders available. Insurance companies that offer both options—purchasing additional coverage in the future and automatic percentage increases in benefits—limit future incremental additions and make sure that they are in line with the earnings of the insured. Such companies often refuse to issue the options if the insured has another policy that already contains such riders or if the base policy was issued on an extra-premium basis due to health problems.

Premium Payments

Premiums for disability income policies are similar to life insurance policy premiums in that they are based on the policyowner's age at the time of policy issuance and remain level for the duration of the coverage. Consequently, an individual can lock in lower premiums by buying a policy at a younger age and keeping it in force.

Premiums can be paid on an annual, semiannual, quarterly, or monthly basis and can be set up on a payroll-deduction basis or an automatic bank draft plan. Premiums must be paid on a timely basis to keep the coverage in force, but the policies do contain a 31-day grace period for late premium payments. Most insurance companies also allow lapsed policies to be reinstated automatically if the premium is paid within 15 days after the end of the grace period.

Most disability income policies automatically include the waiver-of-premium provision. Some companies waive premiums after 90 days of disability, while other companies waive premiums after 60 days of disability. The shorter the elimination period, the higher the premium for the waiver-of-premium provision if it is charged separately. Disability policies differ as to whether the waiver of premium requires consecutive days or allows aggregate nonconsecutive days from short disability periods to satisfy the elimination period.

Some policies waive only future premiums after the waiver-of-premium elimination period has been satisfied; other policies retroactively waive prior premium payments made after the onset of disability but before the waiver-of-premium eligibility requirements have been met. Once the insured individual recovers and no additional disability benefits are payable, premiums will no longer be waived and premium payments must be resumed. Premium waivers generally do not continue beyond age 65 even in policies providing lifetime benefits.

Return-of-Premium Option

Some insurance companies offer on an optional basis a policy provision that returns some portion of premiums at specified intervals such as 5 years or 10 years. For example, one company has an option that returns 60 percent of premiums paid at the end of each 5-year interval if no claims have been made during that period. This particular option can increase premiums by more than 40 percent over the base premium level. Other companies offer variations in the percentage of premium to be returned, such as 70 percent or 80 percent of the premiums paid, and in the duration of the interval over which the coverage must be without claims in order to collect the return of premium.

Rehabilitation Benefits

rehabilitation benefit

Higher-quality disability income policies may include some type of *rehabilitation benefits*, although many insurance policies do not. The policies that do include rehabilitation benefits tend to require the insurance company's prior approval of the rehabilitative program in writing. Some companies limit the amount of rehabilitation benefits to 24 or 36 times the monthly total-disability benefit payable. Receiving rehabilitation benefits generally does not disqualify the individual from collecting total-disability benefits. In other words, the better policies pay the full total-disability benefit and at the same time pay additional rehabilitation expenses over and above the monthly benefit payments. Policy provisions often require rehabilitation programs to be provided by accredited educational institutions, state or local governments, or otherwise licensed and recognized providers of sanctioned rehabilitation training.

Presumptive Disability

presumptive-disability provision

Many disability income policies include provisions setting forth specific losses that qualify for permanent total-disability status. They are referred to as *presumptive-disability provisions* because the individual is presumed to be totally disabled even if he or she is able to return to work or gain employment in a new occupation.

Presumptive-disability provisions generally include loss of sight, loss of speech, loss of hearing, or the total loss of use of or the severance of both hands, both feet, or one hand and one foot. As with other disability coverages, the presumptive-disability benefits cease if the insured individual recovers to an extent that he or she no longer qualifies for the presumptive disability. For example, an individual may lose the use of both hands because of paralysis from a stroke or other causes. If the individual gradually recovers use of one or both of the hands, he or she no longer qualifies for presumptive-disability benefits.

Presumptive-disability provisions differ as to whether the benefits are paid as of the first day presumptive-disability requirements have been met or if the regular elimination period still applies.

Incontestability

The laws of all states require that disability income policies contain incontestability provisions. Generally, the incontestable clause specifies that the policy will remain contestable for 2 years after the date of issue during the lifetime of the individual insured. Some insurance companies, however, include a provision that extends the contestable period for any disabilities occurring during the first 2 years of coverage. Under such a policy, if an individual were disabled for 13 months out of the first 2 years of the policy, the policy would not count the 13 months toward satisfying the 24-month period. This type of extension provision is not found in the better disability income policies available in the marketplace.

Treatment of Organ Donations

Disability income policies differ as to how they treat disabilities intentionally induced by the insured for the purpose of donating vital organs or tissue to other human beings. The most generous policies provide the same disability benefits for such operations as for any other covered disability. The normal elimination period is applicable, and then the appropriate level of benefits is provided. Policies containing this coverage usually require that the policy be in force for a minimum of 6 or 12 months before benefits become payable for such purposes.

Social Security Rider

Social Security rider

Many insurance companies offer an optional provision in the form of a *Social Security rider* that requires a separate extra premium to cover additional benefits payable when the individual is disabled under the base policy but does not qualify for Social Security disability benefits. The supplemental benefit is paid over and above the base disability benefit of the underlying policy. When claiming benefits under this option, the insured is generally required to apply for the Social Security or other social insurance benefits, then supply the insurance company with evidence that the benefits have been denied by the Social Security Administration or other governmental agency (which often use a more stringent definition of disability than the insurance company). Some policies also require that the insured must appeal the government's benefit denial before benefits will be paid under this rider. Under most of these riders, the benefit payments are not retroactive, and the first benefit payment is not dispensed until the insurance company has accepted the denial of government benefits. Therefore, in most cases, the first benefit payment will be 13 or more months after the onset of disability.

The reason for this type of rider is that underwriting guidelines limit the amount of coverage that an individual can purchase to avoid overinsurance. In setting these guidelines, the insurance companies usually take into consideration the level of benefits that might be payable under Social Security for disability purposes. The maximum benefit available in the base policy can be supplemented under this rider so that total benefits collected from the insurance company are essentially the same as would have been collected if the individual qualified for Social Security disability benefits.

Benefits under the Social Security rider terminate for any period that the insured does receive benefits from Social Security or other governmental units specified in the contract. Benefits also terminate at age 65 even if the individual continues to be totally disabled. Election to take early retirement benefits under Social Security also terminates benefits.

Hospitalization Benefits

For an additional premium, some disability income policies provide the option of adding supplemental income benefits for periods of hospitalization.

These additional benefits are made available because the insured's need for income can rise during a period of hospitalization due to deductibles, coinsurance provisions, exclusions, and other benefit limitations in medical expense coverage. The benefit payable is for a stated dollar amount, which under some policies begins with the first day of hospitalization and under other policies is subject to an elimination period that may or may not be the same as that for total-disability benefits. These riders generally contain a limitation on the duration of benefits for any single hospitalization.

Some contracts provide no elimination period at all, and hospitalization benefits are payable from the first day of hospitalization regardless of the length of the elimination period for total-disability benefits. Other contracts have a specified elimination period applicable to the hospitalization rider, which is often the same duration as the elimination period applicable to total-disability benefits, but it may differ.

Dividends

Many insurance companies issuing disability income policies provide participating contracts that pay policyowner dividends. In most cases, little or no dividends are paid during the first 2 years of coverage, while under some policies no dividends are paid during the first 3 years of coverage. The level of dividends payable is a function of the company's profitability on its disability income policies and thus subject to fluctuation. In general, dividends do increase with policy duration. As with dividends in life insurance policies, however, dividends cannot be guaranteed. Any dividend illustration is merely an extrapolation of past experience adjusted for expectations of future results.

Many disability income policies are issued on a nonparticipating basis and pay no policyowner dividends. Purchasers of these policies know the full cost in advance because there is no future reduction in cost through dividends.

Insurance Company Limitations on the Amount of Coverage

Insurance company statistics have shown that the higher the percentage of a person's predisability income that is replaced by disability income benefits, the higher the likelihood that claims experience will exceed claims expected. In other words, high levels of disability benefits tend to stimulate higher aggregate claims. This is especially true if the benefits exceed the cash income available prior to disability. There have been a surprising number of fraudulent claims in disability income insurance where the insured intentionally maimed himself or herself with the express intent of ceasing work and collecting disability income benefits. Some of the more notorious cases have involved medical practitioners who injected painkillers before severing fingers or other extremities of the body. In cases where fraud was detected, the individuals were unable to collect disability income benefits even though they were permanently disabled.

Minimizing Fraudulent Claims

To minimize the motivation for fraudulent claims as well as padding of legitimate claims by malingering, insurance companies limit the amount of coverage they will issue to any individual in relation to that individual's income. Generally speaking, disability income coverage is not available for benefit amounts that exceed 60 or 66 2/3 percent of the individual's gross earned income. In fact, as the level of income increases, the percentage of income replacement that insurance companies will issue decreases. High-income professionals are often limited to less than 50 percent of their income level in setting the maximum benefit level for their disability policies.

Some experts advise that, for individuals providing full disclosure to the insurance company, the appropriate amount of disability income protection to purchase is the maximum amount available from an insurance company that provides quality coverage. Insurance companies will want to know about existing sources of disability protection such as sick-leave plans and group insurance policies through employers, professional associations, or affinity groups. The financial underwriting aspect of disability income policy issuance is just as important as the medical evaluation.

Business owners having financial difficulties and facing bankruptcy present a high risk of adverse selection. A high stress level increases the likelihood of a stroke, heart attack, or other stress-related disability. Stressed individuals with a history of high blood pressure or heart problems present an even higher risk.

The underwriting process for disability income insurance is much more complex than that for life insurance. Although the underwriting for life insurance and for disability insurance coverages has many similarities, disability coverages entail more refined classifications and, therefore, a more involved evaluation process. The evaluation process is more complicated because disability can be, and often is, a recurrent condition throughout an individual's lifetime. For example, an individual with a bad back may require repeated hospitalization and rehabilitation therapy even though he or she may have a long life. Joint problems associated with knees and elbows often start with injuries at a young age and get progressively worse with wear and the onset of arthritis.

The job of underwriting for disability insurance is to correctly classify individuals as to how costly their medical maintenance will be over their lifetime. The individual must be classified appropriately on the basis of existing information so that the premium for that individual and similar individuals adequately covers the cost of claims for that group over the duration of their coverage.

Modifying the Standard Issue

Depending on the insurer, 25 percent to 40 percent of issued policies may require some sort of modification or adjustment from the standard issue. As in life insurance, disability premiums can be increased for individuals presenting a higher level of risk to the insurance company. Another modification in disability insurance is to insist on a longer elimination period for some high-risk insureds, which eliminates more of the short-term problems and disabilities. In some cases, a longer elimination period may be applicable to specified causes or conditions, or the insurance company may insist on a relatively long elimination period that applies to all causes of disability. Such an approach does not preclude coverage for a particular condition, but it limits claim payments to the longer durations. The most limiting modification is an outright exclusion of any benefits associated with disabilities stemming from specified causes or conditions. Although this approach may seem drastic, it at least allows individuals to obtain disability coverage for causes other than the major problem that is preventing them from getting full disability protection.

The disability underwriting process commonly includes one or more requests from the home office for additional information. Although this does delay the issuance of coverage, it does not necessarily indicate that the coverage will not be issued. Disability insurers use many resources in an attempt to accept and insure all applicants who fall within their acceptable risk classifications. Obviously, some risks will not meet the minimum company standards and will be rejected outright. Individual applicants who are rejected by one company may not necessarily be uninsurable; another company may classify risks in a different manner and apply different cutoff standards. Individuals who experience difficulty in obtaining disability insurance should shop for coverage from other insurers on a sequential basis and should not apply for coverage with many insurers concurrently. Certain brokers who specialize in substandard insurance can be helpful in obtaining disability coverage for individuals with serious health problems.

Policy Exclusions

A few exclusions typically appear in disability income policies. Disabilities resulting from war or any sort of military service are nearly always excluded from coverage by a specific policy exclusion provision. This provision often defines war to include declared wars, undeclared wars, and any acts of war. Exclusions also preclude benefit payments for any sickness or injury sustained during military service because they are usually covered by military or veterans' benefits. Some policies exclude benefits for disabilities resulting from a normal pregnancy and disabilities resulting from travel in aircraft if the insured has duties relating to the plane's flight or maintenance.

The total exclusion provision in disability policies is usually rather short. Longer exclusion clauses often indicate that the coverage may be less generous than that provided by premier-quality policies.

Conversion to Long-term Care Coverage

A few insurers allow the insured to convert a disability income policy to a long-term care policy when the insured is no longer working or when the policy duration has reached a point that disability income benefits are no longer available (such as age 65). Such provisions are in the early stages of development and may or may not become more common as the sales of separate long-term care policies (discussed in chapter 15) increase.

The conversion does not require evidence of insurability, and the amount of benefits available is often based on what can be purchased with the same premium that had been paid for the disability income coverage. As a general rule, benefits are more limited than those found in most separate long-term care policies. For example, benefits may be paid only if the insured is confined to a nursing home, whereas many long-term care policies cover other settings for care, including the home.

Federal Income Taxation

Premiums paid by a person for individually owned disability income insurance are not deductible for federal income tax purposes; benefits received are tax free.

BUSINESS USES OF DISABILITY INSURANCE

The disability of business owners or key employees poses a serious risk to a business's financial health. Just as a family suffers from the loss of the income of its breadwinners, a business suffers from the loss of its productive resources. The problems are particularly acute for small enterprises in which the workforce may not be large enough to have a backup for critical tasks that could be interrupted because of disabilities. Good examples of business owners in need of disability insurance are self-employed attorneys, accountants, physicians, and dentists who operate solo practices and employ a support staff of one or more persons. When these business owners become totally disabled, the primary business activities are often halted. However, it is necessary to maintain the business premises and at least a skeletal support staff so that business can be resumed when the business owner recovers from the disability. For example, accounts receivable must still be collected, and ongoing expenses must still be paid.

Business Overhead Expense Insurance

Business overhead expense policies are available to cover many of the ongoing costs of operating a business while the business owner is totally disabled. These policies tend to be limited to benefit durations of one or 2 years and have relatively short elimination periods. The intent is to keep the necessary staff and premises available for the resumption of business if the business owner recovers from the disability.

Insurance companies are extremely cautious in writing this coverage and in keeping the benefit amount in line with established stable costs for previous periods. Consequently, the application for such coverage must be accompanied by supporting financial statements to verify the stability of the business and to establish the appropriate level of insurable expenses. These expenses include such things as salaries for secretaries, nurses, and other staff necessary to resume business upon the business owner's recovery as well as the ongoing expenses for rent, utilities, taxes, accounting services, and so forth. Actual expenses are reimbursed at time of disability up to a maximum monthly indemnity selected at the time of policy issue.

Key Person Insurance

Business entities are dependent on their personnel to carry out their activities and generate revenues and profits. Very often the unique talents and experiences of a few key individuals are crucial to the success of the business entity. The loss of an individual's contributions by reason of disability or death could deal a devastating blow to the financial well-being of the enterprise. In fact, sometimes the dependence is so critical that losing the individual's participation could lead to the bankruptcy or termination of the business. This is particularly true of professionals operating as sole practitioners.

Many business enterprises have recognized the importance of key individuals who make the most critical contributions and have obtained disability income insurance covering these key individuals. Benefits from key employee disability policies are payable to the business entity when the insured key employee is disabled. The justification for such coverage is very similar to that for key person life insurance policies. Proceeds from key person disability policies can be used to replace lost revenue directly attributable to the key person's disability, to fund the search for individuals to replace the insured person, to fund the extra cost of hiring specialized individuals to replace the multiple talents of the insured, and to fund training costs that may be incurred to prepare replacements to carry out the duties the insured performed. The costs of training, hiring, and compensating are usually rather easy to ascertain, whereas estimating lost revenue is a very difficult and complex task. These policies are not designed to provide continuance of salary for the key employee.

Even though a business entity may determine a desired amount of disability income protection for each key individual, it may not be able to obtain that amount of coverage. The underwriting processes of insurance companies limit the maximum amount of coverage available on any one individual. A wide range of guidelines is utilized for setting these limitations, and getting an insurer to waive any of these limitations is usually difficult. Sometimes a business entity is able to make a strong enough argument on both financial and economic grounds to justify an exception and obtain the desired amount even though it exceeds underwriting guideline limitations.

Premiums for a business-owned disability income policy are not deductible for federal income tax purposes if benefits are paid to the business; the receipt of these proceeds by the business is free of any federal income tax liability. Payment of those premiums does not create any taxable income for the insured employee.

Salary Continuation for Owners and Key Employees

Individual disability income policies can be purchased by the business entity to fund formal plans to continue salary for disabled owner or key employees. Formal plans can be set up in two different ways. The corporation can own the policy and be the beneficiary under the policy, or the corporation can pay the premiums on a policy owned by the employee to whom benefits will be paid. When the corporation is both the owner and the beneficiary of the policy, premium payments are nondeductible by the corporation and the corporation receives the insurance proceeds free of any federal income tax liability. Premium payments for such coverage are not considered taxable income to the employee.

When the corporation merely pays the premiums on a policy owned by the employee, the premiums are deductible expenses of the corporation as long as they meet reasonable expense criteria. The premium payments are not considered taxable income to the employee; however, benefits paid under the policy are taxable income to the employee.

In some informal plans to continue salary, the corporation pays a large enough bonus to the employee for the employee to buy an individual disability income policy. If the bonus payments are reasonable compensation, they are deductible by the corporation. The bonus is taxable income to the employee. The premium payments made by the employee are not deductible. Any benefit payments received by the employee has no effect on the corporation and is received free of any federal income tax liability by the employee.

Disability Buy-Sell Funding

A business owner's disability often threatens the viability of that enterprise. Preserving the value of the business often necessitates shifting the business owner's ownership interest to one or more other individuals who can continue conducting the affairs of the business. In cases that involve multiple ownership of the business, the most likely parties to purchase the ownership interest of a disabled owner are the nondisabled co-owners. Unfortunately, few business owners have adequate amounts of liquid assets to make an outright purchase of the ownership interest from the disabled co-owner.

Just as buy-sell agreements triggered by the death of an owner can be funded with life insurance, buy-sell agreements triggered by the disability of an owner can be funded with disability insurance. Special disability policies have been designed specifically for the purpose of funding buy-sell agreements. These policies can fund either an installment purchase or a lump-sum buyout.

The types of buy-sell arrangements are similar to those discussed earlier in this book for situations arising from death. However, some extra care is necessary. The definition used in the disability policy should be the same definition as that specified in the buy-sell agreement. The elimination period for a buy-sell policy is typically one year or longer in order to avoid triggering the buyout for disabilities that last less than one year. Most buy-sell policies pay the benefit in one lump sum.

Although a discussion is beyond the scope of this book, readers should also be aware that different approaches to buy-sell agreements can have significantly different tax implications.

CHECKLIST FOR EVALUATING AND COMPARING DISABILITY INCOME POLICIES

☐   What is the definition of total disability? If the definition of total disability is a two-step definition, how many years apply to own occupation?

☐   What are the amount and frequency of total disability benefits?

☐ What elimination period applies to total disability benefits?

☐ What is the duration of total disability benefits?

☐ Are partial disability benefits covered? If yes,

___ What is the definition of partial disability?
___ What period of total disability is required before benefits are payable?

☐ Are residual disability benefits covered? If yes,

___ What is the benefit amount?
___ How long are they payable?
___ Is a prior period of total disability required?

☐ What is the annual policy premium?

☐ Is there a presumptive disability provision?

☐ Is there coverage for disabilities arising from organ donations?

☐ What cost-of-living increases are available for benefits being paid and coverage in force, and what is the basis on which such increases are made?

☐ Does the policy contain any modifications from standard issue?

☐ What is the renewability provision?

☐ What is the waiver-of-premiums provision?

☐ Is there a return-of-premium option?

☐ What are the rehabilitation benefits?

☐ Does the policy contain riders? If yes,

___ What do they cover?
___ Is there an additional premium for their use?

SOURCES FOR FURTHER IN-DEPTH STUDY

- Sadler, Jeff, *Disability Income: The Sale, the Product, the Market,* 2d ed., Cincinnati, OH: The National Underwriter Company, 1995. Phone 800-543-0874. Web site address www.nuco.com
- Soule, Charles E., *Disability Income Insurance: The Unique Risk,* 5th ed., Bryn Mawr, PA: The American College, 2002. Phone 888-263-7265. Web site address www.amercoll.edu

CHAPTER REVIEW

Answers to review questions and self-test questions start on page 725.

Key Terms

short-term disability income plan	any-occupation
long-term disability income insurance	partial disability
	residual-disability benefits
sick-leave plan	cost-of-living-adjustment (COLA) rider
own-occupation	
waiting period	rehabilitation benefit
buy-up plan	presumptive-disability provision
carve-out (benefit plan)	Social Security rider

Review Questions

14-1.   Describe the need for disability insurance coverage.

14-2.   What are the sources of coverage that may protect your client against financial trouble in case of disability?

14-3.   What is the nature of sick-leave plans?

14-4.   What are the typical eligibility requirements in an insured group disability income plan?

14-5.   Explain how the definition of total disability in group long-term contracts may differ from that found in group short-term contracts.

14-6.   What types of exclusions can be found in group disability income contracts?

14-7.   What types of benefit schedules are found in group disability income plans?

14-8.   Explain how group disability income benefits are coordinated with other benefits.

14-9.   Describe the following additional benefits occasionally found under group long-term disability income contracts:
a.   cost-of-living (COLA) riders
b.   pension supplements
c.   survivors' benefits

14-10.   Describe what the income tax consequences are for each of the following clients who receive disability income benefits from an employer plan:
a.   Kevin receives disability benefits under a fully contributory plan.
b.   Patty receives disability benefits under a noncontributory plan.
c.   Julie receives disability benefits under a partially contributory plan.

14-11.   Describe residual-disability benefits, and explain how they are calculated.

14-12.   What advice might a planner give a client regarding each of the following aspects of individual disability income insurance policies?
a.   ability to keep the coverage in force
b.   when benefits start
c.   recurring disabilities
d.   duration of benefit period
e.   level of benefits payable
f.   premium payments

14-13.   Describe the three approaches used to keep individual disability income policy benefits in step with an increasing income for individuals who are not disabled.

14-14.   Describe how the return-of-premium option works.

14-15.   Explain why it may be a good idea to add a Social Security rider to an individual disability income policy.

14-16.   What are insurance company limits on the amount of coverage that can be provided under an individual income disability policy?

14-17.   Explain how individual disability income policies can be used by business for
a.   paying business overhead expenses
b.   key person protection
c.   salary continuation for owners and key employees
d.   disability buy-sell funding

Self-Test Questions

T   F   14-1.   At all working ages, the probability of being disabled for at least 90 consecutive days is much greater than the chance of dying.

T   F   14-2.   The definition of disability under the Social Security program is less restrictive than that found in most individual or group disability income contracts.

T   F   14-3.   Employer-provided short-term disability income plans typically provide benefits for a limited period of time such as 6 months or less.

T   F   14-4.   It is generally possible to provide disability income protection for up to 100 percent or more of a client's income by purchasing a supplemental policy to coordinate with his or her group long-term policy.

T   F   14-5.   Most employers do not provide long-term disability income coverage for their employees.

T   F   14-6.   Sick-leave plans generally replace all lost income for a limited period of time starting on the first day of disability.

T   F   14-7.   Most sick-leave plans are open to part-time employees.

T   F   14-8.   Most sick-leave plans are coordinated with social insurance programs.

T   F   14-9.   Long-term disability plans often limit benefits to salaried employees because claims experience has traditionally been less favorable for hourly paid employees.

T   F   14-10.   Short-term disability income contracts typically limit coverage to occupational disabilities.

T   F   14-11.   Group disability income contracts typically specify that no benefits will be paid unless the employee is under the care of a physician.

T   F   14-12.   Most group disability income contracts exclude disabilities that result from pregnancy.

T   F   14-13.   Group long-term disability income contracts cannot exclude benefits based on preexisting conditions.

T   F   14-14.   Group short-term disability income contracts generally have 30-day waiting periods.

T   F   14-15.   Group long-term disability income contracts typically require disabled employees who return to work to complete a new waiting period before any benefits can be reinstated if they subsequently decide they are unable to keep working.

T   F   14-16.   Group long-term disability income plans do not provide for any cost-of-living adjustments (COLAs) since they might eventually increase a disabled employee's income to over 100 percent of salary, thus facilitating a moral hazard.

T F 14-17. Planners should advise their clients to buy an any-occupation individual disability income policy because they are very liberal in defining disability.

T F 14-18. Residual-disability benefits focus on how much income reduction has been sustained as a result of the disability rather than on the physical dimensions of the disability itself.

T F 14-19. Planners should advise clients to consider individual disability income contracts that are at least guaranteed renewable to some specified age, such as 65, or even for the insured's lifetime.

T F 14-20. The premium for an individual disability income policy with a 2-year benefit period can be as low as 40 to 50 percent of the premium required to extend the benefits to age 65.

T F 14-21. Insurance companies often require repeated verification that an individual's disability still satisfies the qualifications for benefit eligibility.

T F 14-22. The best way to adjust benefits upward for inflation while the insured is not disabled is to purchase new policies to supplement the in-force policies incrementally as the insured's income increases.

T F 14-23. Most individual disability income policies include a waiver-of-premium provision.

T F 14-24. Individual disability income policies cannot have an incontestability provision because of the potential for fraud.

T F 14-25. Benefits under a Social Security rider continue even after the insured elects to start receiving Social Security retirement benefits.

T F 14-26. The underwriting process for individual disability income insurance is much more complex than for individual life insurance.

T F 14-27. Business overhead expense policies are available to cover many of the ongoing costs of operating a business while the business owner is totally disabled.

T F 14-28. Benefits from key employee disability policies are payable to the wife or husband of the disabled key employee.

T F 14-29. Buy-sell agreements triggered by the disability of an owner can be funded with disability policies.

Long-Term Care Insurance

<table>
<tr><td colspan="2">Learning Objectives</td></tr>
<tr><td colspan="2">An understanding of the material in this chapter should enable the student to</td></tr>
<tr><td>15-1.</td><td>Explain the need for and sources of long-term care.</td></tr>
<tr><td>15-2.</td><td>Describe the development of long-term care insurance, including the NAIC model legislation.</td></tr>
<tr><td>15-3.</td><td>Explain the effect of the Health Insurance Portability and Accountability Act (HIPAA) on long-term care insurance.</td></tr>
<tr><td>15-4.</td><td>Describe the characteristics of individual long-term care policies.</td></tr>
<tr><td>15-5.</td><td>Describe how group long-term care policies differ from individual policies.</td></tr>
</table>

Chapter Outline

Since the early 1980s, long-term care insurance has evolved from being virtually nonexistent to being an important form of insurance product carried by over 5 million persons. The number of insurers with individual long-term care products has gradually increased to over 100, and the major providers of employee benefits now make group products available. Financial planners need to understand this important new market in order to advise their clients.

During its relatively short life, long-term care coverage has been hailed as a major source of financial security and criticized as a coverage that fails to meet consumers' real long-term care needs. State and federal legislation affecting coverage has also been common. In this environment, long-term care products have continued to evolve, with the frequent introduction of newer and more comprehensive products. Long-term care coverage can probably best be described as having grown from infancy to somewhere between the childhood and teenage years. Coverage will change to meet consumer demands and expectations, and the largely untapped market for coverage will continue to grow as the American population ages.

The first portion of this chapter looks at the need for long-term care. This is followed by a brief description of sources of long-term care other than insurance. The chapter continues with a discussion of how and why insurance policies have evolved into the products now being offered. It then contains an analysis of the more common products in the marketplace today—both individual and group. The chapter concludes with a checklist for evaluating and comparing policies.

NEED FOR LONG-TERM CARE

An Aging Population

Long-term care has traditionally been thought of as a problem primarily for the older population. The population aged 65 or over is the fastest-growing age group; today it represents about 11 percent of the population, a figure that is expected to increase to between 20 percent and 25 percent over the next 50 years. The segment of the population aged 85 and over is growing at an even faster rate. While less than 10 percent of the over-65 group is over 85 today, this percentage is expected to double over the next two generations.

An aging society presents changing problems. Those who needed long-term care in the past were most likely to have suffered from strokes or other acute diseases. With longer life spans today and in the future, a larger portion of the elderly are incapacitated by chronic conditions such as Alzheimer's disease, arthritis, osteoporosis, and lung and heart disease—conditions that often require continuing assistance with day-to-day needs. The likelihood that a person will need to enter a nursing home increases dramatically with age. One percent of persons between the ages of 65 and 74 reside in nursing homes, and the percentage increases to 6 percent between the ages of 75 and 84. At age 85 and over, the figure rises to approximately 25 percent. Statistics of the Department of Health and Human Services indicate that persons aged 65 or older face a 40 percent chance of entering a nursing home at some time during the remainder of their lives. Nearly half of the persons who enter nursing homes remain longer than one year, and the average nursing home stay is about 2-1/2 years.

Nursing home statistics tell only part of the story. An even greater percentage of the elderly have age-related conditions that require varying degrees of assistance to enable them to perform normal daily activities. In some cases, this assistance is provided in other types of supportive-living arrangements such as assisted living facilities and adult foster homes. In many cases, however, the elderly remain in their own homes or the homes of relatives and receive their care from relatives, home health agencies, and community-based programs. The latter programs include meals on wheels and adult day care centers.

It should be noted that the elderly are not the only group of persons who need long-term care. Many younger persons are unable to care for themselves because of handicaps resulting from birth defects, mental conditions, illnesses, or accidents.

Increasing Costs

Almost $100 billion is spent each year on nursing home care, and home health care costs exceed $30 billion. These costs, about 11 percent of national health care expenditures, are increasing faster than inflation because of the growing demand for nursing home beds and the shortage of skilled medical personnel. The cost of complete long-term care for an individual can be astronomical, with annual nursing home costs of $30,000 to $60,000 and more not unusual. Costs of $2,500 or more per month can easily be incurred in part-time home health care. By 2030, the annual cost of nursing home care is expected to approximate $200,000 with comparable increases in home care charges.

Inability of Families to Provide Full Care

Traditionally, family members have provided long-term care, often at considerable personal sacrifice and stress. However, it is becoming more difficult for families to provide long-term care for these reasons:

- geographic dispersion of family members
- increased participation in the paid workforce by women and children
- fewer children in the family
- more childless families
- higher divorce rates
- inability of family members to provide care because they, too, are growing old

Inadequacy of Insurance Protection

Private medical expense insurance policies (both group and individual) almost always have an exclusion for convalescent, custodial, or rest care. Some policies do provide coverage for extended-care facilities and for home health care. In both cases, the purpose is to provide care in a manner that is less expensive than care in a hospital. However, coverage is provided only if a person also needs medical care; benefits are not provided if a person is merely "old" and needs someone to care for him or her.

Medicare is also inadequate because it does not cover custodial care unless this care is needed along with the medical or rehabilitative treatment provided in skilled-nursing facilities or under home health care benefits.

SOURCES OF LONG-TERM CARE

There are several sources other than insurance that are available for financing long-term care; however, there are drawbacks associated with each.

One source is to rely on personal financial resources. Few individuals have sufficient retirement income to fully meet their potential long-term care expenses. Unless a person has substantial assets on which to draw, this approach may force an individual and his or her dependents into poverty. It may also mean that the person will not meet the financial objective of leaving assets to heirs.

An often overlooked source of providing or financing long-term care is relatives, or even friends. In some cases, family members may act as caregivers themselves; in other cases, they may give financial support to provide care or pay for long-term care insurance premiums. The support of relatives, however, may not last forever. For example, a spouse may no longer be able to provide care because of his or her own physical condition. And aging children may not have the financial resources to continue the same level of support because of their own long-term care needs.

Another source is to rely on welfare. The Medicaid program in most states provides benefits, which usually include nursing home care and home health care (and possibly assisted living care), to the "medically needy." However, a person is not eligible unless he or she is either poor or has a low income and has exhausted most other assets (including those of a spouse). There is also often a social stigma associated with accepting welfare. One strategy that is sometimes used is to give a person's assets away at the time nursing home care is needed and ultimately rely on Medicaid. (This will work only if income, including pensions and Social Security, is below specified limits.) However, Medicaid benefits are reduced (or their onset postponed) if assets were disposed of at less than their fair market value

look-back period

within a specific time period (called the *look-back period*) prior to Medicaid eligibility. One approach is to purchase long-term care insurance in an amount sufficient to provide protection for the length of the look-back period. If care is needed, a person can rely on the insurance coverage and transfer assets to heirs. When the insurance coverage runs out and the look-back period is over, the person can apply for Medicaid.

Several states have attempted to encourage better coverage for long-term care by waiving or modifying certain Medicaid requirements if a person carries a state-approved long-term care policy. For example, in Connecticut a person can apply for and receive Medicaid benefits without having to exhaust current assets if the individual has maintained an approved long-term care policy and its benefits have run out. In essence, these programs increase the assets that a person can retain and still collect Medicaid benefits, with the increase in the allowable asset threshold related to the amount of long-term care coverage carried and exhausted.

continuing care retirement community

Continuing-care retirement communities (CCRCs), also referred to as life care facilities, are growing in popularity as a source of meeting long-term care needs. Residents in a CCRC pay an "entrance fee" that allows them to occupy a dwelling unit but usually does not give them actual ownership rights. The entrance fee may or may not be refundable if the resident leaves the facility voluntarily or dies. As a general rule, the higher the refund is, the higher the entrance fee is. Residents pay a monthly fee that includes meals, some housecleaning services, and varying degrees of health care. If a person needs long-term care, he or she must give up the independent living unit and move to the assisted-living or nursing home portion of the CCRC, but the monthly fee normally remains the same.

The disadvantages of this option are that the cost of a CCRC is beyond the reach of many persons, and a resident must be in reasonably good health and able to live independently at the time he or she enters the facility. Therefore, the decision to use a CCRC must be made in advance of the need for long-term care. Once such care is needed or is imminent, this approach is no longer viable.

A few insurers now include long-term care benefits in some cash value life insurance policies. Essentially an insured can begin to use these accelerated benefits while he or she is still living. For example, if the insured is in a nursing home, he or she might be able to elect a benefit equal to 25 percent or 50 percent of the policy face amount. However, any benefits received reduce the future death benefit payable to heirs. One potential problem with this approach is that the acceleration of benefits may result in the reduction of the death benefit to a level that is inadequate to accomplish the purpose of life insurance—the protection of family members after a wage earner's death. If benefits are accelerated, there is less left for the surviving family. In addition, the availability of an accelerated benefit may give the insured a false sense of security that long-term care needs are being met when in fact the potential benefit may be inadequate to cover extended nursing home stays.

Some Ways of Paying for Long-Term Care

- Personal income and assets
- Family support
- Medicaid/welfare programs
- Continuing care retirement communities
- Accelerated benefits in life insurance policies
- Long-term care insurance

---

long-term care insurance

Finally, there is *long-term care insurance*, which is the subject of the remainder of this chapter. It is a form of health insurance that usually provides coverage for custodial care, intermediate care, and skilled-nursing care. Benefits may also be provided for other types of care such as home health care, adult day care, and assisted living.

DEVELOPMENT OF INSURANCE COVERAGE

It is common for insurance coverages to evolve over time. However, the evolution of long-term care products has been dramatic with respect to the magnitude of the changes and the speed with which these changes have occurred.

Early Policies

The long-term care policies in existence in the early 1980s were primarily designed to provide care during the recovery period following an acute illness. They seldom met the needs of persons who required long-term care for chronic conditions. The following provisions were characteristic of many of these policies:

- benefit periods of less than one year
- a prerequisite for benefits in a skilled-nursing facility, often a prior hospitalization of 3 to 5 days
- a prerequisite of a higher level of out-of-hospital care before benefits could be received for a lower level of care. For example, home health care might be covered, but only if a person had spent 3 to 5 days in a skilled-nursing facility.
- the exclusion of benefits for care needed as a result of Alzheimer's disease or other organic brain diseases
- no inflation protection to meet higher long-term care costs in the future
- lack of guaranteed renewability provisions

In addition, the sale of early long-term care policies was often accompanied by improper sales practices. Consumers were led to believe that policies were much more comprehensive than they actually were. In effect, policyowners felt that they were purchasing "nursing home" insurance that would cover them anytime nursing home care was needed. Only when such care was needed did many of these policyowners realize that their coverage was very limited.

Finally, for many years, there was no favorable tax treatment given to long-term care insurance. Premiums for coverage were not deductible, and benefits and employer-paid premiums under group plans resulted in taxation to employees.

Evolution of Coverage

Criticism of the early long-term care policies created considerable pressure for change. Consumer groups argued for more government regulation. The federal government conducted studies and held hearings, with the results painting a less than flattering picture of long-term care policies. Change itself, however, resulted primarily from the actions of insurance companies themselves and from the state regulators of insurance. But the threat of federal regulation was always present. The negative publicity about early policies had a dampening effect on the public's perception of long-term care insurance. This led many insurance companies to modify their policies and companies entering the business to offer more comprehensive policies. At the same time, the National Association of Insurance Commissioners (NAIC) began to take a very active interest in long-term care insurance. This culminated in the adoption of the Long-term Care Insurance Model Act in 1987. In 1988, model regulations were issued to enable the states to implement the model act. The act and the regulations have been amended almost every year since. Sometimes these amendments changed previous act provisions; at other times, new issues were addressed. The majority of states have adopted the model act, which is discussed in more detail later. However, the version in force in a given state is not always the latest NAIC version. A few states still have little regulation of long-term care policies, and other states have adopted legislation different from the model act, although it may be similar to that recommended by the NAIC.

Considerable changes have also taken place at the federal level with passage of the Health Insurance Portability and Accountability Act in 1996. This law, referred to as HIPAA, provides favorable tax treatment to long-term care insurance contracts that meet certain standards. These contracts are referred to as *tax-qualified* policies.

The long-term care policies of most insurance companies have gone through many revisions. While coverage is still not always complete, there is little comparison between the early policies and most of what is marketed today. Not only have policies become more comprehensive over the last few years, but premiums have also tended to drop as more credible statistics about long-term claims have become available. Existing policyowners are often able to obtain the enhancements in newer policies but frequently at an increased premium. Some companies allow the policyowner to add the enhanced benefits by paying the new premium based on the policyowner's original age of issue. Other companies may require evidence of insurability and use attained-age rates.

Most companies that write individual policies now issue only the tax-qualified contracts prescribed by HIPAA. Some companies issue both qualified contracts and *non-tax-qualified* contracts, and a few companies issue only non-tax-qualified contracts. While purchasers of these contracts do not receive the new tax advantages, the contracts often include provisions that make it easier to qualify for benefits.

NAIC MODEL LEGISLATION

Because of its widespread adoption by the states, it is appropriate to discuss the NAIC model legislation regarding long-term care. The legislation consists of a model act that is designed to be incorporated into a state's insurance law and model regulations that are designed to be adopted for use in implementing the law. This discussion is based on the latest version of the model legislation, which, as mentioned earlier, seems to be amended almost annually. Even though most states have adopted the NAIC legislation, some states may not have adopted the latest version. However, the importance of the model legislation should not be overlooked. With most insurers writing coverage in more than one state, it is likely that the latest provisions have been adopted by one or more states where an insurer's coverage is sold. Because most insurance companies sell essentially the same long-term care product everywhere they do business, the NAIC guidelines are often, in effect, being adhered to in states that have not adopted the legislation.

Before proceeding with a summary of the major provisions of the NAIC model legislation, it is important to make two points. First, the model legislation establishes guidelines. Insurance companies still have significant latitude in many aspects of product design. Second, many older policies are still in existence that were written prior to the adoption of the model legislation or under one of its earlier versions.

The model legislation focuses on two major areas—policy provisions and marketing. Highlights of the criteria for policy provisions include the following:

- Many words or terms cannot be used in a policy unless they are specifically defined in accordance with the legislation. Examples include adult day care, home health care services, personal care, and skilled-nursing care.
- No policy can contain renewal provisions other than guaranteed renewable or noncancelable.
- Limitations and exclusions are prohibited except in the following cases:
    - preexisting conditions
    - mental or nervous disorders (but this does not permit the exclusion of Alzheimer's disease)
    - alcoholism and drug addiction
    - illness, treatment, or medical condition arising out of war, participation in a felony, service in the armed forces, suicide, and aviation if a person is a non-fare-paying passenger
    - treatment in a government facility and services available under Medicare and other social insurance programs

- No policy can provide coverage for skilled-nursing care only or provide significantly more coverage for skilled care in a facility than for lower levels of care.
- The definition of preexisting condition can be no more restrictive than to exclude a condition for which treatment was recommended or received within 6 months prior to the effective date of coverage. In addition, coverage can be excluded for a confinement for this condition only if it begins within 6 months of the effective date of coverage.
- Eligibility for benefits cannot be based on a prior hospital requirement or higher level of care.
- Insurance companies must offer the applicant the right to purchase coverage that allows for an increase in the amount of benefits based on reasonable anticipated increases in the cost of services covered by the policy. The applicant must specifically reject this inflation protection if he or she does not want it.
- Insurance companies must offer the applicant the right to purchase a nonforfeiture benefit.
- A policy must contain a provision that makes a policy incontestable after 2 years on the grounds of misrepresentation alone. The policy can still be contested on the basis that the applicant knowingly and intentionally misrepresented relevant facts pertaining to the insured's health.

The following provisions of the model legislation pertain to marketing:

- An outline of coverage must be delivered to a prospective applicant at the time of initial solicitation. Among the information this outline must contain is (1) a description of the coverage, (2) a statement of the principal exclusions, reductions, and limitations in the policy, (3) a statement of the terms under which the policy can be continued in force or terminated, (4) a description of the terms under which the policy may be returned and the premium refunded, (5) a brief description of the relationship of cost of care and benefits, and (6) a statement whether the policy is intended to be tax qualified.
- A shopper's guide must be delivered to all prospective applicants.
- The policy must allow policyowners to have a free 30-day look.
- An insurance company must establish procedures to ensure that any comparisons of policies by its agents or other producers are fair and accurate and to prohibit excessive insurance from being sold or issued.
- Applications for insurance must be clear and unambiguous so that an applicant's health condition can be properly ascertained. The application must also contain a conspicuous statement near the place

for the applicant's signature that says the following: "If your answers to this application are incorrect or untrue, the company has the right to deny benefits or rescind your policy." The purpose of these requirements is to control postclaim underwriting.

- No policy can be issued until the applicant has been given the option of electing a third party to be notified of any pending policy lapse because of nonpayment of premium. The purpose of this provision is to eliminate the problem of policy lapse because a senile or otherwise mentally impaired person fails to pay the premium.

NAIC Model Legislation Concerning Marketing of Long-Term Care Insurance

---

- Prospective purchasers must be given an outline of the coverage, a shopper's guide, and a 30-day free look at the policy.
- Procedures for fair and accurate policy comparisons must be established.
- Applications must be clear and unambiguous.
- Applicants must have option to name a third party to be notified of pending lapse due to nonpayment of premium.
- Applicants must be given the right to purchase inflation protection and nonforfeiture benefits.

EFFECT OF HEALTH INSURANCE PORTABILITY AND ACCOUNTABILITY ACT (HIPAA)

The Health Insurance Portability and Accountability Act (HIPAA) made the tax treatment of long-term care insurance more favorable. However, this favorable tax treatment is given only if long-term care insurance policies meet prescribed standards. It should be emphasized that the long-term care changes in the act are primarily changes in the income tax code. States still have the authority to regulate long-term care insurance contracts.

Eligibility for Favorable Tax Treatment

qualified long-term care insurance contract

The act provides favorable tax treatment to a *qualified long-term care insurance contract*. This is defined as any insurance contract that meets all the following requirements:

- The only insurance protection provided under the contract is for *qualified long-term care services*.

- The contract cannot pay for expenses that are reimbursable under Medicare. However, this requirement does not apply to expenses that are reimbursable if (1) Medicare is a secondary payer of benefits or (2) benefits are payable on a per diem basis.
- The contract must be guaranteed renewable.
- The contract does not provide for a cash surrender value or other money that can be borrowed or paid, assigned, or pledged as collateral for a loan.
- All refunds of premiums and policyowner dividends must be applied as future reductions in premiums or to increase future benefits.
- The policy must comply with various consumer protection provisions. For the most part, these are the same provisions contained in the NAIC model legislation and already adopted by most states.

qualified long-term care services

The act defines *qualified long-term care services* as necessary diagnostic, preventive, therapeutic, curing, treating, and rehabilitative services, and maintenance or personal care services that are required by a chronically ill person and are provided by a plan of care prescribed by a licensed health care practitioner.

chronically ill individual

A *chronically ill individual* is one who has been certified as meeting one of the following requirements, often referred to as benefit triggers:

activities of daily living (ADLs)

- The person is expected to be unable to perform, without substantial assistance from another person, at least two *activities of daily living (ADLs)* for a period of at least 90 days due to a loss of functional capacity. The act allows six ADLs: eating, bathing, dressing, transferring from bed to chair, using the toilet, and maintaining continence. A qualified long-term care insurance contract must contain at least five of the six.
- Substantial supervision is required to protect the individual from threats to health and safety because of severe cognitive impairment.

The act also specifies that any contract issued before January 1, 1997, that met the long-term care requirements in the state where the policy was issued will be considered a tax-qualified long-term care contract. If such a contract undergoes a material change, however, the policy must then conform to the HIPAA requirements to retain this status.

Federal Income Tax Provisions

A qualified long-term care insurance contract, typically referred to as tax qualified, is treated as accident and health insurance. With some exceptions, expenses for long-term care services, including insurance premiums, are treated like other medical expenses. That is, self-employed persons may deduct the premiums paid, and persons who itemize deductions can include the cost of long-term care services, including insurance premiums, for purposes of deducting medical expenses in excess of 7.5 percent of adjusted gross income. However, there is a cap on the amount of personally paid long-term care insurance premiums that can be claimed as medical expenses. These limits, which are based upon a covered individual's age and subject to cost-of-living adjustments, are shown for 2003 in table 15-1. Deductions cannot be taken for payments made to a spouse or relative who is not a licensed professional with respect to such services.

TABLE 15-1
Long-Term Care Deductible Limits

Age	Annual Deductible Limit per Covered Individual
40 or younger	$ 250
41–50	470
51–60	940
61–70	2,510
Older than 70	3,130

Any employer contributions for group contracts are deductible to the employer and do not result in any taxable income to an employee. Coverage cannot be offered through a cafeteria plan on a tax-favored basis. In addition, if an employee has a flexible spending account for unreimbursed medical expenses, any reimbursements for long-term care services must be included in the employee's income.

Benefits received under a qualified long-term care insurance contract are received tax free by an employee with one possible exception. Under contracts written on a per diem basis, proceeds are excludible from income up to $220 per day in 2003. (This figure is indexed annually.) Amounts in excess of $220 are also excludible to the extent that they represent actual costs for long-term care services.

CHARACTERISTICS OF INDIVIDUAL POLICIES

For many types of insurance, policies are relatively standardized. For long-term care insurance the opposite is true. Significant variations (and therefore differences in cost) exist from one insurance company to another. An applicant also has numerous options with respect to policy provisions.

The discussion in this section of the chapter focuses on issue age, types of care covered, benefit variations, benefit amounts, benefit duration, the ability to restore benefits, the degree of inflation protection, renewability, and cost. The provisions and practices described represent the norm in that most policies fit within the extremes that are described. However, the norm covers a wide spectrum.

Issue Age

Significant variations exist among insurance companies with respect to the age at which they will issue policies. At a minimum, a healthy person between the ages of 40 and 75 is eligible for coverage from most insurance companies. Most companies also have an upper age in the range of 84 to 89, beyond which coverage is not issued. Restrictive policy provisions and very high premiums often accompany coverage written at age 85 or older, when available.

Considerably more variation exists with respect to the youngest age at which coverage is written. Some companies have no minimum age. Most companies sell policies to persons as young as age 18. Still other companies have a higher minimum age, often age 40.

Types of Care Covered

There are many types of care for which benefits may be provided under a long-term care policy. By broad categories, these can be categorized as nursing home care, assisted-living care, hospice care, Alzheimer's facilities, home health care, care coordination, and alternative sources of care. A long-term care policy may provide benefits for one, several, or all of these types of care.

Nursing Home Care

nursing home care

Nursing home care encompasses skilled-nursing care, intermediate care, and custodial care in a licensed facility. Skilled-nursing care consists of daily nursing and rehabilitative care that can be performed only by, or under the supervision of, skilled medical personnel and must be based on a doctor's orders. Intermediate care involves occasional nursing and rehabilitative care that must be based on a doctor's orders and can be performed only by, or under the supervision of, skilled medical personnel. *Custodial care* is primarily to handle personal needs, such as walking, bathing, dressing, eating, or taking medicine, and can usually be provided by someone without professional medical skills or training.

custodial care

Policies that provide nursing home care often also provide a *bed reservation benefit*, which continues payments to a long-term care facility for a limited time (such as 20 days) if a patient temporarily leaves because of hospitalization or any other reason. Without a continuation of payments, the bed may be assigned to someone else and unavailable upon the patient's release from the hospital.

Assisted-Living Facility Care

assisted-living care

Assisted-living care is provided in facilities that care for the frail elderly who are no longer able to care for themselves but do not need as high a level of care as is provided in a nursing home.

Hospice Care

Hospice care does not attempt to cure medical conditions but rather is devoted to easing the physical and psychological pain associated with death. In addition to providing services for the dying patient, a hospice may offer counseling to family members. A hospice may be a separate facility, but this type of care can also be provided on an outpatient basis in the dying person's home. Most long-term care insurance policies that provide benefits for hospice care make no distinction in the setting.

Alzheimer's Facilities

The states require long-term care insurance policies to cover Alzheimer's disease and related forms of degenerative diseases and dementia under the same terms as they cover other conditions that qualify an individual as chronically ill. Therefore, coverage is provided if an individual receives services in a nursing home, in an assisted-living facility, or at home—as long as the specific type of care is covered in the policy. Most policies, however, have some specific reference to Alzheimer's facilities. In some cases, they are included as part of the definition for assisted-living facilities. In other cases, they are referred to separately but defined as a facility that must meet the policy's definition of either a nursing home or an assisted-living facility.

Home Health Care

Home health care is much broader than just part-time skilled-nursing care, therapy, part-time services from home health aides, and help from homemakers. It may also include benefits for one or more of the following:

- the purchase or rental of needed medical equipment and emergency alert systems
- modifications to the home such as a ramp for a wheelchair or bathroom modifications

- adult day care, which is received at centers specifically designed for the elderly who live at home but whose spouses or families cannot be available during the day
- respite care, which allows occasional full-time care for a person who is receiving home health care. Respite care can be provided in a person's home or by moving the person to a nursing facility for a short stay.
- caregiver training, which is the training of a family member or friend to provide care so that a person can remain at home
- a homemaker companion, who is an employee of a state-licensed home health care agency. The companion may assist with such tasks as cooking, shopping, cleaning, bill paying, or other household chores.
- prescription drugs and laboratory services typically provided in hospitals and nursing homes

Care Coordination

Many policies provide the services of a care coordinator who works with an insured, his or her family, and licensed health care practitioners to assess a person's condition, evaluate care options, and develop an individualized plan of care that provides the most appropriate services. The care coordinator may also periodically reevaluate ongoing plans of care and act as an advocate for the insured. Some long-term care policies mandate that the insured use the services of the care coordinator in order to receive benefits.

Alternative Plans of Care

Many policies provide benefits for alternative plans of care, even though the types of care might not be covered in the policy. For example, a policy covering nursing home care only might provide benefits for care in an assisted-living facility if these benefits are an appropriate and cost-effective alternative to care in a nursing home. As a general rule, the alternative plan must be acceptable to the insurance company, the insured, and the insured's physician.

Benefit Variations

There are almost as many variations among long-term care policies as there are insurance companies writing the product. Much of this variation is related to the types of care for which benefits are provided. These benefit variations fall into three broad categories: facility-only policies, home health care only policies, and comprehensive policies.

Facility-Only Policies

facility-only policy

Many early long-term care policies were designed to provide benefits only if the insured was in a nursing home. This type of policy was frequently referred to as a nursing home policy. Such policies still exist, but they frequently also provide benefits for care in other settings such as assisted-living facilities and hospices. The term *facility-only policy* is often used to describe this broader type of policy, and the term, in its most generic sense, also includes nursing home policies.

Home Health Care Only Policies

home health
 care only policy

Home health care only policies were originally developed to be used either as an alternative to nursing home policies or to complement such policies if more comprehensive coverage was desired. A *home health care only policy* is designed to provide benefits for care outside an institutional setting. Some home health care policies also provide benefits for care in assisted-living facilities, and this is one area in which they often overlap with facility-only policies.

Although some insurers still write stand-alone home health care policies, many other insurers have exited this market and now write the coverage as part of a broader comprehensive policy.

Comprehensive Policies

comprehensive
long-term care
insurance policy

Most long-term care policies written today can be described as comprehensive policies. A *comprehensive long-term care insurance policy*, sometimes referred to as an integrated policy, combines benefits for facility care and home health care into a single contract. However, variations exist within this type of policy with respect to what is covered as part of the standard policy and what is an optional benefit that the applicant may select. For example, some policies cover almost all care settings as part of their standard benefits; other policies provide facility-only coverage as a standard benefit with home health care covered as an option for an additional premium.

Benefit Amounts

When purchasing long-term care insurance, the applicant selects the level of benefit he or she desires up to the maximum level the insurance company will provide. Benefits are often sold in increments of $10 per day up to frequently found limits of $200 or $250 or, in a few cases, as much as $400 or $500 per day. Most insurance companies will not offer a daily benefit below $40 or $50. Some policies base benefits on a monthly (rather than daily) amount that can vary from $1,000 to $6,000 or more.

The same level of benefits is usually provided for all types of institutional care. Most comprehensive policies that provide home health care benefits once limited the daily benefit to one-half the amount payable for institutional stays. However, many insurers now allow applicants to select home health care limits that are as high as 75 percent to 100 percent of the benefit for institutional care; a few insurers even offer limits as high as 125 percent or 150 percent. If a policy provides home health care benefits only, the daily amount of that benefit is what the applicant selected.

Policies pay benefits in one of two basic ways: reimbursement or per diem.

Reimbursement Policies

reimbursement basis

The majority of newer policies pay benefits on a *reimbursement basis*. These contracts reimburse the insured for actual expenses up to the specified policy limit. For example, a policy with a daily benefit amount of $200 will pay only $150 if that was the insured's actual charge for care. Tax-qualified policies that provide benefits on a reimbursement basis must be coordinated with Medicare except when Medicare is the secondary payer of benefits.

Per Diem Policies

per diem basis

Some policies provide benefits on a *per diem basis* once care is actually being received. This means that benefits are paid regardless of the actual cost of care. In this case, a policy with a daily benefit of $200 will pay $200 even if actual long-term care charges for the day are only $150. Per diem contracts are seldom coordinated with any benefits that are payable under Medicare. If home health care benefits are provided, most per diem policies pay benefits regardless of the service provider. In such cases, benefits are paid even if a family member provides care at no charge. Some policies, however, define the type of service provider from whom care must be received.

Note that per diem policies are sometimes referred to as indemnity policies even though the usual insurance meaning of indemnity implies payment of benefits for actual expenses up to policy limits. In this sense, reimbursement policies, not per diem policies, are actually policies of indemnity.

A few insurers offer a variation of the per diem policy that pays benefits as long as the insured satisfies the policy's benefit triggers, even if no long-term care is being received. Such a policy is referred to as a *disability-based policy*.

Period of Benefits

To determine the period of benefits under a long-term care insurance policy, it is necessary to look at the elimination period and the maximum duration of benefits.

Elimination Period

The applicant is required to select a period of time that must pass after long-term care commences but before benefit payments begin. The majority of long-term care insurers refer to this period as an elimination period. However, some insurers call it a waiting period or a deductible period. Most insurers allow an applicant to select from three to five optional elimination periods. For example, one insurer allows the choice of 20, 60, 100, or 180 days. Choices may be as low as 0 days or as high as 365 days.

In a comprehensive policy, there is normally a single elimination period that can be met by any combination of days during which the insured is in a long-term care facility or receiving home health care services.

There are several ways that home health care services can be counted toward the elimination period. Some policies count only those days when actual services are received for which charges are made and that will be covered after the elimination period is satisfied. If an insured receives services 3 days during the week, this counts as 3 days. If the insured's policy has a 60-day elimination period, benefit payments will not begin until the insured had been receiving services for 20 weeks (or 140 days). Some policies count each week as 7 days toward the satisfaction of the elimination period if services were received on any number of days in the week, even one day. In this case, the insured will start receiving benefit payments after 60 days have elapsed from the first service.

Another variation in reimbursement policies is for the insurer to start counting days toward satisfaction of the elimination period as soon as long-term care is certified as being necessary, even if services are received from someone who does not make a charge. Therefore, family members or friends could provide the services until the elimination period is satisfied, and the insurer will then start paying benefits for the services of a paid caregiver.

One final comment about the elimination period concerns its relationship to the requirement that tax-qualified policies cannot pay benefits for the inability to perform ADLs unless this inability is expected to last at least 90 days. Actually, despite what some people think, there is no relationship! If an insured is certified as being unable to perform the requisite number of ADLs for at least 90 days, benefit payments will start after the satisfaction of the elimination period, be it 0, 20, 60, or any other specified number of days. If the insured makes a recovery after the elimination period is satisfied but before the end of the 90-day period, the insured is fully entitled to any benefits received because the period was *expected* to be at least 90 days.

Maximum Duration of Benefits

The applicant is also given a choice as to the maximum period for which benefits are paid, often referred to as the benefit period. This period begins from the time benefit payments start after satisfaction of the elimination period. In addition, the benefit period does not necessarily apply to each separate period for which long-term care services are received. Rather, it is a period that applies to the aggregate time benefits are paid under the policy. When the maximum benefits are paid, the policy will terminate. However, if benefits are only partially exhausted during a course of long-term care, they may be restored under certain circumstances, as explained later. Also, as explained later, the length of the benefit period may actually differ from the period chosen if a policy uses a pool-of-money concept.

Most insurers require the applicant to select the benefit period, and they make several options available. For example, one insurer offers durations of 2, 3, and 5 years as well as lifetime benefits. In most cases, a single benefit period applies to long-term care, no matter where it is received. A few policies, however, have separate benefit periods for facility care and home health care. There are also a few policies, usually the per diem type, that specify the maximum benefits as a stated dollar amount such as $100,000.

There are actually two ways that the benefit period is applied in the payment of benefits. Under one approach, benefit payments are made for exactly the benefit period chosen. If the applicant selects a benefit period of 4 years and collects benefits for 4 years, the benefit payments cease. The other approach, most commonly but not exclusively used with reimbursement policies, uses a *pool of money*. Under this concept, there is an amount of money that can be used to make benefit payments as long as the pool of money lasts. The applicant does not select the amount in the pool of money; it is determined by multiplying the daily benefit by the benefit period selected. For example, if the daily benefit is $200 and the benefit period is 1,460 days (or 4 years), then the pool of money is $292,000 ($200 x 1,460). Several important points about this pool of money should be mentioned:

pool of money

- Daily benefit payments from the pool of money cannot exceed the daily policy benefits.
- Under comprehensive policies, the pool of money is typically determined by using the daily benefit amount for institutional care.
- Adjustments are made to the pool of money during periods of benefit payments to reflect any inflation protection that applies to the policy benefits.

shared benefit

A few insurers use the concept of a *shared benefit* when a husband and wife are insured under the same policy or with the same insurer. Under this concept, each spouse can access the other spouse's benefits. For example, if each spouse has a 4-year benefit period and one spouse has exhausted his or her benefits, benefit payments can continue by drawing on any unused benefits under the other spouse's policy. In effect, one spouse could have a benefit period of up to 8 years as long as the other spouse receives no benefit payments.

Restoration

Many policies written with less than a lifetime benefit period provide for restoration of full benefits if the insured has been out of a nursing home for a certain time period, often 180 days. If a policy does not have this provision, maximum benefits for a subsequent claim are reduced by the benefits previously paid.

Inflation Protection

Most states require that a long-term care policy offers some type of automatic inflation protection. The applicant is given the choice to select this option, decline the option, or possibly select an alternative option. The cost of an automatic-increase option is built into the initial premium, and no additional premium is levied at the time of an annual increase. As a result of the NAIC model act and HIPAA, the standard provision found in almost all policies is a 5 percent benefit increase that is compounded annually over the life of the policy. Under such a provision, the amount of a policy's benefits increases by 5 percent each year over the amount of benefits available in the prior year.

A common alternative that many insurers make available is based on simple interest, with each annual automatic increase being 5 percent of the original benefit amount. Other options that are occasionally found are increases (either simple or compound) based on different fixed percentage amounts such as 3 or 4 percent.

If an automatic-increase option is not selected, some insurers allow a policyowner to increase benefits without evidence of insurability on a pay-as-you-go basis at specified intervals such as every one, 2, or 3 years. Each benefit increase is accompanied by a premium increase that is based on attained-age rates for the additional coverage.

The amount of the periodic benefit increase under a pay-as-you-go option may be a fixed dollar amount, such as a daily benefit increase of $20 every third year, or be based on a specified percentage or an index such as the CPI. Some insurers have an aggregate limit on the total amount of benefit increases or an age beyond which they are no longer available. Failure to exercise a periodic increase or a series of increases over a specified period typically terminates the right to purchase additional benefits in the future.

It is important to note that increases in benefits are often inadequate to offset actual inflation in the annual cost of long-term care, which has been in the double digits over the last decade.

Eligibility for Benefits

Almost all tax-qualified contracts use the same two criteria for determining benefit eligibility, with the insured being required to meet only one of the two. The first criterion is that the insured is expected to be unable, without substantial assistance from another person, to perform two of the six ADLs that are acceptable under HIPAA for a period of at least 90 days due to loss of functional capacity. The second criterion is that substantial supervision is required to protect the individual from threats to health and safety because of severe cognitive impairment.

Non-tax-qualified contracts, on the other hand, have more liberal eligibility requirements. Many of these contracts use the same criteria that are in tax-qualified contracts, except there is no time period that applies to the inability to perform the ADLs. A small number of non-tax-qualified contracts require only the inability to perform one ADL and/or use more than the six ADLs allowed by HIPAA. Finally, some non-tax-qualified contracts make benefits available if a third criterion—medical necessity—is satisfied. This generally means that a physician has certified that long-term care is needed, even if neither of the other criteria is satisfied.

Exclusions

Most long-term care policies contain the exclusions permitted under the NAIC model act. One source of controversy is the exclusion for mental and nervous disorders. This is an area that insurers frequently avoid because of the possibility of fraudulent claims and the controversies that often arise over claim settlements. The usual exclusion is stated as follows: "This policy does not provide benefits for the care or treatment of mental illness or emotional disorders without a demonstrable organic cause." Many policies also specifically stipulate that Alzheimer's disease and senile dementia, as diagnosed by a physician, are considered as having demonstrable organic cause, even though state law frequently requires these disorders to be covered.

Underwriting

The underwriting of long-term care policies, like the underwriting of medical expense policies, is based on the health of the insured. However, underwriting for long-term care insurance focuses on situations that will cause claims far into the future. Most underwriting is done on the basis of questionnaires rather than on the use of actual physical examinations. Numerous questions are asked about the health of relatives. For example, if a parent or grandparent had Alzheimer's disease, there is an increased likelihood that the applicant will get this disease in the future. In addition, the insurance company is very interested in medical events, such as temporary amnesia or fainting spells, that might be an indication of future incapacity.

Underwriting tends to become more restrictive as the age of an applicant increases. Not only is a future claim more likely to occur much sooner, but adverse selection can also be more severe.

Many insurers have a single classification for all acceptable applicants for long-term care insurance, but other insurers have three or four categories of insurable classifications, each with a different rate structure.

Some long-term care policies have a preexisting-conditions provision which specifies that benefits are not paid within the first 6 months for a condition for which treatment was recommended or received within 6 months of policy purchase. However, other policies have no such provision or state that the provision does not apply to preexisting conditions that are listed on the policy application. There is little need for such a provision because insurers are required in most states to underwrite at the time coverage is written and are not allowed to use post-claims underwriting. If properly underwritten at the time of application, claims within the usual preexisting-conditions period are unlikely to occur. Elimination periods for benefits often serve a similar purpose.

Renewability

Long-term care policies currently being sold are guaranteed renewable, which means that an individual's coverage cannot be canceled except for nonpayment of premiums. While premiums cannot be raised on the basis of a particular applicant's claim, they can (and often are) raised by class.

Nonforfeiture Options

Most companies give an applicant for long-term care insurance the right to elect a nonforfeiture benefit, and some states require that such a benefit be offered. With a nonforfeiture benefit, the policyowner will receive some value for a policy if the policy lapses because the required premium is not paid in the future.

The most common type of nonforfeiture option is a shortened benefit period. With this option, coverage is continued as a paid-up policy, but the length of the benefit period (or the amount of the benefit if stated as a maximum dollar amount) is reduced. Under the typical provision, the reduced coverage is available only if the lapse is on or after the policy's third anniversary. The amount of the benefit is equal to the greater of the total premiums paid for the policy prior to lapse or 30 times the policy's daily nursing home benefit.

Some non-tax-qualified policies offer a return-of-premium option, under which a portion of the premium is returned if a policy lapses after a specified number of years. For example, the policy of one insurer pays nothing if a policy lapses before it has been in force for 5 full years. Fifteen percent of the total premiums paid are returned if the policy was in force for 6 years, 30 percent for 7 years, 45 percent for 8 years, 60 percent for 9 years, and 80 percent for 10 or more years.

In some states that require an insurer to offer a nonforfeiture benefit, a policy must contain a *contingent benefit upon lapse* if the nonforfeiture benefit is not purchased. This provision gives the policyowner the right to elect certain options if the premium has increased by a specified percentage since the time of policy issue. The percentage is a sliding scale that is determined by the issue age. For example, the percentage is 110 if the policy were issued when the insured was 50 to 54. The figure drops to 70 percent for an issue age of 60, 40 percent for an issue age of 70, and 20 percent for an issue age of 80. The options are a reduction in benefits to a level sustainable by the current premium or the conversion of the policy to a paid-up status with a shorter benefit period. The policyowner is not required to select either of these options and can continue to pay the higher premium and maintain the current policy benefits.

Premiums

Premium Payment Period

The vast majority of long-term care policies have premiums that are payable for life and determined by the age of the insured at the time of issue. A few insurers, however, offer other modes of payment. Lifetime coverage can sometimes be purchased with a single premium. Some insurers offer policies that have premium payment periods of 10 or 20 years or to age 65, after which time the premium is paid up. These policies are particularly attractive to applicants who do not want continuing premium payments after retirement.

Most long-term care policies have a provision that waives premiums if the insured has been receiving benefits under the policy for a specified period of time, often 60 or 90 days.

Factors Affecting Premiums

Numerous factors affect the premium that a policyowner will pay for a long-term care policy. Even if the provisions of several policies are virtually identical, premiums will vary among companies. For example, the premiums for three similar policies from three different companies are shown in table 15-2. Each policy has a daily benefit of $120 per day, a 0-day elimination period, a lifetime benefit period, and coverage for home health care.

TABLE 15-2
Comparison of Long-Term Care Premiums for Similar Policies

Age	Company A	Company B	Company C
40	$ 391	$ 549	$ 590
50	641	714	832
60	1,104	1,126	1,331
70	2,550	3,157	2,736
75	4,540	5,491	4,763

Age. Age plays a significant role in the cost of long-term care coverage, as shown by the rates in the table. These figures demonstrate that long-term care coverage can be obtained at a reasonable cost if it is purchased at a young age.

Types of Benefits. The benefits provided under a policy have a significant bearing on the cost. Most policies cover care in a long-term care facility. However, many policies also cover home health care and other benefits provided to persons who are still able to reside in their own homes. This broader coverage increases premiums by 60 to 70 percent.

Duration of Benefits. The longer the maximum benefit period, the higher the premium. The longer the elimination period, the lower the premium. With many insurers, a policy with an unlimited benefit period and no elimination period will have a premium about double that of a policy with a 2-year benefit period and a 90-day elimination period.

Inflation Protection. Policies may be written with or without automatic benefit increases for inflation. All other factors being equal, the addition of a 5 percent compound annual increase in benefits can raise premiums by 50 to 100 percent.

Nonforfeiture Benefits. A policy may be written with or without a nonforfeiture benefit. The inclusion of such a benefit can increase a premium by anywhere from 20 to 50 percent or more, depending on type of nonforfeiture benefit and other policy features.

Spousal Coverage. Most insurance companies offer a discount of 10 percent to 15 percent if both spouses purchase long-term care policies from the company.

Nonsmoker Discount. A few insurers offer a discount such as 10 percent, if the insured is a nonsmoker.

GROUP COVERAGE

Success in the individual marketplace led to interest in group long-term care insurance as an employee benefit. The first group long-term plan was written in 1987, and a growing number of employers, mostly large ones, now make coverage available. The number of insurance companies writing coverage has also grown, but it still remains relatively small and is primarily limited to the largest group insurance carriers. However, over 1 million employees and their family members now have group coverage.

For the most part, group long-term care policies are comparable to the better policies that are being sold in the individual marketplace. However, there are a few differences, mostly because of the characteristics of group coverage:

- Eligibility for coverage generally requires that an employee be full-time and actively at work. At a minimum, coverage can be purchased for an active employee and/or the spouse. Some policies also make coverage available to retirees and to other family members of eligible persons such as minor children, parents, parents-in-law, and possibly adult children.
- The cost of group coverage is usually slightly less than the cost of individual coverage. To some extent, this is a result of the administrative services, such as payroll deduction, being performed by the employer.
- An employee typically has fewer choices with respect to benefit amounts, benefit duration, and the length of the elimination period.
- If a participant leaves employment, the group coverage can usually be continued on a direct-payment basis, under either the group contract or an individual contract.

CHECKLIST FOR EVALUATING AND COMPARING LONG-TERM CARE POLICIES

☐ What is the annual policy premium?

☐ Is the policy qualified to receive favorable tax treatment?

☐ Is there a 30-day free look?

☐ What services are covered?

  ___ Nursing home care
  ___ Assisted-living care
  ___ Custodial care
  ___ Home health care
  ___ Adult day care
  ___ Other

☐ How much does the policy pay per day for the following?

  ___ Facility care
  ___ Home health care
  ___ Other

☐ How long will benefits last?

  ___ For facility care
  ___ At home

☐ Does the policy have a maximum lifetime benefit? If yes, what is it?

☐ Does the policy have a maximum length of coverage of each period of confinement? If yes, what is it?

  ___ For facility care
  ___ For home health care

☐ What is the length of time before preexisting conditions are covered?

☐ What is the elimination period before benefits begin?

  ___ For facility care
  ___ For home health care

☐ What is the age range for enrollment?

☐ Is there a waiver-of-premium provision?

  ___ For facility care
  ___ For home health care

☐ What is the confinement period before premiums are waived?

☐ Does the policy offer an inflation adjustment feature? If, yes,

   ___ What is the rate of increase?
   ___ How often is it applied?
   ___ For how long?
   ___ Is there an additional cost?

☐   What nonforfeiture options are available?

SOURCES FOR FURTHER IN-DEPTH STUDY

- Beam, Burton T., Jr., and O'Hare, Thomas P., *Meeting the Financial Need of Long-Term Care,* Bryn Mawr, PA: The American College, 2003. Phone 888-263-7265. Web site address www.amercoll.edu
- Sadler, Jeff, *How to Sell Long-Term Care Insurance*, The National Underwriter Company, 2001. Phone 800-543-0874. Web site address www.nationalunderwriter. com
- Shilling, Dana, *Financial Planning for the Older Client,* 5th ed., Cincinnati, OH: The National Underwriter Company, 2001. Phone 800-543-0874. Web site address www.nationalunderwriter.com

CHAPTER REVIEW

Answers to review questions and self-test questions start on page 725.

Key Terms

look-back period	custodial care
continuing care retirement community	assisted-living care
	facility-only policy
long-term care insurance	home health care only policy
qualified long-term care insurance contract	comprehensive long-term care insurance policy
qualified long-term care services	reimbursement basis
chronically ill individual	per diem basis
activities of daily living (ADLs)	pool of money
nursing home care	shared benefit

Review Questions

15-1. Why is there a need for long-term care insurance?

15-2. Describe the sources for providing long-term care other than insurance.

15-3. Summarize the criteria for policy provisions in the NAIC model legislation for long-term care insurance.

15-4. What are the requirements that a long-term care insurance contract must meet to be "qualified" under the Health Insurance Portability and Accountability Act (HIPAA)?

15-5. What are the requirements that an individual must meet to be certified as a "chronically ill person" under HIPAA?

15-6. Describe the federal income tax treatment of a qualified long-term care insurance contract.

15-7. What are the usual issue ages for long-term care insurance contracts?

15-8. Describe the amounts and duration of long-term care benefits.

15-9. Explain how insurance companies determine whether a long-term care policyowner is eligible for benefits.

15-10. Describe the factors that affect the amount of the premium for a long-term care insurance contract.

15-11. Compare group long-term care insurance with the coverage being sold in the individual marketplace. What differences exist between the two types of coverage?

Self-Test Questions

T   F   15-1. Both group and individual medical expense policies typically cover custodial care in a nursing home.

T   F   15-2. The Medicaid program in most states will provide nursing home care to low-income individuals.

T   F   15-3. NAIC model legislation regarding long-term care policies has become federal law and applies retroactively to older policies.

T   F   15-4. NAIC model legislation regarding long-term care policies requires that a shopper's guide must be delivered to all prospective applicants.

T   F   15-5. Under the Health Insurance Portability and Accountability Act (HIPAA), a "qualified long-term care insurance contract" cannot provide for a cash surrender value.

T   F   15-6. Under HIPAA, a "chronically ill person" must be unable to perform at least four activities of daily living (ADLs).

T   F   15-7. Coverage under a group long-term care insurance contract must be offered through a cafeteria plan to receive favorable tax treatment.

T   F   15-8. One of the benefits that may be available under a long-term care insurance contract is adult day care.

T   F   15-9. Long-term care benefits are typically based on the actual charge for long-term care up to a maximum amount.

T   F   15-10. Most states require long-term care policies to offer some type of inflation protection that the applicant can purchase.

T   F   15-11. Most insurance companies offer a discount if both spouses purchase long-term care policies from the company.

Introduction to Property and Liability Insurance

Learning Objectives
An understanding of the material in this chapter should enable the student to

16-1. Describe the types of property and liability loss exposures faced by families and businesses.

16-2. Explain the basic types of property and liability policies and coverages available to meet the protection needs of families and businesses.

16-3. Briefly explain the taxation of property and liability insurance premiums and loss settlements for individuals and businesses.

Chapter Outline

This is the first of four chapters devoted to property and liability insurance—an area of financial planning that is often either overlooked or given less-than-thorough attention. Financial planners should be equipped to help their clients assess their property and casualty risks. For many individuals, particularly those with good employee benefits paid by their employers, the premiums spent on property and liability insurance exceed those spent on all other types of insurance. It is also a complex subject. Because of many gaps in coverage, policies must be thoroughly analyzed to determine whether client needs are adequately being addressed and the extent to which additional policies or policy endorsements (of which there are many available) are required.

The existence of appropriate property and liability insurance is important in the scheme of overall financial planning. The resources needed to recover from an inadequately insured loss often mean that fewer funds can be devoted to asset accumulation. In addition, the size of some personal emergencies can be minimized with proper insurance protection.

The cost of property and liability insurance also raises several other financial planning issues. For example, significant premium variations exist among companies, and shopping for both price and service is wise. In addition, substantial premium savings can often result through the use of deductibles and the assumption of loss exposures that have the potential for small monetary losses only.

This chapter describes the types of property and liability loss exposures with the methods for settling claims, including the valuation of losses and the duties of the insured. The basic types of policies and their income tax implications are also discussed.

The three following chapters are devoted to a discussion of the types of policies needed primarily by individuals. However, some treatment of the business uses of property and liability insurance is also included.

TYPES OF PROPERTY AND LIABILITY LOSS EXPOSURES

The types of property and liability loss exposures facing families and businesses fall into three broad categories:

- property loss exposures, which include losses to either real or personal property
- liability loss exposures
- consequential or indirect loss exposures that arise as a result of property or liability losses[1]

In some cases, the occurrence of a given peril may result in only one type of loss. For example, the loss of a diamond that falls out of a ring setting is clearly a property loss to the ring owner. However, the owner of the ring is not liable to anyone for the loss, and no consequential losses result unless the time involved in replacing the diamond is taken into consideration.

In other cases, a given situation may result in more than one type of loss. For example, a driver who loses control of a car may have an accident that causes a property loss to the car. In addition, there can be consequential losses associated with the accident such as the cost of renting a substitute vehicle while the car is being repaired. Furthermore, if the accident caused injury or property damage to others or to their property, a liability loss exists. Along with possibly being required to pay a legal judgment, losses in the form of legal fees can also result. Legal fees can also result even if the driver is ultimately found to not be liable.

In this section of the chapter, the three categories of loss exposures are each discussed.

Property Losses

real property

Property losses can occur to either real or personal property. *Real property* is defined as land and anything that is growing on it, erected on it, or affixed to it, and the bundle of rights inherent in the ownership. It includes such items as crops, mineral rights, air rights, buildings, items that are permanently attached to buildings, fences, in-ground swimming pools, driveways, and retaining walls. Condominium units and the unit owners' rights to use common areas are also examples of real property.

personal property

Personal property is defined to include anything that is subject to ownership other than real property. This includes such items as clothes, furniture, dishes, artwork, musical instruments, money, securities, airline tickets, office equipment, business inventory, vehicles, and boats. It also includes intangible property such as copyrights and patents.

In most cases, it is relatively easy to determine whether something is real or personal property. However, in a few cases, the distinction may vary from state to state, and an understanding of the quirks of individual state laws is important in order to determine the proper amounts of insurance. For example, a gas range is generally considered to be real property because it is attached to a building by a gas line. But an electric range, which merely plugs into an electrical outlet, can be considered either real or personal property, depending on the state. Variations also exist for such items as drapes and television antennas.

Covered Perils

Real and personal property are subject to loss from the occurrence of many different perils. However, it is very rare for an insurance policy to cover losses from every peril that might occur. Insurance policies fall into two broad categories with respect to covered perils—named-perils policies and "open-perils" policies.

named-perils policy

Named-Perils Policies. Named-perils policies (also referred to as specified-perils policies) contain a list of the covered perils, which in number may range from one to many, depending on the type of policy. If a peril is not listed, losses resulting from that peril are not covered.

Some policies, particularly those for businesses, are designed for very specific types of losses and cover few perils. For example, there is a policy designed to cover losses to money, securities, and other property only from the peril of computer fraud. On the other hand, named-perils policies can be extremely broad. An example is the personal property coverage under a homeowners 3 (HO-3) policy, which is discussed in more detail in a later chapter. The HO-3 policy contains a list of many covered perils for personal property, ranging from fire to theft to volcanic eruption.

A mere listing of the covered perils in a named-perils policy can be somewhat misleading since the precise meaning of the terms is often established by either legal precedent or specific policy language. For example, the term *fire* is not normally defined in insurance policies because its meaning has long been established by the courts. A fire consists of a rapid oxidation or combustion that causes a flame or glow. Therefore, an item scorched because it was too close to a burner on a stove would not be covered under the peril of fire. In addition, courts have determined that the peril of fire only covers hostile fires, which are those that are outside normal confines. For example, a fire in a fireplace is a friendly rather than a hostile fire. As a result, an item accidentally thrown into a fireplace would not be covered under a named-perils policy covering fire. It should be noted that a fire that spreads beyond the fireplace has turned from a friendly fire into a hostile fire.

Unlike the peril of fire, the meanings of most covered perils are specifically defined in insurance policies. For example, the peril of volcanic eruption in the previously mentioned HO-3 policy is defined to cover volcanic eruptions other than those arising from earthquakes, land shock waves, or tremors.

"open-perils" policy

"Open-Perils" Policies. "Open-perils" policies (sometimes called all-risks policies) cover all losses to covered property unless the loss is specifically excluded. The coverage for real property under the HO-3 policy is an example of a typical "open-perils" policy in that some potentially significant losses are not covered. The policy has exclusions for earth movement and water damage that are broad enough to eliminate coverage for earthquake and flood. In most cases, such perils can be insured for an extra premium under the HO-3 policy or a separate policy. There are also exclusions for perils that are generally uninsurable such as war and nuclear

accidents. Other perils are modified by policy language. For example, while vandalism and malicious mischief to the property are generally covered, the perils are not covered if a building has been vacant for more than 60 days preceding a loss. Similarly, smoke is not a covered peril if it arises from agricultural smudging or industrial operations.

Settling Claims

In many ways, the process of settling claims is more complex for property insurance than for most other types of insurance. The insurance company has various options for settling losses, more duties are placed upon the insured, different bases may be used for valuing losses, other insurance may affect loss payments, and provisions must be made for settling the disputes that often arise over the amount of settlements. Although variations exist among states, insurance companies, and types of policies, the following discussion—based on the HO-3 policy—is typical of the provisions that apply to property insurance.

Duties of the Insured. Several duties are imposed on the insured. These typically include

- giving prompt notice of the loss to the insurer or its agent
- notifying the police in case of a loss by theft
- notifying the credit card or fund transfer card company if a loss involves credit card or fund transfer card coverage
- protecting the property from further damage, which includes making reasonable repairs to the property. The insured must also keep an accurate record of the expenses incurred for repair, which are considered part of the loss.
- preparing an inventory of damaged personal property. This inventory should show the quantity, description, property value, and amount of loss. Any bills, receipts, and related documents that justify the amounts shown in the inventory must be attached.
- cooperating with the insurance company as it reasonably requires. This includes showing the damaged property, providing requested records and documents and allowing copies to be made, and submitting to an examination under oath.
- providing a sworn proof of loss, generally within 60 days of the insurer's request. This form is generally provided by the insurance company and contains the following:
    - the time and cause of loss
    - the interest of the insured and all others in the property involved as well as all liens on the property
    - other insurance that may cover the loss

   –   specifications of damaged buildings and detailed repair costs
   –   an inventory of damaged personal property
   –   information to support any other claims such as consequential
       losses and credit card losses

It is difficult to comply with these requirements without adequate records and documentation. For this reason, an insured should be encouraged to maintain receipts of major purchases. An inventory of personal property should be maintained, along with pictures or videotapes of both personal and real property. Of course, a copy of this information should be kept at a place other than the insured location to prevent the information from also being destroyed should a loss occur there.

Insurance Company Obligations. The insurance company will settle all losses with the policyowner unless some other person is named in the policy or is legally entitled to receive payment. As a general rule, losses are payable 60 days (or whatever period a state requires) after the company receives a proof of loss and one of the following has occurred:

   •   An agreement has been reached with the policyowner.
   •   There is a filing of an appraisal award with the company. (The appraisal process is described later in this chapter.)
   •   There is a final legal judgment. However, no legal action can be brought against the insurance company unless all policy provisions have been complied with and the legal action is brought within some period of time after a loss, usually one year. In addition, the appraisal process may lead to a binding settlement amount.

The insurance company has the right to repair or replace damaged property but is not required to do so. In most cases, the insurer will make a monetary settlement, and the insured is responsible for repairing or replacing the property.

Dealing with Other Insurable Interests. Property insurance policies only pay for the policyowner's insurable interest in a loss, unless some provision has been made in the policy to cover other insurable interests. If two persons own property jointly, they are likely to both be listed as policyowners. However, many lenders have an insurable interest because they have loaned the policyowner money to purchase real or personal property. As a requirement of such loans, these lenders often require the borrower to purchase insurance that also protects the lender's insurable interests and to escrow the premium payments. This is typically accomplished through the use of a mortgage clause or a loss payable clause.

mortgage clause

Mortgage Clause. The *mortgage clause* is used for real property that the policyowner has pledged as collateral for a loan. It is a standard part of many property insurance policies and becomes effective by listing the mortgagee (the lender) in the policy declarations. The policy gives certain rights to the mortgagee but also imposes certain obligations. These include the right to

- receive any loss payments to the extent of their insurable interest in the property. This payment is made even if the policyowner's claim is denied as long as the mortgagee does the following:
  - notifies the insurer of any change in ownership or occupancy, or any increase in risks of which the mortgagee is aware
  - pays any premium due if the policyowner fails to do so
  - provides a sworn statement of loss if the policyowner fails to do so
  - surrenders any claim it has against the policyowner to the extent payment is made
- receive separate notice of cancellation
- sue the insurer in its own name in accordance with policy provisions

The claim check is normally issued jointly to the policyowner and the mortgagee. It is up to these parties to determine how the proceeds are split. In most cases, the mortgagee endorses the check to the policyowner so the property can be repaired or replaced. However, in the absence of any provision in the mortgage loan agreement to the contrary, the mortgagee can apply its share of the loss settlement to the loan principal.

loss payable clause

Loss Payable Clause. The *loss payable clause* is added to a policy as an endorsement and is used for automobiles and other types of personal property that have been financed. The policy gives the lender more limited rights than are found in the mortgage clause. For example, under the clause that is used for automobiles, the lender will still be paid if the policyowner is denied coverage but only because of certain fraudulent acts or omissions. The lender receives notification if the policy is canceled so other provisions can be made to protect its insurable interest. However, the lender cannot pay the premium to keep the coverage in force.

Valuing Losses. Property insurance policies specify the way in which losses will be valued. Historically, most policies have settled losses on an actual cash value basis. This is still true for most losses that involve personal property. However, replacement cost is often used as the settlement basis for many losses to real property and for an increasing number of losses to personal property. In some cases, the type of policy available dictates the standard method for valuing losses. However, alternative policies or endorsements may be available so that the insured can select whether he or she has actual cash value coverage or replacement-cost coverage. When replacement-cost coverage is available, loss settlements will be higher, but such policies also have higher premiums.

A few policies also settle losses on the basis of agreed values and some states have valued policy laws.

Actual Cash Value. The practice of using actual cash value to determine loss payments is based on the principle of indemnity, which means that an insured should not profit from a loss but should be put into approximately the same financial position that existed prior to a loss.

Policies written on an actual cash value basis (such as automobile physical damage and personal property under many homeowners policies) state that losses will be settled at actual cash value at the time of loss but not in an amount greater than the amount required to repair or replace the property.

actual cash value

Although many terms are defined in insurance contracts, *actual cash value* usually is not. As a result, there are varying court interpretations as to its precise meaning. Generally, it is defined as replacement cost less depreciation. As an illustration, assume a 10-year-old refrigerator is destroyed in a fire. It cost $900 when new, but a similar new model now sells for $1,200. The $1,200 amount is the replacement cost. However, according to the principle of indemnity, the insured is not entitled to a new refrigerator since the one that was destroyed was several years old. The issue then becomes the amount of the deduction for depreciation. Insurance companies tend to have depreciation schedules for various items, and refrigerators typically last about 15 years. Therefore, the insurer would probably assume the refrigerator was two-thirds depreciated and offer the insured one-third of $1,200, or $400.

In some states, actual cash value is defined as fair market value, which is the amount a willing buyer would pay a willing seller in a free market. In most cases, this approach leads to a settlement similar to one based on replacement cost less depreciation.

replacement cost

Replacement Cost. When losses are settled on a *replacement-cost* basis (as in most homeowners policies for real property), no deduction is made for depreciation. In the previous example, $1,200 would be paid to purchase a new refrigerator. In the past, it was argued that this method of settlement violated the principle of indemnity because the insured was put into a better position after the loss. However, in many cases, there is no way to put the insured into exactly the same position that existed prior to the loss. For example, if a windstorm blows the shingles off a roof, the insured clearly needs new shingles. However, if the old shingles had already served for a portion of their life expectancy, an actual cash value settlement would require the insured to use additional resources to fully repair the roof. Such a result, obviously, would leave the insured feeling less than fully indemnified.

To alleviate this situation, replacement-cost coverage is commonly written on homes and is often used for personal and commercial property.

A few additional comments need to be made about replacement cost. First, it is based on replacement with materials or items of like kind and quality as that lost. For example, if a kitchen were destroyed, the value of the loss would be determined by characteristics of the old kitchen. The insurance company would pay the cost to replace an old Formica countertop with a new countertop of Formica or something similar. The insured would have to assume the extra cost if he or she wanted a new granite countertop. Similarly, the insurance company would not pay to replace average kitchen cabinets with expensive custom-made cabinets.

Second, the insurance company, with one possible exception, will pay no more than actual cash value until the replacement or repair is completed. The exception involves relatively small losses (such as those under $2,500), for which settlement is on a replacement-cost basis.

Agreed Value. In some circumstances, it is extremely hard to determine values after an item has been totally destroyed or lost through theft. Examples include fine art and antiques. To avoid this dilemma, the insurer and the insured may agree upon a value at the time a policy is written. However, the insurance company will probably want detailed appraisals before it enters into such an agreement. In the event of a total loss to the property, the agreed value is paid.

valued policy law   *Valued Policy Laws.* Some states have a *valued policy law* that can apply to certain types of property losses and/or certain perils. As a rule, this type of law applies to real property and only if a total loss occurs. Under such a law, the full amount of insurance coverage would be paid. For example, $500,000 would be paid for a loss to a building insured for $500,000 even if the actual cash value or replacement cost of the building were lower. The rationale for a valued policy law is that it prevents agents and insurance companies from benefiting from premiums and commissions that are too high because a building is overinsured. Thus, the burden is on the insurance company to either prevent overinsurance or to be bound by the amount of coverage if a loss occurs. It should be noted that most insurers try to avoid overinsurance because of the accompanying moral hazard. In addition, the purchasers of insurance are more likely to be underinsured than overinsured.

Other Insurance and Policy Provisions. Numerous provisions in property insurance policies can affect the amount of a loss that is paid.

Insurable Interest. Policies will not pay an insured more than the amount of his or her interest in property at the time of loss. Assume that two people each have a 50 percent interest in a $100,000 building. If a person buys a policy with only himself or herself as the insured, only $50,000—the person's insurable interest—would be paid in the case of a total loss. The other owner should have his or her own coverage. In most cases, this can be accomplished by having them both named as insureds in the same policy.

Policy Limits. Property insurance policies need to be analyzed carefully to determine the amount of coverage that is in force. If a policy limit is inadequate, the insured might collect less than the full value of a loss.

Some policies do not specify a maximum dollar amount of coverage. For example, the personal auto policy (PAP)—the most common automobile insurance policy—states that the amount of coverage on an insured car is limited to the lesser of actual cash value of the vehicle or the amount required to repair or replace it. Obviously the actual cash value and potential claim varies significantly depending on the type and age of the car insured. However, this is considered in the pricing structure of the policy, whereby someone with a newer and more expensive vehicle will pay a higher premium.

Other policies, such as homeowners policies, have specified amounts of coverage that apply to real property and personal property. However, this does not necessarily mean that the specified limit is the maximum amount that will be paid for a claim. For example, some companies settle claims on real property at replacement cost at the time of loss at amounts in excess of the stated policy limit if certain conditions are met. This might include the stipulation that the insured carry an amount of coverage equal to at least 100 percent of the estimated replacement cost at the time the policy was purchased.

In other cases, less than the full amount of coverage might be paid because of internal policy limits that apply to certain types of personal property. Such limits are common in homeowners policies and are discussed in chapter 17.

Deductibles. Many property insurance policies have deductibles that apply to each loss. In most cases, the deductible is a set dollar amount. Although insurance policies and companies tend to have standard deductibles, such as $250 for collision losses to an automobile, deductibles can usually be increased with an accompanying premium reduction. Deductibles can sometimes be decreased for an additional premium.

A few policies—earthquake coverage is a common example—have percentage deductibles. Under such a policy, the deductible is equal to a percentage, such as 5 percent, of the amount of insurance.

While deductibles minimize attitudinal hazard by making the insured bear a portion of any loss, they also lower premium costs by eliminating the relatively high administrative costs of adjusting small claims. Significant discounts are often available for selecting higher deductibles, and an analysis of this savings should be part of a financial planning analysis.

Underinsurance. Obviously it is important to carry an amount of insurance equal to the full value of property if one expects to be fully indemnified in the event of a total loss. Moreover, the failure to carry "insurance to value" can also result in less-than-full payment for partial losses in many types of property insurance policies.

The rating structure of property insurance policies is often based on the assumption that adequate insurance to value is carried. If it is not, the insured will bear a portion of any loss. The common provision found in many commercial property insurance policies that leads to this result is what is referred to as a *coinsurance* provision. Note that this is a different use of the term than is found in medical expense insurance.

coinsurance (property insurance)

A coinsurance provision requires the policyowner to carry insurance equal to a percentage of the property's insurable value in order to receive full payment for any losses. The percentage is commonly 80, 90, or 100, and the policy will specify whether this is a percentage of actual cash value, replacement cost, or some other value.

The best way to explain coinsurance is to use an example, and the replacement-cost provision that applies to many commercial buildings will be used. It states that if the amount of insurance is 80 percent (or other percentages selected by the policyowner) or more of replacement cost at the time of loss, the loss will be paid on a replacement-cost basis up to the limit of coverage. However, if the amount of insurance is less than 80 percent of replacement cost, the insurer will pay the portion of the cost to repair or replace the damage that the limit of insurance bears to 80 percent (or other selected percentage) of the replacement cost at the time of loss. This is explained by the following formula.

$$\text{Loss payment} = \frac{\text{limit of insurance}}{80\% \text{ of replacement cost}} \times \text{replacement cost of the loss}$$

For example, assume a building has a replacement cost of $200,000 but the policyowner only carries $140,000 of coverage. Also assume a windstorm destroys a roof that would cost $8,000 to replace. Using the above formula:

$$\text{Loss payment} = \frac{\$140,000}{.8 \times \$200,000} \times \$8,000 = \frac{\$140,000}{\$160,000} \times \$8,000 = \$7,000$$

Therefore, $7,000 would be paid (ignoring any deductible).

The same formula is used if losses are settled in an actual cash value basis except that the term replacement cost is replaced by the term actual cash value.

A somewhat similar provision with an 80 percent insurance-to-value requirement is found in most homeowners and businessowners policies for situations when losses to the building and other real property are settled on a replacement-cost basis, but the term coinsurance provision is not used. The same formula described above for commercial property is used, but with one modification. The insurer agrees to pay the actual cash value of the loss if that amount is greater than the amount determined by applying the coinsurance formula.

Example: Alex and Sandra own a home with a replacement value of $200,000. A fire in the kitchen causes a loss with a replacement cost of $10,000 and an actual cash value of $8,000. If the amount of insurance carried is $150,000, how much will Alex and Sandra collect? Since they carried less than $160,000 of insurance (80% of $200,000), they will collect the greater of the following:

- the amount determined by the coinsurance formula

$$\frac{\$150,000}{\$160,000} \times \$10,000 = \$9,375$$

- the ACV of the loss, or $8,000

The possibility of a penalty for underinsurance can be minimized in several ways. In commercial insurance, the coinsurance clause can sometimes be deleted for a price. In homeowners insurance, some insurers provide guaranteed replacement-cost coverage as long as the policyowner carries what the insurer determines is 100 percent of replacement cost. Other homeowners policies may contain provisions to adjust the amount of coverage for inflation.

It should be noted that even if adequate insurance is carried to avoid an underinsurance penalty, an insured will not be indemnified for 100 percent of the value of a total loss of the insured property unless the amount of insurance equals 100 percent or more of replacement cost.

other insurance clause

Other Insurance. Most property and liability insurance policies contain an *other insurance clause* to specify how an insurer's obligation is affected by the existence of other insurance covering a loss.

It was once common to have provisions exonerating an insurer from the payment of a claim if there was another insurance policy covering the property for the same perils. Such restrictions are not widely used now. However, most homeowners policies do not cover losses to personal property that is separately described and specifically insured in another policy or in an endorsement to the homeowner policy. Such coverage often exists when the policyowner has valuable personal property. Because of limited coverage for certain types of personal property in an unendorsed homeowners policy, this property is often separately insured. The rationale is that the separate coverage should be written to cover the entire loss.

In other situations when duplicate coverage exists, two other approaches are often found. The most common approach is for policies to pay on a pro rata basis. For example, if one policy provides $200,000 of insurance on a building and another policy provides $300,000 of insurance on the same building, the first insurance policy will pay two-fifths of any loss, and the second policy will pay three-fifths.

In some cases, policies cover on a primary and excess basis. Such a provision is common for collision losses to automobiles when coverage exists under the policy of the automobile owner and the policy of another person who drives the automobile. In this case, the owner's policy is primary. The other policy only pays if the owner's policy limits are inadequate or the owner's policy provides less adequate coverage. The latter circumstances would exist, for example, if the owner's policy has a $1,000 deductible for collision and the other policy has a $250 deductible. The owner's policy would pay the loss less the $1,000 deductible, and the other policy would pick up $750 of this amount so that a $250 deductible effectively applies to the loss.

Settling Disputes. In most cases, the insurance company and the insured reach a mutually satisfactory settlement of property claims, but disputes do sometimes arise regarding whether coverage exists or concerning the value of the loss. State insurance departments have offices that look into complaints by insureds, and these offices are one avenue for resolving disputes. However, the state insurance departments have little authority to impose a settlement unless an insurer is clearly acting contrary to policy provisions; they are not an arbitration body to resolve legitimate disputes.

Disputes that involve the question of whether coverage exists ultimately may have to be decided by the legal system. However, both parties may agree that a loss is covered but disagree on the value of property or the amount of loss. To resolve this type of dispute, most property insurance policies contain an appraisal provision, which may lead to a binding settlement.

appraisal provision   The typical *appraisal provision* states that either party may make a written demand for an appraisal. If this occurs, each party selects a "competent and impartial" appraiser. The two appraisers then select an umpire. If they cannot agree on the umpire, either appraiser can request that a judge in the court with jurisdiction select the umpire. Each party pays his or her own appraiser; the other costs, including the umpire, are shared equally.

Once the umpire is selected, each appraiser submits his or her opinion on the value of the property and the amount of the loss. Differences are submitted to the umpire. An agreement by any two of the three parties leads to a binding settlement. If none of the three agree, the insured can take the matter to court.

Liability Losses

The second category of loss exposure consists of losses that result from legal liability. Unlike many other countries, the United States has a legal climate that encourages lawsuits. The potential result of these lawsuits puts the entire financial resources of an individual or business in jeopardy because the amount of legal damages is based on the loss to the injured party, not the ability to pay of the party that caused the injury. In addition, legal judgments can lead to the garnishment of future wages or the loss of future profits.

The following discussion looks at the types of liability damages, the basis of legal liability, and the settlement of claims.

Types of Liability Losses

Legal damages fall into several categories, including bodily injury, property damage, personal injury, and contractual liability.

bodily injury

Bodily Injury. *Bodily injury* results when a person suffers bodily harm, sickness, or disease and includes required care, loss of services, and death that results.[2] The injured party may incur tangible losses such as medical bills, lost income, or the need to hire someone to perform services such as cleaning the house or mowing the lawn.

Bodily injury can also result in an award of damages for pain and suffering. In many cases, pain and suffering payments far exceed those paid for medical bills and lost income.

In some cases, additional punitive damages are awarded when a defendant's behavior has been so offensive that the legal system feels an example should be made of the behavior. Some states have taken the position that a defendant should not be relieved of paying punitive damages by an insurance company and prohibit insurance companies from paying this portion of any judgment.

Bodily injury can also result in suits by parties other than the person actively suffering the injury. For example, relatives can sue for wrongful death or loss of companionship.

property damage

Property Damage. The destruction or damage to real or personal property can also result in legal liability. The *property damage* can consist of actual damage to the property but can also arise because of lost income or extra expenses that result from the inability to use the property.

personal injury

Personal Injury. Some types of legal liability occur from situations that involve neither bodily injury nor property damage. One of these situations that is commonly insured is *personal injury*, which can result from such actions as invasion of privacy, defamation of character, malicious prosecution, libel, slander, and the like.

contractual liability

Contractual Liability. Legal liability can also arise from the failure of a person or business to meet contractual obligations. This *contractual liability* may result from breach of contract, responsibility for damage to the property of others in one's possession, and implied warranties.

Basis of Legal Liability

A claim based upon liability imposed by law develops as the result of the invasion of the rights of others. A legal right is more than a mere moral obligation of one person to another; it has the backing of the law to enforce the right. Legal rights impose many specific responsibilities and obligations, such as not invading privacy or property, as well as not harming others.

The invasion of such legal rights is a *legal wrong*. The wrong can be criminal or civil. A *criminal wrong* is an injury that involves the public at large and is punishable by the government.

tort

Civil wrongs are based upon torts and contracts. Contracts can involve legal wrong when implied warranties are violated, bailee responsibilities are not fulfilled, or contractual obligations are breached. *Torts* are wrongs independent of contract (for example, false imprisonment, assault, fraud, libel, slander, and negligence). Although the government takes action with respect to crime, civil injuries are remedied by court action instituted by the injured party in a civil action. The remedy is usually the award of monetary damages. The consequences of a crime are not usually insurable, but the liability for damages growing out of a civil wrong can—and often should be—insured.

Figure 16-1 illustrates the legal basis for liability. Although liabilities include criminal wrongs, the emphasis for liability insurance is on civil wrongs and particularly on the many legal wrongs based upon *torts*. Of greatest importance are torts that result from *negligence* (unintentional acts or omissions), which are said to encompass more than 9 out of 10 claims for bodily injury or property damage to others.

Liability under Contract Law. Liability under contract law is based on the invasion of another's rights under a contract. It occurs only as a result of a contract between one party and another. In contrast, liability under tort law is based on the breach of one's duty to respect the rights of the general public. It can result from either common law or statute.

Breach of Contract. The nonfulfillment of promises that are made in an agreement, or breach of contract, is the most obvious type of civil wrong based on contracts. The failure to honor a warranty expressly contained in a contract is an example of such a breach.

Bailees' Responsibilities. Liability can result when a person or business has intentionally received temporary custody of the property of others. This

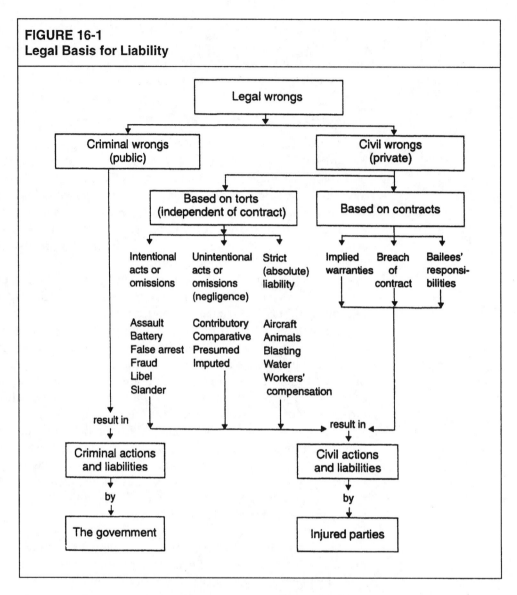

FIGURE 16-1
Legal Basis for Liability

bailment

is referred to as *bailment,* and a bailment is considered a subset of contractual liability even though there might not be a written contract. The degree of care required for this property and the potential for legal liability depends on the circumstances of the bailment. For example, a person who takes care of another's property without compensation while the other person is on vacation would have a lower degree of care imposed than if the property had been borrowed for his or her use. A high degree of care is also required when a business, such as a dry cleaner or repair shop, has possession of customers' property.

Implied Warranties. One of the most common extensions of liability under contract law concerns manufacturers and distributors of products. In connection with sales or a contract to sell, the law imposes certain obligations termed *implied warranties.* Where a buyer reasonably relies on the skill or judgment of the seller, there is an implied warranty that the goods are reasonably fit for the purpose for which they were sold. A seller can also be held liable if products are supplied to a user without giving proper notice of their dangerous qualities.

Liability under Tort Law. Torts include all civil wrongs not based on contracts. As such, they are a broad residual classification of many private wrongs against another person or organization. They occur independently of contractual obligations and can result from (1) intentional acts or omissions, (2) strict liability imposed by law, or (3) negligence.

Intentional Acts or Omissions. Lawsuits sometimes occur because of injuries or damage caused by intentional acts or omissions. One example is battery, which is the offensive or harmful touching of another without his or her express or implied consent. Assault is a second example, and this involves threatened battery. Other examples include fraud, trespass (entry on land of another without permission), and false arrest or detention, which results from the unprivileged restriction of another's freedom of movement. In addition, libel (written) and slander (oral) involve false statements made about someone else. All of these acts are based upon planned or premeditated acts or omissions, although the harmful results may not have been anticipated.

strict liability

Strict or Absolute Liability. The law in particular situations holds persons responsible for injuries or damages no matter how careful they may have been in trying to avoid losses to others. Under what is called *strict liability* or *absolute liability,* certain persons are held liable for damages, regardless of whether or not fault or negligence can be proved against them. Examples include injury from blasting operations by contractors, injury caused by any type of wild animal kept in captivity, and damage done by a release of pressure or weight of water such as a weak dam bursting. Other illustrations of this trend include the absolute liability (up to certain amounts) that airlines have for the safety of their passengers and workers' compensation laws, which hold the employer liable for most employee work-related injuries and diseases.

negligence

Negligence Liability. Negligence is a tort, and most of the liability imposed by law stems from accidents attributable to negligence. If negligence can be shown to be the proximate cause of an injury to another, the negligent party is liable to the injured party for damages. *Negligence* is the failure to exercise the proper degree of care required by circumstances. It can consist of not doing what was required under the circumstances, or of doing something that should not have been done. Behavior in any circumstances that fails to measure up to that expected of a careful, prudent person in like circumstances constitutes negligence. Faulty judgment can result in liability for negligence, even if the motive behind the act was the best.

Four requirements must exist before negligence liability is present. There must be (1) a legal duty, (2) a wrong, (3) a proximate relationship between the wrong and an injury or damage, and (4) an injury or damage.

A *legal duty* to act, or not to act, depends on the circumstances and the persons involved. A bystander has no legal duty to try to prevent a mugging, but a police officer does. Lifeguards have a legal duty to attempt to save a drowning victim, but others usually do not. Whether or not a legal duty is owed to someone else is decided by the courts, and many factors can determine the degree of care required.

A *wrong* is a breach of legal duty, based upon a standard of conduct that is determined by what a prudent person would have done or not done in similar circumstances. To do a wrong, the act or omission must be voluntary. Thus, if a person in the course of avoiding great danger injures another person without intent, there is held to be no voluntary act and hence no liability. Negligence usually involves injury that is unintentional. On the other hand, it is no defense if the act that injures a party was committed without intent to do an injury or if the motive behind the act was good and praiseworthy.

A third requisite for the fixing of liability is found in the rule that the voluntary act of the wrongdoer must have been the *proximate cause* of the injury. For the act to be held a proximate cause, there must have been a continuous succession of events from the act to the final event that caused the injury. If there was an independent and intervening cause, the continuous succession of events is broken. Thus, a fire ignited negligently and spread by the winds is one continuous succession of events. If, however, a third party were deliberately pushed into the flames by someone else and injured, there would not have been a continuous sequence. No liability for the injury would attach to the party responsible for the fire.

The fourth requirement for negligence liability is that there is *injury* or *damage*. The guilty person must pay an amount that reasonably compensates

---

Elements of a Negligent Act

- A certain standard of care is owed to others.
- That standard of care is not met.
- There is injury or damage.
- Failure to meet the standard of care is the proximate cause of the injury or damage.

the injured party for any losses for which the negligence is the proximate cause.

Several modifications, by court cases or statutes, sometimes change the usual rules pertaining to negligence liability. These include *contributory* and *comparative* negligence laws and the doctrines of *presumed* and *imputed* negligence.

Contributory and Comparative Negligence. Except where statutory enactments have modified the common-law rule, anyone who is so negligent as to contribute to his or her own injuries or damage cannot recover from another for these injuries because of *contributory negligence*. Such a person is said to be contributorily negligent and is barred from recovery, no matter how slight the negligence.

contributory negligence

The claimant frequently advances the plea that the alleged contributory negligence did not contribute to the injury, and that if the defendant had exercised reasonable care, the accident could have been avoided. There has developed a rule, known as the *last clear chance doctrine*, which holds that although the claimant is negligent, there is liability if the defendant had a last clear chance to avoid the accident. Today the rule is followed by statute in only a few states. It is, however, a concept often used in defense proceedings, sometimes successfully.

last clear chance doctrine

In its strict application, the old common-law doctrine of contributory negligence does not always produce equitable results. A very slight degree of negligence on the part of an injured person would bar recovery. Many states have enacted statutes that provide that contributory negligence shall not bar recovery for damages. Such statutes apply the idea of *comparative negligence* and provide that damages shall be diminished in proportion to the amount of negligence attributable to the person injured or to the owner or person in control of the damaged property.

comparative negligence

At first glance, there seems to be substantial merit to have each person share the cost of an accident in proportion to their share of negligence. For example, 80 percent of the damages to others is paid if a person has been held 80 percent negligent. In some states, however, under complete comparative negligence, the person who was primarily responsible for the accident would also receive 20 percent of his or her damages if the other party were deemed 20 percent negligent. The critics of the comparative negligence law used in these states point out this drawback. Other states have partial comparative negligence statutes, under which a plaintiff can recover only if the degree of his or her negligence is less than (or in some states not greater than) the defendant's negligence. In the preceding example, the person who was 20 percent negligent would receive 80 percent of his or her damages, and the other party would receive nothing. In actual practice, slight negligence tends to be disregarded, and suit against the party primarily responsible is permitted. Settlements out of court also frequently ignore slight negligence or take it into consideration in making partial payments.

Presumed Negligence. In order to establish a case, the claimant in ordinary circumstances must show a failure to exercise reasonable care on the part of the defendant. The burden of proof therefore is on the claimant. In certain cases, however, presumed negligence can be assumed from the facts. The legal doctrine that applies is *res ipsa loquitur,* meaning "the thing speaks for itself." Negligence is presumed without the need for the injured person to prove it. The burden of proof is shifted to the defendant, an exception to the common-law rule that a plaintiff must prove the defendant's fault.

The doctrine operates when an accident causes an injury (1) if the instrumentality would not normally cause injury without negligence, (2) if inspection and use of the instrumentality is within exclusive control of the party to be held liable, and (3) if the party to be held liable has superior knowledge of the cause of the accident and the injured party is unable to prove negligence. There must be no contributory negligence, and the accident must be of such nature that injury would not ordinarily occur without negligence.

Modern situations to which this doctrine has been applied include automobile injuries (in cases where no witnesses are available), railroad or aviation injuries, medical malpractice claims (such as an operation on the wrong part of the body or on the wrong person), and many damages caused by defective products.

Imputed Negligence. Not only is a negligent person liable for his or her acts or omissions that cause injuries or damage to others, but sometimes the responsibility extends to the negligence of other persons under the concept of **imputed negligence** *imputed negligence.* Courts and statutes have extended the rules of negligence to apply to employers, landlords, parents, automobile owners, and many other parties.

If the negligent party acts in the capacity of employee or agent of another, the wrongdoer and the owner or operator of a property can be held liable. For example, employers can be personally liable for the torts of their employees. Imputed liability is also important in property rentals, where landlords can be held responsible for the actions of their tenants.

Parents, too, although generally not liable for the negligent actions of their children, can be held liable by some state statutes. These statutes usually impose limited liability up to several thousand dollars on the parents for damages caused by their children, but they can extend further for specific types of dangerous instruments (guns, for example) used by minors. A child can also be legally liable for his or her own wrongful acts but is seldom able to pay substantial damages.

Under statutes called *vicarious liability* laws, liability in most states is imputed to automobile owners even though they are not driving or riding in their cars. In addition, under the *family purpose doctrine,* such liability applies particularly to the car owner whose family members negligently use the car, either under the idea of agency (when the car is used for family purposes) or on the basis of using a dangerous instrumentality.

Several dozen states have passed dram shop or liquor liability laws that make taverns, other businesses, and individuals dispensing liquor liable for injuries that may be caused by their intoxicated patrons such as in an automobile accident.

Some states impose liability if children are injured on a premises because they were attracted there by such items as swimming pools, ladders, gasoline, unlocked automobiles, or other *attractive nuisances*. Other states impose liability for injuries from domestic animals even if it would otherwise be difficult or impossible to prove negligence.

Settlement of Claims

Liability policies specify the duties of the insured following losses as well as the obligations of the insurance company.

Duties of the Insured. Most liability insurance policies require the insured to perform duties similar to the following in the case of a covered accident or occurrence:

- Give written notice as soon as practical to the company or its agent. The written notice should include (1) the identity of the policy and the insured, (2) reasonable information on the time, place, and circumstances of the accident or occurrence, and (3) names and addresses of any claimants or witnesses.
- Forward promptly to the insurance company every notice, demand, summons, or other process relating to the accident or occurrence.
- Assist the insurance company, at its request, to do the following:
  - Make settlement.
  - Enforce any of the insured's rights against others who may be liable to the insured.
  - Help with the conduct of suits and attend hearings and trials.
  - Secure and give evidence, and obtain the evidence of witnesses.

Obligations of the Insurance Company. If a claim is made or a suit brought against an insured because of an occurrence to which coverage applies, the insurance company has two primary obligations.

First, the insurer will pay up to the limit of liability for the damages for which the insured is legally liable. Damages include any prejudgment interest awarded against the insured.

Second, the insurer will provide a defense at its expense by a counsel of its choice, even if a suit is groundless, false, or fraudulent. The company typically has the right to settle any claim or suit as it deems appropriate. The choice of whether a settlement is made is at the insurer's option. In some cases, settlements are made because it is less expensive than going to trial. Even though some insureds may view this as admitting their liability when they are convinced they are not liable, there is usually nothing they can do to prevent a settlement. It once was common to let the insured veto a settlement under professional liability policies, but this right has been disappearing in recent years.

Consequential Losses

The final category of loss exposures consists of consequential or indirect losses. These can best be defined as additional expenses and lost income that arise as a result of property and liability losses. Consequential losses can cause significant financial harm and, in some instances, can exceed the direct property or liability loss from which they result. Examples include the following:

- expense of renting substitute facilities during the time it takes to repair a damaged house or business
- rental income lost because a structure has been damaged and cannot be occupied
- extra expenses to keep a business in operation following a loss
- expense of towing a damaged vehicle or renting a substitute vehicle while repairs are being made
- profits that are lost when a business is shut down because of damage to its building
- cost of bail bonds because of an automobile accident
- wages that are lost in order to attend hearings or trials resulting from a liability loss

Consequential loss can occur to a person or individual even when a loss does not directly involve his or her property. For example, an individual may need to find temporary living facilities when authorities prevent his or her return to an area because of a potential explosion due to a gas leak or following a disaster, even though the insured's home has not suffered any damage. Similarly, a business can lose profits when it cannot operate because of its inability to obtain inventory following a loss to a supplier's plant.

At least some consequential loss coverage is contained in most property and liability insurance policies along with the direct property and liability coverage. In fact, this is the primary source of coverage for individuals as separate policies are seldom written. However, unique coverages, such as business income insurance and extra expense insurance, are common commercial insurance policies or endorsements.

TYPES OF PROPERTY AND LIABILITY POLICIES

Property and liability policies can cover only a few types of losses and perils or be comprehensive package policies. However, even the broadest policy contains some exclusions and limitations, which may dictate a need for additional policies or endorsements.

Single Coverages

Historically, property and liability policies focused on relatively narrow types of coverage. Property insurance and liability insurance were seldom written in the same contract. In addition, policies were often written to cover specific types of property losses. Over the years, several changes have taken place. First, more types of losses are covered under a single policy. For example, personal and real property can be insured under one contract.

Second, coverage is now written for a broader number of perils, and it may even be "open-perils."

Third, the consequential losses from a direct loss are not only more likely to be covered, but they are frequently covered in the same policy as the direct losses.

Finally, an increasing amount of insurance is now provided under package policies.

Package Policies

package policy

A *package policy* combines two or more types of insurance—often property and liability insurance—into a single contract. For many individuals, two types of package policies—a homeowners policy and an automobile policy—will cover most of their insurance needs. However, a personal umbrella liability policy will still probably be needed. Over time, these policies have also tended to become relatively standardized among companies.

Package policies are now also the norm for businesses. However, unlike personal policies, which automatically cover a large number of loss exposures, some commercial package policies (particularly those for large businesses) are more likely to require the policyowner to select the appropriate coverage parts to meet the needs of a business or other organization.

Need for Endorsements or Additional Policies

Many individuals think that their package policies cover everything. Unfortunately, this is often far from the truth, and the financial planning process should determine when such policies fall short of adequate protection. In many—but not necessarily all—situations, policy endorsements or separate policies are available to compensate for policy shortcomings or to accommodate special needs.

Coverage in package policies is limited for several reasons. Certain perils—such as war, wear and tear, and intentional destruction of insured property by the insured—are considered uninsurable. Other perils are excluded because the cost of coverage tends to be relatively high and not everyone has a need for the coverage. However, those who want coverage can obtain it at a cost. For example, not all policyowners are susceptible to floods and earthquakes, but such coverage tends to be available for those who need and want it. Flood insurance is usually a separate policy whereas earthquake insurance is often in the form of a policy endorsement. Similarly, an individual with domestic employees or a large boat needs to purchase a workers' compensation policy or a yacht policy, respectively.

The dollar amount of coverage is also limited for certain types of property—certain classes of personal property are a prime example. Again, those who need a higher amount of coverage can obtain it for an additional premium. In addition, the added coverage may be subject to more stringent underwriting (such as a determination of value before a loss occurs) because of the difficulty in determining the value of personal property after it has been destroyed. Examples of types of property with limited coverage under a typical homeowners policy are jewelry, silverware, and collections of coins, stamps, and firearms.

In the remaining chapters on properly and liability insurance, particular attention should be paid to policy limitations so that an insured can be properly advised of the need to tailor coverage to specific circumstances.

TAXATION

The tax implications of premium payments for, and loss settlements from, property and liability policies vary by type of loss and type of taxpayer.

Deductibility of Premium

Premiums paid by individual taxpayers for personal property and liability insurance are not deductible. However, premiums paid for business coverage by individuals, partnerships, or corporations are deductible business expenses.

Taxation of Premiums for Employees

Although group property and liability insurance as an employee benefit is not a wide-spread, it is growing somewhat in use. Such plans typically require an employee to pay the full cost of his or her coverage, and the tax implications are the same as if the employee had purchased an individual policy. If the employer pays any part of an employee's premium, for either individual or group coverage, the employer can deduct this cost as a business expense. However, the employer must report this amount as taxable income to the employee.

Taxation of Benefits

Benefits paid under liability insurance policies do not result in taxable income to the policyowner or insured even if they are paid on their behalf.

Under property insurance policies, benefits paid for direct loss to real or personal property result in a capital gain to the extent that a taxpayer receives reimbursement in excess of his or her basis in the property. However, the situation is treated as an involuntary conversion and the gain can be postponed to the extent that a taxpayer uses the proceeds to purchase replacement property and the purchase amount exceeds the taxpayer's basis in the lost or damaged property.

Example: Erin Poole purchased a diamond ring for $10,000 many years ago. The ring was stolen and she recovered $25,000, which was the current value of the ring. If a replacement ring is not purchased, she will have a capital gain of $15,000, just as if the ring were sold for $25,000. If a replacement ring is purchased at a cost of $25,000 or more, the entire gain is postponed until the future sale of the ring. If she purchases a $22,000 replacement ring, $3,000 of the settlement is taxable as a gain in the year the theft was discovered. The ring would continue to have a tax basis of $10,000, and the remaining $12,000 of the gain is taxable if the ring is later sold for $22,000 or more.

The situation for certain consequential losses is less clear. To the extent that benefits are paid for actual expenses incurred, there is no taxable income. Business interruption coverage, however, will result in ordinary income if it is written on a basis that insures the policyowner against loss of net profits. The rationale for such taxation is that the policy proceeds are merely replacing the net profits that would have been fully taxable if no loss had occurred. However, some forms of business interruption insurance are written to cover loss of use of property rather than lost profits. In such cases, some courts have held this type of settlement to be a part of the property loss and subject to capital-gains treatment to the extent it and the settlement for the direct property loss exceed the cost of replacement property.

Deductibility of Uninsured Losses

The Internal Revenue Code allows a deduction for certain losses to the extent they are not compensated for by insurance. This involves not only losses when there is no insurance but also losses when the insurance provides less than full protection because there are inadequate limits or deductibles. Those losses must arise from fire, storm, shipwreck, or other casualty, or from theft.

Interestingly, the term *casualty* is not defined by the Internal Revenue Code, but IRS and legal interpretations generally consider casualty to be a sudden, unexpected, or unusual event that results in damage, destruction, or loss of property. This definition is very broad and clearly includes losses from such perils as floods, earthquakes, weather-related events, vandalism, fire, motor vehicle accidents, and the like.

Theft is also broadly interpreted to mean loss of money or property resulting from, for example, embezzlement, extortion, larceny, or robbery. Losses from situations caused intentionally by a taxpayer or involving normal wear and tear do not meet the definition.

The maximum amount of the losses for tax purposes is the lesser of (1) the decrease in the fair market value of the property as a result of the casualty or theft or (2) the taxpayer's adjusted basis in the property. Therefore, the amount of the deductible loss for the ring previously discussed would be $10,000 if there were no insurance.

Losses can be deducted in full by businesses and by individual taxpayers if the loss is incurred in a trade or business or any transaction entered into for profit. Other losses of individual taxpayers are only deductible if they itemize income tax deductions and then only to the extent that (1) each separate loss exceeds $100 and (2) the total of all casualty and theft losses for the year exceeds 10 percent of adjusted gross income.

SOURCES FOR FURTHER IN-DEPTH STUDY

- Wiening, Eric A., *Foundations of Risk Management and Insurance* Malvern, PA: American Institute for CPCU/Insurance Institute of America, 2002. Phone 800-644-2101. Web site address www.aicpcu.org
- Wiening, Eric A., Rejda, George E., Luthardt, Constance M., and Ferguson, Cheryl L., *Personal Insurance,* Malvern, PA: American Institute for CPCU/Insurance Institute of America, 2002. Phone 800-644-2101. Web site address www.aicpcu.org

CHAPTER REVIEW

Answers to review questions and self-test questions start on page 725.

Key Terms

real property
personal property
named-perils policy
"open-perils" policy
mortgage clause
loss payable clause
actual cash value
replacement cost
valued policy law
coinsurance (property insurance)
other insurance clause
appraisal provision
bodily injury

property damage
personal injury
contractual liability
tort
bailment
strict liability
negligence
contributory negligence
last clear chance doctrine
comparative negligence
imputed negligence
package policy

Review Questions

16-1. List the three broad categories of property and liability loss exposures that face families and businesses.

16-2. Explain to your client the difference between the coverage provided by a specified-perils (named-perils) policy and an open-perils (all-risks) policy.

16-3. When a property loss occurs,
   a. what duties are typically imposed on the insured?
   b. what obligations does the insurer typically have?

16-4. Jim Smith has a homeowners policy with replacement cost coverage. After a fire at his home, the damage is estimated at $50,000 on an actual cash value basis and $60,000 ignoring depreciation (that is, on a replacement cost basis). The replacement cost of his home at the time of the loss is $300,000. Ignoring the deductible, how much would Jim recover in each of the following situations:
   a. if Coverage A in his policy is $250,000 and Jim repairs the house
   b. if Coverage A in his policy is $250,000 and Jim does not repair the house
   c. if Coverage A in his policy is $220,000 and Jim repairs the house
   d. if Coverage A in his policy is $180,000

16-5. Bill has a property loss of $90,000 and finds that it is covered by two policies—Policy A for $100,000 and Policy B for $80,000. Ignoring deductibles, indicate how much of the loss would be paid by each policy in each of the following situations:

a. if Policy A and Policy B both have pro rata other insurance provisions

b. if Policy A is written on a primary basis and Policy B is written on an excess basis

c. if Policy B is written on a primary basis and Policy A is written on an excess basis

16-6. Billy, a summer employee at Jones Dry Cleaners, was driving the company truck to pick up dry cleaning in the neighborhood when he failed to see a stop sign, glanced off a car that had the right of way, and hit a phone pole. Indicate the type of liability loss if each of the following resulted from the accident:

a. the cost of surgery, loss of income, and pain and suffering for the driver of the car that Billy hit

b. the cost to the phone company to repair its pole

c. the suit by the driver of the other car that resulted from Billy slandering her with foul language in front of witnesses at the accident scene

d. the settlement with the customers whose clothes were burned when the truck caught fire after it hit the phone pole

16-7. What are the four requirements that technically must exist before negligence is present?

16-8. Using the situation in question 6, indicate under what rule of law each of the following can happen:

a. Billy's employer is found liable for the injuries suffered by others that were caused by Billy.

b. Neither Billy nor his employer is required to pay the injured driver of the other car because a police officer at a radar trap indicated that the other driver had entered the intersection at an excessive rate of speed and the court held that the other driver was 20 percent at fault.

c. Billy's employer is required to pay the injured driver of the other car only 80 percent of her damages because a police officer at a radar trap indicated that the other driver had entered the intersection at an excessive rate of speed and the court held that the other driver was 20 percent at fault.

16-9. In the event of a loss under a liability policy, what are the

a. typical duties of the insured

b. obligations of the insurance company

16-10. With the widespread use of package policies, why are endorsements and additional policies often needed to meet a client's property and liability protection needs?

16-11. Explain the basic tax rules that apply to each of the following and point out where differences exist by type of taxpayer and/or type of loss:

> a. deductibility of premium
> b. taxation of premiums for employees
> c. taxation of benefits
> d. deductibility of uninsured losses

Self-Test Questions

T F   16-1. Property losses can occur to either real or personal property.

T F   16-2. "Open-perils" coverage refers to a policy that contains a very long list of named perils.

T F   16-3. A typical property insurance policy requires that whenever a property loss occurs, the insured must give prompt notice to the police.

T F   16-4. The key difference between a settlement on an actual cash value basis and a replacement cost basis is that depreciation is considered in calculating the actual cash value of the loss.

T F   16-5. Deductibles not only minimize attitudinal hazard but also lower premium costs.

T F   16-6. Most property and liability policies contain a provision that specifies how an insurer's obligation is affected by the existence of other insurance that covers a loss.

T F   16-7. A dispute that involves the amount of a property loss that should be paid by the insurance company typically is settled by a lawsuit against the insurer.

T F   16-8. All liability losses involve either bodily injury or property damage.

T F   16-9. Torts can result from negligence or contractual obligations.

T F   16-10. Negligence is the failure to exercise the proper degree of care required by the circumstances.

T F   16-11. If Pete was only 20 percent at fault for an auto accident in a state that relies on the contributory negligence standard, he could collect 80 percent of his damages from the other party.

T F   16-12. People cannot be responsible for the negligent acts of others.

T F   16-13. In a liability insurance policy, the insurance company has two primary obligations: (1) to pay up to the limit of liability for the damages for which the insured is legally liable and (2) to provide a defense at its expense.

T F   16-14. Consequential losses can cause severe financial harm that may exceed the direct property or liability loss from which they result.

T F   16-15. Property and liability insurance premiums paid for business coverage are generally not deductible as a business expense.

NOTES

1. Although consequential losses result from both property and liability losses, the term consequential loss insurance is often used to refer to policies or endorsements that cover consequential losses that result from property losses only.
2. This is typical of the definitions found in insurance policies. The precise legal definition varies from state to state.

Homeowners and Other Personal Property Coverages

Learning Objectives

An understanding of the material in this chapter should enable the student to

17-1.   Briefly describe the nature of a homeowners policy, including who is insured and what locations are insured.

17-2.   Describe the coverages and exclusions contained in Sections I and II of the HO-3 form of the homeowners policy.

17-3.   Explain the coverage provided by HO-2, HO-4, HO-5, HO-6, and HO-8 and the key ways they differ from HO-3.

17-4.   Describe the coverage provided by the various endorsements available to tailor the homeowners policy to individual needs.

17-5.   Explain why property and liability policies other than a homeowners policy may be required to meet the needs of individuals and describe the key policies available.

Chapter Outline

This chapter's primary focus is on the homeowners policy, which is a package policy that provides coverage for a family's home, personal possessions, and liability that arises out of the many activities of family members. However, it is a complex policy with many limitations and exclusions. In some cases, these limitations and exclusions deal with insurable loss exposures; in other cases, the limitations and exclusions can be handled with the proper use of policy endorsements or, occasionally, separate additional polices. These endorsements and separate policies for property insurance—such as flood insurance and title insurance—are also discussed.

Financial planners should be able to alert their clients to potential risk exposures related to their homeowners coverage. Specific recommendations and implementations are usually handled by a property and casualty insurance agent or broker.

HOMEOWNERS POLICIES

homeowners policy

The *homeowners policy* is not a single policy but rather a series of policy forms for different types of situations and with differing degrees of coverages for real and personal property. In this book, the discussion centers around the forms of *ISO (Insurance Services Office)*. ISO is an advisory organization that provides a wide range of services for insurance companies, including the development and filing of standardized insurance policies. Many property and liability companies purchase the services of ISO, and its policy forms are commonly used. Another, but smaller, advisory organization—The American Association of Insurance Services (AAIS)—also has a series of homeowners forms for its member companies. In addition, some insurance companies develop and file their own independent forms. While the AAIS forms and the independent forms are arranged differently and often use different wording, their coverage is very similar to the ISO forms.

ISO (Insurance Services Office)

The ISO forms evolve over time, and the discussion in this chapter is based on the latest forms—referred to as Homeowners 2000.

ISO Forms

There are six standard ISO homeowners forms:

- Homeowners 2—Broad Form
- Homeowners 3—Special Form
- Homeowners 4—Contents Broad Form
- Homeowners 5—Comprehensive Form
- Homeowners 6—Unit-owners Form
- Homeowners 8—Modified Coverage Form

In making reference to these forms, it is common to call them Form 2, Form 3, and so on, or HO-2, HO-3, HO-4, HO-5, HO-6, and HO-8. The latter terminology is used in this book. When one of these forms is added to a declarations page, a homeowners policy is created.

HO-2, HO-3, HO-5, and HO-8 are designed for owner-occupants of one- to four-family dwelling units. Each unit may contain no more than two families or one family and two roomers or boarders. HO-4 is designed for tenants of residential property and also for the owner of an apartment building who occupies one of its units. The building itself may be ineligible for homeowners coverage because it contains too many units. HO-6 is designed for the owners of condominium units.

Each homeowners form has two major sections. Section I provides property coverage, and it is in this section that the forms differ. The liability coverage of Section II is identical in all six forms.

HO-3 is the most common of the forms and appropriate for most owners of homes. It is analyzed in some detail. Following this analysis, the differences in most of the other forms and when their use is appropriate are discussed.

Definitions

The homeowners policy is typical of most property and liability contracts because a list defines terms used throughout the policy. In any such policy, a thorough understanding of what is or isn't covered depends on these definitions.

Because terms can be defined differently among policies, it is important to understand their meaning in a specific policy. Two terms that are particularly important in the homeowners policy are insured and insured location.

Insured

Many persons are classified as insureds under a homeowners policy. For purposes of the entire policy, these include

named insured

- the *named insured*. This is the person listed in the policy declarations and the spouse of the named insured, if not also listed, as long as he or she is a resident of the same household.
- residents of the named insured's household who are relatives
- residents of the named insured's household who are under the age of 21 and in the care of any of the persons previously mentioned
- a full-time student (as defined by the school) who was a resident of the insured's household before moving out to attend school, as long as the student is either
  - (1) under 24 and a relative of an insured or
  - (2) under 21 and in the care of an insured

There are two other categories of persons who are considered an insured for the purposes of the Section II liability coverage. These categories include

- any person or organization responsible for animals or watercraft owned by anyone on the previous list. However, they are insureds only with respect to animals or watercraft to which the policy applies and only if this possession is with the owner's permission and not in the course of any business. For example, a neighbor while caring for a pet because the named insured is on vacation is an insured, but a veterinarian where the pet is boarded is not.
- any person employed by any one of the insureds in the earlier list with respect to any vehicles insured under the policy and other persons using the vehicles on an insured location with the consent of the named insured

Insured Location

An insured location includes the following:

- the residence premises. This includes the one- to four-family dwelling, other structures, and grounds where the policyowner resides as shown in the declaration.
- that part of other premises, other structures, and grounds used by the named insured or spouse as a residence (for example, a vacation home) if it is shown in the declarations or if it is acquired during the policy year as a residence by the named insured
- other premises not owned by an insured but where an insured is temporarily residing
- vacant land, other than farm land, owned by or rented to an insured
- individual or family cemetery plots or burial vaults of an insured
- any part of a premises occasionally rented to an insured for other than business use

HO-3 Property Coverages

Section I of HO-3 contains five categories of property coverage:

- Coverage A for the dwelling
- Coverage B for other structures
- Coverage C for personal property
- Coverage D for loss of use
- Additional coverages that provide protection for assorted situations

The insurance buyer must determine the amount of insurance for Coverage A on the dwelling. The amount of insurance for Coverages B, C, and D are then a percentage of the amount of the Coverage A limit. The standard limit for Coverage B is 10 percent of the Coverage A limit, the Coverage C limit is 50 percent, and the Coverage D limit is 30 percent. The limits for Coverage C and Coverage D, which are adequate for most policyowners, can be increased by selecting a higher amount of coverage and paying an additional premium. The percentage for Coverage C can also be reduced to as little as 40 percent. The limit for Coverage B can also be increased with an endorsement that is described later.

Three points need to be made. First, the limits for Coverages B, C, and D are additional amounts of insurance, not part of the Coverage A limit. For example, if a policyowner has $250,000 of insurance on a dwelling, there is an additional $125,000 of insurance for personal property, and any payment for a personal property loss does not affect the amount of coverage on the dwelling.

Second, it is important that the policyowner have adequate insurance for Coverage A at the time of loss, or a penalty can result.

There are some who argue that maintaining insurance equal to 100 percent of a dwelling's replacement value is not necessary because a total loss is unlikely to occur. For example, a fire probably won't destroy the dwelling's concrete foundation. (However, there are times when a fire damages a foundation so severely that it must be replaced.) Even if less than a 100 percent coverage limit is maintained, the replacement value of the dwelling can increase because of inflation. There is an available inflation guard endorsement, whereby an annual percentage increase is selected and the limit of insurance increases on a pro rata basis of that amount during the policy period.

Third, the replacement cost of the dwelling is not equal to the market value of a dwelling. For example, a 25-year-old property may sell for $400,000. The lot by itself could be worth $100,000. However, the cost to replace the dwelling with new construction might be $500,000. An estimate from a builder or a professional appraiser is probably necessary to pinpoint replacement value with any degree of accuracy.

Coverage A for the Dwelling

Coverage A provides property insurance for the residence premises listed in the declarations page of the policy. The land itself is specifically excluded from coverage. Coverage A also applies to structures attached to the dwelling, such as a garage, decks, or fences, and to materials and supplies located on or next to the residence premises for construction, repair, or alteration of the dwelling or other structures on the residence premises.

Covered Perils and Losses. Coverages A and B are "open-perils," but they do not cover loss arising from the following:

- collapse. However, there is coverage under Additional Coverages for losses from certain perils.
- freezing of (1) a plumbing, heating, air conditioning, or automatic fire protection sprinkler system or (2) a household appliance. In addition, the policy does not cover leakage from within the system unless the insured has taken reasonable care to maintain heat in the building or to shut off the water supply and drain the system and appliances of water. However, if the building is protected by an automatic fire protection sprinkler system, the insured must take reasonable care to continue the water supply and maintain heat in the building.
- freezing, thawing, pressure, or weight of water or ice to items such as fences, pavement, patios, swimming pools, foundations, retaining walls, and docks
- theft in or to a dwelling or of construction materials until a dwelling is finished and occupied

- vandalism and malicious mischief to a dwelling (other than one under construction) that has been vacant for more than 60 consecutive days preceding a loss
- mold, fungus, or wet rot unless it is hidden within or by walls, floors, or ceilings and results from accidental discharge of water or steam from (1) a household appliance or a plumbing, heating, air conditioning, or automatic fire protective sprinkler system on the residence premises or (2) a storm drain, or water, steam, or sewer pipes off the residence premises
- wear and tear, marring, and deterioration
- inherent vice, latent defect, and mechanical breakdown. (Inherent vice is the tendency of something to deteriorate—for example, fabric.)
- smog, rust or other corrosion, or dry rot
- smoke from agricultural or industrial operations
- pollutants unless they are released or escape because of a peril that is covered by one of the named perils that apply to personal property under Coverage C
- settling, shrinking, bulging, or expansion of pavement, patios, foundations, walls, floors, roofs, or ceilings
- birds, vermin, rodents, or insects
- animals owned or kept by an insured

The HO-3 does make two clarifications with respect to these excluded perils. First, if they result in water damage not otherwise excluded, the water damage is covered, but not the system or appliance from which the water escaped. For example, if a water pipe in a bathroom leaks and causes damage to the dwelling, the broken pipe is not covered, but there is coverage for the cost of tearing out any part of the building to repair the water pipe.

Second, any ensuing loss from these perils is covered unless it is otherwise excluded. For example, if a dog chews an electrical cord and a fire results, the damage to the electrical cord is not covered but the fire is.

Exclusions. Numerous exclusions apply, and some of them are significant. The effect of some exclusions can be negated with proper policy endorsements or separate policies.

The exclusions fall into two categories: (1) excluded losses that apply to all Section I coverages and (2) excluded losses that apply to Coverages A and B.

Several types of losses are specifically excluded from all Section I coverages, regardless of any other cause or event that contributes to the loss. These include losses resulting from the following:

- ordinance or law. Except for coverage provided in the Additional Coverages section of the policy or by an optional endorsement, losses that occur from the enforcement of an ordinance or law are excluded. For example, the policy would not pay to install an interior sprinkler system in a residence after a loss if that were now a building code requirement unless such a system was already in the destroyed and damaged dwelling.

- earth movement. Losses from earthquakes and other types of earth movement are excluded. However, any ensuing fire or explosion is covered. Earthquake insurance can be obtained through a policy endorsement or a separate policy.
- water damage. Losses are excluded that are caused by (1) flood, surface water, waves, tidal waves, and overflow or spray from a body of water; (2) water or water-borne material that backs up through sewers or drains; and (3) water or water-borne material below the surface of the ground that exerts pressure on or seeps through a building, sidewalk, driveway, foundation, swimming pool, or other structure. However, any ensuing fire, explosion, or theft resulting from water damage is covered. Coverage for the back-up of water or water-borne material is available by endorsement. Flood coverage requires a separate policy.
- power failure if the power failure occurs off the residence premises. For example, there is no coverage for spoiled food because a tornado destroyed a power plant several miles away. However, if a storm caused a policyowner's tree to fall on the power line entering his or her home, the consequential loss related to power failure would be covered.
- neglect of the insured to use all reasonable means to protect property at and after the time of loss
- war
- nuclear hazards. These include nuclear reaction, radiation, or radioactive contamination.
- intentional losses committed by an insured
- government action, which includes the destruction, confiscation, or seizure of property by a governmental or public authority. However, the exclusion does not apply to acts ordered to prevent the spread of fire.

There are three other types of excluded losses that apply to Coverages A and B. These include losses resulting from the following:

- weather conditions
- acts or decisions, including the failure to act or decide by any person, group organization, or government body
- any of the following that are faulty, inadequate, or defective

- planning, zoning, development, surveying, or siting
- design, specifications, workmanship, repair, construction, renovation, grading, or compaction
- materials used in repair, construction, renovation, or remodeling
- maintenance

However, any ensuing loss to insured property is covered unless it is precluded by some other policy provision.

Example: Faulty zoning allowed homes to be built on a hillside that was subject to landslides and grass fires. Losses resulting from landslides are not covered elsewhere in the homeowners policy, and a policyowner could not expect to be reimbursed by claiming that the cause of loss was faulty zoning rather than landslide. On the other hand, a loss due to a grass fire would be covered, not because of the faulty zoning, but because there is nothing else in the policy that excludes such fire losses.

Basis of Loss Settlement. Losses under Coverage A are settled on a replacement-cost basis.

Coverage B for Other Structures

Coverage B provides insurance for other structures on the residence premises that are set apart from the dwelling by a clear space. If there is no clear space, they are part of the dwelling and insured under Coverage A. Examples of other structures include swimming pools, detached garages, and garden sheds.

There is no coverage if another structure is rented or held for rental to any person not a tenant of the dwelling, unless used solely as a private garage. In addition, there is no coverage if the structure is used for business purposes, with the exception that the garage can be used to store business property owned solely by an insured as long as it does not contain gaseous or liquid fuel other than in a permanently installed fuel tank of a vehicle parked in the structure.

The same perils and exclusions that apply to Coverage A apply to Coverage B, and losses are also settled on a replacement-cost basis.

Coverage C for Personal Property

Coverage C provides insurance for personal property owned or used by any insured while it is located anywhere in the world. In addition, if the named insured or spouse so requests it at the time of loss, coverage is also provided for the property of others while the property is in the residence premises occupied by an insured or for the property of any guest or residence employee while the property is in any residence occupied by an insured.

The amount of coverage for property at a residence other than the residence premises is limited to the greater of 10 percent of the Coverage C limit or $1,000. Note that this 10 percent limitation does not apply to property that is at a location other than another residence such as a self-storage warehouse. In this case, the full amount of Coverage C applies. In addition, the full amount of Coverage C applies to property that is moved from the residence premises because it is being repaired, renovated, or rebuilt and is not fit to live in or to store property in. Finally, there is coverage for 30 days at each location when an insured is moving from one principal residence to another.

Perils Covered. Coverage is written on a named-perils basis. These perils include

- fire or lightning
- windstorm or hail. However, losses from rain, snow, sleet, sand, or dust are not covered unless they are a result of direct wind or hail damage to a building. In addition, damage to watercraft is not covered unless the watercraft is in a fully enclosed building.
- explosion
- riot or civil commotion
- aircraft
- vehicles
- smoke other than that from agricultural smudging or industrial operations
- vandalism or malicious mischief
- theft. This also includes mysterious disappearance, which is the loss of property from a known place when it is likely that it has been stolen. However, several exclusions apply to theft and the following are excluded from Coverage C:
  - theft committed by an insured
  - theft in or to a dwelling under construction, including material and supplies, unless the dwelling is finished or occupied
  - theft from the part of a residence premises rented by an insured to someone other than an insured
  - theft of property from another residence of the insured (such as a vacation home) unless the insured is temporarily living there
  - theft of property belonging to an insured who is a student when the property is at a residence away from home if the student has

not been there at any time during the 60 days immediately preceding the loss
  - theft of watercraft, including furnishings and equipment
  - theft of trailers and campers
- falling objects
- weight of ice, snow, or sleet
- accidental discharge or overflow of water or steam
- sudden and accidental tearing apart, cracking, burning, or bulging of a steam, hot water, air conditioning, or automatic fire protective sprinkler system, or appliance for heating water
- freezing of a plumbing, heating, air conditioning, or automatic fire protective sprinkler system, or household appliance
- sudden and accidental damage from an artificially generated electrical current
- volcanic eruption

Special Limits of Liability. Coverage C limits the amount of insurance available to certain classes of property. In some cases, this limitation is for all perils; in other cases, it is for theft losses only. Several endorsements are available to increase these limits.

These limitations apply to the total loss of property from any single category. They include

- $200 for money, bank notes, bullion, coins, medals, scrip, stored value cards, smart cards, and gold, silver, and platinum other than goldware, silverware, and platinumware
- $1,500 for securities, accounts, deeds, evidences of debt, letters of credit, notes other than bank notes, manuscripts, personal records, passports, tickets, and stamps
- $1,500 for watercraft, including trailers, furnishings, equipment, and motors
- $1,500 for trailers not used with watercraft
- $2,500 for property on the residence premises (and $500 away from the residence premises) used primarily for business purposes
- $1,500 for electronic apparatus and accessories while in a motor vehicle, but only if the apparatus is equipped to be operated by power from the motor vehicle's electrical system while still capable of being operated by other power sources
- $1,500 for electrical apparatus and equipment used primarily for business while away from the insured premises and not in or upon a motor vehicle. However, the apparatus must be equipped to be operated from a motor vehicle's electrical system while still being capable of being operated by other power sources.

- $500 for property away from the residence premises used primarily for business purposes, other than electronic apparatus and equipment as previously described

The following limitations apply to theft but not other perils:

- $1,500 for jewelry, watches, furs, and precious and semiprecious stones
- $2,500 for firearms and related equipment
- $2,500 for silverware, goldware, platinumware, and pewterware

Excluded Property. Some categories and property are excluded from coverage under Coverage C:

- articles insured elsewhere
- animals, birds, and fish
- most motor vehicles
- aircraft
- hovercraft
- property of roomers or borders other than those related to an insured
- property in an apartment rented to others. However, there is some coverage under Additional Coverages.
- property rented or held for rental to others off the residence premises
- business data
- credit cards, electronic fund transfer cards, or access devices used solely for deposit, transfer, or withdrawal of funds. However, there is limited coverage under Additional Coverages.
- water or steam

In a few cases, some limited coverage is provided as an Additional Coverage or under other parts of the policy. In most cases, coverage can also be obtained under separate insurance policies.

Basis of Loss Settlement. Under the standard homeowners policy, Coverage C losses are settled on an actual cash value basis. However, replacement-cost coverage is frequently added through the use of an available endorsement.

Coverage D for Loss of Use

Coverage D provides certain types of consequential loss coverage when the named insured's residence cannot be occupied as a result of a loss covered under Section I of the policy.

additional living expenses

If the named insured and family must live elsewhere while the portion of the residence that they normally occupy is being repaired or rebuilt, the named insured is entitled to benefits for *additional living expenses*. These benefits pay for any increase in expenses necessary to maintain the family's normal standard of living.

Coverage is also provided for the fair rental value, less any noncontinuing expenses, of the portion of the residence premises that is rented to others. Finally, up to two weeks' coverage is provided for the expenses of living elsewhere when civil authorities prohibit the named insured from using the residence premises because neighboring property is damaged by an insured peril. For example, expenses resulting from an evacuation because of a nearby brush fire would be covered, but not the expenses resulting from a threatening flood.

There is no coverage under Coverage D for losses arising out of the cancellation of leases or agreements.

Additional Coverages for Section I

Section I contains several Additional Coverages to fill in some of the gaps of the other four property coverages. In most cases, these provide amounts of insurance in addition to the limits under Coverages A, B, and C. Additional coverages include

- debris removal. Coverage is provided for the removal of debris following a covered loss and for removal of ash resulting from a volcanic eruption that has caused direct loss to a building or property contained therein. The removal of debris is included in the policy limit, but if the actual damage plus the cost of debris removal exceeds the policy limit, an additional 5 percent of the amount of insurance is available for debris removal. The policy will also pay up to $1,000 (but no more than $500 for any one tree) for the removal from the premises of trees that have been felled by windstorm, hail, or weight of ice, snow, or sleet if the trees damage a covered structure, block a driveway, or block an access ramp for a handicapped person.
- reasonable repairs to protect property from further damage after a covered loss occurs
- trees, shrubs, plants, and lawns. An amount of insurance equal to 5 percent of the Coverage A limit (but no more than $500 for any one tree, shrub, or plant) will be paid for damage that results to these items on the residence premises from the following perils: fire, lightning, explosion, riot, civil commotion, aircraft, vandalism, malicious mischief, theft, and vehicles not owned or operated by a resident of the premises.

- fire department service charges. Up to $500 will be paid for charges incurred under a contract or agreement when a fire department is called to save property from a covered peril. The policy deductible does not apply to this additional coverage.
- property removed from the premises because of endangerment by an insured peril such as a forest fire or hurricane. The property is covered elsewhere for up to 30 days against any peril.
- credit card, electronic fund transfer card or access device, forgery, and counterfeit money. Up to $500 is paid for the following losses as long as they do not arise out of business use or dishonesty of an insured:
  - legal obligations resulting from the theft or unauthorized use of an insured's credit card
  - loss resulting from theft or unauthorized use of an insured's electronic fund transfer card or access device. However, coverage does not apply to losses from misuse (1) by a household resident, (2) by anyone who has been entrusted with the card or access device, or (3) if the insured has not complied with the conditions under which the cards are issued or the devices accessed.
  - loss caused by forging or alteration of checks or negotiable instruments
  - loss through acceptance of counterfeit United States or Canadian paper currency
- loss assessments of up to $1,000 for the named insured's share of assessments during the policy period by a corporation or association of homeowners when the assessment is a result of a direct loss by a covered peril to property owned by all members collectively.
- collapse. Coverage is provided for the collapse of a building from (1) the perils insured against in Coverage C, (2) hidden decay, (3) hidden insect or vermin damage, (4) weight of contents, equipment, animals, or people, (5) weight of rain on a roof, and (6) use of defective material or construction methods. This is not an additional amount of insurance but rather the addition of losses from collapse if they result from certain perils.
- glass or safety glazing material that is part of a covered building, storm door, or storm window. Coverage is provided for the breakage of glass or safety glazing material and for any damage caused by the broken glass or safety glazing material as long as a covered building has not been vacant for more than 60 consecutive days.
- landlord's furnishings. Up to $2,500 will be paid for appliances, carpets, and other household furnishings owned by a named insured that are in an apartment on the residence premises rented to others. Coverage is from most of the named perils that apply under Coverage C.

- ordinance or law. An amount equal to 10 percent of the Coverage A limit applies to increased costs of demolition, construction, or repair because of ordinances or laws. For example, new building codes may require the use of more expensive, fire retardant roofing materials if a damaged roof is replaced. However, there is no coverage because of any law that requires the insured to test for, monitor, treat, respond to, or assess the effects of any pollutants.
- grave markers and mausoleums. Up to $5,000 is provided for damage resulting from a peril insured under Coverage C.

HO-3 Liability Coverages

Section II is the same in all homeowners forms. Like Section I, it contains more than one coverage. These are

- Coverage E for personal liability
- Coverage F for medical payments to others
- Additional Coverages that provide some miscellaneous liability and related benefits

As in Section I, coverage is broad but it is also subject to several exclusions, many of which can be covered by endorsements or other policies, including a personal umbrella liability policy.

Coverage E—Personal Liability

Coverage E provides protection for damages for which an insured is legally liable that arise out of bodily injury or property damage. The policy can be endorsed to also provide coverage for personal injury liability, but the personal umbrella policy covers this loss exposure.

The limit of coverage is typically $100,000 per occurrence but can be increased. Although a higher liability limit is usually desirable, many insureds carry only the underlying limit required by their personal umbrella policy, which will provide this additional protection if the homeowners limit is inadequate.

The insurance company also agrees to defend the insured and has the right to settle any suit. These defense costs are in addition to the stated policy limit for personal liability and will be paid even if a suit is groundless, false, or fraudulent.

Although Coverage E is very broad, it is subject to numerous exclusions. Some apply only to Coverage E; others also apply to Coverage F, which is discussed shortly.

Section II contains exclusions for both bodily injury and property damage that

- arises out of motor vehicles if the vehicle is
    - registered (or required to be registered) for use on public roads or property
    - used in an organized race, a speed contest, or some other competition
    - rented to others
    - used to carry persons or cargo for a charge
    - used for any business purpose, except for a motorized golf cart while on a golfing facility

  However, there are some exceptions to the exclusion, and there is coverage for motor vehicles under the following circumstances:
    - The vehicle is in dead storage on an insured location.
    - The vehicle is used solely to service an insured's residence.
    - The vehicle is designed to assist the handicapped or is being used by a handicapped person or parked on an insured location.
    - The vehicle is designed for recreational use off public roads and is not owned by an insured, or is owned by an insured and the occurrence takes place on an insured location.
    - The vehicle is a motorized golf cart either parked or stored on a golfing facility or used to (1) play golf, (2) travel to or from an area where golf carts are parked or stored, or (3) cross public roads at designated points to access other parts of a golfing facility. There is also coverage for the use of golf carts within a private residential community where an insured lives and which is subject to a property owner's association.
- arises out of aircraft or hovercraft
- arises out of watercraft if the watercraft is
    - a nonsailing vessel used in an organized race, speed contest, or other competition
    - rented to others
    - used to carry persons or cargo for a charge
    - used for any business purpose

  If a watercraft is not excluded by these conditions, there is coverage if the watercraft is stored or is a sailing vessel either (1) less than 26 feet in length or (2) not owned by or rented to an insured. If a watercraft is not a sailing vessel, there is liability coverage under the following conditions:
    - The boat has outboard engines or motors with less than 25 total horsepower.
    - The boat has outboard engines or motors of more than 25 horsepower if the boat (1) is not owned by an insured or (2) is owned by an insured and acquired during the policy inception.
    - The boat has outboard engines or motors of more than 25 horsepower and is owned by an insured prior to policy inception

if (1) the boat is declared at policy inception and (2) the intent to insure the boat is reported to the insurer within 45 days after acquisition.

- The boat has inboard-outboard motors or engines of 50 total horsepower or less and is not owned by an insured.
- The boat has inboard-outboard motors or engines of 50 horsepower or more and is not owned by or rented to an insured.

- is expected or intended by an insured
- arises out of or in connection with a business engaged in by an insured. There are some exceptions to this exclusion, however, and Coverage E applies if
  - a house is occasionally rented to others and used only as a residence
  - part of the residence is rented to others
  - part of the residence is rented and used as an office, school, study, or private garage
  - an insured is under age 21 and involved in part-time or occasional self-employed business (for example, lawn mowing) with no employees

  Several endorsements are available to provide limited coverage for businesses on the residence premises, but in many cases, commercial coverage is needed.
- arises out of the rendering or failure to render professional services
- arises out of a location owned or rented by an insured that does not meet the policy definition of an insured location
- is caused by war
- is caused by transmission of communicable disease
- arises out of sexual molestation, corporal punishment, or physical or mental abuse
- arises from the use, sale, manufacture, delivery, transfer, or possession of a controlled substance

Note that the exclusions arising out of locations that are not insured premises and motor vehicles, aircraft, and watercraft do not apply to bodily injury to residence employees in the course of their employment.

There are also more exclusions that apply only to Coverage E. These include liability arising from

- loss assessments charged against members of an association, corporation, or community of property owners. However, there is $1,000 of coverage for this exposure under the additional coverages for Section II.
- any contract or agreement other than written contracts (1) relating to the ownership, maintenance, or use of an insured location or (2) for liability of others assumed by the insured prior to an occurrence

- property damage to property owned by an insured
- damage to property that is rented to, occupied by, or in the care of the insured except for property damage caused by fire, smoke, or explosion
- results in bodily injury to any person who is eligible to receive benefits or who is provided benefits under a state workers' compensation law, nonoccupational disability law, or occupational disease law. Workers' compensation coverage is needed if this loss exposure exists.
- bodily injury arising out of nuclear energy
- bodily injury to any insured. In other words, the policy would not provide coverage if one insured injured another insured.

Coverage F—Medical Payments to Others

Coverage F provides up to $1,000 of coverage (or more if increased by endorsement) per occurrence for the necessary medical expenses of persons other than an insured who are injured while on an insured location with the permission of an insured. Benefits are paid regardless of fault even though this coverage is in the liability section of the policy. Injuries that occur off an insured location are also covered on the same basis if they

- arise out of a condition in an insured location
- are caused by the activities of an insured
- are caused by a resident employee of an insured in the course of employment for an insured
- are caused by an animal owned by or in the care of an insured

In addition to the exclusions previously mentioned that apply to both Coverages E and F, Coverage F does not apply to a residence employee injured off an insured location unless in the course of employment. Other persons regularly residing on an insured premises are also not covered.

| *Example:* | Walter Booth held a birthday party at his home for his 6-year-old son. During the festivities, a deck collapsed, injuring Walter, his son, and six guests. Two other guests were bitten while trying to catch Walter's dog which had also been injured. There is no medical payments coverage for Walter and his son because they are both insureds under Walter's homeowners policy. The six persons injured by the deck collapse will receive medical payments benefits because the collapse arose out of conditions in an insured location. The guests bitten by the dog are also |

covered because their injuries were caused by an animal owned by an insured. (Note that any injuries that exceeded $1,000 would be covered by the Booths' personal liability coverage if they were legally liable.)

Additional Coverages for Section II

Additional Coverages under Section II include the following:

- claim expenses in addition to defense costs
- first aid to others incurred by an insured for bodily injury covered by the policy
- up to $1,000 per occurrence for property damage to the property of others caused by an insured. However, this additional coverage does not apply to losses when
  - the loss is caused intentionally by an insured who is aged 13 or older
  - the property is owned by another insured
  - the property is owned by or rented to a tenant of an insured or a resident of the named insured's household
  - the damage arises out of a business engaged in by an insured
  - the damage arises out of any act or omission in connection with premises owned, rented, or controlled by an insured other than the insured location
  - the damage arises out of ownership or use of aircraft, hovercraft, watercraft, or motor vehicles other than recreational vehicles that are (1) designed for off road use, (2) not by an insured and, (3) not subject to motor vehicle registration

  In addition, there is an offset for any duplicate benefits paid under Section I.
- up to $1,000 for the insured's share of a loss settlement against a corporation or association of property owners for (1) bodily injury or property damage not excluded under Section II or (2) liability that results from the act of an elected and unpaid director, officer, or trustee

OTHER HOMEOWNERS FORMS

As previously mentioned, there are other homeowners forms. The ways in which they differ from HO-3 are discussed below, followed by table 17-1, which provides a side-by-side comparison.

HO-2 Broad Form

HO-2 differs from HO-3 in that Coverages A and B are written on the same named-perils basis as Coverage C. This form is most likely to be used when the cost of coverage is a concern. It is less comprehensive and therefore a little less expensive. Some insurers also use it for policyowners who have had several small losses due to carelessness that have been paid under a prior, more comprehensive HO-3.

HO-4 Contents Broad Form

HO-4 is often referred to as tenants homeowners insurance or renters insurance and is identical to HO-3 except that there is no Coverage A or Coverage B. The policyowner selects a limit for Coverage C, and Coverage D is 30 percent of this amount.

HO-4 is usually written for tenants of a house or apartment unit. There is no requirement that they live in a one- to four-family dwelling. HO-4 is also sometimes written for a policyowner who owns a residential structure that is not eligible for a homeowners policy. For example, the owner lives in one of ten units of an apartment building. The owner needs a commercial policy on the building but could use HO-4 for his or her personal possessions and personal liability.

HO-5 Comprehensive Form

HO-5 differs from HO-3 in that Coverage C is written on an "open-perils" basis.

HO-6 Unit-owners Form

HO-6 is designed to cover the unique loss exposures of a policyowner who lives in a condominium or cooperative unit. It is like HO-3 in that Coverage C is on a named-perils basis. This is also the amount of insurance selected by the policyowner. Coverage D is 50 percent of this amount.

In some cases, the condominium or cooperative association might insure the entire structure, including the fixtures, plumbing, wiring, partitions, and so on, of each unit owner. In other cases, the association's policy provides coverage for only the building structure and the walls that support it. Other real property within each unit, such as bookshelves or wall-to-wall carpeting, is the responsibility of the unit-owner. Consequently, HO-6 does provide $5,000 for Coverage A on a named-perils basis. This amount also applies to other structures, and the amount can be increased if needed. There is no Coverage B.

Coverages A and C can be changed to an open-perils basis by endorsement.

HO-8 Modified Coverage Form

HO-8 is not a widely used homeowners form and has been mostly written on older homes where the replacement cost of a dwelling often significantly exceeds its market value. Providing replacement coverage might create a moral hazard because the policyowner could collect more under an insurance settlement than by selling the house. In addition, the premium for replacement-cost coverage might be beyond the means of many persons who own such homes.

The perils insured against for all coverages are limited to fire, lightning, windstorm or hail, explosion, riot or civil commotion, aircraft, vehicles, smoke, vandalism and malicious mischief, and volcanic eruption. Theft is covered only from the residence premises and up to a limit of $1,000. This limitation reflects the fact that HO-8 is often written in areas where the crime rate is higher than average.

There are also other limitations. Only 10 percent of Coverage C is provided off the insured premises. Additional Coverages are more limited and, for example, do not include collapse or extra expenses because of ordinances or laws.

Loss settlements under Coverages A and B are based on common construction materials and methods that are functionally equivalent to the original construction. Settlements are limited to market value if repairs are not made. (Note, however, that some states require loss settlements to be on an actual cash value basis.)

The issue of functional equivalency is discussed later with respect to the Functional Replacement Cost endorsement.

Comparison of Homeowner Forms

Table 17-1 (see next page) shows a comparison of the homeowners forms.

HOMEOWNERS ENDORSEMENTS—TAILORING THE POLICY TO INDIVIDUAL NEEDS

The homeowners policies are designed for the typical needs of a broad range of homeowners. As a result, an individual homeowner may need to tailor the policy to meet his or her own special needs. These needs can be met in many instances through the use of appropriate policy endorsements that can add or delete coverage, change definitions, or clarify the intent of the insurance company.

While an individual company can design almost any type of endorsement, there are nearly 60 standard endorsements prepared by ISO for use with its homeowners forms. Several of these endorsements are briefly described below. The name used is the actual name of the ISO endorsement.

TABLE 17-1
Homeowners Forms

	HO-2 Broad	HO-3 Special	HO-4 Tenants	HO-5 Comprehensive	HO-6 Unit Owners	HO-8 Modified
Perils Insured Against	Broad named perils	Open perils for dwelling; broad named perils for personal property	Broad named perils for personal property	Open perils	Broad named perils	Limited named perils
Coverage A—Dwelling	Amount selected	Amount selected	—	Amount selected	$5,000	Amount selected
Coverage B—Other Structures	10% of A	10% of A	—	10% of A	—	10% of A
Coverage C—Unscheduled Personal Property	50% of A	50% of A	Amount selected	50% of A	Amount selected	50% of A
Coverage D—Loss of Use	30% of A	30% of A	30% of C	30% of A	50% of C	10% of A
Coverage E—Personal Liability	$100,000	$100,000	$100,000	$100,000	$100,000	$100,000
Coverage F—Medical Payments to Others	$1,000 per person	$1,000 per person	$1,000 per person	$1,000 per person	$1,000 per person	$1,000 per person

Some endorsements apply to the entire policy, others modify only Section I or Section II.

Note that it is not generally necessary to add an endorsement to increase the limits of insurance for Coverages, C, D, E, or F. This is accomplished by listing the higher amount in the policy declaration and paying the necessary additional premium.

Endorsements That Modify Section I and Section II

Additional Insured—Residence Premises

In some cases, persons other than the named insured have an interest in residential property. For example, a sister might occupy a house that she and her brother jointly inherited from their parents. This endorsement adds others (such as the brother) as insureds. However, the additional insured's coverage under Section II is only for liability with respect to the residence premises.

Assisted Living Care Coverage

This endorsement provides coverage for personal property, additional living expenses, and liability for people residing in assisted-living facilities, including nursing homes, who are related to the insured by blood, marriage, or adoption. It is not necessary that the person resided with the insured prior to entering the facility. The insured agrees to act as the person's representative in all matters pertaining to the coverage. There are also special limits of liability for items such as hearing aids ($250), eyeglasses ($100), and walking aids ($250).

Home Business Insurance Coverage

This endorsement provides both business property and liability coverage for certain home businesses owned solely by the named insured or jointly by the named insured and resident relatives. Coverage is provided for the following:

- business property, property of others in the insured's care because of the business, and business property leased by the insured if there is a contractual responsibility to insure it
- accounts receivable and valuable papers and records
- consequential loss coverages for business income and extra expenses
- liability coverage for bodily injury, property damage, personal and advertising injury, products, and completed operations

There is no coverage for liability for the rendering or failure to render professional services.

Home Day-Care Coverage Endorsement

This endorsement is for persons who conduct day-care businesses in their homes, either for children or older adults. It provides coverage for personal property used in the day-care business and extends Section II liability coverage to home day-care services. However, liability is excluded for injuries arising out of motor vehicles, watercraft, and saddle animals. Note that Section II excludes liability arising out of sexual molestation and physical or mental abuse inflicted by an insured or an employee. These are obvious liability loss exposures for a day-care center.

Loss Assessment Coverage

The purpose of this endorsement is to increase the $1,000 limits for loss assessments by a homeowners association. While it can be added to any homeowners form, it is most often needed with HO-6.

Permitted Incidental Occupancies (Residence Premises)

This endorsement deletes many of the homeowners exclusions that pertain to a business conducted on the residence premises. If business is conducted in a separate structure on the premises it is necessary to list that structure under Coverage B and select a limit of property coverage for the building. The $2,500 limit for business property under Coverage C is deleted and the full limit of Coverage C applies to business and personal property. Liability coverage is still excluded for bodily injury to an employee or to a pupil if the injury is a result of corporal punishment.

This endorsement merely extends the existing homeowners coverage. It does not pick up many of the unique business situations covered by the Home Business Insurance Coverage endorsement.

Structures Rented to Others

This endorsement provides both property and liability coverage for structures on an insured premises that are rented to others.

Endorsements That Modify Section I

Additional Limits of Liability—Coverages A, B, C, and D

For use only with HO-2 and HO-3, this endorsement amends the policy to provide replacement-cost coverage for the dwelling at the time of loss, regardless of the stated policy limit. Limits for other property coverages are increased accordingly. As a condition for this protection, the policyowner agrees to maintain insurance at full replacement value and to report any alterations that increase the dwelling's value by 5 percent or more.

Coverage C—Increased Special Limits of Liability

This endorsement can be used to increase coverage for some of the items where limited amounts of protection are available under Coverage C. The limits can be increased for

- money, bank notes, bullion, coins, medals, scrip, stored value cards, smart cards, and gold, silver, and platinum other than goldware, silverware, or platinumware
- securities, accounts, deeds, evidences of debt, letters of credit, and other valuable papers
- jewelry and watches
- firearms
- electronic apparatus for use in a motor vehicle

An increased amount of coverage is selected for each category.

Credit Card, Electronic Fund Transfer Card or Access Device, Forgery, and Counterfeit Money Coverage

This endorsement increases the $500 limit for these types of losses.

Earthquake

This endorsement can be used in most states to add the peril of earthquake as well as tremors that accompany volcanic eruption. In place of the regular deductible, there is an earthquake deductible equal to 5 percent of the limit of insurance that applies to Coverage A or Coverage C, whichever is greater. The deductible percentage can be increased for a premium credit. Coverage for masonry veneer is optional for an extra premium.

The situation is different in the largest market for earthquake insurance—California. The state requires insurers that sell homeowners policies to offer earthquake coverage. However, because of adverse claims experience and the financial inability of insurers to withstand catastrophic claims from future earthquakes, the market for homeowners policies virtually disappeared in the mid-1990s. At that time, many insurers ceased to write new policies or withdrew from the market altogether. As a result, a state agency was formed to make earthquake coverage available. This coverage is now sold by many insurers along with their homeowners policies, but the insurer of the earthquake coverage is the state agency. While there is coverage available for the residence, there is no coverage for other structures and a limited amount of coverage for personal property, debris removal, and additional living expenses. There is a deductible of 15 percent of a home's insured value.

Some insurers still make earthquake coverage available in California as part of their homeowners policies, and other types of insurers specialize in this market with separate policies. In most cases, more comprehensive coverage and lower deductibles are available from these sources.

Functional Replacement Cost Loss Settlement

Older homes often have replacement values far in excess of their market values. An example would be a 100-year-old Victorian house that might sell for several hundred thousand dollars but which would cost several million dollars to replace.

Some insurance companies are unwilling to insure such dwellings for replacement cost because of the potential moral hazard. In addition, property owners may not desire to pay the premium for replacement-cost coverage.

functional replacement cost

The purpose of this endorsement is to change the replacement-cost provision of an HO-2 or HO-3 policy with a provision for *functional replacement cost*. This is defined to mean the cost to repair or replace the damaged dwelling with less costly construction materials and methods that are functionally equivalent to obsolete, antique, or custom construction materials and methods used in the original construction of the dwelling. For example, dry wall would replace plaster walls, composition shingles would replace slate, hollow core doors might replace solid wood interior doors, and wall-to-wall carpeting over plywood might replace hardwood floors. All of this, unfortunately, might result in the loss of a dwelling's unique character.

Note that some states prohibit loss settlements that are less than the actual cash value of a loss. In these states, a modified endorsement is used so that the insured receives the actual cash value when it exceeds the functional replacement cost.

This endorsement has an 80 percent coinsurance provision based on functional replacement cost, which may be as difficult to determine as regular replacement cost.

Increased Limits on Business Property

The endorsement allows a policyowner to increase the $2,500 limit that applies to business property on the premises. The endorsement is of value to a person who has an office at home but does not conduct a business on the premises since personal property is not covered in such a situation.

Increased Limits on Personal Property in Other Residences

Coverage under the homeowners forms for the insured's property at a secondary residence is limited to 10 percent of Coverage C. This endorsement can be used to provide increased coverage. Note, however, that if the insured owns the secondary residence, coverage for its contents can be insured under a policy that also covers that residence.

Inflation Guard

This endorsement provides automatic increases for all Section I coverages by the percentage selected. The increase is effective on a pro rata basis during the policy period.

Multiple Company Insurance

In the case of very large amounts of insurance, the Section I coverage can be divided between two or more insurers if they all agree to such an arrangement. This endorsement specifies the percentage of the total amount of insurance each insurer will pay. Only one of the insurance policies will provide the Section II coverage.

Ordinance or Law—Increased Amount of Coverage

This endorsement can be used to increase the Additional Coverage limit of 10 percent of Coverage A for increased costs of construction because of enforcement of an ordinance or law. These additional costs can be significant when major changes have occurred in building codes such as provisions aimed at minimizing losses due to floods or earthquakes when a structure is rebuilt or undergoes significant repairs.

Other Structures—Increased Limits

This endorsement is used when the amount of insurance for Coverage B is inadequate. It provides additional insurance on structures that are described in the endorsement. For example, an insured with $200,000 of coverage on a dwelling would automatically have $20,000 of insurance for Coverage B. If the insured had a separate structure used as an art studio that had a replacement cost of $35,000, the additional $15,000 of protection could be provided with this endorsement.

Personal Property Replacement Loss Settlement

This endorsement changes the loss settlement basis for personal property from actual cash value to replacement cost. Some property, such as antiques, fine art, and collectibles, is not eligible for replacement-cost coverage.

If the replacement value of a loss is more than $500, repair or replacement must be made before the replacement-cost provision is applicable. The insured can make a claim for the actual cash value at the time of loss and amend it to replacement cost with 180 days.

Premises Alarm or Fire Protection System

This endorsement acknowledges that an insurer-acceptable alarm system or automatic sprinkler system is in place. The policyowner agrees to maintain the system in working order and to let the insurer know promptly if any changes are made to the system or if it is removed. In exchange, the policyowner receives a premium credit.

Refrigerated Property Coverage

This endorsement adds up to $500 coverage (with a $100 deductible) for losses to property in refrigerators or freezers caused by interruption of electrical services (either on or off the premises) or the mechanical failure of the refrigerator or freezer.

Scheduled Personal Property Endorsement

This endorsement is commonly used, particularly by clients who have possessions of high value that are subject to the coverage limitations of the basic homeowners policy. It broadens coverage on specific categories of valuable personal property such as jewelry, furs, cameras, musical instruments, silverware, golfer's equipment, fine art, and stamp and coin collections. Each item is usually listed separately and insured for a specified value, but some coverage can be written on a blanket-basis for certain classes of property.

Coverage is "open-perils" with few exceptions and applies worldwide. There is also coverage for up to 30 days for newly acquired property in a category insured under the endorsement. It is limited, however, to 25 percent of the amount of insurance for that category.

Once property is insured under this endorsement, there is no coverage for it under Coverage C. In addition, the Section I deductible does not apply to scheduled items.

Losses are generally settled on an actual cash value basis. However, fine art is written on an agreed-value basis, and there is another available endorsement that provides coverage for other personal property on an agreed-value basis.

Sinkhole Collapse

Property is sometimes damaged or destroyed when earth collapses because of voids created under limestone or similar rock formations. This endorsement provides coverage for losses from such collapses.

Special Computer Coverage

This endorsement provides "open-perils" coverage on computer equipment and is designed for homeowners or unit-owners who do not already have "open-perils" coverage on their personal property.

Special Loss Settlement

This endorsement lowers the 80 percent insurance-to-value requirement to either 50, 60, or 70 percent. It is used when the replacement cost of a dwelling far exceeds its market value and the insurer is unwilling to write a policy for as much as 80 percent of replacement cost.

Special Personal Property Coverage—HO-4

This endorsement allows tenants to change the named-perils coverage for personal property under HO-4 to "open-perils" coverage like the coverage provided by HO-5.

Unit-owners Coverage A and Unit-owners Coverage C

These endorsements change the named-perils coverage of HO-6 to "open-perils" coverage. If both endorsements are purchased, the condominium owner has a policy much like HO-5.

Endorsements That Modify Section II

Additional Residence Rented to Others

Sometimes a policyowner owns a separate rental property. This endorsement can be used to extend the Section II coverages to liability that arises out of such property as long as it is listed in the endorsement and contains no more than four living units.

Business Pursuits

This endorsement provides coverage for liability that arises out of or in connection with a business engaged in by an insured. An example is a suit against a salesperson who accidentally injured a customer. The endorsement is most commonly used by persons in sales, clerical, and teaching occupations.

Coverage does not apply with respect to a business owned or financially controlled by an insured or in which an insured is a partner. (A commercial policy is needed for this.) In addition, there is no coverage for liability that arises out of professional services, with the exception of teaching. Bodily injury to fellow employees is also excluded.

Farmers Personal Liability

It is not unusual for a person whose principal business or occupation is not farming to own some land where farming operations take place. This endorsement provides Section II coverage for this activity at those locations listed in the endorsement. Several exclusions in the endorsement apply to unique farming activities.

Personal Injury

This endorsement modifies the definition of bodily injury to include personal injury which is defined to include the following:

- false arrest, detention or imprisonment, or malicious prosecution
- libel, slander, or defamation of character
- invasion of privacy, wrongful eviction, or wrongful entry

The coverage does not apply to an insured's conscious violation of criminal law, employment-related injuries, business-related and professional injuries, civic or public activities performed for pay, injury to another insured, or contractual liability other than that relating to the insured's home.

Snowmobiles

This endorsement provides coverage for listed snowmobiles when they are used off the insured premises. However, coverage does not apply if they are

(1) subject to motor vehicle registration, (2) used to carry paying passengers, (3) used for a business purpose, (4) rented to others, or (5) operated in organized competitions.

Watercraft

This endorsement provides coverage for boats that are longer or more powerful than those covered by the standard homeowners coverage. It does not cover liability arising out of (1) racing or speed competitions except for sailboats, (2) injuries to employees who maintain or use the boats, (3) watercraft used to carry persons for a fee, or (4) watercraft rented to others.

THE NEED FOR OTHER POLICIES

Even though the homeowners policy provides broad insurance protection, it does not cover everything; certain personal property and liability loss exposures can create a need for other policies.

The remainder of this chapter focuses on some other policies or programs for insuring real and personal property, primarily when it is ineligible for coverage under a homeowners policy. These include

- other residential forms
- flood insurance
- coverage for hard-to-insure residential property
- floater policies for personal property

OTHER RESIDENTIAL FORMS

The homeowners policy does not cover all types of residential loss exposures. The following discussion briefly describes three other types of residential coverage:

- dwelling policies
- mobilehome[1] insurance
- insurance for farms and ranches

As with homeowners policies, companies may have their own forms or use those developed by ISO or AAIS. As was previously the case, the following discussion is based primarily on the ISO forms.

Dwelling Policies

dwelling policy

A *dwelling policy* is designed primarily for a residence that is ineligible for homeowners coverage for one or more of the following reasons:

- The dwelling is rented to others.
- The dwelling does not meet the insurer's eligibility requirements for homeowners coverage. This may be because of low value, too many living units, the old age of the dwelling, or the poorer-than-average physical condition of the dwelling.

In addition, a few insureds may elect a narrower and less expensive dwelling policy because they do not want all the homeowners coverages or are unwilling or unable to pay the price of a homeowners policy. Under the ISO program, a dwelling policy can also be written for houseboats in some states and for mobile homes, subject to certain restrictions.

Like the homeowners form, ISO has several dwelling forms:

- Dwelling Property 1—Basic Form (DP-1)
- Dwelling Property 2—Broad Form (DP-2)
- Dwelling Property 3—Special Form (DP-3)

DP-2 and DP-3 are similar to the Section I coverages HO-2 and HO-3, respectively. DP-1 is a more limited policy. However, the coverage is slightly less comprehensive. For example, the standard dwelling forms have no coverage for the peril of theft, and off-premises coverage for personal property is limited to 10 percent of Coverage C.

There are five coverages under the forms:

- Coverage A—Dwelling
- Coverage B—Other Structures
- Coverage C—Personal Property
- Coverage D—Fair Rental Value
- Coverage E—Additional Living Expenses (not included with DP-1)

The applicant selects the coverages to purchase and the limits of coverage. Tenants can purchase a policy without Coverages A and B, and landlords can purchase a policy without Coverage C.

The peril of theft can be endorsed to the dwelling forms and, for owner-occupied dwellings, the coverage is similar to that under the homeowners forms. Tenants are eligible only for more limited coverage.

The dwelling forms do not automatically provide liability and medical coverages as do the homeowners forms. However, they can be added by endorsement.

Mobilehome Insurance

mobilehome insurance

Mobilehome insurance can be written in a manner very similar to that of a regular homeowners policy as long as the mobile home is owner-occupied and meets certain other underwriting rules such as a length of at least 40 feet and a width of at least 10 feet.

Nonowner-occupied mobile homes can be insured under dwelling forms, while tenants of mobile homes can purchase an HO-4 policy.

Under the ISO mobilehome program, an endorsement is added to either an HO-2 or HO-3 policy. The endorsement alters certain definitions and amends a few policy provisions to adapt the homeowners form to his different form of living unit. For example, the Coverage C limit of insurance is lowered from 50 to 40 percent of the Coverage A limit because furniture is often built in and part of the mobile home. There is up to $500 of coverage for removal of a mobile home that is endangered by an insured peril, but no coverage is provided for increased costs due to ordinance or law changes.

Losses to the mobile home are generally settled on a replacement-cost basis as long as adequate limits are carried.

Many of the previously described homeowners endorsements can be used for mobile homes and, in addition, a few additional endorsements are available. One endorsement changes the loss settlements basis for the mobile home to actual cash value. This may be required by the insurer, particularly for older mobile homes. Another endorsement can be added for the perils of transportation if the mobile home is subject to being moved. Other endorsements allow the policyowner to increase the $500 limit for removal and to add coverage for increased costs due to ordinance or law changes.

Because mobile homes are particularly subject to windstorm damage, a rate credit is given if the mobile home meets certain criteria, including special anchoring to withstand bad weather.

Farm and Ranch Policies

A large number of persons earn their livelihood by owning farms and ranches and numerous policies are available to provide them with the necessary property and liability protection. Coverage tends to be written by insurers who use their own forms and often specialize in writing coverage for the persons engaged in this type of occupation. Small farms and ranches are often insured under package policies, but as an operation becomes more sophisticated, the likelihood increases that the liability loss exposures will be insured under a commercial policy.

In addition to coverages for the farm or ranch dwelling and household personal property, coverage is needed for farm structures and farm personal property. Other property loss exposures include food spoilage, private power and light poles, pumps, and loss to animals from numerous perils other than sickness or disease. There are also unique liability loss exposures such as animal boarding, injury or sickness from chemicals, and injury to the public if they are allowed to pick fruits or vegetables.

The available policies tend to look much like homeowners policies with additional coverage for many of these and other farming and ranching loss exposures.

FLOOD INSURANCE

National Flood Insurance Program (NFIP)

A major exclusion in almost all insurance policies that cover real property and many that cover personal property is flood, which is the most common type of natural disaster. At one time, coverage was virtually impossible to obtain, but this changed in the late 1960s when Congress passed legislation that enacted the *National Flood Insurance Program (NFIP)*. This program is administered by the Federal Insurance and Mitigation Administration (FIMA). Under the NFIP, the federal government provides limited amounts of flood insurance coverage—often at subsidized rates—for the owners of dwellings, commercial buildings, and the contents of both.

While coverage was once purchased directly from the NFIP, most policies are now written through private insurance companies under the *write-your-own-program*. Under this program, the NFIP reimburses the insurance company for any losses that exceed the sum of premiums collected and any investment income earned on these premiums. Consumers obtain their policies through private insurance agents.

Eligibility

In order for property owners to be eligible for flood insurance, they must live in a community that participates in the program. Such communities must agree to establish and enforce certain land use restrictions to minimize the community's exposure to flood losses. These, for example, might include a prohibition against new construction in flood prone areas.

Unfortunately, even when flood insurance has been available, many consumers have not purchased it, particularly if they were in an area where the chance of flood seems low. To minimize uninsured flood losses, the government prohibits the issuance of federal loans or federally assisted or insured loans to persons in highly flood-prone areas (called *special hazard flood areas*) unless coverage is purchased.

When a community first becomes eligible for flood insurance, it is covered under the emergency program, whereby limited amounts of coverage at subsidized rates are available. The government then prepares maps that identify the flood potential in the community by area. After these maps are prepared and the community establishes appropriate flood control and land use restrictions, property owners can purchase coverage under the regular program. The program is divided into two parts—a basic amount of insurance at often heavily subsidized rates and additional insurance at actuarial rates. Table 17-2 shows the maximum amount of coverage available.

TABLE 17-2
National Flood Insurance Program Coverage Limits

Category of Coverage	Emergency Program	Regular Program	
		At Subsidized Rates	Additional Coverage at Actuarial Rates
1–4 Family Dwellings	$ 35,000*	$ 50,000	$200,000
Other Residential Buildings	100,000*	135,000	115,000
Nonresidential Buildings	100,000	135,000	365,000
Residential Contents	10,000	15,000	85,000
Nonresidential Contents	100,000	115,000	385,000

* Higher limits are available in Alaska, Guam, Hawaii, and the U.S. Virgin Islands.

There is generally a 30-day waiting period before new policies or increases in coverage become effective. This prevents persons in an area predicted to be flooded in the next few days from purchasing insurance for the impending flood. There are exceptions to the 30-day waiting period for flood insurance, including its initial purchase in connection with the sale of property or the making or increasing of a mortgage loan on property. In those cases, coverage is effective at the time of transfer of ownership or date of the mortgage loan as long as the policy was applied for and the premium paid before these dates.

Policy Provisions

The flood insurance policy defines flood as "a general and temporary condition of partial or complete inundation of two or more acres of normally dry land or two or more properties (at least one of which is your property) from overflow of inland or tidal waters from unusual and rapid accumulation or runoff of surface water from any source, or from mudflow." There is no coverage for losses that result from broken or backed-up sewers or from a malfunctioning sump pump.

A policyowner can purchase insurance on the dwelling, its contents, or both. To a large extent, coverage is similar to that provided for other perils under the homeowners policy. However, there are some exceptions, several of which are mentioned below.

Dwelling Coverage

The coverage on the building includes a 10 percent extension to cover a detached garage on the insured premises and coverage for debris removal of or on the insured premises. However, any amount paid for these items is part of the limit of insurance selected rather than an additional amount of insurance.

Losses are settled on an actual cash value basis, but replacement-cost coverage can be endorsed to policies that cover one- to four-family dwellings if they are occupied by the owner for at least 80 percent of the year.

There is up to $20,000 of coverage for the increased cost of repair or reconstruction because of laws or ordinances. This is a significant loss exposure if ordinances require that rebuilt structures be elevated or conform to other flood-prevention guidelines.

There are also exclusions for several categories of property, including land value, lawns, trees, shrubs, plants, swimming pools, docks, boat houses, paved surfaces, wells, and septic systems. Exclusions also apply to most property in basements, including finished floors and most personal belongings. However, there is coverage for items used to service the building such as water heaters, furnaces, and circuit breaker boxes. Washers, dryers, and freezers are also covered under contents coverage if they are in a basement.

A $500 deductible applies separately to the dwelling and its contents, but optional deductibles of up to $5,000 are available.

Contents Coverage

Contents coverage applies only on the residence premises except when property is removed to protect it from flood. There is an extensive list of property not covered under the policy. The list excludes money, securities, valuable papers, animals, birds, fish, aircraft, watercraft, motor vehicles, and property not inside an enclosed building. There is also a $2,500 aggregate limit on items such as artwork, collectibles, jewelry, watches, gold, silver, furs, and business property.

HARD-TO-INSURE RESIDENTIAL PROPERTY

Even though most residential property is eligible for coverage in the standard insurance market, some residential property fails to meet the underwriting guidelines of most insurers. This can occur for a variety of reasons, including the

- high replacement cost of the property relative to its market value
- physical condition of the property
- environment of the property. For example, the neighborhood is one of high crime, or susceptibility to brush fires or severe coastal storms.
- poor reputation of the owner or occupants
- excessiveness of past claims of the applicant
- the use of the property. For example, it may be a remote cabin that is seldom occupied and in an area without fire protection.

Several alternatives for coverage are available, but policies that are written can be more limited than policies written in the normal marketplace. Some companies specialize in the substandard market and write coverage for a variety of properties, but at higher-than-normal premiums.

FAIR (Fair Access to Insurance Requirements) plans

Many states have taken a variety of actions to make coverage available, often at subsidized rates. Over 30 states have *FAIR (Fair Access to Insurance Requirements) plans*. These plans originally began as a result of urban riots in the 1960s, which made property insurance very difficult to obtain in many major cities. The current plans are state-run programs to provide insurance for buildings and their contents if the property owner is unable to obtain coverage in the standard insurance market, for whatever reason. In most cases, coverage is written by a pool or syndicate of private insurers who are assessed for any losses of the plan if premiums are inadequate.

Each state has its own FAIR plan, and they do differ. However, a few generalizations can be made. Some types of property are still largely uninsurable. These may include ones that are vacant, poorly maintained, subject to unacceptable hazards (such as the manufacture of fireworks), or not built in accordance with safety and building codes. Coverage is usually written under forms that are more limited than homeowners policies. Often the perils insured against are only fire and a limited number of other perils. Coverage is also subject to maximum limits and mandatory deductibles.

FAIR Plans

- Plans vary from state to state.
- They are designed to make residential property insurance available to applicants who can't meet normal underwriting standards of insurers.
- Coverage is provided by a pool of insurers who share premiums and losses.
- Coverage is more limited than under homeowners or dwelling forms.
- Only a few types of applicants are ineligible for coverage.

Some states, primarily in the Southeast and on the Gulf Coast, have beachfront and windstorm plans to provide protection that insurers are unwilling to write because of the loss exposure to hurricanes. Some of these plans only cover the perils of windstorm and hail, and property owners obtain protection for other perils in the normal insurance market.

Finally, there is the situation of the expensive home. In some cases, the amount of insurance needed exceeds the limit an insurer is willing to write. In other cases, replacement cost substantially exceeds market value. Some insurers specialize in this market and have their own policies to meet the needs of the well-to-do. Other insurers tailor standard homeowners forms (such as

HO-3 with endorsements that were previously described). These include the ones for multiple company insurance and functional replacement cost.

TITLE INSURANCE

title insurance

Title insurance is designed to protect the purchaser of real estate against defects in title that can result in the loss of ownership or that can be corrected only after certain costs are incurred. These defects can arise from many sources, including forged titles, invalid wills, inaccurate property descriptions, and undisclosed liens and easements. To provide protection against loan defaults, lenders of funds for the purchase of real property usually require the purchase of title insurance by a borrower.

One method of protection against a defective title is to have an abstract of title prepared (often by an attorney) prior to the purchase of the property. This abstract, based on public records, lists all liens, mortgage loans, easements, and the like. If any previously unknown condition is found, the potential purchaser can either have the situation rectified, renegotiate, or back out of the transaction. It should be noted that property is often purchased subject to existing mortgage loans, liens, or easements, and the real purpose of the abstract is to find circumstances about which the purchaser had no knowledge.

While an abstract of title provides a great deal of protection, unknown situations that have existed may become known in the future such as the appearance of a long-lost heir that has a legitimate claim to the property. An abstract of title does not provide any indemnification to the property owner, and suits against the attorney or other person preparing the abstract are usually not a recourse unless negligence can be shown. Title insurance, however, is designed to protect against this loss. It is almost always required by lenders who finance property purchases and also frequently obtained when cash purchases are made.

The title insurance company conducts a title search and then issues a policy to provide protection against losses that arise from circumstances other than the items already found in the title search and listed in the policy.

Some characteristics of title insurance include the following:

- The policy provides protection only against unknown title defects that have occurred prior to the effective date of the policy but are discovered after the effective date.
- The policy is written on the assumption that losses will not occur since most title defects are known and listed in the policy.
- The policy term is indefinite and continues until title to the property is again transferred. At that time, the new owner will need to purchase a new title insurance policy since the existing policy is not assignable.
- The premium is paid only once—when the policy is issued—and the policy cannot be canceled by either party.

- The insured is indemnified up to the policy limits if a loss occurs. However, there is no guarantee that possession of the property will be retained.
- The amount of insurance is usually the initial purchase price of the property and a potential loss in the future can be much higher than the policy limit because of inflation.

FLOATER POLICIES

floater

Several policies are available to provide broad insurance protection on a wide variety of personal property. These policies are commonly referred to as *floaters* because the insured property is often subject to being moved or "floating around" rather than remaining at a fixed location.

With the broadening of the homeowners forms over the years and the development of endorsements to meet specialized needs, the use of personal floater policies has diminished. However, they are still written for persons who are not eligible for homeowners policies or who for some reason prefer to have the property insured separately.

Personal Articles Floater

personal articles floater

The *personal articles floater* is used to provide "open-perils" coverage for certain scheduled and valuable items of personal property. It is essentially the same as the scheduled personal property endorsement to the homeowners policy that was discussed earlier in the chapter.

Personal Property Floater

personal property floater

The *personal property floater* is designed primarily to provide "open-perils" coverage for unscheduled personal property on a worldwide basis. The endorsement essentially provides the same coverage on personal property that is available under an HO-5 policy or under an HO-4 or HO-6 policy that has an endorsement for "open-perils" coverage on personal property. The floater may be appropriate for persons who are not eligible for a homeowners policy. For example, the floater could be used by a couple who sold their home and stored their personal property with a friend while taking an around-the-world trip for a year. It may also be appropriate for an itinerant person, such as an actor, who does not maintain a permanent home.

Personal Effects Floater

personal effects floater

The *personal effects floater* is designed to provide "open-perils" worldwide coverage on property such as baggage, clothes, cameras, and sports equipment typically worn or carried by tourists. However, it does not provide coverage for such items as money, passports, and tickets. Without any endorsements, a homeowners policy would only cover this property on a named-perils basis.

CHECKLIST FOR EVALUATING AND COMPARING HOMEOWNERS POLICIES

☐ What is the homeowners form?

    ___ HO-2
    ___ HO-3
    ___ HO-4
    ___ HO-5
    ___ HO-6
    ___ HO-8

☐ If the policy is not an ISO form, how does it differ?

☐ What is the annual policy premium?

☐ What is the Section I deductible?

☐ Does the policy automatically contain endorsements that are optional with other insurers?

☐ What are the limits for the various coverages?

    ___ Coverage A—Dwelling
    ___ Coverage B—Other Structures
    ___ Coverage C—Personal Property
    ___ Coverage D—Loss of Use
    ___ Coverage E—Personal Liability
    ___ Coverage F—Medical Payments to Others

☐ Are the coverage limits adequate?

☐ What provisions, if any, are there for increasing policy limits?

☐ Does the insured own personal property subject to special limits of liability?

☐ Is personal property covered for replacement cost?

☐ Are there, or is there any need for, any of the following endorsements?

    ____ Additional insureds
    ____ "Open-perils" computer coverage
    ____ "Open-perils" personal property coverage
    ____ Business pursuits
    ____ Credit card, electronic fund transfer card, forgery, and counterfeit money
    ____ Earthquake
    ____ Higher limits for certain types of personal property
    ____ Home business insurance coverage
    ____ Home day-care coverage
    ____ Increased ordinance or law coverage
    ____ Increased loss assessment coverage
    ____ Increased property limits on business property
    ____ Personal injury
    ____ Premises alarm or fire protection system credits
    ____ Scheduled personal property coverage
    ____ Sinkhole collapse
    ____ Snowmobile
    ____ Watercraft
    ____ Other property loss exposures
    ____ Other liability loss exposures

☐ Is the flood peril adequately covered in another policy?

SOURCES FOR FURTHER IN-DEPTH STUDY

- *FC&S Bulletins,* Personal Lines Volume, (loose-leaf and/or CD-ROM service updated monthly), Cincinnati, OH: The National Underwriter Company. Phone 800-543-0874. Web site address www.nuco.com
- Hamilton, Karen L., and Ferguson, Cheryl L., *Personal Risk Management and Property-Liability Insurance*, American Institute for CPCU/Insurance Institute of America, 2002. Phone 800-644-2101. Web site address www.aicpcu.org
- Wiening, Eric A., Rejda, George E.; Luthardt, Constance M.; and Ferguson, Cheryl L., *Personal Insurance,* Malvern, PA: American Institute for CPCU/Insurance Institute of America, 2002. Phone 800-644-2101. Web site address www.aicpcu.org

CHAPTER REVIEW

Answers to review questions and self-test questions start on page 725.

Key Terms

homeowners policy	National Flood Insurance
ISO (Insurance Services	Program (NFIP)
Office)	AIR (Fair Access to Insurance
named insured	Requirements) plans
additional living expenses	title insurance
functional replacement cost	floater
dwelling policy	personal articles floater
mobilehome insurance	personal property floater
	personal effects floater

Review Questions

17-1.   Frank and his wife Janet own a home. Also living in the house is their oldest daughter, Elaine, who returned home after finishing college 8 years ago. Their 21-year-old daughter, Destiny, is currently at college living in an on-campus dorm room. What members of the family would be covered under Frank's homeowners policy?

17-2.   What locations are typically listed as insured locations in a homeowners policy?

17-3.   Nathan's home is covered for $250,000 (Coverage A) under an HO-3 policy. Which of the following losses would be covered under Nathan's HO-3 policy?

   a.   vandalism to Nathan's home

   b.   damage to the inside walls and hardwood floors of Nathan's home caused by rain water that blew in when he accidentally left the window open during a storm

   c.   damage to the family room couch and end tables inside Nathan's home caused by rain water that blew in when he accidentally left the window open during a storm

   d.   earthquake damage to the walls of Nathan's home

   e.   stains on the wall-to-wall carpet inside Nathan's home due to housebreaking the new family pet plus the hole in the outside of Nathan's home cut by a woodpecker

   f.   theft of the $2,000 cast aluminum porch furniture from the back deck of Nathan's home

   g. $1,500 in cash burned in a fire in Nathan's home

   h. $2,000 of damage to Nathan's wife's furs as a result of a fire

       i. $1,000 of additional expense incurred while Nathan's family had to live elsewhere for a day and one-half after a small fire loss

       j. $2,000 of windstorm damage to the detached garage at Nathan's home

17-4.   Which of the following losses would be covered under Sarah's HO-3 policy?

    a.   Sarah's guests received bodily injuries and the side of her neighbor's house received property damage when a gas grill exploded during a cookout at her house.

    b.   While running to a meeting at work, Sarah accidentally injured a coworker.

    c.   While at the local mall, Sarah carelessly backed out of a parking space and damaged another shopper's car.

    d.   Sarah's 3-year-old son Matthew ripped out some of the neighbor's flowers for a Mother's Day gift.

    e.   Sarah's daughter injured a team member when she tossed a bat into the bat rack and it bounced off and hit the teammate, cutting her head.

17-5.   Describe how each of the following homeowners property coverages differs from the HO-3 property coverages:

    a.   HO-2

    b.   HO-4

    c.   HO-5

    d.   HO-6

    e.   HO-8

17-6.   Describe the nature of the coverages added to the homeowners policy by these commonly used endorsements:

    a.   home day-care coverage

    b.   increased special limits

    c.   earthquake

    d.   inflation guard

    e.   personal property replacement loss

    f.   scheduled personal property

    g.   business pursuits

17-7.   Describe the coverage provided by the National Flood Insurance Program (NFIP) and explain how a client can obtain such coverage if needed.

17-8.   Briefly explain the alternatives available for obtaining property coverage for clients who fail to meet the underwriting guidelines of most insurers.

17-9.   Describe the characteristics of title insurance.

Self-Test Questions

T   F   17-1.   Regardless of which of the six property forms is included in a homeowners policy, the liability section is identical for all forms.

T   F   17-2.   Children over the age of 21 are no longer covered under their parents' homeowners policy even if they continue to reside in their parents' household.

T   F   17-3.   The limits for homeowners Coverages B, C, and D are part of the Coverage A limit.

T   F   17-4.   Damage to an attached garage is covered under Coverage A in an HO-3 policy, but damage to a detached garage is covered under Coverage B.

T   F   17-5.   An HO-3 policy covers damage to the insured's residence against "open-perils" including earthquake and flood.

T   F   17-6.   In a homeowners policy, losses under all property coverages are settled on a replacement cost basis.

T   F   17-7.   In an HO-3 policy, the personal property of any insured is covered while located anywhere in the world.

T   F   17-8.   In a homeowners policy, the amount payable for the loss of money and securities is limited only for theft.

T   F   17-9.   A homeowners policy has coverage for additional living expenses incurred while a family lives elsewhere during repairs for a covered property loss.

T   F   17-10. If Jim moves his remaining furniture to a storage locker after his house is damaged by a tornado and two weeks later the furniture in the locker is damaged by flood waters, Jim's homeowners policy will cover the loss.

T   F   17-11. The liability coverage contained in an unendorsed homeowners policy provides protection against suits for bodily injury, property damage, and personal injury.

T   F   17-12. Liability coverage in an unendorsed homeowners policy excludes coverage for liability arising out of business and professional activities as well as the use of an automobile.

T   F   17-13. Benefits under the medical payments coverage in the homeowners policy are paid only to persons other than an insured.

T   F   17-14. A person who lives in a condominium should carry an HO-4 Contents Broad Form, because the association covers the building and detached structures.

T   F   17-15. Clients with expensive jewelry and silverware should consider adding a scheduled personal property endorsement to their homeowners policy.

T   F   17-16. Most flood insurance policies are now written through private insurance companies.

T   F   17-17. To provide a better spread of risk, flood insurance is now available to property owners regardless of where they live.

T   F   17-18. Title insurance provides protection against all title defects regardless of when they occur or are discovered.

NOTE

1. The term *mobile home* is two words. However, insurance for such property is written as a single word.

18

Personal Automobile and Umbrella Liability Insurance

Learning Objectives

An understanding of the material in this chapter should enable the student to

18-1. Describe the problems associated with automobile accidents and the methods of compensating the victims.

18-2. Describe the basic elements of the Personal Auto Policy.

18-3. Explain the coverage provided by Parts A, B, C, and D of the Personal Auto Policy.

18-4. Describe the key endorsements available to tailor the Personal Auto Policy to other common client needs.

18-5. Describe the potential sources of automobile insurance coverage available for hard-to-insure drivers.

18-6. Explain the key factors to be considered by a client in shopping for automobile insurance.

18-7. Briefly describe the policies available for insuring watercraft and aircraft.

18-8. Describe the need for and general features of personal umbrella liability insurance.

Chapter Outline

This second chapter on personal property and liability insurance focuses on two other important types of coverage—automobile insurance and umbrella liability insurance. The insuring of loss exposures that arise out of other modes of transportation, such as watercraft and airplanes, is also discussed.

Financial planners should be able to alert their clients to potential risk exposures related to automobile and excess liability coverage. Specific recommendations and implementation are usually handled by a property and casualty insurance agent or broker.

AUTOMOBILE INSURANCE

During the 1990s, the most prominent public policy issues involving personal insurance seem to have centered on health insurance. However, for several prior decades the insurance topic of primary consumer and legislative importance was arguably automobile insurance. The discussion of automobile insurance begins with a look at some of the problems associated with automobile accidents and automobile insurance and continues with a history of the methods of compensating automobile accident victims. A description of the personal auto[1] policy (PAP) and insurance for high-risk drivers follows.

Problems Associated with Automobile Accidents and Automobile Insurance

Given the severe financial consequences that can arise from automobile accidents, automobile insurance is viewed as a necessity by most Americans both for themselves and for the other drivers who might injure them. Yet there are many problems in providing automobile insurance to everyone at an affordable price.

These problems center around the

- large number of automobile accidents
- high cost of automobile accidents

- uninsured and underinsured drivers
- difficulty that some individuals have in obtaining automobile insurance

Large Number of Automobile Accidents

Automobile accidents occur frequently (over 6 million were reported to police in 2000[2]). Young drivers have a disproportionate number of accidents, and regardless of the driver's age, speeding and/or substance abuse are often involved.

High Cost of Automobile Accidents

The costs associated with automobile accidents each year in the United States are staggering. The annual insurance payments for automobile accidents is estimated to be over $125 billion for property damage, medical expenses, lost income, and defense costs. This loss far exceeds losses from fires and natural disasters. Automobile accidents kill over 40,000 persons each year and account for approximately half of the country's accidental deaths. Statistics indicate that close to 40 percent of these automobile deaths are alcohol related.

Uninsured and Underinsured Drivers

While there are variations from state to state, the number of persons without automobile insurance is estimated at between 5 and 30 percent. Even in states with compulsory insurance laws, there is no perfect mechanism to prevent an uninsured, or even unlicensed, driver from getting behind the wheel.

When uninsured drivers are involved in accidents, they can rarely pay for the property damage and bodily injury they have caused themselves or others. Another problem is the underinsured driver. The minimum amount of automobile liability insurance needed in most states (usually no more than $25,000 for any injured person) is often below the amount necessary to adequately compensate an innocent victim for his or her injuries.

Because of uninsured and underinsured drivers, innocent victims of automobile accidents may be inadequately compensated for their injuries, and society must often bear some of the burden. As a result, states have undertaken various actions to minimize these problems.

Difficulty of Some Persons in Obtaining Automobile Insurance

Automobile insurance can be difficult to obtain. High-risk drivers (for example, younger persons or drivers with serious or multiple traffic violations) are often unable to find coverage in the standard insurance market. An increasing number of insurers are willing to write these substandard applicants, and many states have passed legislation that makes coverage available through a residual market plan.

There is also the problem of affordability. Automobile insurance is expensive and accounts for about half of the premiums collected by property and liability insurers. This is a result of both the high frequency and high severity of claims. For example, the average claim paid for bodily injury in an automobile accident is approximately $10,000. Even with premiums that are often considered too high by consumers, automobile insurance has not generated large profits for insurers. Some of the automobile insurance legislation mentioned later in this chapter attempts to control automobile insurance costs and therefore make it more affordable.

Methods of Compensating Automobile Accident Victims

Since the early days of automobiles, there has been significant societal concern over the number and severity of automobile accidents and the methods of compensating automobile accident victims.

Numerous laws and regulations have been passed—often with strong support from the insurance industry—to control the number of automobile accidents and to lessen the number of injuries and deaths. Among these are

- federal design and safety standards for automobiles
- highway design standards
- seat belt laws
- drunk-driving laws
- tightening of licensing standards for young drivers
- license retesting for older drivers

Over time there has also been concern over the compensation of automobile accident victims, particularly those who were not at fault. Historically, their compensation was under the traditional tort liability system, which was discussed in an earlier chapter. Because contributory negligence laws made it difficult for many mostly innocent victims to collect for damages, most states enacted one of the variations of comparative negligence that were previously discussed. In addition, various other methods of ensuring compensation have been developed over the years. These include

- compulsory insurance
- financial responsibility laws
- unsatisfied judgment funds
- uninsured motorists coverage

- underinsured motorists coverage
- no-fault automobile insurance

Not every method exists in every state, and none of these methods is exactly the same in all states where it is used. It should also be noted that most of these methods do not alter the concept of tort liability but are aimed at increasing the likelihood that a source of monetary recovery exists for innocent victims.

Compulsory Insurance

Almost all states and the District of Columbia have some type of compulsory insurance law that requires the owners of automobiles to carry liability insurance before a vehicle can be registered. While this is almost always in the form of a policy from an insurance company, the law can usually be satisfied on a self-insured basis by the posting of a cash deposit, bond, or other form of security. Unfortunately, such laws are far from perfect for several reasons:

- The compensation must come through traditional legal channels and can be delayed by an overburdened legal system.
- There is no guarantee that an innocent victim will be compensated. Some drivers may not license their vehicles; others may drop insurance after a vehicle is licensed. In addition, a person may be injured by a hit-and-run driver, an out-of-state driver without insurance, a driver of a stolen car, or a driver of a fraudulently registered automobile.
- The required liability limits are relatively low and rarely exceed $20,000 or $25,000 for bodily injury to any one person, $40,000 or $50,000 in the aggregate for all bodily injury claims in an accident, and $10,000 or $15,000 for property damage claims.

Financial Responsibility Laws

financial responsibility law

All states have some type of *financial responsibility law*. These laws require proof of future financial responsibility by the carrying of insurance (or the posting of a cash deposit, bond, or other security) under the following circumstances:

- after an automobile accident involving bodily injury or property damage that exceeds a specified limit
- after conviction of a serious offense such as drunk driving or reckless driving
- after loss of a driver's license because of repeated motor vehicle violations

- failure to pay a legal judgment that arose from an automobile accident

Failure to comply with financial responsibility laws results in the revocation or suspension of a person's driving privileges.

The major criticism of financial responsibility laws is that they only become effective after an accident or serious offense and do not provide any compensation to the innocent victims of that accident. In addition, the same limitations that apply to compulsory automobile insurance also apply to financial responsibility laws.

Unsatisfied Judgment Funds

unsatisfied judgment fund

A few states (all of which also have compulsory insurance requirements) have *unsatisfied judgment funds*, which are established by the state to compensate persons who are unable to collect a legal judgment that results from an automobile accident. The injured person—in addition to obtaining a legal judgment against the negligent party—must show that the judgment cannot be collected. The maximum amount that can be collected from the fund is usually limited to the state's minimum compulsory insurance requirement and is reduced by collateral sources of recovery such as workers' compensation benefits or insurance.

The negligent driver must repay the fund for payments made to the injured person or lose his or her driver's license until repayment is made.

The process of collecting from unsatisfied judgment funds is slow and cumbersome. In addition, some funds have had financial problems as a result of inadequate funding, which usually comes from fees levied on insured drivers or insurance companies that write automobile insurance in the state.

Uninsured Motorists Coverage

uninsured motorists coverage

In most states, insurers that write automobile insurance are required to offer *uninsured motorists coverage*. However, the policyowner can voluntarily waive the coverage in writing. In a few states, uninsured motorists coverage must be included in any automobile insurance policy.

Under uninsured motorists coverage, the insured is able to collect the amount he or she would have collected from the insurer of an insured driver if that driver had been carrying insurance. In effect, the insured's own company acts as the insurer of the uninsured driver. The term *uninsured* is broadly defined to include not only uninsured drivers, but also the drivers of hit-and-run vehicles and persons whose insurer cannot pay because the insurer has become insolvent. Uninsured motorists coverage, however, does not apply if the negligent party carries insurance that has inadequate limits to fully indemnify the innocent party. Uninsured motorists coverage is analyzed in more detail when the personal auto policy is discussed.

Limitations to uninsured motorists coverage include the following:

- The limits of coverage are equal only to a state's compulsory insurance or financial responsibility limits unless the policyowner has purchased higher limits.
- The insured must establish that the other party was legally liable.
- The coverage usually applies to bodily injury only. States vary as to whether the coverage applies to property damage.
- The cost of the coverage is borne by the innocent victim, not the uninsured driver.

Underinsured Motorists Coverage

underinsured motorists coverage

Underinsured motorists coverage provides protection to automobile accident victims when a negligent driver has insufficient insurance limits to pay for the damages for which he or she is responsible. For example, assume a negligent driver causes bodily injury of $30,000 to another person but only carries $25,000 of insurance, which is the minimum state requirement. If the innocent victim has $100,000 of underinsured motorists coverage, the additional $5,000 can be collected from his or her own company.

Underinsured motorists coverage is a policy endorsement in about half the states and can only be purchased if the policyowner also carries uninsured motorists coverage with the same limit. However, in most other states, underinsured motorists coverage must be included along with uninsured motorists coverage and for the same limits.

No-fault Automobile Insurance

The traditional insurance and tort systems for compensating automobile accident victims have been subject to criticism for many years. These criticisms center around the following issues:

- Many innocent persons are unable to collect anything for their injuries under the traditional tort system because injuries are caused by uninsured and hit-and-run drivers.
- Injuries from automobile accidents are a societal problem for all insured parties whether they are negligent or not.
- It is often difficult or impossible to determine who is at fault in an accident.
- The traditional tort system has resulted in many serious claims being underpaid because of inadequate insurance limits. However, there is evidence that many small claims are overpaid for the sake of a quick settlement.

- Under the traditional insurance and tort systems, a large portion of premium dollars are used to pay claims costs and attorneys' fees.
- The traditional tort system is slow. In some states, delays of 3 to 5 years between an accident and a resulting trial are common.

The result of these shortcomings to the traditional systems of compensating automobile accident victims has lead to the passage of some type of no-fault law in many states. The concept of no-fault is not new, having been originally proposed in the 1930s. However, the first such law was enacted in Massachusetts in 1971, and most existing laws date to the 1970s. A few additional states passed laws in the 1980s and early 1990s, but a few others also terminated these existing laws. Today 23 states, in addition to the District of Columbia and Puerto Rico, have no-fault laws.

The slow growth of no-fault in additional states results from many arguments against no-fault laws such as the following:

- They have not resulted in lower premiums, probably because the right to sue is only modified for relatively minor injuries.
- The traditional systems of compensating automobile accident victims work well with most cases being settled relatively quickly and out of court.
- The inability in some states to sue for pain and suffering has not been popular with plaintiffs' attorneys and many drivers, who feel such suits are their right.
- There are ways to modify the current tort systems such as limiting attorneys' fees and increasing the use of arbitration rather than trials.
- Some of the costs of automobile accidents tend to be shifted from negligent parties to innocent victims.

Types of No-fault Laws

pure no-fault

The original proposals for no-fault automobile insurance were based on the principle that the tort liability system would be abolished for automobile accidents. Under such a *pure no-fault* system, each owner of an automobile would be required to carry first-party insurance that compensated all persons injured in automobile accidents involving that vehicle. The right to sue a negligent party, even for pain and suffering, would not exist. No state has gone as far as adopting a pure no-fault law. The types of laws that do exist fall into three broad categories—modified no-fault laws, add-on plans, and choice no-fault laws.

modified no-fault

Modified No-fault Laws. The most common form of no-fault legislation, used in 11 jurisdictions,[3] limits the right of an injured party to recover damages from a negligent party but does not eliminate it. States with *modified no-fault* laws have taken two approaches in allowing suits. Some states have a *dollar threshold*, which may vary from $400 to $5,000 dollars. If a person's injuries are below this amount, he or she must collect from first-party no-fault benefits and cannot sue. However, suits are allowed once the threshold is reached. The injured party can still receive no-fault benefits, but his or her insurer is reimbursed to the extent any amount from a legal judgment duplicates any no-fault benefits received. Other states have a *verbal threshold* and allow suits when there is a fatal injury, serious injury, or serious disfigurement. What constitutes a serious injury or disfigurement varies among these states.

Types of No-Fault Laws

- Pure no-fault: right to sue negligent party would be eliminated.
- Modified no-fault: right to sue negligent party exists only if injuries exceed a dollar or verbal threshold.
- Add-on no-fault: right to sue negligent party exists in addition to right to collect first-party no-fault benefits.
- Choice no-fault: right to sue negligent party is an alternative to collecting under a modified no-fault plan, at option of the injured person.

---

add-on plan

Add-on Plans. Under an *add-on plan*, there is no restriction on the right to sue a negligent party, but first party no-fault type benefits are available. The insurer that pays these benefits has subrogation rights against the negligent party. (Note that there are some persons who argue that add-on plans should not be referred to as a type of no-fault since the traditional tort system has not been altered.)

Ten jurisdictions use add-on plans.[4] In some states, both liability insurance and no-fault benefits are compulsory; in other states, liability insurance is compulsory, but the no-fault benefits are optional. In still other states, both liability insurance and no-fault benefits are optional.

choice no-fault

Choice No-fault Laws. A *choice no-fault* law, used in three states[5] gives the injured person two choices: coverage under the traditional tort liability system or coverage under a modified no-fault law at a reduced premium. Depending on the jurisdiction, a person who elects to retain the right to seek damages under the traditional liability system may or may not be able to purchase no-fault type benefits in a manner similar to an add-on plan.

Types of No-fault Benefits

personal injury protection (PIP) endorsement

No fault benefits are provided by adding an endorsement to an automobile insurance policy. This endorsement varies from state to state to conform to each state's no-fault law. Usually, it is referred to as the *personal injury protection (PIP) endorsement*.

Benefits are normally subject to dollar or time limits, and some states require insurers to make larger-than-required benefits available. Some states also require insurers to offer optional deductibles to reduce or eliminate certain no-fault benefits. The use of these deductibles can make sense to the extent the no-fault benefits duplicate other medical expense or disability income insurance. No-fault benefits in most states include

- medical expenses
- rehabilitation expenses
- loss of earnings (or some proportion thereof)
- expenses for essential services such as house or yard work that an injured person can no longer perform
- funeral expenses
- survivors' benefits arising from death in an automobile accident

No-fault benefits are typically available to the policyowner and relative members of his or her household riding in any vehicle, as well as to other persons riding in the policyowner's vehicle. State law varies as to which policy pays when a person is eligible for benefits as an injured passenger in someone else's automobile and also under his or her own automobile insurance policy.

Note that the PIP endorsement does not change the liability coverage available under an automobile insurance policy. However, its existence does result in fewer liability claims being filed.

THE PERSONAL AUTO POLICY

The discussion of automobile insurance focuses on the most common automobile policy—ISO's personal auto policy, often referred to as the PAP. Like the homeowners policy, it is a package policy that provides both property and liability insurance for family members. As is the case with the ISO homeowners policy, some insurers use their own policy forms. However, these forms tend to be similar to the PAP.

The following discussion looks at the basic format of the PAP, eligibility, some definitions that apply throughout the policy, and the policy territory. This is followed by an analysis of the various coverages in the policy. Finally, some of the more common endorsements are briefly described. Like the homeowners policy, the basic PAP does not meet everyone's needs and often must be modified.

Format of the PAP

Following a declarations and definitions section, the PAP provides four types of insurance coverage:

- Part A—Liability Coverage
- Part B—Medical Payments Coverage
- Part C—Uninsured Motorists Coverage
- Part D—Coverage for Damage to Your Auto

In states with no-fault laws, Part B is replaced with an endorsement that provides the required no-fault benefits.

The policy also contains two other sections—Part E and Part F—that spell out the duties of an insured following a loss and other policy provisions. These provisions have largely been discussed in prior chapters.

Eligibility

A PAP can be written on eligible vehicles owned or leased by an individual or by a husband or wife residing in the same household. Vehicles with other forms of ownership (such as a father and a son) can also be insured with an endorsement. A vehicle rented to others or used as a public or livery conveyance is not eligible and must be insured under a commercial policy.

Eligible vehicles include private passenger automobiles such as cars, vans, and sports utility vehicles, owned by the policyowner or leased under a written contract of six continuous months or longer. Pickups are also eligible vehicles if their gross weight is less than 10,000 pounds. However, vans and pickups are ineligible for coverage if they are used for the transportation or delivery of goods and materials except when (1) they are used for farming or ranching or (2) their use is incidental to the named insured's business of installing, maintaining, or repairing furnishings or equipment. An example of the latter would be a van of an electrician or appliance repair person.

Other vehicles, such as motor homes, motorcycles, golf carts, and snowmobiles, can also be insured by endorsement in most states.

Finally, the policy can be endorsed to provide automobile insurance to a person who drives automobiles but does not own any vehicles eligible for coverage under a PAP. This might be a person who frequently rents a car or has use of a company car on a regular basis.

Definitions

Like the homeowners policy, the PAP contains numerous definitions. One important definition—*insured*—is different for different parts of the policy and is discussed later. However, some definitions are used throughout the policy. These definitions include *covered auto*, *you*, *family members*, and *occupying*.

Covered Auto

covered auto

A *covered auto* (referred to in the PAP as "your covered auto") is any vehicle listed in the policy declarations. In addition, it includes three other categories of vehicles: newly acquired autos, trailers, and temporary substitute vehicles.

newly acquired auto

Newly Acquired Autos. A *newly acquired auto* is one that meets the eligibility requirements previously described but which is acquired after the effective date of the policy.

If the new automobile replaces an existing vehicle, it is automatically insured for the broadest Parts A, B, and C coverages that apply to any vehicle listed in the declarations. There is no need to notify the insurance company, though it is a good idea to do so. If the new automobile is an additional vehicle, the same automatic coverage applies only if the policyowner asks the insurance company to insure the vehicle within 14 days of purchase.

The situation is different for damage to the automobile (Part D). There is automatic insurance for the broadest Part D benefits provided to any vehicle in the declarations only if the insurance company is notified within 14 days of purchase. There is also coverage for newly acquired automobiles even if Part D is not in effect on any vehicles listed in the declarations, but only if the insurance company is notified within four days of purchase that such coverage is wanted. If the four-day notification is satisfied, any loss prior to insurance company notification is subject to a $500 deductible.

Example: Tom Howard's car is insured under a PAP for Coverages A, B, C, and D. Tom trades his car in for a new one. Tom's Coverages A, B, and C apply to the new car automatically, with no necessity to notify the insurer.

Tom's Coverage D also applies to the new car automatically, but only if Tom notifies the insurer within 14 days.

Trailers. A *trailer* is a vehicle designed to be pulled by a private passenger automobile or van. It also includes a farm wagon or farm implement while it is being towed.

temporary substitute vehicle

Temporary Substitute Vehicles. A *temporary substitute vehicle* is one not owned by the insured while it is used temporarily in place of a vehicle listed in the declarations if that vehicle is out of normal use because of breakdown, repair, servicing, loss, or destruction.

Note that this definition of a covered auto only applies to Parts A, B, and C of the PAP.

You

The terms *you* and *yours* are used throughout the PAP. They refer to the named insured shown in the policy declaration and the spouse of the named insured if a resident of the same household.

If the spouse ceases to be a resident of the same household, the spouse is still a "you" or "your" until the earliest of the following:

- the end of 90 days following the spouse's change of residency
- the effective date of another policy that lists the spouse as a named insured
- the end of the policy period

Family Member

A *family member* is any person related to "you" by blood, marriage, or adoption who is a resident of the same household. This includes a ward or foster child.

Occupying

Occupying means in, upon, and getting in, on, out of, or off a vehicle.

Policy Territory

The PAP applies only to accidents and losses that occur in the United States, its territories or possessions, Puerto Rico, or Canada. Coverage also applies if a covered auto is being transported between these locations.

Coverage can be endorsed or other policies purchased when a covered auto is in another country such as Mexico.

PART A—LIABILITY COVERAGE

The discussion of Parts A, B, and C of the PAP focuses on answering four questions:

- What is covered?
- Who are the insureds?
- What exclusions apply?
- What happens when there is other insurance covering a claim?

What Is Covered?

Part A of the PAP provides bodily injury and property damage liability protection to any insured who is legally responsible for an automobile accident. As with other liability policies, the insurer agrees to pay defense costs until the limit of liability has been exhausted by payment of judgments or settlements.

The liability limits are selected by the applicant and apply to each covered accident. The latest version of the PAP is written with split limits, but it can be endorsed to provide single limit coverage. With *split limits*, there are three separate dollar amounts, such as $25,000/$50,000/$10,000, that apply to each accident. The first limit is the maximum amount that will be paid to any one person for bodily injury; the second limit is the maximum that will be paid for all bodily injury claims; and the third limit applies to total property damage claims. With a single limit, there is one amount that applies in the aggregate to all bodily injury and liability claims arising from an accident. The limits available often range from $50,000 to $500,000 or more.

split limits

Example: Gary Rock's PAP provides split limits under Part A of $500,000/$1,000,000/$50,000. In an auto accident, Gary injures two people in another car. One is awarded damages of $750,000 and the other is awarded damages of $300,000. Their car, worth $60,000, is totally demolished.

The insurer will pay only $500,000 of the $750,000 award because that is the per person policy limit for bodily injury. The policy will pay the full $300,000 to the other person. In addition, the policy will only pay $50,000 for the damage to the car because that is the policy's property damage limit.

In most cases, policyowners will carry the amount needed to satisfy the required underlying limits of an umbrella liability policy (usually in the range of $250,000/$500,000/$50,000). The umbrella liability policy is discussed later in this chapter.

The PAP specifies that the insurer's limit of liability shown in the declarations is the most the company will pay regardless of the number of insureds, claims made, vehicles or premiums shown in the declarations, or vehicles involved in any accident. For example, if a son has an accident while driving a family car, the son and both parents might be sued. The policy limits only apply once, not three times. An identical provision applies to Part B and Part C of the PAP. In addition, the policy specifies that no one is entitled to receive duplicate payments for the same elements of loss under more than one of Part A, Part B, and Part C of the policy. For example, an injured passenger who sued an insured could not receive a liability payment under Part A for specific medical expenses and medical payments under Part B for the same medical expenses.

The PAP also contains a provision that adjusts the limits of liability to those required in a state where an accident occurs if it is a state other than the one where the insured vehicle is principally garaged. Any other required coverage, such as no-fault benefits, are also provided for out-of-state accidents.

The PAP also provides certain supplementary payments for expenses arising from an accident covered by the policy. These payments, like defense costs, are in addition to the stated liability limits. They are

- up to $250 for bail bonds
- premiums on appeal bonds and bonds to release attachments
- interest occurring after a judgment
- up to $200 per day for loss of earnings because of attendance at hearings or trials
- other reasonable expenses incurred at the insurer's request

Who Are the Insureds?

The insureds under Part A include several categories of persons. From the policyowner's standpoint, the most important category is probably the named insured, spouse, and family members for legal liability arising out of the ownership, maintenance, or use of any automobile or trailer. There is also coverage for any other person using a covered auto.

In addition, other persons or organizations may have coverage because of their legal liability arising from the actions of any of the parties previously mentioned. For example, if the named insured is driving a vehicle as part of his or her job or while doing work for a charity, it is possible that the employer or charity could also become a party to a legal action. They are insured under the policy as long as they do not own or hire the vehicle.

What Exclusions Apply?

There are several situations in which the PAP does not provide liability coverage. One exclusion denies coverage for anyone who intentionally causes an accident. However, other insureds still have coverage if they are sued because of that person's actions. Another exclusion denies coverage to any insured, other than a family member using the covered auto, who uses a vehicle without a reasonable belief that he or she is entitled to do so.

Several exclusions pertain to business situations. The primary purpose for these exclusions is that certain expenses should be covered under a commercial auto policy rather than the PAP. One of these denies coverage for the ownership or operation of a vehicle if it is used as a public or livery conveyance, which is a vehicle hired out to carry persons or property. Note, however, that this exclusion does not apply to situations where expenses of carpooling or a vacation are shared.

Another exclusion pertains to persons engaged in the business of selling, repairing, servicing, storing, or parking vehicles designed for use mainly on public highways. For example, a named insured while engaged in this type of business would not have coverage when driving other people's vehicles nor would another person engaged in this type of business (such as an auto repair person) have coverage driving the named insured's automobile. However, the exclusion does not apply to the use of the covered auto by the named insured, spouse, or a family member, or any partner, agent, or employee of the insured, spouse, or a family member. Another somewhat similar exclusion denies liability coverage when the named insured is using certain other vehicles in the course of any business (other than farming or ranching). However, this exclusion does not apply to a private passenger automobile, pickup, or van, or to a trailer used with any of the three types of vehicles.

A final business-situation exclusion applies to bodily injury to employees of any insured. However, this exclusion applies to domestic employees only if they either are or should be covered under a workers' compensation policy.

There are also some exclusions that apply to property damage, to property being transported by an insured, or property (other than a residence or private garage) rented to, used by, or in the care of any insured. There may be some coverage for these loss exposures under a homeowners policy.

There is no liability coverage for vehicles with fewer than four wheels or vehicles designed mainly for off-road use except trailers, nonowned golf carts, or vehicles used in an emergency. If a policyowner needs to insure such vehicles as motorcycles or mopeds, coverage can be added by an endorsement.

A significant exclusion for many insureds is one that applies to any vehicle, other than the covered auto, that is either owned by the named insured or spouse or furnished for his or her regular use. If the vehicle is owned, it should be listed and insured along with other owned vehicles. If a vehicle is furnished for regular use, such as an employer-provided car, it should either be insured by the employer or this exclusion should be modified by endorsement. A similar exclusion applies to vehicles owned by or furnished for the regular use of family members. However, this exclusion does not apply to the named insured or spouse. For example, assume a 22-year-old son living at home owns an uninsured car. He would be insured under his parents' policy for driving other cars, but as a family member, he would not have "free" coverage for driving his own vehicle. However, his parents would have coverage if they drove his car on an occasional basis, as long as it was not available to them for regular use.

Finally, there is no liability coverage for vehicles located inside a facility for racing when they are competing in or practicing or preparing for any type of organized racing or speed contest.

Other Insurance

In some cases, more than one PAP might provide coverage. The most common example occurs when a person drives a friend's car. The first person is a named insured under his or her own PAP while driving another automobile. He or she is also an insured under the friend's PAP as a person using the covered auto.

The other insurance provision in the PAP states that the policy will pay its pro rata share of any loss, based on its policy limit as a percentage of the total of all policy limits applicable to the loss. However, the PAP also says that coverage provided for a vehicle that an insured does not own is excess insurance. Therefore, in the previous situation, the friend's policy is primary because it covers an "owned vehicle," and the driver's insurance is secondary or excess because he or she is driving a "nonowned vehicle." The driver's policy will only pay on an excess basis after the limits of the owner's policy are exhausted.

PART B—MEDICAL PAYMENTS COVERAGE

What Is Covered?

Part B of the PAP provides payment for the reasonable and necessary medical expenses of an insured as a result of an automobile accident. Only those expenses that result from medical services that are rendered within 3 years of the date of an accident are covered. Benefits are paid regardless of fault.

The benefit limit, typically in the range of $1,000 to $10,000, is selected by the applicant and applies separately to each person injured in an accident. As previously mentioned, no one can collect for the same expenses more than once under Part A, Part B, and Part C. If an insured incurred $10,000 of medical expenses when struck by a hit-and-run driver, duplicate payments for the same expenses would not be paid under medical payments coverage and uninsured motorists coverage. For example, if the medical payments coverage paid its limit of $5,000, only $5,000 more could be collected under Part C for the actual medical expenses. However, additional amounts might be collected because of pain and suffering from the injuries received in the accident.

Note that in most states with no-fault laws, Part B is replaced by an endorsement that provides the no-fault benefits.

Who Are the Insureds?

The insureds under Part B include the named insured, spouse, and any family members (1) while occupying either a motor vehicle designed for use on public roads or a trailer or (2) when struck as a pedestrian by such a vehicle or trailer.

Any other person who is injured while occupying a covered auto is also an insured.

What Exclusions Apply?

With a few minor exceptions, the exclusions that apply to Part B are the same as those for Part A. That is, if liability coverage would not apply to an accident, medical payments coverage would likewise not be available.

Other Insurance

The other insurance provision that applies to medical payments coverage is similar to the one for liability coverage. The policy pays on a pro rata basis except when the other insurance is on a nonowned vehicle. That coverage is excess over other collectible automobile insurance that provides payments for medical or funeral expenses.

PART C—UNINSURED MOTORISTS COVERAGE

What Is Covered?

Part C of the PAP provides *uninsured motorists coverage* (and underinsured motorists coverage in many states). Under Part C, the insurer agrees to pay compensatory damages that an insured is legally entitled to recover from the owner or operator of an *uninsured motor vehicle* because of bodily injury (and property damage in a few states) sustained by an insured and caused by an accident. The coverage applies to claims for medical expenses, lost wages, and pain and suffering but does not include punitive or exemplary damages.

There typically is a minimum amount of coverage that must be purchased in accordance with a state's financial responsibility law. Above that, the applicant can purchase an amount of coverage as high as the liability limits that apply under Part A.

The insurance company has no legal obligation to pay an uninsured motorists claim unless the owner or operator of the uninsured vehicle is legally responsible for the insured's damages. The insured must file a claim against his or her own insurer and, in the ideal situation, the insured and the insurer will reach a satisfactory settlement. If not, the matter is subject to an arbitration provision. Note that the results of a suit against the uninsured party are not binding on the insurer if it is brought without the insurer's written consent.

For purposes of Part C, an uninsured vehicle is more than one without insurance. It also includes

- a vehicle that is insured for less than the limits of the financial responsibility laws of the state where the covered auto is principally garaged
- a hit-and-run vehicle whose operator cannot be identified and that hits the
  (1) named insured, spouse, or family member,
  (2) a vehicle that any of these insureds are occupying, or
  (3) a covered auto
- a vehicle to which insurance applies at the time of the accident, but the insurance company either denies coverage, is insolvent, or becomes insolvent. Coverage might be denied, for example, because an insured intentionally caused an accident.

Uninsured Vehicle

- One with no insurance
- One with liability limits lower than the applicable state law
- One driven by a hit-and-run driver
- One whose insurer denies coverage or becomes insolvent

Part C, however, specifically excludes certain vehicles from the definition of an uninsured vehicle. These are vehicles that are

- owned by or furnished for the regular use of any family member
- owned or operated by a self-insurer under an applicable motor vehicle law unless the self-insurer is or becomes insolvent
- owned by any government agency unit
- operated on rails or crawler treads
- designed mainly for use off public roads
- located for use as a residence or premises

Who Are the Insureds?

The insureds under Part C include the named insured, spouse, and any family members. They also include any other persons that occupy a covered auto. In addition, anyone else who is entitled to recover damages because of bodily injury to any of the previously mentioned persons is an insured. This would include, for example, the spouse of a passenger injured while riding in the covered auto if a claim was brought for loss of consortium.

What Exclusions Apply?

The PAP excludes uninsured motorists coverage if an insured is injured while occupying or struck by an automobile that is owned by the insured but which is not insured under the policy. However, a few state courts have said this exclusion is not enforceable because the intent of the law was to protect injured persons, and a claim must be paid as long as one automobile is insured under the policy.

There are also exclusions similar to those previously discussed for use of the covered auto without permission or as a public or livery conveyance.

Other Insurance

As with Part A and Part B, losses are settled on a pro rata basis except that coverage on a nonowned vehicle is primary to coverage on a vehicle that an insured owns. Under Part A and Part B, the insured in effect has insurance equal to the combined limit of all policies covering a loss. This is not true under Part C. If more than one policy provides coverage, the recovery for damages under all policies may not exceed the highest limit for any one vehicle under any of the policies.

For example, assume one policy provides $25,000 of uninsured motorists coverage and a second policy provides $50,000 of coverage. The maximum amount of coverage is then $50,000 and the entire claim would be paid under that policy if it was the primary policy. If the first policy was primary, it would pay the first $25,000 of a claim, and the second policy would pay the next $25,000.

PART D—COVERAGE FOR DAMAGE TO YOUR AUTO

The questions to be answered for Part D are somewhat different because the focus is on damage to automobiles rather than on injuries to people.

What Is Covered?

Part D is the portion of the PAP that provides coverage for physical damage to the covered auto and to certain other nonowned automobiles. There are actually two coverages: (1) *collision* and (2) *other than collision*. Other than collision was formerly called comprehensive and this terminology is still frequently used colloquially and in commercial policies, although it is not a term in the PAP. The policyowner can elect both coverages or only other-than-collision coverage; collision coverage cannot be purchased alone. In addition, the policyowner can elect not to purchase any Part D coverage—a decision that is often made with respect to older vehicles whose value has diminished.

Deductibles that can be selected by the policyowner apply to each coverage. Frequently, a lower deductible is purchased for other-than-collision coverage than is purchased for collision coverage because of the significant cost savings by selecting a larger deductible for the latter.

Part D also provides certain additional coverages, referred to as *transportation expenses*.

Collision

collision

Collision is defined as the upset of the covered auto or any nonowned auto or their impact with another vehicle or object.

Other than Collision

other than collision

The PAP never specifically defines the term *other than collision*. Technically, if a loss is not caused by a collision, it must be a result of other than collision. Together these two coverages give an insured "open-perils" coverage on an insured automobile, subject to the various policy exclusions.

In some cases, it is difficult to determine when a loss results from collision or other than collision. The PAP has a specific list of sources of loss that are considered other than collision. These are

- missiles and falling objects
- fire
- theft or larceny
- explosion or earthquake
- windstorm
- hail, water, or flood
- malicious mischief or vandalism
- riot or civil commotion
- contact with a bird or animal

- breakage of glass. However, the policyowner can consider this part of the collision loss if it is caused by collision.

For example, a car damaged in a collision by a thief who stole it would be a theft loss and covered under other than collision. In many cases, this is the most advantageous place for coverage because other-than-collision coverage is sometimes purchased without collision coverage, and the deductible is often lower. Similarly, if a car is swept into a tree by flood, the damage is covered as a flood loss under the other-than-collision coverage.

Transportation Expenses

The PAP also pays up to $600, without application of the policy deductible, for temporary transportation expenses because of a loss to a covered auto or because of a loss to a nonowned auto for which the named insured or spouse is legally responsible. However, this benefit is only paid for a collision loss if the policyowner has purchased collision coverage. Similarly, it is paid for an other-than-collision loss only if other-than-collision coverage is in effect.

The amount of the benefit is limited to $20 per day and is payable beginning 48 hours after a theft loss and ending when the vehicle is returned to use or the insurer pays for its loss. For other types of losses, the benefit begins when the vehicle is withdrawn from use for more than 24 hours and is limited to the period of time reasonably required to repair or replace the vehicle.

What Vehicles Are Covered?

Part D applies to both covered autos and nonowned autos. The term *covered auto* was previously defined and applies throughout the PAP. The term *nonowned auto* for purposes of Part D, however, is defined differently and includes either of the following:

- any private passenger automobile, pickup, van, or trailer not owned by or furnished or available for the regular use of the named insured, spouse or any family member while in the custody of or being operated by the named insured, spouse, or any family member
- any automobile or trailer not owned by the named insured or spouse that is used as a temporary substitute for a covered auto that is out of normal use because of breakdown, repair, servicing, loss, or destruction

Assume that a son lives with his parents and owns a car without collision coverage. If one of his parents borrows his car, their collision coverage would not apply to an accident they might have as a result of using the car merely because it was at the end of the driveway. Under their PAP, it does not fit the definition of either a covered auto or a nonowned auto. If, on the other hand, the son's car were borrowed because one of the parents' cars was in the shop for service, the parents' collision coverage would apply because the use of the vehicle now brings it under the definition of a nonowned auto.

The coverage for nonowned autos applies to vehicles that are rented on a temporary basis, such as when an insured is on a trip, but the policy deductible applies. However, if the insured purchases the loss damage waiver from the car rental company, there will be no deductible. In addition, the administrative hassle of resolving the matter might be minimized. These potential advantages of purchasing the loss damage waiver must be balanced by its relatively high cost—possibly $15 or $20 per day. It should be pointed out that some credit cards pick up the cost of the loss damage waiver for certain vehicles if the card is used to pay for the rental.

Coverage for a nonowned auto is the broadest coverage applicable to any covered auto under the policyowner's PAP.

What Exclusions Apply?

Numerous exclusions apply to Part D. Some of these are similar to the exclusions previously discussed in connection with other parts of the PAP. For example, losses to any vehicle are excluded if it was used as a public or livery conveyance or in competition or for practice inside a racing facility. Losses to nonowned autos are excluded when used without a reasonable belief that an insured is entitled to use them or when the vehicle is used by anyone in the business of selling, repairing, servicing, storing, or parking vehicles designed for use on public highways.

Several exclusions apply to various types of property under certain circumstances. For example, there is no coverage for

- electronic equipment (including accessories) designed for the reproduction of sound. However, this exclusion does not apply if the equipment is permanently installed in an automobile. It also does not apply if the equipment is removable from a housing unit that is permanently installed as long as the equipment is (1) solely operated by power from the automobile's electrical system, and (2) in an automobile at the time of loss.
- electronic equipment that receives and transmits audio, visual, or data signals (including accessories). Examples of such equipment include citizens band radios, telephones, two-way mobile radios, scanning monitor receivers, television monitor receivers, video-cassette recorders, audiocassette recorders, or personal computers. However, this exclusion does not apply to equipment that is necessary for the normal operation of an automobile or the

monitoring of an automobile operating system. It also does not apply to permanently installed telephones (or their accessories) designed to be operated by use of power from the automobile's electrical system.

- loss to tapes, records, discs, or other media used with equipment described in the two previous exclusions
- loss to equipment designed or used for the detection or location of radar or laser
- loss to a trailer, camper body, or motor home (including facilities or accessories used with them) not shown in the policy declarations. However, this exclusion does not apply to nonowned trailers or trailers acquired during the policy period as long as the insurer is asked to insure them within 14 days of acquisition.
- loss to any custom furnishings or equipment in or upon a pickup or van. However, this exclusion does not apply to a cap, cover, or bedliner in or upon a covered auto that is a pickup.

How Are Losses Settled?

The insurer's limit of liability is generally the lesser of (1) the actual cash value of stolen or damaged property or (2) the amount necessary to repair or replace the property with other property of like kind and quality. However, $500 is the maximum payment for loss to a nonowned trailer, and $1,000 is the maximum payment for equipment designed solely for the reproduction of sound that is installed in locations not used by the automobile manufacturer for the installation of such equipment.

The insurance company has the right to pay losses in money or to repair or replace damaged or stolen property. They also have the option of returning stolen property to the named insured and paying any damage that results from the theft, or of keeping all or part of the property and paying the insured an agreed or appraised value. Loss payments in the form of money include applicable sales tax.

The policy contains an appraisal provision that applies to situations when the insurer and insured cannot agree on the amount of a loss.

If there is other insurance, losses are settled on a pro rata basis except that coverage on a nonowned auto is excess over other collectible insurance.

PAP ENDORSEMENTS

As with the homeowners policies, there are several ISO endorsements that can be added to the homeowners policies to better meet the needs of certain individuals. Some endorsements apply to more than one of the four coverages previously discussed; others apply to one specific coverage only. Several of these endorsements are briefly described.

Some of these endorsements are automatically included in PAPs by some insurance companies.

Extended Nonowned Coverage

One significant exclusion in the PAP for many policyowners applies to liability and medical payments coverage for vehicles furnished or made available for the regular use of the named insured and family members. This exclusion, for example, eliminates coverage if an insured regularly drives a company car.

Extended Nonowned Coverage can be used to delete this exclusion in the PAP. However, any person who needs this coverage must be specifically listed in the endorsement. For example, if only the named insured is listed, there is no coverage for a spouse or other family member who might drive the vehicle.

The endorsement also deletes the exclusions that apply to (1) a nonowned vehicle used in business as long as the business is not the automobile business, and (2) a nonowned vehicle used as a public or livery conveyance.

The addition of this endorsement also results in coverage if the insured is sued by a fellow employee as a result of an accident while driving a vehicle covered by the endorsement. This coverage is often excluded under business policies of the employer of the driver and fellow employee.

Named Nonowner Coverage

This endorsement is for use by persons who do not own an automobile but want to have protection when they drive nonowned vehicles. Parts A, B, and C of the PAP are available.

If the named insured acquires an automobile, there is coverage for 30 days to give the insured time to specifically insure the vehicle.

Miscellaneous Type Vehicle Endorsement

This endorsement is used to cover miscellaneous types of owned vehicles such as motor homes, motorcycles and similar type vehicles, all-terrain vehicles, dune buggies, and golf carts. Each vehicle is listed in a schedule, and the same coverages that apply to automobiles in the PAP can be purchased.

Liability for bodily injury to anyone who occupies an insured vehicle can be excluded. This results in a reduced premium, but it is appropriate only if passengers are never carried.

Snowmobile Endorsement

An endorsement similar to the Miscellaneous Type Vehicle Endorsement can be used to insure snowmobiles.

Limited Mexico Coverage

Without an endorsement, the PAP does not provide coverage when an insured is driving in Mexico. It is necessary that acceptable coverage be obtained through a licensed Mexican insurance company before a trip is taken to Mexico. To drive in Mexico without such coverage is a criminal offense. Coverage can be purchased at the border. Alternatively, it may be possible to add this protection to an existing PAP if an insurance company is a member of a foreign insurance association.

However, this is not the purpose of Limited Mexico Coverage. The endorsement is primarily used by people who live near the border and occasionally take brief trips to Mexico. All policy coverages can be purchased for losses that occur in Mexico within 25 miles of the United States' border and the coverage applies only while the insured is in Mexico for 10 days or less. The insurer will only defend the insured under the liability coverage if the original suit is brought in the United States and if the suit does not involve a Mexican citizen or resident. Repairs to a covered auto are not covered if they are made in Mexico unless the vehicle cannot be driven in its damaged condition.

It is important to point out that the endorsement is effective only if the insured has also purchased liability insurance through a Mexican insurer, and coverage is excess over that policy. The main advantage of the endorsement is the ability to have higher liability limits than the Mexican insurance as well as other policy coverages.

Coverage for Damage to Your Auto (Maximum Limit of Liability)

Insurers are often reluctant to write Part D coverage on antique or restored vehicles because of the difficulty in determining value when a loss occurs. This endorsement lists a stated amount, which becomes the maximum that the insurer will pay for a loss. However, this does not mean that the stated amount is automatically paid if a total loss occurs. The insurer's maximum limit of liability is the smallest of three amounts (less the applicable deductible):

- the stated amount selected
- the actual cash value of the stolen or damaged property
- the amount necessary to repair or replace the property with property of like kind and quality

Joint Ownership Coverage

This endorsement is used to modify the definition of insured when individuals are not married, reside together, and jointly own one or more vehicles. It can also be used when related persons jointly own a vehicle but do not live together.

Auto Loan/Lease Coverage

In some cases, the total loss to a leased vehicle or a financed automobile results in the insured's being required to pay the lessor or lending company an amount that exceeds the actual cash value of an insured vehicle. The purpose of this endorsement is to fill that gap.

The endorsement provides indemnification for any unpaid lease or finance amounts other than the following: overdue payments at the time of loss, financial penalties under a lease for excessive use or abnormal wear and tear, security deposits not refunded by a lessor, costs for extended warranties or life and health insurance purchased, and carryover balances from previous leases or loans.

Towing and Labor Costs Coverage

This endorsement pays for towing and labor if a covered auto or nonowned auto is disabled for any reason. The limit of coverage is a stated amount such as $25, $50, or $100 per disablement. The labor costs of repair work (such as changing a flat tire) are covered only at the place of disablement.

This endorsement can be used only for automobiles that are already covered under Part D of the PAP. It is not unusual for the towing and labor coverage to be a standard part of an insurance company's PAPs if collision coverage is purchased.

Other Endorsements

There are several other endorsements that provide coverage either for property that is excluded under the PAP or where the amount of coverage is limited. These endorsements are very briefly described below:

- Optional Limits Transportation Expense Coverage. The $20 per day and $600 maximums that apply to transportation expenses are increased to $30 and $900, respectively, under this endorsement.
- Customizing Equipment Coverage. This endorsement can be used to insure custom furnishings and/or equipment in a pickup or van.
- Audio, Visual and Data Equipment and Media. This endorsement provides coverage for electronic equipment other than that designed solely for reproduction of sound. The equipment must be (1) permanently installed or (2) removable from a permanently installed housing unit and designed to operate solely from the

vehicle's electrical system. There is a limited amount of coverage ($200) for tapes, records, discs, and other media.

- Covered Property Coverage. This endorsement provides coverage for awnings, cabanas, and other similar equipment designed for use with insured vehicles such as vans, camping trailers, or motor homes.

HARD-TO-INSURE DRIVERS

Not all persons can readily obtain automobile insurance in the standard marketplace. These hard-to-insure drivers include persons with poor driving records and often include those who are youthful or who have little driving experience. Statistics clearly show that these groups have a high probability of being involved in future accidents.

Another category of hard-to-insure drivers consists of persons with very high-powered and/or expensive automobiles. However, there are insurers that specialize in this market, particularly for individuals who have good driving records.

The number of hard-to-insure drivers varies significantly from state to state with the number being much higher in those states where insurance companies lose money on their automobile insurance business. This usually results from the state insurance department's unwillingness to grant desired rate increases.

Insuring Hard-to-Insure Drivers

- Specialty high-risk auto insurers
- State automobile insurance (assigned risk) plans
- Joint underwriting associations
- Reinsurance facilities

---

residual market

Hard-to-insure drivers can usually find some coverage in what is referred to as the *residual market* (sometimes referred to as the *shared market* or *substandard market*). This market consists of specialty insurers and state programs to make insurance available, though not necessarily affordable. However, a small number of drivers with very poor driving records (for example, several drunk driving convictions) may still be unable to obtain insurance from either of these sources in some states.

Specialty Insurers

There are insurers who specialize in writing coverage for high-risk drivers. They charge substantially higher premiums than in the standard marketplace and often provide more limited coverage. For example, the limits for liability coverage are sometimes only those specified in a state's financial responsibility or compulsory insurance law. However, it is not unusual to have optional higher limits available.

Medical payments coverage can also be limited, and collision coverage, if written, is often subject to a high deductible.

State Programs

State programs for hard-to-insure drivers also tend to have higher-than-normal premiums (often much higher) and more limited coverage than the standard marketplace, but significant variations exist among the states. The state programs usually follow one of three models:

- automobile insurance plans
- joint underwriting associations
- reinsurance facilities

Automobile Insurance Plans

automobile insurance plan

An *automobile insurance plan* is the type of program that exists in most states. To be eligible, an applicant must show that he or she has been unable to obtain coverage within a recent specified period of time.

Each automobile insurer in the state is then assigned its proportionate share of the drivers in the plan based on the total volume of automobile insurance written in the state. Because of this procedure, these plans were once known as *assigned risk plans*, but this terminology is no longer in vogue because of its perceived negative connotation.

The company to which the policy is assigned issues and services it. It also receives any profits or absorbs any losses from the policies it writes.

Joint Underwriting Associations

Under this arrangement, there is an association of automobile insurers, and all business of the association is placed in a pool. Any underwriting losses are shared by the insurance companies in proportion to the automobile insurance premiums written in the state.

A limited number of companies are designated to issue and service policies on behalf of the association.

Reinsurance Facilities

Under this approach, insurers must accept all applicants who have a valid driver's license, and they issue and service policies for these applicants.

However, if an applicant is considered high-risk, the insurer has the option of assigning the premiums for the applicant to the reinsurance facility. All underwriting losses from this type of business are shared by all automobile insurance companies in the state in proportion to automobile insurance premiums written.

SHOPPING FOR AUTOMOBILE INSURANCE

The cost of automobile insurance varies significantly in a highly competitive market. In fact, studies by some state insurance departments show that the premium for a hypothetical insured can be two to four times higher if purchased from certain insurance companies rather than others. Therefore, it pays to shop around. Of course, as previously stated, factors such as the financial strength of the insurer and the service from the company and its agents also need to be evaluated.

Many factors affect automobile insurance rates, and some of them are not readily within the control of the insured at the time automobile insurance is purchased. These factors include the age, sex, and marital status of drivers, the use of the insured vehicles (that is, driving to work, pleasure, or business), and the geographic territory where vehicles are normally used and garaged.

Other factors are subject to some control by the insured but not necessarily at the moment a policy is purchased. These include driving record and the type and age of vehicles owned. The latter is particularly significant for physical damage coverage where the Part D premium can be several times higher for a new luxury automobile than a van that is several years old.

Even though these previously mentioned factors are commonly used by most companies to determine premiums, they can be applied differently among companies. For example, premiums are higher if a family has a teenager who drives. If the teenager primarily or solely drives the old family van, many companies will rate this vehicle for the teenager. However, other companies will assign the teenage driver to the highest-rated vehicle even if he or she does not use it.

Other factors can also affect automobile insurance premiums for one or more policy coverages. Many companies give discounts for at least some of the following:

- a driver education course for young drivers
- a student with good grades
- a defensive driving course
- senior citizens, but the discount may require the periodic attendance of a classroom program on driver education
- nonsmoking

- anti-theft devices in a vehicle
- airbags or automatic seat belts in a vehicle
- reduced use of a vehicle by a student who is away at school over a specified distance from home, provided the student does not have an insured vehicle at school
- no accidents for some period of time such as 3 years
- other policies with the same company. For example, some insurers give a discount if they write both automobile insurance and homeowners insurance for a policyowner.

Another important factor in the cost of automobile insurance is the coverages selected, their limits, and deductibles. For policyowners with an umbrella liability policy, the limits for liability insurance only need to be those required by the umbrella policy. If a policyowner and family have an adequate medical expense insurance plan, it is probably unnecessary to carry any more Part B coverage for medical payments than might be required in a state. However, it should be pointed out that this coverage applies to more than just family members and also covers funeral expenses. Similarly, if a policyowner and family members have adequate medical expense and disability income insurance, the need to carry other than minimally required no-fault benefits should be evaluated.

Financial planners often disagree over the appropriate limit of uninsured/underinsured motorists coverage. Some argue that it should be the same as a policy's liability limits. Others argue that this is unnecessary if other insurance exists that will pay for a family's medical expenses and lost wages. However, higher limits do give an insured the right to collect damages for pain and suffering.

Finally, there are ways to lower Part D premiums. Higher deductibles, particularly on collision coverage, can result in significant savings over a period of years. In addition, a policyowner must evaluate the need for coverage on an older vehicle. For example, there are those who argue that it is probably not cost-effective to carry physical damage coverage on a vehicle that is worth as little as $3,000 or $4,000. Obviously this threshold amount varies by factors such as the net worth and risk tolerance of an individual.

INSURING WATERCRAFT AND AIRPLANES

It is common for individuals to own watercraft. For some watercraft, liability coverage is available under a homeowners policy, but that policy provides no protection for larger boats and little physical damage protection for any boat. As a result, many insurers market various types of watercraft policies to meet the insurance needs of boat owners. There is no single common policy such as the ISO forms for homeowners and automobile insurance.

Some individuals own private aircraft for their personal or business use. Coverage for aircraft is very specialized and is usually obtained from a small number of aviation pools that underwrite and manage such insurance for their member companies.

Watercraft Policies

There are several types of watercraft policies. Some insurers have policies designed primarily for small boats such as those no longer than 20 or 22 feet. These typically provide physical damage coverage to the boat, motor, equipment, and trailer and contain a deductible. These policies can also be used to provide liability and medical payments coverage.

There are two common types of package policies for boats—the boatowners policy and the yacht policy. The boatowners policy is typically used for boats under a particular length such as 26 or 30 feet, whereas the yacht policy is used for larger boats. The boatowners policy is generally written by an insurer's personal lines department, while the yacht policy is often written by the insurer's ocean marine department. As a result, the policies tend to use different wording, but the coverage is largely the same.

Boatowners and yacht policies are similar to automobile policies in that they contain

- liability coverage, often referred to as *protection and indemnity insurance*
- medical payments coverage
- uninsured boaters coverage
- physical damage coverage, often referred to as *hull insurance*. This provides protection not only for the boat but also for equipment, accessories, motors, and trailers. Coverage can usually be written on either a named-perils or "open-perils" basis.

As a general rule, the exclusions that apply to these coverages also parallel those found in automobile insurance policies.

Other coverages are also available in boatowners and yacht policies. These include coverage for the

- legal obligation of the policyowner to remove a wrecked or sunken vessel
- liability arising out of transportation of the boat on land
- costs of towing and assistance if the boat is disabled
- liability to crew members and other maritime workers covered under various federal acts

Boatowners and yacht policies frequently contain warranties. Failure to comply with these warranties can result in the denial of coverage or higher premiums, depending on the precise policy provision. The common warranties are that the boat will

- be used for pleasure
- not be used during specified seasonal periods unless the policyowner obtains permission from the insurance company and pays any additional premium
- be operated only in the navigational area described in the policy

It is also becoming increasingly common to find a warranty that requires at least two occupants in a boat when it is used for waterskiing.

Aviation Policies

Aviation policies for private aircraft are similar to automobile insurance with respect to liability insurance in that coverage pays for bodily injury that arises out of the insured's ownership, maintenance, or use of insured aircraft. Coverage also applies to bodily injury liability arising out of the location where the insured aircraft is stored. Exclusions similar to those in automobile insurance policies apply. In addition, there are exclusions for damage or injury from noise and pollution.

Medical payments coverage is also available to cover passengers. Crew members can also be covered for an additional premium.

The physical damage coverage, also referred to as *hull coverage*, is "open-perils" and can be written to apply to the following: (1) all losses, (2) only losses that occur while the plane is not in flight, or (3) only losses that occur while the plane is not in motion.

PERSONAL UMBRELLA LIABILITY INSURANCE

umbrella liability policy

In today's litigious society, it is important to carry broad liability insurance of sufficiently high limits. Without this coverage, many individuals face the possibility of having assets and/or income seized to pay a legal judgment. The personal *umbrella liability policy* substantially accomplishes this task for individuals. However, it still contains limitations and exclusions and does not provide liability protection for every situation that might confront an individual.

While once thought of as a policy only for the wealthy with large asset accumulations and/or high incomes, the magnitude of today's legal awards makes this policy appropriate for many middle-income individuals as well.

Unlike homeowners insurance and automobile insurance, there was historically no standard personal umbrella liability policy, and each insurer that offered this type of insurance developed its own policy. The situation has changed somewhat with the recent development of an ISO policy. While insurers can now adopt the ISO policy, most continue to use their own policies. Unfortunately, this results in significant variations among policy forms. As a result, the following discussion is general in nature. However, it is important to remember that the appropriate policy for a particular individual is the one that best covers his or her specific loss exposures, and a thorough evaluation of policies is often appropriate.

The following discussion looks at the general nature of personal umbrella liability policies, the underlying coverage requirements, the persons insured, and the exclusions that often exist.

General Nature

The personal umbrella policy is designed primarily to provide liability coverage for catastrophic legal claims or judgments. The smallest limit of coverage available from most insurers is $1 million, and limits up to $5 or $10 million are often available. The policy covers not only bodily injury and property damage liability but also personal injury liability.

The personal umbrella policy requires the policyowner to carry certain underlying liability coverages of specified minimum amounts. These normally include automobile liability insurance, watercraft liability insurance for large owned watercraft, and personal liability insurance under a homeowners or other policy. If a claim is made under an underlying policy, the umbrella policy will pay only after the limits of the underlying policy are exhausted. The umbrella policy is excess and will pay up to its limits so that the insured effectively has an amount of coverage equal to the sum of the limits of the umbrella policy and the underlying coverage.

Example:	Charlene Smith has a $1 million umbrella policy and an automobile liability policy of the required underlying limit of $250,000 per person. If a legal judgment of $700,000 is obtained against her by an injured party, the underlying auto policy will pay $250,000 and the umbrella policy will pay the remaining $450,000.

self-insured retention

If an underlying policy does not cover a loss that is not excluded from a personal umbrella policy, the umbrella policy is the primary insurer and will cover the loss subject to a *self-insured retention* (SIR). The SIR is like a deductible and requires the policyowner to pay the first portion of the loss—typically $250. However, SIR amounts vary by company and can be $500 or $1,000 or even higher. The SIR is not applicable to losses covered by underlying policies. Note that the term *drop-down coverage* is often used to describe the situation when an umbrella policy covers a loss not covered by underlying insurance. In effect, it drops down to cover the entire loss, other than the SIR, rather than act as excess coverage.

Figure 18-1 shows the relationship of a typical personal umbrella policy to the underlying policies.

In addition to paying liability claims, most personal umbrella policies pay defense costs that are not payable by underlying policies and provide various other supplementary coverages similar to those in the homeowners and PAP policies (premiums on appeal bonds, expenses incurred at the company's request, and so on).

Finally, some states require that the policyowner be given the right to extend coverage under a personal umbrella policy to uninsured and underinsured motorists coverage.

FIGURE 18-1
Relationship of Personal Umbrella Policy to Underlying Policies

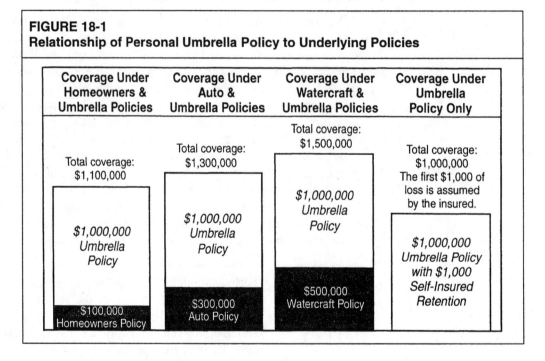

Underlying Coverage Requirements

A requirement of the personal umbrella policy is that the policyowner maintain certain underlying coverages of specified minimum amounts. Some insurers also require that these underlying coverages be purchased for them.

At a minimum, the following underlying coverages are required, and the amounts shown, while they vary from company to company, are not unusual.

- Automobile liability insurance: $250,000/$500,000/$50,000 or $300,000 to $500,000 single limit

- homeowners liability insurance: $100,000 or $300,000
- watercraft liability insurance if the policyowner owns a boat: $300,000 or $500,000

Other underlying coverages for recreational vehicles, aircraft, and employer liability may also be required, particularly if liability from these vehicles or situations is covered under the personal umbrella liability policy.

If the policyowner fails to maintain the required underlying coverages, the insurer will pay only the amount it would have been required to pay if the underlying policies had been in force. In the previous example, if the insured's liability limits had been $50,000, rather than the required $250,000 limit, the umbrella policy would still only pay $450,000. The auto policy would pay $50,000 and the insured would have an uninsured loss of $200,000.

A premium reduction may apply if the underlying limits are greater than those required by the personal umbrella policy.

Who Are the Insureds?

Personal umbrella policies provide coverage for the named insured, spouse, and family members living in the household. Other residents of the household who are under the age of 21 and in the care of an insured are usually covered.

Other persons or organizations who are driving a named insured's or spouse's automobile or who are liable because of actions of an insured with respect to an automobile are also usually covered in a manner similar to coverage under the PAP. Coverage for these persons or organizations may or may not exist with respect to watercraft and recreational vehicles.

Most policies also extend coverage to persons or organizations who have custody of an insured's animals other than businesses such as kennels, veterinary hospitals, and stables.

What Exclusions Apply?

At one time, personal umbrella policies were relatively inexpensive and contained few of the exclusions found in homeowners and automobile policies. However, claims experience over the years has lead to increased premiums and more numerous exclusions. In fact, some umbrella liability policies now have almost the same exclusions that are in homeowners and automobile policies. However, the number and nature of the exclusions vary significantly among companies, and exclusions should be evaluated carefully when selecting a personal umbrella policy.

For example, an individual who is actively involved in recreational boating might frequently operate watercraft owned by other persons. Some policies cover damage to such watercraft when an insured is liable; other policies exclude coverage for nonowned watercraft that are in the insured's care, custody, or control.

Some of the exclusions often found in personal umbrella policies include liability that arises from the following:

- intentional injury unless it results from actions to prevent or eliminate danger or to protect persons or property
- government programs such as workers' compensation
- damage to property owned by an insured
- damage to certain types of nonowned property in an insured's care, custody, or control. There is seldom a blanket exclusion for all property of this type, but damage to certain classes of property (for example, automobiles, watercraft, and aircraft) is often excluded. In addition, damage to property for which an insured has assumed contractual liability is also often excluded. The insured should have some type of property insurance in such situations.
- the use of watercraft, and possibly other recreational vehicles, unless underlying coverage applies
- the use of aircraft
- business pursuits, other than those arising out of a personal automobile or when underlying coverage exists
- the rendering or failure to render professional services. A few insurance companies will cover this loss exposure for an additional premium.
- directors' and officers' activities, other than those performed for a not-for-profit organization but only if the insured receives no compensation other than reimbursement of expenses
- transmission of communicable diseases
- sexual molestation, corporal punishment, and physical or mental abuse

CHECKLIST FOR EVALUATING AND COMPARING PERSONAL AUTOMOBILE INSURANCE POLICIES

☐ What are the limits for each of the following coverages?

___ Part A—Liability
___ Part B—Medical Payments Coverage or no-fault benefits
___ Part C—Uninsured Motorists Coverage
___ Part D—Coverage for Damage to Your Auto

☐ Are the coverage limits adequate?

☐ If the policy is not an ISO form, how does it differ?

☐ Does the policy automatically contain endorsements that are optional with other insurers?

☐ What is the annual policy premium?

☐ Is the policyowner taking advantage of all possible discounts?

☐ What deductible applies to Part D?

☐ Are low-valued vehicles unnecessarily insured under Part D?

☐ Are there, or is there any need for, any endorsements for the following?

    ___ Extended nonowned coverage
    ___ Miscellaneous type vehicles
    ___ Snowmobiles
    ___ Underinsured motorists
    ___ Limited Mexico coverage
    ___ Joint ownership
    ___ Antique or restored vehicles
    ___ Auto loan/lease coverage
    ___ Towing and labor costs
    ___ Customizing equipment
    ___ Auto, visual, and data equipment and media
    ___ Awnings, cabanas, and the like

CHECKLIST FOR EVALUATING AND COMPARING PERSONAL UMBRELLA LIABILITY INSURANCE POLICIES

☐ What are the policy limits?

☐ What is the self-insured retention?

☐ Does the policy provide uninsured or underinsured motorists coverage?

☐ What is the annual policy premium?

☐ What are the underlying coverage requirements and are they satisfied?

    ___ Automobile liability insurance
    ___ Homeowners liability insurance

___ Watercraft liability insurance
___ Other

☐ What persons are insured?

☐ What types of exclusions apply?

SOURCES FOR FURTHER IN-DEPTH STUDY

- Hamilton, Karen L., and Ferguson, Cheryl L., *Personal Risk Management and Property-Liability Insurance*, American Institute for CPCU/Insurance Institute of America, 2002. Phone 800-644-2101. Web site address www.aicpcu.org
- *FC&S Bulletins*, Personal Lines Volume, (loose-leaf and/or CD-ROM service updated monthly), Cincinnati, OH: The National Underwriter Company. Phone 800-543-0874. Web site address www.nuco.com

CHAPTER REVIEW

Answers to review questions and self-test questions start on page 725.

Key Terms

financial responsibility law	covered auto
unsatisfied judgment fund	newly acquired auto
uninsured motorists coverage	temporary substitute vehicle
underinsured motorists coverage	split limits
pure no-fault	collision
modified no-fault	other than collision
add-on plan	residual market
choice no-fault	automobile insurance plan
personal injury protection (PIP)	umbrella liability policy
endorsement	self-insured retention

Review Questions

18-1. Describe the key problems associated with automobile accidents and automobile insurance.

18-2. Explain to your client why he or she should consider purchasing uninsured and underinsured motorists coverage even though the state has a compulsory liability insurance law.

18-3.   Briefly explain the methods of compensating automobile accident victims (include the shortcomings of those methods).

18-4.   While driving his car, John sustained medical expenses and lost wages due to bodily injury when a drunk teenager driving his own car ran a red light and hit him. John in no way contributed to the accident through his own fault. Explain how the settlement would be handled in each of the following situations:
   a.   if John's bodily injuries equaled $40,000 and the accident occurred in a state with compulsory liability insurance
   b.   if John's bodily injuries equaled $40,000 and the accident occurred in a state with a modified no-fault law containing a $5,000 threshold

18-5.   What vehicles are eligible for coverage under the personal auto policy?

18-6.   Pete pays cash for a new car and when he drives it off the dealer's lot he hits another car driving along the street in front of the dealership. The accident is Pete's fault. He injures the driver of the other car and damages both his car and the other driver's car. Pete had $100,000 of liability coverage for bodily injury and property damage (Part A) and collision coverage (Part D) with a $250 deductible on the old car he just traded in as part of the purchase of his new car. What coverage, if any, would Pete have for this accident?

18-7.   Tom falls asleep at the wheel of his car while driving on the interstate, runs across the median, and causes a tractor trailer truck to flip over while trying to avoid a head-on collision with Tom. The truck driver has a claim for $5,000 of bodily injury, while damage to his truck and its contents is $150,000. How much would Tom's personal auto policy pay, if Part A— Liability coverage were
   a. $100,000/$300,000/$50,000?
   b. $300,000?

18-8.   Your client, Betty, mentions that she frequently uses cars in connection with her business and asks whether her personal auto policy provides liability coverage in the following situations:
   a.   when she drives her family car for business purposes
   b.   when she drives the company car furnished to her for her regular use
   c.   when she helps to drive her friend's car to a business meeting in another state

18-9.   A client, who frequently borrows her friend's car, asks whose liability insurance would cover a liability claim that resulted from an accident while she was driving the friend's car.

18-10. A client, whose wife frequently gives rides to several other children attending their daughter's nursery school, asks whether there is any coverage available under their personal auto policy in case the children are injured in an accident that is not his wife's fault.

18-11. On a family vacation, you rent a car and turn down the loss damage waiver offered by the rental company. Which coverage in your personal auto policy would provide you with coverage for damage to the rental car (less any deductible) in the following situations:

    a. the rental car is damaged when you hit a phone pole while swerving to avoid another vehicle

    b. the rental car is scratched by vandals while it is parked in the hotel parking lot

    c. the rental car is badly dented when you hit a deer while you are driving at night

18-12. A client who enjoys recreation asks how he can get liability coverage for his use of his motorcycle, dune buggy, and snowmobile.

18-13. During a meeting to review her financial plan, your client, Celeste, mentions that she and her family plan to vacation driving around Mexico this year. What should you explain to her about auto insurance coverage for the trip?

18-14. Where might automobile coverage be obtained for clients who are hard-to-insure drivers?

18-15. What factors should be considered by clients when shopping for automobile insurance?

18-16. Describe the coverages available to meet the needs of clients who own watercraft and/or airplanes.

18-17. A client, who has rather high limits of liability in her personal auto and homeowners policies, asks why she should consider also purchasing a personal umbrella liability policy.

Self-Test Questions

T   F   18-1. Uninsured and underinsured motorist coverages are unnecessary in states with compulsory liability laws.

T   F   18-2. Financial responsibility laws require owners of automobiles to carry liability insurance before a vehicle can be registered.

T   F   18-3. In uninsured motorist coverage, the term uninsured includes drivers of hit-and-run vehicles.

T   F   18-4. Under most no-fault laws, the right to sue the negligent party, even for pain and suffering, does not exist.

T   F   18-5. No-fault benefits in most states are limited to medical expenses.

T   F   18-6. In most states, clients' motorcycles and snowmobiles can be insured under the personal auto policy (PAP) by endorsement.

T   F   18-7.   A 25-year-old child living at home is covered under her parents' PAP while she is driving the family car or a friend's car.

T   F   18-8.   If a client has $100,000/$300,000/$50,000 limits of liability in her PAP, she would be fully covered if sued for $150,000 for bodily injury and $20,000 for property damage by the driver of the other car as a result of an auto accident that was the client's fault.

T   F   18-9.   If a client has a $300,000 single limit of liability in his PAP, he would be fully covered if sued for $150,000 for bodily injury and $20,000 for property damage as a result of an auto accident that was his fault.

T   F   18-10. If Jim rented a car, damaged it, and was sued by the rental company, he would be covered under the liability coverage of his PAP for the property damage to the rental car.

T   F   18-11. If Jim has an accident while driving his friend's car and is sued for $250,000 for bodily injury and property damage, the friend's liability insurance would pay first and Jim's liability coverage would be excess and thus pay only if needed.

T   F   18-12. Like the homeowners policy, medical payments under the PAP do not cover the insureds, just other people riding in the insured's car.

T   F   18-13. The insurance company has no legal obligation to pay an uninsured motorist claim unless the owner or operator of the uninsured vehicle is legally responsible for the insured's damages.

T   F   18-14. If a client hits a deer, the damage to his car would be paid under the collision coverage.

T   F   18-15. A client driving to Mexico should be advised to look into purchasing liability coverage from a Mexican insurer.

T   F   18-16. Most states handle hard-to-insure drivers through joint underwriting associations.

T   F   18-17. Because of the highly competitive market, the cost of automobile insurance differs little from company to company.

T   F   18-18. Two common package policies for boats are the boatowners policy for smaller boats and the yacht policy for larger boats.

T   F   18-19. Boatowners and yacht policies frequently contain warranties.

T   F   18-20. In addition to covering bodily injury and property damage liability, the personal umbrella policy also covers personal injury liability.

T   F   18-21. If John has an umbrella policy with a $1 million limit and a $250 self-insured retention, and he is sued for $100,000 for an act covered under the umbrella policy but not under the required underlying coverages, the umbrella policy would pay all but $250 of the judgment.

T   F   18-22.   Personal umbrella policies commonly cover situations excluded under the required underlying coverages such as sexual molestation and failure to render professional services.

NOTES

1. Many discussions of *automobile* insurance use the colloquial term *auto*. In fact, the major automobile insurance policy—the personal auto policy—also uses this terminology.
2. These and other statistics in this chapter are based on material in *The Fact Book, 2002,* which is published by the Insurance Information Institute.
3. Colorado, Florida, Hawaii, Kansas, Massachusetts, Michigan, Minnesota, New York, North Dakota, Utah, and Puerto Rico.
4. Arkansas, Delaware, Maryland, New Hampshire, Oregon, South Dakota, Texas, Virginia, Washington, and Wisconsin.
5. Kentucky, New Jersey, and Pennsylvania.

19

Business Uses of Property and Liability Insurance

Learning Objectives

An understanding of the material in this chapter should enable the student to

19-1. Briefly explain the key types of commercial property and liability insurance available to meet the protection needs of businesses.

19-2. Describe the general features of the commercial package policy and the businessowners policy.

Chapter Outline

This final chapter on property and liability insurance is devoted to its business uses. A financial planner may be asked to make specific recommendations about coverages for a business owner, but the task of implementing this coverage is usually left to a property and liability insurance agent or broker who works in the business market.

However, a financial planner needs an overview of this area of insurance. In addition, individuals sometimes need a few of these business coverages—often referred to as *commercial lines*. For example, a person may need workers' compensation coverage for household employees or occasionally need to purchase a surety bond. It is also important for a financial planner to determine whether a business client has appropriate liability insurance to adequately protect personal assets if a suit or legal judgment occurs.

The chapter begins with a brief discussion of the common lines or types of commercial property and liability insurance. It concludes with a description of the two common types of package policies available to businesses—the commercial package policy and the businessowners policy, which is designed for small- and medium-size businesses. Most of the loss exposures of a business can be insured under one of these policies, but certain loss exposures will require separate policies. For example, a dentist might have a commercial package policy to cover most of his or her property and liability loss exposures, but will also need separate policies to cover (1) professional liability and (2) workers' compensation and employers liability.

TYPES OF COMMERCIAL PROPERTY AND LIABILITY INSURANCE

Numerous policy forms and endorsements for commercial property and liability insurance are available. A precise breakdown of the types of coverage into categories is somewhat difficult because terminology and insurance company practices are not uniform. In this chapter, the discussion is categorized as follows:

- commercial property insurance
- business income insurance
- crime insurance
- inland marine insurance
- boiler and machinery insurance
- farm insurance
- commercial general liability insurance
- commercial automobile insurance
- workers' compensation and employers liability insurance
- professional liability insurance
- excess and umbrella liability insurance
- surety bonds

Certain other types of commercial coverages, such as coverage on ships and aircraft (ocean marine and aviation insurance, respectively), are beyond the scope of this book and are not discussed.

The focus in most of the following discussion is on the forms used by ISO for its commercial package policy. Each of these forms can also be the basis for a single-coverage, or "monoline," policy.

Commercial Property Insurance

commercial property insurance

In the broadest sense, the term *commercial property insurance* refers to the coverage of losses to real and personal property. These losses can result from many sources, including the explosion of boilers, crime, and perils of transportation. However, specific types of insurance, which are discussed later, have been developed for losses that arise from these types of perils. In addition, property such as automobiles and watercraft are also covered under separate types of insurance. Therefore, the term as used here and in common business practice is somewhat narrower and does not include insurance for these types of perils or property.

Covered Property

Commercial property insurance can be used to cover one or more of the following classes of property:

- buildings
- business personal property of the named insured
- personal property of others in the care, custody, or control of the named insured

Each of these classes is specifically defined and subject to various exclusions, some of which can be deleted, or "bought back," by using an endorsement. Other exclusions can be countered by the use of other policies.

As with the homeowners policy, there are various extensions of coverage, a few of which are debris removal, pollution cleanup after a loss, newly acquired property, and the cost of research to reconstruct valuable papers and records that have been damaged or destroyed.

Covered Perils

Commercial property can be insured against various perils on either a named-perils basis or a more comprehensive "open-perils" basis. In all cases, these forms can be expanded with endorsements to cover losses that might arise, for example, from earthquake or the enforcement of ordinances or laws. There is also an endorsement that provides excess coverage over what is available through the National Flood Insurance Program.

Forms for Specific Types of Property

Commercial property insurance forms are flexible enough to be used by most types of businesses. However, some forms have been developed for use in specific situations. These include

- Builders Risk Coverage Form. This form provides protection for buildings under construction and covers the unique loss exposures associated with these types of structures.
- Condominium Association Coverage Form. This form covers property for which a residential or commercial condominium association is responsible. It not only covers property owned by the association but also furniture, fixtures, alterations, and appliances of unit owners if the association agreement requires the association to insure them.
- Condominium Commercial Unit-Owners Coverage Form. This form covers the interest of the owner of a commercial condominium unit. Note that an owner of a residential condominium unit can protect his or her interest under an HO-6 policy.

Loss Settlement

Losses under commercial property forms are settled on an actual cash value basis. However, replacement-cost coverage is often elected. Losses are subject to a deductible that, depending upon available options, can be selected by the policyowner.

The settlement of losses is subject to a coinsurance provision that is often 80 percent but can vary. To provide protection against a coinsurance penalty, the policyowner has the option to elect an agreed amount of coverage or an inflation guard endorsement that automatically increases coverage limits.

One problem for many businesses is that property values, particularly inventory, are subject to wide fluctuations. Various types of forms have been developed to address this problem so that premiums charged reflect the varying loss exposures, and, at the time of loss, there is adequate insurance to properly indemnify the policyowner and avoid a coinsurance penalty. These forms include value reporting forms, which require periodic reporting of values, and peak season endorsements that modify policy limits during certain specified periods of the year.

Business Income Insurance

A business can suffer significant consequential, or indirect, losses after the occurrence of a direct physical damage loss to business property that causes a suspension of business operations. Policy forms are available to cover this loss exposure, and the purchase of this coverage can make the difference between the success and failure of a business.

business income insurance

This type of coverage is *business income insurance* (formerly called business interruption insurance). Note, however, that business income insurance is not only for businesses, but can be used by nonprofit organizations and governmental entities as well. For coverage to apply, the indirect loss must result from an insured peril, usually the same perils as those for which the direct property loss is insured.

Business income insurance covers the following types of losses:

- reduction in net income (This is the difference between the net income the business would have earned had no loss occurred and the net income the business did earn after a loss.)
- extra expenses to minimize or avoid the suspension of operations such as rent at a temporary location and the cost of obtaining services such as data processing that can no longer be handled in-house

Policy Forms

ISO forms include two types of business income coverage and an extra expense only form:

- Business Income (and Extra Expense) Coverage Form
- Business Income (without Extra Expense) Coverage Form
- Extra Expense Coverage Form

The two business income forms cover the sum of (1) net profit or loss that would have been earned or incurred during a period of business suspension and (2) normal continuing business expenses, including payroll, during the suspension. The Business Income (and Extra Expense) Coverage Form also covers extra expenses to avoid or minimize the suspension of operations, even if they do not otherwise reduce the business income loss. The Business Income (without Extra Expense) Coverage Form also covers extra expenses but only to the extent they reduce the loss that is otherwise payable.

Several endorsements are designed to adapt these forms to the particular needs of policyowners. Some of these are

- Ordinary Payroll Limitation or Exclusion Endorsement. By laying off certain noncritical employees, organizations can minimize expenses during prolonged periods of business suspension. This endorsement deletes coverage on the amount of the payroll for these employees and results in a premium reduction.
- Ordinance or Law—Increased Period of Restoration Endorsement. The business income forms only cover losses for the period of time needed to repair damaged property with reasonable speed and like-quality materials. Ordinances or laws can effectively extend this period, for example, if a frame building must be torn down and

replaced with a masonry fire-resistive building. The endorsement provides coverage during this additional period of time.

- Business Income from Dependent Properties Endorsement. Some firms are so dependent on a single supplier or customer that a loss at the supplier's or customer's location would result in the suspension of the firm's operations. This endorsement covers the loss of income that results from direct damage at these other locations.
- Utilities Services—Time Element Endorsement. This endorsement extends coverage to loss of earnings that results from off-premises interruptions of utilities and communications services.

extra expense insurance

The Extra Expense Coverage Form is designed to provide *extra expense insurance* for organizations that must remain in operation after a property loss and, therefore, are unlikely to have a significant decrease in revenue. However, the extra expenses of remaining open can be significant. Businesses that might purchase only extra expense insurance include banks, hospitals, newspapers, insurance agencies, and financial planning firms. In most cases, however, these businesses also have a business income loss exposure, and in such cases the Business Income (and Extra Expense) Coverage Form is the better way to obtain extra expense coverage.

Other specialized forms include tuition fees insurance for schools, convention cancellation insurance, lease cancellation insurance, and weather insurance that covers losses due to weather conditions such as excessive rain that results in cancellation or poor attendance at an outdoor event.

Loss Settlement

Loss settlements for business income insurance are often more difficult than settlements for direct property losses, because it is impossible to know precisely what business income might have been. The policy form provides that the amount of the loss is determined by the following:

- the net income of the business before the loss occurred
- the probable net income of the business if no loss had occurred
- the operating expenses that must continue during the period of restoration so the policyowner can resume operations with the quality of service that existed prior to the loss
- other relevant sources of information

Disputes regarding the amount of loss are settled in accordance with an appraisal clause.

As a general rule, the business income forms pay for losses continuing up to 30 days after business is resumed. However, the revenue of many businesses will not return to normal for longer periods of time, and coverage can be extended by endorsement beyond this 30-day period.

Loss payments are subject to a coinsurance provision. However, the variation in length of business suspensions and the difficulty in estimating future net income and expenses make it difficult to select the proper amount of insurance and the coinsurance percentage. As in property insurance, there are various endorsements that can be used to eliminate or suspend the coinsurance provision.

Crime Insurance

While various other types of commercial coverages provide some limited insurance for losses that result from criminal acts, many crime loss exposures are inadequately covered. The primary reason for this limited coverage results from the fact that crime loss exposures are subject to significant variations among policyowners, and insurers often want to underwrite these loss exposures separately.

Crime insurance provides coverage for various types of property from various causes of loss.

Covered Property

Commercial crime forms typically cover one or more of three broad classes of property:

- money, which includes currency, coins, bank notes, checks, and money orders
- securities, which include both negotiable and nonnegotiable instruments, contracts that represent money or other property, tokens, tickets, stamps, and charge slips
- tangible property other than money or securities. Examples are inventory and office equipment. Intangible property, such as a copyright, is not included in this class of property for purposes of crime insurance. In addition, there are exclusions for certain types of property, for which adequate coverage can be obtained under other types of insurance.

Causes of Loss

Crime coverages are written to provide protection from various causes of loss. These include the following terms, which are not necessarily the same as legal definitions:

burglary

- *burglary*, which is the taking of property from inside an insured premises by a person who enters or leaves the premises unlawfully as evidenced by marks of forcible entry or exit

- computer fraud, which is a type of theft of property relating to the use of a computer to fraudulently transfer property from its rightful owner to someone else
- disappearance and destruction, which includes unknown causes of loss. This is in contrast to burglary, robbery, and theft, which involve losses from a known location at a known time.
- extortion, which is the surrender of property away from the insured premises as a result of a threat to do bodily harm to someone who is, or allegedly is, being held captive
- forgery and alteration. Forgery is the creation of a document or signature that is not genuine, while alteration involves changes to a document in a manner that is neither authorized nor intended.
- *robbery*, which is the taking of property from one person by someone else who has either caused harm or threatened to cause harm to the person. It also includes situations in which property is taken in an unlawful act that a person has witnessed.
- safe burglary, which is burglary from a locked safe or vault or the removal of a safe or vault from inside a building
- *theft*, which is a broad term that includes robbery, burglary, shoplifting, and any other act of stealing

robbery

theft

Policy Forms

In mid 2000, ISO introduced new crime forms in most states. There are two primary forms, with the difference being whether the form is written on a loss-sustained basis or a discovery basis. When written on a loss-sustained basis, the only losses covered are those that occur during the policy period and are discovered within a specified period after the coverage expires. Subsequent coverage will respond to losses if the specified discovery period has expired as long as there has been continuous coverage.

When written on a discovery basis, the current coverage pays all losses discovered while the coverage is in force, whether or not there was previous coverage. However, insurers may use an endorsement to eliminate coverage for losses that occurred prior to a specified retroactive date.

The new forms contain eight optional insuring agreements. None of the insuring agreements is mandatory, and the insured may select one or more by inserting a limit for each one selected on the declarations page:

- employee theft of money, securities, and other property
- forgery or alteration of an organization's checks (including drafts and promissory notes) by parties other than the organization's owners, employees, directors, or representatives

- theft of money and securities from inside the insured's premises or banking premises. There is also coverage for damage to the premises during the actual or attempted theft and to items on the premises such as locked safes and cash registers.
- robbery and safe burglary of other property inside the insured's premises
- theft, disappearance, or destruction of money outside the insured's premises when in the custody of a messenger and robbery of other property in the possession of a messenger
- computer fraud to transfer money, securities, or other property from the insured's premises or bank to somewhere else
- funds-transfer fraud for losses resulting from fraudulent instructions to a financial institution to transfer money from the insured's account to someone else
- the acceptance of counterfeit money orders or currency. The acceptance must be in the United States or Canada, but the currency can be that of any country.

Numerous endorsements can be added to the primary forms to provide most additional types of crime coverage than an insured might need. A few examples of these coverages are the following:

- dishonest acts of employees while they are working on client's property
- extortion payments because of threats to people and threats to damage property
- theft of other property from within the insured's premises
- theft, burglary, robbery, and vandalism of the insured's property while stored in a safe deposit box or vault in a depository premises
- legal liability for losses involving damage to guests' property while in safe deposit boxes or inside the insured's premises

Unique Policy Provisions

Some provisions are common to many crime forms:

- There is no coverage for losses caused by the named insured or any of its directors, trustees, or authorized representatives. In addition, there is no coverage for losses caused by employees except under the forms that specifically cover employee theft.
- Coverage is for direct losses only. There is no coverage available for consequential losses that might result from criminal acts.
- Most of the forms require the policyowner to notify the police if there is a reason to believe that the loss results from a violation of law.

- The forms specify how settlements are valued. Money is valued at its face value. If the money is foreign, the insurer can pay the face value in the foreign currency or at its equivalent value in United States currency. Securities are valued as of the close of the business day a loss is discovered. The insurer can pay the value of the securities or replace them in kind. The insurer also has the option of paying the cost of a bond that is required for the issuance of replacement securities. Other property is valued at its cash value, and any disputes over value are settled by arbitration.

Inland Marine Insurance

Historically, marine insurers wrote insurance on ships and their cargoes and fire insurance companies wrote insurance on property at fixed locations. As other types of transportation became more common, a hybrid type of insurance—*inland marine insurance*—evolved.

inland marine insurance

Today inland marine policies and forms are used to write coverage for the following:

- goods in domestic transit
- property held by bailees
- mobile equipment and property
- property of certain dealers
- instrumentalities of transportation and communication
- difference in conditions exposures

Inland marine insurance is largely characterized by coverage for specific situations. It is often written on an "open-perils" basis but can also be named perils. It should be pointed out that property insurance forms often provide some coverage for loss exposures that could also be covered under inland marine forms, usually as additional coverages.

Goods in Transit

Inland marine policies are used to cover domestic goods in transit by mail, rail, truck, or aircraft. It is common for these policies to only cover shipments within and between the continental United States, Alaska, and Canada, but coverage can be endorsed, for example, for shipments to Mexico. Shipments to overseas locations (including Puerto Rico and Hawaii) by either ship or plane are typically insured under ocean marine policies.

Depending on the terms of sale, the responsibility for goods being shipped can fall on the shipper of the goods, the carrier of the goods, or the recipient of the goods. Any of these parties can buy insurance as needed.

The owners of property can purchase transit policies to provide property damage to their goods while in the course of transit by common carriers, contract carriers, or their own vehicles. A trip transit policy covers only the particular shipment specified in the policy. An annual transit policy covers all shipments during an annual period.

There are also policies, called motor truck cargo insurance that common carriers or contract carriers can use to cover customer's goods when the carrier is legally liable for the damage. These policies do not cover damage for which the carrier is not liable such as those arising from acts of God, war, or neglect of the cargo owner.

Mobile Equipment and Property

There are several inland marine forms that are designed to insure property that is often moved from one location to another. The floater policies described in chapter 17 are examples of personal forms for this purpose. Examples of property that can be insured under commercial floater forms include the following:

- contractors' mobile equipment
- agricultural equipment
- cameras
- computer equipment
- farm animals
- fine art
- musical instruments
- physicians' and surgeons' equipment
- property on exhibition
- sales samples
- signs
- theatrical property

Property Held by Bailees

Bailees such as dry cleaners, repair shops, and public warehouses often have possession of significant amounts of customers' goods. A bailee liability policy can be purchased to cover damage to these goods when the bailee is legally liable. However, many bailees, for the sake of goodwill, purchase a bailees customers policy, which provides coverage whether or not the bailee is legally liable.

Property of Certain Dealers

Certain types of dealers in property have a significant amount of inventory that is likely to be transported. Special policies have been developed for these businesses that pick up not only the transportation loss exposure, but also provide coverage for merchandise in a store, furniture and fixtures of the dealer, and property of others in the dealer's care, custody, or control. These policies, often referred to as *block policies* because they cover a block of unique loss exposures, are often written for dealers in jewelry, furs, fine art, cameras, musical equipment, stamps, coins, and mobile and agricultural equipment.

block policy

Difference in Conditions

difference in conditions (DIC) insurance

Difference in conditions (DIC) insurance is a separate policy that provides "open-perils" coverage to fill in the gaps left by a policyowner's other commercial insurance policies. Traditionally, it was used to provide "open-perils" coverage to policyowners whose basic policies provided named-perils protection. Even though "open-perils" coverage is now relatively common, the DIC policy is still used as a method of either providing earthquake and flood coverage or providing higher limits than are otherwise obtainable. It is also used to cover loss exposures not in basic policies such as property in transit and the consequential losses that result from its damage or destruction. Another use is to provide coverage on overseas property that is broader than is available under the policies that can be purchased in many other countries.

The DIC policy is a broad policy that can be tailored to meet most any specific property insurance need of a policyowner.

Instrumentalities of Transportation and Communication

Inland marine forms are used to insure instrumentalities of communication on either a named-perils or "open-perils" basis. These types of property include bridges, tunnels, pipelines, television towers, satellite dishes, and power lines.

Boiler and Machinery (Equipment Breakdown) Insurance

Commercial property and business income insurance forms exclude damage caused by steam boiler explosion, electrical breakdown, or mechanical breakdown. The Equipment Breakdown Protection Coverage Form provides insurance for these types of losses. Insurers that write this type of coverage provide extensive inspection and loss control services to prevent losses, and these insurance company inspections are often accepted by governmental organizations that require periodic inspections of boilers and certain types of machinery.

Boiler and machinery coverage (referred to as equipment breakdown coverage by some insurers) agrees to pay for direct damage to covered property as a result of a breakdown to covered equipment. *Covered equipment* includes (1) equipment built to operate under internal pressure or vacuum other than weight of contents, (2) electrical or mechanical equipment that is used in the generation, transmission, or utilization of energy, (3) communication equipment, (4) computer equipment, and (5) equipment of the types previously mentioned that is owned by a utility and used solely to provide utility services to the insured's premises. *Covered property* is not just the covered equipment but includes any real or personal property that is (1) owned by the named insured or (2) in the named insured's care, custody, or control and for which the named insured is legally liable. A *breakdown* is a direct physical loss to covered equipment that necessitates its repair or replacement and which arises from one of the following causes: (1) failure of pressure or vacuum equipment, (2) mechanical failure including rupture or bursting caused by centrifugal force, or (3) electrical failure including arcing.

This coverage also agrees to pay the reasonable costs of temporary repairs and expediting repairs or the permanent replacement of damaged property. Boiler and machinery coverage can also be written to provide business income and extra expense coverage as well as coverage for spoilage to raw materials, property in process, or finished products if the spoilage is caused by the lack or excess of power, light, heat, steam, or refrigeration that results from a breakdown to covered equipment.

Farm Insurance

As mentioned in chapter 17, there are homeowners-type policies available for small- and medium-size farm operations. However, large farms and commercially owned farms are more likely to be insured under commercial forms. In many ways, these forms are similar to other commercial insurance forms except that they are modified to meet the unique loss exposures of farmers. There are property forms that can be written on either a named-perils or "open-perils" basis for various types of farm property, including livestock. There is also an endorsement to cover loss of farm income if real or personal farm property is damaged or destroyed by an insured peril. A farmowner's home and personal property can also be insured under these forms.

There is also a form to cover the liability loss exposures of farmers. It essentially combines commercial general liability insurance, homeowners liability insurance for the farmowner's personal needs, and other insurance coverages unique to farming operations.

A special need of many farmowners is insurance on crops. Insurers offer crop hail insurance, which covers losses due to hail and can sometimes be endorsed to cover additional perils such as windstorm or damage by livestock. These policies may also cover crops while being transported to places of storage. Broader crop insurance is written through the Federal Crop Insurance Corporation, and the federal government subsidizes the cost of this coverage. It provides insurance if a farmer's production of a crop is less than the farmer's actual production history for most any reason, including drought, excessive moisture, and bad weather.

Another special need for some farmers is animal mortality insurance. This is essentially term life insurance on animals and is used for animals such as valuable horses, registered cattle, or breeding stock. This type of coverage can also be purchased on racehorses, circus animals, show cats and dogs, and laboratory animals. These animals are generally covered for death from most any cause as well as theft.

Commercial General Liability Insurance

commercial general liability (CGL) insurance

Commercial general liability (CGL) insurance is designed to cover a wide variety of liability loss exposures that can face an organization, including

- premises liability. An owner or tenant can be liable if someone is injured or property is damaged because of a condition in or arising out of premises that are owned or occupied.
- business operations liability. A business can be liable if bodily injury, personal injury, or property damage results from the activities of the business owner or an employee. These activities can take place on or away from the business location.
- products liability. Legal liability often arises from bodily injury or property damage caused by a defective product that is manufactured or sold by a business.
- completed operations liability. Similarly, legal liability can arise out of work that has been performed. For example, a fire can start as a result of an improperly installed gas line.
- contractual liability. In many cases, a business, through written or oral contracts, assumes liability for the acts of others.
- contingent liability. This is liability that a business can face because of work performed by independent contractors such as a subcontractor hired by a firm.

However, CGL coverage forms do not cover all types of business liability. Because of exclusions in policy forms, there is little or no coverage for (1) liability for injury to employees, (2) liability that arises from the rendering or failure to render professional services, or (3) liability that arises from aircraft, automobiles, or watercraft. Coverage for several of these loss exposures is discussed later in this chapter.

The CGL Coverage Form has three coverages:

- Coverage A—Bodily Injury and Property Damage Liability
- Coverage B—Personal and Advertising Injury Liability
- Coverage C—Medical Payments

In addition to a separate discussion of each coverage, the definition of insured is described. For the most part, policy provisions and conditions are similar to other types of liability insurance. However, a few provisions are discussed.

Coverage A—Bodily Injury and Property Damage Liability

Coverage A applies to legal liability and defense costs that arise from bodily injury and property damage.

In addition to exclusions that apply to workers' compensation, employers liability, aircraft, automobiles, and watercraft, policyowners must be aware of other significant exclusions, including the following:

- bodily injury or property damage that is expected or intended from the insured's standpoint except when it results from reasonable force to protect persons or property.
- certain contractual assumptions of liability. These include contractual assumptions made after bodily injury or property damage has occurred, some contracts with railroads, and some contracts with architects, engineers, and surveyors that involve their errors and omissions in performing professional duties.
- liquor liability of insureds who are in the business of manufacturing, distributing, selling, serving, or furnishing alcoholic beverages. Liquor liability arises from (1) causing or contributing to the intoxication of a person, (2) furnishing of alcoholic beverages to underage persons, and (3) statutes pertaining to the sale, gift, distribution, or use of alcoholic beverages. However, addition of the Liquor Liability Coverage Form will cover this loss exposure.
- pollution. The CGL Coverage Form excludes coverage for most pollution liability, including clean-up costs that arise from pollution. However, there are numerous endorsements and other forms that can be used to cover this loss exposure.
- property damage to certain classes of property including
    - property owned, rented, or occupied by the named insured
    - property loaned to the named insured
    - personal property in the care, custody, or control of the insured
    - premises that have been sold, given away, or abandoned, except property built by the named insured for sale and never occupied, rented, or held for rental
    - the part of real property being worked on by the named insured or a subcontractor if the damage arises from the work
    - the part of any property that must be restored, repaired, or replaced because the named insured's work was incorrectly performed on it

The first three items can be insured under property and inland marine forms.

- damage to the insured's product that arises out of the product. For example, if a generator that the insured sold exploded, the cost to replace it would not be covered, but any damage to other property is covered.

- damage to the insured's work. For example, if the named insured repaired a generator, there would no be coverage for damage to the insured's work if the completed work led to an explosion. However, liability coverage would exist for damage to other property as a result of the explosion.

- damage to impaired property or property not physically injured. This exclusion eliminates coverage to property that has not been physically damaged because of the insured's defective product, poor workmanship, or failure to perform a contractual agreement. For example, a building that cannot be occupied because the electrical work performed by the named insured did not meet building code specifications. There is no physical damage to the building, but its owner can suffer a significant loss before the faulty work is corrected.

- product recall. Products are sometimes recalled voluntarily or because of government action. Claims for damages that arise from such actions are excluded. In addition, the manufacturer or distributor of the product can incur significant recall expenses. These loss exposures can be insured through specialty insurers.

- employment-related practices. Most insurers now exclude employment-related practices from CGL coverage. These practices include wrongful termination, discrimination, and sexual harassment. Because coverage is also often limited under other types of liability policies, many employers purchase separate employment practices liability insurance for these loss exposures.

- professional liability. The CGL Coverage Form does not provide coverage for employees for liability that arises out of their providing or failure to provide professional health care services. In addition, insurers frequently exclude the professional liability of certain classes of business. Such an exclusion applies not only to employees but also to the named insured. Professional liability is covered in a later section of this chapter.

Coverage B—Personal and Advertising Injury Liability

Coverage B provides protection for personal injury liability, which has been discussed in earlier chapters. However, the definition of personal injury liability in the CGL includes advertising injury liability. Advertising injury can arise out of the following:

- oral or written publication of material that slanders or libels a person or organization or disparages their goods, products, or services
- oral or written publication of material that violates a person's right of privacy
- the use of another's advertising idea in your advertisement
- infringement upon another's copyright, trade dress, or slogan in your advertisement

Among the Coverage B exclusions are liability that arises out of (1) publication of material if the insured knows it is false, (2) willful violation of a penal statute or ordinance, (3) the failure of goods, products, or services to conform with advertised quality or performance, or (4) the wrongful description of the price of goods, products, or services.

Coverage C—Medical Payments

Coverage C is very similar to the medical payments coverage of the homeowners policy. It pays medical expenses for bodily injury to persons injured on premises that the named insured owns or rents and because of the named insured's operations.

The coverage does not apply to the following persons:

- any insured other than a volunteer worker
- anyone hired to do work for or on behalf of any insured or a tenant of any insured
- a person injured on that part of a premises that the person normally occupies
- a person entitled to collect workers' compensation or disability benefits for the injury
- a person injured while taking part in athletics

Who Is an Insured?

Several categories of persons are insureds under the CGL Coverage Form. These include (1) the named insured and others with a family or business relationship to the named insured, (2) employees of the named insured, and (3) certain other persons or organizations.

The Named Insured and Others. The named insured can be an individual, a partnership, a joint venture, a limited liability company, any other organization, or a trust.

- If the named insured is an individual, the insureds include the named insured and spouse with respect to the conduct of a business of which the named insured is a sole owner.
- If the named insured is a partnership or joint venture, the insureds include the named insured, partners, members, and their spouses with respect to conduct of the business.
- If the named insured is a limited liability company, the insureds include the named insured, members with respect to the conduct of the business, and managers of the business with respect to their duties.
- If the named insured is any other type of organization, such as a corporation, the insureds include the named insureds, executive officers and directors with respect to the duties, and stockholders with respect to their liability as stockholders.
- If the organization is a trust, the insureds include trustees with respect to their duties as trustees.

Employees. Employees and volunteer workers of the named insured are also insureds while they are acting within the scope of their employment or performing duties related to the conduct of the business. However, some exclusions apply. For example, the CGL Coverage Form does not cover employees for liability to

- the named insured
- partners or members of the insured
- co-employees or volunteer workers while in the course of their employment or while performing duties related to the conduct of the business
- relatives of co-employees as a consequence of injuries described in the previous exclusion

Other Insureds. Several other persons or organizations are insured under certain circumstances. These include real estate managers, legal representatives, mobile equipment operators, and newly acquired organizations.

Policy Provisions

Three specific policy provisions will be mentioned. These pertain to coverage territory, the events that trigger coverage, and policy limits.

Coverage Territory. Claims under the CGL Coverage Form are covered only if they take place in the coverage territory. For most claims, this includes the United States, its territories or possessions, Puerto Rico, and Canada. There is also coverage in international waters or airspace as long as travel is between the above locations. In addition, coverage is worldwide for products made or sold in the previously mentioned locations, for activities of persons who are away from these locations for short periods of time on business trips, and for personal and advertising injury offenses that take place through the Internet or similar electronic means of communication. Firms with broader business territories need to arrange appropriate coverage.

Events that Trigger Coverage. The more commonly used CGL Coverage Form is written on an occurrence basis. This means that a liability claim is covered only for injury or property damage that occurs during the policy period. In other words, the policy that responds to a claim is the one that is in effect when the injury or property damage occurs, even if a claim is made several years later.

The other CGL Coverage Form is written on a claims-made basis. This means that the policy that responds to a claim is the one in force when a claim is made, regardless of when the injury or property damage occurred.

The distinction between these two types of triggering events is discussed further in the section on professional liability insurance, for which claims-made coverage is more common.

CGL Coverage Forms

- Occurrence basis: coverage applies to bodily injury or property damage that occurs during the policy period, regardless of when claims for damages are made.
- Claims-made basis: coverage applies to claims made while the policy is in force, regardless of when the loss-causing events occur.

Limits of Liability. The CGL Coverage Form has several different limits of liability. Note that defense costs are payable in addition to these limits.

There are two aggregate limits that apply for an annual policy period and once they are exceeded, the insurer has no further obligations to pay or defend claims. However, the limits are reinstated when a policy is renewed. One of these limits is a general aggregate amount that applies to all amounts paid under Coverages A, B, and C, except for claims that arise out of products or completed operations. These two types of liability are together subject to a second aggregate limit.

There are several sublimits. One of these applies to each occurrence for the sum of amounts paid under Coverage A and Coverage B. Another limit applies on an annual basis to personal and advertising liability.

Finally, a Coverage C limit applies to medical payments for any one person during a year and another limit applies to any damage to a premises that a business rents or temporarily occupies.

Commercial Automobile Insurance

Three types of commercial automobile policies are as follows:

- Business Auto Coverage Form
- Garage Coverage Form
- Motor Carrier Coverage Form

Business Auto Form

The Business Auto Coverage (BAC) Form is the most common type of commercial automobile insurance and is similar to the Personal Auto Policy with respect to the coverages that can be purchased.

Coverages

Available coverages include liability, medical payments, no-fault benefits, uninsured motorists, underinsured motorists, collision, comprehensive, specified causes of loss, and towing and labor. Comprehensive is equivalent to the personal auto policy's other-than-collision coverage. Specified causes of loss coverage is a more limited named-perils alternative to comprehensive coverage.

The definition of *auto* is very broad and includes any land motor vehicle, trailer, or semitrailer designed for use on public roads except mobile equipment.

Covered Automobiles

There are nine classifications of automobiles that can be insured under the BAC Form, and different classifications of automobiles can be insured for each type of coverage. For example, one classification of automobiles might be insured for liability, while a different classification might be insured for collision. The nine classifications each have a symbol (numbers 1–9) that is entered in the declarations section of the form by the appropriate coverage. The nine classifications are:

- symbol 1—any auto
- symbol 2—owned autos only
- symbol 3—owned private passenger autos only
- symbol 4—owned autos other than private passenger autos
- symbol 5—owned autos subject to no-fault

- symbol 6—owned autos subject to compulsory uninsured motorists law
- symbol 7—specifically designated autos
- symbol 8—hired autos only
- symbol 9—nonowned autos only

A *nonowned auto* is an auto owned by a named insured's employee or a member of his or her household but only while used in the named insured's business or personal affairs. A *hired auto* is an auto, other than a nonowned auto, that is leased, hired, rented, or borrowed by the named insured. Many businesses own no automobiles but have a loss exposure from accidents that involve nonowned and hired autos.

There also are some policy extensions. For example, mobile equipment is covered for liability insurance while it is being carried or towed by a covered auto. Other liability that arises from mobile equipment is covered under the CGL Coverage Form. An inland marine floater can cover damage to the equipment itself.

Temporary substitute autos, other than ones owned by the named insured, are also covered for liability coverage if the autos are used in place of a covered auto because of its breakdown, repair, servicing, loss, or destruction.

Who Is an Insured?

The definition of insured is similar to that found in the PAP. It includes the named insured, most other persons driving owned autos, and persons or organizations liable because of the acts or omissions of any of the previously mentioned persons. While the business would have coverage, partners of a partnership, members of a limited liability company, and employees are not insured with respect to an auto owned by that person or a member of his or her household.

Exclusions

There are several exclusions in the BAC Form, but many of them merely exclude situations that are covered under workers' compensation and employers liability insurance and the CGL Coverage Form. There is no coverage for property that is owned by or is in the care, custody, or control of an insured. However, this property can be insured under the appropriate property and inland marine forms. Claims that arise from pollutants that are carried by covered autos are also excluded, but separate coverage is available.

Limit of Liability

Liability coverage under the BAC Form is a single limit of insurance that applies to all bodily injury, property damage, and covered pollution costs or expenses that arise from a single accident, and there is no aggregate annual limit. Defense costs are paid in addition to this limit. Split liability limits can be added by endorsement.

Losses for physical damage are limited to the lesser of (1) the actual cash value of the property at the time of loss or (2) the cost of repairing the property with other property of like kind and quality.

Other Commercial Auto Forms

There are other commercial auto forms, each designed for specific types of businesses.

The Garage Coverage Form is designed to meet the special needs of auto dealers. It is actually more than just an auto policy since it also provides liability coverage comparable to what is available under the CGL Coverage Form. It also provides an option for insuring the dealer's autos.

The Motor Carrier Coverage Form is designed for businesses that provide transportation by vehicles in the furtherance of commercial enterprise. These include common carriers, contract carriers, and private carriers who transport their own property. The coverage is similar to the BAC Form with modification for the unique needs of motor carriers.

Workers' Compensation and Employers Liability Insurance

An employer faces a significant loss exposure for liability that arises from injuries to employees or their deaths—either under tort law or because of government statutes. Coverage for this loss exposure is largely excluded under other liability policies and is usually insured under the Workers Compensation and Employers Liability (WC&EL) Insurance Policy. The policy form used in a majority of states is one developed by the National Council on Compensation Insurance. Note that some employers operate in states with monopolistic state funds for workers' compensation benefits, and coverage must be purchased from the state fund. Other employers may be large enough that they are able to self-fund workers' compensation benefits. In these cases, they may still need employers liability insurance, and variations of the WC&EL Policy are available to meet their needs. The following discussion assumes that this policy is used to insure both the workers' compensation and employers liability loss exposures.

The WC&EL Policy contains three insuring agreements:

- Part One—Workers Compensation Insurance
- Part Two—Employers Liability Insurance
- Part Three—Other States Insurance

Each part is discussed below. However, the order of the discussion switches the last two parts since Part Three also pertains to workers' compensation insurance. Some common endorsements are also described.

Part One—Workers' Compensation Insurance

workers' compensation insurance

The states to which Part One applies are listed in the policy declarations. The *workers' compensation insurance* coverage then agrees to pay all compensation and benefits required of the insured by the workers' compensation law of any state listed. These benefits vary from state to state and were discussed in chapter 7. The insurer also agrees to pay any defense costs that arise out of a workers' compensation claim and certain other expenses the insured might incur as part of a claim.

The policy explains that the insured is responsible for any penalties under a workers' compensation law because of (1) willful misconduct, (2) illegal employment, (3) failure to comply with health and safety laws and regulations, and (4) discrimination against employees who file claims. If the insurer pays any of these penalties, the policyowner must reimburse the insurer.

The policy does not specify the benefits to be paid except by reference to the fact that it will pay what the workers' compensation law requires. If the policy and the law conflict, the policy agrees to conform to the law.

There is no specified dollar limit of liability for Part One. The policy will pay the state-mandated benefits to any and all employees who are injured and their survivors.

Part Three—Other States Insurance

This part of the WC&EL Policy provides coverage when an employer expands operations to include other states listed in the policy declarations for which Part Three applies. In many cases, the declarations list all states except those with monopolistic state funds or in which the insurer is not licensed to do business. The policyowner must notify the insurer when operations begin in these states.

Part Two—Employer Liability Insurance

employers liability insurance

Part Two of the WC&EL Policy—*employers liability insurance*—is a traditional form of liability insurance that protects an employer when it can be sued because of injuries to employees. Such suits occasionally arise for various reasons, including the following:

- An injured employee is not covered under a workers' compensation law.
- A spouse or family member sues for loss of services because of an employee's injury or death.

- An employee sues the employer in a capacity other than as an employer. For example, an employee injured by a faulty product of the employer may be able to bring suit against the employer as a manufacturer rather than as an employer.
- A spouse or family member sues because of bodily injury as a consequence of the injury or death of an employee. For example, a husband may have a heart attack after learning that a disgruntled coworker has killed his wife.
- The manufacturer of a product that injures one of the employer's workers can be sued by the worker and in turn sue the employer for improper maintenance of the product. This is referred to as a *third-party-over suit*.

The insuring agreement under Part Two agrees to pay damages and defend the insured because of bodily injury by accident or disease to an employee. For bodily injury by accident, the policy that covers an injury is the one in effect when the injury occurs. For bodily injury by disease, it is the policy that is in effect on the employee's last day of last exposure to the conditions causing or aggravating the injury.

The Part Two coverage contains three limits of liability, all of which can be selected by the policyowner. One limit of liability applies to bodily injury by accident and is the maximum amount that will be paid for any one accident, regardless of how many employees are injured. There is no annual limit for bodily injury by accident. Two limits of liability apply to bodily injury by disease. One is per employee, and the other is an aggregate limit for the policy period.

Part Two contains several exclusions. Some exclusions eliminate coverage for claims that arise out of state workers' compensation laws and various federal acts. Workers' compensation claims are covered under Part One and endorsements, as described later, can be used to cover liability imposed by federal acts.

There is no coverage outside the United States, its territories or possessions, and Canada except for employees temporarily working in these locations.

Other exclusions eliminate coverage for

- most contractual liability. However, contractual liability is largely covered under the CGL Coverage Form.
- punitive damages for injury or death of illegally employed persons
- bodily injury to employees employed in violation of the law and with the knowledge of the insured or any executive officer
- damages that arise out of employment practices. As discussed later, this can be insured elsewhere.
- fines or penalties imposed for violation of federal or state law

Endorsements

Several endorsements are available to broaden the coverage of the WC&EL Policy.

The Voluntary Compensation and Employers Liability Coverage Endorsement obligates the insurance company to pay an amount equal to what is available under a state's workers' compensation law to employees who are not covered under the law. If an injured employee who is entitled to benefits brings suit, the coverage provided by the endorsement reverts to the employers liability coverage. A few insurers sell an additional endorsement to provide benefits for United States citizens hired to work abroad for indefinite periods. The benefits paid are those of the specific act or state listed in the endorsement.

Several federal acts either require the payment of workers' compensation benefits to certain groups of employees or allow certain groups of employees to sue employers regardless of state limitations on employee suits. Endorsements are available for employees with loss exposures that might arise out of the following acts:

- United States Longshore and Harbor Workers' Compensation Act (for most maritime workers other crew members of vessels)
- Jones Act (for crew members of vessels)
- Defense Base Act (for civilian employees working at foreign military bases or working abroad for agencies of the United States government)
- Outer Continental Shelf Lands Act (for workers engaged in exploration of natural resources)
- Nonappropriated Fund Instrumentalities Act (for civilian employees of certain operations on military facilities)
- Migrant and Seasonal Agricultural Worker Protection Act
- Federal Employers' Liability Act (for employees of interstate railroads)

Professional Liability Insurance

professional liability insurance

The term *professional liability insurance* covers a wide variety of insurance policies. It includes policies for many occupations and can best be defined as insurance to protect against liability for the failure to use the degree of skill expected of a person in a particular occupation. While the terms tend to be used interchangeably, professional liability insurance is often referred to as *malpractice insurance* for those occupations in which professional liability is likely to result from bodily injury and *errors and omissions insurance* for other occupations.

Several other types of insurance are also increasingly referred to as professional liability even though the organizations that buy them might not provide professional services to others. These are directors' and officers' liability insurance, employee benefits liability insurance, fiduciary liability insurance, and employment practices liability insurance.

Policies for Various Occupations

In the absence of any endorsements to the contrary, the professional liability exposures of many occupations would be covered, or partially covered, under a CGL Coverage Form. However, there are two major exceptions. First, as previously mentioned, the CGL excludes liability of employees that arises out of providing or failing to provide health care services. Second, the policy would only cover claims that could be classified as bodily injury, property damage, personal injury, or advertising injury. Certain types of claims do not fall under those policy definitions. For example, a client might suffer a financial loss because a financial planner failed to carry out an investment transaction or because an attorney missed a deadline for filing a suit.

The fact that an endorsed CGL Coverage Form might or might not cover a professional liability claim is often of little significance because insurers will add an endorsement to exclude the professional liability loss exposure of many professions and/or professional activities. A few of these include

- physicians and other health care providers
- attorneys
- barber shops
- cemeteries
- computer manufacturers
- electronic data processing operations
- engineers and architects
- financial planners
- health clubs
- insurance agents and companies
- stockbrokers
- tattoo parlors
- veterinarians

This points out the importance of reading policy endorsements. If professional liability is excluded, there is a need for separate coverage for this loss exposure.

Professional liability policies have been developed for many occupations. For some occupations, several insurers write coverage; for other occupations, the number of insurers in the market may be only one or a small number. Businesses and employees both need these policies; in some cases, the business policy also covers employees. For example, a stockbrokerage firm might have a policy that covers it as well as the representatives it employs. However, in other cases, the employee may need to obtain his or her own coverage. While coverage is often obtained directly through an insurance agent, professional associations are often a source of group coverage or plans of mass-marketed individual insurance.

While ISO has developed standard policies for some occupations, individual insurers develop many professional liability policies. Policy variations exist among professions and insurers and should be evaluated with respect to limits, covered acts, defense coverage, coverage triggers, exclusions, and coverage territory.

Covered Acts. Professional liability policies differ in the exact wording of their insuring agreements. At a minimum, they cover acts, errors, or omissions that arise out of the rendering of professional services. For many professions, they also cover claims that result from the failure to render appropriate services.

Professional liability policies are not designed to cover business activities, such as the maintenance of an office premises, and do not eliminate the need for a CGL or auto policy to cover the many business activities that do not involve professional services.

Defense Coverage. Professional liability policies cover defense costs. Some policies provide this benefit in addition to the stated policy limits, but most policies include these costs as part of the policy limits. In many policies, the insurer agrees to conduct the defense and has the right to appoint the defense attorney; in some policies, the insurer allows the policyowner to select the attorney subject to insurer approval.

Most insurers now reserve the right to defend and settle claims as they see fit, but some policies still require the insurer to obtain the insured's consent before a claim is settled. If the insured does not consent to a settlement that has been recommended by the insurance company, many insurers limit policy benefits to the amount for which the claim could have been settled.

Coverage Triggers. The majority of professional liability policies are written on a claims-made basis. This means that the policy in force when a claim is made is the policy that covers the claim, not the policy in force when the event that caused the claim occurred. As long as a series of policies remains in force, the professional continues to have coverage for prior acts.

A series of claims-made professional liability policies typically ceases to pay claims if coverage is no longer carried unless the last policy contains an extended reporting period. In most policies, the extended reporting period is not automatic but must be requested and paid for. Some insurers only make extended periods of one to 3 years available, but some insurers offer an unlimited extended period. The latter is of particular importance to someone such as a retired obstetrician who might be sued for a birth defect many years after a child is delivered.

Some insurers make extended reporting periods available if either the insurer or the policyowner terminates a policy. Other insurers only make coverage available if the insurer terminates the policy by cancellation or nonrenewal.

A few professional liability policies do consider claims to have been made during the policy period as long as the insured, during the policy period, reports any circumstances of an event that might result in a future claim.

Significant gaps in coverage can occur if a policyowner switches from a policy written on a claims-made basis to one written on an occurrence basis and vice versa. Such changes should be made with care, and proper endorsements to eliminate any gaps should be obtained.

Exclusions. Professional liability policies commonly exclude dishonest, criminal, or malicious acts, contractual liability, and punitive damages. Policies that cover errors and omissions also typically exclude bodily injury and damage to tangible property—which normally are, or should be, covered by a CGL.

Other exclusions may apply to professional liability insurance of a particular occupation.

Coverage Territory. Some professional liability policies cover claims that occur from activities anywhere in the world. Suits may or may not have to be brought in the United States or Canada. Other policies are written for a more restrictive territory such as the United States and Canada.

Directors and Officers Liability Insurance

Directors and officers of a corporation can be held personally liable for breaches of their corporate duties. Stockholders, creditors, competitors, governments, and others can bring suits. In today's litigious environment, many qualified persons are unwilling to sit on corporate boards unless the corporation provides them with protection against these suits.

directors and officers (D&O) liability insurance

Directors and officers (D&O) liability insurance is purchased by a corporation, but the corporation (unless it is a nonprofit organization) is often only the policyowner and not an insured; the insureds are the officers and directors.

There are at least two insuring agreements in D&O policies. The first agreement covers the directors and officers for their personal liability as directors and officers that results from wrongful acts such as any breach of duty, neglect, errors, misstatements, misleading statements, omissions, and other acts. However, benefits are usually not paid to the extent that the corporation has indemnified an officer or director.

The second insuring agreement reimburses the policyowner for any sum that it is required or permitted by law to pay to the directors and officers as indemnification.

Some D&O policies have a third insuring agreement that covers the corporation for its liability arising from the acts of officers and directors.

D&O policies commonly exclude coverage for situations that are covered under a firm's other liability policies such as bodily injury or damage to tangible property. Other exclusions often include claims because of

- fraudulent acts
- acts that result in personal gain to which a director or officer is not entitled
- violations of certain securities laws
- failure to maintain adequate insurance for the corporation
- suits that involve one director or officer against another (with some exceptions)
- service on boards not affiliated with the corporation, but this coverage can be obtained if the corporation wants to encourage such service

Because of the high cost of D&O suits, defense costs are often subject to policy limits. In addition, D&O policies may have both an initial deductible and a percentage of participation above the deductible amount. For example, the insured (or the corporation) may be responsible for the first $25,000 of any claim and 5 percent of any remaining amount.

Employment Practices Liability Insurance

employment practices liability insurance

As previously mentioned, employment-related claims are often excluded from CGL policies. These claims can be covered by *employment practices liability insurance*.

An employment practices liability policy covers only those employment practices specified in the policy. These can include discrimination, sexual harassment, wrongful termination, breach of employment contract, failure to employ or promote, and wrongful discipline.

The insured is usually the business, its officers and directors, and some or all of its employees and former employees. Like the D&O policy, there may be both a deductible and percentage participation above the deductible.

Employee Benefits Liability Insurance

employee benefits liability insurance

Employee benefits liability insurance covers claims that arise out of improper advice or other errors or omissions in the administration of employee benefit plans. The insured is usually the business, its directors and stockholders, and officers and directors who are authorized to administer a plan. There is usually a per employee policy limit as well as an aggregate limit for the policy period. Most policies have a deductible. The coverage is typically provided as an endorsement to the CGL policy for little extra premium.

Fiduciary Liability Insurance

fiduciary liability insurance

Fiduciary liability insurance arises from the offering of employee benefit plans but involves claims that result from the breach of fiduciary duties such as pension plan losses because of improper investments. In some cases, employee benefits liability coverage is incorporated into a fiduciary liability policy. Some policies cover all breaches of duties; other policies cover only breaches of duties imposed by ERISA. The insureds usually consist of the employer sponsoring a benefit plan, the plan itself, and past, present, and future directors, officers, and employees in their plan capacities as fiduciaries, administrators, or trustees.

Excess and Umbrella Liability Insurance

The need for individuals to have additional liability insurance coverage under a personal umbrella policy was discussed in chapter 18. This same need exists for businesses. While the concept is the same, the situation is more complex for several reasons and a careful analysis is necessary to determine the appropriate policy in order to avoid unintentional gaps in coverage. First, the insured has a choice between an excess policy and an umbrella policy. Second, the underlying commercial policies are likely to be less uniform than the underlying personal policies. Third, commercial excess and umbrella policies are not standardized, and each insurer that writes coverage has its own form. As a result, significant variations exist.

The following discussion briefly describes excess liability insurance and then goes into more detail on commercial umbrella liability policies.

Excess Liability Insurance

excess liability insurance

An *excess liability insurance* policy is written to provide additional liability limits for claims that are covered under specified underlying coverages. There is no drop-down coverage for claims excluded by the underlying coverages. Excess liability insurance is often used to obtain larger limits for loss exposures such as directors' and officers' liability when a firm's umbrella policy does not cover that particular loss exposure.

There are two basic types of excess liability policies, but a policy can combine these two approaches. Under the first approach—referred to as a *following form*—the excess policy incorporates the policy provisions and conditions of the underlying policies. Therefore, there are always additional limits available if a claim is covered by the underlying insurance. Under the second approach—referred to as a *self-contained policy*—the excess policy is subject to its own policy provisions and conditions. This can result in coverage gaps since a claim is paid by the excess policy only if it is covered under the provisions of the underlying policies *and* the excess policy.

Some excess policies combine these two approaches by incorporating the provisions and conditions of the underlying policies and then making modifications for certain situations.

Commercial Umbrella Liability Insurance

Commercial umbrella policies operate much like the personal umbrella policies discussed in chapter 18. Unlike excess policies, there is often coverage for claims that are excluded by the underlying policies. However, each insurer that sells commercial umbrella policies has its own form and differences exist. Therefore, it is important to look at several policy provisions, including required underlying limits, insuring agreements, policy limits, events that trigger coverage, exclusions, and coverage territory. Adding to the complexity that can result from analyzing these variations is the terminology used by insurers. For example, some insurers that sell umbrella policies refer to them as excess policies.

Required Underlying Limits. The following are typical of required underlying limits:

- CGL
    - $1 million each occurrence
    - $2 million general aggregate
    - $2 million completed operations aggregate
- Business Auto Liability
    - $1 million single limit
- Employers Liability
    - $100,000 bodily injury each accident
    - $100,000 bodily injury by disease each employee
    - $500,000 disease aggregate

Depending on the insurer, the type of policyowner, and the breadth of the umbrella policy, other underlying limits may be required for loss exposures such as liquor liability, watercraft, and aircraft.

The self-insured retention for claims not covered by the underlying policies may be as low as $500 for small businesses or as high as $25,000 or more for large businesses.

Insuring Agreements. Umbrella policies often have a single insuring agreement that applies to all covered losses. For example, a policy can agree to pay up to $10 million for any claim in excess of the underlying limits for which the insured is liable for bodily injury, property damage, personal injury, or advertising injury. A policy can have a broader insuring agreement or separate insuring agreements to pick up other specialized loss exposures, such as professional liability, if the insurer is willing to cover them.

Policy Limits. Policy limits are selected by the insured, subject to insurer standards, and can be many millions of dollars. Most policies now have an aggregate limit that applies for the policy period. Defense costs can be included in the policy limit or in addition to it.

Events that Trigger Coverage. Umbrella policies are usually written on an occurrence basis, but some underlying policies can have a claims-made trigger. This can result in coverage gaps. Some insurers write umbrella policies with both types of triggers in the same policy and use the same trigger that applies to a claim under the underlying coverages.

Exclusions. While commercial umbrella policies provide broader coverage than the underlying policies, they contain exclusions, and it is important to evaluate these exclusions when obtaining coverage. In some cases, the exclusions are like those in the underlying policies such as intentional injury and damage to the insured's product and work. In other cases, exclusions in the underlying policies are omitted from the umbrella policy or made less restrictive. However, the exclusions in an umbrella policy can be more restrictive. For example, it is not unusual to see an exclusion for punitive damages even though they may be covered by the underlying policies.

Coverage Territory. Most umbrella policies provide worldwide coverage. However, some policies require that suits be brought in the United States, its territories or possessions, or Canada.

Surety Bonds

surety bond

Surety bonds are used in situations when an individual or organization wants a guarantee of indemnity if a second party fails to perform a specified act or fulfill an obligation. There are three parties to a surety bond:

- the *principal* is the party who buys the bond and who agrees to perform certain acts or fulfill certain obligations
- the *obligee* is the party who is reimbursed for damages because of the failure of the principal to uphold the agreement
- the *surety* is the party who agrees to indemnify the obligee for damages because of the principal's failure to uphold the agreement. This indemnity can be in the form of cash or the fulfillment of the

principal's obligation. The surety could be any person or organization but is usually an insurance company.

Parties to Surety Bond

- Principal: the one obligated to perform
- Obligee: the one for whom the principal is obligated to perform
- Surety: the one who compensates the obligee for the principal's failure to perform

---

Characteristics of Surety Bonds

Surety bonds have several unique characteristics. These pertain to the liability of the principal, the expected losses, the coverage period, the bond limit, and the statutory nature of some bonds.

Liability of the Principal. Unlike an insured under an insurance contract, a principal who defaults on a bond is liable to the surety to the extent of any expenditure the surety incurs. The surety can require the principal to post collateral to repay the surety if the principal defaults.

Expected Losses. A surety generally expects to pay few losses and underwrites in a strict manner to determine whether the principal is capable of meeting any obligations. The surety will carefully scrutinize the financial resources of the principal and the principal's character and ability to perform.

Coverage Period. The coverage period under most surety bonds is indefinite, and the premium for the bond is paid only once. In most cases, neither the surety nor the principal can cancel the bonds.

Bond Limit. A surety bond is written for a dollar limit, and that is the maximum amount of the surety's obligation to the obligee. Some bonds, however, pay court costs and interest on judgments in addition to the bond

Most surety bonds only pay the obligee's actual loss if it is less than the bond limit, but some bonds are written on a basis that requires the forfeiture of the entire bond limit if the principal defaults.

Statutory versus Nonstatutory Bonds. Governmental ordinances, regulations, or statutes require many bonds, and the provisions of these statutory bonds and the obligations of the parties are established by law. The obligations of the parties under nonstatutory bonds are established by contract between the obligee and the principal.

Types of Surety Bonds

There are many categories of surety bonds, and each is briefly described below.

Contract Bonds. Contract bonds guarantee that the principal will fulfill a commitment according to the provision of a contract. They are most often required of contractors and suppliers.

License and Permit Bonds. State and local governments often require persons who engage in many types of occupations to obtain licenses. They also frequently require permits for various types of activities. Various bonds are often required in connection with these licenses and permits. For example, a license or permit bond might guarantee that the principal will pay required taxes, including remittance of sales taxes collected, or that the principal will provide a means of indemnity for persons injured by its activities.

Public Official Bonds. Statutes often require that persons who are elected or appointed to certain positions be bonded. These bonds guarantee that the principal will uphold the promise made to faithfully and honestly perform the official duties of his or her office. These bonds terminate when a successor takes office.

Judicial Bonds. Numerous bonds are required by courts, and these can be divided into three broad categories—fiduciary bonds, litigation bonds, and bail bonds.

Fiduciary bonds are often required of persons who act as administrators, trustees, and guardians. They guarantee that a person who is responsible for the property of another will faithfully exercise his or her duties, give proper accounting of any property received, and make proper indemnification if the court determines that the principal is responsible for any financial loss that relates to the property.

The purpose of litigation bonds, also referred to as court bonds, is to require a person or organization who is seeking a court remedy to protect other parties from damages if the party seeking the remedy does not prevail.

There are also bonds required in many other legal activities, some of which are garnishment of wages, seizure of a tenant's personal property for back rent, suits to recover property, and removal of mechanic's liens and injunctions.

Finally, a bail bond guarantees that the bonded person will appear in court at the appointed time. Failure to do so can result in the forfeiture of the entire bail amount.

Federal Surety Bonds. Many federal agencies require businesses they regulate to carry bonds. These bonds guarantee that the business will comply with federal standards, including the payment of taxes and duties.

Credit Enhancement Insurance. Also referred to as financial guarantee insurance, this coverage is actually a form of surety bond that guarantees that principal and interest will be paid to the purchasers of debt instruments. The issuer of the debt, such as a municipality or a corporation, purchases the bond to enhance its audit rating.

There has been concern by regulators over the highly catastrophic nature of losses that could occur in case of a major economic downturn, and many states limit the writing of such bonds to specialty companies that are specifically licensed for this type of business.

Miscellaneous Bonds. Numerous other types of bonds do not fit into the previous categories. For example, an employer that self-insures its workers' compensation exposure will need to post a bond to guarantee that statutory benefits will be paid to employees.

Issuers of securities are often required to post a lost instrument bond to replace securities or other valuable papers that have been lost or stolen. The bond guarantees that the principal will reimburse the issuer if the original securities turn up and their holder is able to collect on them.

PACKAGE POLICIES

There are two common types of package policies for businesses that incorporate many of the coverages described in this chapter. These are the commercial package policy and the businessowners policy. However, separate policies, such as the following, are often needed to cover some loss exposures:

- workers' compensation and employers liability
- professional liability
- excess and umbrella liability insurance
- ocean marine insurance
- aviation insurance
- surety bonds

The following description is of the ISO policies; the policies of insurers that use other forms can differ. These differences are often very significant for businessowners policies.

Commercial Package Policy

commercial package policy

Any type or size of business can use a *commercial package policy*. The format developed by ISO consists of three major components. The first component is a common declarations page that applies to the entire policy and contains the policy number, the name of the insurer, the name and address of the policyowner, the policy period, and premium amounts.

The second component is a section of common policy conditions, which again applies to the entire policy. These conditions pertain to matters such as cancellation, policy changes, transfer of policy rights, and the insurer's rights to inspect the policyowner's premises and operations and to examine and audit books and records that pertain to the policy coverage.

The last component of the policy consists of various sections of coverages that a policyowner can select, and at least two of the sections must be selected. These sections are

- commercial property
- comprehensive general liability
- crime
- boiler and machinery
- inland marine
- auto
- farm

There is a separate declarations page that applies to each coverage and a variety of coverage forms that can be added. These forms include the ones described earlier in this chapter.

Businessowners Policy

**businessowners
policy (BOP)**

The *businessowners policy (BOP)* is designed for small- to medium-size businesses and organizations that meet certain eligibility requirements. It is more like the homeowners policy than the commercial package policy in the sense that it is designed to meet most of the needs of an average policyowner. While some options and endorsements are available, a policyowner with many additional insurance needs will probably use the commercial package policy. The following discussion is based on the ISO policy, but a number of insurers have their own policy forms that may provide broader or narrower coverage. For example, these policies may not have an insurance-to-value requirement and may provide higher limits for the additional coverages mentioned later.

Eligibility

The BOP can be used to insure various types of real property. These vary by insurer but usually include apartment buildings, office buildings, and residential condominiums below a certain size. For example, apartment buildings must have no more than sixty units, and office buildings must not exceed six stories or 100,000 square feet.

Other commercial properties are eligible provided the type of business is eligible, the business location does not exceed 25,000 square feet, and annual gross sales at the location do not exceed $3 million.

Many types of businesses are eligible for coverage under the BOP, but several are specifically ineligible. These include garages, automobile dealers, parking lots, bars, restaurants with extensive cooking operations, contractors, places of amusement, and banks.

Policy Coverages

The BOP provides open-perils coverage on property, but the coverage can be changed to named perils by endorsement. Losses are paid on a replacement-cost basis, and there is an 80-percent-to-value requirement like the one in the homeowners policy. In other respects, the coverage for buildings and personal property is similar to the coverage under the commercial package policy. The BOP has several additional property coverages, some of which include coverage for

- debris removal
- business income for up to 12 months following a loss, but ordinary payroll is only covered for 60 days
- extra expenses for up to 12 months following a loss
- up to $10,000 per year at each location for pollutant cleanup and removal
- up to $1,000 per loss for acceptance of counterfeit money and money orders that are not paid by the issuer
- up to $2,500 per loss for forgery and alteration of a check, draft, promissory note, bill of exchange, or similar promise to pay in money
- up to $10,000 for increased cost of construction

For additional premiums, the policyowner can also extend coverage to

- newly acquired or constructed buildings, with a $250,000 limit
- personal property at newly acquired premises, with a $100,000 limit
- personal property off premises, with a $5,000 limit
- outdoor property, with a $2,500 limit
- personal effects, with a $2,500 limit
- valuable paper and records, with a $5,000 limit or higher selected limit
- accounts receivable, with a $10,000 limit or a higher selected limit

The policyowner can also purchase certain optional coverages with the premiums depending on the amount of insurance selected. These include

- money and securities if open-perils coverage is purchased (More limited burglary and robbery coverage is available if named-perils is purchased.)

- employee dishonesty
- mechanical breakdown of boiler and pressure vessels and air-conditioning units

In most respects, the BOP liability coverage is similar to that provided by the CGL Form. Professional liability is specifically excluded in the policy, but endorsements may be available for some professions to add this coverage.

Automobiles owned by the business must be insured under a separate policy. However, businesses that have no owned automobiles can provide coverage for hired and nonowned automobiles by endorsement.

SOURCES FOR FURTHER IN-DEPTH STUDY

- *The CPCU Handbook of Insurance Policies*, 5th ed., Malvern PA: American Institute for CPCU/Insurance Institute of America, 2003. Phone 800-644-2101. Web site address www.aicpcu.org
- *FC&S Bulletins*, Commercial Liability Volume and Commercial Property Volume, (loose-leaf and CD-ROM service updated monthly), Cincinnati, OH: The National Underwriter Company, Phone 800-543-0874. Web site address www.nuco.com
- Malecki, Donald S., and Flitner, Arthur L., *Commercial Liability Insurance and Risk Management*, 5th ed., Malvern, PA: American Institute for CPCU/Insurance Institute of America, 2001. Phone 800-644-2101. Web site address www.aicpcu.org
- Trupin, Jerome, and Flitner, Arthur L., *Commercial Property Insurance and Risk Management*, 7th ed., Malvern, PA: American Institute for CPCU/Insurance Institute of America, 2003. Phone 800-644-2101. Web site address www.aicpcu.org
- Flitner, Arthur L., and Trupin, Jerome, *Commercial Insurance*, Malvern, PA: American Institute for CPCU/Insurance Institute of America, 2002. Phone 800-644-2101. Web site address www.aicpcu.org

CHAPTER REVIEW

Answers to review questions and self-test questions start on page 725.

Key Terms

commercial property insurance	robbery
business income insurance	theft
extra expense insurance	inland marine insurance
burglary	block policy

difference in conditions (DIC)
  insurance
commercial general liability
  (CGL) insurance
workers' compensation insurance
employers liability insurance
professional liability insurance
directors and officers (D&O)
  liability insurance

employment practices liability
  insurance
employee benefits liability
  insurance
fiduciary liability insurance
excess liability insurance
surety bond
commercial package policy
businessowners policy (BOP)

Review Questions

19-1.   A client has just purchased a building and started a small parts manufacturing business. Without getting into too much detail about the specifics of his business, you recommend that he see an insurance agent who specializes in commercial property and liability coverages. He replies, "I know I need insurance on the building, the equipment, and my inventory, but what other coverages do I need to see an agent about?" What important coverages might he need?

19-2.   What are the three common types of business income insurance forms and what coverage does each provide?

19-3.   What are the three broad classes of property covered alone or in various combinations by commercial crime insurance forms?

19-4.   Briefly explain the rather unique policy provisions common to many crime insurance forms.

19-5.   Describe the situations in which inland marine policies and forms are used to provide coverage today.

19-6.   Indicate what type of commercial liability coverage you should recommend to a client in each of the following situations:
  a.   a client who may be sued for a defective product that is manufactured or sold
  b.   a client who is concerned about being sued by a person who is injured or whose property is damaged by ongoing business activities at the person's home
  c.   a client who is concerned about being sued by a customer who is injured or whose property is damaged because of a condition in his store (such as a wet floor)
  d.   a client who is concerned about being sued by a person who is injured or whose property is damaged by work already performed
  e.   a general contractor who is concerned about being sued for poor work done by a subcontractor

    f.   a client who is concerned with having to pay a judgment against the railroad if the railroad is sued by the parents of a child who is injured while playing on the side track on the client's business property

    g.   a client who is concerned about being held liable for the employees who drive her company's delivery trucks

    h.   a client who is concerned about being sued by an injured employee not covered by the workers' compensation law, or by an employee's spouse or family member because of the employee's injury or death

    i.   a dentist who is concerned about being sued by one of his patients

    j.   an insurance agent who is concerned about being sued by a client for bad advice about the appropriate coverages to purchase

    k.   a client who is concerned about members of the board of directors of her corporation being sued for breaches of corporate duty

    l.   a client who is concerned about his business being sued for discrimination or sexual harassment

19-7.   What are the similarities and differences between excess liability insurance and commercial umbrella liability insurance?

19-8.   What are the unique characteristics of surety bonds?

19-9.   Describe the key features of the package policies commonly available for businesses.

Self-Test Questions

T F   **19-1.** Commercial property insurance covers only buildings and business personal property of the insured.

T F   **19-2.** Commercial property insurance can be written on either a named-perils or "open-perils" basis.

T F   **19-3.** Loss of income, continuing expenses, and extra expenses while a business is closed following a direct physical damage loss can be covered under business income insurance.

T F   **19-4.** A client can purchase crime insurance to cover the client's business against losses due to employee theft as well as burglary and robbery.

T F   **19-5.** Inland marine insurance provides coverage against a variety of losses including those to domestic goods in transit by truck, customers' clothes at a dry cleaner, fine art, and television towers.

T F   **19-6.** An electrical contractor who works on residential construction and repairs requires mainly premises and products liability coverages to cover his business liability loss exposures.

T   F   19-7.   Although the comprehensive general liability coverage form excludes coverage for most liability from pollution, numerous endorsements and other forms can cover the pollution loss exposure.

T   F   19-8.   Advertising injury liability cannot be covered under the comprehensive general liability coverage form.

T   F   19-9.   Most commonly, comprehensive general liability coverage is written on a claims-made basis.

T   F   19-10.   The comprehensive general liability coverage form has two aggregate limits that apply for an annual policy period.

T   F   19-11.   The most common type of commercial automobile insurance is the business auto coverage form, which is very similar to the personal auto policy with respect to the coverages that can be purchased.

T   F   19-12.   Due to workers' compensation laws, employers are not subject to suits for injuries to employees.

T   F   19-13.   Most professional liability policies are written on an occurrence basis.

T   F   19-14.   Although the directors and officers (D&O) liability policy is purchased by a corporation, the insureds are generally the officers and directors and not the corporation.

T   F   19-15.   Both excess liability policies and commercial umbrella policies include drop-down coverage for claims excluded by the underlying coverages.

T   F   19-16.   Surety bonds are three-party contracts in which a principal who defaults on a bond is liable to the surety to the extent of any expenditure the surety incurs.

T   F   19-17.   Any type or size of business can use a commercial package policy.

T   F   19-18.   A businessowners policy is designed for small- to medium-size businesses in the sense that it can meet most of the needs of an average policyowner.

a priori reasoning • reasoning with conclusions that are based on self-evident propositions (also known as *deductive reasoning*). As an example, one can reason deductively, or *a priori*, that the probability of a result of tails in the flip of a balanced coin is one chance in two. *Compare* inductive reasoning

AAIS (American Association of Insurance Services) • an advisory organization that provides various services to its member companies, including the development and filing of standardized insurance forms

absolute liability • *See* strict liability

accelerated benefits provision • a provision in a life insurance policy that allows death benefits to be paid to the policyowner prior to the insured's death under certain circumstances such as if the insured is terminally ill

accidental death • a death that is caused by an unintentional event that is sudden and unexpected

accidental death benefit • a life insurance rider that increases the death benefit, usually doubling it, if the insured dies accidentally

accumulation period • the period of time in a deferred annuity during which the purchase price is deposited with the insurer and accumulated at interest. It ends with the start of the liquidation period.

accumulation unit • a unit of a variable annuity that is purchased during the annuity's accumulation stage

actively-at-work requirement • a provision in a group insurance master contract specifying that the employee is not eligible for coverage if he or she is not active on the job on the otherwise effective date of coverage. Coverage commences when the employee returns to work.

activities of daily living (ADLs) • activities such as eating, bathing, and dressing. The inability to perform a specified number of these activities triggers eligibility for benefits in a long-term care insurance contract.

actual cash value • a process for valuing property losses. Usually it is defined as replacement cost minus depreciation but in some states is defined as fair market value.

add-on plan • a no-fault type of system that provides first-party benefits but does not restrict the right to sue for damages

additional living expenses • benefits under a homeowners policy to pay the extra costs of maintaining a family's standard of living while the family's residence is being repaired or rebuilt following a covered loss

adjustment bureau • an adjusting organization that is not owned by an insurance company and operates on a regional or national basis

adult day care • day care at centers specifically designed for the elderly who live at home but whose spouses or families cannot stay home to care for them during the day

advance-premium mutual • a mutual company that collects the full premium for coverage at the start of the policy period

adverse selection • selection against the insurance company. It is the tendency for those who know that they are highly vulnerable to specific pure risks to be most likely to acquire and to retain insurance to cover that loss.

advertising injury liability • liability that can arise out of (1) oral or written publication of slanderous or libelous material or (2) material that violates a person's rights of privacy. It also includes liability that arises through the misappropriation of advertising ideas or styles of doing business and infringement of copyright, title, or slogan.

advisory organization • an organization that assists member insurance companies in such areas as gathering and analyzing statistical information for rate-making purposes and drafting recommended policy language

age set back • an assumption for rating purposes that an annuitant is some years younger than his or her actual age

agent • a legal representative of an insurance company with express, implied, and sometimes apparent authority to act on behalf of the insurer

agreed value • the practice of determining value prior to a possible property loss. The agreed value is paid in the case of a total loss.

aleatory contract • a contract in which the values exchanged are not necessarily equal. Insurance is an aleatory contract inasmuch as an insured may pay a large amount in premiums and receive no proceeds from the policy. Conversely, an insured may pay only a small amount of premium and receive a large claim settlement from the insurer.

alien insurer • an insurer that is formed in a country other than the United States but that writes business in the United States

all-risks policy • *See* open-perils policy

alteration • the act of making changes to a document in a manner that is neither authorized nor originally intended

Alzheimer's facility • a facility with a high level of staffing and other capabilities to provide the personal assistance individuals with Alzheimer's disease need. It may be a stand-alone facility or part of a nursing home or assisted-living facility.

American Agency System • *See* independent agency system

American Lloyds association • the term used to characterize Lloyds associations that are formed in the United States

annual exclusion • the amount of a gift exempt from federal transfer taxation. Currently it is $10,000 annually for gifts to any one person. This can be increased to $20,000 if the donor is married and the donor's spouse elects to split the gift on a timely filed gift tax return.

annual transit policy • a type of inland marine insurance policy that covers all shipments during an annual period

annuitant • the person whose life governs the duration of benefit payments under a life annuity

annuity • a periodic payment to begin at a specified or contingent date and to continue for a fixed period or for the duration of a designated life or lives

annuity certain • an annuity with benefit payments that continue for a definite period of time without being linked to the duration of a specified human life

annuity principle • the concept of many persons pooling their funds to provide annuities to all while they live or for some period certain. Each person receives annuity payments consisting of the annuitants' principal, the unliquidated principal of other annuitants who die early, and investment income on these funds.

annuity unit • a measure for valuing a variable annuity during its liquidation stage. The dollar value of each unit fluctuates with the investment performance of the separate account underlying the annuity.

antigag clause rules • legislation that prevents managed care organizations from including provisions in contracts with doctors that prevent them from discussing with patients treatment options that may not be covered under their plans or from referring extremely ill patients for specialized care outside of their plans

any occupation • a strict definition of disability which requires a person to be so severely disabled that he or she cannot engage in any occupation

apparent authority • authority that, in the absence of contrary action by the principal, appears to a reasonable person to be possessed by the principal's agent

applicant • the person or organization that applies for insurance

appraisal provision • a provision in a property insurance policy that can lead to a binding settlement regarding the value of property or the amount of a settlement. It is used only if there is no disagreement regarding the existence of coverage.

Archer medical savings account • an alternative to first-dollar coverage under a medical expense plan. An employee is given medical expense coverage that has a high deductible, and money is deposited into the Archer medical savings account so that the employee can pay for expenses below the deductible amount. Any monies not used at the end of the year are paid to the employee.

assessment mutual • a mutual company that reserves the right to levy assessments on its policyowners to cover adverse underwriting experience

assignment provision • a clause that specifies the conditions under which a policyowner can transfer some or all of his or her ownership rights in the policy to another

assisted-living care • long-term care benefits for facilities that provide care for the frail elderly who are no longer able to care for themselves but who do not need the level of care provided in a nursing home

assumption-of-risk doctrine • a common-law defense available to employers under which a worker cannot recover damages for an injury if he or she knowingly assumed the risks inherent in the job

attained age rate • the insurance rate at the insured's attained age, used for attained-age term conversions and sometimes for long-term care insurance upgrades

attitudinal hazard • a condition of carelessness or indifference on the part of an individual as to whether a loss occurs and/or the size of a loss if one does occur

attorney-in-fact • the individual who directs a reciprocal exchange

automatic premium loan option • an option associated with a cash value life insurance policy whereby, if a renewal premium is not paid by the end of the grace period, the insurer creates a loan against the cash value in the amount of the unpaid premium

automatic reinsurance • *See* treaty reinsurance

automobile insurance • a package property and liability insurance policy that provides (1) liability coverage for losses that arise out of the use, operation, or maintenance of an automobile, (2) medical payments benefits, (3) uninsured motorists benefits, and (4) physical damage coverage to owned and certain nonowned vehicles

automobile insurance plan • a state plan that assigns drivers who have been unable to obtain automobile insurance to insurance companies in proportion to their volume of business in a state. Formerly called *assigned risk.*

aviation insurance • insurance policies to provide liability, physical damage, and medical payments coverage for the owners of aircraft

backdating • issuance of a life insurance policy as if it had been purchased when the insured was younger in order to obtain a lower periodic premium

bail bond • a bond that guarantees that the bonded person will appear in court at the appointed time

bailee • a person or organization in temporary custody of the property of another for some reason such as for service or repair of the property

bailees customers policy • an insurance policy for customers' goods whether or not a bailee is liable for their loss or destruction

bailees liability policy • an insurance policy for customers' goods if a bailee is liable for their loss or destruction

bailment • the situation in which a person or business has temporary custody of the property of others

bail-out provision • a clause in an annuity contract that allows the purchaser to surrender the contract without a surrender charge if the interest rate being credited falls below a specified but nonguaranteed minimum

bed reservation benefit • a benefit under a long-term care insurance policy that continues to pay a long-term care facility for a limited time if a patient must temporarily leave because of hospitalization. Without a continuation of benefits, the bed might be rented to someone else and unavailable upon the patient's release from the hospital.

beneficiary • the person or entity designated to receive the death proceeds of a life insurance policy

binder • a written or oral agreement between an agent and an applicant for insurance whereby the principal-insurer is committed to provide the desired insurance, at least on a temporary basis

birthing center • a facility, separate from a hospital, designed to provide a homelike atmosphere for the delivery of babies. Deliveries are performed by nurse-midwives, and mothers and babies are released shortly after birth.

blackout period • the period during which no Social Security benefits are payable for a surviving spouse, extending from the time the youngest child reaches age 16 until the spouse is age 60

block policy • a property insurance policy designed to pick up the exposures of a dealer in such items as jewelry, cameras, fine art, musical equipment, furs, stamps, and coins. The policy covers inventory while at a fixed location or while being transported. There is also coverage for the furniture and fixtures of the dealer and property of others in the dealer's care, custody, or control.

Blue Cross and Blue Shield plans • organizations formed for the purpose of prepaying subscribers' medical care expenses. Blue Cross plans provide coverage primarily for hospital expenses, and Blue Shield plans provide coverage primarily for physicians' services.

boatowners policy • a package policy that provides liability and physical damage coverage for small- and medium-size boats

bodily injury • bodily harm, sickness, or disease. It includes required care, loss of services, and death that results.

boiler and machinery insurance • commercial property and liability insurance that provides coverage for damage caused by steam boiler explosion and electrical or mechanical breakdown; referred to as equipment breakdown coverage by some insurers

branch manager • an insurance company employee who heads up a branch office for the marketing of the insurer's products in a given geographic area

branch office system • in life insurance, a marketing system whereby insurers establish branch offices in the areas where they write business. The offices are headed by branch managers.

broker • a marketing intermediary between the insurer and policyowner who represents not the insurance company but the policyowner

builders risk insurance • commercial property insurance that provides protection for buildings and construction and the unique exposures associated with these types of structures

burglary • the removal of property from inside an insured premises by a person who enters or leaves the premises unlawfully as evidenced by marks of forcible entry or exit

business income insurance • insurance that covers business losses after the occurrence of a direct physical damage loss that results in the suspension of business operations. The three basic types of losses covered include net income, normal ongoing business expenses, and extra expenses. Formerly called *business interruption insurance*.

business insurance • the category of insurance used by businesses and other organizations

business interruption insurance • *See* business income insurance

business operations liability • bodily injury, personal injury, or property damage liability that results from the activities of a business owner or employee

business overhead expense insurance • a policy available to cover many of the ongoing costs of operating a business while the business owner is totally disabled

businessowners policy (BOP) • a common type of package policy designed to meet the property and liability needs of certain small- and medium-size businesses

buy-sell agreement • a contract binding the owner of a business interest to sell the business interest for a specified or determinable price at his or her death or disability and a designated purchaser to buy at that time

buy-up plan • an employee benefit plan under which a covered person can purchase additional coverage (for example, life insurance or disability income insurance) at his or her own expense. Also referred to as a *supplemental plan*

cafeteria plan • an employee benefit plan under which an employee can use a specified amount of employer funds and/or salary reductions to design his or her own benefit package from an array of available benefits

calendar-year deductible • a deductible that applies to medical expenses incurred within a calendar year. A new deductible must be satisfied in a subsequent calendar year.

cancelable • a contract feature that allows the insurance company to terminate the coverage at any time (and perhaps for any reason) during the term of coverage by notifying the insured

capital needs analysis • a system for determining how much life insurance a client needs if the principal sum is to be preserved in the process of meeting the financial objectives for his or her survivors

captive agent system • *See* exclusive agency system

captive insurer • an insurance company owned by a parent company and formed primarily to insure the loss exposures of the parent company

care coordination • the use of a licensed health care practitioner to assess a person's condition, evaluate care options, and develop an individualized plan of care that provides the most appropriate services

carryover provision • a provision in a medical expense plan that allows any expenses applied to the deductible and incurred during the last 3 months of the year to also be applied to the deductible for the following year

carve-out (benefit plan) • the practice of excluding certain classes of employees from a benefit plan and providing benefits to them under an alternative arrangement. Carve-outs are generally used to contain employee costs or provide broader or tax-favored benefits to key employees and executives.

carve-out (medical expense insurance) • coverage under a medical expense plan that has been singled out for individual management by a party other than the employer or the employee's primary health plan provider

cash option • an option that allows an annuitant, at the start of the liquidation period, to withdraw the funds in cash, rather than as an annuity

cash refund annuity • a refund annuity that specifies if the annuitant dies before receiving total benefit payments equal to the purchase price of the annuity, all or a stated percentage of the difference will be refunded in cash

cash value • the savings element that builds up in a permanent life insurance policy, an endowment policy, or an annuity contract

cash value accumulation test • a test to determine whether an insurance policy meets the definition of a life insurance policy for federal income tax purposes. To qualify as such, the cash value must not exceed the net single premium that would be needed to fund the policy's death benefit.

cash value life insurance • a type of life insurance under which premiums are sufficient not only to pay the insurer's death claims and expenses but also to build up a savings fund within the policy

casualty loss • usually considered a loss that is sudden, unexpected, or unusual and which results in damage, destruction, or loss of property

catastrophic benefits rider • a disability income insurance rider that makes additional benefits available if the insured suffers a severe disability that includes cognitive impairment or the inability to perform two or more of six activities of daily living

cede • the transfer of a portion of the amount of insurance written by a primary or original insurer to a reinsurer

certificate of insurance • a description of the group insurance coverage provided to employees. Although it is given to the employees, it is not part of the master contract.

choice no-fault • a modified no-fault law that allows a person to elect traditional tort coverage at a reduced premium

chronically ill individual • a person who, for purposes of long-term care insurance, is expected to be unable to perform at least two activities of daily living (ADLs) for at least 90 days or who needs substantial services to protect the individual from threats to health and safety due to substantial cognitive impairment

civil wrong • a legal wrong other than a criminal wrong. It is based upon torts or contracts.

claims adjusting • the basic insurance function of loss payment

claims-made policy • a liability insurance policy that only covers claims that are first reported during the policy period as long as the event that caused the claims occurred after a specified retroactive date in the policy

class rate • an average price of insurance that applies to a category or classification of similar insureds

closed-panel plan • a benefit plan under which covered persons must obtain services from practitioners selected by the provider of benefits

COBRA • a provision of the Consolidated Omnibus Budget Reconciliation Act of 1985 that requires group health plans to allow employees and certain beneficiaries to extend their current health insurance coverage at group rates for up to 36 months following a qualifying event that results in the loss of coverage. The provision applies only to employers with 20 or more employees. In addition, a person electing COBRA continuation can be required to pay a premium equal to as much as 102 percent of the cost to the employee benefit plan for the period of coverage for a similarly situated active employee to whom a qualifying event has not occurred.

coinsurance (medical expense insurance) • the percentage of covered expenses under a major medical plan that is paid by the insurance company once a deductible is satisfied. The most common coinsurance is 80 percent.

coinsurance (property insurance) • a provision whereby a property owner must share in a loss if the amount of insurance carried is less than a specified percentage of value

collateral assignment method • the technique used with split-dollar life insurance whereby the employee owns the policy and has the responsibility for paying the premium. The employers' share of the policy proceeds is secured by an assignment.

collision • the term used in an automobile insurance policy that refers to the upset of an automobile or its impact with another vehicle or object

combination dental plan • a dental plan under which diagnostic and preventive services are covered on a usual-and-customary basis but other dental services are covered on the basis of a fee schedule

commercial general liability (CGL) insurance • commercial liability insurance designed to cover a wide variety of liability loss exposures that can face an organization, including premises, business operations, products, completed operations, contractual, and contingent liability

commercial insurance • as contrasted with personal insurance, a category of insurance—particularly of property and liability insurance—that is purchased by businesses and other organizations

commercial package policy • a common type of package policy that covers many of the property and liability loss exposures of a business

commercial property insurance • coverage for losses to real and personal business property. As commonly used, the term applies to policies that cover losses from most perils other than those that relate to crime, transportation, and boiler explosion. There are numerous forms that cover various classifications of property from specified perils or on an open-perils basis.

common accident provision • a provision in a major medical expense contract whereby if two or more members of the same family are injured in the same accident, the covered medical expenses for all family members will, at most, be subject to a single deductible, usually equal to the individual deductible amount

comparative negligence • the legal principle whereby an injured party can recover a portion of the damage for his or her injuries if he or she were also negligent. In some jurisdictions, a plaintiff can recover only if his or her negligence is less (or not more) than the defendant's negligence.

completed operations liability • bodily injury or property damage liability caused by work that has been performed

comprehensive coverage • *See* other than collision

comprehensive dental plan • *See* nonscheduled dental plan

comprehensive long-term care insurance policy • a long-term care insurance policy that combines benefits for facility care and home health care services into a single contract. *Also known as* an integrated policy

compulsory insurance law • a law in most states that requires the owners of automobiles to carry liability insurance before a vehicle can be registered

computer fraud • theft of property that relates to the use of a computer to fraudulently transfer property from its rightful owner to someone else

concealment • failure by one party to a contract to affirmatively disclose to the other party all of the important facts that are the exclusive knowledge of the first party. Even if it is not intentional or fraudulent, concealment can make an insurance contract voidable.

condition precedent • a condition in an insurance contract that must be fulfilled by the policyowner before the insurer can be held liable for a loss

condition subsequent • a condition in an insurance contract that must be fulfilled by the policyowner after the insurer has become liable in order to avoid the insurer's release from liability

conditional contract • an agreement in which one party's obligation to perform is subject to the performance of specified acts by the other party to the agreement

conditional receipt • a receipt given to an applicant for life insurance in exchange for the payment of the first premium in which the insurer, through its agent, specifies that the coverage will be effective as of the date of the receipt, subject to the condition that the proposed insured later be found to have been insurable as of the date the receipt was issued

condominium commercial unit-owners coverage • commercial property insurance that covers the interest of the owner of a commercial condominium unit

consequential loss • *See* indirect loss

consideration • a right or something of value given to another party in exchange for the assumption of an obligation by the other party. Consideration is a requirement for a valid contract.

consumer-directed health care • an approach to medical expense insurance that requires employees to make financial decisions involving their health care

contingent beneficiary • the person or entity designated to receive the death proceeds of a life insurance policy if the primary beneficiary predeceases the insured

contingent liability • legal liability that arises because of work performed by an independent contractor such as a subcontractor of a business

contingent payee • in life insurance, the person or entity designated to receive the remaining death proceeds if the beneficiary dies after the insured but before the beneficiary has received the full amount of the proceeds payable

continuing care retirement community • a facility that provides lifetime care for older adults. Initial occupancy is in an independent living unit, but a resident must move to an assisted-living or nursing home unit if health deteriorates.

contract of adhesion • a characteristic of a contract that is prepared in all of its details by one party, rather than having its terms bargained over between the parties to the contract. Because insurance policies are generally contracts of adhesion, if ambiguity exists in the terms, the courts are likely to rule in favor of the insured and against the insurer (the party that drew up the contract).

contractual liability • the assumption of legal liability of others through a written or oral contract

contributory negligence • the legal principle whereby an injured person cannot recover damage for injuries from another negligent party if the injured party was also negligent

contributory plan • a type of employee benefit plan in which the insured pays a portion of the premium cost

conversion • a provision in a group benefit plan that gives an employee whose coverage ceases the right to convert to an individual insurance policy without providing evidence of insurability. The conversion policy may or may not be identical to the prior group coverage.

convertibility • a feature in term life insurance that allows the insured to replace the term coverage with permanent individual life insurance without having to show evidence of insurability. In group insurance, the right is available only at certain times, including termination of the insured from the group or from an eligible class within the group.

coordination-of-benefits provision • a provision in most group medical expense plans under which priorities are established for the payment of benefits if an individual is covered under more than one plan. Coverage as an employee is generally primary to coverage as a dependent. When parents are divorced, the plan of the parent with custody is primary, the plan of the current spouse of the parent with custody is secondary, and the plan of the parent without custody pays last. Other rules apply to other situations.

copayment • *See* percentage participation

cost-of-living adjustments (COLA) • increases in benefit levels because of changes in some index such as the CPI. These increases apply to Social Security income benefits and sometimes to benefits under private insurance and retirement programs.

cost-of-living rider • a rider to an insurance policy, such as individual disability income insurance, that allows an insured to purchase against inflation

cost shifting • the attempt by employers to control benefit costs by shifting these costs to employees. Examples include the requirement of larger employee contributions and increased deductibles.

counteroffer • an offer made by an offeree to the original offeror in lieu of acceptance of the original offer

countersignature law • a law that requires that property insurance contracts covering property in a particular state be signed by an agent who is a resident of that state

covered auto • a vehicle specifically listed in the policy declarations of an automobile insurance policy

credibility • the degree of reliability one can place on past results as an indicator of likely future results

credit enhancement insurance • a form of surety bond that guarantees that the principal and interest will be paid to the purchasers of a debt instrument; also known as *financial guarantee insurance*

crime insurance • various insurance coverages for losses that arise from illegal activities such as burglary, robbery, extortion, forgery, employee dishonesty, and theft

criminal wrong • an injury that involves the public at large that is punishable by the government

critical illness insurance • a form of supplemental medical expense insurance that provides a substantial one-time lump-sum cash benefit for listed critical illnesses

cross-purchase agreement • a business buy-sell agreement in which the surviving co-owners will be the purchasers of the business interest of a deceased owner

current assumption whole life insurance • a nonparticipating whole life insurance policy in which premium rates are redetermined by the insurer periodically, based on its then current assumptions as to mortality, interest, and expenses

currently insured • an insured status under Social Security that requires a person to have credit for at least 6 quarters of coverage out of the 13-quarter period ending with the quarter in which death occurs

custodial care • care given to help with personal needs such as walking, bathing, dressing, eating, or taking medicine. Such care can usually be provided by someone without professional medical skills or training.

declarations • factual statements that are a part of an insurance policy and that identify the specific person, property, or activity being insured, the parties to the insurance transaction, and other descriptive information about the insurance being provided

decreasing term insurance • a form of term life insurance in which the amount of insurance systematically decreases from year to year

deductible • the initial amount or portion of an insured loss that is borne by the insured, rather than by the insurance company

deductive reasoning • *See* a priori reasoning

deferred annuity • an annuity for which benefit payments begin more than one payment interval after the date of purchase

defined-contribution plan • in medical expense insurance, a plan under which the employer makes a fixed contribution that an employee can use toward paying the cost of medical expense coverage, regardless of the premium

definitions • explanations of the meaning of key terms in an insurance policy to clarify the coverage

Delta Plans • service plans sponsored by state dental associations for the purpose of providing dental benefits. They are also called Delta Dental Plans.

demutualization • the process of converting a mutual insurance company into a stock company

dental health maintenance organization (DHMO) • an HMO that provides dental care only

dependent • most commonly defined under a group medical expense plan to include an employee's spouse who is not legally separated from the employee and any other unmarried dependent children (including stepchildren and adopted children) under age 19 or, if full-time students, age 23

difference in conditions (DIC) insurance • a separate insurance policy that provides open-perils coverage to fill in the gaps left by the insured's other commercial property insurance policies

direct loss • loss that arises first or immediately following the occurrence of a peril. For example, the cost to repair a dented fender is a direct loss following an automobile accident.

direct recognition • in life insurance, the practice of paying smaller dividends on policies that have outstanding policy loans than on other policies

direct-selling system • a method of marketing insurance without the intermediary of an agent or broker

directors and officers (D&O) liability insurance • insurance that covers directors and officers of a corporation and that is purchased by a corporation. The policy covers directors and officers for their personal liability as directors and officers that results from wrongful acts and also covers reimbursement to the policyowner for any sum that it is required or permitted by law to pay to the directors and officers as indemnification.

disability income insurance • insurance to partially replace income of persons unable to work because of sickness or accident

disability insured • the insured status under Social Security necessary to receive disability benefits. It requires that a worker (1) be fully insured and (2) have had a minimum amount of work under Social Security within a recent period.

disability-based policy • a long-term care insurance policy with a per diem basis of payment that provides benefits even if no care is being received as long as the insured satisfies the policy's benefit trigger

diversification • a method of risk control that involves the duplication of assets or activities at different locations

dividend options • a set of provisions in a participating life insurance policy that describe how the policyowner can use the dividends, usually to reduce the premium payment, to buy additional paid-up permanent insurance, to accumulate at interest, to buy term insurance, or to make the policy a paid-up policy at an earlier age than originally planned

divisible surplus • that portion of an insurer's surplus that is declared as a dividend to be distributed to policyowners and/or stockholders of the insurer

domestic insurer • an insurer formed in the state in which it does business

double indemnity provision • *See* accidental death benefit

dram shop laws • laws that impute liability to taverns and other businesses that serve liquor for injuries that may be caused by intoxicated patrons

dread disease insurance • *See* specified disease insurance

dwelling policy • one of a series of policies for the insurance of dwellings. The forms are somewhat less comprehensive than homeowners policies and can be used for dwellings that do not meet certain homeowners standards.

dynamic risk • a possibility of loss that results from changes in society or in the economy. An example of a dynamic risk is the possibility that a retailer's inventory will become obsolete because of a sudden change in consumer tastes.

earnings test • the process for determining whether income benefits of Social Security beneficiaries under age 65 should be reduced because of wages that exceed a specified amount that is subject to annual indexing. Prior to 2000, the test also applied to beneficiaries aged 65–69.

earthquake insurance • a homeowners endorsement or separate policy that covers property for earthquake as well as tremors that accompany volcanic eruption. The coverage has a large deductible such as 5 percent of the limit of insurance.

elimination period • *See* waiting period

employee benefits liability insurance • insurance that covers claims that arise out of improper advice or other errors or omissions in the administration of employee benefit plans

employee dishonesty • a dishonest act by an employee, whether known or not and whether the employee acts alone or in collusion with others. The employee must intend to cause the employer a loss and to obtain a financial gain for the employee or someone else.

employers liability insurance • a type of liability insurance that protects an employer when it can be sued because of injuries to employees

employment practices liability insurance • a liability policy that covers specified employment practices such as discrimination, sexual harassment, and wrongful termination

endorsement • a provision added to a property or liability insurance policy, sometimes for an extra premium charge, by which the scope of the policy's coverage is clarified, restricted, or enlarged

endorsement method • the technique used with split-dollar life insurance whereby the employer owns the policy and has the primary responsibility for paying the premium

endowment life insurance • a type of life insurance policy that pays the face amount if the insured dies during a specified period of time and also pays the face amount if he or she lives to the end of that period

entire contract provision • in life and health insurance, a provision that specifies that the policy and the attached application constitute the entire agreement between the parties

entity agreement • a business buy-sell agreement in which the business itself is the designated purchaser of the deceased's business interest

equipment breakdown insurance • *See* boiler and machinery insurance

equity-indexed annuity • an annuity that guarantees a minimum fixed rate of interest credits but also provides higher credits if a specified common stock index rises sufficiently

errors and omissions insurance • a type of professional liability insurance for those in occupations such as real estate appraising and accounting, where the professional's acts or omissions are unlikely to result in bodily injury

estate tax • a tax imposed upon the right of a person to transfer property at death. The federal government and many states levy such taxes.

evidence of insurability • documentation or other evidence submitted to the insurance company regarding the physical condition or other attributes of the applicant for insurance coverage, which is taken into account when the insurer determines whether to accept the risk

excess liability insurance • a policy written to provide additional liability limits for claims that are covered by specified underlying coverage

excess line broker • a broker who is authorized to place insurance with nonadmitted insurers in certain circumstances. Also known as a *surplus line broker*

exclusion ratio • the ratio used to determine the portion of the benefit payment from an annuity that is tax free as a return of the investment in the contract. It is the ratio of the total amount invested to the total amount expected to be received.

exclusions • provisions in an insurance contract that indicate what the insurer does not intend to cover. Exclusions can apply to certain perils, certain types of losses, certain types of property, or certain types of activities.

exclusive agency system • a marketing system in property and liability insurance in which the agent represents only one insurer (or group of affiliated insurers), and the insurer has ownership rights over the business written by the agents

exclusive-provider organization (EPO) • a variation of a preferred-provider organization in which coverage is not provided outside the preferred-provider network, except in those infrequent cases where the network does not have an appropriate specialist

exposure unit • the unit of measurement for which an insurance rate is developed. Examples are each $1,000 of life insurance protection or each $100 of property value.

express authority • authority specifically granted by a principal to an agent by means of an agency agreement

extended care facility • a health care facility for a person who no longer requires the full level of medical care provided by a hospital but does need a period of convalescence under supervised medical care. Also known as a *skilled-nursing facility*

extended nonowned coverage • an automobile insurance endorsement for persons who have a vehicle that is made available for their regular use

extended term insurance • paid-up term life insurance purchased through the use of a life insurance policy's cash value as a single premium

extension of benefits • a provision in a medical expense plan under which benefits are extended for any covered employee or dependent who is totally disabled at the time coverage would otherwise terminate. The disability must have resulted from an injury or illness that occurred while the person was covered under the group contract. The length of the extension generally ranges from 3 to 12 months.

external adjuster • an independent business or person whose job is to adjust claims on a fee basis for insurers

extortion • the surrender of property away from the insured premises as a result of bodily harm to someone who is, or is allegedly, being held captive

extra expense insurance • commercial insurance that provides coverage for expenses to avoid or minimize the suspension of operations

extra percentage tables • tables used in treating substandard applicants for life insurance in which separate, higher-than-normal mortality rates are used in calculating the premium for the coverage

extraterritoriality • the application of one state's regulatory requirements to all of the business written by a company licensed in that state, rather than to just the business it writes in that state

facility-only policy • a long-term care insurance policy that provides benefits for care in a nursing home and other settings such as an assisted-living facility and hospice

factory mutual • a type of mutual company that writes property insurance on large, highly protected industrial exposures

facultative reinsurance • reinsurance that is optional for both the primary insurer and the reinsurer

FAIR (Fair Access to Insurance Requirements) plan • a state-run program to provide property insurance, within limits, if a property owner is unable to obtain coverage in the standard marketplace. The actual coverage is usually written by a pool or syndicate of private insurers.

family deductible • a provision in a major medical plan that waives future deductibles for all family members once a specified aggregate dollar amount of medical expenses has been incurred or after a specified number of family members have satisfied their individual deductibles

family purpose doctrine • a legal principle that imputes liability to motor vehicle owners for the negligence of family members who use the motor vehicle

federal surety bond • a bond that guarantees that a business will comply with federal standards, including the payment of taxes and duties

fee schedule • a list of covered benefits and the maximum fee that will be paid to the provider of benefits. Such a schedule is found in many surgical expense policies, dental policies, vision care plans, and group legal expense plans.

fellow-servant doctrine • a common-law defense available to employers under which a worker cannot collect if an injury resulted from a fellow worker's negligence

fiduciary bond • a bond that guarantees that a person who is responsible for the property of another faithfully exercises his or her duties, gives proper accounting of any property received, and makes proper indemnification if the court determines that the principal is responsible for any financial loss that relates to the property. It is often required of persons who act as administrators, trustees, or guardians.

fiduciary liability insurance • insurance that covers claims that result from the breach of fiduciary duties such as pension plan losses because of improper investments

field underwriting • the initial screening of applicants for insurance performed by the agent or broker

fifth dividend option • a provision in cash value life insurance whereby dividends can be used to purchase term insurance

50 percent refund annuity • a refund annuity that pays a benefit to a beneficiary if the annuitant dies before receiving benefits equal to half the cost of the annuity. Installments continue until the total benefits paid equal half the cost of the annuity.

FSA • *See* flexible spending account (FSA)

file-and-use law • a law regulating insurance rates that allows insurers to file their rates with the regulatory authority and then begin to use those rates unless/until the regulatory authority disapproves the rates

financial guarantee insurance • *See* credit enhancement insurance

financial institution bond • a bond that is designed to pick up the unique loss exposures faced by financial institutions such as stockbrokerages, investment banks, banks, credit unions, savings and loan associations, and insurance companies

financial needs analysis • a system for determining how much life insurance a client needs if the principal sum is to be liquidated in the process of meeting the client's financial objectives for his or her survivors

financial responsibility law • a law that exists in most states that requires proof of future automobile insurance after certain circumstances occur. These can include an automobile accident, conviction for certain traffic offenses, or failure to pay a legal judgment that arises from an automobile accident.

financial risk • a category of risk for which the possibility of loss involves a decrease or a disappearance of monetary value, usually in an unexpected or relatively unpredictable manner

fire • rapid oxidation or combustion that causes a flame or glow

first-to-die policy • *See* joint-life policy

fixed-amount option • a life insurance settlement option under which the death proceeds are distributed in level installments consisting of principal and interest for as long as the proceeds last

fixed annuity • an annuity that provides a stated dollar benefit, regardless of the insurer's investment return

fixed-period option • a life insurance settlement option under which the death proceeds are distributed in installments consisting of principal and interest over a specified period of time

flat extra premium • a method of treating substantial life insurance applicants by charging a specified extra premium per $1,000 of insurance regardless of age

flexible benefit plan • *See* cafeteria plan

flexible premium life insurance • various types of life insurance in which the premium is flexible, either at the option of the insurer or the policyowner

flexible spending account (FSA) • a cafeteria plan provision that allows an employee to fund certain types of expenses other than insurance premiums on a before-tax basis

flex-rating law • a law regulating insurance rates that requires prior approval of rates only if they differ from the existing rates by at least some specified percentage such as 5 or 10 percent

floater • a property insurance policy to provide broad insurance protection on property that is subject to being moved

following form • a basic form of an excess liability policy that incorporates the policy provisions and conditions of an underlying policy, thus providing additional coverage only if a claim is covered by the underlying insurance

foreign insurer • an insurer that writes business in a state but which is incorporated in another state

forgery • the creation of a document or signature that is not genuine

fraternal insurer • a nonprofit insuring organization that writes mainly life insurance on members of a fraternal society

fraud • intentional deception or intentional misleading of another person. In order to constitute fraud, intent must be shown, and the information concealed or misrepresented must be relied upon by and injure the other party.

free-look provision • a clause found in some lines of insurance contracts that gives the policyowner a specified period of time, such as 10 days, to return the policy after acceptance and receive a full refund of the premium paid

full advance funding • a funding method for insurance by which taxes or premiums are set at a level to fund all promised benefits from current service for those making current contributions

full retirement age • the age at which a worker can retire under Social Security and receive nonreduced benefits equal to his or her primary insurance amount (PIA). Also referred to as *normal retirement age*

fully insured • an insured status under Social Security. This status requires one of the following: (1) 40 quarters of coverage or (2) credit for at least as many quarters (but a minimum of 6) of coverage as there are years elapsing after 1950 (or after the year in which age 21 is reached, if later) and before the year in which a person dies, becomes disabled, or reaches age 62, whichever occurs first.

functional replacement cost • the cost to repair or replace damaged real property with less costly construction materials and methods that are functionally equivalent to the old construction

fundamental risk • a loss possibility that can affect a large segment of society at the same time. An example is the possibility of widespread unemployment during an economic downturn.

gambling • the deliberate creation of a speculative risk by betting on an uncertain outcome. Playing poker for money is an example of gambling.

garage insurance • insurance designed to meet the special needs of businesses engaged in selling, servicing, storing, or parking vehicles

gatekeeper PPO • a preferred-provider organization that requires a participant to select a primary care physician in the manner of an HMO subscriber. However, at the time medical service is needed, the participant can elect to go outside the PPO network.

general agency system • in life insurance marketing, the term used to describe a marketing system whereby a general agent is granted a franchise by an insurer to build an agency force for the marketing of the insurer's products in a given geographic area

general agent • in the legal sense, an agent who has the authority to bind insurance for a client

gift • for federal gift tax purposes, a completed transfer and acceptance of property for less than full and adequate consideration

gift tax • a tax imposed on transfers of property by gift during the donor's lifetime

grace period • an additional period of time, usually 31 days, granted in some types of insurance for the policyowner to pay the premium after it has become due. During the grace period, the coverage remains in force.

gross estate • for federal estate tax purposes, the property of a decedent that passes by will and by other means

gross rate • an insurance rate that includes a margin for loading as well as a provision for expected future loss costs

group insurance • in contrast with individual insurance, all types of private insurance that cover many people under one master contract issued to a sponsoring organization such as an employer

group-model HMO • a closed-panel HMO under which physicians and other medical personnel are employees of another legal entity that has a contractual relationship with the HMO to provide medical services for its subscribers

guaranteed purchase (insurability) option • a rider to a life insurance policy that gives the insured the right to buy additional insurance in specified amounts at specified times or ages without having to provide evidence of insurability

guaranteed renewable • a characteristic of an insurance contract in which the insured retains the right to renew the coverage at each policy anniversary date, usually up to a stated age. Also, the insurer is not allowed to cancel the coverage during the period of protection. However, the insurer does retain the right to raise the rates for the coverage for broad classes of insureds.

guaranty fund • a state fund that at least partially protects consumers against the insolvency of insurers. The typical fund assesses solvent insurers to pay the unpaid claims of insolvent companies.

guideline premium and corridor test • a two-pronged test to determine whether an insurance policy meets the definition of a life insurance policy for federal income tax purposes. The test relates to both the size of the total premium paid and the size of the death benefit relative to the cash value.

hazard • an act or condition that increases the likelihood of the occurrence of a peril and/or increases the severity of a loss if a peril does occur. The three types of hazards are physical hazards, moral hazards, and attitudinal hazards.

health association • an organization that provides medical expense coverage to members. Examples include HMOs and Blue Cross and Blue Shield plans.

health insurance • a generic term that applies to all types of insurance for losses that result from bodily injury or illness. These include medical expense insurance, long-term care insurance, dental insurance, and disability income insurance.

Health Insurance Portability and Accountability Act (HIPAA) • federal legislation, passed in 1996, that reforms the health care system through numerous provisions. The act's primary purpose is to make insurance more available, particularly when an employed person changes jobs or becomes unemployed.

health maintenance organization (HMO) • a managed system of health care that provides a comprehensive array of medical services on a prepaid basis to voluntarily enrolled persons living within a specific geographic region. HMOs both finance health care and deliver health services. There is an emphasis on preventive care as well as cost control.

Health Maintenance Organization Act • a federal act in 1973 that introduced the concept of the federally qualified HMO

health reimbursement account • an account funded with employer dollars from which an employee can withdraw amounts to pay medical expenses that are not covered under a high-deductible medical expense plan

hedging • a procedure by which two compensating or offsetting transactions are used to ensure a position of at least "breaking even." An example of hedging is the simultaneous taking of a "long" position and a "short" position in shares of common stock.

high-risk pool • a state-run insurance pool to provide medical expense coverage for persons who have been rejected in the normal marketplace

HIPAA • *See* Health Insurance Portability and Accountability Act

hired auto • in commercial automobile insurance, an automobile, other than a nonowned auto, that is leased, hired, rented, or borrowed by the named insured

HMO • *See* health maintenance organization

hold-harmless agreement • an agreement in which one party, such as a tenant, accepts the responsibility of another party, such as a landlord, for losses that would otherwise fall on that other party

home health care • care that is received at home and includes part-time skilled nursing care, speech therapy, physical or occupational therapy, part-time services from home health aides, and help from homemakers or chore workers

home health care policy • a long-term care insurance policy designed to provide benefits only for care outside an institutional setting, although some policies may provide benefits for care in assisted-living facilities

homeowners policy • a package policy that provides coverage for a family's home, personal possessions, and liability that arises out of the many activities of family members. There are several homeowners forms that provide varying degrees of coverage for different types of homeowners and tenants.

homogeneity • the quality or state of being of the same or a similar kind or nature

hospice care • a health care facility or service that provides benefits to terminally ill persons. The emphasis is on easing the physical and psychological pain associated with death rather than on curing a medical condition.

hospital indemnity insurance • a medical expense policy that pays a fixed dollar amount for each day a person is hospitalized, regardless of other insurance

hospital-surgical policy • an individual medical expense policy that provides limited coverage for hospital, surgical, and certain other medical expenses. It is less comprehensive than a major medical policy.

HRA • *See* health reimbursement account

hull insurance • the term often applied to physical damage coverage in watercraft and aviation policies

human life value • the present value of that portion of a person's estimated future earnings that will be used to support dependents

immediate annuity • an annuity with benefit payments that begin one payment interval after the date of purchase

implied authority • the authority that an agent has as necessary to carry out acts needed to exercise his or her express authority

implied warranty • an obligation imposed by law on the manufacturer or distributor of products

imputed negligence • legal responsibility extended by the courts to persons other than those who cause injury

incident of ownership • any right to the economic benefits of a piece of property such as a life insurance policy

incontestable clause • a provision in life and health insurance that specifies that, except for nonpayment of the premium, the insurer will not contest the policy after it has been in force for a specified period (usually 2 years) during the insured's lifetime

indemnity • a principle underlying most insurance contracts whereby the insurance seeks to reimburse the insured for approximately the amount lost, no more and no less

independent adjuster • an adjuster who is not an employee of an insurance company and who operates as an individual within a limited area

independent agency system • a marketing system in property and liability insurance in which an agent represents several insurers or groups of insurers and has ownership rights over the business written by the agency

indeterminate premium whole life insurance • *See* interest-sensitive whole life insurance

indirect (consequential) loss • a loss that occurs only as a secondary result following the occurrence of a peril. An example is the additional living expenses a family might incur in order to pay for substitute living accommodations following fire damage to their home.

individual equity • the principle that insurance benefits are actuarially related to contributions

individual insurance • all types of insurance that are purchased by individuals and families

individual practice association • an HMO under which participating physicians practice individually or in small groups in their own offices. In many cases, these physicians also accept non-HMO patients on a traditional fee-for-service basis.

inductive reasoning • reasoning in which a generalized conclusion is derived from particular instances. Inductive reasoning is based on statistical analysis. *Compare* a priori reasoning

inflation guard endorsement • a homeowners endorsement that provides an automatic increase for property coverages. The policyowner selects the annual percentage increase.

initial deductible • a deductible that must be satisfied before any benefits are paid under a medical expense plan

inland marine insurance • a specialized type of transportation insurance used for goods in transit, property held by bailees, mobile equipment and property, property of certain dealers, and instrumentalities of transportation and communication

inside build up • the increase in the cash value or investment fund of a permanent life insurance policy

installment refund annuity • a refund annuity specifying that, if the annuitant dies before receiving total benefit payments equal to the purchase price of the annuity, the difference will be refunded in the form of continuing benefit payments

insurable interest • a right or relationship with regard to the subject matter of an insurance contract such that the insured will suffer financial loss from damage, loss, or destruction to that subject matter

insurable risk • a risk that substantially meets the following requirements: (1) the amount of the loss must be important, (2) the loss must be accidental in nature, (3) future loss must be calculable, (4) the loss must be definite, and (5) the risk cannot be associated with an excessively catastrophic loss

insurance • an economic system for reducing financial risk through a transfer and combination (pooling) of losses • a social device in which the losses of a few are paid by many

insurance commissioner • the state official responsible for the regulation of the business of insurance

insurance contract • the agreement that transfers financial risk from a policyowner to an insurer. It may begin with an oral agreement but then is usually converted to written form.

insurance equation • an equation which shows that an insurance company's receipts (premiums, investment earnings, and other income) equal its cost factors (losses, expenses, and profit)

insurance management • the process of determining when, how, how much, and where to insure risks. It is a more narrow term than risk management.

insurance policy • *See* insurance contract

insured • a person whose life, health, or property is covered under an insurance contract. The policyowner may or may not also be an insured.

insuring agreement • that part of an insurance contract that spells out the basic promise of the insurance company to pay benefits according to the terms of the policy

interest option • a life insurance settlement option under which the death proceeds are retained by the insurer temporarily, with only the interest earnings thereon distributed to the beneficiary

interest-sensitive whole life insurance • a current assumption whole life insurance policy under which a low initial premium is guaranteed for a period of time, often 3 or 5 years. After that time, the premium is recalculated on the basis of current mortality, interest, and expense assumptions.

interinsurance exchange • *See* reciprocal exchange

intermediate care • care that involves occasional nursing and rehabilitative care that must be based on a doctor's orders and can be performed only by or under the supervision of skilled medical personnel

international travel medical insurance • interim medical insurance for international travelers. It is usually folded into a broader policy to cover many non-health-related travel contingencies.

irrevocable beneficiary • a beneficiary that cannot be changed by the policyowner without the beneficiary's permission '

ISO (Insurance Services Office) • an advisory organization that provides various services to insurance companies, including the development and filing of standardized insurance forms

joint annuity • an annuity with benefit payments that continue only until the first death among specified lives

joint-and-last-survivor annuity • an annuity with benefit payments that continue until the last death among specified lives

joint-and-two-thirds annuity • a joint-and-survivor annuity with periodic benefit payments that drop to two-thirds of the former amount following the first death among the annuitants

joint-life (first-to-die) policy • a type of life insurance policy covering two or more persons in which the proceeds are payable on the death of the first one to die

joint underwriting association • an association, or pool, of automobile insurers that writes hard-to-place drivers in some states

judicial bond • a bond required by courts, including fiduciary bonds and litigation bonds

jumbo risk policy • a policy with extremely large potential losses

key employee • a person in an organization whose capital, technical knowledge, skills, experience, business connections, or other attributes make him or her highly valuable to the organization's financial success

key employee (person) insurance • insurance designed to protect a business firm against the loss of income that results from the death or disability of a key employee

last clear chance doctrine • the legal principle that holds that, although a claimant is negligent, the defendant is liable if he or she had the last clear chance to avoid an accident and failed to take advantage of that chance

late remittance offer • an offer made by an insurer to the owner of a lapsed life insurance policy that invites him or her to pay the premium and reinstate the coverage without having to provide evidence of insurability

law of large numbers • a mathematical principle stating that, as the number of independent trials or events is increased, the actual results from those trials or events will come closer and closer to the results that one would expect to occur based on the underlying probability

legal reserve • the minimum amount of the reserve, as specified by state law, that must be maintained by a life insurer to meet its assumed future claim costs under a block of policies. It is discounted for future premium and investment income under those policies.

legal wrong • the invasion of a legal right. It can be either criminal or civil.

less value statute • a state law that prohibits a life insurer from promising something on the face of the policy while taking it away in the "fine print," such as by offering a settlement option of less value than the policy's death proceeds

liability risk • a possibility of loss as a result of being held legally responsible for an injury to another, usually for bodily injury or damage to his or her property

license bond • a bond that is often required by state and local governments for persons in many types of occupations that need licensing

lien • a method of treating substandard applicants for life insurance in which the policy is issued as standard except that the death proceeds are reduced if death occurs within the first few years of coverage

life annuity • an annuity whose benefit payments continue for the duration of a designated life

life annuity certain • a life annuity that provides a guaranteed minimum number of benefit payments whether the annuitant lives or dies. It is a combination of an annuity certain and a pure deferred life annuity.

life-care facility • *See* continuing care retirement community

life income option • a life insurance settlement option, and in some insurance policies a nonforfeiture option, under which the proceeds are distributed over the lifetime of the recipient, perhaps subject to some type of minimum guarantee as to the aggregate amount to be paid

life insurance • insurance that provides for payment of a specified amount at the insured's death or, possibly, at a specified date if the insured is still living

limited agent • an agent who does not have the authority to bind the insurance company to provide coverage for an applicant

limited-payment life insurance • a form of whole life insurance for which premiums are based on the assumption that they will be paid for only a specified number of years or until a specified age of the insured

line • a type of insurance such as life, medical expense, disability income, homeowners, or automobile liability

liquidation • the process of dissolving a financially troubled insurance company by an insurance commissioner

liquidation period • the period of time during which annuity benefit payments are made

liquidity • an asset characteristic that describes the extent to which the asset can be converted into cash quickly without loss of value

litigation bond • a bond whose purpose is to require a person or organization who is seeking a court remedy to protect other parties from damages if the party seeking the remedy does not prevail

Lloyd's association • an association of individual insurers in which insurance is underwritten by its members rather than by the association itself

Lloyd's of London • a British organization made up of and regulating the activities of members, both individual and corporate, who act as insurers. The organization itself does not write insurance.

loading • that portion of an insurance rate or premium that covers the insurer's expenses, profit, and contingency margin

long-term care insurance • a form of health insurance that usually provides coverage for custodial care, intermediate care, and skilled-nursing care. Benefits may also be available for home health care, adult day care, and assisted living. Benefits are usually limited to a specified dollar amount per day.

long-term disability income insurance • disability income coverage that provides extended benefits after a person has been disabled for a period of 6 months or longer

look-back period • a specific time period prior to Medicaid eligibility during which Medicaid benefits are reduced (or their onset postponed) if assets were disposed of at less than their fair market value

loss assessment coverage • a coverage in many property and liability insurance policies that pays the insured's share of losses levied against members of a homeowners or condominium association

loss exposure • a loss that prospectively might occur

loss frequency • the number of losses that occur within a given time period among a given number of units exposed to that loss possibility

loss payable clause • a clause used to protect a lender's insurable interest in personal property. If a loss occurs, the lender receives payment to the extent of its insurable interest.

loss prevention • activities that are designed to reduce loss frequency or the chance that a loss will occur

loss ratio • most commonly, the ratio of losses and loss adjustment expenses to premiums earned

loss ratio method of rate making • a method in which the actual loss ratio is compared to the desired or expected loss ratio to determine the change needed in an existing insurance rate

loss reduction • a category of activities that is designed to reduce loss severity or the size of a loss if it should occur

loss reserve • in property and liability insurance, an insurer's liability for losses that have already occurred but that have not yet been paid or otherwise settled

loss severity • the size of a loss or the average size of a group of losses

lost instrument bond • a bond which guarantees that the principal will reimburse the insurer of lost securities if the original securities turn up and their holder is able to collect on them

major medical insurance • a medical insurance plan designed to provide substantial protection against catastrophic medical expenses. There are few exclusions and limitations, but deductibles and coinsurance are commonly used.

malpractice insurance • a type of professional liability insurance for those in occupations where an act or omission is likely to result in bodily injury

managed care • a process to deliver cost-effective health care without sacrificing quality or access. Common characteristics include controlled access to providers, comprehensive case management, preventive care, risk sharing, and high-quality care.

marital deduction • an unlimited amount that can be taken as a deduction against the federal gift and estate tax for transfers to the donor's spouse

mass • as a characteristic of a statistical group or an insured group, sufficient size within such a group as to allow the true underlying probability to emerge

master contract • a contract issued to someone other than the persons insured that provides benefits to a group of individuals who have a specific relationship to the policyowner

material • a condition or circumstance that is so important as to affect whether an insurer will accept an applicant or the terms under which it will accept the applicant

maximum possible loss • the worst loss that could happen

maximum probable loss • the worst loss that is likely to happen

Medicaid • a joint federal and state program to provide medical expense benefits for certain classes of low-income individuals and families

medical expense insurance • protection against financial losses that result from medical bills because of an accident or illness

Medical Information Bureau (MIB) • an organization sponsored by its member life insurance companies to gather and maintain principally medical information disclosed by applicants for life insurance

medical payments coverage • a coverage in many liability policies that pays the medical expenses of persons injured on an insured premises or because of the actions of an insured. Payments are made, regardless of fault, in the hope of reducing liability claims. • in automobile insurance, a coverage that pays medical and funeral expenses incurred by a covered person in an automobile accident

medical savings account (MSA) • an alternative to first-dollar coverage under a medical expense plan. An employee is given medical expense coverage that has a high deductible, and money is deposited into the medical savings account so that the employee can pay for expenses below the deductible amount. Any monies not used at the end of the year are paid to the employee.

Medicare • the health insurance portion of the Social Security program that is available to persons aged 65 or older and limited categories of persons under age 65

Medicare carve-out • an employer-provided medical expense plan for persons over age 65 under which benefits are reduced to the extent that they are payable under Medicare for the same expense

Medicare+Choice • the option that allows beneficiaries to select HMOs and other alternatives to the traditional Medicare program

Medicare secondary rules • regulations that specify when Medicare will be secondary to an employer's medical expense plan for disabled employees and active employees aged 65 or older

Medicare SELECT policy • a medigap policy that pays benefits for nonemergency services only if care is received from network providers

Medicare supplement • an employer-provided medical expense plan for employees aged 65 or older under which benefits are provided for certain specific expenses not covered under Medicare. These can include a portion of expenses not paid by Medicare because of deductibles, coinsurance, or copayments, and certain expenses excluded by Medicare such as prescription drugs. • Also, an individual policy to supplement Medicare. *See* medigap insurance

medigap insurance • an individual health insurance contract that covers certain expenses not covered by Medicare. These expenses include such items as deductibles, copayments, and noncovered services such as prescription drugs.

Mental Health Parity Act • federal legislation that requires annual and lifetime dollar limits on mental health benefits to be on par with limits that apply to other medical conditions. The act applies to employers with more than 50 employees.

misappropriation • the unlawful retention of funds that belong to someone else

miscellaneous type vehicle endorsement • an automobile insurance endorsement to insure vehicles such as all-terrain vehicles, dune buggies, golf carts, motor homes, motorcycles, and the like

misrepresentation • a false and material statement made by an applicant for insurance. It is the basis for the insurer to make the contract voidable.

misstatement of age or sex clause • a life insurance policy provision that specifies that, if the insured's age or sex has been misstated, the benefits payable under the policy will be adjusted to what the premium paid would have purchased at the correct age or sex

mixed-model HMO • an HMO that has characteristics of two or more of the basic HMO forms. It occurs most often when one HMO purchases a different type of HMO or when an HMO expands its capacity or geographic region by adding other medical care providers under a different type of arrangement.

mobilehome insurance • insurance coverage, somewhat similar to homeowners insurance, that provides coverage to owner-occupants of mobile homes

modified cash refund annuity • a refund annuity sometimes used in contributory pension plans that specifies that if the employee dies before receiving total benefit payments equal to his or her share of the purchase price, the difference will be refunded in cash

modified endowment contract (MEC) • a life insurance policy that fails to meet the Internal Revenue Code's 7-pay test. Distributions, therefore, receive less favorable tax treatment than other life insurance contracts receive.

modified no-fault • a no-fault system with the right to sue another party once certain monetary thresholds are exceeded

modified whole life insurance • a form of whole life insurance in which a level premium lower than that for conventional whole life insurance is charged for the first few policy years and a higher level premium is charged thereafter

moral hazard • a dishonest tendency that is likely to increase loss frequency and/or severity

mortality table • a table that shows the number of persons living or dying at specified ages. It is used to calculate life insurance and annuity premiums.

mortgage clause • a clause used to protect a lender's insurable interest in real property. If a loss occurs, the lender receives payments to the extent of its insurable interest, even if a policyowner's claim is denied.

motor carrier insurance • insurance designed for businesses that provide transportation by vehicles in the furtherance of a commercial enterprise

motor truck cargo insurance • a type of inland marine insurance policy used by common carriers or contract carriers to cover customers' goods when the carrier is legally liable for damage

MSA • *See* medical savings account (MSA)

mutual holding company • a holding company controlled by policyowners that owns a stock insurance company

mutual insurance company • a not-for-profit insurance company owned by its policyowners, who elect its board of directors

NAIC • *See* National Association of Insurance Commissioners

name • a member of Lloyd's of London

named insured • the term often applied to the owner of an insurance policy, particularly in property and liability insurance. If not also a policyowner, the term usually includes the spouse if living in the same household.

named nonowner coverage • an automobile insurance endorsement for persons who want coverage but do not own a covered auto

named-perils policy • an insurance contract that covers only losses that arise from one of a series of listed perils. If the peril is not listed, it is not covered by the policy.

National Association of Insurance Commissioners (NAIC) • a voluntary association of state insurance regulatory officials which is involved in financial examinations of insurers and which develops model insurance laws and regulations

National Flood Insurance Program (NFIP) • a federal program that provides subsidized insurance for the peril of flood

negligence • an unintentional tort in the form of an action or omission that leads to the injury of another party

net amount at risk • in a life insurance policy, the difference between the policy's face amount and the reserve at any point in time

net level annual premium • in life insurance, the actuarial spreading of the net single premium on a level basis over a policy's premium-paying period

net payment cost index • a method of estimating the net cost of life insurance on a time-value-adjusted basis assuming that the policy's death benefit will be paid at the end of a specified time period

net single premium • in life insurance, the amount needed today for all insureds in a classification, together with future investment earnings, to pay all claims within that class of insureds

network-model HMO • an HMO that contracts with two or more independent groups of physicians to provide medical services to its subscribers

newly acquired auto • in personal automobile insurance, an automobile that otherwise meets the definition of a covered auto but is acquired after the effective date of the policy

no-fault automobile insurance • a modification of the traditional tort liability system that provides first-party benefits to injured persons and imposes some restrictions on their rights to sue negligent parties

nonadmitted asset • an asset of an insurer that is not permitted by regulatory authorities to be counted as an asset for annual statement purposes

nonadmitted insurer • an insurer that does not have a license to conduct insurance business in a particular state

nonassessible policy • a policy where the initial premium is the final premium (other than reductions for dividends). There can be no assessment of the policyowner if the premium is inadequate.

noncancelable • in an insurance contract, the right of the insured to renew the coverage at each policy anniversary date, usually up to some stated age. The coverage may not be terminated by the insurer during the term of coverage. Also the rates for the coverage are guaranteed in the contract, although they are not necessarily level.

nonfinancial risk • a category of risk for which the possibility of loss does not represent a reduction in monetary value, although sometimes such losses are compensated by the award of money. An example is pain and suffering.

nonforfeiture options • a set of choices available regarding how a life insurance policyowner can use the policy's cash value. These choices include the options to surrender for cash, buy a reduced amount of paid-up whole life insurance, or buy extended term insurance. For long-term care insurance, an optional benefit provides extended benefits or a cash refund if a policy lapses after it has been in force for a specified number of years.

noninsurance transfer • the contractual transfer of risk by a contract other than an insurance contract. Subcontracting is an example.

nonoccupational disability laws • *See* temporary disability laws

nonowned auto • in personal automobile insurance, a vehicle not owned by or furnished for the regular use of the insured or any family member • in commercial automobile insurance, an automobile owned by a named insured's employee or a member of his or her household, but only while used in the named insured's business or personal affairs

nonparticipating policy • a type of insurance policy that pays no dividends to the policyowner

nonscheduled dental plan • a dental plan that pays benefits on the basis of reasonable-and-customary charges. However, there may be a schedule of covered dental services.

non-tax-qualified policy • a type of long-term care insurance contract that fails to meet certain standards of the Health Insurance Portability and Accountability Act for favorable tax treatment

notice of loss • the process by which the insurer is notified that a loss has occurred. This begins the loss adjustment process. The actual process of notification is spelled out in a policy and varies by line of insurance.

nursing home care • a term that encompasses skilled-nursing care, intermediate care, and custodial care in a licensed facility

OASDHI • the old age, survivors, disability, and heath insurance program of the federal government. This program consists of Social Security and Medicare.

OASDI • the old-age, survivors, and disability insurance portion of the OASDHI program, commonly referred to as Social Security

obligee • the party to a surety bond who is reimbursed for damages because of the failure of the principal to uphold an agreement

occurrence policy • a liability insurance policy that covers claims that arise out of occurrences that take place during the policy period, regardless of when claims are made

open competition law • a law that relies mainly on competitive forces in the insurance marketplace to produce acceptable insurance rates

open-ended HMO • an HMO that allows a subscriber to go outside the HMO network of medical care providers

open-panel plan • a benefit plan under which covered persons can obtain services from any practitioner or may have to select one from a limited list of practitioners who have agreed to the plan's terms and conditions

open-perils policy • an insurance contract that covers all types of losses except those that are specifically excluded by the policy's terms

opportunity cost • the benefit given up by taking one course of action rather than another—for example, the investment income that is lost when funds are kept as cash rather than invested

optionally renewable • an insurance contract in which the insurer reserves the right to refuse to renew the coverage at each policy anniversary date, either for specified reasons or for any and all reasons

ordinance or law coverage • insurance to provide coverage to comply with extra costs to bring damaged property in conformity with current building codes or ordinances

ordinary life insurance • a form of whole life insurance for which premiums are based on the assumption that they will be paid until the insured's death and which provides a guaranteed cash value

other insurance clause • a provision in property and liability insurance policies that specifies how losses are shared if more than one policy covers a loss

other than collision • the term used in automobile insurance to refer to physical damage to a vehicle that is not caused by collision (formerly referred to as *comprehensive*)

ownership provision • in life insurance, a clause that specifies that the insured is the owner of the policy, (unless the application states otherwise), and that the owner can change the beneficiary (unless named irrevocably), assign the policy, and exercise other ownership rights

own occupation • a definition of total disability that requires a disabled person to be unable to perform each and every duty (or material duties) of his or her regular occupation

package policy • an insurance policy that combines two or more types of insurance, often property and liability insurance, in a single contract

paid-up additions • additional amounts of permanent life insurance purchased on a single-premium basis through the use of the policy's dividends

pain and suffering • intangible losses arising from bodily injury

parol evidence rule • a legal principle that specifies that oral contemporaneous evidence is inadmissible to contradict or to vary the terms of a valid written contract

partial advance funding • the funding method used by Social Security and Medicare whereby taxes are more than sufficient to pay current benefits and also to provide some accumulation of assets for the payment of future benefits

partial disability • the inability to perform some stated percentage of job duties or to take a longer-than-normal amount of time in which to complete job duties

participating policy • a type of insurance policy that can pay dividends to the policyowner

participation rate • in an equity-indexed annuity, the percentage (always less than 100 percent) of the increase in the stock index that is used to credit the account of the annuity contract owner

particular risk • a loss possibility that affects only individuals or small groups of individuals at the same time, rather than a large segment of society. An example is the possibility of loss due to the theft of one's wallet.

pay-as-you-go financing • a funding method for insurance whereby taxes are set at a level to provide just enough income to pay future benefits

per diem basis • a method of paying under long-term care insurance policies in which the insured receives a specified daily or weekly benefit amount regardless of the actual cost of care

percentage participation • the percentage of covered medical expenses that must be paid by a person receiving benefits and that will not be paid by a medical expense plan

peril • an event that causes a loss. Fire, earthquake, and flood are examples.

permanent life insurance • *See* cash value life insurance

permit bond • a bond often required by state and local governments for persons engaged in various types of activities for which a permit is needed. This guarantee, for example, is in compliance with laws or payment of taxes.

personal articles floater • an open-perils policy for certain scheduled and valuable items of personal property

personal auto policy (PAP) • the most common automobile insurance policy for individuals. It is a package policy that can provide liability, medical, no-fault, uninsured motorists, and physical damage coverages.

personal effects floater • a policy to provide open-perils worldwide coverage for baggage, clothes, cameras, and other items commonly worn or carried by tourists

personal injury • a type of legal liability that is neither bodily injury nor property damage. Examples include libel, slander, invasion of privacy, false arrest, and defamation of character.

personal injury protection (PIP) endorsement • the usual name that is applied to an endorsement that provides a state's no-fault benefits

personal insurance • insurance purchased by individuals and families rather than by businesses and other organizations

personal producing general agent (PPGA) • an agent of a life insurance company who is the insurer's general agent in a given territory but whose primary task is to sell the insurer's products, rather than to build an agency force for the insurer

personal property • a tangible asset, other than real estate, that is subject to ownership

personal property floater • a policy to provide open-perils coverage for unscheduled personal property on a worldwide basis

personal risk • a loss possibility associated with death, injury, illness, old age, and unemployment

physical hazard • a physical condition relating to location, structure, occupancy, exposure, and the like

plan change provision • an insurance policy provision which states that the parties may agree to change the terms of the contract

point-of-service (POS) plan • a hybrid arrangement that combines aspects of a traditional medical expense plan with an HMO or a PPO. At the time of medical treatment, a participant can elect whether to receive treatment within the plan's network or outside of the network.

policy loan • an advance of money available to a life insurance policyowner from the policy's cash value

policyholder • *See* policyowner

policyowner • the person or entity that owns an insurance policy. The policyowner generally has the right to change, renew, or cancel the policy and the obligation to comply with policy conditions such as premium payments.

portability • the ability to continue employer-provided or employer-sponsored benefits after termination of employment • the concept of allowing an employee to use evidence of prior medical expense coverage to eliminate or reduce the length of any preexisting-conditions provision when the employee moves to another medical expense plan

POS plan • *See* point-of-service plan

PPO • *See* preferred-provider organization

preadmission certification • a requirement under many medical expense plans that a covered person or his or her physician obtain prior authorization for any nonemergency hospitalization

preexisting-conditions provision • a provision that excludes coverage, but possibly only for a limited period of time, for a physical or mental condition for which a covered person in a benefit plan received treatment or medical advice within a specified time period prior to becoming eligible for coverage

preferred-provider organization (PPO) • a group of health care providers that contracts with employers, insurance companies, union trust funds, third-party administrators, or others to provide medical care services at a reduced fee. PPOs can be organized by the providers themselves or by organizations such as insurance companies, the Blues, or groups of employers.

premises liability • bodily injury or property damage liability of an owner or tenant because of a condition in or arising out of premises that are owned or occupied

premium • the price charged for a period of coverage provided by an insurance policy and found by multiplying the rate by the number of units of coverage

premium-conversion plan • a cafeteria plan provision that allows employees to elect a before-tax salary reduction to pay for their contributions to an employee-sponsored health plan or certain other types of employee benefits

premium tax • a tax levied by a state on gross insurance premiums

prescription drug expense benefits • basic medical expense benefits for the cost of prescription drugs. These benefits are often separate from other medical expense coverage because of techniques that can be used to contain costs.

presumed negligence • negligence that can be assumed from the facts of certain situations. It can occur if (1) the action would not normally cause injury without negligence, (2) the action is within the control of the party to be held liable, and (3) the party to be held liable has superior knowledge of the cause of the accident or the injured party is unable to prove negligence.

presumptive-disability provision • a provision in a disability income contract by which an individual is presumed to be totally disabled as long as certain circumstances exist. Examples include loss of sight or one hand. A person with a presumed disability may in fact be able to return to work.

primary beneficiary • the beneficiary in a life insurance policy who, if living at the time of the insured's death, is entitled to receive the policy proceeds upon the insured's death

primary insurance amount (PIA) • the amount a worker will receive under Social Security if he or she retires at full retirement age or becomes disabled. It is also the amount on which all other Social Security income benefits are based.

principal • the entity for whom an agent acts such as an insurance company • the party to a surety bond who buys the bond and who agrees to perform certain acts or to fulfill certain obligations

prior approval law • a law regulating insurance rates that requires that proposed rates be approved by the regulatory authority before they may be used by the insurer

probate estate • all property interests possessed by a decedent that pass to others by will or under a law of intestacy

probationary period • in group insurance, a period at the start of a person's employment during which the person is not eligible to participate in the group insurance plan

products liability • bodily injury or property damage liability caused by a defective product that is manufactured or sold by a business

professional liability insurance • insurance that protects against liability for the failure to use the degree of skill expected of a person in a particular occupation

prohibited provisions • certain provisions that states do not allow insurers to include in their contracts

proof of loss • a statement that details the specifics of a loss. It can be a sworn written statement or, in life insurance, a death certificate. The specifics are spelled out in policies and vary by line of insurance.

property damage • destruction or damage to real or personal property

property risk • a loss possibility associated with the loss or destruction of property

prospectus • a highly detailed document accompanying the sale of securities, including variable life insurance, variable universal life insurance, and variable annuity contracts, providing full disclosure of all of the provisions of the contract

protection and indemnity insurance • the term often applied to liability coverage in watercraft policies

proximate cause • one requirement for proving negligence. There must be a continuous succession of events from the negligent act to the final event causing injury.

public adjuster • a person who represents a claimant in negotiating the settlement of a claim against an insurance company

public official bond • a bond often required of persons who are elected or appointed to certain public positions and that guarantees that the principal will uphold the promise made to faithfully and honestly perform the official duties of his or her office

punitive damages • damages awarded in addition to bodily injury or property damage when a defendant's behavior is so severe that the legal system feels an example should be made of the behavior

pure annuity • a life annuity that provides no guaranteed minimum number of benefit payments or refund of the purchase price

pure (net) rate • that portion of an insurance rate that is designed to cover future loss costs

pure no-fault • a no-fault system with no right to sue a negligent party

pure premium method of rate making • a method in which a pure or net rate is calculated, after which a loading is calculated and added to the pure or net rate

pure risk • a possibility of loss that involves only two outcomes, loss or no loss

qualified beneficiary • any employee, spouse, or dependent child who, on the day before a qualifying COBRA event, was covered under the employer's group health plan

qualified long-term care insurance contract • a long-term care contract that meets specified standards and qualifies for favorable tax treatment under the Health Insurance Portability and Accountability Act. *Also called* tax-qualified policy

qualified long-term care services • services that must be provided by a qualified long-term care insurance contract. These include necessary diagnostic, preventive, therapeutic, curative, treatment, and rehabilitative services and maintenance or personal care services that are required by a chronically ill individual and are provided by a plan of care prescribed by a licensed health care practitioner.

qualifying event • in life insurance, a condition or event that triggers the payment of accelerated benefits such as an illness that is expected to reduce the insured's life expectancy to 24 months or less • under COBRA, an event that triggers eligibility to elect continuing coverage

quarters of coverage • the basis on which eligibility for benefits under the OASDI portion of Social Security is determined. Credit for up to 4 quarters of coverage may be earned in any calendar year.

rate • the price charged for each unit of insurance coverage

rate making • the process of determining insurance rates. It involves the determination of future loss costs and adding the necessary margins for expenses and profit.

rate-up age method • a method of treating a substandard applicant for life insurance that bases the premium rate and policy values on an age older than the actual age

real property • land and anything that is growing on it, erected on it, or affixed to it, and the bundle of rights inherent in the ownership

reasonable-and-customary charge • a charge that falls within the range of fees normally charged for a given procedure by physicians with similar training and experience in a geographic region. It is usually based on some percentile of the range of charges for specific medical procedures.

rebating • the usually illegal practice of returning a part of the premium paid to the policyowner (except as a dividend) as a price-cutting sales inducement

reciprocal exchange • a not-for-profit unincorporated mutual association managed by an attorney-in-fact. Each member of the reciprocal is both an insured and an insurer of the other members.

reentry term insurance • a form of renewable term life insurance under which one rate schedule is used if the insured can prove continuing insurability. A higher schedule is used if the insured cannot prove continuing insurability.

refund annuity • a life annuity that promises to return in some manner a portion or all of the purchase price or to provide a guaranteed minimum number of benefit payments

rehabilitation • the process, overseen by an insurance commissioner, of restoring an insurance company to financial stability

rehabilitation benefit • a benefit under workers' compensation laws or disability income plans that provides rehabilitative services for disabled workers. Benefits may be given for medical rehabilitation and for vocational rehabilitation, including training, counseling, and job placement.

rehabilitation provision • a provision in a disability income contract that allows a person to receive reduced benefits during trial work periods in rehabilitative employment. The original benefit is resumed if the person is unable to perform the rehabilitative employment.

reimbursement basis • the method of paying long-term care insurance benefits that reimburses the insured for actual expenses incurred up to the specified benefit amount

reinstatement provision • in life insurance, a clause giving the owner of a lapsed policy the right to reacquire the coverage under certain conditions

reinsurance • an arrangement in which an insurance company transfers to another insurance company some or all of the risks it has taken on through the writing of primary insurance

reinsurance facility • a system of providing automobile insurance to high-risk drivers. Insurers write coverage but assign premiums to a statewide reinsurance pool. All insurers in the state share the pool's losses and expenses.

renewability • a feature frequently found in individual term life insurance that allows the policyowner to renew the policy for another period of protection, up to a stated point in time, without having to show evidence of insurability

replacement • the replacing of one life insurance policy with another. To prevent financial harm to the policyowner, agents and insurers must follow prescribed procedures.

replacement cost • the method of valuing property losses where no deduction is made for depreciation

representation • a statement made by an applicant to the insurer at the time of or prior to the formation of a contract that, if false and material, may provide a basis for the insurer to make the contract voidable

reserve • an amount that must be maintained by an insurance company in order to meet definite future obligation. *See also* legal reserve, loss reserve, unearned premium reserve

residual-disability benefits • a provision for the replacement of lost earnings due to less-than-total disability. The benefit is based on a person's reduction in earnings rather than his or her physical condition.

residual market • the market that consists of specialty insurers and government programs to provide insurance for hard-to-insure drivers or property

respite care • occasional full-time care at home for a person who is receiving home health care. Coverage for such care under a long-term care insurance policy enables family members (or other persons) who are providing much of the home care to take a needed break.

restoration of benefits • a provision in long-term care insurance that provides for a restoration of used benefits after a period without claims

return-of-premium option • a provision in disability insurance that provides for the return of some portion of premiums at specified intervals, such as 5 years or 10 years, if no claims have been made during that period

revocable beneficiary • a beneficiary that can be changed by the policyowner without the beneficiary's permission

rider • the term used in life insurance in place of the term endorsement

risk • the possibility of loss

risk and insurance survey form • a tool in the form of a questionnaire or checklist used to identify the risks that confront a family or organization

risk avoidance • a risk control method that involves avoiding situations that include certain types of risks

risk control • a program to minimize losses through such activities as avoidance, separation, diversification, combination, loss prevention and reduction, and some noninsurance transfers of responsibility for loss

risk financing • a program to pay for losses through such means as risk retention in various ways and risk transfer, including insurance

risk identification • the process that involves the careful and systematic discovery of all the risks that confront a household or organization

risk management • a coordinated program for treating risks based on risk identification, risk measurement, choice and use of methods of treatment, and administration

risk retention • a method of risk financing that involves assuming the financial consequences associated with risk

risk-tolerance level • the degree to which an individual is attracted to or averse to the possibility of loss

risk transfer • a method of risk financing that involves the shifting of the financial consequences of risk to someone else

robbery • the removal of property from one person by someone else who has either caused harm or threatened to cause harm to the person. It also includes situations in which property is taken in an unlawful act that a person has witnessed.

salary continuation plan • *See* sick-leave plan

savings bank life insurance • life insurance allowed to be written by mutual savings banks in Connecticut, Massachusetts, and New York on residents of, and persons regularly employed in, those three states

schedule rating • the process of developing specific insurance rates by applying a schedule that measures the relative quantity of fire hazard to the particular loss exposure

scheduled dental plan • a dental plan under which benefits are paid up to the amount specified in a fee schedule

second surgical opinion • a cost-containment strategy under which covered persons are encouraged or required to obtain the opinion of another physician after certain categories of surgery have been recommended. If a second opinion is mandatory, benefits are reduced if the second opinion is not obtained. Benefits are usually provided for the cost of a third opinion if the opinions of the first two physicians are in disagreement.

second-to-die policy • *See* survivorship life policy

Sec. 79 plan • a group term life insurance plan that qualifies for favorable federal income tax treatment under the Internal Revenue Code

segregation • a risk control method that involves the separation or dispersion of items or lives susceptible to loss

self-insurance • a formal program of risk retention usually characterized by factors necessary for a sound insurance enterprise, including funding based on actuarial calculations

self-insured retention • the initial portion of a loss under an umbrella policy that must be assumed by the policyowner when there is no underlying policy to cover the loss

service representative • a salaried specialist of an insurance company or large agency who assists agents in writing more complex lines of insurance

settlement options • ways in which a life insurance policy's death proceeds can be taken, typically in cash, under an interest option, under a fixed-period or fixed-amount option, or under a life-income option

7-pay test • a test to determine if a particular life insurance contract is or is not a modified endowment contract. If the total premium paid into the policy in the first 7 years or in the 7 years following a material change in it exceeds the sum of the net level premiums that would be needed to pay up the policy in 7 years, the policy is an MEC.

shared market • *See* residual market

shopper's guide • a state-approved booklet that must be provided to potential purchasers of certain types of insurance to enable them to better evaluate the benefits and costs of the insurance

short-term disability income plans • disability income coverage with a duration of 6 months or less. Such plans may be insured or uninsured.

sick-leave plan • an uninsured arrangement to replace lost income for a limited period of time, often starting on the first day of disability

single premium annuity • an annuity paid with a single premium rather than with installment payments

skilled-nursing care • daily nursing and rehabilitative care that can be performed only by or under the supervision of skilled medical personnel and that must be based on doctors' orders

skilled-nursing facility • *See* extended care facility

social adequacy • a principle emphasized by social insurance programs in which benefits are designed to provide a minimum floor of income to all beneficiaries, regardless of their economic status. Social adequacy also is reflected in the provision of disproportionately large benefits relative to contributions for some groups of beneficiaries, particularly lower-income groups.

social insurance • government-run or government-regulated insurance programs designed primarily to solve major social problems that affect a large portion of society. Distinguishing characteristics are compulsory employment-related coverage, partial or total employer financing, benefits prescribed by law, benefits as a matter of right, and emphasis on social adequacy.

Social Security • the term commonly used to identify the old-age, survivors, and disability (OASDI) program of the federal government

Social Security rider • a policy amendment to provide additional disability income benefits payable when an individual is disabled but does not qualify for Social Security disability benefits

Social Security Statement • a statement issued by the Social Security Administration that enables an employee to verify his or her contributions to the Social Security and Medicare programs. The statement also contains an estimate of benefits that will be available because of retirement, disability, or death.

specific (schedule) rate • a rate that is created for an individual insured based on that insured's particular risk characteristics

specified disease insurance • a type of medical expense coverage that provides benefits for persons who have certain specified diseases or medical events, such as cancer or heart attacks. The policy may pay for actual medical expenses or, more likely, may pay a specified dollar amount regardless of actual medical expenses and without regard to other coverages.

specified-perils policy • *See* named-perils policy

speculative risk • a possibility of loss with three possible outcomes: loss, no loss, or gain

split-dollar carve-out arrangement • a plan whereby life insurance is provided to selected employees under a split-dollar arrangement that is superimposed on a group life insurance plan for employees in general

split-dollar life insurance • a plan under which two parties, usually an employer and an insured employee, share the premium costs, death proceeds, and perhaps cash value of a life insurance policy pursuant to a prearranged agreement

split limits • in liability insurance, separate limits that apply to any one person for bodily injury, to the aggregate for all bodily injury claims, and to property damage

staff adjuster • an employee of an insurance company whose full-time job is adjusting claims for that insurer

staff-model HMO • an HMO that owns its own facilities and hires its own physicians. It may also own hospitals, laboratories, or pharmacies, or it may contract for these services.

standard policy provisions laws • state laws that require life and health insurance policies to include certain provisions but allow insurers to select the actual wording as long as it is at least as favorable to the policyowner as the statutory language

static risk • in contrast with dynamic risk, a possibility of loss that exists even in the absence of changes in society. Hurricanes are an example.

step-rate annuity • an annuity for which future benefits increase, possibly at a compound annual rate. Step-rate annuities are often used in structured settlements.

stock insurance company • a profit-seeking insurance company owned by its stockholders

stop-loss limit • the maximum amount of out-of-pocket medical expenses that a covered person must pay in a given period (usually one year). After this limit is reached, future copayments and deductibles are waived for the remainder of the period.

straight life annuity • *See* pure annuity

strict compliance rule • a legal principle that specifies that a written contract will normally be enforced on the basis of strict conformity with the terms contained in that contract

strict liability • liability under law regardless of whether fault or negligence can be proved

structured settlement • an agreement to pay a specified set of periodic benefits in lieu of (or in addition to) a single, lump-sum amount

subrogation • a process by which an insurer takes over the legal rights its insured has against a responsible third party

substandard annuity • an annuity whose benefit payments are larger per dollar of purchase price than those of a standard annuity because of the annuitant's impaired health

substandard market • *See* residual market

suicide provision • a life insurance policy provision that specifies that if the insured, whether sane or insane, commits suicide during the first one or 2 years of the policy, the insurer will be liable only for a return of the premium

supplemental plan • *See* buy-up plan

surety • the party to a surety bond who agrees to indemnify the principal for damages because of the obligee's failure to uphold an agreement

surety bond • a bond used when an individual or organization wants a guarantee of indemnity if a second party fails to perform a specified act or to fulfill an obligation

surplus line broker • *See* excess line broker

surrender charge • a fee imposed on the owners of certain types of life insurance policies and annuities at the time they surrender their contracts

surrender cost index • a method of estimating the net cost of life insurance on a time-value-adjusted basis, assuming the policy will be surrendered at the end of a specified time period

survivorship (second-to-die) life policy • a type of life insurance policy that covers two or more persons in which the proceeds are payable on the death of the last person to die

target premium • the level renewal premium that the insurer suggests be paid for a universal life insurance policy

tax-qualified policy • a long-term care insurance contract that meets the requirements of the Health Insurance Portability and Accountability Act for favorable income tax treatment

temporary disability law • a law in a few states that requires employers to provide short-term disability income benefits to employees for non-work-related disabilities. Such a law is often referred to as a nonoccupational disability law.

temporary life annuity • an annuity whose benefit payments continue until the earlier of the death of a designated person or the end of a specified period of time

temporary medical insurance • short-term medical insurance that generally provides coverage for periods between 30 days and one year while a person is between permanent medical expense plans

temporary substitute vehicle • in personal auto insurance, a vehicle not owned by the insured while it is used temporarily in place of a covered auto that is out of normal use because of breakdown, repair, servicing, loss, or destruction

term life insurance • a form of life insurance in which the death proceeds are payable in the event of the insured's death during a specified period and nothing is paid if the insured survives to the end of that period

theft • a broad term that encompasses robbery, burglary, shoplifting, and any other act of stealing

third-party-over suit • a suit that can result when the manufacturer of a product that injures one of the employer's workers is sued by the worker who, in turn, sues the employer for improper maintenance of the product

title insurance • protection for the purchaser of real estate against defects in title that occurred prior to the effective date of coverage but are discovered after the effective date

tort • a civil wrong other than breach of contract

transfer-for-value rule • a rule that specifies that, subject to certain exceptions, if a life insurance policy is transferred from one owner to another for valuable consideration, the death proceeds will be subject to federal income taxation

transfer tax • a tax on gifts, estates, or generation-skipping transfers

treaty reinsurance • reinsurance that is obligatory for the original or primary insurer and the reinsurer with respect to every loss exposure covered by the treaty or agreement

trip transit policy • a type of inland marine insurance policy that covers only the particular shipment specified in the policy

twisting • the illegal practice in life insurance of using misrepresentation to induce a policyowner, to his or her disadvantage, to replace a life insurance policy with a new one

umbrella liability insurance • a personal or business liability policy that provides high limits for a broad range of liability situations. The policyowner is required to have underlying liability coverage of specified amounts. Claims not covered by the underlying insurance are subject to a self-insured retention.

uncertainty • a state of mind that arises from the presence of risk and that is characterized by not being sure about something. Uncertainty often is characterized by worry and fear.

underinsured motorists coverage • an automobile insurance coverage that enables an insured to collect from his or her own insurance company for bodily injuries (and property damage in a few states) that are caused by a legally liable but underinsured driver. The recovery is equal to the difference between the limit of the underinsured motorists coverage and the amount of the automobile liability insurance carried by the underinsured driver.

underlying coverage • the underlying policies and limits required by an insurer that provides umbrella liability insurance. If not carried, the insured must absorb this amount of any claim before the umbrella policy pays.

underwriting • the selection (or rejection) and classification of applicants for insurance

unearned premium reserve • in property and liability insurance, an insurer's liability for future claims or premium refunds under a policy as measured by the proportion of the written premiums for those policies that has not been earned by the insurer through the provision of protection for the full policy period

unemployment insurance • joint federal and state programs to provide income benefits to unemployed workers who meet the specific program requirements. In most states, these programs are financed entirely by employer contributions.

unified credit • a cumulative credit that can be taken against a taxpayer's liability for federal gift and/or estate taxes

Uniform Premium Table I • an IRS table used to determine the amount of taxable income from group term life insurance

unilateral contract • a contract in which only one of the parties to it makes a binding promise that, if broken, gives rise to an action against that party for breach of contract

uninsured motorists coverage • an automobile insurance coverage that enables an insured to collect from his or her own insurance company for bodily injuries (and property damage in a few states) that are caused by a legally liable but uninsured driver

universal life insurance • a type of life insurance policy characterized by flexible premiums, a shift of some of the investment risk to the policyowner even though the policyowner is not allowed to direct the investment portfolio, and a choice of death benefit designs

unsatisfied judgment fund • a fund in some states to compensate automobile accident victims who are unable to collect a legal judgment that results from an automobile accident. The maximum amount that can be received is usually equal to a state's financial responsibility limits.

use and file law • a rating law with which rates are filed with the insurance commissioner within a specified time after the rates are first used. The insurance commissioner may, however, disapprove the rates if they are not in compliance with the law.

utilization review • the process of reviewing the appropriateness and quality of medical care provided to patients. It can be conducted on a prospective, concurrent, or retroactive basis.

valued policy • a policy in which the full amount of insurance is paid for a total loss under certain circumstances, regardless of the actual amount that has been lost by the insured

valued policy law • a law in some states that makes valued policies mandatory for insurance on homes or other real estate property. Valued policy laws apply only when property is totally destroyed and only by certain perils.

vanishing premium whole life insurance • a type of current assumption whole life insurance designed so that, if experience is favorable, the accumulation account equals or exceeds the net single premium necessary to pay up the contract

variable annuity • an annuity with benefit payments that vary depending on the performance of selected blocks of the insurer's invested assets

variable life insurance • a type of life insurance policy in which the policyowner directs how the cash value will be invested, and thus bears the investment risk, and in which the death benefit is linked to the investment performance of the policy

variable universal life insurance • a type of life insurance policy that combines the premium flexibility features of universal life insurance with the policyowner-directed investment aspects of variable life insurance

viatical settlement provider • the party who purchases a policy from a viator under a viatical settlement purchase agreement

viatical settlement purchase agreement • contract arranging for the sale of a life insurance policy by a viator to a viatical settlement provider

viator • the policyowner who sells a life insurance policy to a third party

vicarious liability • imputed liability to, for example, owners of vehicles

vision care expense benefits • benefits for vision care expenses that are not usually covered under other medical expense plans. Benefits are provided for the cost of eye examinations and eyeglasses or contact lenses.

void contract • a contract that is entirely without legal effect and, therefore, unenforceable by either party. In essence, a void contract never was a contract.

voidable contract • a contract that can be affirmed or rejected at the option of one of the parties but is binding on the other party

voluntary benefits • a plan offered to employees under which they may purchase insurance coverages with premiums paid through payroll deductions. The employer does not share in the premium cost.

voluntary compensation and employers liability coverage endorsement • an insurance policy endorsement that obligates the insurance company to pay an amount equal to what is available under a state's workers' compensation law to employees who are not covered under the law

waiting period (elimination period) • a period of time that an employee must be disabled before benefits commence under an employee benefit plan, such as disability income insurance, Social Security, and workers' compensation insurance

waiver-of-premium provision • a rider under which, if the insured becomes totally disabled, the insurer will waive the premiums on the policy during the continuance of the disability. It is commonly used in life and health insurance.

warranty • a statement that becomes a part of an insurance contract and that must be strictly complied with. A warranty, if false, makes the policy voidable, even if the false statement is not material.

watercraft insurance • insurance policies to provide liability, physical damage, and medical payments coverage for boat owners

whole life insurance • a form of life insurance that provides death benefits upon the death of the insured, no matter when that occurs, if the policy is kept in force by the policyowner

withdrawal • the right, in some life insurance policies, to take part of the cash value without it being treated as a loan. It is commonly found in forms of universal life insurance.

workers' compensation insurance • insurance under which the insurer agrees to pay all compensation required by workers' compensation laws

workers' compensation law • a type of law enacted in all states under which employers are required to provide benefits to employees for losses that result from work-related accidents or diseases. Benefits include medical care, disability income, income for survivors, and rehabilitative services.

yacht policy • a package policy that provides liability and physical damage coverage for large boats

yearly renewable term insurance • a plan that provides a level amount of insurance for one year, renewable for a stated number of years, with the premium at each renewal date rising at an increasing rate consistent with the rise in the mortality rate over time

Answers to Review Questions and Self-Test Questions

Chapter 1

Answers to Review Questions

1-1. For purposes of this book, *risk* is defined as the *possibility of loss*. Uncertainty is the state of mind of being unsure. As a consequence, uncertainty can vary significantly from one person to another, even when each is confronted with the same set of facts, the same objective reality, or the same risk.

1-2. A fire can cause direct and indirect losses. The damage to the printing equipment and paper are examples of direct losses. The loss of income from having to close temporarily and the extra expense of having to rent other premises at a higher cost are examples of indirect loss. If the fire was a result of Jim's negligence, any damages awarded for bodily injury or property damage to others are examples of direct loss; any income Jim lost while attending court proceedings is an indirect loss.

1-3. a. the possibility of Sally's children losing her financial support
      b. death
      c. her high blood pressure, which increases the chance of loss

1-4. a. physical hazards
      b. attitudinal hazard (carelessness)
      c. moral hazard

1-5. a. Although the probability of death for a woman aged 29 is quite small, she is only one person, and knowledge of the probability is no help in measuring the risk (possibility of loss) she alone faces. If she dies, her family will suffer a loss of her future income that would have been available for their support. The financial loss to her family would be severe even though the chance of loss is small. This situation of low probability but high severity is where insurance works most effectively and efficiently.
      b. Life insurance companies measure their probabilities by observing large numbers (mass) of similar (homogeneous) exposures (females aged 29 insured in the past) in the statistical group from which they make their estimate of the probability of a female dying at age 29. But they also apply this estimate to a large number (mass) of (homogeneous) exposures (females aged 29 insured at present) in estimating the percentage of the currently insured females aged 29 who will die during the year. However, the insurer cannot measure any better than Janet what the probability is that any particular individual in the group will die this year. The probability has meaning in predicting the outcome only when applied to a large number of similar exposure units.

1-6. a. Particular risks are loss possibilities that affect only individuals or small groups of individuals at the same time, rather than a large segment of society. Fundamental risks, in contrast, are loss possibilities that can affect large segments of society at the same time.
      b. Dealing with particular risks is generally thought to be the responsibility of the individuals who are exposed to them. However, some social insurance programs also deal with particular risks. Fundamental risks, on the other hand, are not the fault of any specific individual, and dealing with them is generally thought to be the responsibility of society as a whole through government action.

1-7. Homeownership can give rise to
      a. pure risk by providing a possibility of loss from fire, windstorm, theft, and many other property-related perils as well as from legal liability (for example, the possibility of someone falling down your shaky stairs to the basement).
      b. speculative risk by providing a possibility of a gain or a loss when the home is sold.

1-8. Insurance is concerned mainly with the economic problems created by pure risks where there is only the potential for loss or no loss. The pure risks confronting individuals and businesses are ordinarily divided into three categories: risks involving the person, risks involving loss of or damage to property, and risks involving liability for injury or damage to persons or the property of others.

1-9.   Gambling creates risk, while insurance transfers or reduces a risk that already exists.

1-10. A risk must substantially meet the following five requirements:
- The amount of the loss must be important.
- The loss must be accidental in nature.
- Future losses must be calculable.
- The loss must be definite.
- The risk cannot be associated with an excessively catastrophic loss.

Many insurance risks do not meet each of the requirements perfectly, but when considered as a whole, they may meet the requisites adequately.

1-11. *Risk-tolerance levels* vary from person to person, situation to situation, and risk to risk. Based on research on the risk tolerance of individuals, we know that:
- Most people are more risk averse than they are risk tolerant.
- Risk taking in physical or social activities does not necessarily correlate with high risk tolerance in financial matters.
- The way in which questions about a risk are worded or posed to a person can influence the person's attitude toward that risk.
- Emotions can severely limit a person's ability to make rational decisions about a risk.
- People tend to overestimate low-probability risks and underestimate higher-probability risks.
- People tend to be risk averse if the major impact of a possible loss will fall on them or their loved ones, rather than mainly on strangers.
- Most people have a greater fear about risks with which they are unfamiliar than about risks with which they are familiar.

1-12. Because pure risks generally produce either losses or no losses, they represent a cost to society with little or no offsetting benefit. Losses could cripple a business or cause an individual or family great financial hardship. Direct physical loss, such as fire damage, results in several billion dollars of property loss each year in the United States. Indirect loss is also considerable such as lost profits following a direct loss. Billions of dollars are lost, too, because of the loss of human life values due to such perils as death and disability. Even if no losses ever occur as anticipated, at least three factors add to the costs of risks: (1) fear and worry, (2) less-than-optimum use of resources, and (3) expenses of treating risks.

1-13. a.   Insurance reduces risk by transfer and combination.
       b.   Insurance transfers risk by payment of a premium by the policyowner to the insurer in a contract of indemnity.
       c.   Insurance shares risk by transferring risk from individuals and businesses to a financial institution specializing in risk.
       d.   Insurance collectively bears losses by using group members' contributions to pay losses suffered by some group members.
       e.   Insurance predicts and distributes losses using actuarial estimates based on principles of probability.

1-14. Benefits include: encourages peace of mind, pays losses, increases marginal utility of assets, provides a basis for credit, stimulates saving, provides investment capital, offers advantages of specialization, and fosters loss prevention. The costs of insurance include: operating costs, profits, opportunity costs, increased losses, and adverse selection.

1-15. Social insurance programs tend to have the following characteristics: compulsory employment-related coverage, partial or total employer financing, benefits prescribed by law but not uniform for everyone, benefits as a matter of right, and emphasis on social adequacy rather than individual equity.

1-16. Individual insurance is usually owned by the person or entity who is insured or who owns the property. Group insurance is issued as a single contract to someone other than the person insured and provides coverage to a number of persons.

Individual insurance coverage normally begins with the inception of the contract and ceases with its termination. Under group insurance, individual members may become eligible for coverage long after the inception of the contract or lose their eligibility status long before the contract terminates.

Individual insurance underwriting typically requires the individual to show evidence of insurability. Under group insurance, underwriting is focused on the characteristics of the group, and individual members are usually not required to show evidence of insurability when initially eligible for coverage.

Individual insurance does not use experience rating, while under group insurance, the group may be experience rated.

Answers to Self-Test Questions

1-1.   True.
1-2.   False. Risk is the possibility, not the probability or chance, of loss.
1-3.   False. This is an *indirect* loss.
1-4.   True.
1-5.   False. Perils are causes of loss. Hazards are acts or conditions that increase the chance or amount of loss caused by a peril.
1-6.   False. Attitudinal hazards are evidenced by carelessness or indifference. Moral hazards are evidenced by dishonest tendencies.
1-7.   True.
1-8.   False. An individual cannot use the probability of a loss to measure the risk he or she faces—the individual either will or will not suffer a loss. Statistical probabilities have no relevance in this case. In order to use a probability to measure risk, a large number of similar exposures would be needed.
1-9.   False. This would be true only if the number of insureds is also large.
1-10. True.
1-11. False. Because pure risks involve only loss or no loss, they cannot be handled effectively with hedging. Because speculative risks involve *gain* as well as loss, they can be handled effectively with hedging.
1-12. False. The fact that risk is an existing condition is what removes insurance from the category of a gambling risk. Insurance does not create risk—gambling does.
1-13. True.
1-14. False. In addition to the actual loss that takes place, the costs associated with pure risk include fear and worry, less-than-optimum use of resources, and the expenses of treating risks.
1-15. True.
1-16. True.
1-17. True.
1-18. False. Social insurance emphasizes social adequacy rather than individual equity.
1-19. True.

Chapter 2

Answers to Review Questions

2-1.   Steps are identification, measurement, choice and use of methods to treat each identified risk, and administration.
2-2.   Many risk managers might say that the objective is to "preserve the assets and income of my organization or household by providing protection against the possibility of accidental loss." More specific risk management goals might include: (1) survival, (2) peace of mind, (3) lower costs (or higher net income), (4) stable earnings, (5) minimal interruption of business operations or personal life, (6) continued growth, and (7) satisfaction of social responsibility with a good public image.
2-3.   The risk manager's responsibilities and authority in a large organization are quite broad and cut across many of the organization's activities. The risk manager of a larger firm has, in a majority of cases, full responsibility in the property and liability area for (1) identifying and evaluating risks, (2) selecting insurers, (3) approving insurance renewals and amounts, (4) negotiating insurance rates, (5) seeking competitive insurance bids, (6) keeping insurance records, (7) choosing deductibles, and (8) handling insurance claims. The risk manager usually shares authority for (1) deciding whether or not to insure or retain (including self-insuring) financial risks, (2) selecting insurance agents and brokers, (3) instituting safety programs, and (4) reviewing contracts other than insurance. In some organizations, the risk manager also has some responsibility for life and health insurance programs, while in others these programs fall within the scope of the human resources or personnel department.

Sometimes, particularly in small- and medium-size firms, an insurance agent, broker, or consultant serves as the risk manager, because the organization has no one person assigned to these responsibilities. Larger agencies and brokerages, especially, offer to serve in this capacity. Care must be taken to see (1) that the services are much broader than mere insurance coverages and include loss prevention and other risk treatment alternatives, and (2) that the insurance agency or brokerage representative or consultant knows the firm's special individual needs.
2-4.   Risk control methods attempt to reduce the possibility of losses, focusing on minimizing losses that might occur to assets and income. Risk financing methods facilitate paying for losses that do occur.

2-5.   Although some unusual risks with a high chance of loss can be avoided, realistically, risk avoidance is only an alternative for a limited number of risks. Some risks may be impossible to avoid; others may not be economically desirable to avoid because of the high costs of doing so or because avoiding one risk may create another.

2-6.   *Unplanned risk retention* is the result of lack of planning, or lack of knowledge concerning the exposure. Unplanned risk retention can also result from unintentional or irrational action or from passive behavior due to lack of thought, laziness, or lack of interest in discovering possibilities of loss. Reasons for planned risk retention are (1) necessity, when other alternatives are not possible, (2) control or convenience, and (3) cost. The first reason demands that risk retention be used; the second and third result from a conscious effort to analyze the benefits of retention in terms of control, convenience, or cost, and the ability of individuals or business firms to handle their own risks effectively.

2-7.   Deductibles lower insurance premiums by eliminating the relatively high claims costs associated with small losses. From the insurer's perspective, deductibles also minimize moral hazards by making an insured responsible for a portion of any loss.

2-8.   Retention through the use of deductibles generally provides a more cost-effective method of handling high-frequency, low-severity losses than the purchase of insurance for those losses. With insurance, Sam's premium would not only contain a charge for expected losses (close or equal to actual losses in the case of high-frequency, low-severity losses), but he would also be charged for insurance company expenses and profit. Instead, by using a deductible and keeping the freed-up premium dollars invested, Sam not only can save the charge for insurance company expenses and profit, but he also can earn a return on his money until it is needed to pay the high-frequency, low-severity losses.

2-9.   Absorption in Current Operating Expenses or Family Budgets.
       Funding and Reserves.
       Self-Insurance through a formal program of risk retention.
       Captive Insurers, separate subsidiary insurance companies established to write the parent company's insurance.

2-10. (a) The equality between the receipts taken in and what is paid out. The receipts include (1) premiums (or insurance payments from policyowners), (2) investment earnings, and (3) other income. The cost factors that enter into what is paid out are as follows: (1) the cost of losses, (2) the cost of doing business, or expenses, and (3) the cost of capital, or profits.

       (b) Probability measures the chance of occurrence of a particular event. In the field of insurance, the theory of probability has proved to be of great importance in measuring (predicting) losses. The probability of loss is expressed algebraically in a fraction whose numerator is the number of unfavorable outcomes and whose denominator is the total number of all possible outcomes. The insurer can reduce the sum total of all the uncertainties to a reasonable degree of certainty. Within calculable limits, the insurer can foresee the normal losses and estimate losses from catastrophes in order to compute the premium necessary to pay all losses, as well as to cover expenses and profits.

       (c) As the number of independent events increases, the likelihood increases that the actual results will be close to the expected results. Insurance is concerned with the number of times an event, or loss, can be expected to happen over a series of occasions. Certain events occur with surprising regularity when a large number of instances is observed. The regularity of the events increases as the observed instances become more numerous.

       (d) Use of the mathematical laws of probability and large numbers requires adequate statistical data. Unless accurate statistical information is available, predictions in the form of probabilities will be defective. In each of the lines of insurance, carefully compiled statistics are assembled to accumulate experience as a basis for rate making.

       The goal is to reduce judgment factors to a minimum and to set rates scientifically, based on the use of statistical data in applying known laws of probability, variability, and large numbers. Insurance applies mathematical tools to statistical data on groups to achieve better predictions than individuals can make.

2-11. *Survey Forms.* Although most often used in business situations, survey forms are also appropriate for nonprofit organizations, as well as for individuals and families. In the business sector, small- and medium-sized businesses need good risk and insurance surveys as much as larger firms do. The smaller businesses, in fact, are particularly vulnerable to financial ruin as the result of a mistake or omission regarding insurance protection. Risk and insurance survey forms involve risk detection, identification, and classification. Sometimes they also include estimates of the possible loss values, which are part of risk measurement.

       Financial Statement Analysis. In financial statement analysis, each account in the balance sheet, the profit and loss statement, and other financial statements is listed separately and analyzed to determine the potential perils that might cause losses. A comprehensive analysis of a firm's financial statements thus becomes a very useful method for identifying both direct and indirect losses. As for a business, these financial records can reveal many of the risks confronting a household.

Flowcharts. Charts that show the entire business operation in detail are prepared, and each step in the production and distribution of goods and services is analyzed to consider the potential losses that might occur at each point or location in the process.

Personal Inspections. Personal inspections of a business or a household by insurance consultants or agents are a significant source of information about possible losses.

2-12. At the level of the household or small business organization, the choice of the best technique or combination of techniques is likely to be determined by such less quantifiable factors as the following:

- the maximum probable loss associated with a particular risk in comparison with the household's or firm's financial and other capacities for bearing risk
- the legal restrictions that may force or preclude the use of one or more of the available techniques
- the extent to which the household or firm is able to exert control over the loss frequency or severity associated with the risk
- the loading fees (expense charges) associated with the available risk management techniques
- the value of ancillary services that may be provided as part of the risk treatment technique, especially the insurance technique
- the time value of investable funds that may be gained or lost by using certain of the available techniques
- the federal income tax treatment of losses under the various techniques
- the possible unavailability of certain techniques for dealing with some pure risks

2-13. A review of insurance priorities first assumes that, for each of the pure risks that have been identified and measured in the risk management process, insurance will be used if it is available. The most suitable policy and its cost are listed for each risk as a benchmark against which to evaluate other possible techniques. Listing insurance policies also clarifies which risks must be treated by means other than insurance—that is, the risks for which no insurance policy is available.

Next, insurance coverages are grouped into priority categories such as

- essential (for example, insurance required by law or losses of possibly disastrous results for the household or business)
- desirable (for example, losses that would seriously impair but not totally wipe out the financial position of the household or business)
- available (all other types of insurance coverage)

Finally, each insurance coverage is compared with the other available techniques for treating the particular risk.

A different approach to selecting the most appropriate technique is to group the most logical techniques based on the probable frequency and severity of the losses associated with each pure risk confronting the family or organization.

2-14. (a) *Social Insurance.* The first building block is several social insurance programs, each of which is designed to provide a floor of protection against certain perils. For example, Social Security (OASDI) covers the perils of old age, death, and disability.

(b) *Employer-Sponsored Insurance.* The second building block is various insurance programs made available at work. Group insurance programs can provide specified types of coverage such as group life insurance, group medical expense insurance, and a pension plan.

(c) *Individual Insurance.* The third building block, individual insurance, should fill in coverage gaps left by social insurance and employer-sponsored insurance and increase total coverage amounts to the necessary levels.

Answers to Self-Test Questions

2-1. True.

2-2. False. The risk management process considers all the alternatives for treating risks.

2-3. True.

2-4. True.

2-5. False. Self-insurance is generally appropriate only for large businesses that can act like an insurance company for their own risks.

2-6. False. Other noninsurance risk transfer methods also can be used to handle pure risks—for example, extended warranties and hold-harmless agreements.

2-7. False. Premiums plus investment earnings plus other income must equal losses, expenses, and profits.

2-8. True.

2-9. False. The first step is risk identification.

2-10. True.

2-11. False. The most useful concept is maximum *probable* loss.

2-12. True.

Chapter 3

Answers to Review Questions

3-1. Both the stock and mutual insurance companies are corporations. The stock company is owned by stockholders who elect the board of directors and who typically receive any dividends. The mutual company is owned by policyowners who elect the board of directors and who typically receive any dividends.

3-2. a. Probably the most important reason for demutualization is to enable the insurer to raise capital quickly. A second and often related reason is to enable the insurance company to diversify its activities by acquiring other insurers or other types of financial institutions through the issuance or exchange of stock. A third reason for demutualization is to facilitate payment of certain types of noncash compensation to the insurance company's key executives and board members. A fourth reason is to gain federal income tax savings.

b. The time, cost, and complexity may be enormous due to the difficult regulatory, tax, legal, and accounting problems that must be overcome. Of particular importance is the regulatory requirement that the policyowners of the company seeking to demutualize be compensated adequately for loss of their ownership rights. A second disadvantage of demutualization is that, as a stock company, the insurer might become vulnerable to a hostile takeover. Third, as a stock insurer, the company would have to meet SEC and state rules relating to its equity securities. Fourth, demutualization represents a major change in corporate philosophy in the introduction of an explicit profit motive, a change that may be very difficult for senior executives and other long-standing employees of the former mutual company to accept.

3-3. a. Lloyd's itself does not directly issue insurance policies; rather, insurance is written by underwriting members who sign "each for himself and not for another." The insurer, then, is not Lloyd's but the underwriters at Lloyd's. A policyowner insures *at* Lloyd's but not *with* Lloyd's.

b. The function of the corporation of Lloyd's is purely to supervise transactions and to guard the institution's reputation.

c. Underwriting members supply capital but do not work at Lloyd's. These members are organized into syndicates, with membership varying from a few to more than 1,000 in each. Each syndicate is operated by an underwriting agent, who commits the members of that syndicate to the risks from the business written. There are also a number of firms of authorized Lloyd's brokers.

d. Lloyd's of London is licensed directly in only two states—Illinois and Kentucky—although Lloyd's brokers and agents operate throughout the United States and the rest of the world.

e. In the United States, state excess and surplus line laws allow coverage to be placed at Lloyd's (or any other nonadmitted insurer) if the desired coverage is not available from licensed insurers. Although the usual household or small business would have little need for insuring at Lloyd's of London, businesses can insure at Lloyd's to obtain needed high liability limits, special coverages such as worldwide package policies, or difficult-to-obtain protection for unusual perils or very large amounts of insurance.

f. American Lloyd's associations write primarily fire and allied lines and automobile physical damage insurance. In the American associations, each member is ordinarily liable for only a specified maximum, and the strict regulations of Lloyd's of London that govern membership, deposits, and audits are not present. Each American Lloyd's organization depends on the financial strength of its individual members within their limited liability.

3-4. a. The reciprocal exchange is not a mutual insurer in the legal sense because the individual subscribers assume liability as individuals, not as a responsibility of the group as a whole. Another basic difference from mutual insurers is that reciprocal exchanges are not incorporated but are formed under separate laws as associations under the direction of an attorney-in-fact.

    b. Reciprocal exchanges differ from Lloyd's associations in that Lloyd's associations are (1) proprietary or profit seeking, and (2) the Lloyd's insurer is not also a policyowner, whereas every insurer in a reciprocal exchange is a policyowner.

3-5. First, financial planners are in many cases active participants in the marketing process, deriving some of their compensation from being participants. Second, working with consumers of insurance, financial planners may gain a better understanding about the choices among insurers and agents that clients must make in buying insurance. Finally, the marketing process is a key function in insurance operations, and the methods companies use to sell and service insurance contracts are significant in determining their costs and usefulness.

3-6. The agent's powers are governed by his or her agency contract with the insurer. The agency contract spells out the agent's express authority. The agent also has implied or incidental authority to carry out those acts needed to exercise his or her express authority. However, an agent's acts may bind the principal even if (1) those acts are outside the scope of the agent's express or implied authority, or (2) the acts are within the agent's apparent authority. This type of authority arises when the agent, without contrary action by the principal, performs an act that appears to a reasonable person to be within the agent's express or implied authority.

    Among the legal duties an agent owes to his or her principal are the duty to be loyal to the principal, the duty not to be negligent, and the duty to obey instructions given by the principal. Duties the principal owes to the agent include the duty to give the agent an opportunity to work, to compensate the agent, to keep accounts of amounts owed to the agent, and to reimburse the agent for authorized payments the agent makes and liabilities he or she incurs while working for the principal.

3-7. a. Life insurance companies customarily limit the authority to issue or modify life insurance contracts to salaried company officers. Life insurance agents, even those called general agents, are thus limited agents. Generally speaking, life insurance agents are authorized to solicit, receive, and forward applications for the contracts written by their companies. Agents are authorized to receive the first premiums due on applications but not subsequent premiums. The life insurance agent's authority is also limited in the ability to accept business or bind the coverage. The life insurer issues the contract after receiving the written, signed application and, often, a medical examination report. The agent may not cover the policyowner immediately, nor may contract modifications be made later without the insurance company's approval.

    b. Agents appointed to represent property and liability insurers are often granted the powers of a general agent. The limitations on their authority are set forth in the agency agreement. General agents may bind their companies for a client's coverage in certain cases. This is done by an oral or written binder, which is temporary evidence of coverage until the full insurance policy is issued by the insurance company. Among their other responsibilities, these agents inspect and collect initial (and sometimes renewal) premiums. Some general agents even issue contracts in their own offices for automobile or homeowners policies. Contracts for other lines of insurance may have to be issued by the insurer in the home office or a branch office.

3-8. a. Tom would be covered immediately by XYZ Insurance Company under the homeowners policy. Property and liability agents typically have express authority to bind their companies for most cases involving a homeowners policy. However, even if the agent didn't have express authority to bind the company in this case, the company would be bound by the agent's apparent authority exercised when the agent told Tom he was covered.

    b. Tom would not be covered immediately by ABC Life. A life insurance agent does not have the authority to cover the applicant immediately.

3-9. a. The agent (often referred to as a producer) is a representative of the insurance company (called the principal in agency law). The broker acts on behalf of the applicant for insurance or the policyowner after the insurance goes into effect.

    b. The insurance agent is acting under specific and delegated authority from the insurer and is sometimes authorized to bind coverage within specific limits. The broker, on the other hand, has no such authority. In fact, because the broker represents the applicant or policyowner, the applicant or policyowner is bound by the broker's acts.

3-10. a. Historically, a general agent was an individual entrepreneur granted a franchise by an insurer to market the insurer's products in a specified geographic area. The general agent represented only that one insurer, and he or she was responsible for hiring, training, motivating, and supervising agents. The general agent was compensated solely by commissions on business the agency produced and was fully responsible for all expenses of operating the agency. In more recent times, however, insurance companies have typically given some form of financial assistance to the general agent, perhaps paying some of the costs involved in hiring and training new agents and/or providing an allowance to cover some of the operating agency's expenses.

b. In the branch office or managerial system, the insurer establishes branch offices in the areas where it writes business, with each branch headed by a manager who is a salaried employee of the insurance company. Again, the manager is responsible for hiring, training, motivating, and supervising agents for the company, but the insurer bears all costs of operating the branch. The branch manager may also receive a bonus as part of his or her compensation, depending on the quantity and quality of business the branch writes. Payment of bonuses to branch managers, together with coverage of some general agency operating expenses, has tended to blur somewhat the historical distinctions between the two agency systems.

c. A variation of the general agency system that has become significant in some life insurance companies is the personal producing general agent (PPGA) system. In this system, the insurer hires an experienced agent with a proven record of sales success as its general agent in a given territory. Unlike a traditional general agent, however, the PPGA's main responsibility is to sell the insurer's products, rather than to build an agency force for the company. The PPGA often receives higher commissions than other agents to help cover his or her own operating expenses. The PPGA may be expected to meet certain sales quotes for the company, but he or she may also be allowed to represent other insurers.

3-11. a. Under the independent agency system, several companies or groups of companies are represented, while under the exclusive agency system, only one company is represented.

b. Under the independent system, the agency is an independent business organization and pays its own operating expenses; under the exclusive system, the insurer may cover the agent's operating expenses, particularly for new agents.

c. Agents in the independent system are compensated mainly through commissions on business written by the agency; also, these agents may receive contingent commissions if good business is submitted and may receive fees for other services provided.

d. Under the exclusive agency system, compensation is mainly from commissions on the sale of new business. In the independent agency system, commission rates are generally the same for renewing policies as for the sale of new policies, while in the exclusive agency system, lower commission rates are paid for renewals than for new business.

e. The independent agent generally has ownership, use, and control of policy and expiration data; under the exclusive system, the insurer has these rights.

f. The independent agent generally collects premiums and settles small claims (although the trend is toward the insurer performing these functions). Under the exclusive system, the insurer generally performs these duties, although the agent may collect initial premiums and settle some small claims.

Answers to Self-Test Questions

3-1. False. Foreign insurers are organized in another state; alien insurers are incorporated in another country.

3-2. False. While stock insurers are owned by stockholders who elect the board of directors, mutuals are owned by their policyowners who elect the board of directors.

3-3. True.

3-4. False. Neither stocks nor mutuals are inherently superior from a consumer's standpoint. The real issue for the insurance consumer is which specific insurer to select, not which type to select.

3-5. False. The trend is for mutual companies to demutualize.

3-6. False. Insurance is written by the underwriters at Lloyd's. The corporation of Lloyd's is purely to supervise transactions and to guard the reputation of the institution.

3-7. True.

3-8. True.

3-9. True.

3-10. False. An insurance agent has implied and apparent authority as well as the express authority spelled out in the agency contract.

3-11. False. From a legal standpoint, nearly all life insurance agents, even those called general agents, are granted the powers of a limited agent.

3-12. True.

3-13. True.

3-14. True.

3-15. False. Independent agents traditionally receive the same commission rate for renewing a policy as for initially selling the policy, whereas exclusive agents generally receive renewal commissions that are considerably smaller than their initial commissions.

Chapter 4

Answers to Review Questions

4-1. a. With adverse selection, the insurer's actual losses and expenses on insurance written would far exceed the expected losses and expenses built into its premium rates, and its underwriting losses would tend to be substantial. The first function of underwriting, selection, is to choose applicants for insurance so that the insurer's actual losses and expenses on insurance written would approximate the expected losses and expenses built into its premium rates. This would leave an acceptable margin for profit (or at least a small enough loss so that it could be offset by investment income).

b. In the second function of underwriting, classification, applicants who are not rejected in the selection phase are assigned to the class that best fits with their hazards and are charged the rate for that class. Therefore, an applicant with greater hazards is likely to be assigned to a class with a higher rate than an applicant who brings fewer hazards to the insurance company.

4-2. The applicant for an insurance contract often makes both written and oral statements. Signed written statements are normal procedures in life and health insurance, and the application becomes a part of the contract. Automobile and business insurance applicants also frequently prepare written statements as a means of giving the insurance company basic underwriting details. Agents in many kinds of insurance give their companies reports, opinions, and recommendations that are valuable aids to the insurers in selecting or rejecting applications. Many insurers maintain separate inspection departments to provide the underwriters with physical inspection and engineering reports on applicants' properties. The insurer's claims department, too, can be a source of important underwriting data for renewal decisions.

Insurers also combine efforts to maintain bureau or association lists of insurance applicants, for example, the Medical Information Bureau (MIB). In many kinds of insurance, companies use outside agencies to supplement the information gathered from the applicants, agents, and other insurer representatives. Sources include physicians, financial rating services, credit investigators, motor vehicle reports, court orders, and inspection agencies.

4-3. The primary purpose of reinsurance is to enable the insurer to spread or diversify losses. Reinsurance also reduces the ceding company's reserve requirements, which drain surplus and restrict growth. In addition, reinsurers offer many technical advisory services to new insurers or those expanding to new types of insurance or territories.

4-4. Facultative reinsurance is optional for both the insurer and the reinsurer. Each facultative reinsurance contract is written on its own merits and is a matter of individual bargaining between the primary insurer and the reinsurer. In treaty, or automatic, reinsurance, the primary insurer agrees in advance to transfer some types of loss exposures and the reinsurer agrees to accept them.

4-5. The objective of both insurers and claimants is to arrive at a fair and equitable measure of the loss.

4-6. In property insurance, some agents have their companies' authority to settle a claim with the policyowner immediately. For large agencies and experienced agents, the authority can extend to actually issuing checks in the name of their company. In life insurance, the agent is often involved in loss payment as an intermediary but not as an adjuster. The life insurance agent usually forwards the death notice and certificate to the insurer, and the check is issued by the company for delivery by the agent to the policyowner's beneficiary. For larger policies, the agent may need to explain various installment payment options in place of a lump-sum cash payment.

4-7. (1) The notification to the insurer must be provided as spelled out in the policy. Often, the time frame is specified as "immediately," "promptly," or "as soon as practicable," and a few types of policies may be more specific.

(2) The investigation of the claim is designed to determine whether a loss occurred and, if so, whether it is covered by the policy. In life insurance, this process is usually quite simple, but complicating factors occasionally arise.

(3) The third step in the process of adjusting a claim is filing a proof of loss. In life insurance, proof of loss may be in the form of a death certificate. In other lines, a written and sworn statement may be required that details all the specifics of the loss.

(4) Finally, the amount to be paid must be determined in one of three ways: denial of the claim, payment of the claim in full, or payment of a lesser amount than the claimant seeks. Once again, life insurance claims are

usually simpler because there are no partial losses. There can, however, be some complicating factors that affect the amount to be paid, including an accidental death benefit provision, a misstatement-of-age-or-sex clause, or a settlement option selected by the policyowner or by the beneficiary.

In other lines of insurance, the amount to be paid, if any, can be a very troublesome issue. Numerous policy provisions may be applicable. These include provisions that deal with other insurance covering the same loss; provide for a deductible; specify that recovery will be affected by the amount of insurance carried relative to the value of the covered property; give the insurer the choice of two or three methods of calculating the amount of the loss; stipulate the use of appraisers to establish the amount of the loss; and impose a specific limit on the insurer's liability for certain types of losses.

4-8.   a.   The insurance rate is the *unit* cost for the coverage; the insurance premium is the price charged for the *total* coverage provided by the policy. The insurance premium is determined by multiplying the rate by the number of exposure units (number of units of coverage).

       b.   An insurance rate is typically developed using the pure premium method, which first requires an estimate for the future loss costs per unit of coverage during the policy period. This portion of the rate is called the pure or net rate and involves a statistical analysis of past loss data with a projection of that experience into the future policy period. Added to the pure rate is a loading factor, which covers the insurer's anticipated expenses and provides a margin for profit and contingencies. The sum of the pure rate and the loading is called the gross rate, which is the rate applied to an insured.

Answers to Self-Test Questions

4-1.   False. The general purpose of underwriting is to select insureds who on average will produce actual loss experience comparable to the expected loss experience incorporated into the premium rates.

4-2.   True.

4-3.   False. Under treaty reinsurance, the insurer agrees in advance to transfer some types of risks, and the reinsurer agrees to accept those risks. With facultative reinsurance, the insurer is under no obligation to offer the risk to the reinsurer, and the reinsurer is under no obligation to accept.

4-4.   True.

4-5.   False. A life insurance agent may become involved as an intermediary delivering a death proceeds check to a beneficiary but not as an adjuster with authority to settle a claim.

4-6.   False. As with staff adjusters, independent adjusters and adjustment bureaus represent insurers. Public adjusters represent the public.

4-7.   False. In calculating the insurance premium, the gross rate (composed of the pure rate plus a loading for expenses, profit, and contingencies) is multiplied by the number of units of coverage.

4-8.   True.

4-9.   True.

Chapter 5

Answers to Review Questions

5-1.   The general purpose of insurance regulation is to protect the public against insolvency or unfair treatment by insurers. From the state's viewpoint, regulation is also important as a revenue producer through state taxes on insurance premiums. The insurance business is among the types of private enterprise subject to much government regulation because it is generally classed as a business that is "affected with a public interest." Although competition is an effective regulator for some businesses, uncontrolled competition in insurance could work a hardship on the buyers of insurance, most of whom do not understand insurance contracts.

5-2.   Three basic methods of providing insurance regulation that the government uses are: (1) legislative action, (2) administrative action, and (3) court action. Legislation is the foundation of insurance regulation because it creates the insurance laws. The insurance laws of each state are often combined in an insurance code. Administrative action refers to the application and enforcement of insurance laws, which is the responsibility of the insurance commissioner in each state. Court action has great value because it provides detailed interpretations of troublesome parts of the law.

5-3.   The regulation of insurers falls into the following categories.

       Formation and Licensing of Insurers. Insurance companies must meet specific standards of organization that are often higher than those set for general business organizations. Standards are necessary to ensure the solvency, competence, and integrity of the insuring organization. The first step is incorporation, an introductory process in which the state recognizes and approves the existence of a new legal identity.

The next step, licensing, is a check on the insurer's financial condition to ascertain that it has the required initial capital and surplus for the kinds of insurance permitted in the license. The objective of licensing is to provide a preliminary method of lessening the chance of the insurer's financial insolvency, particularly during the difficult formative years.

Insurer Operations. The states exercise some control over many phases of the operations of insurers. Most obligations of insurers extend years into the future, so the state provides supervision to see that the promises in the contracts are fulfilled. The ways in which insurer operations are supervised are strikingly different among the states and among the various kinds of insurance. Most states do provide some regulation of the following types: contracts and forms, rates, reserves, asset and surplus values, investments, agents' licensing and trade practices, claims practices, and taxation.

Rehabilitation and Liquidation of Insurers. The insurance commissioner of a state presides over the insurance company's liquidation. Some liquidations may occur due to financial insolvency; others are voluntary in order to effect a corporate reorganization or merger. All outstanding liabilities and contracts may be reinsured so that no loss results to policyowners.

5-4. a. *Contracts and Forms.* Because insurance policies are complex legal documents that are often not fully understood by consumers, they could be used to mislead or unfairly treat policyowners. Consequently, in many lines of insurance, policy forms must be approved by, or at least filed with, the insurance commissioner.

Life and health insurance contracts are not standard contracts in the sense that similar forms or benefits are required. Most states do, however, provide some uniformity by requiring a number of standard provisions in life and health contracts pertaining to such items as the grace period, loan and surrender values, and the like. Examples of little regulation over contracts are found in the transportation insurance field. Except for a few required provisions, these contracts are among the most nonuniform of insurance contracts and should be carefully studied by policyowners in order to determine what benefits, conditions, and exclusions they contain.

   b. *Rates.* The price of insurance contracts is controlled to a varying degree in the different lines of insurance. In some lines of insurance, such as aviation insurance, practically no regulation exists in the states. In life insurance, regulation involves maintaining minimum reserves, rather than setting the prices that must be charged. Most other major kinds of insurance are subject to some direct rate regulation.

The statutory standards to be met are set forth in an insurance rating law. Basic standards recognized by rating laws usually require (1) that rates be reasonable and adequate for the class of business to which they apply, (2) that no rate be unfairly discriminatory, and (3) that consideration be given to the past and prospective loss experience and a reasonable underwriting profit. Rates are considered reasonable (not too high) and adequate (not too low) when, along with investment income, they can be expected to produce sufficient revenue to pay all losses and expenses of doing business, and, in addition, produce a reasonable profit.

Instead of direct regulation of insurance prices by required rate approval, some state laws supervise the cost of life insurance by limiting the portion of the premium that can be used for expenses rather than claims.

   c. *Reserves.* The states require insurers to maintain (as a liability) a minimum reserve considered adequate to meet policy obligations as they mature. In life insurance, the legal reserve is an amount that, augmented by premium payments under outstanding contracts and interest earnings, is sufficient to enable the life insurer to meet its assumed policy obligations. Minimum reserve requirements are also thought to indirectly regulate life insurance rates, at least by reducing the likelihood of inadequate rates.

In the field of property insurance, the unearned premium reserve must at all times be adequate to pay a return premium to policyowners in the event of cancellation of a policy before it expires.

A second type of reserve required of property and liability insurers is the loss reserve. Since many contracts do not involve immediate payment of all losses that have occurred, a reserve must be set up to ensure their payment.

   d. *Asset and Surplus Values.* The value of assets appearing in the balance sheets of insurers must be correct and conservative in order that liabilities, reserves, and residual surplus items have true meaning. Securities held by insurers are valued according to practices adopted by a committee of the NAIC. Stocks are usually given year-end market values, while most bonds are carried at amortized values. Some assets of insurance companies are not allowed to be carried on their balance sheets as assets. These *nonadmitted assets* are thought to be of marginal quality or of little liquidity for policyowners if their insurers should get into financial difficulty.

    e. *Investments.* To protect the solvency of insurers, most states have laws governing the types of securities that may be purchased for investment. The strictest regulations apply to life insurers, which are subject to vigorous supervision of their investment portfolios. Bonds and common stocks are the prime investments in the portfolio of life insurers, although most states grant some limited permission for certain other investments such as stocks as a percentage of assets or of surplus. Real estate holdings, especially commercial properties, are also limited to a maximum in various states.

        The investment of assets by property and liability insurers is also supervised, although the laws are more lenient and vary greatly among the states. The general practice aims at requiring the safest types of investments for all assets held as reserves (unearned premium and loss reserves) and other liabilities. Cash, bonds of high grade and specified experience, and perhaps preferred stocks of proven quality may be permitted for such assets. The remainder of assets (representing capital and surplus) may be invested in a wider range of securities, including common stocks meeting certain standards. Limitations on real estate holdings, on the size of single investments in relation to total assets or surplus, and on investments in foreign companies, as well as many other restrictions, are also common.

    f. *Agents' Licensing and Trade Practices.* An important control of insurer operations is maintained through laws in all states that require licensing for insurance agents and brokers. The insurance departments usually administer these laws, with the objective of permitting insurers to use only competent and trustworthy representatives. The standards vary tremendously, from little more than payment of a license fee to a comprehensive written examination following required attendance in insurance courses approved by the department. The examinations are often divided into separate tests for different lines of insurance. The examinations for insurance brokers are usually more difficult and extensive than those given to agents. Some adjusters and consultants also must be licensed in a few states. Almost all states now require continuing education as a condition for license renewal.

        Unfair trade practices in insurance are made illegal in all states under laws similar to the Federal Trade Commission Act. These laws aim at retaining jurisdiction for the states (under the provisions of Public Law 15) in preventing fraudulent and unethical acts of agents and brokers. They provide fines and, more important, suspension or revocation of licenses as penalties for violations.

        The insurance commissioner has broad powers to prevent unfair practices and exercises this authority by investigating complaints as well as by initiating investigations of any questionable acts of insurers or their representatives.

    g. *Claims Practices.* Most states now have enacted laws patterned after the NAIC's model acts and regulations pertaining to unfair claim settlement practices. Some of the practices that are regarded as unfair are the following:

- failing to investigate claims promptly
- failing to communicate with or acknowledge communications from clients on a timely basis
- failing to provide a reasonable explanation as to why a claim has been denied
- failing to maintain procedures for complaint handling about claims
- misrepresenting pertinent policy provisions affecting claims
- failing to try to settle a claim once the insurer's liability has become clear
- attempting to settle a claim for far less than a reasonable person would expect to receive based on the insurer's advertising material

5-5. In recent years, all 50 states have adopted insurance guaranty fund plans to at least partially protect consumers against the insolvency of insurers. The plans are administered on a state-by-state basis, but usually they assess solvent insurers in order to pay the unpaid claims of an insolvent company and to return unearned premiums to its policyowners. Insurers each pay a proportional share of the losses, based on their premium volume in the state.

        The guaranty funds appear to protect the consumer reasonably well. In some states, several improvements have been adopted concerning (1) giving the guaranty funds immediate access to assets of the insolvent insurer (rather than waiting until liquidation proceedings are completed), (2) giving the guaranty funds priority before general creditors to obtain assets of the insolvent insurer, and (3) permitting a tax offset against premium taxes to solvent insurers for money paid into the guaranty funds. Even with these improvements, however, problems remain in the areas of lengthy delays before consumers receive their money and dollar limits on some types of claims that will be paid.

5-6. Advocates of state regulation of insurance have pointed out such reasons as (1) the local nature of many insurance transactions, for which any difficulties can best be resolved on a state basis; (2) the reasonable success of state regulation for many years, during which insurance has become an important and sound business; (3) the value of regulation on a state-by-state basis, which permits gradual changes and innovations in regulation without applying them to the entire country all at once; and (4) the help of the NAIC in recommending model legislation to the states in order to achieve some uniformity in insurance regulation. While recognizing that state regulation is not perfect, its supporters claim that federal regulation would be cumbersome, expensive, less effective, and fragmented among dozens of agencies.

Proponents of federal regulation of insurance have criticized state regulation on many points, emphasizing (1) inconsistencies and lack of uniformity in regulation of insurers; (2) inadequate funding for the important tasks of the insurance commissioners, and the short-term and political aspects of their term of office; (3) greater standardization needed in insurance contracts to cover many interstate exposures; and (4) increased competition desired in order to ensure availability and lower and fairer prices for insurance. Implicit in these criticisms of the present state of insurance regulation is the idea that federal regulation would be better.

5-7. Probably the single most important criterion to be applied is the insurer's financial strength. Selection of an insurer should also be based on its willingness to pay claims.

Another criterion that should be used in evaluating insurers is service. The insurer's ability to provide proper protection for the applicant is essential. As part of the evaluation of an insurer's service, the applicant is interested in knowing whether or not the insurer is liberal with respect to underwriting. The insurer's facilities for loss-prevention recommendations that may reduce insurance costs are also important to the consumer.

Another important criterion in the evaluation of an insurer, of course, is the cost of the products it offers. Initial costs are only part of the necessary analysis; final costs over a longer period of protection must be considered, including possible rate changes, dividends, assessments, or premium adjustments under some types of rating plans.

5-8. Some of the criteria include:

Knowledge and Ability. The agent must have the background and experience necessary to identify, analyze, and treat risk properly.

Willingness. If qualified, can and will the agent also take the time to apply his or her knowledge with an attitude of conscientiousness that will result in the full appraisal of all the client's needs and alternatives? The agent must be able and willing to take the time to see that services (including those of agency staff and insurance companies) are performed in the most effective way possible.

Integrity and Character. Agents or brokers must be able to command the confidence and trust of the policyowner.

Representation. Good agents generally do not represent poor insurers. They must represent or have contacts with one or many insurers that can provide the required protection and services for the policyowner. All the necessary coverages, including even special or unusual ones, must be available through the agent(s) in a prompt and efficient manner and at a reasonable cost. The insurer or insurers represented should be capable of writing many different kinds of insurance with a progressive attitude toward newer coverages and forms designed to meet the particular needs of individual buyers.

Answers to Self-Test Questions

5-1. True.

5-2. True.

5-3. True.

5-4. False. Life insurance is not subject to direct rate regulation. Instead, some states supervise the cost of life insurance by limiting the portion of the premium that can be used for expenses rather than claims. Also, life insurance rates are indirectly regulated through the minimum reserve requirements.

5-5. True.

5-6. False. Most states prohibit rebating and twisting as unfair trade practices.

5-7. False. Most premium taxes paid by insurers to the states are used for revenue purposes rather than to pay for the cost of insurance regulation.

5-8. False. Financial strength is determined by the insurer's ability to pay claims.

5-9. True.

5-10. False. Some of the criteria for evaluating an agent include knowledge and ability, willingness, integrity and character, and representation.

Chapter 6

Answers to Review Questions

6-1.   Unlike most of the physical goods that one purchases for immediate enjoyment, insurance provides *future* benefits when loss payments are made. However, the relief from anxiety and freedom from worry about financial losses are immediate and continual benefits throughout the period of protection.

Insurance has a *contingent* nature in that benefits are paid based on particular events. Policyowners buy insurance against many perils despite a feeling that such perils will not really cause losses to them. Insurance can be considered a service contract or a bundle of services, rather than a single physical product.

Financial *risk* is a final characteristic that differentiates insurance from other goods and services. The basis of the insurance contract is uncertainty about many perils that may cause accidental loss. Insurance transfers the financial risk of such losses to the insurer, a professional risk bearer. Other service contracts may be future and contingent, but they do not involve payment for the occurrence of such unexpected perils as fire, windstorm, disability, and death.

6-2.   a.   *Offer and Acceptance.* A legally binding agreement, or contract, requires both an offer by one party and an acceptance by another party. In insurance, the offer is usually made in a request for coverage by the prospect, or applicant.

Before a contract is effective, acceptance of the offer is necessary. In property and liability insurance, the agent often has authority to bind, or accept, the offer even without receiving any payment from the applicant. In life insurance, written application with the first premium payment is usually considered the offer to the insurer. Acceptance is held by most courts to occur when the applicant meets the normal underwriting standards of the insurer, and coverage becomes effective as of the time of the application and premium payment. If the premium was not paid with the application, the offer to insure is made by the insurer. The insurance is accepted when the contract is delivered to the applicant while the applicant is in good health and the premium is paid. If the applicant does not meet the underwriting standards of the insurer, the insurer may make a counteroffer with a different contract, which the prospect may accept or reject upon delivery by the agent.

b.   *Legal Purpose.* A legally binding contract must have a legal purpose or object. The courts will not enforce a contract that has an illegal purpose or is contrary to public policy.

c.   *Competent Parties.* Valid contracts require that the party making the offer and the one accepting the offer be legally competent to make the agreement. In insurance, the most common problem arises in connection with applicants who are under the age of legal majority. Some insurance contracts are voidable by applicants who are minors, and these applicants would receive a full return of the premiums paid if they later decide to make them void. Some states have made exceptions for life, health, and auto insurance contracts by establishing special age limits of 14 or 16; beyond this age, minors are considered to have the legal capacity to insure themselves, and a contract is binding on them.

A similar problem may occur in insurance written for insane or intoxicated persons. They cannot make legal contracts because they fail to understand the agreement.

Insurers, too, must be competent to enter into a legal contract by meeting charter and license requirements of the states. In cases where such legal capacity is lacking, many courts have nevertheless held the contracts binding on the insurer, or on its corporate officers personally, rather than penalizing a good-faith purchaser of the coverage.

d.   *Consideration.* The final requirement for a valid contract is some consideration exchanged by both parties to the agreement—a right or something of value given up, or an obligation assumed. In insurance, the applicant typically makes a premium payment, or the contract may become effective on the basis of the applicant's promise to pay and to meet other conditions of the contract. The insurer's consideration is its promise to pay for specified losses or to provide other services to the policyowner.

6-3.   a.   *Unilateral Nature.* The insurance contract is a unilateral one because only one party, the insurer, makes a legally enforceable promise. If the company fails to fulfill the promises it makes, such as to pay the specified benefits at the death of the insured, the insurer may be held legally liable for breach of contract. The insured makes no such promises after the contract comes into force (although, of course, failure to live up to policy conditions like paying the premiums may release the insurer from the contract).

    b. *Personal Nature.* The insurance contract is personal and follows the person rather than the property concerned. Insurance provides repayment of a loss arising out of an undesired happening by indemnifying the person who has incurred the loss.

    c. *Conditional Nature.* The obligation to perform on the part of one of the parties to an agreement may be conditioned upon the performance of the second party. A clause in an insurance contract requiring such performance is usually referred to as a *condition.* Failure of one party to perform relieves the other party of his or her obligation.

6-4. a. Insurance contracts are contracts of adhesion and, as a general rule, are not subject to negotiation and bargaining.

    b. As a general rule, the benefit of doubt in an insurance contract goes to the insured if the terms are unclear.

    c. Sue is bound by the contract whether she read it or not. A planner should take great care to explain the contract to his or her client because the chances are good the client will not read and/or understand it.

    d. Under the parol evidence rule, oral evidence cannot be used to modify the contract.

6-5. The common law concept of indemnity, modified by state statute, means that an insured is entitled to payment only to the extent of financial loss or legal liability. In other words, the insured should remain in the same financial position that existed prior to a loss and should not be allowed to profit from the loss. Of course, an insured is only indemnified up to the policy limits and is subject to policy provisions and limitations such as deductibles.

    Not all insurance policies are considered policies of indemnity under common law and state statutes. The major example of this exception is life insurance. The courts have determined that it is impossible to place a value on a human life, even though this is done by judges and juries in wrongful death suits. In addition, courts have held that most life insurance contracts are also investment contracts rather than solely insurance contracts. Therefore, the amount of the investment should be protected. The major significance of life insurance not being a contract of indemnity is that the insurer must pay the policy limit if the insured dies.

6-6. The purposes of requiring an insurable interest in insurance contracts are to prevent gambling, to decrease moral hazard, and to help measure the actual loss. Without an insurable interest, a contract is a wager or gambling contract. It also could be an undesirable incentive for some persons to cause losses or injuries on purpose. When an insurable interest exists, no profit results because policyowners merely receive repayment for the loss they have suffered.

6-7. a. An insurable interest exists because your client may suffer a financial loss if his debtor friend dies before repaying the loan.

    b. An insurable interest exists because an automobile owner or driver can be held responsible for losses caused by his or her car.

    c. No insurable interest exists because your client did not own the precious stone at the time it was destroyed. For property to be insurable, an insurable interest must exist at the time of the loss.

6-8. The common law doctrine of subrogation gives the insurer whatever rights the insured possessed against responsible third parties. It is basically a process of substitution, the insurer taking over the legal rights of the insured that existed at the time of the loss. Therefore, from the time of the loss, the insured may not release any rights that might prove beneficial to the insurer.

    In common law, it is a matter of equity that, on paying the insured the amount of the loss, the insurer has a right of action against any other person who may have caused the loss.

    The right of the insurer against other negligent persons usually does not rest on any contractual relationship, but arises out of the nature of the contract of insurance as one of indemnity. If the insured is indemnified, it would be inequitable for him or her also to try to collect from the party responsible for the loss. If the insured were permitted to do this, a double collection of the loss from both the insurer and the party responsible might result in a profit to the insured. Subrogation also holds wrongdoers responsible for the results of their wrongful actions, instead of permitting them not to pay only because an insurance contract bought by someone else was in force. The overall cost of the insurance to policyowners is also reduced in this manner.

6-9. A fundamental doctrine of insurance law is that neither party may practice concealment. This doctrine makes mandatory the disclosure to the insurer of all material or important facts that are the exclusive knowledge of the applicant.

    In general, the concealment of a material fact need not be intentional or fraudulent in order to make a policy voidable, and it is no defense to plead mistake or forgetfulness.

A *representation* is a statement made by an applicant to the insurer at the time of, or prior to, the formation of a contract. A misrepresentation on the part of the applicant of any material fact has the same effect as a concealment and affords a basis for making the contract voidable by the insurer.

The difference between concealment and misrepresentation is that the applicant conceals if a silence is maintained when there is an obligation to speak; he or she misrepresents if a statement is made that is not true.

6-10.   a. Declarations are factual statements that identify the specific person, property, or activity being insured and the parties to the insurance transactions; they also provide descriptive information about the insurance being provided.

        b. The definitions section carefully defines what the policy wishes to cover or not cover. Since ambiguities in the contract are likely to be construed against the insurer, this section of the policy is a major help in making the insurer's intentions precise.

        c. The insuring agreements spell out the basic promises of the insurance company.

        d. Every insurance policy has exclusions—items that the insurer does not intend to cover. The exclusions usually apply either to certain perils, types of losses, types of property, or types of activities.

        e. The insuring agreement is not an absolute promise by the insurer with "no strings attached." Instead, the promise is a qualified one, enforceable only if the policyowner fulfills a number of conditions that are spelled out in the policy.

6-11.   Both noncancelable and guaranteed renewable policies give the policyowner the right to renew the coverage at each policy anniversary date, although possibly only to some stated age such as age 65. These policies may not be terminated by the insurer during the period of coverage. A truly noncancelable policy gurantees future rates for the coverage in the contract itself. In a guaranteed renewable policy, the insurer does not guarantee future rates for the coverage. Instead, the insurer retains the right to raise the rates for broad classes of insureds, but not just for individual insureds with poor claims experience.

6-12.   a. Under the initial deductible, the insurer will pay claims to the extent they exceed a specified amount. The deductible amount may apply to each claim, as is common in property insurance policies, or to a period of time, such as a calendar year, in medical expense policies.

        b. A loss-sharing provision known as a coinsurance clause, or a percentage participation clause, is found in major medical and other types of medical expense coverage. Under this type of provision, the insured is required to assume a percentage of certain covered expenses.

6-13.   As a general legal principle, whenever the wording in an endorsement or rider conflicts with the terms of the policy to which it is attached, the endorsement or rider takes precedence. The assumption underlying this principle is that an alteration of the basic agreement between the policyowner and insurer more accurately reflects the true intent of the parties than does the basic agreement itself.

Answers to Self-Test Questions

6-1.   False. Policyowners realize the immediate benefit of relief from anxiety and freedom from worry about financial losses.

6-2.   True.

6-3.   False. A written application and the first premium payment are usually submitted by the applicant as the offer to the insurer through the agent, who issues a conditional receipt.

6-4.   False. Clients under the age of 21 (18 in some states) are considered minors and can void many types of insurance contracts and get a full refund of premiums paid. However, state laws may hold legal capacity for 16-year-olds who enter into auto insurance contracts.

6-5.   False. An insurance contract is a unilateral contract.

6-6.   False. Property and liability insurance policies are not freely assignable by policyowners. They must obtain the insured's approval in order to effectuate a transfer. Life insurance policies, however, are freely assignable by policyowners.

6-7.   False. This is an example of a condition subsequent.

6-8.   True.

6-9.   True.

6-10. False. Under the general rule of indemnity, if the property is valued at $25,000 and insured for $50,000, the insurance company would only pay $25,000. An insured is entitled to payment only to the extent of financial loss or liability, and should not be allowed to profit from the loss.

6-11. False. Life insurance contracts are valued contracts and are not based on the principle of indemnity.

6-12. True.

6-13. False. The misrepresentation or concealment of a material fact by an applicant for insurance will not void the contract but will make it voidable by the insurer.

6-14. False. Fraud involves an active *intent* to deceive. The applicant making the statement must know that it is false or make the statement in reckless disregard of whether it is true or false.

6-15. True.

6-16. True.

6-17. False. Under an initial deductible, the insurer will pay for losses only after they exceed a specified amount. The insured must absorb all losses up to that specified amount.

6-18. True.

Chapter 7

Answers to Review Questions

7-1. In 2003, an employee and his or her employer pay a tax of 6.2 percent each on the first $87,000 of the employee's wages for Social Security. The employee and employer also pay the Medicare tax rate of 1.45 percent on employee wages. The tax rates are currently scheduled to remain the same after 2003, but the wage bases are adjusted annually for changes in the national level of wages.

Part B of Medicare is financed by a combination of monthly premiums paid by persons eligible for benefits and contributions from the federal government. Part A of Medicare and all the benefits of the Social Security program are financed through a system of payroll and self-employment taxes paid by all persons covered under the programs. In addition, employers of covered persons are also taxed. (These taxes are often referred to as FICA taxes because they are imposed under the Federal Insurance Contributions Act.)

7-2. a. Evelyn does not meet the first test, as she has not earned credit for 40 quarters. However, she does qualify as fully insured under the second test. Evelyn is 38 this year, 2003, so she was born in 1965. She was age 21 in 1986, so would require 15 quarters from 1987 to 2002 to be fully insured, and she has 28 quarters.

b. Because Evelyn is fully insured, she is also currently insured.

c. Although Evelyn is fully insured, she is not disability insured because she does not have the minimum number of quarters within a recent time period.

7-3. A worker who is fully insured under Social Security is eligible to receive monthly retirement benefits as early as age 62. However, the election to receive benefits prior to the full retirement age results in a permanently reduced benefit. Beginning in 2003, the age at which full benefits are payable will increase in gradual steps from age 65 to age 67. Workers born in 1960 or later will wait until age 67 for their full retirement benefits.

7-4. If a deceased worker was either fully or currently insured at the time of death, the following categories of persons are eligible for benefits:

- dependent, unmarried children under the same conditions as for retirement benefits
- a spouse (including a divorced spouse) caring for a child or children under the same conditions as for retirement benefits

If the deceased worker was fully insured, the following categories of persons are also eligible for benefits:

- a widow or widower aged 60 or older. However, benefits are reduced if taken prior to full retirement age. This benefit is also payable to a divorced spouse if the marriage lasted at least 10 years. The widow's or widower's benefit is payable to a disabled spouse at age 50 as long as the disability commenced no more than 7 years after the (1) worker's death or (2) end of the year in which entitlement to a mother's or father's benefit ceased.
- a parent aged 62 or over who was a dependent of the deceased worker at the time of death

7-5. a. The definition of disability requires a mental or physical impairment that prevents the worker from engaging in any substantial gainful employment. The disability must also have lasted (or be expected to last) at least 12 months or be expected to result in death. A more liberal definition of disability applies to blind workers who are aged 55 or older. They are considered disabled if they are unable to perform work that requires skills or abilities comparable to those required by the work they regularly performed before reaching age 55 or becoming blind, if later.

b. Certain family members not otherwise eligible for Social Security benefits may be eligible if they are disabled. Disabled children are subject to the same definition of disability as workers. Disabled widows or widowers must be unable to engage in any gainful (rather than substantial gainful) employment.

7-6. a. The primary insurance amount (PIA) is the amount a worker receives if he or she retires at full retirement age or becomes disabled, and it is the amount on which benefits for family members are based. If a worker is retired or disabled, benefits are paid to family members, as follows. The spouse at full retirement age, or a spouse at any age caring for a disabled child or a child under 16 receives 50 percent of the worker's PIA. Each child under 18 or disabled also receives 50 percent of the worker's PIA. If a worker dies, benefits are paid to family members, as follows. The spouse at full retirement age receives 100 percent of the worker's PIA. A spouse at any age caring for a disabled child or a child under 16 receives 75 percent of the worker's PIA. Each child under 18 or disabled also receives 75 percent of the worker's PIA. Additionally, a sole dependent parent receives 82.5 percent, while two dependent parents receive 75 percent each. However, the full benefits described above may not be payable because of a limitation imposed on the total benefits that may be paid to a family.

       b. If the total amount of benefits payable to family members exceeds the family maximum, the worker's benefit (in the case of retirement and disability) is not affected, but the benefits of other family members are reduced proportionately.

7-7. If a worker elects to receive retirement benefits prior to full retirement age, benefits are permanently reduced by 5/9 of one percent each of the first 36 months that the early retirement precedes full retirement age and 5/12 of one percent for each month in excess of 36. Workers who delay applying for benefits until after full retirement age are eligible for an increased benefit for each month of late retirement until age 70.

7-8. Beneficiaries under full retirement age are allowed earnings of up to $11,520 in 2003, and this figure is subject to annual indexing for later years. If a beneficiary earns more than this amount, then his or her Social Security benefit is reduced by $1 for each $2 of excess earnings. There is one exception to the test: The reduction is $1 for every $3 of earnings in excess of $30,720 (in 2003) in the calendar year a worker attains the full retirement age, for earnings in months prior to such age attainment.

7-9. Social Security benefits are increased automatically each January if there was an increase in the CPI for the one-year period ending in the third quarter of the prior year. The increase is the same as the increase in the CPI since the last cost-of-living adjustment, rounded to the nearest 0.1 percent.

7-10. a. *Hospital Benefits.* Part A pays for inpatient hospital services for up to 90 days in each benefit period (also referred to as a spell of illness). A benefit period begins the first time a Medicare recipient is hospitalized and ends only after the recipient has been out of a hospital or skilled-nursing facility for 60 consecutive days. A subsequent hospitalization then begins a new benefit period.

          Skilled-Nursing Facility Benefits. In many cases, a patient may no longer require continuous hospital care but may not be well enough to go home. Consequently, Part A provides benefits for care in a skilled-nursing facility if a physician certifies that skilled-nursing care or rehabilitative services are needed for a condition that was treated in a hospital within the last 30 days. In addition, the prior hospitalization must have lasted at least 3 days. Benefits are paid in full for 20 days in each benefit period and for an additional 80 days with a daily copayment charge.

          Home Health Care Benefits. If a patient can be treated at home for a medical condition, Medicare will pay the full cost for an unlimited number of home visits by a home health agency. To receive these benefits, a person must be confined at home and be treated under a home health plan set up by a physician.

          Hospice Benefits. Hospice benefits are available under Part A of Medicare for beneficiaries who are certified as being terminally ill with a life expectancy of 6 months or less.

       b. *Hospital Benefits.* In each benefit period, covered hospital expenses are paid in full for 60 days, subject to an initial deductible ($840 in 2003). This deductible is adjusted annually to reflect increasing hospital costs. Benefits for an additional 30 days of hospitalization are also provided in each benefit period, but the patient must pay a daily copayment ($210 in 2003) equal to 25 percent of the initial deductible amount. Each recipient also has a lifetime reserve of 60 additional days that may be used if the regular 90 days of benefits have been exhausted. However, once a reserve day is used, it cannot be restored for use in future benefit periods. When using reserve days, patients must pay a daily copayment ($420 in 2003) equal to 50 percent of the initial deductible amount.

          Skilled-Nursing Facility Benefits. Benefits are paid in full for 20 days in each benefit period and for an additional 80 days with a daily copayment ($105 in 2003) that is equal to 12.5 percent of the initial hospital deductible.

          Home Health Care Benefits. There is no charge for these benefits other than a required 20 percent copayment for the cost of such durable medical equipment as oxygen tanks and hospital beds.

          Hospice Benefits. There are modest copayments for some services.

c. Exclusions under Part A of Medicare include the following:

- services outside the United States and its territories or possessions. However, there are a few exceptions to this rule for qualified Mexican and Canadian hospitals. Benefits will be paid if an emergency occurs in the United States and the closest hospital is in one of these countries. However, persons living closer to a hospital in one of these countries than to a hospital in the United States may use the foreign hospital even if an emergency does not exist. Finally, there is coverage for Canadian hospitals if a person needs hospitalization while traveling the most direct route between Alaska and another state in the United States. However, this latter provision does not apply to persons vacationing in Canada.
- elective luxury services such as private rooms or televisions
- hospitalization for services not necessary for the treatment of an illness or injury such as custodial care or elective cosmetic surgery
- services performed in a federal facility such as a veterans' hospital
- services covered under workers' compensation

In addition to the exclusions, there are times when Medicare will act as the secondary payer of benefits.

7-11. a. Part B of Medicare provides benefits for most medical expenses not covered under Part A. These can include physicians' and surgeons' fees, diagnostic tests, physical therapy, drugs and biologicals that cannot be self-administered, radiation therapy, medical supplies, rental of medical equipment, prosthetic devices, ambulance service, mammograms and Pap smears, diabetes glucose monitoring and education, colorectal cancer screening, bone mass measurement, prostate cancer screening, pneumococcal vaccine and its administration, and home health care services as described for Part A when a person does not have Part A coverage or when Part A benefits are not applicable.

b. With some exceptions, Part B pays 80 percent of the approved charges for covered medical expenses after the satisfaction of a $100 annual deductible. Annual maximums apply to outpatient psychiatric benefits ($450) and physical therapy in a therapist's office or at the patient's home ($400). A few charges are paid in full without any cost sharing. These include (1) home health services, (2) pneumococcal vaccine and its administration, (3) certain surgical procedures that are performed on an outpatient basis in lieu of hospitalization, (4) diagnostic preadmission tests performed on an outpatient basis within 7 days prior to hospitalization, (5) mammograms, and (6) Pap smears.

c. A list of exclusions includes most drugs and biologicals that can be self-administered, most routine examinations, routine foot care, most immunizations, most cosmetic surgery, most dental care, custodial care, and eyeglasses, hearing aids, and orthopedic shoes.

7-12. The new Medicare+Choice plans include HMOs as previously allowed, PPOs, PSOs, private fee-for-service plans, private contracts with physicians, and Archer medical savings accounts. These plans must provide all benefits available under Parts A and B. They may include additional benefits as part of the basic plan or for an additional fee.

7-13. a. All payroll taxes and other sources of funds for Social Security and Medicare are deposited into four trust funds: an old-age and survivors fund, a disability fund, and two Medicare funds. Benefits and administrative expenses are paid out of the appropriate trust fund from contributions to that fund and any interest earnings on accumulated assets. The trust funds have limited reserves to serve as emergency funds in periods when benefits exceed contributions such as in times of high unemployment.

b. The solution lies in doing one or both of the following: increasing revenue into the trust funds or decreasing benefit costs.

7-14. Benefits received in the form of monthly income under Social Security are partially subject to income taxation for some Social Security recipients. If the modified adjusted gross income is $25,000 or less for a single taxpayer ($32,000 or less for a married taxpayer filing jointly), Social Security benefits are not taxable. If the modified adjusted gross income is between this amount and $34,000 ($44,000 for a married taxpayer filing jointly), up to 50 percent of the Social Security benefit is includible in taxable income. If the modified adjusted gross income exceeds $34,000 ($44,000 for a married taxpayer filing jointly), up to 85 percent of the Social Security benefit is includible in taxable income. The exact amount of the taxable Social Security benefit is determined by complex formulas that are beyond the scope of this discussion. Medicare benefits and any lump-sum Social Security benefits are received tax free.

7-15. a. The objectives of unemployment insurance are to provide periodic cash income to workers during periods of involuntary unemployment and to help the unemployed find jobs.

      b.   Unemployment insurance programs are financed primarily by unemployment taxes levied by both the federal and state governments.

      c.   The right to benefits depends on the worker's attachment to the labor force within a prior base period. During this base period, the worker must have earned a minimum amount of wages or worked a minimum period of time, or both. The right to benefits is also contingent on an unemployed worker's being available for work, and both physically and mentally capable of working.

7-16.   Temporary disability laws enable employees to collect disability income benefits regardless of whether their disability begins while they are employed or unemployed. These laws are generally patterned after the state unemployment insurance law and provide similar benefits.

7-17.   a.   Workers' compensation laws were enacted to require employers to provide benefits to employees for losses resulting from work-related accidents or diseases.

      b.   Medical care benefits for medical expenses are usually provided without any limitations on time or amount. Disability income benefits are a function of an employee's average weekly wage over some time period. Death benefits provide burial allowances in a flat amount, varying by state; death benefit cash income payments to survivors are a function of the worker's average wage prior to the injury resulting in death. Rehabilitation benefits are payable for medical rehabilitation and vocational rehabilitation.

7-18.   Unemployment insurance benefits and benefits received under temporary disability laws are included in a recipient's gross income. Workers' compensation benefits are received free of income taxation.

Answers to Self-Test Questions

7-1.   True.

7-2.   False. A person born in 1962 will be eligible to receive full Social Security benefits when he or she reaches age 67.

7-3.   True.

7-4.   True.

7-5.   True.

7-6.   True.

7-7.   False. There is no earnings test reduction for workers older than the full retirement age.

7-8.   True.

7-9.   False. Part A of Medicare pays the inpatient hospital services for an uninterrupted stay of up to 90 days plus another 60 lifetime reserve days.

7-10.   False. A new 90-day benefit period begins after an individual has been out of a hospital or skilled-nursing facility for 60 consecutive days.

7-11.   True.

7-12.   True.

7-13.   True.

7-14.   True.

7-15.   True.

7-16.   False. In almost all cases, the full cost of providing workers' compensation benefits is borne by the employers, not the employees.

7-17.   False. Workers' compensation benefits are received free of income taxation.

Chapter 8

Answers to Review Questions

8-1.   When an income producer's family is completely dependent on his or her personal earnings for subsistence and the amenities of life, and the income earner dies, the unrealized portion of his or her total earnings potential is lost. Life insurance can enable the family to retain the same economic position that they would have enjoyed had the income earner lived.

8-2.   The annual premium under the yearly renewable term plan must (along with interest earned during the year) pay the policy's share of death claims each year for the group (class) to which the insured has been assigned. The death rate rises at an increasing rate as age increases for the class from year to year so the overall premium also rises at an increasing rate.

Premiums under the level premium plan are constant throughout the premium paying period. In the early years, the level premium is larger than the policy's share of the death claims. In the years when the level premiums are more than sufficient to meet the policy's share of the death claims, the excess premiums are accumulated at interest in a reserve to help pay the policy's share of the death claims in later years when (in most cases) the policy's share of the death claims is larger than the policy's level premium. With cash value insurance, the reserve increases over the years and equals the face amount of the policy at the maturity of the policy.

The term plan provides protection for the face amount of the policy, while the level premium plan provides protection for the net amount at risk, equal to the face amount of the policy minus the reserve. The term plan provides no cash value, while the level premium plan builds cash value (except for short-term level premium term policies, where the reserve is very small).

8-3. a. (1) Term insurance provides temporary death protection for the policy period. With whole life insurance, there is permanent death protection as long as the policy remains in force.

(2) If the insured lives beyond the end of the policy period with term insurance, no benefit is paid. For a whole life policy, if the insured is still alive at maturity age (usually age 100), the policy matures, and the face amount (for tax purposes, the cash value) is paid.

(3) With yearly renewable term insurance, the full gross premium is used to pay mortality costs, expenses, contingencies, and profit. With level premium policies, whether term or whole life, the early year premiums are greater than needed (along with interest) to pay mortality costs, expenses, contingencies, and profit. The excess premium is accumulated at an assumed rate of interest in a reserve.

b. If you buy a 10-year *renewable* term policy, you may extend it at the end of 10 years, without proof of insurability. You'll pay the new higher level premium that reflects the higher death rates in the next 10 years. If your policy was not renewable term, you would have to reapply for insurance and prove your insurability again.

c. If you buy a 10-year *convertible* term policy and then need a more permanent form of insurance, you can switch it to whole life insurance or another form of permanent insurance sold by the insurer in the future without proof of insurability.

d. A decreasing term policy is appropriate for funding the balance of your mortgage when you die.

e. (1) There is no difference.

(2) With an ordinary life policy, the premium is paid as long as the insured lives (up to the assumed mortality age 99), the premium outlay will be smaller per year than that for limited-payment whole life policies of the same face amount. With limited-payment whole life policies, the shorter the premium payment period, the larger the amount of premium outlay per year.

(3) Because limited-payment whole life policies have higher premiums for the same death benefit as ordinary life policies, their reserves and cash values are larger than for ordinary life policies.

8-4. Participating (par) policies provide for the payment of dividends to the policyowner. These policies anticipate charging a small extra margin in the premium with the intent to return part of the premium as policyowner dividends depending on the extent to which the insurer has favorable experience from interest, mortality, and/or expenses. Nonparticipating policies do *not* provide for the payment of policyowner dividends and policyowners share in the insurer's experience via changes in premiums and/or cash values.

8-5. a. An endowment policy pays the death benefit at the death of the insured, or the end of the policy period, whichever comes first. The endowment policy requires a much higher premium than whole life and has a savings element much larger relative to the protection element for whole life insurance.

b. A 1984 tax law change eliminated the tax-free buildup of cash values for most newly sold endowment policies, so endowment purchases do not make sense today.

8-6. a. A variable life insurance policy provides no interest rate guarantee and no minimum cash value.

b. The SEC requires variable life policies to be registered and all sales to be subject to the requirements applicable to other registered securities. Policy sales may be made only after the prospective purchaser has had a chance to read the policy prospectus. The SEC also requires that the insurance company be registered as an investment company and that all sales agents be registered with the SEC for the specific purpose of variable life insurance policy sales. Agents who sell variable life insurance policies must be licensed as both life insurance agents and securities agents.

c. Variable life insurance policies give the purchaser several investment options into which the funds can be directed. The policyowner is free to put all of the funds into one of these choices or to distribute the funds among the options in whatever proportions he or she desires. Some insurance companies have more than a dozen funds to choose from in their current product offering.

d. Variable life insurance contracts include mortality charges for the death benefits they provide. Consequently, the return on the invested funds within a variable life insurance contract will never equal that of a separate investment fund that does not provide death benefits but invests in assets of a similar type and quality.

e. There are two basic ways used to link a policy's death benefit to the associated portfolio's investment performance—the level additions method or the constant ratio method. Regardless of the linkage design, a minimum death benefit is guaranteed. The purchaser selects a target level of investment performance as a benchmark against which actual investment performance will be measured. Performance in excess of the target level is used to fund incremental increases in the death benefit; performance below the target amount requires downward adjustments in the death benefits to make up for the deficit.

f. After administrative charges, the balance of the premium payment goes into the cash value account. Cash value accounts are further diminished by mortality charges to support the death benefits. The actual value of the cash component is determined by the net asset value of the separate account funds that make up the policy portfolio. The cash value of a variable life policy fluctuates daily. Each day's net asset value is based on the closing price for the issues in the portfolio on that trading day. Variable life insurance policies usually limit maximum policy loans to a slightly smaller percentage of the total cash value than is traditionally available in whole life policies.

g. The prospectus must contain a full disclosure of all the contract provisions, including expenses, investment options, benefit provisions, and policyowner rights under the contract. Other information includes information regarding all of the expense charges levied by the insurance company against variable life insurance contracts, surrender charges, and investment portfolio information.

8-7.   a. Premiums are flexible after the first year—the only time that a minimum level of payment is required.

b. The higher the amount or proportion of prefunding through premium payments, the more investment earnings will be credited to the policy and utilized to cover mortality and administrative costs. All premium suggestions are based on some assumed level of investment earnings, and the policyowner assumes the possibility that actual investment earnings will be less than necessary to support the suggested premium. Even though investment earnings cannot go below the guaranteed rate, a long-term shortfall may necessitate either an increase in premiums or a reduction in coverage at some future point. The accumulations from prefunding are credited to the policy's cash value and are quite visible to the policyowner. The earnings rates applied to those accumulations are also clearly visible as they fluctuate with current economic conditions.

c. The policyowner can make partial withdrawals from the policy's cash value without incurring indebtedness. There is no obligation to repay those funds, nor is there any interest incurred on the amount withdrawn. Withdrawals do affect the policy's future earnings because the fund still intact to earn interest for future crediting periods is reduced by the amount of the withdrawal. The effect on the death benefit depends on the type of death benefit in force.

d. The target premium amount is the suggested premium to be paid on a level basis throughout the contract's duration, or for a shorter period of time if a limited-payment approach was originally intended to fund the policy. The target premium amount is a suggestion and carries no liability to the insurer if it is inadequate to maintain the contract.

e. (1) The level death benefit design is much like the traditional whole life design. The death benefit stays constant, the cash value increases over time, and the net amount at risk decreases.

(2) Under the increasing death benefit design, a constant net amount at risk is superimposed over the policy's cash value. As the cash value increases, the total death benefit also increases. A reduction in the cash value will reduce the death benefit. At the insured's death, the policy's stated face amount plus its cash value are paid.

f. Most insurance companies credit current interest rates on the universal life cash value as long as there are no policy loans outstanding. Once the policyowner borrows funds from the cash value, the insurance company usually credits a lower interest rate or earnings rate to the portion of the cash value associated with the policy loan.

g. From each premium dollar paid for universal life insurance, deductions are made for expenses and mortality. In addition, the universal life cash value account is increased at the current crediting rate to reflect investment earnings on that cash value. These dollars help to reduce the policyowner's current and future out-of-pocket premium expenses. The actual rate is credited at the insurer's discretion and tends to fluctuate, reflecting current economic conditions.

8-8.   If just enough premium is paid each year to cover policy expense and mortality charges for the year, the universal life policy will essentially be the equivalent of yearly renewable term insurance providing pure protection for the year with no cash value (savings). As the amount of premium paid in each year is increased (with the policy death benefit unchanged), the universal life policy will provide protection and savings *comparable* to that available with longer and longer term insurance, then an ordinary life policy, and finally limited-payment whole life insurance with a shorter and shorter premium payment period.

8-9.   a.   Federal income tax law requires that to meet the tax law definition of life insurance, a specified proportion of the death benefit must be derived from the amount at risk (for tax purposes, that is the death benefit minus the cash value). Whenever the cash value in the contract becomes high enough that the proportion is no longer satisfied, the death benefit of the universal life policy starts increasing, even though the contract has a level death benefit design.

       b.   With the increasing benefit design, a constant amount at risk is superimposed over the policy's cash value. Thus the total death benefit payable equals the policy's stated face amount plus its cash value. If the cash value decreases (for example, because of premium payments being skipped), the death benefit will likewise decrease.

8-10. a.   Variable universal life insurance is similar to variable life insurance in that it gives policyowners several options for directing the investments. The policyowner can reposition the portfolio at any time. Like variable life, variable universal life has no interest rate or cash value guarantee. Variable universal life like variable life is technically classified as a security and is subject to regulation by the SEC. In addition, sales of both variable universal life and variable life policies require a prospectus.

       b.   Variable universal life insurance incorporates all of the premium flexibility, death benefit design, and partial withdrawal features like those under universal life policies. Like universal life policies, variable universal life policies have no guarantee that once the cash value is large enough to carry the policy, it will always be able to do so.

8-11. a.   A joint-life or first-to-die policy is written on the lives of two or more persons and is payable on the death of the first person to die. These policies are common for funding business buy-sell agreements.

       b.   A survivorship or second-to-die policy is written on two or more lives and payable on the death of the last insured to die. These policies are used to fund federal estate taxes of wealthy couples whose wills provide for maximum tax deferral at the first death.

8-12. a.   To be eligible, an employee must be in a covered classification of workers, work on a full-time basis, and be actively at work. He or she may be required to fulfill a probationary period and, in some cases, to show insurability and meet premium contribution requirements.

       b.   Most group life coverage is provided without individual evidence of insurability. However, this evidence is required in some cases such as when an employee decides after the expiration of the eligibility period that he or she wants the coverage after all.

       c.   The amount of group life insurance on each covered worker is normally set according to a schedule, most commonly based on earnings or position. In an earnings schedule, the amount of insurance is often equal to some multiple of earnings, such as two times the employee's annual earnings, rounded up to the next $1,000 and subject to a maximum benefit. In a position schedule, differing benefit amounts are provided based on each employee's position within the firm.

       d.   Any employee whose group life insurance ceases has the right according to the master contract to convert to an individual insurance policy. Conversion does not require proof of insurability and must occur within the first 31 days of eligibility to convert. The individual policy may be any type the insurer offers except term insurance, and the face amount may not exceed the amount of group life insurance. The premium for the individual policy is based on the employee's attained age as of the time of conversion.

       e.   Additional amounts of insurance may be made available to some or all classes of employees. Proof of insurability is usually required to obtain the additional amount, except when the amount of coverage is small, and the employer does not usually pay any part of the premium for it.

            Dependent life insurance also may be available. Coverage is usually optional, with the employee paying the entire cost. The amount of insurance is usually modest, and the employee usually is not allowed to select which of his or her eligible dependents will be covered but must decide on an all-or-none basis.

Self-Test Questions

8-1.   False. In some cases, child support and alimony are court ordered to continue even beyond the provider's death.

8-2.   True.

8-3.   True.

8-4.   True.

8-5.   False. Insurers offering term insurance on an individual basis often place a limit on the period during which the insurance can be renewed, in order to protect against adverse selection.

8-6.   True.

8-7.   False. The policyowner/insured would be permitted to renew the policy regardless of the insured's health.

8-8.   False. Decreasing term represents a substantial portion of the term insurance used for financial planning purposes, especially mortgage coverage.

8-9.   True.

8-10.   False. Both of these policies provide protection for the lifetime of the insured (until the assumed mortality age).

8-11.   True.

8-12.   False. Federal income tax reform in 1984 eliminated the tax-free buildup of cash values in most endowment policies, so few endowment policies are sold today.

8-13.   True.

8-14.   False. Both the cash value and the level of death benefits reflect investment performance.

8-15.   True.

8-16.   True.

8-17.   False. Under the level death benefit design, death benefits are level unless the cash value gets too close to the death benefit to comply with the federal income tax law, in which case the death benefit will start increasing. However, under the increasing death benefit design, the death benefit will increase or decrease with the cash value.

8-18.   True.

8-19.   False. A joint-life policy is payable on the death of the first of two or more lives insured under the single contract. A survivorship or second-to-die policy is payable on the death of the last of two or more lives insured under the single contract.

8-20.   True.

Chapter 9

Answers to Review Questions

9-1.   The declarations page of most life insurance contracts contains the name of the insurance company, specific policy details, a general description of the type of insurance provided by the policy contract, a statement about the policy's free-look provision, and the insurer's promise to pay.

9-2.   a. *Grace Period:* Life insurance policies include a grace period, during which an overdue premium may be paid without a lapse in coverage. The standard length of the grace period is 31 days. Frank's coverage is still in force.

        b. *Policy Loan Provision:* The policy loan provision gives the policyowner access to the cash value that accumulates inside the policy without terminating the policy. The policyowner requests a loan, and the life insurer lends the funds confidentially. The loan provisions in the policy specify the portion of the cash value that is available for loans and how interest will be determined. In most policies, over 90 percent of the cash value is available for loans.

        c. *Incontestable Clause:* The incontestable clause provides that once the policy has been in force for 2 years during Frank's lifetime, the insurer cannot deny payment to the beneficiary because of concealment or misrepresentation in the application.

        d. *Dividend Options:* In addition to reduction in premiums (and cash), participating whole life policies generally offer:

        • *accumulation at interest.* The insurer retains the dividends in the equivalent of a savings account with a minimum guaranteed rate of interest, although a higher rate may be credited if conditions warrant. The accumulated dividends may be withdrawn at any time. If not withdrawn, they are added to the death proceeds or to the nonforfeiture value if the policy is surrendered.

- *purchase of paid-up additions.* Each dividend purchases a small amount of additional, fully paid whole life insurance on an attained-age basis. The purchase premium does not contain expense loading, and no evidence of insurability is required.
- *purchase of term insurance ("fifth dividend").* Some insurers use a portion of the dividend to buy one-year term insurance equal to the policy's then cash value, with the remainder used to buy paid-up additions or to accumulate at interest. Alternatively, other insurers use the entire dividend to buy one-year term insurance. In either case, the term insurance is purchased on the basis of the insured's attained age.

e. *Misstatement of Age:* The insurer would adjust the death benefits payable to the beneficiary to that amount which the premium paid would have purchased at the correct age.

9-3. The policyowner has the option of taking a reduced amount of paid-up whole life insurance, payable upon the same conditions as the original policy. The amount of the paid-up insurance is the amount that can be purchased at the insured's attained age by the net cash value (cash value, less any policy indebtedness, plus any dividend accumulations) applied as a net single premium. The paid-up insurance is purchased at net rates.

The other option provides extended term insurance in an amount equal to the original face amount of the policy, increased by any dividend additions or deposits and decreased by any policy indebtedness. The length of the term is that which can be purchased at the insured's attained age with the net cash value applied as a single premium. If the insured fails to elect an option within a specified period after default of premiums, this option is usually the one that automatically goes into effect.

9-4. The types of settlement options, in addition to the lump-sum or cash option, most commonly found in life insurance policies are as follows:

- *interest option.* Death proceeds are retained temporarily by the insurer, and only the interest is paid to the beneficiary periodically. A minimum interest rate is guaranteed in the policy, although insurers frequently pay a higher rate if investment earnings warrant. Death proceeds are paid at a specified later date at the request of the beneficiary, or on the occurrence of a specified event such as the death of the beneficiary.
- *fixed-period option.* Installment payments consisting of both the death proceeds and interest are made to the beneficiary over a specified period of time. A minimum interest rate is guaranteed. If the insurer pays a higher rate than the guaranteed rate, the amount of the installment payment is increased accordingly.
- *fixed-amount option.* Level periodic installments of a specified amount are paid to the beneficiary. The payments consist of a portion of the death proceeds and interest, and continue for as long as the funds held by the insurer last. Unlike the fixed-period option, excess interest earnings under the fixed-amount option do not increase the size of the periodic payments but instead extend the length of time during which the payments will continue.
- *life income options.* Death proceeds are applied as a single premium to purchase an annuity for the beneficiary. Various forms of annuities may be available, most commonly straight life income, a life income with a period certain, a life income with some type of refund feature, and a joint-and-survivor life income.

9-5. a. The primary beneficiary is the person or organization that is to receive the proceeds if he, she, or it survives the insured. The estate of the insured may be named primary beneficiary, although this is usually unwise because it subjects the proceeds to transfer taxes and costs that can be avoided.

A contingent beneficiary is a person or organization that is to receive the proceeds only if the primary beneficiary predeceases the insured or loses entitlement to any of the proceeds for some other reason. If the primary beneficiary is eligible to receive the policy proceeds, the rights of the contingent beneficiary to proceeds are extinguished.

b. If a beneficiary is named revocably, the policyowner can change the designation at any tim insured's death without the beneficiary's consent. If the beneficiary is named irrevocabl' must obtain the beneficiary's consent before changing the beneficiary. Normally, an requires the beneficiary's consent to the exercise of various other ownership r surrendering for cash or borrowing against the nonforfeiture value.

9-6. Yes. While most insurance contracts do not provide coverage for a death by su after the policy is issued, they do cover suicide after the exclusion period has e\

9-7.   Some insurers permit the insured to withdraw policy death benefits under certain circumstances. These accelerated benefits or living benefits provisions state that if the insured develops a medical condition that renders the insured terminally ill, then he or she may withdraw a portion of the policy's death benefit. According to the NAIC Accelerated Benefits Model Regulation, the condition that permits the payment of the accelerated benefits must be a medical condition that drastically limits the insured's normal life span expectation (for example, to 2 years or less). Therefore, Harold may be able to draw his policy's death benefits due to his poor prognosis.

9-8.   Double indemnity may give the illusion of "double coverage." However, certain conditions must be satisfied in order for the insurer to pay double the face amount. One requirement is that death must occur as a result of an accident.

9-9.   The guaranteed purchase option, also called the guaranteed insurability option, helps policyowners protect themselves against the possibility that the insured might become uninsurable. Under the typical option, the owner may purchase additional insurance in specified amounts at specified times or ages of the insured. Typically, this provision allows additional purchases every 3 years, upon marriage, and after the birth of a child, provided the events occur before the insured reaches a specified maximum age (often age 45). No evidence of insurability is required in order to exercise the option. Also, the new coverage is normally not subject to a new suicide provision or a new incontestability clause.

Self-Test Questions

9-1.   False. While certain provisions must be included, insurers can select the actual wording as long as it is at least as favorable to the policyowner as the statutory language.

9-2.   False. If the insured dies 2 weeks after the premium was due but not paid, the policy remains in force under the grace period provision, and the life insurance company must pay the beneficiary an amount equal to the full death benefit (possibly minus one month's premium).

9-3.   True.

9-4.   True.

9-5.   True.

9-6.   False. The company would lower the death benefit to the amount that the premium paid would have purchased at the correct age. The incontestable clause does not apply to a misstatement of age.

9-7.   False. If the premium for a whole life insurance policy is not paid by the end of the grace period, the policy will lapse and automatically go under a nonforfeiture option, usually extended term. The policyowner then has a period of time to decide to keep the policy under the automatic option, surrender it for its cash value, or switch to the paid-up whole life option.

9-8.   False. The death proceeds from Sarah's policy will be paid to her children as contingent beneficiaries. Upon her husband's death, the right to receive the death proceeds from Sarah's policy transfers to the children as contingent beneficiaries.

9-9.   True.

9-10. False. This person is the policyowner.

9-11. False. Accidental death benefit riders do not pay for deaths caused by disease.

9-12. True.

Chapter 10

Answers to Review Questions

10-1. Life insurance planning includes a determination both of how much insurance is needed and of the proper type of insurance. The first of these tasks is usually completed based on an analysis of the client's needs. The second task begins with a decision between temporary versus permanent coverage and proceeds to the selection of a particular type of policy.

10-2. In the financial needs analysis, first, an estimate must be made of the family financial needs in the event of the client's death. An estimate is made of lump-sum needs at death, which include, for example, final medical expenses not covered by insurance, repayment of debt, estate taxes, final expenses, probate costs, attorneys' fees, ongoing short-term household operational expenses, and an emergency fund. Information needed to determine the lump-sum needs includes knowing the spending habits of the surviving dependents, as well as the level of liquid or near-liquid assets available at the death of the client.

Ongoing income needs also must be estimated. These needs are estimated for four time periods: (1) the readjustment period immediately after the client's death; (2) the period following the readjustment period continuing until the youngest child becomes self-sufficient; (3) the blackout period between the time that the youngest child becomes self-sufficient and the surviving spouse becomes eligible again for Social Security; and (4) the period after the surviving spouse becomes eligible again for Social Security and for any other pension benefits. Then sources of income are identified that can offset the ongoing income needs. Information needed to determine the sources of income include estimating the Social Security retirement benefit, identifying other employer-provided plan benefits, and estimating the surviving spouse's earnings. Then the present value of the income shortfall is calculated and added to the lump-sum needs at death that are not covered by liquid or near-liquid assets.

10-3.   The financial needs analysis approach, which involves the liquidation of principal, calculates the amount of additional life insurance needed by computing the gap between the needs of the client's dependents and the resources available to meet those needs in the event of the client's death. In this case, $50,000 of additional life insurance would be needed to meet the lump-sum needs ($300,000 minus $250,000 from existing insurance and savings). Another $200,000 of life insurance would be needed to meet the children's income support needs after taking into account their Social Security benefits after their mother's death. Thus, Janet would need an additional $250,000 ($50,000 plus $200,000) of life insurance to meet her family's needs in the event of her death.

10-4.   Unlike the capital liquidation approach, which assumes that policy proceeds will provide a life income through annuitization, the capital needs analysis approach assumes that the income benefits can be provided from the investment income only. First, family financial needs are determined in the same manner as in the capital liquidation approach. Then a personal balance sheet of the client is prepared. From the total assets are subtracted all the liabilities, immediate cash needs, and all assets that do not produce income. The remainder is the client's present income-producing capital. Finally, the amount of additional capital needed to achieve the desired income objective net of all other income sources is computed. The amount of additional capital needed to meet the desired objective is found by dividing the amount of additional income needed by the applicable interest rate that represents the after-tax rate of investment return anticipated on the capital sum.

10-5.   Regarding safety of principal, the life insurance industry has compiled a solvency record over the years that is unmatched by any other type of business organization. It has survived war, depression, and inflation; losses to policyowners have been relatively rare. Even the few companies seized by the regulators in recent years have been able to honor most of their policyowners' contracts.

Life insurance companies unquestionably obtain the highest possible yield commensurate with the standard of safety they have set for themselves and the regulatory constraints within which they operate. It is highly questionable that the typical life insurance policyowner can, over a long period, earn a consistently higher yield than a life insurance company without taking on a greater degree of speculative investment risk. Annual increases in cash values are not subject to federal income taxes as they accrue, while the earnings from a separate investment program are often taxed as ordinary income.

With respect to the third objective of an investment program, the liquidity of a life insurance contract is unsurpassed. The policyowner's cash value can be taken out at any time with no loss of principal. This can be accomplished through surrender for cash, through policy loans, or through partial withdrawals (in many newer life insurance products). In traditional products, the insured virtually never faces the possibility of liquidating his or her assets in an unfavorable market; nor can the insured's policy loans be called because of inadequate collateral.

10-6.   Among the distinguishing characteristics that may make one type preferable over another for a particular client are the following:

- length of the planned premium-paying period.
- emphasis on saving versus protection. If very heavy emphasis is to be placed on the savings element, consider a very short premium-paying period (perhaps even single-premium whole life) or an endowment (though some of the advantage of the tax-deferred buildup of the savings element can be lost).
- time when death benefits are needed. If the principal need for funds is at the death of the main income-earner, a single-life policy is appropriate. However, if the principal need for funds is to provide estate liquidity when the surviving spouse dies, consider a joint or survivorship life (second-to-die) policy.
- desire for inflation protection. Variable life, universal life, or variable universal life insurance can provide increasing amounts of death benefit protection.

- importance of yield versus safety in the savings component. If the client's risk-tolerance permits, variable, universal, or variable universal life may be appropriate as a way to achieve a higher yield.
- unbundling of cost components. If the client wants to know where his or her premium dollars go, consider variable, universal, or variable universal life insurance.
- premium-payment flexibility. If this is an important consideration, universal life or variable universal life can be appropriate recommendations.

10-7.   a. The surrender cost index indicates the cost of surrendering the policy and withdrawing the cash value at some future point in time such as 20 years. The result is the average amount of each annual premium, in this example, $7.35 per $1,000 of coverage, that is not returned if the policy is surrendered for its cash value.

To compute the surrender cost index, the usual steps are as follows:

(1) Assume that each annual premium is placed in an account to accumulate at 5 percent interest until the end of a 20-year period.

(2) Assume that each annual dividend is placed in an account to accumulate at 5 percent interest until the end of the 20-year period.

(3) Subtract the 20th year cash value and the result of step (2) from the result of step (1).

(4) Divide the result of step (3) by the future-value-of-an-annuity-due factor for 20 years and 5 percent. The result represents the estimated level annual cost of the policy.

(5) Divide the result of step (4) by the number of thousands of dollars in the policy's death benefit. The result is the estimated level annual cost per $1,000 of coverage.

b. The net payment cost index is useful when the main concern is with the death benefit, rather than the cash value to be paid at some future point in time such as the end of the 20th year. The procedure for calculating this index is identical to that for the surrender cost index, except that in step (3) there is no subtraction of the 20th year cash value.

c. The calculations must take into account the time value of money. The future value of all premium payments is compared to the eventual cash value plus future value of dividends accumulated. The net shortfall, or future value of net costs, is then annuitized across the payment period.

10-8.   a. In recent years, with sometimes higher interest rates and improved mortality experience, a policyowner may be able to substantially improve his or her situation by replacing an existing policy in either the same or a different company.

b. The Unfair Trade Practices Act contains prohibitions against misrepresentation, including misrepresentations to induce the lapse, forfeiture, exchange, conversion, or surrender of any life insurance policy.

c. The replacing agent must state whether the policy is a replacement at the time of application. For a replacement, the agent must give the applicant a prescribed notice alerting the applicant to the need to compare the existing and the proposed benefits carefully and to seek information from the agent or insurer from whom he or she purchased the original policy.

The replacing insurer must advise the other insurer of the proposed replacement and provide accurate information on the new policy. The replacing insurer must also give the applicant at least a 20-day free look at the new policy, during which time he or she has an unconditional right to a full refund of all premiums paid if he or she decides not to retain the policy.

The existing insurer or agent has 20 days to furnish the policyowner with accurate information on the existing policy, including its premium, cash values, death benefits, and dividends.

10-9.   A group that is rated as substandard by an insurer is expected to produce a higher mortality rate than a group of normal lives. If 1,000 persons, each of whom is engaged in a hazardous occupation, are granted insurance, it is certain that the death rate among them will be greater than the death rate among a group of people the same age who are not engaged in a hazardous occupation. To allow for the higher death rates (called extra mortality) that will certainly occur within the substandard group, the company must collect an extra premium from—or impose special terms on—all who are subject to the extra mortality, because it is not known which of the members of the group will be responsible for it. Every member of the group is not expected to survive for a shorter period than the normal life expectancy. In fact, it is a certainty that this will not be the case; it is known merely that a larger proportion of the people in a standard group will attain normal life expectancy.

10-10. The methods used by life insurers for handling substandard risks include:

Increase in age. Under this method, the applicant is assumed to be a number of years older than his or her real age, and the policy is written accordingly. This method of dealing with substandard applicants is often used when the extra mortality is decidedly increasing and will continue to increase indefinitely.

Extra percentage tables. If an applicant presents an increasing hazard, the life insurer may charge premiums that reflect the appropriate increase in mortality. Depending on company practice and state law, surrender values may be based on the special mortality table or may be the same as surrender values under policies issued to standard applicants.

Flat extra premium. Under this method, the life insurer increases the standard premium by a specified number of dollars per $1,000 of insurance. The flat extra premium method is normally used when the hazard is thought to be constant (deafness or partial blindness, for example) or decreasing (as with a family history of tuberculosis or the aftermath of a serious illness or surgical operation, in which case the flat extra premium is usually temporary). The flat extra premium is widely used to cover the extra mortality associated with certain occupations and avocations. The flat extra premium is not reflected in policy values and dividends.

Liens. When the extra mortality to be expected from an impairment is of a distinctly decreasing and temporary nature, such as that associated with convalescence from a serious illness, an insurer might agree to create a lien against the policy for a number of years, the amount and term of the lien depending on the extent of the impairment. If such a method is utilized, the policy is issued at standard rates and is standard in all respects except that, should death occur before the end of the period specified, the amount of the lien is deducted from the proceeds otherwise payable.

Other Methods. When the degree of extra mortality is small, or when its nature is not well known, the life insurer may make no extra charge but, if the policy is participating, may place all of the members of the group in a special class for dividend purposes, adjusting the dividends in accordance with the actual experience. Another approach is to deal with the impairment by merely limiting the plan of insurance to one with a high savings component.

10-11. The major benefit is that cash will be available to the policyowner to fund for the insured's final needs. However, the surviving family will no longer be provided for by the policy. Other pitfalls include potential loss of social benefits based on need and the lack of regulation regarding privacy. Furthermore, state regulation is not uniform and may be nonexistent, information regarding the provider's financial strength may be unavailable, and fraudulent practices taint the industry.

10-12. a. A business can purchase life insurance on Betty, a key employee, to cover the possibility of an income loss and/or increase in expenses resulting from her death. Term insurance can be purchased if the primary concern is the key employee's dollar value to the business. Decreasing term might be appropriate because the key employee loss exposure decreases as the insured approaches retirement. Key employee insurance, however, is usually coupled with some other purpose such as providing a retirement benefit for the key employee. Permanent life insurance is typically purchased to meet this objective.

b. Suzie can set up a buy-sell agreement with the two minor shareholders so that upon Suzie's death, her shares will be sold to the surviving owners of the business. The agreement may be funded with life insurance and should indicate how such life insurance will be structured and paid for. If an entity arrangement is used, the firm itself enters into an agreement with each owner specifying that, on the death of an owner, the firm will buy and the deceased's estate will sell the business interest of the deceased. The firm carries life insurance on each owner, with the firm as beneficiary, to provide the money to fund the agreement. If a cross-purchase approach is used, each stockholder is both a seller and a purchaser. On the death of one owner, the decedent's estate will sell, and the other owners will buy, the deceased's interest. To fund this type of agreement, each owner should carry and be the beneficiary of insurance on the lives of the other owners.

c. The company can provide group term life insurance to participating employees under a Sec. 79 benefit plan. This plan allows the employer a tax deduction for premium payments on behalf of a participant unless the premium amounts cause the tax code's reasonable compensation test to be exceeded (an unlikely event). If the coverage provided by the plan is nondiscriminatory, the first $50,000 of coverage is provided tax free to all plan participants.

d. The company can provide split-dollar life insurance, a form of permanent life insurance frequently used as an executive compensation benefit. In a traditional split-dollar plan, a corporation and an employee split a life insurance policy covering the life of the employee. The corporation contributes an amount equal to the annual increase in the cash surrender value, while the executive pays the remainder of the annual premium. At the death of the insured, the corporation receives a return of its contributions, which equals the cash surrender value, while the beneficiary named by the policyowner receives a death benefit equal to the net amount at risk.

10-13. a. Subject to some exceptions, proceeds paid under a life insurance contract by reason of the insured's death are excludible from gross income for federal income tax purposes. The basic requirement for the income tax exclusion for life insurance proceeds is that they be paid by reason of the death of the insured. Current law also extends the exclusion to certain accelerated death benefits made on behalf of an insured who is terminally ill and expected to die within 24 months. The most important exception to the general rule of exclusion of life insurance death proceeds from federal income taxation is the transfer-for-value rule, which provides that if a policy is transferred from one owner to another for valuable consideration, the income tax exclusion is lost. There are some exceptions to the transfer-for-value rule.

b. Death proceeds distributed as a series of payments under a settlement option generally include an element of interest earned, which is taxable. However, the portion of a settlement option payment that represents principal (the policy's face amount) still qualifies for the income tax exclusion.

c. Policy dividends are treated as a nontaxable return of premium and reduce the policyowner's basis. If total dividends paid exceed total premiums, dividends are taxable to that extent. If dividends are used to reduce premiums or otherwise paid back into the policy (for example, to buy paid-up additions), the basis reduction caused by the payment of the dividend is offset by a corresponding basis increase when the dividend is reinvested in the policy because it is then treated as an additional premium payment.

d. The inside buildup (increase in the cash value or investment fund) of a permanent life insurance policy is not subject to taxation as long as it is left inside the policy.

e. If a policyowner withdraws funds from a policy's cash value, the general rule is that the withdrawal is first treated as a nontaxable return of basis. The excess, if any, of the amount of the withdrawal over the policyowner's current basis is taxable in the year of withdrawal. However, there are important exceptions, including certain withdrawals from universal life policies and withdrawals from policies classified as modified endowment contracts.

   One exception typically occurs in a universal life contract. If a cash value withdrawal results in a reduction in the policy's death benefit during the first 15 years of the policy, the withdrawal may first be taxed as income to the extent of income earned within the contract. This income first or LIFO (last in, first out) method of taxation is the reverse of the general rule of basis first or FIFO (first in, first out) taxation that life insurance typically enjoys.

f. Loans from a policy are not taxable unless the policy is a modified endowment contract (MEC).

g. Any life insurance policy that falls under the definition of an MEC is subject to an income first or LIFO tax treatment with respect to loans and most distributions from the policy. A 10 percent penalty tax also generally applies to the taxable portion of any loan or withdrawal from an MEC unless the taxpayer has reached age 59½. With respect to loans (not withdrawals) from an MEC, the policyowner does receive an increase in basis in the policy equal to the amount of the loan that is taxable. However, the nontaxable portion of a loan from an MEC will not affect the policyowner's basis. A nontaxable portion of a withdrawal, on the other hand, will reduce basis.

h. The general rule is that premium payments for individual life insurance policies are not deductible for federal income tax purposes. This rule applies regardless of who owns the policy and whether it is used for personal or business purposes. However, in certain situations, life insurance premiums can be deductible because they also fit the definition of some other type of deductible expense, not because they are premium payments—for example, because they are for a policy written for the benefit of a charitable organization or because the premium is a corporate expense or part of an alimony payment.

10-14. a. The federal gift tax applies only if there has been a completed transfer and acceptance of property and the transfer was for less than full and adequate consideration.

b. Qualifying gifts of $11,000, the annual exclusion, or less may be made by a donor to any number of donees without gift tax consequences. The annual exclusion amount is indexed to inflation, and it will increase in $1,000 increments. To qualify for an annual exclusion, the gift must provide the donee with a present interest.

c. Two types of gifts are fully deductible from the gift tax base. First, the marital deduction provides that unlimited qualifying transfers made by a donor to his or her spouse are fully deductible from the gift tax base. Second, qualifying gifts to a legitimate charity are deductible.

10-15. The starting point in the federal estate tax calculation is determining the property included in the decedent's gross estate, which includes all property that passes under the deceased's will or, in the absence of a valid will, under the state intestacy law, as well as property transferable by other means by the decedent at death. Then certain items are deductible from the gross estate for estate tax calculation purposes such as legitimate debts of the decedent, reasonable funeral and other death costs of the decedent, and the reasonable cost of estate settlement, such as the executor's commission and attorney fees. Qualifying transfers to a surviving spouse and transfers to qualifying charities are also deductible from the estate tax base. Then the unified credit, if it has not been exhausted to shelter lifetime gifts, is applied against transfers made at death. The state death tax credit provides a dollar-for-dollar reduction (with certain limits) against the federal estate tax for any state death taxes paid by the estate. The state death tax credit is limited, and the maximum state death tax credit available to a particular estate is provided for by a progressive rate schedule in the federal tax code.

10-16.   a. Life insurance proceeds payable to or for the benefit of the insured's estate are includible in the estate, regardless of who owned the contract or who paid the premium.

      b. When insurance proceeds are paid to a named beneficiary other than the insured's estate, incidents of ownership in the policy at the time of death are the key criteria for determining inclusion. As in this case, because the insured held an incident of ownership at the time of his or her death, the policy is included in his gross estate. The decedent had retained the right to change the beneficiary.

      c. Although the decedent had transferred all rights to the policy to his wife, his transfer occurred within 3 years of his death. Under the 3-year rule, life insurance transferred to a third party for less than full consideration within 3 years of the insured's death is automatically includible in the insured's gross estate.

10-17.   Life insurance can serve as an estate enhancement in order to provide for the basic needs of the decedent's heirs. This is particularly true for young clients, clients with family members dependent on their income, and/or clients with small to moderate-sized estates. Also, insurance can provide estate liquidity/wealth replacement for older clients or clients with large estates, providing coverage for probate expenses, death taxes, and estate liquidity needs.

Answers to Self-Test Questions

10-1.   True.

10-2.   True.

10-3.   False. With the capital needs analysis approach, the amount of additional life insurance needed is determined by subtracting the resources already available from the resources needed by the survivor's dependents if the client should die today, assuming that future income payments can be comprised solely of investment earnings on a capital sum. With the financial needs analysis approach, the amount of additional life insurance needed is determined by subtracting the resources already available from the resources needed by the survivor's dependents if the client should die today, assuming that future income payments can be comprised of a combination of investment earnings and liquidation of the capital sum.

10-4.   False. A major advantage of the financial needs analysis approach is that it does take into account factors that would be available in the event of the insured's death such as Social Security benefits and future earnings by a spouse.

10-5.   False. In addition to a number of needs that can and should be met with term insurance, various types of permanent insurance, not just whole life, should be considered in determining how to best meet a client's life insurance needs.

10-6.   True.

10-7.   True.

10-8.   False. Only those life insurance policy replacements involving agent or insurer distortion or misrepresentation of facts constitute twisting. Sometimes a policyowner can substantially improve his or her situation by replacing an existing policy in either the same or a different company.

10-9.   True.

10-10.   False. The most common method of dealing with risks that present an increasing hazard is to use extra percentage tables. A flat extra premium is normally used when the hazard is thought to be constant or decreasing.

10-11.   True.

10-12.   False. Viaticals are not deemed securities and are not subject to SEC regulation.

10-13.   False. There are no federal privacy laws regarding viatical agreements.

10-14.   False. One of the common uses of life insurance in business is to serve as a method of funding, not of replacing, a properly designed buy-sell agreement.

10-15.   False. In a traditional split-dollar plan, the corporation contributes an amount equal to the annual increase in the policy's cash surrender value, while the executive pays the remainder of the annual premium.

10-16.   False. In general, and subject to some exceptions, proceeds paid under a life insurance contract by reason of the insured's death are excludible from gross income for federal income tax purposes.

10-17.   True.

10-18. False. The federal gift tax applies when there has been a completed transfer and acceptance of property, and the transfer was for less than full and adequate consideration.

10-19. True.

10-20. True.

10-21. False. Life insurance can provide estate enhancement for young clients as well as estate liquidity/wealth replacement for older clients.

Chapter 11

Answers to Review Questions

11-1.　a.　The primary function of life insurance is to create an estate or principal sum; the primary function of an annuity is to liquidate a principal sum, regardless of how it was created.

　　　　b.　Life insurance and annuities are based on the same fundamental pooling, mortality, and investment principles. First, both insurance and annuities use the pooling technique. In insurance, all make contributions so that the dependents of those who die prematurely are partially compensated for loss of income. In annuities, those who die prematurely contribute on behalf of those who live beyond their life expectancy and would otherwise outlive their income. Second, both life insurance and annuity costs are based on probabilities of death and survival as reflected in a mortality table. Finally, under both arrangements, premiums are discounted for the compound interest that the insurance company will earn.

11-2.　If the annuitant is willing to pool savings with those of other annuity owners, the administering agency can provide all the participants with an income of a specified amount as long as they live—regardless of longevity. This arrangement implies the willingness of participants to have all or a portion of their unliquidated principal at the time of death used to supplement the principal of those who live beyond their life expectancy. Therefore, each payment under an annuity is composed partly of the annuitant's principal, the unliquidated principal of other annuitants who die early, and investment income on these funds.

11-3.　a.　The annuity can be distributed on a *pure annuity* basis providing periodic income payments that continue as long as the annuitant lives but that terminate at that person's death. A *refund annuity* is any type that promises to return, in one manner or another, a portion or all of the purchase price of the annuity.

　　　　b.　The annuity may cover a single life or it may cover two or more lives. A joint annuity provides that the income ceases at the first death among the lives covered. A joint-and-last-survivor annuity provides that the income ceases only at the last death among the lives covered.

　　　　c.　An *immediate annuity* makes the first benefit payment one payment interval after the date of purchase. Under a *deferred annuity*, more than one payment interval will elapse after purchase before the first benefit payment is due.

　　　　d.　Deferred annuities can be purchased with either single premiums or periodic premiums.

　　　　e.　Annuity payments may be fixed, providing a fixed number of dollars for each benefit payment, or may be variable, providing payments based on the investment performance of the assets underlying the annuity.

11-4.　a.　While deferred annuities can be purchased with either single premiums or periodic premiums, immediate annuities can only be purchased with single premiums because the first benefit payment is made at the end of one payment period from the purchase date of the annuity.

　　　　b.　While all annuities have a liquidation period, deferred annuities also have an accumulation period when funds are accumulated with the insurance company to provide the annuity income benefits during the liquidation period.

11-5.　Jim should purchase a deferred annuity on a periodic premium basis (flexible premiums in case he wants to contribute more or less in some periods). To protect against loss of purchasing power, he should use a variable annuity product. When he reaches retirement, he can choose a joint-and-last-survivor option to guarantee an income to him and his wife as long as either is living. At that time, he can also decide whether he wishes to keep the annuity in a variable mode or switch to fixed payments during the liquidation period. He can also decide at retirement whether he wants any additional guarantees (for example, 10-years certain).

11-6.　a.　The annuity payments cease.

　　　　b.　Annuity payments will continue to Ann's beneficiary for the remainder of the 20 years, in this case, for 19 years and 10 months.

　　　　c.　Payments will continue to Ann's beneficiary until the insurer has paid out the purchase price of $300,000.

11-7.　During the accumulation period of a deferred variable annuity, premium deposits are applied to the purchase of accumulation units. The accumulation unit is assigned an arbitrary value, such as $10, at the inception of the plan, and the initial premiums purchase accumulation units at that price. Thereafter, the units are revalued each month to reflect changes in the market value of the common stock that constitutes the company's variable annuity portfolio. On any valuation date, the value of each accumulation unit is determined by dividing the market value of the common stock underlying the accumulation units by the aggregate number of units. Dividends are usually allocated periodically and applied to the purchase of additional accumulation units, although they may simply be reinvested without allocation and permitted to increase the value of each existing accumulation unit. Capital appreciation or depreciation, both realized and unrealized, is always reflected in the value of the accumulation units, rather than in the number of units. A portion of each premium payment is deducted for expenses, and the remainder is invested in accumulation units at their current market value.

At the beginning of the liquidation period, the accumulation units are exchanged for annuity units. The number of annuity units that will be acquired by the annuitant depends on the company's assumptions as to mortality, dividend rates, and expenses, and on the market value of the assets underlying the annuity units. In essence, the number of annuity units is determined by dividing the dollar value of the accumulation units by the present value of a life annuity at the participant's attained age in an amount equal to the current value of one annuity unit. The number of annuity units remains constant throughout the liquidation period, but is revalued each year, reflecting the current market price of the common stock and the mortality, investment, and expense experience for the preceding year. The dollar income payable to the annuitant each month is determined by multiplying the number of annuity units owned by the annuitant by the current value of one unit.

11-8. Key features of equity-indexed annuities include:
- *participation rate formula.* This formula defines the potential return of the annuity, based on increases in the value of a stock index.
- *term period.* Most contracts anticipate a series of terms of uniform length; however, some contracts reserve the insurer's right to modify the term period available for continuation at the expiration of any existing term.
- *participation rate.* The participation rate is used in the participation rate formula to determine the amount of the index gain that can be applied (if any) to produce more than the guaranteed yield. Higher participation rates may be available from some insurers if the purchaser accepts a lower guaranteed interest rate.
- *cap on the crediting rate.* Some contracts cap the crediting rate that is applied to the accumulated value of the contract, preventing full formula participation in times of very rapid index increases.
- *minimum crediting rate.* As a protection on the downside, most contracts specify a floor of zero percent as the minimum extra interest crediting rate applicable to the accumulated value. This prevents the application of a negative percentage in the formula to reflect plunges in the index value and ensures that the fixed-interest-rate guarantee is the worst possible outcome.
- *no SEC regulation.* Equity-indexed annuities currently are regarded as fixed annuities and may be sold by agents who are not licensed to sell variable products.
- *minimum guarantees.* The minimum guarantees under equity-indexed annuities are lower than those for traditional fixed-interest annuities, and the rates actually guaranteed apply to less than the full amount paid as a premium. The specified interest rate applied each year to the contract value is set forth in the contract and remains fixed unless a negotiated change is later agreed to by both the contract owner and the insurance company.

11-9. Life insurance companies cope with problems of adjusting annuity prices for anticipating future increases in life expectancy in three ways:
- Compute annuity premiums on the basis of mortality tables that reflect annuitants' lower mortality. This current approach has replaced an earlier technique of using age setbacks.
- Use a low-interest assumption in the premium formula. Intensified competition among insurance companies and between insurance companies and investment media, however, has caused companies to adopt interest assumptions closer to the level of their actual investment earnings.
- Compute the premiums and/or benefits on a participating basis, which enables the insurance company to use conservative assumptions.

11-10. The usual structured settlement uses an annuity to provide periodic payments that meet the recipient's financial needs as much as possible. The periodic payments of income are received tax free by the claimant during his or her life and by the claimant's beneficiaries thereafter for the balance of any guarantee period. All timing decisions, as well as the exact amount of money, are predetermined by the defendant and its insurer, who are the legal owners of the annuity.

11-11. Advantages of structured settlements include the following:

For the injured party: The structured settlement provides financial security for the lifetime of the injured party. The use of periodic payments reduces the possibility of dissipation of funds through mismanagement, imprudent investment, unwise expenditures, misuse, or neglect by claimants and their families or guardians. Payments represent personal injury damages, which are excluded from income tax.

For the plaintiff attorney: Attorneys are assured that the settlement is guaranteed and will not be subject to dissipation as is a lump-sum settlement. Some attorneys believe that recommending a structured settlement insulates them from exposure to legal malpractice because attorneys do not take a sizable portion of the total value of the entire benefit payable as a lump sum at the time of settlement.

For the judge: Guaranteed lifetime periodic payments assure the plaintiff of financial security regardless of when he or she dies. Unlike the lump-sum settlement, the judge or jury does not need to determine how much money the plaintiff will need to fund for the rest of his or her life.

For the public: The injured party does not become a ward of the state and is assured of a guaranteed income and proper care. The delay of prolonged litigation is avoided, reducing court costs and placing fewer burdens on an overloaded judicial system. Disadvantages can arise from the insurer's insolvency, resulting in delayed and/or reduced benefits. Also, the annuitant will absorb losses in excess of any state guaranty fund limitations. Also, the annuitant cannot accelerate or decelerate future payments, so problems can occur if more immediate cash is needed than the stream of payments provides.

Answers to Self-Test Questions

11-1.   True.

11-2.   False. Annuities serve the function of liquidation of principal sum regardless of how it was created. Life insurance creates an estate or principal sum.

11-3.   False. Jack should purchase a deferred annuity with periodic premiums. Immediate annuities do not provide for accumulation and cannot be purchased with periodic premiums.

11-4.   False. If Rachel is still alive at the end of 20 years, her annuity benefit payments would continue until her death.

11-5.   False. An installment refund annuity pays installment benefits to the annuitant and/or beneficiary until the total equals the purchase price of the annuity.

11-6.   True.

11-7.   False. During liquidation, a variable annuity pays a fixed number of annuity units of variable value each payment period.

11-8.   False. Equity-indexed annuities offer a minimum guaranteed interest rate.

11-9.   False. Annuity considerations are not calculated using the same mortality rates as those used in calculating life insurance premiums.

11-10. True.

Chapter 12

Answers to Review Questions

12-1.   Renewal rates for employer-provided medical expense plans are increasing at a high percentage, and high percentage increases are predicted to continue. A large majority of Americans are satisfied with their own health care plan, and dissatisfaction is higher among plans with the greatest degree of managed care. Surveys indicate that Americans are becoming less satisfied with and less confident about the health care system, despite satisfaction with their own coverage. There is a growing backlash against managed care, particularly HMOs. There is bipartisan disagreement about what should be done regarding federal health care legislation.

12-2.   a. She is covered. Hospital expense benefits are typically payable for a period of from 31 to 365 days.

        b. She is not covered. Cosmetic surgery is generally not covered unless it is needed to correct a condition resulting from an accidental injury.

        c. She is covered. Extended care facility benefits typically are provided to people who have been hospitalized for a period of at least 3 days. Confinement in the extended care facility must usually be for the same or a related condition for which the covered person was hospitalized. An extended care facility typically furnishes room and board and 24-hour-a-day skilled-nursing care under the supervision of a physician or a registered professional nurse.

d. She is not covered. Home health care benefits are not designed for custodial or rest care. They are designed for those situations when the necessary part-time nursing care ordered by a physician following hospitalization can be provided in the patient's home.

e. Major medical plans give broad coverage for necessary expenses incurred for medical services and supplies that a physician has ordered or prescribed, including prescription drugs.

12-3. The exclusion for preexisting conditions found in many major medical plans differs from the other exclusions found in major medical plans in that it applies only for a limited time, after which the condition will no longer be considered preexisting and will be covered in full, subject to any other contract limitations or exclusions.

A preexisting condition is typically defined as any illness or injury for which a covered person received medical care during a 3-month period prior to the person's effective date of coverage. Usually, the condition is no longer considered preexisting after the earlier of (1) a period of 3 consecutive months during which no medical care is received for the condition or (2) 12 months of coverage under the contract by the individual.

Some insurers provide limited coverage rather than exclude coverage for preexisting conditions.

12-4. a. The initial deductible is the amount that a covered person must pay for covered expenses before the plan will pay any insurance benefits.

b. The family deductible is a provision that waives future deductibles for all family members once a specified aggregate dollar amount of medical expenses has been incurred or after a specified number of family members have satisfied their individual deductibles.

12-5. Peggy's out-of-pocket expenses are calculated as follows:

$1,500   of covered medical expenses
− 250   deductible (out-of-pocket expense)
$1,250
x   .20   (percentage Peggy is required to pay)
  $250   (out-of-pocket expense)

Therefore, Peggy will have to pay $500 of her medical expenses out-of-pocket, and the insurance company will pay the remaining $1,000.

12-6. A true managed care plan should have five basic characteristics: controlled access to specialists and hospitals, emphasis on case management, encouragement of preventive care and healthy lifestyles, sharing by medical care providers in the financial consequences of medical decisions, and careful selection and monitoring of medical providers.

12-7. HMOs act like insurance companies and the Blues in that they finance health care. However, unlike insurance companies and the Blues, they also deliver medical services. HMOs offer their subscribers a comprehensive package of health care services, generally including benefits for outpatient services as well as for hospitalization. Subscribers usually get these services at no cost except the periodically required premium and in some cases, a copayment. HMOs emphasize preventive care and provide such services as routine physicals and immunizations. HMOs provide for the delivery of medical services, which in some cases are performed by salaried physicians and other personnel employed by the HMO. Although this approach is in contrast to the usual fee-for-service delivery system of medical care, some HMOs do contract with providers on a fee-for-service basis. Subscribers are required to obtain their care from providers of medical services who are affiliated with the HMO.

12-8. PPOs typically differ from HMOs in several respects. First, the preferred providers are generally paid on a fee-for-service basis as their services are used. However, fees are usually subject to a schedule that is the same for all similar providers within the PPO contracts, and providers may have an incentive to control utilization through bonus arrangements. Second, employees and their dependents are not required to use the practitioners or facilities that contract with the PPO; rather, a choice can be made each time medical care is needed, and benefits are also paid for care provided by nonnetwork providers. However, employees are offered incentives to use network providers; these incentives include lower or reduced deductibles and copayments as well as increased benefits such as preventive health care. Third, most PPOs do not use a primary care physician as a gatekeeper, so employees do not need referrals to see specialists.

12-9. A POS plan is a hybrid arrangement that combines aspects of a traditional HMO and a PPO. With a POS plan, participants in the plan elect, at the time medical treatment is needed, whether to receive treatment within the plan's tightly managed network, usually an HMO, or outside the network. Expenses received outside the network are reimbursed in the same manner as for nonnetwork services under PPO plans. One type of POS plan, the open-ended HMO, consists of traditional HMO coverage with an endorsement for nonnetwork coverage. The other type of POS plan, the gatekeeper PPO, requires the PPO participant to elect a primary care physician in the manner of an HMO participant. This physician acts as a gatekeeper to control utilization and refer members to specialists within the PPO network. However, at any time care is needed, a covered person can elect to go outside the network.

12-10.   Benefit carve-outs can be used to contain costs via managed care techniques. A well-managed specialty provider may also provide a higher quality of care.

12-11.   a.   The typical prescription drug plan covers the cost of drugs (except those dispensed in a hospital or in an extended care facility) that are required by law to be dispensed by prescription. Drugs for which prescriptions are not required by law are usually not covered even if a physician orders them on a prescription form, with the frequent exception of injectable insulin, which is generally covered. Most plans have a copayment, which may vary depending on whether the drug is generic or brand-name; other plans have a three-tier structure for generic drugs, formulary drugs, and brand-name nonformulary drugs.

         b.   Normally, a benefit schedule is used that specifies the type and amounts of benefits and the frequency with which they will be provided. If the plan is written by a provider of vision services, a discount for costs incurred with the provider that are not covered by the schedule of benefits may be available. Benefits are generally provided for eye examinations by either an optometrist or an ophthalmologist, and larger benefits are sometimes provided if the latter is used.

         c.   Behavioral health programs offer treatment for mental health, alcoholism, and drug addiction, and should use case management to design and coordinate treatment plans and to monitor the follow-up needs, have a referral mechanism, have a provider network, and provide patient access to care on a 24-hour basis.

12-12.   Eligible dependents usually include an employee's spouse who is not legally separated from the employee and any unmarried dependent children (including stepchildren, adopted children, and children born out of wedlock) under the age of 19. However, coverage may be provided for children to age 23 or 26 if they are full-time students. In addition, coverage may also continue (and is required to be continued in some states) for children who are incapable of earning their own living because of a physical or mental infirmity. If an employee has dependent coverage, all newly acquired dependents (by birth, marriage, or adoption) are automatically covered.

12-13.   HIPAA's provisions put limitations on preexisting-conditions exclusions and allow an employee to use evidence of prior insurance coverage to reduce or eliminate the length of any preexisting-conditions exclusion when the employee moves to another employer-provided medical expense plan.

12-14.   The plan of the stepparent who is the spouse of the parent with custody takes priority over the father's plan.

12-15.   Unless an employee elects otherwise, the employer's plan is primary and Medicare is secondary. Except in plans that require large employee contributions, it is doubtful that employees will elect Medicare to be primary because employers are prohibited from offering active employees or their spouses a Medicare carve-out, a Medicare supplement, or some other incentive not to enroll in the employer's plan.

         Medicare is the secondary payer of benefits when persons who are eligible for Medicare benefits receive treatment for end-stage renal disease with dialysis or kidney transplants. Medicare provides these benefits to any insured workers (either active or retired) and to their spouses and dependent children, but the employer's plan is primary during the first 30 months of treatment only; after that time Medicare is primary and the employer's plan is secondary.

         Medicare is also the secondary payer of benefits to disabled employees (or the disabled dependents of employees) under age 65 who are eligible for Medicare and who are covered under the medical expense plan of large employers (defined as plans with 100 or more employees). Medicare, however, does not pay anything until a person has been eligible for Social Security disability income benefits for 2 years. The rule applies only if an employer continues medical expense coverage for disabled persons; there is no requirement for such a continuation.

12-16.   a.   A strong likelihood—one characteristic of dental insurance seldom found in medical expense plans is the inclusion of benefits for routine diagnostic procedures, including X rays

         b.   A strong likelihood—treatment for diseases of the dental pulp within teeth, such as root canals, is covered under the category of endodontics

         c.   Almost no likelihood—a common exclusion in dental plans is the replacement of lost, missing, or stolen dentures

         d.   Almost no likelihood—a common exclusion in dental plans is services that are purely cosmetic, which would include teeth whitening

         e.   Some likelihood—some dental plans include benefits for orthodontics, which involves the prevention and correction of dental and oral anomalies through the use of corrective devices such as braces

12-17.   Additional medical and dental benefits for executives may include reimbursement for deductibles and coinsurance under the employer's plan; coverage for annual physicals and the extra cost of private hospital rooms; and extra coverage for mental or emotional treatment, hearing care, vision care, and dental work.

12-18.   A portion of an employee's contribution for coverage may be tax deductible as a medical expense if that individual itemizes his or her income tax deductions. Under the Internal Revenue Code, individuals are allowed to deduct certain medical care expenses (including dental expenses) for which no reimbursement was received. This deduction is limited to expenses (including amounts paid for insurance) that exceed 7.5 percent of the person's adjusted gross income.

Answers to Self-Test Questions

12-1.   True.

12-2.   False. The Pregnancy Discrimination Act requires that benefit plans of employers with 15 or more employees treat pregnancy, childbirth, and related conditions the same as any other illness.

12-3.   True.

12-4.   True.

12-5.   True.

12-6.   False. Basic extended care facility benefits do not cover rest or domiciliary care for the aged. They are for people who require convalescence under supervised skilled nursing.

12-7.   False. Hospice care does not attempt to cure medical conditions but tries to ease the physical and psychological pain associated with the death of terminally ill patients.

12-8.   True.

12-9.   False. HMOs may operate in a geographic area no larger than a single metropolitan area, and most HMOs offer "out-of-area coverage" only in the case of medical emergencies.

12-10.   False. By providing and encouraging preventive care, HMOs attempt to detect and treat medical conditions at an early stage, thereby avoiding expensive medical treatment in the future.

12-11.   False. The EPO does not provide coverage outside the preferred-provider network, except in those infrequent cases when the network does not contain an appropriate specialist.

12-12.   True.

12-13.   False. For the most part, PPOs pay benefits for the same medical procedures, whether they are performed by a network or nonnetwork provider. However, a few procedures may be covered only if they are received from network providers.

12-14.   True.

12-15.   True.

12-16.   False. Drugs for which prescriptions are not required by law are usually not covered, even if a physician orders them on a prescription form.

12-17.   True.

12-18.   False. Any unmarried dependent children who are full-time students are only covered up to age 23.

12-19.   True.

12-20.   False. Employers with 20 or more employees must make coverage available under their medical expense plans to active employees aged 65 or older. Unless the employee elects otherwise, the employer's plan is primary and Medicare is secondary.

12-21.   True.

12-22.   False. Premium contributions by an employer to group medical and dental coverage for an employee do not create any income tax liability for the employee.

Chapter 13

Answers to Review Questions

13-1.   a.   The term *group health plan* as used in the Act is broad enough to include medical expense plans, dental plans, vision care plans, and prescription drug plans, regardless of whether benefits are self-funded or provided through other entities such as insurance companies or HMOs. Long-term care coverage is not subject to COBRA rules.

   b.   Under the Act, each of the following is a qualifying event if it results in the loss of coverage by a qualified beneficiary:

- the death of the covered employee
- the termination of the employee for any reason except gross misconduct
- a reduction of the employee's hours so that the employee or dependent is ineligible for coverage
- the divorce or legal separation of the covered employee and his or her spouse
- for spouses and children, the employee's eligibility for Medicare
- a child's ceasing to be an eligible dependent under the plan

    c. A *qualified beneficiary* is defined as any employee, or the spouse or dependent child of the employee, who on the day before a qualifying event was covered under the employee's group health plan. In addition, the definition includes any child who is born to or placed for adoption with the employee during the period of COBRA coverage.

13-2. The Health Insurance Portability and Accountability Act (HIPAA) encourages states to adopt mechanisms for helping individuals find alternative coverage. If the state does not have its own plan, the state alternative must provide a choice of health insurance coverage to all eligible individuals, impose no preexisting-conditions restrictions, and include at least one form of coverage that is either comparable to comprehensive health coverage offered in the individual marketplace or comparable to (or a standard option of) coverage available under the group or individual laws of the state.

    If a state fails to adopt an alternative to federal regulation, then insurance companies, HMOs, and other health plan providers in the individual marketplace must make coverage available on a guaranteed-issue basis to individuals with 18 or more months of creditable coverage and whose most recent coverage was under a group health plan, although coverage does not have to be provided to an individual who has other health insurance or who is eligible for COBRA coverage, Medicare, or Medicaid. No preexisting-conditions exclusions can be imposed.

13-3. The basic benefits that must be included in all medigap plans consist of the following:

- hospitalization. This is the coinsurance or cost sharing of Part A benefits for the 61st through the 90th day of hospitalization and the 60-day lifetime reserve. In addition, coverage is extended for 365 additional days after Medicare benefits end.
- medical expenses. This is the Part B insurance for Medicare-approved charges for physicians' and medical services.
- blood. This is the payment for the first three pints of blood each year.

13-4. Persons aged 65 or older may buy any available Medicare supplement policy, regardless of health status, at any time during the 6-month period after initial enrollment for Medicare Part B benefits. If a person initially elects a managed care option in lieu of regular Medicare benefits, the person will be eligible to purchase a Medicare supplement policy, without evidence of insurability, if he or she leaves the managed care option during the first 12 months of coverage and returns to regular Medicare benefits. Similarly, a person who drops Medicare supplement coverage and elects a managed care option can regain Medicare supplement coverage if he or she decides to drop the managed care option during the first 12 months of coverage. Also, a person can obtain a medigap policy on a guaranteed-issue basis because an employer-provided plan that supplements Medicare terminates, because a Medicare+Choice plan no longer provides coverage, or because the person loses eligibility by moving out of the plan's service area.

13-5. a. Temporary medical insurance provides coverage for periods between 30 days and one year to under-age-65 individuals and their dependents who are between permanent medical plans. The plans are similar to individual major medical policies, with applicants usually having a choice of deductibles and coinsurance percentages.

    b. International travel medical insurance provides coverage ranging from a minimum of 15 days to a maximum of one year, with optional renewal of some policies for up to 5 years. Benefits cover the expenses of inpatient and outpatient hospitalizations as well as medical and related services. Deductibles are selected, and coinsurance levels are frequently available at 80 percent up to a specific dollar amount, with 100 percent payable thereafter to the policy maximum. Coverage typically ceases when a person returns to his or her home country.

    c. Hospital-surgical policies typically provide coverage for a limited number of days of hospitalization, and the daily benefit can be less than the cost of semiprivate accommodations. Surgical benefits are usually paid on a fee-schedule basis. Depending on the policy, benefits may be available for expenses associated with physician's visits, maternity, and extended care facilities. These policies are typically inadequate for prolonged sicknesses, serious accidents, or the significant medical expenses that can arise outside a hospital setting that normally a major medical policy would cover.

d. Hospital indemnity insurance provides the insured with a fixed daily cash benefit during a covered hospitalization. A spouse or dependent child is usually eligible for coverage, although benefits may be reduced. The policy provides daily benefits in the event of hospital confinement in a specified dollar amount for a defined period, and additional benefits are available as a standard feature or as a rider.

e. Specified disease insurance provides benefits to insured individuals and covered family members upon the diagnosis of or medical events related to the treatment of a disease named in the policy. Benefits vary, and provisions may utilize a combination of three payment structures: per-day or per-service, expense-incurred, or a lump-sum payment. Benefits are contingent on a diagnosis of the specified disease, but payments will cover the first day of care or confinement even though the diagnosis is made at some later date.

f. Critical illness insurance provides a substantial one-time lump-sum cash benefit for listed critical illnesses. Some of these conditions result from injury as well as disease and include specified major surgeries. The policyowner selects a maximum benefit amount, which can range from $10,000 to several hundred thousand dollars. The maximum benefit is payable only once—upon the first diagnosis of a condition or specified surgical treatment that is covered.

13-6. Two types of individuals are eligible:

- an employee (or spouse) of a small employer that maintains an individual or family high-deductible health plan that covers the individual. These persons will establish their Archer MSAs under an employer-sponsored plans.

- a self-employed person (or spouse) who maintains an individual or family high-deductible health plan that covers himself or herself. These persons will need to seek out a custodian or trustee for their Archer MSAs.

13-7. a. Either the account holder or the account holder's employer, but not both, may contribute to an Archer MSA. Contributions by an employer are tax deductible to the employer and are not included in an employee's gross income or subject to Social Security and other employment taxes. Employee contributions are deductible in computing adjusted gross income. The amount of the annual deductible contribution to an employee's account is limited to 65 percent of the deductible for the health coverage if the MSA is for an individual, 75 percent if the MSA covers a family. Employeee contributions must generally be made by April 15 of the year following the year for which the contributions are made.

b. An individual can take any part or all of the account balance from an MSA at any time. Subject to some exceptions, distributions of both contributions and earnings are excludible from an account holder's gross income if used to pay medical expenses of the account holder and the account holder's family as long as these expenses are not paid by other sources of insurance. For the most part, the eligible medical expenses are the same ones that would be deductible, ignoring the 7.5 percent of adjusted gross income limitation, if the account holder itemized his or her tax deductions. Distributions for reasons other than paying eligible medical expenses are included in an account holder's gross income and are subject to a 15 percent penalty tax unless certain circumstances exist.

13-8. Noncancelable policies are rare because of the uncertain nature and cost of future medical claims.

Answers to Self-Test Questions

13-1. False. The term group health plan as used for COBRA purposes is broad enough to include dental plans and vision care plans, but not long-term care plans. Long-term care coverage is not subject to the COBRA rules.

13-2. True.

13-3. False. COBRA coverage is not automatic but must be elected.

13-4. True.

13-5. True.

13-6. True.

13-7. True.

13-8. False. ERISA exempts noninsured plans from state insurance mandates. This exemption includes a self-funded, employer-provided medical expense plan.

13-9. False. Because of the emphasis on first-dollar coverage and preventive medicine, HMO coverage for individuals is typically more expensive than an individual major medical policy.

13-10.   False. Estimates indicate that about two-thirds of Medicare recipients have some type of coverage to supplement Medicare.

13-11.   True.

13-12.   False. Insurance companies are allowed to exclude benefits for no more than 6 months because of preexisting conditions. In fact, some policies immediately provide benefits for preexisting conditions or have an exclusion period shorter than 6 months.

13-13.   True.

13-14.   True.

13-15.   True.

13-16.   False. Either the account holder or the account holder's employer, but not both, may make a contribution to an Archer MSA.

13-17.   False. Individuals who itemize deductions for income tax purposes are allowed to deduct most unreimbursed medical expenses to the extent that the total of such expenses exceeds the threshold of 7.5 percent of adjusted gross income.

Chapter 14

Answers to Review Questions

14-1.   At all working ages, the probability of being disabled for at least 90 consecutive days is much greater than the chance of dying. About half of all employees will have a disability that lasts at least 90 days during their working years, and one out of every ten persons can expect to be permanently disabled prior to age 65. In terms of its financial effect on the family, long-term disability is more severe than death. In both cases, income ceases. In the case of long-term disability, however, family expenses—instead of decreasing because the family has one less member—may actually increase due to the cost of providing care for the disabled person.

14-2.   The sources of coverage that may protect your client against financial trouble in case of disability include the Social Security program, workers' compensation, state temporary disability laws, unemployment compensation, employer-provided short-term disability plans, employer-provided long-term disability plans, individual disability income insurance, and sick-leave plans.

14-3.   Sick-leave plans (often called salary continuation plans) are usually uninsured and generally fully replace lost income for a limited period of time, starting on the first day of disability. Almost all sick-leave plans are limited to permanent full-time employees. Most sick-leave plans are designed to provide benefits equal to 100 percent of an employee's regular pay. Most plans, however, provide a reduced level of benefits after an initial period of full pay. The most traditional approach used in determining the duration of benefits credits eligible employees with a certain amount of sick leave each year such as 10 days.

14-4.   In addition to being in a covered classification, an employee must usually work full-time and be actively at work before coverage commences. Any requirements concerning probationary periods, insurability, and premium contributions must also be satisfied. Long-term disability plans often limit benefits to salaried employees; some long-term plans also exclude employees below a certain salary level. Long-term plans sometimes require that the employee be on the job for an extended probationary period (such as 30 days) without illness or injury before coverage becomes effective.

14-5.   Group short-term disability plans typically define disability as the total inability of the employee to perform each and every duty of his or her regular occupation (an "own occupation" definition). In contrast, group long-term disability plans contain a dual definition under which benefits will be paid for 24 (or 36) months, "as long as an employee is unable to perform his or her regular occupation." After that time, benefits will be paid only if the employee is unable to engage in any occupation for which he or she is qualified by reason of training, education, or experience. The purpose of this dual definition is to require and encourage a disabled employee who becomes able after a period of time to adjust his or her lifestyle and earn a livelihood in another occupation. Under the short-term disability plan, coverage for nonoccupational disabilities and different definitions of disabilities for different classes of employees are unlikely, with those characteristics more likely under the long-term disability plan.

14-6.   Common exclusions under both short-term and long-term disability income contracts specify that no benefits will be paid for any period during which the employee is not under the care of a physician, for any disability caused by an intentionally self-inflicted injury, and for any disability that commenced while the employee was not covered under the contract. Additionally, employers with fewer than 15 employees may exclude pregnancy disabilities unless they are subject to state laws to the contrary.

Long-term contracts commonly deny benefits for disabilities resulting from
- war, whether declared or undeclared
- participation in an assault or felony; some insurers have expanded this to include the commission of any crime
- mental disease, alcoholism, or drug addiction
- preexisting conditions

14-7.   Benefit schedules classify employees and, for each class of employee, specify the amount of disability income to be provided, indicate the length of time that benefits are payable, and coordinate benefits with other available types of disability income. Benefits may be expressed as either flat-dollar amounts, varying dollar amounts by classification, or a percentage of earnings. Short-term disability income contracts commonly contain a waiting, or elimination, period. The typical short-term contract has no waiting period for disabilities resulting from accidents, but a 1–7 day waiting period for disabilities resulting from sickness. Long-term disability income plans have elimination periods of 3 to 6 months. The waiting periods for sicknesses and accidents are the same under the long-term contract. Long-term disability income benefits may be paid for as short a period as 2 years or as long as the lifetime of the disabled employee.

14-8.   To minimize the possibility of an employee receiving total benefits higher than his or her predisability earnings, disability income plans commonly stipulate that benefits be integrated with other sources of disability income. Benefits under short-term plans are generally integrated with (1) workers' compensation benefits if the plan covers occupational disabilities; (2) temporary disability laws if they are applicable; and (3) Social Security benefits if the maximum benefit period is longer than 5 months.

Long-term disability income benefits are usually integrated with benefits provided under the following:
- Social Security
- workers' compensation laws
- temporary disability laws
- other insurance plans for which the employer makes a contribution or payroll deduction
- pension plans for which the employer has made a contribution or payroll deduction to the extent that the employee elects to receive retirement benefits because of disability
- sick-leave plans
- earnings from employment, either with the employer or from other sources

To prevent the integration with other benefits from totally eliminating a long-term disability benefit, many plans provide (and some states require) that a minimum benefit be paid. Most plans also contain a provision freezing the amount of any Social Security reduction at the initial level that was established when the claim began.

14-9.   a. A disability income plan may have a COLA to prevent inflation from eroding the purchasing power of disability income benefits being received. Under the typical COLA formula, benefits increase annually along with changes in the consumer price index.

   b. A firm may treat disabled employees as if they were still working and accruing pension benefits. Such a provision requires that contributions on behalf of disabled employees be made to the pension plan, usually from the employer's current revenues. However, some disability income contracts stipulate that the contributions necessary to fund a disabled employee's accruing pension benefits will be paid from the disability income contract.

   c. Some long-term contracts continue payments to survivors after the death of a disabled employee. The disability income payments are continued, possibly at a reduced amount, for periods ranging up to 24 months to eligible survivors, who commonly are the spouse and unmarried children under age 21.

14-10. a. The benefits are received by Kevin free of income taxation.

   b. The benefits are included in Patty's income for tax purposes.

   c. Benefits attributable to contributions by Julie are received free of income taxation. Benefits attributable to employer contributions are includible in Julie's income for tax purposes.

14-11. Residual-disability benefits replace lost earnings due to less-than-total disability. The focus of the benefit is on the income reduction rather than on the physical dimensions of the disability. Policies providing residual-disability benefits usually specify a fraction (representing the proportion of lost income) that is multiplied by the stated monthly benefit for total disability to derive the residual benefit payable. The numerator of that fraction is usually income prior to disability minus earned income during disability; the denominator of the fraction is income prior to disability. The definitions of each form of income differ from one insurance company to another, and persons subject to income fluctuation should insist on a definition allowing the greater of two different base periods so that they are not unduly penalized as a result of a single base period applied during a slump in income. Most of the definitions either explicitly or implicitly include not only income earned from work activities but also pension or profit-sharing contributions made on behalf of the individual. Additionally, a minimum benefit clause specifies that the minimum benefit payable for residual-disability periods is at least 50 percent of the benefit payable for total disability.

14-12.   a. Guaranteed renewable contracts, which are high-quality contracts, give the policyowner the right to continue the coverage in force by paying the premium due. The premium may be increased on a class basis for all guaranteed-renewable policies in the classification, but cannot be increased on an individual basis. The highest quality contracts, noncancelable disability contracts, guarantee that the individual can keep the policy in force by paying the premium and that the premium will not increase. Low-quality cancelable disability insurance contracts offer very questionable protection for the insured because the insurance company can refuse renewal or increase the premium.

    b. Disability income policies generally have an elimination period before benefit payments begin. When selecting the elimination period for a disability income policy, the insured should consider his or her ability to pay living costs and other expenses during the elimination period, and whether the insured has other sources of funds available during short-term disabilities. Residual-disability benefits specify a qualification period, which indicates the number of days of total disability that must be sustained before residual-disability benefits are payable.

    c. Most disability policies define a specified period of recovery (usually measured by return to work) that automatically separates one disability from another. For disability policies with a limited benefit period, it can be advantageous to have each relapse classified as a new disability, which then starts with a full benefit period.

    d. Disability income policies differ according to the duration of benefits that they provide once the individual becomes disabled. Disability contracts often provide choices such as 2 years, 3 years, 5 years, to age 65, or even for the insured's lifetime. Policies with short benefit durations do not provide comprehensive protection against disability, but their main appeal is the premium savings associated with the relatively short maximum benefit period. Some policies differentiate between disabilities caused by injury and disabilities caused by illness. These policies may provide lifetime benefits if the disability results from injury but limit benefits to age 65 if the disability stems from illness.

        Even policies purporting to provide lifetime benefits for disability include limitations on disabilities occurring after specified ages such as 50, 55, or 60. Disabilities with their first onset after the specified age are often limited to benefit periods of 2 or 5 years or may terminate at a specified age such as 65, 68, or 70.

        Insurance companies are more restrictive in writing longer benefit duration policies than they are in writing policies of short benefit duration. Fewer occupations qualify for policies with long benefit durations than for policies of short benefit durations. Policies with long benefit durations are rarely available to any occupation that involves physical labor or direct involvement in dangerous processes.

    e. Disability income policies specify the amount of monthly benefits payable during periods of total disability after the elimination period has been satisfied. At the time of policy issuance, the stated monthly benefit amount should be in line with the insured's income and provide fairly complete protection. However, over time, the stated benefit amount is likely to become inadequate as the insured's income increases because of both inflation and job promotions. Disability income policies are available with provisions to counteract such erosion in benefit levels.

    f. Premiums for disability income policies are based on the policyowner's age at the time of policy issuance and remain level for the duration of the coverage. Consequently, an individual can lock in lower premiums by buying a policy at a younger age and keeping it in force. Premiums must be paid on a timely basis to keep the coverage in force, but the policies do contain a 31-day grace period for late premium payments.

14-13.   Increased predisability benefits consist of provisions aimed at increasing the benefit level while the coverage is in force, but the insured is not disabled. There are basically three approaches to keeping disability income benefits in step with increased income for insured individuals who are not disabled:

- Purchase new policies to supplement the in-force policies incrementally as income increases. This is the oldest and least attractive method, with the drawback that evidence of insurability is required every time incremental amounts of coverage are obtained. If the individual's health deteriorates, additional coverage may not be available at any price.

- Adjust predisability benefit levels through a rider that guarantees the right to purchase additional coverage at specified future intervals up to some specified maximum age such as 45, 50, or 55. This approach is similar to the first one in that additional coverage must be purchased every time an adjustment is needed, but the additional amounts can be acquired at the specified intervals regardless of the health of the insured. However, these incremental purchases are subject to underwriting requirements regarding the individual's current income.

- Use riders that automatically increase the base benefit amount on a formula basis such as a stated flat-percentage amount at each policy anniversary. This is the most attractive way to adjust benefits upward for inflation while the insured is not disabled, but even this approach requires purchasing additional coverage, and the premium will be increased appropriately. As with the second approach, the additional increment of coverage is purchased at premium rates based on the insured's attained age at the time it is added to the policy. The real advantage to this approach is that the changes are automatic unless they are refused by the policyowner.

14-14. Some insurance companies offer on an optional basis a policy provision that returns some portion of premiums at specified intervals such as 5 years or 10 years. For example, one company has an option that returns 60 percent of premiums paid at the end of each 5-year interval if no claims have been made during that period. This particular option can increase premiums by more than 40 percent over the base premium level. Other companies offer variations in the percentage of premium to be returned, such as 70 percent or 80 percent of the premiums paid, and in the duration of the interval over which the coverage must be without claims in order to collect the return of premium.

14-15. Many insurance companies offer an optional provision that requires a separate extra premium to cover additional benefits payable when the individual is disabled under the base policy but does not qualify for Social Security disability benefits. The supplemental benefit is paid over and above the base disability benefit of the underlying policy. The maximum benefit available in the base policy can be supplemented under this rider so that the total benefits collected from the insurance company are essentially the same as would have been collected if the individual qualified for Social Security disability benefits.

14-16. In order to minimize the motivation for fraudulent claims as well as padding of legitimate claims by malingering, insurance companies limit the amount of coverage they will issue to any individual in relation to that individual's income. Generally speaking, disability income coverage is not available for benefit amounts that exceed 60 or 66 2/3 percent of the individual's gross earned income. In fact, as the level of income increases, the percentage of income replacement that insurance companies will issue decreases. High-income professionals are often limited to less than 50 percent of their income level in setting the maximum benefit level for their disability policies. Some experts advise that, for individuals providing full disclosure to the insurance company, the appropriate amount of disability income protection to purchase is the maximum amount available from an insurance company that provides quality coverage.

14-17.   a.   Overhead expense policies cover many of the ongoing costs of operating a business while the business owner is totally disabled. These policies tend to be limited to benefit durations of one or 2 years and have relatively short elimination periods. The intent is to keep the necessary staff and premises available for the resumption of business if the business owner recovers from the disability. The application must accompanied by supporting financial statements to verify the stability of the business and to establish the appropriate level of insurable expenses. Actual expenses are reimbursed at time of disability up to a maximum monthly indemnity selected at the time of policy issue.

   b.   Benefits from key employee disability policies are payable to the business entity when the insured key employee is disabled. Proceeds from key person disability policies can be used to replace lost revenue directly attributable to the key person's disability, to fund the search for individuals to replace the insured person, to fund the extra cost of hiring specialized individuals to replace the multiple talents of the insured, and to fund training costs that may be incurred to prepare replacements to carry out the duties the insured performed. The costs of training, hiring, and compensating are usually rather easy to ascertain, whereas estimating lost revenue is a very difficult and complex task. These policies are not designed to provide continuance of salary for the key employee.

   c.   Individual disability income policies can be purchased by the business entity to fund formal plans to continue salary for disabled owner or key employees. Formal plans can be set up in two different ways. The corporation can own the policy and be the beneficiary under the policy, or the corporation can pay the premiums on a policy owned by the employee to whom benefits will be paid. In some informal plans to continue salary, the corporation pays a large enough bonus to the employee for the employee to buy an individual disability income policy.

   d. Buy-sell agreements triggered by the disability of an owner can be funded with disability insurance specifically designed for this purpose. These policies can fund either an installment purchase or a lump-sum buyout. The disability definition in the policy should be the same definition as that specified in the buy-sell agreement. The elimination period for a buy-sell policy is typically one year or longer, in order to avoid triggering the buyout for disabilities that last less than one year. Most buy-sell policies pay the benefit in one lump sum.

Answers to Self-Test Questions

14-1. True.

14-2. False. While most employed persons are potentially eligible for disability benefits under the Social Security program, the definition of disability used is more restrictive than that found in most individual or group contracts.

14-3. True.

14-4. False. Insurance companies that offer disability income policies are very concerned about overinsurance and the accompanying moral hazard, and, consequently, limit the amount of benefits relative to the individual's income. As a result, many individuals with coverage through other sources are ineligible for additional disability income protection.

14-5. True.

14-6. True.

14-7. False. Almost all sick-leave plans are limited to permanent full-time employees.

14-8. True.

14-9. True.

14-10. False. The majority of short-term disability contracts limit coverage to nonoccupational disabilities because employees have workers' compensation benefits for occupational disabilities.

14-11. True.

14-12. False. Most group disability income contracts cover disabilities that result from pregnancy because it is illegal under federal law for an employer with 15 or more employees to exclude these disabilities. Employers with fewer than 15 employees may still exclude pregnancy disabilities unless they are subject to state laws to the contrary.

14-13. False. Group long-term disability income contracts commonly deny benefits for disabilities resulting from preexisting conditions. This exclusion is designed to counter adverse selection and control costs.

14-14. False. Group short-term disability income contracts typically have no waiting period for disabilities that result from accidents, but a waiting period of one to 7 days for disabilities that result from sickness.

14-15. False. Most insurers include a rehabilitation provision in their long-term disability income contracts as an incentive to encourage disabled employees to return to active employment as soon as possible. This provision permits employees to enter a trial work period. If the trial work period indicates that the employees are unable to work, the full benefits will be reinstated without the employees having to satisfy a new waiting period.

14-16. False. Some disability income plans have COLAs to prevent inflation from eroding the purchasing power of disability income benefits received. Under the typical COLA formula, benefits increase annually along with changes in the consumer price index.

14-17. False. Any-occupation policies are too restrictive and generally should not be purchased. Most individual policies use a dual definition of disability under which benefits are first paid accordingly to an own-occupation definition of disability, and then under a definition that looks to the individual's training, education, or experience.

14-18. True.

14-19. True.

14-20. True.

14-21. True.

14-22. False. The most attractive way to adjust benefits upward for inflation while the insured is not disabled is to use riders that automatically increase the base benefit amount on a formula basis.

14-23. True.

14-24. False. The laws of all states require that disability income policies contain incontestability provisions.

14-25. False. Benefits under the Social Security rider terminate when the insured elects early retirement benefits under Social Security.

14-26. True.

14-27. True.

14-28.   False. Benefits from key employee disability policies are payable to the business entity when the insured key employee is disabled. These policies are not designed to provide continuance of salary for the key employee.

14-29.   True.

Chapter 15

Answers to Review Questions

15-1.   Some of the reasons why there is a need for long-term care insurance include the following:
- demographics—the population aged 65 and over is the fastest-growing age group
- increasing costs—annual nursing home costs can range from $30,000 to $60,000
- inability of families to provide care—geographic dispersion, women in the workforce, and fewer children are just some of the reasons why it is increasingly difficult for families to provide full care
- inadequacies of Medicare and medical expense insurance—custodial care is not covered well, if at all, under these coverages

15-2.   There are several other sources for providing long-term care other than insurance:
- personal savings. Unless a person has substantial resources, this approach may force an individual and his or her dependents into poverty. It may also mean that the person will not meet the financial objective of leaving assets to heirs.
- relatives and friends. These individuals may provide caregiving themselves or furnish financial support to purchase care.
- welfare. The Medicaid program in most states will provide benefits, which usually include nursing home care, to the "medically needy." However, a person is not eligible unless he or she is either poor or has a low income and has exhausted most other assets (including those of a spouse).
- state programs. These programs have attempted to encourage better coverage for long-term care. One aspect of these experiments has been to waive or modify certain Medicaid requirements if a person carries a state-approved long-term care policy. These programs increase the assets that a person can retain and still collect Medicaid benefits, with the increase in the allowable asset threshold related to the amount of long-term care coverage carried and exhausted.
- life-care facilities. These facilities require an "entrance fee" that enables residents to occupy a dwelling unit but usually does not give them actual ownership rights. Residents pay a monthly fee that includes meals, some housecleaning services, and varying degrees of health care. If a person needs long-term care, he or she must give up the independent living unit and move to the nursing home portion of the facility, but the monthly fee normally remains the same. The disadvantages of this option are that the cost of a life-care facility is beyond the reach of many persons, and a resident must be in reasonably good health and able to live independently at the time he or she enters the facility.
- long-term care benefits in cash value life insurance policies. Some companies provide this benefit, which enables an insured to use a portion of death benefits while he or she is still living. However, any benefits received reduce the future death benefit. The benefit acceleration may result in the reduction of the death benefit to a level inadequate for accomplishing the purpose of life insurance—the protection of family members after a wage earner's death. In addition, the availability of an accelerated benefit may give the insured a false sense of security that long-term care needs are being met when in fact the potential benefit may be inadequate to cover extended nursing home stays.

15-3.   Highlights of the criteria for policy provisions include the following:
- Many words or terms cannot be used in a policy unless they are specifically defined in accordance with the legislation, for example, *adult day care, home health care services, personal care,* and *skilled-nursing care.*
- Renewal provisions must be either guaranteed renewable or noncancelable.
- Limitations and exclusions are prohibited except in the cases of preexisting conditions; mental or nervous disorders (but Alzheimer's disease cannot be excluded); alcoholism and drug addiction; illness, treatment, or medical condition arising out of war, participation in a felony, service in the armed forces, suicide, and aviation if a person is a non-fare-paying passenger; and treatment in a government facility and services available under Medicare and other social insurance programs.
- No policy can provide coverage for skilled-nursing care only or provide significantly more coverage for skilled care in a facility than for lower levels of care.

- The definition of preexisting condition can be no more restrictive than to exclude a condition for which treatment was recommended or received within 6 months prior to the effective date of coverage. In addition, coverage can be excluded for a confinement for this condition only if it begins within 6 months of the effective date of coverage.
- Eligibility for benefits cannot be based on a prior hospital requirement or higher level of care.
- Insurance companies must offer the applicant the right to purchase coverage that allows for an increase in the amount of benefits based on reasonable anticipated increases in the cost of services covered by the policy. The applicant must specifically reject this inflation protection if he or she does not want it.
- Insurance companies must offer the applicant the right to purchase a nonforfeiture benefit. If the applicant declines the nonforfeiture benefit, the insurer must provide a contingent benefit upon lapse that is available for a specified period of time following a substantial increase in premiums.
- A policy must contain a provision that makes a policy incontestable after 2 years on the grounds of misrepresentation. The policy can be contested on the basis that the applicant knowingly and intentionally misrepresented relevant facts pertaining to the insured's health.

15-4.   The act provides favorable tax treatment to tax-qualified long-term care insurance contracts, which are defined as insurance contracts that meet all the following requirements:
- The only insurance protection provided under the contract is for qualified long-term care services.
- The contract cannot pay for expenses that are reimbursable under Medicare.
- The contract must be guaranteed renewable.
- The contract does not provide for a cash surrender value or other money that can be borrowed or paid, assigned, or pledged as collateral for a loan.
- All refunds of premiums and policyowner dividends must be applied as future reductions in premiums or to increase future benefits.
- The policy must comply with various consumer protection provisions. For the most part, these are the same provisions contained in the NAIC model act and already adopted by most states.

15-5.   A person who has been certified as *chronically ill*:
- Is expected to be unable to perform, without substantial assistance from another person, at least two ADLs for a period of at least 90 days due to a loss of functional capacity, or
- Requires substantial services to protect the individual from threats to health and safety due to substantial cognitive impairment.

15-6.   With some exceptions, expenses for long-term care services, including insurance premiums, are treated like other medical expenses. Self-employed persons may deduct the premiums paid. Persons who itemize deductions can include long-term care insurance premiums, up to an annual limit, for purposes of deducting medical expenses in excess of 7.5 percent of adjusted gross income. Limits are based on a covered individual's age and subject to cost-of-living adjustments. Employer contributions for group contracts are deductible to the employer and do not result in taxable income to an employee. Benefits received under a qualified long-term care insurance contract are received tax free by an employee with one possible exception. Under contracts written on a per diem basis, proceeds are excludible from income up to $220 per day in 2003. (This figure is indexed annually.) Amounts in excess of $220 are also excludible to the extent that they represent actual costs for long-term care services.

15-7.   Most companies have an upper age in the range of 84 to 89, beyond which coverage is not issued. Some companies have no minimum age, while others have a minimum age such as age 40.

15-8.   The amount of benefits is usually limited to a specified amount per day that is independent of the actual charge for long-term care. The same level of benefits is usually provided for all levels of institutional care. The applicant can select home health care limits from one-half to 150 percent of the benefit amount payable for institutional stays. The policyowner is usually given a choice regarding the maximum duration of benefits, which can range from one year to the insured's lifetime.

15-9.   Under a tax-qualified plan, the insured must meet one of the following criteria:
- The insured is unable, without substantial assistance from others, to perform two of the six ADLs acceptable under HIPAA for at least 90 days due to loss of functional capacity.
- Substantial services are required to protect the individual from threats to health and safety due to substantial cognitive impairment.

Many non-tax-qualified plans use the same criteria that are in tax-qualified contracts, except no time period applies to the inability to perform ADLs. Some non-tax-qualified plans require the inability to perform only one

ADL, or extend the definition of ADLs beyond the six allowed by HIPAA. Finally, some non-tax-qualified plans make benefits available when a physician certifies medical necessity, regardless of whether other criteria are satisfied.

15-10. Factors that affect the premium include age, types of benefits, duration of benefits, inflation protection, waiver-of-premium, spousal coverage, and nonsmoker discount.

15-11. Differences between individually purchased long-term care insurance and group long-term care insurance include:
- Eligibility for group coverage generally requires that an employee be full-time and actively at work. At a minimum, coverage can be purchased for an active employee and/or the spouse. Some policies also make coverage available to retirees and to other family members of eligible persons such as minor children, parents, parents-in-law, and possibly adult children. There may be a maximum age for eligibility, but it is often age 80 or 85.
- The cost of group coverage is usually slightly less than the cost of individual coverage.
- An employee typically has less choice in benefit levels and the duration of benefits under a group policy. The amounts and duration of benefits are selected by the employer and normally apply to all employees. However, some policies do allow choice but to a lesser extent than is allowed under individual policies.
- If a participant leaves employment, the group coverage usually can be continued on a direct-payment basis, under either the group contract or an individual contract.

Answers to Self-Test Questions

15-1. False. Both group and individual medical expense policies exclude custodial care.

15-2. True.

15-3. False. The NAIC model legislation establishes guidelines that have been adopted by several states (not federally). Furthermore, older policies that are still in existence and were written prior to the adoption of the model legislation or one of the later revisions may be unaffected.

15-4. True.

15-5. True.

15-6. False. Under HIPAA, a chronically ill person must be unable to perform only two activities of daily living.

15-7. False. Coverage under a group long-term care insurance contract cannot be offered through a cafeteria plan to receive favorable tax treatment.

15-8. True.

15-9. False. Benefits are usually limited to a specified amount per day that is independent of the actual charge for long-term care.

15-10. True.

15-11. True.

Chapter 16

Answers to Review Questions

16-1. The three broad categories are property loss exposures, which include losses to either real or personal property; liability loss exposures; and consequential or indirect loss exposures that arise as a result of property or liability losses.

16-2. Named-perils policies contain a list of the covered perils. If a peril is not listed, losses resulting from that peril are not covered. In contrast, open-perils policies cover all losses to covered property unless the loss is specifically excluded.

16-3. a. Duties imposed on the insured typically include:
- giving prompt notice of the loss to the insurance company or its agent
- notifying the police in case of a loss by theft
- notifying the credit card or fund transfer card company if a loss involves credit card or fund transfer card coverage
- protecting the property from further damage, which includes making reasonable repairs to the property, and keeping an accurate record of the expenses incurred for repair
- preparing an inventory of damaged personal property
- cooperating with the insurance company as it reasonably requires
- providing a sworn proof of loss, generally within 60 days of the insurer's request

b. As a general rule, the insurer will settle all losses within 60 days (or whatever period a state requires) after the company receives a proof of loss and either: (a) an agreement has been reached with the policyowner, (b) there is a filing of an appraisal award with the company, or (c) there is a final legal judgment.

16-4. a. If Coverage A in his policy is $250,000 and Jim has the house repaired, Jim would receive $60,000, the replacement cost of the loss, because he carries insurance greater than 80 percent of the replacement cost of his home at the time of the loss (.80 x $300,000 = $240,000).

b. If Coverage A in his policy is $250,000 and Jim does not have the house repaired, he would be paid $50,000, the actual cash value of the loss.

c. If Coverage A in his policy is $220,000 and Jim has the house repaired, he would be paid only $55,000 because his amount of insurance is less than the 80 percent required ($240,000) but the amount calculated by the following formula is greater than the actual cash value of the loss:

$$\frac{\text{Insurance carried}}{80\% \text{ of replacement cost of the house}} \times \frac{\text{Replacement cost}}{\text{of the loss}} = \frac{\$220,000}{\$240,000} \times \$60,000 = \$55,000$$

d. If Coverage A in his policy is $180,000, Jim would receive the actual cash value of the loss, $50,000, because it is larger than the amount produced by the underinsurance formula.

$$\frac{\text{Insurance carried}}{80\% \text{ of replacement cost of the house}} \times \frac{\text{Replacement cost}}{\text{of the loss}} = \frac{\$180,000}{\$240,000} \times \$60,000 = \$45,000$$

16-5. a. If Policy A and Policy B both have pro rata other insurance provisions, Policy A would pay 55.56 percent ($100,000/$180,000) of the loss or $50,000 and Policy B would pay 44.44 percent ($80,000/$180,000) of the loss or $40,000.

b. If Policy A is written on a primary basis and Policy B is written on an excess basis, Policy A would pay first up to a maximum of its limit and then Policy B would pay any unpaid loss up to a maximum of its limit. In this case, Policy A would pay $90,000 (the entire loss) and Policy B would not be required to pay.

c. If Policy B is written on a primary basis and Policy A is written on an excess basis, Policy B would pay $80,000 (its limit) and then Policy A would pay the remaining $10,000 of the loss.

16-6. a. The cost of surgery, loss of income, and pain and suffering for the driver of the car that Billy hit are bodily injury liability losses.

b. The cost to the phone company to repair its pole is a property damage liability loss.

c. The suit by the driver of the other car that resulted from Billy slandering her with foul language in front of the witnesses at the accident scene is under personal injury liability.

d. The need for Jones Dry Cleaners to settle with the customers whose clothes were burned when the truck caught fire after hitting the phone pole is under contractual liability due to bailment.

16-7. There must be (1) a legal duty to act, or not to act, depending on the circumstances and the persons involved; (2) a wrong, or voluntary breach of legal duty, based on a "prudent person" standard of conduct; (3) a proximate relationship between the wrong and an injury or damage, where a continuous succession of events occurred, from the act to the final event that caused the injury; and (4) an injury or damage.

16-8. a. Under imputed negligence, legal responsibility for injuries or damage is extended to other persons such as employers. In this case, because the negligent party, Billy, acted in the capacity of employee or agent of Jones Dry Cleaners, both the wrongdoer and the owner of the property can be held liable.

b. Under contributory negligence, anyone who is so negligent as to contribute to his or her own injuries or damage cannot recover from another for these injuries.

c. Under comparative negligence, damages are diminished in proportion to the amount of negligence attributable to the person injured or to the owner or person in control of the damaged property.

16-9. a. Duties imposed on the insured typically include the following:
   - Give written notice as soon as practical to the company or its agent.
   - Forward promptly to the insurance company every notice, demand, summons, or other process relating to the accident or occurrence.
   - Assist the insurance company, at its request, to (a) make settlement, (b) enforce the insured's rights against others who may be liable to the insured, (c) help with the conduct of suits and attend hearings and trials, (d) secure and give evidence, and (e) obtain the evidence of witnesses.

b. First, the insurer will pay up to the limit of liability for the damages for which the insured is legally liable. Second, the insurer will provide a defense at its expense by a counsel of its choice, even if a suit is groundless, false, or fraudulent.

16-10. Policy endorsements or separate policies can be used to compensate for shortcomings in currently owned policies or to accommodate special needs. A policy endorsement or separate policy may cover perils excluded in the package policy or provide higher amounts of coverage.

16-11. a. Premiums paid by individual taxpayers for personal property and liability insurance are not deductible. However, premiums paid for business coverage by an individual, partnership, or corporation are a deductible business expense.

b. Group property and liability insurance as an employee benefit typically requires that an employee pays the full cost of his or her coverage, and the tax implications are the same as if the employee had purchased an individual policy. If the employer pays any part of an employee's premium, for either individual or group coverage, the employer can deduct this cost as a business expense. However, the employer must report this amount as taxable income.

c. Benefits paid under liability insurance policies do not result in taxable income to the policyowner or insured even if they are paid on their behalf. Under property insurance policies, benefits paid for direct loss to real or personal property result in a capital gain to the extent that a taxpayer receives reimbursement in excess of his or her basis in the property. However, the situation is treated as an involuntary conversion, and the gain can be postponed to the extent that a taxpayer uses the proceeds to purchase replacement property, and the purchase amount exceeds the taxpayer's basis in the lost or damaged property.

The situation for certain consequential losses is less clear. To the extent that benefits are paid for actual expenses incurred, there is no taxable income. Business interruption coverage, however, will result in ordinary income if it is written on a basis that insures the policyowner against loss of net profits.

d. The Internal Revenue Code allows a deduction for certain losses to the extent they are not compensated for by insurance. Those losses must arise from fire, storm, shipwreck, or other casualty, or from theft. The maximum amount of the losses for tax purposes is the lesser of (1) the decrease in the fair market value of the property as a result of the casualty or theft or (2) the taxpayer's adjusted basis in the property. Losses can be deducted in full by businesses and by individual taxpayers if the loss is incurred in a trade or business or any transaction entered into for profit. Other losses of individual taxpayers are only deductible if they itemize income tax deductions and then only to the extent that (1) each separate loss exceeds $100 and (2) the total of all casualty and theft losses for the year exceeds 10 percent of adjusted gross income.

Answers to Self-Test Questions

16-1. True.

16-2. False. Open-perils coverage refers to a policy that covers all losses to covered property unless the loss is specifically excluded. Some named-peril policies contain a very long list of named perils.

16-3. False. A typical property insurance policy requires that whenever a property loss occurs, the insured must give prompt notice to the insurance company or its agent. Notice to the police is required in the case of loss by theft only.

16-4. True.

16-5. True.

16-6. True.

16-7. False. A dispute involving the amount of a property loss that should be paid by the insurance company typically is settled by an appraisal.

16-8. False. All liability losses involve either bodily injury, property damage, personal injury, or contractual liability.

16-9. False. Torts can result from negligence, intentional acts or omissions, and strict or absolute liability.

16-10. True.

16-11. False. If Pete was only 20 percent at fault for an auto accident in a state that relies on the contributory negligence standard, he could collect none of his damages from the other party.

16-12. False. People can be responsible not only for their own negligent acts but also for those of others. For example, employers can be personally liable for the torts of their employees. In states with vicarious liability laws, the owner of an automobile can be liable for the acts of another person driving the car.

16-13. True.

16-14. True.

16-15. False. Property and liability insurance premiums paid for business coverage are generally deductible as a business expense.

Chapter 17

Answers to Review Questions

17-1.   Frank and Janet are covered, as the named insured and spouse. Elaine is covered as a relative residing in the named insured's household. Destiny, who is temporarily residing at college, is also a covered person.

17-2.   An insured location includes:

- the residence premises. This includes the one- to four-family dwelling, other structures, and grounds where the policyowner resides as shown in the declaration.
- that part of other premises, other structures, and grounds used by the named insured or spouse as a residence if it is shown in the declarations or if it is acquired during the policy year as a residence by the named insured
- other premises not owned by an insured but where an insured is temporarily residing
- vacant land, other than farm land, owned by or rented to an insured
- individual or family cemetery plots or burial vaults of an insured
- any part of a premises occasionally rented to an insured for other than business use

17-3.   a.   Damage to Nathan's home done by vandals is covered under the open-perils Coverage A (as long as the house has not been vacant for more than 60 consecutive days preceding the loss).

      b.   Damage to the inside walls and hardwood floors caused by rain water that blew in when Nathan accidentally left the window open during a storm is covered under the open-perils Coverage A because it is not excluded.

      c.   Damage to the family room couch and end tables caused by rain water that blew in when Nathan accidentally left the window open during a storm is not covered under the "named-perils" Coverage C because the windstorm peril does not cover the damage from rain that was not a result of direct wind or hail damage to the building.

      d.   Damage to the walls of the house caused by an earthquake is excluded under Coverage A. Nathan would have to obtain coverage via a policy endorsement or a separate policy.

      e.   Stains on the wall-to-wall carpet due to housebreaking the new family pet and the hole in the outside of the house cut by a woodpecker are excluded under Coverage A.

      f.   Theft of the $2,000 cast aluminum porch furniture from the deck off the back of Nathan's home is covered under Coverage C, which includes the peril of theft.

      g.   Only $200 of the $1,500 in cash burned in a fire in Nathan's home is covered under the typical HO-3 policy due to the special limits of liability for Coverage C.

      h.   The damage to Nathan's wife's furs as a result of a fire is covered under the special limits of liability under Coverage C that apply specifically to theft of furs and jewelry to the limit of $1,500.

      i.   The $1,000 of additional expense incurred while Nathan's family had to live elsewhere for a day and one-half after a small fire loss is covered under Coverage D. The limit for Coverage D is 30 percent of Coverage A (or $75,000 for Nathan).

      j.   The $2,000 loss would be included under Coverage B, which provides insurance for other structures on the residence premises that are set apart from the dwelling by a clear space such as Nathan's detached garage. Coverage B is open-perils and windstorm damage is not among the exclusions.

17-4.   a.   The bodily injuries to Sarah's guests and the property damage to the side of the neighbor's house when Sarah's gas grill exploded during a cookout at her house would be covered up to the limit of Coverage E (and up to the $1,000 limit of Coverage F for medical payments stemming from the injuries to guests). The policy would also pay Sarah's defense costs in addition to the stated limit of liability.

      b.   There was no coverage when Sarah accidentally injured a coworker when running to a meeting while at work because both bodily injury and property damage arising out of or in connection with a business engaged in by the insured are excluded under Coverage E and Coverage F.

      c.   There was no coverage when Sarah damaged another shopper's car at the mall while carelessly backing out of a parking space because there is an exclusion for this type of loss that would be covered by automobile liability insurance.

      d.   Although intentional acts by an insured are excluded under Coverage E, there would be limited coverage under the additional coverages for Section II when Sarah's 3-year-old son Matthew ripped out some of the neighbor's flowers to make a Mother's Day gift.

      e.   Without regard to fault, there was medical expense coverage under Coverage F for the injury to a team member when Sarah's daughter tossed a bat into the bat rack, it bounced and hit the teammate, cutting her head. Coverage E would also apply if a lawsuit were involved.

17-5. a. HO-2 differs from HO-3 in that HO-2 Coverages A and B are written on the same named-perils basis as Coverage C. HO-2 is less comprehensive and therefore a little less expensive.

 b. HO-4 is often referred to as tenants homeowners insurance or renters insurance and is identical to HO-3 except that there is no Coverage A or Coverage B. The policyowner selects a limit for Coverage C, and Coverage D is 30 percent of this amount.

 c. HO-5 coverage, unlike HO-3 coverage, is written on an open-perils basis.

 d. HO-6 is designed to cover the loss exposures of a policyowner who lives in a condominium or cooperative unit. It is like HO-3 in that Coverage C is on a named-perils basis. This is also the amount of insurance selected by the policyowner. Coverage D is 50 percent of this amount. HO-6 provides $5,000 for Coverage A on a named-perils basis. This amount also applies to other structures and can be increased if needed. There is no Coverage B.

 e. HO-8 has been mostly written on older homes where the replacement cost of a dwelling often significantly exceeds its market value. Providing replacement coverage might create a moral hazard because the policyowner could collect more under an insurance settlement than by selling the house. Perils insured against for all coverages are limited to fire, lightning, windstorm or hail, explosion, riot or civil commotion, aircraft, vehicles, smoke, vandalism and malicious mischief, and volcanic eruption. Theft is covered only from the residence premises and up to a limit of $1,000. There are also other limitations. Loss settlements under Coverages A and B are based on common construction materials and methods that are functionally equivalent to the original construction. Settlements are limited to market value if repairs are not made, although some states require loss settlements to be on an actual cash value basis.

17-6. a. Home day-care coverage is for persons who conduct day-care businesses in their homes either for children or older adults. The endorsement provides coverage for personal property used in the day-care business and extends Section II liability coverage to home day-care services. However, liability is excluded for injuries arising out of motor vehicles, watercraft, and saddle animals and for liability arising out of sexual molestation and physical or mental abuse inflicted by an insured or an employee.

 b. The increased special limits of liability endorsement can be used to increase coverage for some of the items where limited amounts of protection are available under Coverage C. Examples of items for which coverage can be increased include currency, securities, jewelry and watches, firearms, and electronic apparatus for use in a motor vehicle.

 c. An earthquake endorsement can be used in most states to coverage for earthquake and tremors that accompany volcanic eruption. In place of the regular deductible, there is an earthquake deductible equal to 5 percent of the limit of insurance that applies to Coverage A or Coverage C, whichever is greater. In California, earthquake coverage is sold by many insurers along with homeowners policies, but the insurer is a state agency established to make earthquake coverage available to homeowners.

 d. The inflation guard endorsement provides automatic increases for all Section I coverages by the percentage selected.

 e. The personal property replacement loss endorsement changes the loss settlement basis for personal property from actual cash value to replacement cost. Certain property, such as antiques, fine art and collectibles, is not eligible for replacement-cost coverage.

 f. The scheduled personal property endorsement broadens coverage on specific categories of valuable personal property. Coverage is open-perils with few exceptions and applies worldwide except for fine art that is covered only in the United States and Canada. There is also limited coverage for up to 30 days for newly acquired property in a category insured under the endorsement. Losses, except for fine art, are generally settled on an actual cash value basis.

 g. The business pursuits endorsement provides coverage for liability that arises out of or in connection with a business engaged in by an insured, and is most commonly used by persons in sales, clerical, and teaching occupations. Coverage does not apply with respect to a business owned or financially controlled by an insured or in which an insured is a partner. There is no coverage for liability that arises out of professional services, with the exception of teaching.

17-7. In order for property owners to be eligible for flood insurance, they must live in a community that participates in the NFIP. Such communities must agree to establish and enforce certain land use restrictions to minimize the community's exposure to flood losses. There is generally a 30-day waiting period before new policies or increases in coverage become effective.

 A homeowner can purchase insurance on the dwelling, its contents, or both. Coverage is similar to that provided for other perils under the homeowners policy, with some additional exceptions. Losses on the dwelling are settled on an actual cash value basis, but replacement-cost coverage can be endorsed under some circumstances. Contents coverage applies only on the residence premises except when property is removed to protect it from flood, and there is an extensive list of property that is not covered under the policy.

17-8.   Several alternatives for coverage are available, but policies that are written can be more limited than policies written in the normal marketplace. Some companies specialize in the substandard market and write coverage for a variety of properties, but at higher-than-normal premiums.

Many states have taken a variety of actions to make coverage available often at subsidized rates. State-run FAIR programs provide insurance for buildings and their contents if the property owner is unable to obtain coverage in the standard insurance market, for whatever reason. In most cases, coverage is written by a pool or syndicate of private insurers who are assessed for any losses of the plan if premiums are inadequate. Each state has its own FAIR plan, and the plans differ.

Some states, primarily in the Southeast and on the Gulf Coast, have beachfront and windstorm plans to provide protection that insurers are unwilling to write because of the loss exposure to hurricanes. Some of these plans only cover the perils of windstorm and hail, and property owners obtain protection for other perils in the normal insurance market.

Finally, the amount of insurance needed on an expensive home may exceed the limit an insurer is willing to write. In other cases, replacement cost substantially exceeds market value. Some insurers specialize in this market and have their own policies to meet the needs of the well-to-do. Other insurers tailor standard homeowners forms (such as HO-3 with endorsements that were previously described).

17-9.   Some characteristics of title insurance include the following:

- The policy provides protection only against unknown title defects that have occurred prior to the effective date of the policy but are discovered after the effective date.
- The policy is written on the assumption that losses will not occur because most title defects are known and listed in the policy.
- The policy term is indefinite and continues until title to the property is again transferred. At that time, the new owner will need to purchase a new title insurance policy because the existing policy is not assignable.
- The premium is paid only once—when the policy is issued—and the policy cannot be canceled by either party.
- The insured is indemnified up to the policy limits if a loss occurs. However, there is no guarantee that possession of the property will be retained.
- The amount of insurance is usually the initial purchase price of the property and a potential loss in the future can be much higher than the policy limit because of inflation.

Answers to Self-Test Questions

17-1.   True.

17-2.   False. Regardless of age, children are covered under their parents' homeowners policy as long as they continue to reside in their parents' household.

17-3.   False. The limits for homeowners Coverages B, C, and D are additional amounts of insurance and do not affect the amount of coverage (Coverage A) on the dwelling.

17-4.   True.

17-5.   False. An HO-3 policy covers damage to the insured's residence against open-perils but excludes, among other things, earthquake and flood.

17-6.   False. In a homeowners policy, losses to the dwelling under Coverage A are settled on a replacement-cost basis while losses under personal property Coverage C are settled on an actual cash value basis (unless an endorsement is added for replacement cost).

17-7.   True.

17-8.   False. In a homeowners policy, the amount payable for the loss of money and securities is limited for all perils.

17-9.   True.

17-10. True.

17-11. False. The liability coverage contained in an unendorsed homeowners policy provides protection against suits for bodily injury and property damage, but excludes intentional acts (personal injury). However, the policy can be endorsed to provide coverage for personal injury liability as well.

17-12. True.

17-13. True.

17-14. False. A person who lives in a condominium should carry an HO-6 Unit-owners Form because the association covers the building and detached structures. A renter should buy an HO-4 Contents Broad Form.

17-15. True.

17-16. True.

17-17. False. Flood insurance is now only available to property owners who live in a community that participates in the National Flood Insurance Program. It is not available to other property owners.

17-18. False. Title insurance provides protection only against unknown title defects that have occurred prior to the effective date of the policy but were discovered after the effective date.

Chapter 18

Answers to Review Questions

18-1. Key problems include the large number of automobile accidents, the high cost of automobile accidents, uninsured and underinsured drivers, difficulty of some persons in obtaining automobile insurance, and the affordability of that insurance.

18-2. Even in states with compulsory insurance laws:

- The compensation must come through traditional legal channels and can be delayed by an overburdened legal system.
- Some drivers may not register their vehicles; others may drop insurance after a vehicle is registered.
- A person may be injured by a hit-and-run driver, an out-of-state driver without insurance, a driver of a stolen car, or a driver of a fraudulently registered automobile.
- The required liability limits are relatively low, leaving some motorists underinsured.

18-3. Compulsory insurance requires the owners of automobiles to carry liability insurance (or to post a cash deposit, bond, or other security) before a vehicle can be registered. Shortcomings of this system were discussed in question 18-2.

Financial responsibility laws require proof of future financial responsibility by the carrying of insurance (or the posting of a cash deposit, bond, or other security), but only after some triggering event. Financial responsibility laws have the same shortcomings as compulsory insurance, and in addition, only become effective after an accident or serious offense and do not provide any compensation to the innocent victims of that accident.

Unsatisfied judgment funds are established by the state to compensate persons who are unable to collect a legal judgment resulting from an automobile accident. The injured person must obtain a legal judgment against the negligent party and show that the judgment cannot be collected. The maximum claim is usually limited to the state's minimum compulsory insurance requirement and is reduced by collateral sources of recovery. The collection process is slow and cumbersome, and some funds are inadequately funded.

Uninsured motorists coverage provides the insured with the amount he or she would have collected from the insurer of an uninsured driver had that driver been carrying insurance. Uninsured motorists coverage does not apply if the negligent party carries insurance that has inadequate limits to fully indemnify the innocent party. The limits of coverage are equal only to the state's compulsory insurance or financial responsibility benefit unless the policyowner has purchased higher limits, and the insured must establish that the other party was legally liable. The coverage usually applies to bodily injury only. The cost of the coverage is borne by the innocent victim, not the uninsured driver.

Underinsured motorists coverage provides protection to automobile accident victims when a negligent driver has insufficient insurance limits to pay for the damages for which he or she is responsible. Shortcomings are similar to those of the uninsured motorist coverage.

No-fault automobile insurance provides first-party benefits to injured persons and imposes some restrictions on their rights to sue negligent parties. No-fault has not resulted in lower premiums, restricts the right in some states to sue for pain and suffering, and shifts some costs of automobile accidents from negligent parties to innocent victims.

18-4. a. In a state with compulsory liability insurance, John would sue the driver of the other car and, given the assumptions with regard to fault, receive payment for the $40,000 in bodily injury plus any pain and suffering to the extent of the liability coverage on the other car. If the teenager had no liability coverage or less than the amount of John's uninsured and underinsured motorist coverages, those coverages in John's own policy would respond.

b. If the accident occurred in a state with a modified no-fault law containing a $5,000 threshold, John's own insurer would pay for lost wages and medical expenses from benefits available under his no-fault coverage (even if he is from a state without no-fault, his PAP will automatically provide no-fault coverage when he is driving in a no-fault state). Because his bodily injuries exceed the $5,000 threshold, he can sue the other driver for bodily injury losses including pain and suffering. His insurance company would be reimbursed to the extent that any of the amount from the legal judgment duplicates the no-fault benefits received. If the teenager had no liability coverage or less than the amount of John's uninsured and underinsured motorist coverages, those coverages in John's own policy would respond for the amount unpaid in excess of the no-fault benefits.

18-5. A PAP can be written on eligible vehicles owned or leased by an individual or by a husband or wife residing in the same household. Vehicles with other forms of ownership can be insured with an endorsement. Eligible vehicles include private passenger automobiles, such as cars, vans, and sports utility vehicles, owned by the policyowner or leased under a written contract of six continuous months or longer. Also eligible are newly acquired autos, trailers, temporary substitute vehicles, and pickups with a gross weight of less than 10,000 pounds. Vans and pickups are ineligible for coverage under some circumstances when used for the transportation or delivery of goods and materials. Other vehicles, such as motor homes, motorcycles, golf carts, and snowmobiles, can be insured by endorsement in most states.

18-6. Pete would be covered up to a total of $100,000 for bodily injury to the other driver and property damage to the other driver's car. Pete's own car would be covered by the collision coverage subject to the deductible as long as he notifies his company that he wants collision coverage on the new car within 14 days of purchase.

18-7. a. With split limits, Tom's policy would pay the claim for $5,000 of bodily injury, but only $50,000 of the property damage to the truck and its contents. Tom would have to pay the remaining $100,000 out of his pocket unless he has an umbrella liability policy.

b. With a single limit of $300,000, all $155,000 of claims for bodily injury and property damage would be paid by Tom's personal auto policy.

18-8. a. Unless Betty's business involves use of the vehicle as a public or livery conveyance, hired out to carry persons or property, her liability coverage applies.

b. Betty has liability coverage only if the employer-provided car is insured by the employer, or if Betty has added an endorsement to her PAP to include liability coverage on this car.

c. The friend's policy is primary because it covers an "owned vehicle," and Betty's insurance is secondary or excess because she is driving a "nonowned vehicle." Betty's policy will only pay on an excess basis after the limits of the owner's policy are exhausted.

18-9. When a person drives a friend's car, the first person is a named insured under his or her own PAP while driving another automobile. He or she is also an insured under the friend's PAP as a person using the covered auto. In this situation, the friend's policy is primary because it covers an "owned vehicle," and the driver's insurance is secondary or excess because he or she is driving a "nonowned vehicle." The driver's policy will only pay on an excess basis after the limits of the owner's policy are exhausted.

18-10. Part B of the PAP provides payment for the reasonable and necessary medical expenses of an insured as a result of an automobile accident. Benefits are paid regardless of fault. The insureds under Part B include the named insured, spouse, and any family members (1) while occupying either a motor vehicle designed for use on public roads or a trailer or (2) when struck as a pedestrian by such a vehicle or trailer. Any other person, such as a child being transported, who is injured while occupying a covered auto is also an insured.

18-11. a. Coverage under Part D, Coverage for Damage to Your Auto, applies to nonowned vehicles that are rented on a temporary basis such as when an insured is on a trip. Damage to the nonowned auto caused by the impact of that auto with an object is covered under Part D's collision coverage.

b. Damage to the nonowned auto caused by malicious mischief or vandalism is covered under Part D's other-than-collision coverage.

c. Damage to the nonowned auto caused by the contact of that auto with an animal is covered under Part D's other-than-collision coverage.

18-12. A miscellaneous type vehicle endorsement is used to cover miscellaneous types of owned vehicles, including motorcycles and dune buggies. Each vehicle is listed in a schedule, and the same coverages that apply to automobiles in the PAP can be purchased. Likewise, a snowmobile endorsement can be used to insure snowmobiles.

18-13. Without an endorsement, the PAP does not provide coverage when an insured is driving in Mexico. Acceptable coverage must be obtained through a licensed Mexican insurance company prior to the trip. Driving in Mexico without such coverage is a criminal offense. Coverage can be purchased at the border. Alternatively, it may be possible to add this protection to an existing PAP if an insurance company is a member of a foreign insurance association; however, this endorsement is primarily used by people who live near the border and occasionally take brief trips to Mexico. The endorsement is effective only if the insured has also purchased liability insurance through a Mexican insurer, and coverage is excess over that policy. The main advantage of the endorsement is the ability to have higher liability limits than the Mexican insurance as well as other policy coverages.

18-14. Hard-to-insure drivers can usually find some coverage in the residual market, which consists of specialty insurers and state programs to make insurance available, though not necessarily affordable. State programs usually follow one of three models: automobile insurance plans, joint underwriting associations, or reinsurance facilities. A small number of drivers with very poor driving records may still be unable to obtain insurance from any of these sources in some states.

18-15. Clients should evaluate the cost of coverage, the financial strength of the insurer, and the service from the company and its agents.

18-16. For some watercraft, liability coverage is available under a homeowners policy, which provides no protection for larger boats and little physical damage protection for any boat. Boatowners policies, for smaller boats, and yacht policies, for larger boats, contain liability coverage, medical payments coverage, uninsured boaters coverage, and physical damage coverage. Also available are coverages for the legal obligation of the policyowner to remove a wrecked or sunken vessel, for liability arising out of transportation of the boat on land, for costs of towing and assistance if the boat is disabled, and for liability to crew members and other maritime workers.

Aviation policies for private aircraft pay for bodily injury liability that arises out of the insured's ownership, maintenance, or use of insured aircraft. Coverage also applies to bodily injury liability arising out of the location where the insured aircraft is stored. Medical payments coverage is available to cover passengers, and crew members can be covered for an additional premium. Physical damage coverage is open-perils.

18-17. The personal umbrella policy is designed to provide liability coverage for catastrophic legal claims or judgments. Without broad liability insurance of sufficiently high limits, individuals face the possibility of having assets and/or income seized to pay a legal judgment. The umbrella policy covers bodily injury and property damage liability as well as personal injury liability. Most personal umbrella policies also pay defense costs that are not payable by underlying policies and provide other supplementary coverages similar to those in the homeowners and PAP policies (premiums on appeal bonds, expenses incurred at the company's request, etc.).

Answers to Self-Test Questions

18-1. False. Even in compulsory liability states, there are uninsured and even unlicensed drivers. Also, many drivers only carry the limits required by law and thus are underinsured. Therefore, uninsured and underinsured motorist coverages are necessary even in states with compulsory liability laws.

18-2. False. Compulsory insurance laws require owners of automobiles to carry liability insurance before a vehicle can be registered. Financial responsibility laws only require proof of future financial responsibility under certain circumstances.

18-3. True.

18-4. False. Under most no-fault laws, the right to sue the negligent party exists once a dollar or verbal threshold has been met. No state has adopted a pure no-fault law.

18-5. False. No-fault benefits in most states include rehabilitation expenses, loss of earnings, expenses for essential services, funeral expenses, and survivors' benefits as well as medical expenses.

18-6. True.

18-7. True.

18-8. False. If a client has $100,000/$300,000/$50,000 limits of liability in her PAP, she would be fully covered for the $20,000 of property damage, but would only be covered to the extent of $100,000 of the other driver's bodily injury claim.

18-9. True.

18-10. False. If Jim rented a car, damaged it, and was sued by the rental company, he would be covered under the collision or other-than-collision coverages of his PAP for the property damage to the rental car. Liability coverage excludes damage to property rented to the insured.

18-11. True.

18-12. False. Unlike the homeowners policy, medical payments under the PAP cover the insureds as well as other people riding in the insured's car. Insureds are covered while occupying a motor vehicle designed for use on public roads or when struck as a pedestrian.

18-13. True.

18-14. False. If a client hits a deer, the damage to his car would be paid under the other-than-collision coverage.

18-15. True.

18-16. False. Most states handle hard-to-insure drivers through automobile insurance plans.

18-17. False. Despite the highly competitive market, the cost of automobile insurance differs significantly from company to company.

18-18. True.

18-19. True.

18-20. True.

18-21. True.

18-22. False. Personal umbrella policies commonly exclude sexual molestation and failure to render professional services.

Chapter 19

Answers to Review Questions

19-1. In addition to commercial property insurance on the building, the equipment, and inventory, the client is likely to need, or at least should consider the need for, the following:

- business income insurance to cover lost profits, continuing expenses, and/or extra expenses to minimize the suspension of business after the occurrence of a direct physical damage loss to business property
- crime insurance, especially to cover burglary and employee dishonesty
- inland marine insurance to cover goods in transit
- boiler and machinery insurance to cover repairs or replacement of machinery that breaks down
- commercial general liability insurance to cover premises liability and products liability
- commercial automobile insurance for company vehicles
- workers' compensation and employer's liability insurance to provide protection for injuries to employees
- directors and officers liability insurance (if the business is incorporated)
- employment practices liability insurance

19-2. The Business Income (without Extra Expense) Coverage Form covers the sum of (1) net profit or loss that would have been earned or incurred during a period of business suspension and (2) normal continuing business expenses, including payroll, during the suspension. The Business Income (and Extra Expense) Coverage Form provides for the same expenses as well as expenses incurred to avoid or minimize the suspension of operations, even if they do not otherwise reduce the business income loss. The Extra Expense Coverage Form provides extra expense insurance for organizations that must remain in operation after a property loss and, therefore, are unlikely to have a significant decrease in revenue. However, the extra expenses of remaining open can be significant.

19-3. First, commercial crime forms typically cover money, which includes currency, coins, bank notes, checks, and money orders. These forms also typically cover securities, which include both negotiable and nonnegotiable instruments, contracts that represent money or other property, tokens, tickets, stamps, and charge slips. Finally, these forms also typically cover tangible property other than money or securities; however, there are exclusions for certain types of property for which adequate coverage can be obtained under other types of insurance.

19-4. The following provisions are common to many crime forms:

- There is no coverage for losses caused by the named insured or any of its directors, trustees, or authorized representatives. In addition, there is no coverage for losses caused by employees except under the forms that specifically cover employee dishonesty.
- Coverage is for direct losses only. There is no coverage available for consequential losses that might result from criminal acts.
- Most of the forms require the policyowner to notify the police if there is a reason to believe that a loss results from a violation of law.
- The forms specify how settlements are valued. Currency is valued at its face value. If the currency is foreign, the insurer can pay the face value in the foreign currency or at its equivalent value in United Stated currency. Securities are valued as of the close of the business day a loss is discovered. The insurer can pay the value of the securities or replace them in kind. The insurer also has the option of paying the cost of a bond that is required for the issuance of replacement securities. Other property is valued at its cash value, and any disputes over value are settled by arbitration.

19-5.   Today inland marine policies and forms are used to write coverage for:
   - goods in domestic transit, by mail, rail, truck, or aircraft. Commonly, these policies cover shipments within and between the continental United States, Alaska, and Canada, but coverage can be endorsed, for example, for shipments to Mexico. Depending on the terms of sale, the responsibility for goods being shipped can fall on the shipper, the carrier, or the recipient. Any of these parties can buy insurance as needed. Owners of property can purchase transit policies to provide property damage to their goods while in the course of transit by common carriers, contract carriers, or their own vehicles. Certain policies, such as motor truck cargo insurance, are used by common carriers or contract carriers to cover customer's goods when the carrier is legally liable for the damage. These policies do not cover damage for which the carrier is not liable such as those arising from acts of God.
   - mobile equipment and property for property that is often moved from one location to another.
   - property held by bailees, such as dry cleaners, repair shops, and public warehouses, who often have possession of significant amounts of customers' goods. A bailee liability policy can be purchased to cover damage to these goods when the bailee is legally liable. Many bailees purchase a bailees customers policy, which provides coverage regardless of whether the bailee is legally liable.
   - property of certain dealers who own a significant amount of inventory that is likely to be transported such as jewelry, furs, fine art, cameras, musical equipment, stamps, coins, and mobile and agricultural equipment.
   - instrumentalities of transportation and communication, which include bridges, tunnels, pipelines, television towers, satellite dishes, and power lines.
   - gaps left by a policyowner's other commercial insurance policies. The differences in conditions (DIC) insurance provided open-perils coverage that can be used to provide earthquake and flood coverage, to provide higher limits than are otherwise obtainable, or to cover loss exposures not in basic policies.

19-6.   a.   commercial general liability insurance (products liability)
   b.   commercial general liability insurance (business operations liability)
   c.   commercial general liability insurance (premises liability)
   d.   commercial general liability insurance (completed operations liability)
   e.   commercial general liability insurance (contingent liability)
   f.   commercial general liability insurance (premises liability)
   g.   commercial auto coverage (liability)
   h.   workers' compensation and employer liability policy (employer liability under part 2)
   i.   professional liability insurance, also known as malpractice insurance
   j.   professional liability insurance, also known as errors and omissions insurance
   k.   directors and officers liability insurance
   l.   employment practices liability insurance

19-7.   Both excess liability insurance and commercial umbrella liability insurance provide additional liability limits for claims that are covered under specified underlying coverages. Under the excess liability policy, there is no drop-down coverage for claims excluded by the underlying coverages. Unlike excess policies, commercial umbrella liability insurance often covers claims excluded by the underlying policies.

19-8.   Unique characteristics of surety bonds include:
   - *liability of the principal.* Unlike an insured under an insurance contract, a principal who defaults on a bond is liable to the surety to the extent of any expenditure the surety incurs. The surety can require the principal to post collateral to repay the surety if the principal defaults.
   - *expected losses.* a surety generally expects to pay few losses and underwrites in a strict manner to determine whether the principal is capable of meeting any obligations.
   - *coverage period.* The coverage period under most surety bonds is indefinite, and the premium for the bond is paid only once. In most cases, neither the surety nor the principal can cancel the bond.
   - *bond limit.* A surety bond is written for a dollar limit, and that is the maximum amount of the surety's obligation to the boligee. Some bonds, however, pay court costs and interest on judgments in addition to the bond limit.
   - *statutory versus nonstatutory bonds.* Governmental ordinances, regulations, or statutes require many bonds, and the provisions of these statutory bonds and the obligations of the parties are established by law. The obligation of the parties under nonstatutory bonds is established by contract between the obligee and the principal.

19-9.   A commercial package policy consists of three major components. The first component is a common declarations page that applies to the entire policy and contains the policy number, the name of the insurer, the name and address of the policyowner, the policy period, and premium amounts. The second component is a section of common policy changes, transfer of policy rights, and the insurer's rights to inspect the policyowner's premises and operations and to examine and audit books and records that pertain to the policy coverage. The last component of the policy consists of seven sections of coverages that a policyowner can select, of which at least two must be selected.

The businessowners policy is designed for small- to medium-size businesses and organizations that meet certain eligibility requirements. Two property forms are available, named-perils coverage and open-perils coverage. Losses are paid on a replacement-cost basis, and there is no coinsurance provision.

Answers to Self-Test Questions

19-1.   False. Commercial property insurance covers personal property of others in the care, custody, or control of the insured as well as buildings and business personal property of the insured.

19-2.   True.

19-3.   True.

19-4.   True.

19-5.   True.

19-6.   False. An electrical contractor who works on residential construction and repairs requires mainly business operations liability and completed operations liability coverages to cover his business liability loss exposures.

19-7.   True.

19-8.   False. Advertising injury liability is covered under Coverage B of the comprehensive general liability coverage form.

19-9.   False. Most commonly, comprehensive general liability coverage is written on an occurrence basis.

19-10. True.

19-11. True.

19-12. False. Even with workers' compensation laws, employers are subject to suits for injuries to employees.

19-13. False. Most professional liability policies are written on a claims-made basis.

19-14. True.

19-15. False. Excess liability policies do not include drop-down coverage for claims excluded by the underlying coverages, but commercial umbrella policies often do provide such coverage.

19-16. True.

19-17. True.

19-18. True.

Index